John W. Diggle

The Lancashire Life of Bishop Fraser

John W. Diggle

The Lancashire Life of Bishop Fraser

ISBN/EAN: 9783743338296

Manufactured in Europe, USA, Canada, Australia, Japa

Cover: Foto ©Lupo / pixelio.de

Manufactured and distributed by brebook publishing software (www.brebook.com)

John W. Diggle

The Lancashire Life of Bishop Fraser

Photographed by DEBENHAM & GABELL.

Yours affectionately,
J. Manchester.

THE
LANCASHIRE LIFE
OF
BISHOP FRASER

BY

JOHN W. DIGGLE, M.A.

Vicar of Mossley Hill, Liverpool; Hon. Canon of Liverpool; Rural Dean of Childwall.

AUTHOR OF "GODLINESS AND MANLINESS"; "TRUE RELIGION"; "RAINBOWS," ETC.
EDITOR OF "BISHOP FRASER'S SERMONS."

WITH TWO ILLUSTRATIONS

SECOND EDITION.

LONDON:
SAMPSON LOW, MARSTON, SEARLE & RIVINGTON
LIMITED,
St. Dunstan's House,
FETTER LANE, FLEET STREET, E.C.
1889

117763
DEC 1 2 1984

TO

THE WORKING PEOPLE OF ALL CLASSES IN LANCASHIRE

THE LANCASHIRE LIFE

OF

BISHOP FRASER

Is Dedicated.

PREFACE.

"It would be quite incompatible," says Judge Hughes in his Memoir of James Fraser, "within the limits which have been fixed for this book, to attempt anything like a detailed account of the work of Bishop Fraser in his diocese. Our space will be all too small for even a compressed narrative of what may be called the Bishop's work of supererogation." The aim of the present volume is to supply, by way of supplement, a more detailed account of the "Work in his Diocese," *i.e.*, of the *Lancashire Life*, of Bishop Fraser, than the limitation of space permitted to Judge Hughes. The story is told, as far as possible, in the Bishop's own words, as they occur in his public utterances and private correspondence. As, however, the story gives no account of Bishop Fraser before he came to Lancashire, it seemed desirable to introduce him to the reader by attempting to gather into focus the most striking personal features of his character. The Chapter upon "Personal Characteristics," with which the volume opens, is intended, therefore, as an introductory sketch of the Bishop.

The Charges of Bishop Fraser, having been separately published, are not reproduced in this volume, though extracts from them will be found in various Chapters. Nor has the strict chronological sequence of events been adhered to. In a life like Bishop Fraser's, in which the same topics are again and again dealt with, the chronological method of narrative would have led to much confusion. While, therefore, the order of time has been preserved as far as possible, yet each Chapter of the Book aims at presenting the separate story of some particular department of the Bishop's work; and the Author can but humbly hope that from the combination of the Chapters a true picture of Bishop Fraser's *Lancashire Life* will form itself in the reader's mind :—a picture full of light, yet not without shadows.

The Author desires to thank—(1) all those who have placed the Bishop's letters to them at his disposal; (2) all those who (like the Venerable Archdeacons Norris, Anson, and Hornby; the Revs. Canon Maclure, James Lonsdale, and H. B. Hawkins; most of all, Mrs. Fraser and Mr. Chancellor Christie) have assisted him with important suggestions, and the revision of large portions of the manuscript; (3) his Assistant-Curate, the Rev. H. P. Cronshaw, by whom the Index has been compiled.

The Author has sometimes been inclined to relinquish his task, under the sense of his inability to do anything like justice to the subject of it; but the encouragements of his many correspondents—particularly of Mrs. Fraser—united to his own strong desire to pay his tribute to one for whom he feels an ever-deepening sense of affection, have induced him to persevere; and he now submits the results of his labours to the kindly consideration of those for whose sake it was chiefly undertaken, viz., the people of Lancashire, earnestly trusting that it may help to bring back to their recollection some memories of one who loved to spend himself for their sakes.

THE VICARAGE, MOSSLEY HILL, LIVERPOOL.
June 18*th*, 1889.

CONTENTS.

CHAPTER I.

SOME PERSONAL CHARACTERISTICS.

Personal Appearance and Bodily Strength—Bodily Health—Moral Health—Impulsiveness—Dignity—Courtesy—Industry—Speech at Shrewsbury School—Frankness — Truthfulness — Unselfishness— Intellectual Roominess — Earnestness—Power of Observation— Geniality—Hospitality—Simplicity of Habits — Directness—The Citizen-Bishop—Politics—Churchmanship—Theology—Belief in Providence—Practice of Prayer—Knowledge of the Bible—Love of Righteousness—Righteousness and Ritualism—Love of Liberty —Summary 1

CHAPTER II.

APPOINTMENT TO MANCHESTER.

Offer of Bishopric—Letters of Advice—Dean Church's and other Letters—Acceptance of Bishopric—Congratulations . . . 41

CHAPTER III.

ARRIVAL IN MANCHESTER.

Consecration—First Sermon—His Preaching—Pulpit and Press — Mauldeth Hall—His Mother's Diary 52

CHAPTER IV.

AT WORK: MANCHESTER MISSION.

Introduction—Bishop Lee—Organization of Diocese—Summary of Work —Description of Diocese—The Mission—Pastoral Letter—Sacerdotalism—Medical Students—Railway Employés—Cab-drivers— Slaughtermen — Theatre Employés— Bishop's Address in the Theatres—Baroness Burdett Coutts's Letter—Private Theatricals —Letters to the Bishop—The Bishop's Letter on Theatres—Conclusion of Mission 64

CHAPTER V.

THE LANCASHIRE STRIKE.

The Bishop and Strikes—A Strike an Industrial War—Sermon on Strikes—Letter to Mr. Broadhurst—Causes of Strike—Proposed Remedies—Commencement of Strike—Letters and Sermon at Leigh—The Lock-out—The Riot—Letter to Weavers' Association—Sermons at Rishton and Halliwell—Proposed Compromise—The Bishop's Letter to the Manchester and London Press—Termination of Strike 91

CHAPTER VI.

COMMERCIAL DEPRESSION.

Commercial Distress—The Panic—The Bishop's Letter—The Relief Committee—Indiscriminate Benevolence—Savings Banks—Social Christianity—Improvidence—The Elberfeldt System—Organized Charity—The Organization of Relief—Thrift—Commercial Righteousness 119

CHAPTER VII.

CO-OPERATION—SOCIAL SCIENCE.

The Co-operative Movement—Co-operative Congress—Co-operation and Agriculture—Co-operation and the Church—Social Science—Population of Cities—Education—Gradation of Schools—Health—The Interment of the Dead—Thrift and Providence—Recreation—Social Science and Religion 136

CHAPTER VIII.

DIOCESAN SYNODS AND CONFERENCES.

Institution of Conferences—Diocesan Synod, 1874—Constitution and Purpose of Diocesan Conference—Religious Teaching in Day Schools—Temperance—Public Worship Regulation Act—Candidates for Ministry—Church and People—Definite Belief—Church of Rome—Ceremonialism—Ceremonial Innovations—Simplicity of Belief—The Church and Nonconformity—The Church and the Masses—Sermons—The Diocesan Synod, 1881—The Admonition . 156

CONTENTS. ix

CHAPTER IX.

LAMBETH CONFERENCE—CONVOCATION—CHURCH CONGRESSES.

PAGE

The Lambeth Conference—Convocation—The Ornaments Rubric—
The Athanasian Creed—Christianity and the Masses—Church
Congresses—Sheffield Congress—The Church and the Stage—
Brighton Congress—Impure Literature—Newcastle Congress . 181

CHAPTER X.

CONFIRMATIONS AND ORDINATIONS.

Confirmations—Accrington Confirmation, 1877—Confirmation Addresses
—Ordinations—Ordination Address s—The Work of the Ministry—
Notes of Ordination Addresses—Standards for Examination—
Ordination Sermons—Cardinal Newman's Letter 204

CHAPTER XI.

OBITER DICTA.

Religion—Formalism—Dogmatism—Comprehension—Benefits of Discussion—Ecclesiastical Drugs—Family Religion—Education—
Denominational Schools—Sunday Schools—Prize-giving—Desultory Education—Education and Youth—Self-made Men—Education of Women—Eloquence—Power of Plain Preaching—Curates
and Clerical Incomes—Improvident Marriages—Heredity and
Marriage—Cookery—Church Choirs—Hymns—Hymns and Music
—Country Parsons—High Art—Sunday Opening of Museums—
Funeral Reform—Cremation—The Volunteer Movement—Temptations of Youth—The Opium Trade—Fashionable Religion—
Following Christ—Personal Salvation—The Prince Imperial—
Dean Stanley—Dean Stanley and Lord Hatherley—Death of
General Garfield—Dr. Pusey—Death of Dr. Tait, the Archbishop
of Canterbury—Death of the Duke of Albany—General Gordon . 226

CHAPTER XII.

THE BISHOP OF ALL DENOMINATIONS.

Churchmanship—Simplicity in Religion—Worship—Reverence—Sympathetic Christianity—Intelligent Christianity—Interpretation of
Scripture—Truth and Holiness—Comprehension—Absolution—
The Holy Eucharist—The Priestly Office—Historic Churchmanship—Apostolic Succession—Establishment and Endowment—

Disestablishment—Purchase of Livings—Voluntaryism and Endowment—Defence against Disestablishment—Church Reform—Nonconformity and the Church—The Bishop and Nonconformists—Religious Tolerance—The Bishop of the Jews—Testimony of Nonconformists 265

CHAPTER XIII.

THE CITIZEN BISHOP.

Religion and Politics—Bishops in Parliament—Clergy and Laity—Civil and Religious Liberty—Christian Socialism—Religion and Morals—Licentiousness—Purity—National Prosperity—National Decay—Christianity and Citizenship—Christianity and Patriotism—Christianity and War—Phœnix Park Murders—Assassinations in Ireland—The Irish Question—Greatness of Manchester—The Thirlmere Water Scheme—The Town Hall—The Bishop and the Press 302

CHAPTER XIV.

THE BISHOP AND THE WORKING CLASSES.

Incidents in the Bishop's Relationships to the Working Classes—Modern Christianity—Modern Society—Classes and Masses—True Happiness—Religious Enthusiasm—Religious Fervour—Religion of Working Classes—Kearsley Colliery Explosion—Clifton Hall Explosion—The Bishop's Sympathy—Duty—Athletics—Luxury—High Aims—Bishop and Railway Men—Evidences of Christianity—Patriotism—Extravagance and Thrift—The Bishop and the Poor—Letters to Working Men—Church and People 330

CHAPTER XV.

SECULARISM—SCIENCE—FAITH.

Atheism—Infidelity—Social Christianity—Religion and Science—Reason and Faith—Christianity and Atheism—Science and Conscience—Mr Darwin—The Bishop and Professor Huxley—Religion and Knowledge—Bishop of all Classes—Belief in All Truth . . 376

CHAPTER XVI.

MILES PLATTING AND CHEETHAM HILL.

Story of Miles Platting—Bishop's Refusal to ordain Mr. Cowgill to Miles Platting—Vestments, Incense, Mixed Chalice—Letters and Petitions in reference to Ceremonial at Miles Platting—Charges against Mr.

CONTENTS.

Green—Principles involved in Miles Platting Case—Imprisonment of Mr. Green—Bishop's Letters to Mr. Green—Mr. Green's Replies—Correspondence with Mr. Gladstone, Lord Selborne, &c.—Bishop's Application for Mr. Green's Release—Vacancy of Living—Nomination of Mr. Cowgill—Issues at Stake—Bishop's Memorandum—Trial and Verdict—St. John's, Cheetham Hill—Statement of Case—Bishop's Letter—Mr. Gunton—Conclusion . . . 397

CHAPTER XVII.

LETTERS 430

CHAPTER XVIII.

HOME LIFE.

The Bishop's Devotion to his Mother and his Home—Miss Duncan—The Betrothal — Mrs. Duncan's Death — Domestic Economy — Constancy of Mind—Rumours of Marriage—The Bishop's Marriage—Dean Stanley's Address—*Punch's* Letter—Return Home—Home Happiness—Hospitality 490

CHAPTER XIX.

CLOSING SCENES.

Home Life—Wedding Gifts—Statistics of Diocese—His Lancashire Work—Premonitions of Death—Last Visit to Ufton Nervet—Last Letter—Last Illness—Death—Funeral—Ufton Nervet—Ufton Church—The Burial—After Death 519

INDEX 553

BISHOP FRASER'S LANCASHIRE LIFE.

CHAPTER I.

SOME PERSONAL CHARACTERISTICS.

Personal Appearance and Bodily Strength—Bodily Health—Moral Health—Impulsiveness—Dignity—Courtesy—Industry—Speech at Shrewsbury School—Frankness—Truthfulness—Unselfishness—Intellectual Roominess—Earnestness—Power of Observation—Geniality—Hospitality—Simplicity of Habits — Directness — The Citizen-Bishop — Politics — Churchmanship—Theology—Belief in Providence—Practice of Prayer—Knowledge of the Bible—Love of Righteousness—Righteousness and Ritualism—Love of Liberty—Summary.

THE Bishopric of Manchester was offered to the Rev. James Fraser, M.A., Rector of Ufton Nervet, Berkshire, on January 3, 1870. Mr. Fraser was then in robust middle life, having been born on August 18, 1818, at Oakland House, in the parish of Prestbury, Gloucestershire. Nature had bestowed upon him a fine physical constitution. His frame was tall, broad, erect, well built, muscular. His chest was ample and deep; his forehead massive and open; his chin large and firm; his eyes clear, shining, and wide apart; his nose prominent and strong; his lips distinct and thin; his countenance, in action, bright and sympathetic; but, in repose, pensive, almost to sadness; his voice a sweet, penetrating tenor, capable of almost every variety of expression, from the joy of laughter to the sorrow of tears; while, by the shake of his hand, he could convey an electric current of friendliness and goodwill. There was something in Mr. Fraser's very tread which attracted attention; his step was elastic and long—the step of health, of purpose, and of power. "Along with an active step," writes the Rev. James Lonsdale, "it seemed almost as if he carried a bright light with him; those that he passed or met seemed not so much to be paying respect to a bishop and a gentleman, as with happy and cheery looks to be answering to his happy countenance. The prophet speaks of 'all faces gathering blackness;' here it was the opposite, all faces gathered brightness. Men looked at him as if they were saying to themselves, 'There goes one who is perfectly sincere, one whose business it is to make others happy, whose vocation is to spread joy.'" In his early days he had been very fond of horses, a first-rate rider and a good whip. Soon after his ordination he gave up the practice of hunting, but he continued to appreciate the points of a horse till the close of his life. In an address to working men at the Sheffield Church Congress, October 3, 1878, he said :

"Though no one admires horses more than I do—and I think I understand the points of a horse as well as a man can who comes from a southern county—I must say that the modern style of horse-racing does not commend itself to me as an element in our progress and development as a nation."

Upon one occasion, after the Bishop came to Manchester, he wanted to buy a horse. The Archdeacon of Lancaster, the Venerable William Hornby, was staying with the Bishop when the dealer brought a horse on approval. "We must try him," said the Bishop to the Archdeacon; and forthwith his lordship mounted the horse and cantered round the field. Upon his return, pulling up opposite the Archdeacon, he said, " Now, Hornby, let me see *you* have a gallop; I don't ride as I used to do; for one thing the apron bothers me."

In a letter dated June 12, 1877, the Bishop said :

" As for riding, fond as I used to be of it—and no one could be prouder of his horses than I used to be; it was my only serious extravagance—I always would keep two good nags in my stable, one for myself and one when occasion arose for a friend—*now* I have only been on a horse's back twice since I have been a bishop. Once was two years ago when I paid a short visit to the Archbishop of Canterbury at Addington, and rode with him one afternoon about his beautiful park; and I don't suppose I go into my stable (where, however, I still have two good horses) once in three months."

From head to foot Bishop Fraser's whole physical frame overflowed with strength; the strength of natural constitution, well preserved by exercise, by moderation, by industry. As you looked at him, you felt he had all the energy of a man, and all the simplicity of a child. His face was square, his countenance ruddy; the colour and the form combined to produce an impression of freshness and power, of innocence and resolution. He seemed to possess at once a remarkable massiveness, and a singular tenderness. He was a rare and mighty man, with head, heart, health, all upon a grand scale.

For Bishop Fraser was no less healthy in moral feeling than in physical frame, being an admirable specimen of the *Mens sana in corpore sano*. His conscience was as true as his face; and his heart as robust as his body. He might make mistakes; a man of his metal generally makes frequent mistakes. Mr. Phelps has admirably said, "A man who never makes mistakes seldom makes anything," but Bishop Fraser's mistakes were always of the head, never of the heart. He was a being of strong impulses.

"People tell me," he said, "I have the courage of my opinions. It would be more true to say that I have the courage of my impulses. When, *e.g.*, I hear or read of the clergy as a class being described as tyrants, despots, bigots, who 'wish to keep the villagers of England in the deep ditch of poverty and ignorance,' I confess, as Sam Slick says, my 'dander rises,' and I feel more tempted to wax angry than is perhaps becoming in a bishop."—*Speech at Salt Schools, Shipley*, 1884.

Now and again he was tempted into keen controversies; but in his most pugilistic moments he never hit beneath the belt. He would stand with his back against the wall and fight, but he never violated the rules of the contest; and never cherished animosity against his antagonist after the contest ended. Upon one occasion he held an animated discussion concerning his use of patronage with one of his disappointed clergy, who, in the heat of debate, said some hard things to the Bishop. In his turn the Bishop said some hard things back again; but the next morning, the clergyman, who was poor, and had just been put to the expense of changing houses, found upon his breakfast table a £10 note from the Bishop, to help in defraying the cost of removal. Grasping the hand of an antagonist, upon another occasion, he said, with great goodwill, "You have hit me hard, but you have hit me fair."

It used to be said that "the Church of England is dying of dignity." Bishop Fraser was naturally dignified, but he has done much to put off the death, and to strengthen the life of the Church of England.

There is dignity and dignity. There is the pompous dignity of the mere official, a symptom of emptiness and decay; and the princely dignity of the born ruler—an evidence of the richness and fulness of life. It is the false dignity of the pompous official which kills religion; the true dignity of the sovereign man quickens religion into life. Bishop Fraser had none of the false dignity of the pompous official. He always insisted on carrying his own bag: a habit which occasionally provoked adverse comment. In a speech delivered at Keighley, October 8, 1879, he said in defence of the habit:

"There are false standards in society of gentility, of respectability, and the like. Some people seem to think that it is beneath my dignity as a bishop to carry my own bag. What indignity is there in carrying a bag, I want to know? If I am strong and healthy, why shouldn't I carry my own bag?"

His friendliness, graciousness, courtesy, were simple and remarkable. After staying at a house he would sometimes lay his hand upon the shoulder of a servant and say "So much obliged to you for all your goodness." He had the royal gift of recollecting names and faces; he could pat a child on the head; and shake a collier by the hand; and convoy a poor woman across a street. Travelling in the train upon one occasion with Mr. E. P. Charlewood, his secretary, when the railway porter shut the door of the carriage, Mr. Charlewood said, "Thank you." "That's right Charlewood," at once rejoined the Bishop, "I always like to hear people say 'Thank you.'" A friend tells me that he once sent the Bishop a present of game, and, to spare him the trouble of acknowledging the gift, he only put his initials on the label; but in a few days he received a letter of thanks from the Bishop who had taken great pains to discover the anonymous donor. So resolute was the Bishop's habit of courtesy! In the presence of women his courtesy rose into chivalry. To all women he was chivalrous, not because they were beautiful, or fascinating, or rich, but because they were women. His devotion to his mother had glorified and consecrated all womanhood for him.

From a child James Fraser had cultivated the habit of regular strenuous industry. His industry, moreover, had the merit of not springing out of sheer necessity or indigence. All industry has something laudable in it; but the industry of compulsion is less laudable than the industry of free-will. James Fraser was never, in the narrow sense of indigence, poor. His father—a Forfarshire man, one of the Frasers of Durris—had been successful as a merchant in India; his mother was the daughter of a leading solicitor in the town of Bilston in Staffordshire. When Fraser was only fourteen years of age, his father died; and before his death had the misfortune to sink the greater part of his money in unproductive mines. It was, therefore, something of a struggle for the widowed mother, in her reduced circumstances, to maintain and educate her six sons; and James, the eldest, was never weary of telling the touching story of his mother's self-denying nobleness. In an address delivered at the Keighley School of Art, October, 1879, the Bishop made the following beautiful and pathetic allusion to his aged mother:

"When I was fourteen years of age I lost my father. He had engaged—having come home from India comparatively a young man, with what was then considered a good fortune—in iron speculations in the Forest of Dean, in the course of which he lost the greater part of his property; and died, I really believe, a broken-hearted man, leaving his wife to bring up a family of seven children, of whom I was the eldest, with small resources. My mother was not a clever woman, but a woman of sound sense, and one who would do anything for the benefit of her children. Five of her children grew to be men. She said, 'I can't give them a large fortune, but, by denying myself, I can give them a good education.' She gave them a good education; I do not know how she managed it. Three went out to India, two of them laid down their lives for their country—one in the Indian Mutiny. Another was the Head of the Department of Public Works under the Government, and you know what I myself am, and I simply say that, if my brothers who are dead could rise up, they would all, along with those who are living, call their mother blessed for the sacrifices that she made in order that they might have careers open to them in the world. By God's good providence I have that dear mother still spared to me, and, although she is paralysed and speechless and helpless, yet every day, when I go into the room and see her sweet face, I think of all I owe to her."

The manly and beautiful tribute of a successful son to his self-sacrificing mother, but a tribute which must not be permitted to mislead the judgment in forming a true estimate of the real character of that son's industry! For Fraser's industry was never in need of being quickened by the lash of penury. It was the industry of praiseworthy ambition, of filial gratitude, of conscientious principle. The pecuniary losses of Fraser's father had reduced the family below the rank of affluence; but all through his life Fraser was in circumstances which are generally considered comfortable. He was able to go to Oxford upon a scholarship worth only £38 a year, and to spend while in Oxford £200 annually, without incurring any debts. Directly he gained his Fellowship he set up a horse. When Rector of the small college living of Cholderton—where he also took pupils—he contributed £100 to the new church, £300 to new schools, and nearly £200 to rebuilding barns, coach-houses, &c. His mother, who assisted him most liberally in all his parochial schemes, also paid £200 per annum towards house expenses, "so that," as he himself said, "I have a considerable surplus—and shall be able and, I think, justified in putting by £100 a year towards decorating my little country church." He once told a Manchester friend, "It is comparatively easy for me to give donations to good objects, because all my life I have happily been able and accustomed to give."

"James Fraser," writes one well acquainted with the Bishop's personal affairs and manner of life, "was always a most careful man and never wasted a halfpenny, and was a wonderfully sound and clear-headed man of business. When I went through his papers after his death I was struck with his excellent investments, and also with the fact that many of them were in his name as of Oriel, Cholderton, Ufton Nervet, &c., showing that from the time he supported himself he laid by something every year."

He was as economical as he was generous; by never wasting he could both freely give and reasonably accumulate.

No estimate of Bishop Fraser's character can be valuable; no attempt to penetrate to the essence of his life, and to set forth that life, as an inspiration to others, can be thorough, which fails to recognize the true nature of his continuous industry. He was among the most simple and most industrious of men; but neither his simplicity nor his industry was the result of the straitened circumstances of his early life. Both sprang from a source nobler than necessity. When he was working ten hours a day for "the Ireland," * his aim was not the £30 a year, but the University distinction and the fulfilment of a plain duty; and, perhaps, most potent of all, the longing to gratify his widowed mother. "I am reading as hard as I can," he writes, in reference to the approaching examination for an Oriel Fellowship, "but with little prospect of success." When his success was announced, the first letter he wrote began thus:—"My dearest mother, I am delighted to be able to inform you, that you may congratulate your first-born on being this day elected Fellow of Oriel." This incident is typical of Bishop Fraser's whole course of life. When he saw anything to be done he did it; any duty to be performed he performed it; whether the sphere of the duty was small or large. At his first ordination, one of the Archdeacons was asking an old friend of the Bishop's how he accounted for the hold which the Bishop, even then, had taken of the diocese. "The great point about Fraser," was the friend's reply, "is, that if he sees anything needs doing, and he can do it, he does it!" At that moment the door of the room opened, and the Bishop

* Dean Ireland founded his scholarships in Oxford for the "promotion of classical learning and taste." They are worth £30 a year for four years, and are among the Blue Ribands of an Oxford career. A French journal, commenting upon Fraser's appointment to Manchester, in connection with the circumstance that he had been an *Ireland* scholar, said, "Such an appointment is another instance of Mr. Gladstone's desire to conciliate Ireland!"

appeared carrying a coal-scuttle in his hand. He had seen that the fire needed replenishing, and, instead of asking any one else, he got the coals himself. "That," whispered the Bishop's old friend, "is an example of what I mean." This habit of industry and promptitude of action he carried into every department of his Lancashire life.

"Oh," said the Bishop of Carlisle, "how constantly and how cheerfully and manfully he worked! How he made his influence or rather the influence of Christ felt through the mighty city of Manchester and the whole country round! How men who know better than most what work means wondered at him, who seemed to work harder than all and to be never weary, always ready for every effort of intellect, every call of charity, every ecclesiastical or evangelical duty!"

Preaching in 1882 at the public opening of the new buildings of Shrewsbury School, where he had once been himself a pupil, he said—and the utterance is evidently a page of autobiography unfolding the secret motives of his untiring industry, even from the days of boyhood:

"This never was a school for idlers. In my day it was almost Spartan in the fewness of its comforts, the hardness of its discipline. I do not know that it was any the worse preparation for after-life on that account. If we lacked culture in its modern idea, we did not lack earnestness, industry, and a praiseworthy ambition ourselves to contribute something to the reputation of the school. I remember how those honour-boards in the head-master's old room stirred our young hearts with the hope that some day our names too might be enrolled there. How we counted up the distinctions won at the university by some Kennedy or Hillyard, and wondered whether we should ever be able to rival those brilliant careers. And I remember well the boys who were the salt of the school in my time, who made us ashamed of telling a lie or practising a deceit, of being a coward, of meanness of any and every kind. I know what I myself owe, in the way of influence and example, to those boys of stronger and better natures than my own. Arnold's great principle of governing his school through the Sixth Form was not developed among us; but still the best, and bravest, and truest boys were the acknowledged leaders of the rest... And now, boys, I bid you farewell and a 'God speed.' Determine that the New School shall suffer no declension in fame or character at your hands. Be jealous for it, almost, to use a phrase of Paul's, 'with a godly jealousy.' I know you are proud of its reputation; add to that fame new laurels. Above all, maintain among yourselves a high and generous tone. Be real, earnest, brave, truthful, pure. Dark days seem to be threatening our country, and the hope of England in dark days must be in the public spirit of her sons. A genuine patriotism; more purity of domestic and personal life; more simplicity of public manners; more sympathy between class and class; more surrender of private aims to public interests; quicker recognition of the calls of duty—these, and such as those, are qualities we need to sustain the fair name of England, and to hand on to them that come after the noble heritage we have received. Keep these aims before you, as the lode-star of your lives; and you too shall be remembered in your turn as those who, in their generation, added another honourable page to the famous record of the old school."

The Boy-Fraser was the sapling out of which the Bishop-Fraser grew; the same qualities which characterized him at Shrewsbury characterized him also in Manchester. In essence there was no difference between the boy and the Bishop; the difference was only in the stage of development and the sphere of action. The boy was the seed of the Bishop, and the Bishop the fruit of the boy. The Bishop was only the boy upon a large scale. It has been said of Judge Hughes's memoir of him that it is "Tom Brown in Lawn Sleeves." Few biographers have earned so robust a compliment; no Bishop has more richly deserved it. The boy, who was as salt in his school, grew into the Bishop, who was as salt in his church; a Bishop of indefatigable industry, of simplicity of manners; a Bishop who surrendered private aims to public interests, who cultivated sympathy between class and class, who was quick to recognize the calls of duty and careless in measuring the consequences to himself; a thoroughly healthy Bishop, as fresh and straightforward in inward principle as he was strong and erect in outward presence.

It was this open-air healthiness of moral sentiment which made Bishop Fraser almost irresistibly charming. He never had an *arrière pensée*. You might disapprove of what he said and did, but you could not cherish any feeling of vexation against him; for he was always perfectly open and transparent, never keeping anything back.

"When he came to Lancashire," writes a correspondent, "what struck every one was the openness, frankness, almost boyishness—if one may use the term—of his manner and speech. He was utterly unconventional—completely unlike the usual style of bishop. His views and ideas were all his own; and he always spoke evidently from his heart. It was the same in his set speeches and sermons as in his unstudied conversations. He was impulsive in speech, perhaps injudicious and unguarded. He sometimes said things which he afterwards regretted, and sometimes used expressions hastily which he would have afterwards withdrawn. But he seldom or never got into any scrapes by this impulsiveness; because it was evidently so genuine and honest and hearty, that men felt he had a kind of right to say what he liked and to say it as he liked. He was absolutely frank—seemingly careless—in expressing his opinion about people, no matter what their position might be. But somehow his frank speeches never appeared to give offence or to do any harm."

"Perhaps," writes Chancellor Christie, "the most striking point in his character was his absolute and transparent truthfulness. It not only never entered his mind to go a hair's breadth beyond the absolute and perfect truth on every occasion, but he could never bear even to conceal the smallest matter. It was in expressing his own opinions that this characteristic was especially apparent. Whatever his opinion was, and whether it was right or wrong, he was prepared, in season or out of season, to express it in his earnest and most sound manner, nor could he ever be prevailed upon in the slightest degree to modify the open expression of his opinion by representations that it was inexpedient so to state it. I have more than once endeavoured, but unsuccessfully, to induce him in letters to insert some vague phrases of a complimentary nature, but unless they commended themselves to him as entirely and absolutely truthful he never would insert them; he never would use the most trifling conventional phrase unless it expressed in the clearest way his real opinion, nor could he ever be induced in his speeches at societies or committees to speak words of praise or approval such as the promoters or committees desired to be spoken except he was thoroughly satisfied that they were deserved; and, as the habit of his mind was critical as regards details, the promoters of a meeting were always a little nervous when he got up to speak, lest the expected blessing should turn out to be a curse. Of balance sheets and accounts he was an expert critic, not always to the satisfaction of those who had drawn them up, and though his criticisms were never unfair they were always sound."

In season and out of season this truthfulness asserted itself. He could not address a temperance society without confessing that the day before he had been much the better for a glass of bitter beer. If he addressed the Education Union, after stating (with unquestionable truth) that the vast majority of parents desire a religious education for their children, and that the "religious difficulty" was in practice an infinitesimal one, he added: "If a better or simpler formulary than the Church catechism can be found, I am prepared to accept it." On some disputed social questions he was warned that "a dignified neutrality" was the proper attitude for a Bishop; he replied promptly, "A dignified neutrality is not my attitude on any question I think important." But, while the Bishop always expressed in the simplest, clearest, and most decided manner his own opinions, it never entered into his mind to be offended with the like criticisms of his own sentiments made by others. "On one occasion I remember," writes Chancellor Christie, "something he had said at a meeting had been warmly criticised by a gentleman present. A few days after he showed me a note from the gentleman in question, expressing his hope that the Bishop would not be offended by his adverse criticism. The Bishop handed me the letter to read with a smile, saying in his usual off-hand way: 'Why should this fellow think that I should be offended at what he said? he has as much right to his opinions as I have to mine.'"

Closely allied to his open frankness and unhesitating truthfulness was his manifest unselfishness. Had he been more selfish, he must, by the law of correlations in human nature, have been less frank: had he had any aims and ambitions of his own to conceal, the habit of concealment would have induced a habit of greater reserve. But, because he was transparent and all upon the surface himself, he treated other people with a generous candour which postulated that they were transparent and all upon the surface too. To use his own words:

"I do not believe in self-seeking. I have never found a self-seeker either a really happy or a successful man. Men do not like to see a man succeed who in his success thinks of nothing and nobody but himself. I am thankful to know that in these northern counties, more than anywhere else in England perhaps, the public recognition of the heart of a good and right-minded people follows the men who sacrifice themselves for the good of others. I know that the men most honoured in Manchester, for instance, are the men most bent on doing good to their fellow-citizens."

These qualities of unselfishness and truthfulness with which Bishop Fraser was naturally endowed, and which he diligently cultivated to a rare degree, imparted to his conduct the charm of a genuine altruism. He threw himself spontaneously, apparently without effort and yet irresistibly, into the griefs and joys, the needs and interests of others. He had the happy gift of taking everybody to his heart. He was never inattentive. As you talked to him you always felt he was listening and really trying to understand your case. In the light of sympathy you saw yourself reflected in the mirror of his heart.

"You felt sometimes," writes one of his clergy, "almost as if he must have a special liking for you; he was so kind and so much interested in your affairs; yet you knew he was the same towards all men. And how he remembered our names, and our children, and any little incidents he had heard of us!"

Nor did he forget you when you were gone from sight. His was not the cheap sympathy of an outward manner, but the true emotion of the inward self. To your surprise, when you had left Bishop Fraser with a sense of shame at having occupied, in your interview, so much of his overcrowded time, you would find the next morning a letter upon your table giving his fuller and more mature opinion of your plans or course of action. "Out of sight," you were not with Bishop Fraser "out of mind." Indeed, some of his kindest actions, as his correspondence shows, were done to people whom he had never seen, but of whose necessities he had indirectly heard. Not being engrossed with schemes and ambitions of his own, his heart was at leisure from itself to soothe and to sympathize with the sorrows and necessities of others. Even at the meridian of his joys he was thoughtful and compassionate. The following letter was written by him two days after his marriage to a young friend whom he seldom saw and who had no sort of claim, either of kinship or neighbourhood, upon the Bishop's sympathy:

BELGRAVE HOTEL, TORQUAY, *January* 17, 1880

MY DEAR YOUNG FRIEND,—With what sorrow, in the midst of my own deep and strong joy, did I read that announcement in the *Times* of yesterday of the dark sad shadow that has fallen upon that which I so well remember as your bright and happy home, bearing as it did in every detail the impress of that gentle womanly presence which now it knows no more.

It is no mere form of words when I say you have my own and, I may add, my wife's true sympathy. She knows of you and has heard of you, through that Mrs. M———, to whose husband you were so kind a friend, as I believe you have since been to her. Our feelings for you were awakened together as I read aloud after breakfast this morning the sad lines in the *Times* announcing your wife's death. Thank God, one's own sense of happiness is not always of a selfish character; and this is perhaps why at this moment my heart seems especially touched by the sorrow of one called to give up a treasure, the preciousness of which he knew, and which I have so recently gained. May He, Who alone can, give you of His exceeding and sufficing comfort. Believe me, my dear young friend, yours sincerely and affectionately,

J. MANCHESTER.

This complete unselfishness gave Bishop Fraser great *intellectual roominess*. Roominess (if the term be admissible) was one of his most remarkable characteristics. His hospitable mind could supply room and lodgment for everything; from the cedar in Lebanon to the hyssop on the wall. No subject came amiss to him. To-day he presides over a Diocesan Conference, to-morrow he goes upon a trip with the Mayor of Manchester to survey the Thirlmere watershed, and the next day he sits as arbitrator in some wage-dispute between employers and employed. Many-sidedness of intellectual interest is not unfrequently a source of intellectual feebleness and dissipation; breadth being unaccompanied by depth, variety relaxing tenacity, and largeness of view ending in shallowness of penetration. When a man spreads his intellect over many things, of necessity he sometimes spreads it very thin. This was Bishop Fraser's danger: nor was he always successful in escaping it. He himself would have been the first to acknowledge this infirmity. Many of his utterances were ephemeral: they were as sparks in the forge, showers of radiant coruscation, pleasant and beautiful for the moment, but soon lost in darkness and forgotten. Indeed he never posed as a profound thinker. His career at Oxford was successful, almost brilliant; but, in after life, he laid little claim to the erudition of a scholar.

He knew Greek well; but he was among the last men in the world to have composed a laborious theme upon Greek particles. He was often, and by the necessity of his much speaking, superficial; but he was never, by purpose or intention, a smatterer. No man could have set himself more determinedly against intellectual softness and frivolity; or have insisted more strenuously upon the importance of discipline, hardness, and concentration of mind than Bishop Fraser.

If sometimes his information was superficial, yet his feeling was always profound. From his lips people liked to hear the repetition even of commonplace sentiments, because of the earnestness and singleness of purpose with which his sentiments were invariably inspired. The University Church was always crowded when he preached in Oxford; and in the vast congregations could be seen, eagerly listening, many of Oxford's ripest scholars and profoundest thinkers—men at whose feet he himself would humbly have sat as a disciple. One of these great scholars being asked why he always went to hear Bishop Fraser preach, replied, " We go to hear Fraser not for *information*, but for *inspiration. He is an inspiring man.*" His evident seriousness of purpose, his contagious enthusiasm for humanity, his downright belief in God, redeemed his many-sidedness from its frequently accompanying vices. There was no indifference, no aimlessness, no half-belief in him—his intellect was broad, but his heart was deep.

"I am not at all sure," he said, "that the very highest form of greatness, though not perhaps the most brilliant, is not that which elevates mankind not materially, nor intellectually, nor even politically and socially, but *morally.* The greatness that is felt as an influence on the side of goodness; that vindicates virtue; that represses vice; that makes men hear the voice—or, if they will not hear the voice, makes them feel the sting—of conscience; that keeps in awe the scoffer, the ribald, the foul-tongued, the scurrilous, the infidel—*that*, in my judgment, is true greatness."

Another characteristic which distinguished Bishop Fraser in a remarkable degree was his faculty of observation.

Nothing was too trivial to escape his notice and care. He kept all his accounts to a penny; he took an interest in all the arrangements of the house; he was particular about his dress. And the same faculty which made him observant of his own person and home made him observant also of the persons and homes of others. The moment he laid his eye upon you, you felt he had scanned you completely from head to foot. When he entered your house he seemed to see everything without noticeably looking at anything. If you sent him a report of an institution or society, he appeared, by a sort of instinct, to perceive immediately the important details. When he came to preach in your church he generally made you feel, by some gesture or remark, what his opinion of your service was; and whether your church was slovenly or well tended. His observation, however, was not the observation of the critic, far less of the cynic; it was simply the observation of the keen and interested man. This habit of quickly noticing and kindly commenting upon everything made you soon and completely at ease and at home with him. You could not feel strange or aloof from the man who laid his hand on your shoulder and began the conversation by genially advising you "to get a new hat"; or asking "who painted your picture," and "where you got that pretty little vase from." As a guest in the house he was perfectly delightful. It occasionally happens that Bishops are not easy persons to entertain; the very look of a Bishop is, at times, oppressive and silencing. But Bishop Fraser soon succeeded in making you forget his lawn-sleeves, his apron and hat, by his obvious interest in you and your affairs. He was a singularly interesting, because a singularly interested, man. If he stayed a day in your house he knew all about you, your children, your servants, your pictures, your garden, your stables, before he went away. He dandled children upon his knee. "What would you like to be, my little man?" he once asked a rosy-cheeked boy of four years old who was riding on his knee. The boy, undismayed by either apron or gaiters, and simply charmed by their wearer, replied: "I should like to be a bishock." "A Bishop!" laughed Fraser. Then the pensiveness gathered over his face and he added: "If you had tried it for ten years, I think you would change your mind." In the same simple way he would talk to your wife about all her domestic interests, walk with her in the garden and tell her "not to plant her peas so deep;" and to "pick off the faded rhododendron flowers;" and when he was gone she would tell you "the Bishop was the most courteous, the most charming guest she had ever entertained."

He was as genial in the street as in the house. His open face, and dignified yet pleasant bearing, as he strode along the streets of Manchester, bag in hand, won for him hundreds of friends, who never had an opportunity of speaking a single word to him. If you happened to walk with him through the streets of a Lancashire town—a feat not easy to accomplish unless you were a quick walker—it was almost pathetic to watch the eyes of the passers-by, upturned to their Bishop, not in idle curiosity, but in admiring love. When he said "Good morning," there was a ring in his voice, which made music in your heart. His "How-do-you-do?" was irresistible. It was true good-nature and simplicity. It was not the mere salutation of "Hail, fellow! well met," which often means nothing; but the "All-hail" of true greeting, which implies a sense of esteem and brotherhood. His popularity arose, not so much from heartiness of manner, as from the conviction that his heartiness of manner was the index of his good and generous feeling.

"He did not morbidly meditate on his own feelings; being a man mainly of action. Nor did he fight against his natural bent to joy as though it were sinful to be joyous; but took thankfully the gift of God and made the most of it for his own sake and that of others. By keeping his child's heart to the end in spite of the cares and troubles of a diocese, both large and responsible, he continued to be, though ever gaining in grace, in the main the same man, and will be remembered for many a day as the 'joyous Bishop.'"

Bishop Fraser's hospitality was like his greeting; it had nothing conventional about it, and nothing forced. It was a great treat to spend a few days at Bishop's Court. This volume will unfold at a later page the exquisite naturalness of his home-life; but an introductory sketch of his personal character would be notably incomplete which made no mention of his hospitality. His was the genuine hospitality of the heart. He ran to meet you at the door, helped you to take off your coat, stirred the fire, and poured out the tea for you. And how he chatted! It was wonderful to listen to the ease, the variety, the vigour of his conversation. Upon his shoulders lay the weight of the second largest diocese in England; yet so remarkable was his power of mental detachment that, amid many cares and responsibilities, he had all the lightness and all the grace of a leisurely country gentleman. His table was ever most generously supplied; but it never groaned beneath the weight of luxuries or dishes out of season.

Luxury was one of his deepest aversions. He saw clearly the demoralization caused by luxury, and, both in word and act, he set his face steadfastly against luxury in every form. He delighted in bounty, in refinement, in elegance; but he simply hated all vulgarity of display. His estimation of things was fixed not by their market-value, but by their intrinsic worth. He preferred to take a dish of tea with a poor curate who was unselfishly struggling amid poverty to elevate his flock, than to dine off gold plate with a self-indulgent, extravagant millionaire. Upon one occasion he said:

"I never visit the Peel Park at Manchester without thinking what an amount of wisdom there is in the few words inscribed on the statue of Mr. Joseph Brotherton, who had been member for Salford—'My wealth consisted not in the largeness of my means, but in the fewness of my wants.' I am quite certain there is no system of life more likely to lead to disappointment than to surround ourselves with things which to begin with are luxuries, but soon get to be necessities. Many of us have been so long in the habit of surrounding ourselves with luxuries that if we were deprived of them we should think we were actually suffering a wrong; although perhaps twenty years ago they were luxuries beyond our reach, even in our wildest dreams."

Again, in an address delivered to an overflow meeting of

working men at the Sheffield Church Congress, October 3, 1878, he said:

"I am quite sure that the simpler our lives are the happier they will be. I am sure that no man ever made his life really richer or brighter or happier by surrounding himself with artificial wants and superfluous luxury. What is a luxury to-day becomes a necessity to-morrow. Those who are your true friends regret more than anything else that habits of thrift have not yet made their way amongst the working classes of this country to the same extent as in almost every other country. I am afraid there is a very large number who are unthrifty. When times were good and wages were running high, perhaps you spent too much money on things which you once never dreamt of, and which now, I dare say, you can hardly do without. The wealthiest, as well as the poorest, classes in this country may have some very severe strains put upon them in the course of the years that are coming on; may have to leave the country, or to live harder lives than they have been accustomed to live, and may have to cut off a great many of those superfluities in which they have of late years been indulging. During the last five or six years all classes in this country have been spending a great deal too much money."

One story in relation to simplicity of life, associated with largeness of heart, Bishop Fraser was very fond of telling. The following account of the story has been supplied by the pen of a trustworthy correspondent:

"I remember well, soon after Bishop Fraser came into the diocese, that he had to consecrate one of the finest, handsomest churches in South Lancashire, built at a cost of £20,000. A week or two afterwards, I met him at the dinner-table of a friend. He was lost in amazement at what he called an extraordinary peculiarity of the Lancashire character, *i.e.* the simplicity and homeliness of the lives of many of those who made large gifts for public and religious charities.

"'I got out at B—— Station,' he said, 'and after a sharp walk of twenty minutes came in sight of the church at the distance of about a mile. I was struck even then with its nobility. "Can you tell me where Mr. W—— lives," I inquired of a pedestrian, "the gentleman who has built this noble church?" "Oh, ay, it's yon cottage against yon bank." Thinking there was some mistake, I went on, and presently overtook a girl in Sunday attire, "Can you tell me where Mr. W—— lives, who built this noble church?" "That's it," she replied pointing to the same unpretentious cottage, "I'm going to th' consecration."

"'Still I considered there was an error somewhere, but made my way to the door. An old woman, simply but respectably dressed, answered my knock. I dared not ask if Mr. W—— was in! I repeated my question, "Can you tell me where Mr. W—— lives, who built this noble church?"

"Oh, you're the Bishop are you? He's bein' expecting on you—Come forrard, you'll find him i' th' kitchen." Ushered into the kitchen I found an old, but fine-looking man sitting by the fire smoking a churchwarden pipe. "So you've come, have you," said the smoker, "Nowt like being in good time—There'll be a snack of something when you've done." "You have done nobly by the district, Mr. W——," I said, seizing his hand and giving it a hearty grasp. He gave me an equally hearty squeeze, but seemed surprised. "Naw, naw," he said, "I made the population with my mills, so I mun do my duty by them."'

"'In the South of England,' continued the Bishop, 'such a gift, and such a function would have brought the whole county society together, and the donor would have been the recipient of unbounded admiration and praise. It was a new experience.'"

Few men have dreaded more deeply than Bishop Fraser the weakening and deteriorating effect of self-indulging wealth, and the absolute necessity, in the interests of moral and spiritual growth, for cultivating simplicity of habits and bounteousness of liberality in proportion to the increase and accumulation of goods. His robustness and healthiness of mind, his keen sense of proportion both in morals and religion, preserved him from the rigours and extravagances of asceticism. No one could have been less of an ascetic, either by temperament or conviction, than Bishop Fraser; yet he was, both by nature and upon principle, a plain, simple, self-restraining man. "The more simply I live myself," he said, "the better able I shall be to encourage simplicity of living in others."

At the close of a sermon preached in Westminster Abbey June 2nd, 1878, he said:

"O you, who would be valiant for truth, good soldiers of Christ, doing something to stay the inroads of selfishness and frivolity and vice, practise simplicity, and do not cease to believe in goodness—not the mere ethical goodness of the heathen schools (though that was not wholly impotent to produce results), but the same faculty of the human soul when it has been touched by, and conformed to, the example of Him who went about doing good and healing every one that was oppressed. If once the hearts of men, under the over-mastering influences of a self-idolizing and luxurious age, cease to recognize the beauty of this Divine Ideal, and to be attracted by it, then indeed peace, like the fabled Astræa, will be found only in heaven, and the earth must be left to its self-created confusions from which every pure and quiet soul will desire to flee away.

"The Church must go forth to meet the problems of the future. I have no theory for solving them. But I have unlimited faith in the power of simple goodness, trusting in an arm stronger than its own."

Bishop Fraser's simplicity was closely connected with his directness. He had a strong distaste for anything roundabout. He loved to go straight to the point. Sometimes his way of going straight to the point was perplexing to his friends. His questions generally admitted of but one answer, either a simple "Yes," or a simple "No." It was impossible to be with the Bishop for any length of time without being asked, often suddenly, and always directly—"What do you think of ——? Isn't he rather idle? Does he get on well with his people? Would he do well for such a parish?" By the road-side, in the railway-carriage, at the dinner-table, he was always bent upon picking up information by direct questions which it was difficult to shirk. As events proved, the information thus acquired occasionally misled him in his estimation of persons. There is a charm about a direct question; but a sudden answer often needs much salting.

Bishop Fraser hated fencing and qualifications. He had few twilight fancies; most facts were either bright as day or black as night to him. Niceties of philosophic speculation, the cloud-shadows of poetic feeling, the refinements of theological doctrine had no charm for him; they were either unintelligible to him or disagreeable. This characteristic directness had both its disadvantages and advantages. Among its disadvantages were a partial inability to understand minds less clear and prompt than his own; a natural impatience of speculative and doctrinal distinctions; a somewhat rough-and-ready way of disposing of difficulties. But his directness brought the advantage of rendering his own nature and purposes lucid and transparent. He might misunderstand others; but no one had any excuse for misunderstanding him. His whole self lay open as the day. This was among his greatest charms, and especially with the poor. His utterances were plain and direct; they were shorn of all the mystic drapery which delights the philosopher and theologian; but they set forth truth visibly and boldly to the common people. Bishop Fraser might be mistaken in his views; but he was never obscure. Right or wrong, he was always clear. He never darkened counsel with words, or used language as a cloak to cover intention. In all he said he had a direct and practical aim. Soon after he was ordained, he wrote to his mother:

> "I wish you and Aunt Lucy would give me your candid opinion about my sermons; do you think the language plain and intelligible to ordinary minds, as well as sufficiently definite and practical? how far do you think my sermons adapted to awaken a hearer, and lead him to apply what is said to himself? I want my sermons to be useful to others, and not a display of any learning or eloquence of my own."

Bishop Fraser was very successful in achieving this aim —the aim of inducing his hearers to apply his sayings to themselves. A very thoughtful, well-educated man being asked, "What is the effect of Bishop Fraser's preaching on you?" "The general effect," he replied, "is, that I go from Church resolving to try *and practise* in my life what he preaches."

Bishop Fraser is well said by Professor Bryce, himself a keen observer of men and intimately associated with Mr. Fraser in educational work, to have "created a new and admirable type of English bishop." There are several distinct types of bishop. There is the old Court-Bishop: the highly cultivated gentleman, with exquisite refinement of manner, polished and elegant, quietly and gracefully dignifying religion in the high places of the earth. There is the Grammar-Bishop: profound upon particles and various readings, industrious in deciphering manuscripts, proud of his store of literary curiosities, but more at home among books than men. There is the Gladiator-Bishop: the mere party man, the pugilist of the platform, the advocate of a school, who has lost in the hot conflicts of theological battle both the power of large sympathy and the irresistible sweetness of a reasonable mind. There is the Schoolmaster-Bishop: more accustomed to command than persuade, whose chief concern is good discipline, and with whom familiarity is of the nature of offence. There is the Statesman-Bishop: the man capable of instituting reforms, wise in administration, long-sighted in suggestion, weighty in Parliament, trusted by the people. There is the Saint-Bishop: the man of deep inward piety, of sweet, lofty yearnings, not always worldly-wise, but always spreading around him a rich, hallowing influence. Bishop Fraser did not belong to any of these well-known and frequently recurring types of bishop. Bishop Fraser was the *Citizen-Bishop:* the lawn-sleeved citizen, the prince and leader in every movement of civic improvement, civic elevation, civic righteousness. This was his distinguishing characteristic as a bishop. He was not only the Chief Churchman in Manchester—he was also Manchester's Premier Citizen. He threw himself, heart and soul, into the *civic* life of his diocese. Mayors and Corporations were not less interesting to him than Archdeacons and Rural Deans. He cared for well-ventilated rooms and good drainage and pure water, as well as for church-building and lay-readers and mission-women. He threw the spirit of religion into every manner of good and useful work. With him things secular were not on one side of the hedge and things sacred on the other; both were comprised in the one field of a good citizen's interest.

"With Fraser," writes Professor Wilkins, "body, head, and heart were alike in the nineteenth century. He was always ready to bear his witness for the Christian faith; but it was almost always as bringing the only solution to those social problems which pressed upon his heart so heavily. He spoke of it as an evil hour when the Church thought itself obliged to add to or develop the simple articles of the Apostles' Creed. 'Without relaxing my hold,' he said, 'on what I believe to be the great truths of Christianity, I still feel that the great function of Christianity is to elevate man in his *social* condition.'"

No cause came amiss to him, if so be it were only good. He was to be found at all sorts of meetings, promoting all manner of civic interests, talking upon any topic which bore upon the welfare of the community. The newspapers soon found him out and insisted upon reporting him. The mass of newspaper-cuttings which record his utterances is simply enormous—probably all the bishops on the English Bench taken together did not fill the same amount of newspaper space from 1870-1885 as he filled singly and alone. Not that he courted the newspapers; they courted him. The reporters called him, among themselves, by the familiar name of "Jemmy," because they loved him. Reporters see a great deal of the vanity of human nature, and are apt to be incredulous of mankind; but they believed in Bishop Fraser; they saw him almost every day, and they trusted him. He was perpetually going in and out among the people. Whenever he was announced to speak they flocked to hear; whatever speech was reported they read with interest, because it was rare to find any speech of his not inspired by some breath of true and noble citizenship.

Bishop Fraser's conspicuous devotion to the civic welfare was partly the result of natural taste and temperament, and partly the result of assiduous training. Few men have had so remarkable a preparation for the episcopate as Bishop Fraser. His was not the preparation of the schoolmaster or the college don; of the country rector, or the metropolitan preacher; it was pre-eminently the preparation of the parliamentary commissioner. He worked upon four commissions; each commission being associated with the question of education. In the course of his inquiries he became acquainted with the minds of men and the condition of things, both in England and America. Each succeeding commission broadened his interests in the life of the nation, and enlarged his knowledge of that life. The result of the four commissions was to thoroughly humanize and laicize his sympathies. Such work as this, done with his thoroughness, and in his spirit, raised him to the greatness of the public-spirited citizen. As the mind of the young statesman is emancipated by travel in distant countries, and residence at foreign courts, from a too severe bondage in the fetters of political party, so, judging from the beneficent result in Bishop Fraser's case, it would seem well that the young clergyman should be set, for a while, to some layman's work, or some civic task, that his mind may be strengthened against the narrowing influences of clericalism. If Bishop Fraser's training had been purely theological, it is scarcely doubtful that his episcopate would have been both less famous and less useful. It was his knowledge of men and acquaintance with affairs, and splendour of public spirit, that made his Lancashire Life so grand and strong. He merged his distinction as a Bishop in his devotion as a Citizen. The Bishop's heart was with the people, and the people's heart was toward their Bishop. In a great community like the English Church there is room and need for more than one type of bishop; but if the type created by Bishop Fraser is largely cultivated the perils besetting the English Church will be largely diminished. A candidate for parliamentary honours, who, for some time, had been wooing a constituency in south-east Lancashire, in the interests of the Liberation Society, is reported to have relinquished all hopes of success on the ground that the Liberation programme was dead in south-east Lancashire. Being asked, "Who killed it?" he gave the emphatic reply, "Fraser!"

But, although Bishop Fraser was a keen-spirited citizen enthusiastically interested in every department of civic life, yet he seldom engaged in the conflicts of political parties. In an address delivered to the *employés* of the London and North-Western Railway in the Goods' Station, London Road, Manchester, April 25th, 1871:

"My complaint against politics is their extreme unfairness—men do not give others credit for the same sincerity they ask for themselves. Political articles in the newspapers too frequently fail to give credit for fair dealing and sincerity. I will tell you what politics properly mean. They do not mean being a Conservative or a Radical, belonging to a Liberal or a Tory club; but they mean seeking the best interests of the nation, the greatest happiness of the greatest number, by every legitimate means. That was what political science meant when Plato and Aristotle taught it. And Christianity teaches such things as these: it teaches public spirit, patriotism, and obedience to the law. Above all things, it teaches men to be fair towards their opponents, and to discountenance all mean and pitiful ambitions. What does it matter who is prime minister of England so long as whoever fills that high position is seeking the best interests of the people? I am neither a Conservative nor a Liberal; I hardly ever gave a vote at an election in my life; but I do desire that the country shall be governed by men, come from what side of the House they may, who are trying to promote the greatest happiness of the greatest number. Do you think Christ would say that a man who offered or took a bribe was acting in the spirit of His Gospel? He would have spurned such a man from His presence. Christianity, if more widely diffused, would purge our political atmosphere, as it has purged our moral and social atmosphere."

Again, in his Presidential Address, delivered at the Salt Schools, Shipley, Yorkshire, November 27th, 1884:

"As I have been speaking of politics, I will say a word, which I have said before in other places, about political clubs. Of course, the leaders of parties profess to rejoice at their establishment, and make grand speeches when they are opened. But knowing what political clubs have done in other constitutions, both in ancient and modern times, in the democracy of Athens and in the democracy of Paris, I cannot pretend to share the satisfaction. Of course their usefulness consists in their being a machinery to enable the wirepullers of a party to have greater command over those who follow their leaders like sheep; but even in this aspect I doubt if they tend to develop, I will not say political moderation—for that they do not pretend to do—but even political intelligence. And in too many instances I know—as is the case with many working men's clubs, from which I once hoped better things—they degenerate into mere haunts for a class of loafers, who want a place where they can booze, or smoke, or bet, or play billiards; and only at the time of a contested election is their political influence, such as it is, felt or exercised at all. I cannot but regard them as hindrances, and not helps, in the way of forming the temper which I have called 'fairness of mind.'"

It must be admitted that there is a better and nobler side of politics and political clubs than the side here exposed, and in an address delivered to working men at the Sheffield Church Congress, October 3rd, 1878, Bishop Fraser clearly confessed this nobler side, and duly claimed for the clergy their right to take a share in political matters; at the same time warning them against the peril of sinking to the level of mere political partizanship:

"The clergy are but men, and I dare say a majority of them—I am not sure it is not also true of the majority of the working classes in Sheffield—belong to the conservative party, because they have a good thing to conserve; and everybody who feels he has got a good thing to conserve must be a conservative. I don't mean to say that the clergy have always been enlightened in their political views, or even in their social aims. Since I have been in Manchester I have had a very difficult part to play. There is nothing that I have endeavoured to keep more clear of than party politics. But I do feel that there are great questions of political principles which it does seem to me that Christianity, if it is to touch human life at one of its most salient points, ought to concern itself, and with which I have had no scruple to meddle, whether wisely or unwisely. I felt I was in my place, as bishop, in taking a little part in the movement connected with the agricultural labourers; and I also do not think I was moving out of my sphere when I tried, perhaps not successfully, to bring to an end, upon terms of mutual confidence and sympathy, the unhappy strike which for nine weeks last spring made so many looms and spindles in Lancashire silent. These questions surely are questions in which the clergy have a right to meddle; but at the same time I should be extremely sorry—in fact, it has been a reproach, justly or unjustly, levelled at the Church of England—to see the clergy of the Church of England as a body, decidedly and emphatically, political partizans. I don't think you want them to be that. I don't think that people go to church on Sundays to be indoctrinated with partizan politics. But I do think that in view of, we will say, a contested election, it is a perfectly legitimate thing for a clergyman to place before his people those great outlines of national duty and true patriotism which ought to make a man ashamed of selling his vote for a bribe, or giving it otherwise than according to the best of his understanding, or the guidance of his conscience. That is not a question of partizan politics."

And as in political, so also in ecclesiastical affairs, Bishop Fraser eschewed the narrowness of mere partizanship. He belonged exclusively to no single party in the Church.* In the early part of his ministerial life he was chaplain and chancellor to the saintly, and High Church, Bishop Hamilton of Salisbury; among his most intimate friends he counted the comprehensive and Broad Church Dean Stanley of Westminster; while some of his most thoroughly trusted and warmly esteemed clergy, during the period of his Episcopate, belonged to the Evangelical School. Wherever Bishop Fraser saw goodness, reverence, truth, he recognized and loved it. He was pre-eminently an Evangelical High Churchman with Broad Church sympathies. He admired the width and progressiveness of the Broad Church

---

* "I wish you were not so Low," he laughingly said to the late Canon Bardsley. "And I wish your lordship were not so Broad," was the merry rejoinder.

leaders; he inculcated the liturgical and reverential spirit of the High Church leaders; he was jealous, after a godly sort, of the spirituality of temper which characterizes the Evangelical leaders. He attached himself to no single one of the three great parties of the English Church lest he should, by so doing, weaken in his own character the distinctive qualities belonging to the other two. He was, in the best and highest sense of the term, a simple Catholic Churchman; and the result upon his diocese of his appreciative catholicity was remarkable.

"When Bishop Fraser was consecrated at the cathedral," writes a Manchester correspondent, "the minds of the clergy were largely exercised as to whether they should wear surplices or gowns. *Nous avons changé tout cela.* There is now a united diocese. Clergy and people are one in their interest in Church matters. There are practically no Church parties in the diocese now. There are a few extreme men on both sides still among us—but they are few in number and of no practical influence. We are Churchmen now, Churchmen pure and simple without any distinguishing partizanship. All this change was the work of Bishop Fraser."

In simple, comprehensive, earnest Churchmanship, Bishop Fraser seemed to find the strongest anchor for Christianity amid the storms which are perpetually raging on every side:

"I see," he said, "advancing on the one side with gigantic strides the spirit of scepticism and infidelity, and on the other side with almost equally rapid strides that gigantic system of spiritual domination of which we have the highest example in the Church of Rome, and which some, I fear, are more or less endeavouring to introduce into the Church of England. In face of these great and menacing dangers, I think that Englishmen will do well to consider how far their national Church, with her historic faith, with her apostolic organization, with her simple and beautiful forms of worship, with her sober, calm, and moderate mind—how far she may not be the safest meeting-ground for earnest and devout men who would gather together and present a firm and serried front; men whose faith is grounded upon a reasonable interpretation of God's word and a rational adhesion to historic evidence; men who desire to oppose on one side the spirit of latitudinarianism, scepticism, and infidelity, and on the other side the spirit of priestcraft, sacerdotalism, and spiritual aggression and domination.

"To those who appreciate the value of a solid basis for unity—of a primitive and apostolic form of government—of the security that is given to law by freedom—of a ritual at once sober and reverent—of a liturgy breathing the very spirit of a devout and chastened piety—of a parochial system which, if truly carried out, would be the perfection of an ecclesiastical organization—the Church of England can commend herself on solid and sufficient grounds."

"Bishop Fraser,"* says Professor Bryce, "usually struck one as a moderate High Churchman of the older and distinctly non-Roman type, a High Churchman unconsciously verging towards what would be called a Broad Church position; with no great taste either for scientific theology or ecclesiastical history; always maintaining the claim of the Anglican Church to undertake the education of the people, and upholding her status as an establishment, but dwelling very little on minor points of doctrinal difference, and seeming to care still less for external observances or matters of ritual."

There were few sentences more frequently upon his lips than the opening sentence of Keble's Advertisement to 'The Christian Year':

"Next to a sound rule of faith, there is nothing of so much consequence as a sober standard of feeling in matters of practical religion: and it is the peculiar happiness of the Church of England to possess, in her authorized formularies, an ample and sure provision for both."

As Bishop Fraser's Churchmanship was comprehensive rather than exclusive, so his theology was spiritual rather than scientific:

"Christianity," he said, "has been too much elaborated into a system or a philosophy. Erudite treatises, forcible arguments may have done much in support of the faith; but a holy life does more.

"Grant me a right to believe in a personal God—in a living Christ—in an indwelling spirit; and, like that ship driven up and down in Adria, upon which no small tempest lay, I shall have, as it were, my four anchors cast out of the stern, while I wait for the day.

"As I survey the phenomena of the age, the chief fear in my mind for the future of religion is lest it should get dissevered from morality; lest it should become a matter of dogma and ritual, that is, of opinion and sentiment rather than a principle of conduct. It has been truly said that 'Conduct is three-fourths of life.' It is the main affair. Orthodoxy is good, but morality is better. We have need to close our ranks in defence of virtue. Morals and religion have more to fear from those who attempt to discredit the Sermon on the Mount than from those who express (not always, it is true, in such measured language as one could desire) their dislike of the seeming hardness of some of the statements of the Athanasian Creed. Do not suppose that to preach morality is to empty the Gospel of the grace of God of its proper power, or to supplement the work of Christ by a righteousness of our own. The moral nature of

* Judge Hughes' 'Memoir of James Fraser,' p. 395.

man is the true subject of grace: and Christ is only truly Lord when He is thoroughly obeyed."

In his address to working men at the Sheffield Church Congress, Bishop Fraser said:

"I just want to bring before you, as plainly as I can, what seem to me at any rate the fundamental principles of Christianity. They are very few. Men have multiplied them, no doubt; and there are those who say that there are something like seven hundred theological propositions in the thirty-nine Articles of the Church of England; and I suppose there are a great many more than seven hundred theological propositions in the Westminster Confession; and certainly there are in the dogmatic statements of other religious communities. When my Bible tells me that Christ came to make a simple way to heaven, in which a wayfaring man, though a fool, should not err; when we are told that He came to preach the Gospel to the poor, and that the common people heard Him gladly; when we read the practical utterances preserved in the 5th, 6th, and 7th chapters of St. Matthew, or even the deeper and mysterious utterances in the Upper Chamber of Jerusalem—will any one attempt to persuade me that it is necessary for any man, for the life of his soul, to subscribe to seven hundred theological propositions? When men have lost all sense of proportion, sometimes that which is minutest and least important is made more of than the principle that covers and embraces all. When Paul would tell me what is the gospel I ought to preach if I would be a follower of him, he speaks of the fundamental principles of repentance towards God and faith towards Christ—matters about which no living Christian men have two opinions; and we ought to labour to bring men back to the simplicity which is in Christ Jesus, and to the rudimentary truths which all acknowledge, though they do not obey them. I want to see Christianity more human. I want to see it dealing less with pictures of hell and heaven; and more with the difficulties and trials and temptations of this present life. I know very little about the world beyond the grave. I do not know as much as I wish to know about this world in which I am living and moving. I want to see Christianity a good deal more human than in these later days it has been made to be. Christianity in Christ's hands was profoundly human; profoundly sympathetic; profoundly helpful. It was only now and then He threw aside the curtain, and pictured to us a state of bliss equal to the angels—no more death, and the like. Just now and then the curtain was for a moment drawn aside, and we are, as it were, permitted to see a few of the mysteries of the life of the world to come. But even then those revelations are veiled in language which we cannot understand. I do not know what an angel is, therefore I cannot very well understand what is meant by 'equal to an angel.' I do not know what God is like. No human eyes have ever seen Him; and therefore I cannot pretend to say I understand what is meant when it is told me, 'I shall be like God.' I believe in some respects I am like God now, in all the better portion of my nature; in all my highest thoughts; in all my noblest yearnings. If I am not like God, then what am I like? Surely not like the devil, when I am reaching after truth and righteousness? Surely I am not like my own feeble nature, left to itself, when I am struggling, and struggling successfully, against temptation? I may not know what it is to be like God, but I seem to know, it is a truth written most plainly on my heart, that if I am reaching after whatever things are true, and holy, and of good report, then, certainly, I am reaching after that image, at any rate, of the Redeemer which He came in His love and compassion to set before the world. Many other things may be uncertain, but there is one thing of which I seem to be certain. It is that moral truth is a higher thing than speculative truth; that righteousness is a nobler and grander thing than orthodoxy; and what we have to strive after is, if we can, and God helping us we can, to make the world happier and nobler, by making it better and purer."

Yet, although Bishop Fraser was rendered averse to narrow dogmatism by the quality of his temperament, the course of his training, the nature of his interests, and the simplicity of his faith, still he had a clear and strong perception of the value of dogma both to the organization of the Church and the stability of her life. He was not an analytic, speculative, Churchman; but he was a decidedly doctrinal Christian. He clung most tenaciously to what Scotchmen call "the fundamentals," and was ever ready to do battle on their behalf. To him the very idea of Christianity without creed appeared untenable; a creedless Church, he thought, was amorphous, unstable, impotent. His favourite description of Christianity was a "simple, reasonable faith, having also a dogmatic basis."

Preaching at Holmfirth in December, 1875, he said:

"I think we must see that on either side men are running into extremes, between which the Church of England has chosen the middle path, which I think is the path of truth and soberness. The two extremes on either side of the Church of England are the extremes which are represented by the Church of Rome on the one hand, and the extremes which are represented—I hope I am not going to offend, because I do not mean it in the spirit of offensiveness—by the principle of Nonconformity on the other. Take the extreme represented by the Church of Rome. By the decree of its Vatican Council five years ago, it concentrated the claims of infallibility in the person of its chief bishop. I need not remind you that this is an extreme from which St. Paul most distinctly shrank when he told the Corinthians that he did not claim to have dominion over their faith. On the other hand, there is the extreme which I call the principle of Nonconformity. If I understand that principle aright, it is this, that everybody is at liberty to believe whatever he pleases in matters of religion. The liberty of private judgment, as proclaimed by the Reformation, was a great principle; but it is an unfettered and irresponsible liberty of private judgment that is claimed, so far as I understand the matter, by the principle of Nonconformity, because, if, as they say, conscience is the ultimate tribunal, it is perfectly plain that no one has a right to come in and interfere with that final court of judicature. Now, the Church of England has not maintained the absolute and irresponsible liberty of private judgment. Of course, the final appeal must ultimately be to the man's own individual reason and conscience; but conscience and reason are governed by many considerations. I should not set up my judgment in the matter of medicine, which I have not studied, against the judgment of a competent medical practitioner. If I were called in by a man of business to give an opinion upon the strength of materials or the best mode of carrying out a complicated piece of engineering, I should feel myself most utterly incompetent to give a judgment, and should submit my reason to those who are better informed upon the subject. In other words, if there is such a thing as theology, if Christianity is represented as a scientific form of truth, if it is not a mere floating mass of feeling and emotion, if it has a history, a development, and a "law of progress," it is perfectly plain that everybody, well-informed and ill-informed alike, is not equally competent to pass a judgment upon matters of such momentous concern: and therefore the Church of England holds that the Church has authority in controversies of faith. I remember noticing not long ago an utterance of an eminent Nonconformist minister in my own diocese, who said that no one attending his chapel was ever called upon to utter the words 'I believe'; in other words, every man's individual belief was a matter of his own concern, and the Church did not put before him as an historic fact that Christianity had any creed at all. Now, I think that upon that basis it is perfectly plain the result must ultimately be chaos. I think that the disintegration of Christian belief amongst us is largely due to the acceptance of this principle."

In a similar strain he spoke at St. Mary's Church, Crumpsall, in April, 1876:

"It has been said that the day has gone by for creeds, that the invention of printing has sealed their doom, that they are the products of darkness and of ignorance, and that now it is only necessary to put the Scriptures into the hands of the people. But as Churchmen we feel we need a creed —something which should put in simple language what we believe. It is not the positiveness of ignorance but the desire to have a definite standing-ground for faith that has given birth to creeds. No doubt creeds have been used as battle cries, but that is not their proper purpose. They are meant to be the bonds of brotherhood, the seals of Christian unity, the watchwords of a common faith and a common hope, the *qui va là*, as it were, by which in the darkness of the night one recognizes a brother and a friend. There is a wide difference between the creeds of Nice and Constantinople, and the Westminster Confession and the Thirty-nine Articles, and if there is to be re-union of Christendom it must be by going back to primitive simplicity, and peremptorily refusing to allow opinions to claim the same authority as the Catholic faith."

But, though Bishop Fraser was a comparatively unskilled theologian, he was a really great Christian. He had an immovable belief in the guiding hand of an ever-present, all-ordering Providence. In a letter dated April 24th, 1877, he says:

"A very *providential* mercy happened to me last Friday. I was confirming at night in a church at Accrington. There have been for some time rumours—I believe ill-founded—of its stability. There were about four hundred candidates and a congregation in all of about 1500, filling the church in all parts. In the middle of the service a large piece of plaster fell from the ceiling of the gallery, and in a moment the congregation was in a panic—the women began screaming, rushing from their places, &c., and I was afraid a serious catastrophe might ensue. Happily the clergy and the churchwardens kept cool, and in a few moments we got the people calm and in their seats again. But for the *special* mercy of God many lives might have been lost in wild efforts to escape. I have seldom felt more truly thankful to God."

One of his favourite topics for Ordination Addresses was, "Moved by the Holy Ghost to take upon you this office;" and he urged the candidates to trace God's hand in the simpler ways of life; in the way it had been made possible for them to go to college, in the sustaining of their desire to be ministers, and the like.

"I do not wish," he said upon one occasion to the candidates, "to put any exaggerated or unreal interpretation upon these words, that you are 'inwardly moved by the Holy Ghost.' I think that God seldom calls men now to that work in the way He called, for instance, the prophet Samuel, the prophet Isaiah, or the prophet Jeremiah in the olden times; but God comes to us imperceptibly in the ways of His Providence, and in the order of His grace. He calls with a still small voice, not by earthquakes, or wind, or fire. If you in your hearts feel within yourselves a perfect steadfast purpose to serve God, if you feel your hearts and consciences really brought into this work which you are about to undertake, inasmuch as every good thought and every pious aspiration comes alone from God—

then I say you may, without the least unreality or hypocrisy, profess to believe that you are inwardly moved by the Holy Ghost to take upon you this office of ministering."

To Bishop Fraser the whole world was full of divine forces, physical, moral, political, all obeying one will; so that every event of life, whether great or small, appeared to him to be working the "One and Self-same Spirit." This simple-hearted faith in the all-ordering Providence of God was part of his nature—to have changed it would have been to have altogether changed the man. So, when the offer of the Bishopric was made, it found him responsibly ready, but not ambitious, to accept it. He accepted Manchester not because he desired any prominent position—he had already refused Calcutta—but because he believed it was God's will that he should take it.

"My dear ——," he said, to a clergyman who wanted his help in getting a deanery, "do not seek any office. The responsibilities and anxieties are weighty enough if the office has come unsought. They would be overpowering, indeed, if one had gone out of his way to obtain the office."

Even in his last illness it was just the same. The constancy of his absolute trust in the Providence of God never for a moment forsook him. Among his last words were these: "I am content either way. God knows best. I must leave it in His hands. We must wait. I am in good hands."

And, as the Bishop was a firm believer in the ordering of Providence, so was he a diligent observer of the practice of prayer. He had cultivated the habit of daily prayer from very early years. When a boy at Shrewsbury, he had noticed that a schoolfellow who occupied the same room as himself was in the habit of kneeling at his bedside every night in earnest, fervent prayer. At Whitsuntide, 1884, Bishop Fraser preached a sermon to the boys in the chapel of his old school upon "The duty and privilege of prayer." As an illustration he recalled the incident of his own school-days, and told "how deep an impression the example of his own earnest, praying school-fellow had made upon him, how

D

it had given a turn to him for good, had made a lasting improvement in his character, and a corresponding increase in his happiness." Not only in Luther's sense of *laborásse est orásse* was Bishop Fraser a "man of prayer"; he was a man of petitioning, as well as of labouring, prayer. Like his great model, St. Paul, he was wont "in everything with prayer and supplications to make his requests known unto God." It was of the nature of a privilege to hear him read prayers with his household; he seemed to throw so much simplicity, pathos, childlike fervour into every sentence. When at home (and in the days of her solitude and illness he was seldom absent for a night), he always went up to his aged, deeply loved, deeply venerated mother's room to say together their evening prayer. And afterwards his daily delight was the simple morning and evening prayer read quietly with his wife. "I do so enjoy our little office together," he said. "It strengthens and refreshes me."

Another characteristic mark of Bishop Fraser was his knowledge of the Bible, especially of the Pauline epistles— a knowledge which, for its fulness and accuracy, was most remarkable.

"It is curious to trace," writes one correspondent, "in an old Greek Testament which the Bishop used and marked as a boy and a young man, how his attention had been drawn to the very same lines of thought that were his delight in his maturity. The self-same texts which were his favourites when he was bishop are underlined in the Greek Testament of the schoolboy. But when one speaks of favourite texts one remembers that all texts seemed favourites. He seemed equally familiar with the whole Bible: as some one who often heard him preach remarked, 'The Bishop isn't fair; he is always quoting texts that no one else even heard of.' Many a time has the Bishop said before service, 'I really don't know what to preach about. I have been so knocked about from pillar to post that I have had no time to think.' And then he would go into the pulpit and preach a sermon full not only of deep spiritual thought, but also of Scriptural references, giving chapter and verse for all. Fortunately for the Church, he had had time to read and think, to lay his foundations deep, and to make his knowledge firm, before he came to Manchester. After he came to Manchester his work left him little opportunity for reading or research. What time and quiet he could secure he needed and he used for the inner life of his own soul."

At the close of one of his village sermons, he exclaims:

"Oh, that we would all read our Bible with more teachable hearts, with more determined will to find out what it has to say to us about our calling here, our destiny hereafter; that we would store up its *precepts* in our memory, to be our strength in the moment of temptation, its *examples* in our imagination, to be the pattern and model of our daily lives! Do not think that having a Bible, or reading a Bible, is any good, except so far as we live by the Bible. The Bible is the rule of *life* as well as of *faith*, of what we are to *do*, as well as of what we are to *believe*."

This exhortation was uttered by Mr. Fraser in 1853 to his country congregation at Cholderton, and it is interesting to compare with it a passage from an address delivered by him to a Men's Bible Class at Lytham in October 1884, near the close of his episcopate. The comparison is suggestive, as setting forth the essential continuity of the Bishop's character and his lifelong habit of reading the Bible for the definite purpose of making it "a lamp to his feet and a lantern to his path." After stating that—

"By reason of his office" (an evident allusion to the well-remembered vows made at his ordination) "he was bound to make himself well acquainted with the Bible, and that, although he did not profess to be fully able to understand the theory of inspiration, yet he almost seemed to see a special providence watching over God's Word, and that until some one could show him a teaching which could lead him straighter along the path of life than the Bible, he was content, notwithstanding every difficulty and objection which might be suggested against the Bible, to accept the Bible;" the Bishop proceeded, "I should not think any worse of you as members of a Bible class if you could not tell me how long the old patriarchs lived, or give me them in succession. These things are not of much more importance than the tracing of a family pedigree. They are interesting, but no one would for a moment say that they ranked in importance with the account of Christ's life, or the Sermon on the Mount, or the record of the conversations in the Upper Chamber at Jerusalem. The history of the kings of Egypt does not differ much from the history of the kings of England. To know what king of Israel invaded Egypt and how many men he came with and what cities he took, does not differ much from the account of the invasion of France by King Edward III., unless in these things we endeavour to see that it is righteousness which alone makes a nation really strong. I need not tell you that your attending this Bible class, unless you desire to make this Word of God your rule and guide of life, is not much good. Our knowledge will only add to our condemnation if, after we understand and see the full force of the sacred volume, we do not let it govern our lives, making us more dutiful sons, better parents, more kindly affectioned husbands. There is a matchless beauty in the Bible's precepts and a rich blessedness in keeping them; but if we do not keep them our studying them is comparatively worthless. All this Bible reading ought to create in us a desire to do 'something for the Master's cause in this world,' else familiarity with the Bible is no evidence of our living faith in Christ. Contemplation and reading, apart from conduct and righteousness, are of little service to man."

The thought of righteousness was the ever-present, ever-dominant thought in Bishop Fraser's mind; the righteousness of nations, of churches, of individual men. He was fervent in any cause which "made for righteousness"; if the cause did not make for righteousness, he was indifferent to it; if it made against righteousness, he hated it. His lifelong interest in the progress of education was based upon the conviction that education was the helpmeet of righteousness, and ignorance the source of much iniquity. His aversion to partizanship of every sort, whether ecclesiastical or political, arose from the dread lest the dust of party strife should blind the eyes of men to the fair pleadings of righteousness. The reason why "politics seemed to him a miserable game as played just now was, that one party vilified the other continually, whereas each ought to be studying the well-being, the happiness, and the prosperity of the nation." His hostility to ritualism (for it is impossible to gainsay that he was very hostile to the most recent developments of ritualism) arose not from any lack of love for devoutness in demeanour, and reverence in worship; nor from any slackness in realizing the great work done by the Ritualists for the promotion of this reverence and devoutness; but from the deep-rooted and fast-growing fear lest a too intense concentration of thought upon outward ceremonial should result in the peril of inattention to the culture of inward righteousness.

"There is," he said, "ritualism and ritualism. Divine worship cannot be performed without some ritualism—some acts and words and postures and ceremonies. And the more these conduce to reverence, devotion, and a proper conduct of Divine Service, the more they seem to me to be after the mind of that Great Apostle who tells the disorganized Church in Corinth that all 'things done in God's house should be done decently and in order.' Ritualism means in itself nothing more than the form or rite with which a religious service is conducted. It may be a high ritualism or a low ritualism; a histrionic ritualism or an intelligible, pious, reverend ritualism. Any ceremonial in the act of worship which really conduces to edification is a reasonable service and a justifiable act of worship; but any ritualism that is simply a superstition, or that is introduced for the purpose of veiling doctrines which are not the legitimate doctrines of the Church of England, is an unreasonable service, an illegitimate service, and cannot be defended by any reasonable man. . . . I am quite sure that where there is true inner spiritual life it will express itself outwardly in a reverent ritual: I quite admit that an irreverent man is not really penetrated by the spirit of worship: and that we are a long way from becoming too reverent or too devout in our worship in our churches; . . . but, on the other hand, I am not at all equally sure that a gorgeous ceremony is a proof of, or will help to generate, that holiness without which in the ordinance of divine worship no man can really see God. There is a ritualism creeping here and there in the English Church which does seem to me a most distinctly superstitious ritualism, and as such has no place in our worship. If anything can stifle all true spirituality of soul, it must be the mechanical habit of uttering so many words, or taking part in so many acts of devotion merely as a form. Another thing we have to dread is the theory of sacerdotalism destroying or obscuring the power of true religion in the individual life or in the individual conscience: substituting body worship for spirit worship, and intruding upon the immediate communion which ought to exist between our souls and God.* . . . There is a sad fact which we can neither hide from others nor ignore ourselves —viz., the fact that excessive ceremonialism is often attended by moral torpor and religious decay. Can history point to a single age, from the womb of time, in which an excessive addiction to ceremonialism and the externals of religion was not accompanied by a corresponding dulness of the conscience and a proportionate deadness to the higher forms of duty?" †

Bishop Fraser greatly loved a reverent and well-ordered service. He was, in his own high sense of the word, a genuine ritualist. He advocated every act, and posture, and symbol which could contribute towards the exaltation and hallowing of worship; but he felt a shrinking, which amounted to a horror, of the dissociation of ceremonial from conscience, of devoutness from duty, of ritualism from righteousness.

Bishop Fraser's attitude towards freedom of thought was very similar to his attitude towards ceremonialism in worship. As he had a reverent fondness for devout ceremonialism, so

* Sermon at St. Andrew's Church, Ashton-on-Ribble, January 19, 1871.
† 'University Sermons,' p. 200.

he had a profound affection for intellectual liberty. He rejoiced in every kind of freedom, but most of all in freedom of mind. He felt no jealousy of the "scientific temper."

"It is the prevalence of the scientific temper," he said, "more than anything else, which has redeemed religion from superstitious corruptions. The philosophic has taught the religious inquirer the proper frame of mind in which every inquiry, if it is to have a good result, must be pursued. The philosopher has often shown more faith than the theologian in the conviction embodied in the maxim, ' *Magna est veritas et prævalebit.*' He has seldom been willing to *enforce* his conclusions on those whom he cannot *persuade*. He seeks to impose no creed by mere authority. He feels that dogmas must rest upon sure, or at least probable, warrants before they can be thoroughly received. And he would be no wise man who would wish to return to the bondage of superstition in order to escape from the possible perils of scepticism. . . . The Church of Christ has been slow to claim her high prerogative as a child not of the bondwoman but of the free. She has too often been the slave of antiquity, of precedent, of stereotyped ideas. What we want in this nineteenth century is the liberty of which Paul spoke." *

But, as Bishop Fraser's love of religious ceremonial did not hinder him from seeing clearly the dangers attendant on it, neither did his devotion to intellectual liberty make him blind to the excesses into which this liberty occasionally runs :

"Admitting and deploring the failures of the Gospel—weeping at the very thought that a thing so mighty as Christ's Gospel might have been for the regeneration of man, for the healing of the grievous sores and the sad sorrows to which humanity is liable, has been frustrated by the faint-heartedness and half-heartedness, the lethargy, the indifference and the fashionableness of men and women—admitting all this with the sadness of shame, I yet must confess that I do not exactly see the reason why clever men should seem to find so exquisite a pleasure and so much delight in destroying high ideals. The Gospel puts before man high ideals : it tells him what he is and to what image he may hope, by patience, goodness, and holiness to attain. I can never be brought to believe that the principle of reason is contrary to the principle of faith ; or that the liberty to think is synonymous with the licence to deny."

In every department of life, and thought, and action Bishop Fraser pleaded for liberty ; but it was the liberty of the good and earnest man, not the licence of the merely clever, or the disdainfully selfish man.

* Sermon in Manchester Cathedral, December 1875.

"I hope," he said, "I am not narrow in my sympathies: but with this epicurean cynicism, cruelly mocking at life, itself secure; abjuring every high aim in the lofty pursuit of personal comfort; checked by no moral considerations whatever in its froward path of pure selfishness; carelessly wrecking woman's honour; wickedly shattering simple faith; discussing the most solemn verities—at least the most solemn questions—toothpick in hand, over olives and wine; with this unhappy, but only too legitimate offspring of an age that has resolved religion into phrases, and God's service into a gorgeous ceremonialism, I do not feel disposed to hold either truce or terms. Christ can have no concord with Belial, nor he that believeth with this type of infidel." *

Such were some of the personal characteristics of the man whose *Lancashire Life* the following pages will endeavour to tell. A simple, brave, hard-working, God-fearing man; a man full of faith, but void of superstitions; a reverent and a righteous man; an advocate of the utmost freedom of mind so long as the freedom was earnest and unselfish; a lover of all things honest, beautiful, true, and of good report; fond of exercise, horses, and the open air; no particularist in religion, but of a piety penetrating to every detail of life; a loyal, ardent Churchman, with a hand stretched out to every one who names the Name of Christ and departeth from iniquity; a strong, healthy man whose eye was moistened and his heart warmed by every thought of another's sadness, or sorrow, or suffering; a Bishop independent of all party trammels, whether political or ecclesiastical, with more thought of the duties than the dignity of his office; a people's Bishop, understood by the people, believed in by the people, loved by the people; a Citizen-Bishop, with an earnest devotion to the civic welfare; a Bible-loving disciple of his Master, working in prayer, and praying in work, with a steadfast faith in the providence of God, and a keen sense of the necessity of labour; spiritual but not ascetic; intensely devout and sagaciously practical; a pure-minded, noble-hearted, high-souled man; a Bishop whose pleadings from the University pulpit with the undergraduates of Oxford, to gird themselves for the work of life, are evidently the echoes of his own aspirations and resolves.

* 'University Sermons,' p. 202.

"There are lives worth living to be lived in England; even in this unromantic age. In country villages, in manufacturing towns, in the metropolis, in trade, in commerce, in the clerisy, at the bar, in Parliament, England needs as emphatically as ever men who will do—will try to do—their duty. Who will bind the red cross on his arm in a cause nobler than any old crusade, and follow Christ through all the perils and swayings of the fight, strong in the conviction that the cause of righteousness must prevail, and that there are yet powers in the Living Word of God, which, far from being exhausted, have as yet hardly been tried?"

CHAPTER II.

APPOINTMENT TO MANCHESTER.

Offer of Bishopric—Letters of advice—Dean Church's and other Letters—Acceptance of Bishopric—Congratulations.

THE offer of the Bishopric of Manchester was made by Mr. Gladstone to the Rector of Ufton Nervet in the following letter:

HAWARDEN CASTLE, *January 3rd,* 1870.

DEAR MR. FRASER,—I write to place the See of Manchester at your disposal. I will not enumerate the long list of qualifications, over and above entire devotedness to the sacred calling, for which I earnestly seek in the selection of any name to submit to Her Majesty with reference to any vacant bishopric. But I must say with perfect truth that it is with reference to qualifications only that I make the present overture. As respects the particular see, it is your interest in, and mastery of, the question of public education which has led me to believe that you might perform at Manchester, with reference to that question, a most important work for the Church and for the country. Manchester is the centre of the modern life of the country. I cannot exaggerate the importance of the see, or the weight and force of the demands it will make on the energies of a Bishop, and on his spirit of self-sacrifice. You will, I hope, not recoil from them, and I trust that strength to meet them all will be given you in abundance. Believe me, faithfully yours,

W. E. G.

It would be difficult to imagine, and more difficult to describe, the emotions which such a letter, worded in generous terms, and charged with lifelong issues, would vividly arouse in a nature like Mr. Fraser's; a nature simple and intense, a nature slow to accept promotion, yet still more slow to shrink from labour. Not in conventional humility, but with a profound sense both of his own unworthiness, and of the magnitude of the task set before him, Mr. Fraser begged for the grace of a week's opportunity to consider the proposal; and to consult a few of his wisest and most trusted friends.

To the Right Hon. W. E. GLADSTONE.

UPTON, *January 5th,* 1870.

DEAR SIR,—Your letter, and the utterly unexpected offer it contains, has profoundly moved me. Am I making an unreasonable request, in asking to be allowed a week to consider the answer I ought to give to it? My first impulse was, from a most real and unaffected consciousness of unworthiness, to decline. But probably every one to whom such an offer was made would have the same feeling at first; and my life, as I read it, seems to have been such a succession of providences, that my second thought was, that by refusing to enter on a wider sphere of usefulness I might be drawing back from a call. Happily I have no desire for either wealth or rank, nor any ambition beyond that of wishing to be as useful a citizen, both of the realm of England and of the Kingdom of our Lord, as I have the power to be. I quite feel all that you so justly say about the noble opportunities offered by such a diocese as Manchester. All I mistrust is my own adequacy to them. I should therefore wish for time to take counsel with some of my friends, who have known me longest, and by whose judgment I should like to be guided in a matter of this kind—my Provost, Dr. Hawkins, Church, Liddon, Edward Hamilton, etc., for time also to think over so important a step—important not only to my own happiness, but to the highest interests of an imperilled Church at an anxious time—calmly with my own family, and earnestly as in the sight of God. I humbly trust I shall be guided aright. At present I need say no more, than that I will not allow any merely personal consideration of ease, or comfort, or ambition to determine my resolve. With a deep sense of not only what is implied in your offer, but of the manner in which it has been conveyed, I beg to remain, my dear sir, yours most faithfully,

JAMES FRASER.

To the Rev. JAMES FRASER.

HAWARDEN, *January 7th,* 1870.

MY DEAR SIR,—I have received your letter, which does you so much honour in every sense, and I accede of course to your request, only adding that I am sure you will render the interval as short as you possibly can. I am, etc., etc.,

W. E. GLADSTONE.

To the Rev. T. H. TOOKE.

[*Private.*]   UPTON, *January 6th,* 1870.

I am in a grave perplexity, and want the honest counsel of sincere friends. Gladstone, in a most touching and generous way, has offered me the Bishopric of Manchester. On all personal grounds, I should at once shrink from such a perilous responsibility; but second thoughts tell me that, in doing so, I might be shrinking from a call, and that personal considerations ought to be over-balanced by the claims of public duty. So I have asked for a week to consider the matter calmly as before God, and to take counsel with my friends. Without any undue or affected depreciation of my own powers, I am profoundly sensible of my inadequacy to the work of a Bishop at the present time. The perfect conception of a Bishop is of one who can lead men, inspire and sustain work, repair breaches, reconcile differences, mitigate bitterness, help men to the solution of the problems that hold the reason, and even the conscience sometimes, in suspense. No one can be more aware of my unfitness for the more difficult parts of such work than I am myself. But *who is* sufficient? At any rate, if you know any cause or just impediment—and you know me *intus et in cute*—don't let me take a step, which must be irrevocable; and which may be full of the gravest consequences, not to myself merely, but to the Church of Christ; don't let me take the step unwarned. We have known one another long enough to speak the truth face to face, and I have no such hankering after rank, or wealth, or a more conspicuous station, as to desire to be placed in a post the duties of which I should be found unequal to discharge. Keep this communication in confidence till I have made up my mind, help me with your counsel, and pray for me that I may be guided to a right conclusion."

"Besides writing to his distant friends," says Judge Hughes,* "he went over to consult Sir John Mowbray."

"He came directly after breakfast, with Mr. Gladstone's letter in his hand," Sir John writes, "looking as pale as a sheet. I read it, and said 'You are the very man for the place.' He expressed, in very strong terms, his unfitness. I replied, 'Mr. Gladstone and I seldom agree on any subject, but our coincidence on this is remarkable. If you will come into the drawing-room, and see my wife, she will tell you that I said, years ago, "if I were Prime Minister I would make Fraser a Bishop, and send him to Lancashire or the Black Country, as I think he is eminently qualified to influence such a population."' And when, in 1867, Lord Derby made George Selwyn Bishop of Lichfield, I said to my wife, 'There is Manchester still left for Fraser.' I pressed him most strongly to accept, and he said he would take a week to consult Church, Liddon, and others."

The two following letters, typical of many others, show the nature of the advice which Mr. Fraser received.

The Very Rev. Dr. Church (the venerated Dean of St. Paul's) wrote:

My dear Fraser,—I must begin by saying that I am very glad, and that I am *not* surprised, that Gladstone should have made the offer. I will say next that I am not surprised either that you should hesitate. The time is critical and dark; and men ought not lightly to be accused of shrinking from responsibilities, if they feel the burden too much for them. I think there may be as much courage shown in resisting the

* 'Memoir of Fraser,' pp. 186, 187.

opinion of too kind friends as in undertaking what one dreads. And now, as you have asked me, I will venture to submit why I should wish to see you accept the charge. (1) I think you have the great qualification of having seen and known many men and many ways; and with this wide experience, much wider than that of most men, you have joined an independence and moderation of judgment which has made that experience fruitful. (2) Next, I think you would be a generous, fair, sympathizing, warm-hearted Bishop, having your own opinions, and courageous in speaking out, but able to allow for much that you do not perhaps like, and to make people feel that you understand them, even when you have to go against them or check them. (3) You have power of work, and power of saying what you want to say, which all men have not. (4) You have had an example, both of what a Bishop ought to be, and of what a Bishop ought to guard against, in the good and single-hearted man with whom you were so closely connected at Salisbury; and it seems to me a great thing for a man to have had such a lesson, and to have studied it with deep sympathy and admiration, yet with a judgment of his own. For these reasons, I hope earnestly that the Church may be able to have your services.

Though I am sure that in all great matters we are agreed, probably in opinion, still more surely in sympathy, yet I dare say that there are points, perhaps points which may become trying ones, in which my line would be, what would be called, a narrower one than yours. I find myself continually still clinging to conclusions, for which the reasons commonly paraded and dwelt upon seem to me poor or bad; and I don't pretend to be one to find better. But, to me, one lesson of advancing age is the increasing sense of the difficulty of exact and clear truth in such matters. And I think that High Churchmen, who care for the Church and not for their party under that name, ought to wish above all things to see, not their own views, but *those qualities* represented in our Bishops, *without* which opinions are worthless and *with* which we ought to be able to bear differences of view—single-mindedness, generosity, earnest faith, courage. So I wish what I said.

The Rev. Canon Liddon, a very old friend of Mr. Fraser's, wrote:

MY DEAR FRASER,—I hope that you *will* see your way to accepting the Bishopric of Manchester. In saying this, I do not lose sight of the differences to which you allude in so kind a way, and of which perhaps, from the intellectual necessities of the case, I am obliged to take a more serious view than you do. They do not, however, oblige me to close my eyes to the predominating reasons which I have for wishing to see you at Manchester. On moral and social grounds (I mean the moral and social interests of religion), I should hail your going to Manchester with downright enthusiasm. I would rather see you there, I think, than any man whom I know. There must be plenty of latent heart in that vast population to be enlisted on the side of God, which nobody, as yet, has attempted to touch. And your moral force, your business habits, your sympathy with popular life and popular interests—not least your command of the Education Question, are very strong reasons, as it seems to me, for your being in your right place there. I feel sure Bishop Hamilton would have thought and said this; he would have said that you were the very man to win the respect, or rather the heart, of such a diocese. The clergy, I suppose, are generally ultra-Puritan; and, if this be so, and they are not to have a Bishop of that kind, you would have a much better chance of getting them to give up controversy in favour of hard work than a High Churchman would.

I cannot help thinking or hoping that, in offering you the bishopric, Mr. Gladstone is desirous of showing his respect and affection to our late Bishop, in whose life and heart you held so foremost a place. For this minor reason, I hope that you will accept it; but I hope so, chiefly and sincerely, because your doing so would be, I believe, under our existing circumstances, a real blessing to the Church of England.

Pressed upon all sides, and with a large variety of reasons, Mr. Fraser began to feel (though, as will afterwards appear, reluctantly and with a heavy heart), that the plain road of duty lay in the direction of accepting Mr. Gladstone's offer. But, before finally accepting it, he wrote, with characteristic directness and practical business-like capacity, to Mr. Ryder, the Registrar of the diocese, making definite inquiries concerning the condition of the See of which he was being so strongly urged to accept the charge. The nature of his inquiries is evident from the response which Mr. Ryder gave to them.

MY DEAR FRASER,—I can only say that I sincerely hope you will find yourself able to accept the offer, and I need not say how cordially I shall welcome your arrival. Now as to your questions.

(1.) With regard to the state of the diocese. The late Bishop up to within a few days of his death was working. He consecrated a church six days before he died. There are very few arrears to make up except with regard to confirmations, which he was obliged to discontinue, only because he had finished his list; but in so populous a diocese they are numerous.

(2.) With regard to the clergy, I think they, as a general rule, are united among themselves. Party spirit produces less dissension here than in many other dioceses; the reason being, as I have heard many say, that they have too much real work to have time to fight among themselves.

(3.) The laity are, I think, remarkably disposed to support the Church in every way, i.e. of course those who belong to our Church. As you may suppose, rich Dissenters abound, but, as a rule, *they* are tolerant and more than tolerant when they are not abused.

(4.) I thoroughly believe and am convinced that one not a partizan, but such a Bishop as you describe, would be not only acceptable but be warmly supported and followed by the best and most important of the laity of the diocese.

(5.) There is a considerable amount of locomotion required, but railways will carry you to almost every place you have to visit. The correspondence is not excessive, but even what there is may be reduced by the system of the Bishop's levées at Manchester which have been weekly, and might be oftener, for at least a part of the year.

(6.) Mauldeth Hall is five miles from Manchester—access either by railway or road. It is a large handsome house with perhaps thirty acres of land round it; but the holding of this number, more or less, would be a matter of arrangement with the Commissioners. The Bishop has had about eight servants with gardeners, but I think the establishment might be less. You could hardly decide upon this matter without seeing the place. Possibly there might be reasons for asking the Commissioners to provide another house of more moderate dimensions. I will send you a Manchester Church Calendar to-morrow and shall be only too happy to give you any further information I can. Yours most sincerely,

T. D. RYDER.

Without further delay Mr. Fraser wrote to Mr. Gladstone the following letter, definitely accepting the appointment:

UFTON, *January* 8, 1870.

MY DEAR SIR,—There is no advantage in prolonging unnecessarily a period of suspense, and it will be even a relief to me, as well as an act of due consideration to yourself, to apprise you of my resolve, as soon as formed. I consulted nine of my most valued friends, upon the soundness of whose judgment I thought I could rely, with reference to this solemn trust you have offered me, and I have yesterday, and to-day, received answers from them all. Though men of very different views and positions, they unite in telling me that I ought not to shrink from the responsibilities even of such a bishopric as Manchester; and encourage me to believe, that, with the good hand of my God upon me, I may be found not unequal to its charge. And so, although I cannot quell the throbs and misgivings of my own heart, I seem to have no alternative but to accept the trust you are willing to commit to me. It will be my desire, if called upon to administer this great diocese, to do so in a firm and independent, but at the same time generous and sympathizing spirit. I never was, and never could be, a partizan. Even when seeing my way most clearly, I am always inclined to give credit to others, whose views may be different from my own, for equal clearness of vision, certainly for equal honesty of purpose. As little of a dogmatist as it is possible to be, I yet see the use, and indeed the necessity, of dogma; but I have always wished to narrow, rather than to extend, its field; because, the less peremptorily articles of faith are imposed or defined, the more hope there is of eliciting agreements rather than differences. Especially have I been anxious to see the Church adapt herself more genially and trustfully to the intellectual aspirations of the age, not standing aloof, in a timorous or hostile attitude, from the spirit of scientific inquiry, but rather endeavouring (as in her functions), to temper its ardour, with the spirit of reverence and godly fear. And finally, my great desire will be, without disguising my own opinions, or wishing one set of minds to understand me in one sense, and another in the opposite, to throw myself on *the heart* of the whole diocese, of the laity as well as of the clergy, of those who differ from the Church as well as those who conform to her. I have a high ideal of what a Bishop of the Church of England ought to be—an ideal which, for fifteen years of my life, it was my happy privilege to see very nearly realized; and, though I am never likely to attain to it, I can at least keep it steadily before my eyes, and reach after it. If after this frank statement of what I desire to be, you still think me qualified for the administration of such a diocese, and as the adviser of the Crown to recommend me to Her Majesty, I shall be prepared, though not without deep anxiety, to undertake the office, and will endeavour, by the help of God, to do my duty. In the event of my promotion, the next presentation to the living which I now hold (which is in the patronage of Oriel College) will, of course pass, to the Crown. I shall be glad to communicate any particulars respecting it which may be desired. I may briefly say here, that few livings can unite in themselves greater advantages. With a deep sense of the motives which you say have led you to single me out for this appointment, and a humble hope that I may not disappoint your expectations, I remain yours most faithfully,

JAMES FRASER.

Mr. Gladstone replied:

HAWARDEN, *January* 10, 1870.

DEAR MR. FRASER,—I have received your letter, and read it with sympathy and admiration. Your appointment is settled as far as Her Majesty is concerned, and the steps will now be taken for the *congé-d'élire*. Should you be in town after the 20th or 21st, I shall be happy to see you, although the transaction between us as one of mere business is concluded. Believe me, sincerely yours,

W. E. G.

In due course the appointment was publicly announced through the authorized channels; and letters of congratulation poured in upon Mr. Fraser with a flood.

The Dean of Westminster (Dr. Stanley), wrote:

"I am delighted to hear you have accepted Manchester. I have always desired to see you a Bishop, and, in some respects, Manchester is most suitable to you; and it would have been very difficult to have found any one more suitable for Manchester. It is a splendid field, in one sense, the most splendid of all the bishoprics, because it contains within itself more of the germs of the future. Pray do not take, or, at least, indulge a desponding view. I consider the total collapse of the opposition to Temple (out of 20,000 clergy and 25,000,000 of laity a petition signed by 1500) and the enthusiastic reception which he has met at Exeter, a proof both of the superiority of the mass of the clergy and their party leaders, and also of the thorough appreciation of real worth in a bishop by the public at large. There are great dangers, no doubt, but these are very much increased by the dismal forebodings of those who ought to encourage and cheer as friends. I do indeed wish and pray all blessings for you,—above all, that you may still retain your power of speaking out your own mind and of acting independently of your order—and, therefore, in its highest interest. The only drawback, to my mind, is that you will not be in the southern convocation."

Bishop Temple (newly appointed to the see of Exeter) wrote :

"I cannot help writing a line of most warm welcome to you on your entrance into the Episcopal Body. Gladstone could not have made a better choice, and I am sure that you will be most useful, and give all parties the greatest satisfaction. *No one will call you a heretic!*"

Lord Lingen wrote :

"I congratulate you very sincerely. Manchester lies on one of the outer orbits of life, and passes through much more space in the same time than Ufton Nervet. The change has something about it far more desirable than pleasure. The greatest results have been achieved by men who bring body and mind unbroken from comparative quiet to the front rank of affairs at a time of life which implies experience, but not decay. All the reading, all the thinking, all honest application (down to the minutest detail) is so much action *in posse*, ready to be energized when the call comes. I shall perhaps see you a sadder man, if we both live ten years longer, but I shall be much out in my reckoning if I don't see you a man who has made his mark upon his time. No man is better able to take things as he finds them ; but you are now in a position where this great element of success co-exists with the responsibility of being one of the foremost not only to wish them, but to make them, better. I hope you won't think this too little of a cheery letter. I really feel very cheery about you. But going to the wars is never all laughter on the part of the soldier's friends."

Professor Bryce wrote :

"Will you let me congratulate you most heartily on the nomination to the See of Manchester? It is what your friends have been looking for for some time and hoping for, not more because it will give you a worthy sphere of activity than for the sake of the Church of England herself. Knowing Lancashire pretty well, and knowing how much is to be done there for education in particular which you will enjoy doing, I am especially glad that it is to the diocese of Manchester you are going, the rather too as I may hope oftener to see you there than one could hope for in other parts of England."

The Venerable Archdeacon Norris wrote:

"I rejoice unfeignedly to see that you go to Manchester—knowing Manchester well and that North Country, belonging to Cheshire and Lancashire πατρόθεν and μητρόθεν. There is in Lancashire an immense amount of real good honest Churchmanship which has never been properly developed. May God help you to carry it home to them that the Church of England inherits simply the traditions of the 'Acts of the Apostles,' and knows no other Churchmanship, and you will rally them round you as one man!"

It must have been a source of great encouragement and strength to Mr. Fraser to receive the multitude of letters, of which those quoted are only a very small and typical selection. He alone seems to have been doubtful and fearful; all his friends were bright and confident. The idea of becoming a bishop was not new to him. Ten years previously he had refused the Metropolitan See of Calcutta. His friends had often talked to him of the probability of his elevation to the English Episcopate. He had been "very near" Oxford. When Salisbury and Exeter were vacant he was thought, by a large number of persons, to be "the very man" for those dioceses. And probably, had one of these southern sees been offered him, he would have felt less hesitation in accepting it. For although Mr. Fraser had "seen and known many men and many ways"; had been upon four occasions a Royal Commissioner; had contributed, perhaps, as much as any single man in England to form public opinion upon the great question of National Education; yet he was essentially a man of southern England. All his clerical life had been spent in the Dioceses of Oxford and Salisbury. He was, by taste and preference, a country parson. More than once he had been pressed to undertake a London parish; but he seemed to have a strong and deep shrinking from the hurry and bustle, the smoke and streets, of large and crowded towns. He was never a man of the cloister or the cell, but all his life he

E

had been a lover of the meadow and the village. Left to himself, Manchester is probably one of the very last places he would have chosen spontaneously as his sphere of work. But

> "There's a divinity that shapes our ends,
> Rough-hew them how we will."

Bishop Fraser had a firm and tenacious faith in this ever-guiding, ever-ruling providence of God. In a speech at Bacup, 1870, he said : " I have come to Manchester, trusting simply to this, that I am following a call of Providence, and that the same strength which has sufficed me in the past will suffice me in the future." He had asked his friends not only for their advice, but also for their prayers. Some of them " had done what they could for him on their knees." By his mother's side he himself had knelt to ask for leading and for light ; and when the way seemed clear, this country parson of the southern England, who had avoided towns and clung to the country-side, bravely, though not without tears, accepted the spiritual oversight of the most smoky, most busy, most crowded diocese of the northern England. A stranger, he came amongst strangers—with the one brave and noble determination to spend himself for " those strangers' " good.

"Bishop Fraser," writes the Rev. James Lonsdale, "stayed a few days at my house after he had accepted the Bishopric of Manchester. His having been nominated to be Bishop had not made the least difference in his simple and friendly nature, except that he appeared to be at times somewhat depressed by the thought of what by the advice of various friends he had undertaken. There was in him a contending Nolo and Volo: a Nolo for the dignity and appendages of a bishopric, a Volo for the enlarged means it might give of doing good. One thing I remember his saying was, '*I do hope that I shall always be straightforward.*'"

At the closing meeting of the Manchester Missionary Exhibition (which was the occasion of Mr. Fraser's first public appearance in Manchester), January 11, 1870, he spoke of his appointment in the following terms:

"I am not at all familiar with platforms, nor am I in the habit of addressing crowded audiences. I have always lived in a little quiet country parish, and nothing was further from my hopes, I may unaffectedly and honestly say, and nothing further from my desires, than to be made a Bishop of the Church of England in these troublous times. I shrink from the possibility of failure. But the whole course of my life has been a succession of providences. Whatever I have been and whatever places I have filled have been given to me, and I have never once gone in search of them. The call to become Bishop of this diocese came to me on a Monday morning, as I took up my letters from the breakfast table, having no idea of the contents of any one of them; but I saw in the corner of one letter the name of the Premier, and that the letter was 'to be forwarded.' A sort of presentiment told me what the letter contained, and on opening it I found that it contained the offer of the Bishopric of Manchester. I can only say that, if there is any one who doubts the perfect loyalty and allegiance of the great statesman who is now directing the destinies of this country to the true interests of the Church of England, I can only wish that such person could have read the letter in which Mr. Gladstone communicated the offer of the See of Manchester to me. I asked Mr. Gladstone to allow me a week to consider the offer, telling him that my first impulse was at once to decline it; but that, as I felt I might by declining the offer be drawing back from a call to a position of more usefulness, I would take counsel with my most trusted friends and be guided by the advice they gave me. Not one of those friends gave me so much as an excuse for drawing back, and so here I am, coming to the work in fear and much trembling, but hoping that I may be sustained in my efforts to promote the glory of God and the welfare of His Church. I feel sure that I shall receive a warm welcome from the warm-hearted people of Lancashire, and I trust that during my episcopate, whether it be long or short, though I may make, and am certain to make, some mistakes, you will give me credit for honest purposes and straightforward motives, and will construe my failures leniently, and give me good advice, which will be always welcome, to show me the course on which I ought to go."

These simple words, simply spoken, together with his manly bearing and open countenance, at once drew to him the heart of Manchester, and prepared the way for the work which he was destined to accomplish in his *Lancashire Life*.

CHAPTER III.

ARRIVAL IN MANCHESTER.

Consecration—First Sermon—His Preaching—Pulpit and Press—
Mauldeth Hall—His Mother's Diary.

" I SHALL be glad when the present transition state is over; for work is bracing; and when the mind is occupied, it has not leisure to be moody." Bishop Fraser's words in this instance, as in many others, are a clear mirror of Bishop Fraser's self. He had immense power of work; to him work was bracing; he gloried in work. As a boy he had been a great worker; as a country parson he worked harder still; as a Bishop he worked hardest of all. In a speech at Bacup, 1870, he said:

"I have always felt great pleasure in working. I have never lived the life of an idle man. Even in my small Berkshire country parish I found I had abundant opportunities for the exercise of all the talents which God had given me. The only fear I had about myself in Lancashire was that I should be found wanting perhaps in some of those qualities of judgment and discretion—for my nature is somewhat apt to be impulsive—which I feel are emphatically required in any one that pretends to be a leader of the people."

Upon another occasion he said:

"When I left my Berkshire parish, the other day, with only 370 people living in it, how did I leave it in respect of education? I left it with seventy children at the day school, and an average daily attendance of more than sixty; and I had twenty-five agricultural clodhoppers, as they are called, coming to me three nights a week, making themselves smart and tidy, and walking, perhaps, two miles to the school after a hard day's work following the plough over miry fields."

Work kept him cheery. In his leisure moments he was inclined to be pensive, and occasionally despondent; but in harness, and pulling hard, he was spirited, almost prancing.

Wherever he went every one recognized and honoured his love of work. He possessed many fine qualities which especially endeared him to the working classes; not least of these qualities was this hearty, happy devotion to work. Critics called him "the talking Bishop"; the masses called him "our working Bishop."

But, like many ardent workers, Mr. Fraser was somewhat impatient of waiting. The more he loved work, the less he loved waiting; suspense and transition were a burdensome load to his impetuous nature. It was, therefore, with a sense of relief, not unmingled with solemnity, that he saw the dawn of the day of his consecration, Friday, March 25, 1870. The assemblage in "Th' Owd Church," as the Manchester Cathedral is affectionately termed by the Manchester people, was enormous; many persons being grievously disappointed that there was no corner left into which they could squeeze themselves: for, during the interval between Mr. Fraser's nomination and consecration, the tidings had gradually spread through Manchester of the manner of man who was coming to be Bishop. When it was first announced that Mr. Fraser, a Berkshire country parson, had been nominated to the Bishopric of Manchester, the Manchester people inquired wonderingly, "Who is he?" Nobody seemed to know. But, as the history of his life appeared, it was made evident that the new Bishop would be a power. From his photographs the Manchester people had caught an impression of his honest face, his manly bearing, his massive strength, his natural gentleness. Expectation was on the tip-toe; and the day of Mr. Fraser's consecration is a day long to be remembered in Manchester.

The consecrating prelates were Dr. Thomson, the Archbishop of York, Dr. Jacobson, the Bishop of Chester, and Dr. Bickersteth, the Bishop of Ripon. The Mayor of Manchester (Mr. John Grave), Alderman Nicholls, and the Town Clerk (Sir Joseph Heron), represented the City Council and sat in the Corporation pew; the clergy completely filled the chancel; and the nave was thronged with representatives of every class of the general public. The sermon was preached by the Rev. Professor Lonsdale, from St. Luke i. 33: " He shall reign over the house of Jacob for ever; and of His kingdom there shall be no end."

It is narrated by several witnesses that during the entire service the new Bishop seemed wrapt in deep, calm thought, but that the calm was occasionally broken by an intense, quivering expression of responsibility which burst across his face and compelled the tears down his cheek. One who was present at his consecration writes that the clear and decided utterance of the Bishop's answers in the Ordinal will remain with him to his dying day, as will also the manifest fervour with which he, in each answer, implied his strong and firm reliance on the Divine assistance, "The Lord being my helper," "So help me God."

When the Bishop retired to the vestry to complete his robing, at the close of the first portion of the consecration service, Mr. Bridge played upon the organ, with an instinct almost prophetic, Handel's most beautiful anthem, "He shall feed His flock like a shepherd." Henceforward, Bishop Fraser was to be, during the term of his life on earth, the chief human shepherd of the Church in the Diocese of Manchester.

With characteristic promptitude and energy he soon set himself to work. On the Saturday morning, the day following his consecration, he was quietly, and without any public announcement, enthroned in his cathedral; a special prayer being offered "that he might long continue Pastor of that Church, and Bishop of the Diocese of Manchester, and by word and good example set forward the glory of God—so presiding over and governing that Church that in the end he, with the people committed to his charge, might obtain eternal life."

Upon the following day, Sunday (and again quietly without any public announcement), he preached his inaugural sermon at the cathedral from St. John xiv. verses 1–7, in which the following noteworthy passages occur. The passages are given at length, because they strike the keynote of Dr. Fraser's *Lancashire Life*; his manly simplicity, his all-enfolding sympathy, his robustness in religion, his deep spirituality.

"The Gospel of Christ has been the fullest and final revelation of God's will and purposes towards the creatures of His hands. In the Gospel of Christ has been made known the fullest revelation of the righteousness of God and of that eternal principle upon which He administers the moral government of the world. In the Gospel of Christ has been made known the fullest revelation of man's duty and man's destiny. The Gospel of Christ has been a source of calm and peace in a world of unrest and disturbance—a spring of steadfastness amid perpetual change, a stream of joy that brightens and lightens up the darkest hours to strangers and pilgrims and weary wanderers, and reveals to them what the Lord Jesus calls in the text 'the mansions;' that is a rest and home. The world is a world of unrest, anxiety, and change. Watch those crowded streets of yours and the multitudes of those who traverse them; mark their faces as they hurry to and fro, the men of business and the hard-handed sons of toil; notice the lines on their faces as they reach to manhood—lines that have been drawn by care and labour, lines telling us that they want the feeling—the feeling of the blessedness of rest. And so the Gospel emphatically was preached to the poor; to those whose lot in life was hard; to those who knew most what that unrest means—short hurried sleep, broken rest, scanty meals, and the pinches of poverty; those to whom, if their hearts had not grown callous and insensible, the message of rest, remaining for the people of God, must be most dear. Also the Gospel is preached as a message of rest to the sinner. Yes, to him who has trespassed against his brother and against his God, not seven times only but it may be seventy times seven. Christ is not weary of calling even though we have grown weary of hearing; Christ still searches where the wearied are to be found; Christ still knocks at the door often, though we are slow to open it. He came to call sinners to repentance; theirs is the painfullest unrest of all. There is no trouble so great as that of a broken heart lying crushed and bruised under the burden of sin, and no joy so great as that which hears and obeys the invitation, 'Come unto Me all ye that labour and are heavy laden, and I will give you rest.' Yes, rest, even here in this world of sin and strife; and rest, in all its fulness and completeness, there where strife and sin have passed away. Do not suppose, dear friends, that this rest in Christ and Christ's Gospel, either here or there, is identical with sloth. Little as we know of that life in the world to come, and in which we profess to believe, if it be life, if it be not lethargy, it must be activity, and it probably will be progress. Here in this world we are expressly told that we are to *labour* to enter into God's rest. The worst of all forms of unbelief into which a man can fall, to my mind—worse far than any mere speculative doubt, for which, perhaps, many an excuse can be found—is the unbelief expressed by an idle, unprofitable, and wasted life—a life which has added nothing to God's glory, and contributed nothing to the furtherance of any of the high interests of man. It is what I venture to call practical atheism, an abnegation of all duty to the Supreme Governor of the world. Of all the doctrines of devils, none seems to me so earthly, so sensual, so devilish as that which teaches that a man can do just as he wills with his own, and live as best pleaseth himself in this present world. Against such an atheistic theory of life the life of the Lord Jesus is a most emphatic protest. That life is, and ever must be, an ideal of human life, rising into and mingling itself with the Divine. And, so that we may lead this higher life and realize its blessedness, the apostle tells us that we must believe in God, and in that Son and His love. He is the Way, and the Truth, and the Life; no man cometh to the Father but by Him; or, as St. Paul changes it into his own phrase, 'We are complete in Him, and by Him we have all access, through One Spirit, to the Father.' And of this Jesus, the Saviour of God's people from sin and from the power of sin, as well as from the consequences of sin, I love to think there are many ways. He is the One Way to the Father, but I love to think—because then I can welcome and bid God-speed to every good work that seems to savour of Christ or reflects faithfully the mind of Christ—that to Him there are many ways. Some come to Him in a faith that may be called their own; some are brought by others, and let down as it were from the roof where He is teaching; some humbly come behind and touch the border of His garment and are made whole; some, bolder in faith, but not always with like success, venture to go out to the ship and meet His approaching form on the waters; to some He comes uninvited, to others He is almost an unwelcome guest; some He calls, and some, at first, He seems almost to repel; some He humbles by rebukes, as Peter once was humbled; and others He lifts up by encouragement, as Peter again was lifted up; some find Him most readily in the duties of active life, as Martha did; some like Mary at Bethlehem, sitting at His feet; some like the disciples, when they withdrew themselves from the crowd, and spent the night on the lone mountain in prayer; some, when there are two or three together in a little congregation, and He in the midst of them; and to some He makes Himself only truly known in the breaking of bread. But what matter how we come, or in what company—though in some companies we may find Him more likely than in others—so long as we do come, and so long as we find Him? Yes, it is my unshaken belief that He will be found by all who seek for Him earnestly. Let us not lay down peremptorily exclusive narrow landmarks. Better allow something for human infirmity, human differences, human peculiarities, human freedom; better urge all to seek than attempt to define beforehand the precise mode, time, or place in which they can find Him. In God's home are many resting-places. In the great tower of Babylon the sightseers mounted from terrace to terrace by flights of stairs, and there were many sitting-places; so, even in the great flight of stairs by which we have to ascend to heaven, there may be resting-places at lower levels for those who fail to attain the highest summits of possible happiness. Christ is preparing a place for us; and more than that, and better than that, He is preparing us for the place. He is not only the Way, but the Truth and the Life. Not only where He is there will His servants be, but they are to be *like Him.* Even the body of humiliation which we bear with us now shall yet be fashioned like unto His glorious body by His mighty and regenerative power. He assumes that we know the way. We may know the way without knowing the precise whither. If I see, for instance, a finger-post pointing to Manchester, I may travel on securely in that direction though I may never yet have seen Manchester or pictured to myself what manner of city it is. In God's providence there are direction posts set up at all uncertain turnings and by-paths, so that only a blind or careless traveller can miss the road. With his face—as his Master's face was once set—steadfastly towards Jerusalem, the traveller may travel securely on. And, should you ever be in doubt for a moment as to your road, look, I pray you, whether you cannot see, somewhere close by you, under your very feet almost—certainly within range of your eye—footprints that look like the footprints of Jesus—some trail that seems as if the Cross had been borne along the road, through the gateway, up the rising hill; or if you fail to discern these—though, if you look for them, you will not fail to discern them—still if, in your blindness, you fail to discern these, see whether in God's providence there be not about you, almost within hand's-reach, some of those who have companied with Jesus, who wear His livery, who belong to His household—the household of faith—who call themselves by His name, and if such you find, inquire of them. Personal influence and the power of a good example are in my judgment the most potent instruments which the Holy Spirit most commonly uses for the salvation of souls. I love to think of Andrew bringing his brother Peter, and of Philip conducting his friend and companions, to the Messiah, the Jesus whom they found. According to the words of Paul, which sank deep into my ears last Friday, *to help to save those* who hear them is the very work of Christian bishops and Christian ministers. And this, my friends, is the work that I desire to the utmost of my poor ability to do. I never sought this high office to which I have been called. But yet I have accepted it—accepted it with a profound sense of all its perilous responsibilities and of my own manifold insufficiencies. Yet, as I have always found my happiness hitherto in an honest attempt to discharge my duty as a minister of Christ's Gospel, so I trust it may be still. I have been deeply touched by, and feel profoundly grateful for the warmth of the kindness, the generosity, and the confidence with which, as yet, I have been received. I humbly hope I may not prove undeserving of all this. Specially do I desire to keep ever printed in my memory that picture of a Christian Bishop which Paul has drawn: A servant of the Lord must be gentle unto all men, apt to teach, patient, in meekness instructing those who oppose themselves, avoiding foolish questions which engender strife, following with all them that call on the Lord Jesus out of a pure heart, righteousness, faith, and charity and peace. I desire to be a Bishop in the old Pauline and not in the pontifical sense—' a true servant of the Son of God.' Let me in these my first days—days of inexperience—be often remembered in your prayers."

Thus spake, for the first time in a Manchester church, the voice which was destined soon to send forth its utterances, with responsive echo, not through the churches only, but through the assembly halls, the exchange rooms, the clubs, the workshops, the mills, the homes of Lancashire. It is sometimes said that Bishop Fraser "did not know how to preach; that his sermons were speeches, and his preaching was lecturing; that to him the pulpit was what the platform is to other men." Doubtless the Bishop's temptation, as a preacher, lay in the direction thus indicated; and, as his episcopate proceeded, the temptation was increased by the deepening pressure upon his time, which left less and less opportunity for preparation.

But the accounts of his sermons which appeared, sometimes daily, in the public press, give an entirely erroneous impression of the true character of his preaching, and through no fault of the public press. As a rule, and not including that portion of the press avowedly religious, the daily press of England does not report sermons at all. The aims and functions of the pulpit and the daily press are partly mutual, yet largely distinct. When the pulpit ascends above this world, penetrates through the limits of time into the infinitudes of eternity, deals with man not in relation to his brother men, but to his Father, God—(deals with man, *i.e.*, in his spiritual rather than in his social capacity) their functions are distinct; but, in so far as religion is identified with morals, and goodness with godliness, and the world which now is with that world which is to come, their functions are mutual (*i.e.*, throughout the whole extent of that large rich field of man's present domestic, civic, social life which it is the duty of Christianity to cultivate and fertilize).

And one reason why the press takes so little note of the pulpit is, because the pulpit fails to occupy, as it should, this region of the present life which belongs to itself in common with the press, and confines its utterances too exclusively to other-worldliness. In Bishop Fraser, however, the press soon discovered a preacher who did not ignore the message

of Christianity to this present life; a preacher whose
sermons, in some part of them, pursued a path in which the
press could follow—the path which is common to both
civilization and Christianity—or, rather, the path which
Christianity has, of itself, prepared for civilization. In every
sermon of Bishop Fraser's there were portions relating
either to Scriptural exegesis, or distinctive dogma, or personal religion, or eternal hope, or the judgment to come;
but there were portions also directly bearing upon social
manners, or civic duties, or economic problems, or ecclesiastical interests, or national righteousness.

"I remember," writes Canon Maclure, "his asking me one Whit Sunday
what he should preach about. I said, 'I want you to preach *a sermon.*'
'Of course,' he said, 'I have come for that.' I replied, 'You do not
always *preach*; we want nothing about cotton sizeing,' &c. He asked for
pen and paper, and went into my study, afterwards producing a most
powerful sermon on the work of the Holy Spirit, the subject I had
suggested. Characteristically enough, at the end of it he went off into a
little aside in some practical references to a passing event, and this latter,
not anything in the sermon itself, appeared in the morning's newspaper."

The newspaper reports of his sermons were often introduced with some such sentence as this: "The early part
of the Bishop's sermon was of a purely religious description,
but, towards the conclusion of his remarks, he said . . ."
Then follows the account of those portions of the sermon
which were eagerly seized upon by the press, because they
dealt with topics common to both the preacher and the
press. Such utterances were recorded, printed, circulated
in the columns of dozens of newspapers. They were the
message of the Church to the world; and the world read
them, quoted them, was grateful and better for them.
But the other portions of the sermon—the sermon proper
as some may think—the sermon on its spiritual side,
the daily press naturally omitted to record. These portions
lay outside its proper scope and region. None the less
were they the pith and marrow of the sermon; and the
multitudes who flocked, and flocked in ever-growing
numbers, to hear Bishop Fraser preach, would soon have
turned aside from him if his sermons had consisted solely

of the portions recorded in the daily press. People do not go to church to hear the same utterances which they take up the newspapers to read. Their attitude towards the pulpit and the press is different. Both pulpit and press are agents of incalculable influence; the modern world can dispense with neither; but, as the pressman would fail who spoke only as a preacher, so the preacher would fail who spoke only as a pressman. That Bishop Fraser's power as a preacher continued, and increased, to the very end of his life, is in itself a proof that his preaching touched chords in human nature, aroused apprehensions and kindled aspirations, which belong to the dominion of the pulpit alone.

There was something in the very face of Bishop Fraser— a sweet sadness; a clouded, yet intense, hopefulness; a gentle severity; a chastened affection; a brave sympathy; a calm joy; a spiritualized sagacity; a tender manliness, which won the listener's heart. "It is as good as a sermon to look at him," was a common expression. His look was always eloquent, even when his utterances were ordinary. "I always liked to *see* the Bishop," writes the Rev. R. Judson, "when he was preaching. There was something in *his eye* which had quite a remarkable power over me. I feel unable to describe it, but its influence was a very holy one." He seldom had leisure to play the orator; but he never failed to be the plain-speaking man. To the multitude his plainness of speech was a great attraction. "I can't understand our curate," said a church-going artizan in Manchester; "his sermons are too learned for me; but I can always understand the Bishop, he preaches plain." But prayer was a greater power with him than plainness of speech. "Let me be often remembered in your prayers," was the first and chief favour he begged from his diocese; for "to help *to save* those who hear them is the very work of Christian bishops."

But while Bishop Fraser was entreating his diocese for their prayers, and proclaiming that "the very work of a Christian bishop is to help to save those who hear him," thus showing forth the spiritual side of his character, he was also "setting his house in order," and corresponding with his registrar and the Ecclesiastical Commissioners, about selling Mauldeth Hall (the palace of his predecessor, five miles from Manchester) and obtaining a residence within easy reach of the centre of his work, and accessible to his clergy everywhere, thus showing forth the practical and common-sense side of his character.

Upon May 25, 1871, the Bishop wrote to the Rev. W. H. Parker:—

"I hear of no purchaser of Mauldeth, and I am afraid that I shall have to take up my residence there next year. How I shall get on in that big place without a wife, I don't know; and I have no time to look out for one. The gossiping world some time ago gave me away to a lady whom at that time I had never seen!"

Again, on June 6, 1872:—

"I am getting anxious about my house at Manchester. If I cannot sell Mauldeth this summer I mean to resign the see, as I cannot live there and work the diocese, nor can I afford to have on my hands a big house like that, unoccupied, and with the responsibility of repairs resting upon me. My mother and aunt, I am happy to say, are very fairly well for two old ladies of 79 and 82."

At length, however, a purchaser for Mauldeth Hall appeared in the person of Mr. W. Romaine Callender; and Broughton House, afterwards called Bishop's Court, was purchased. There the Bishop took up his abode on December 18, 1872, having resided since April, 1870, at St. Luke's Rectory, Cheetham Hill, which he had obtained, at a yearly rent, through the kindness of the Rev. J. Chippendale, M.A.

Bishop's Court is a convenient roomy dwelling, with about three acres of garden, upon the slope looking westward from Broughton across the valley of the Irwell on to the not unpleasing prospect of Kersal Moor, and the opposite heights of Pendlebury; and is situate within two miles of the central parts of Manchester upon the Bury New Road—the trams passing the gates every seven minutes, thus enabling the Bishop and his clergy to be in easy and constant communication with each other. Some additions were made to the house, with the intention of rendering it more appropriate and more serviceable for the special requirements of a Bishop's residence; the chief of these additions being the private chapel—the windows in the apse being given by the Dean and Chapter—with a room underneath for the examination of candidates for ordination.

Upon their first arrival in Manchester, the Bishop, with his "dear old ladies" (as he fondly called his mother and aunt), had felt keenly the greatness of the change from their quiet life in the country to the rushing life of the city. "I was never meant to be a Bishop in a town like this," said the Bishop to an old schoolfellow; "I am at heart a country parson." "The ladies, my Lord," said another, "will feel it a great change to come from the quiet country side to this busy, bustling place." "Yes," replied the Bishop, "they feel it very much. They came last night, and *we all had a good cry over it.*"

The following extracts from the diary of Bishop Fraser's mother, for the year 1870, may fitly close this chapter.

Wednesday, Jan. 5, 1870.—Dearest James has charming letter from Mr. Gladstone offering him in most handsome way the Bishopric of Manchester. James begs in reply a week's reflection ere he decide: he writes to several tried friends on subject of his fitness. J. B. H. is delighted; but it has cast a sad gloom on dear James's bright face, of anxiety and responsibility of the sacred charge. Dear James writes to ask many of his old tried friends and advisers who know him well whether they think him qualified for so important a diocese.

Thursday, Jan. 6.—James receives some beautiful replies to his letters, all telling him that he is not only fit for the sacred office, but that *duty* earnestly "calls," and he cannot refuse the "call." James has night school.

Saturday, Jan. 8.—James has a great many most interesting letters in reply to his enquiries, *one* and *all* in the same tone urging him to accept the bishopric as a *duty* to God and the Church: Providence still bidding him on to a higher sphere in *His* service. He writes Mr. Gladstone to-night a beautiful letter accepting.

Saturday, Jan. 22.—Dear James returns very low in spirits from his visit to Manchester, fearing he's made a sad mistake in accepting bishopric, which makes us feel very sad and low to see him. He had kind welcome and reception at Manchester, but could not endure Mauldeth Hall Palace, and would not live there!

Sunday, Jan. 23.—After tea James seems again disturbed at the thought of his position; can't throw it off his mind, fearing he has made a great mistake, but recovers a little after talking it over.

Tuesday, Jan. 25.—James returns safely, rather more cheered: sees Mr. Gladstone, who tells him "John Bright was pleased with his appointment": had his photo taken in Baker Street, and seemed tired to death fagging about London. A bad cold to boot.

Friday, March 25.—Our beloved James consecrated at Manchester Cathedral.

Tuesday, March 29.—Letter from A. B. telling how dear James had won all hearts at Manchester, and what a magnificent sermon he gave in the cathedral on Sunday morning.

Tuesday, April 19.—Arrive at St. Luke's Parsonage with all our things. *Most* miserable first evening. Find James well, but very low and uncomfortable.

CHAPTER IV.

AT WORK: MANCHESTER MISSION.

Introduction—Bishop Lee—Organization of Diocese—Summary of Work—Description of Diocese——The Mission—Pastoral Letter—Sacerdotalism—Medical Students—Railway Employés—Cab-Drivers—Slaughtermen—Theatre Employés—Bishop's Address in the Theatres—Baroness Burdett Coutts's Letter — Private Theatricals—Letters to the Bishop — The Bishop's Letter on Theatres—Conclusion of Mission.

In some great lives the man makes his opportunity; in others, the opportunity brings out the man. Occasionally both the opportunity and the man appear so to combine that each makes the other greater and more fruitful than either could have been singly of itself; the man magnifies the opportunity, and the opportunity magnifies the man. This was eminently the case with Bishop Fraser and Manchester. His *Lancashire Life* is an illustrious instance of the man splendidly developed by his opportunity, and of the opportunity splendidly developed by the man. If Bishop Fraser was just the man for Manchester, so also Manchester was just the sphere for Bishop Fraser. If no other bishop could have better suited Manchester, neither could any other diocese have better suited the Bishop. He had been, as one correspondent puts it, "within an ace" of the Bishoprics of Exeter, Salisbury, and Oxford. Had his lot fallen upon any of these three dioceses, it is almost certain that both the character and the measure of his influence would have been entirely different, and, probably, enormously less. The man himself would, of course, have remained the same in all essential points and qualities. He would, in himself, have been just as simple and industrious, as truth-loving and outspoken, as sympathetic and catholic in any of these dioceses as he was at Manchester; but, probably, in none of them would these qualities have found so free and large a scope as they found in Manchester.

The character of the diocese is varied in its several parts —but its dominating feature is business; and the bulk of its population is gathered in towns. So extraordinary has been its commercial prosperity, and the corresponding growth of its population—chiefly congregated in mining districts and manufacturing centres—that, in the forty years of the existence of the diocese (1847-1887) the number of its inhabitants has increased by more than a million. The population of the city of Manchester, and its neighbourhood, during the episcopate of Bishop Fraser, was as large as the population of the whole diocese at the commencement of his predecessor's reign. And besides the great central city "there are probably a dozen towns of more than 50,000 inhabitants within easy reach of Manchester, and at least three times as many so-called 'villages,' larger than most south of England towns, each with its various institutions, religious and secular, denominational and undenominational, in full activity."

Into the midst of this active, energetic population Bishop Fraser was thrown in his 52nd year. His predecessor, Dr. James Prince Lee, the first Bishop of the diocese, had been (says a writer in *The Edinburgh Review* *) a man

"who had won for himself a high reputation as Head-Master of King Edward's School, Birmingham, and had left behind him an enduring testimonial in the fact that three at least of the most distinguished living Churchmen were among his pupils, Archbishop Benson, Bishop Lightfoot, and Canon Westcott. He was a finished scholar, a vigorous ruler, and a man whose persuasive influence few could resist. In some respects he was admirably qualified to bring into order the new diocese over which he was called upon to preside. He gave a great impulse to the building of churches, which was an urgent need of the time. One hundred and sixty-three new parishes and ecclesiastical districts were formed during his episcopate Unhappily his temper was imperious, easily irritated, and not easily appeased. Bad health aggravated this infirmity, and during the latter part of his episcopate he withdrew much from his clergy and people, living in a retired corner of his diocese, near the borders of Derbyshire."

In the judgment of Bishop Fraser, never a niggard of his

* No. ccexxxiv. (April 1886), p 294

F

praises when he could bestow them with justice and truth, the administration of Bishop Lee was "an effective administration":

"I cannot pretend," he said, in one of his earliest Lancashire speeches, "to equal your late Bishop in ability and intellectual power, or in attainments of scholarship, perhaps hardly in firmness, yet I trust I shall never be wanting in fairness. . . . I believe that the strength of the Church of England will be found to lie, as the strength of every other institution established for the public weal must be always found to lie, in the extent to which she is proved to be ministering to the spiritual wants of the nation; working not only for the people but with the people; realizing their wants and endeavouring to satisfy them; not setting herself, in the persons of her ministers, against the mighty currents of public opinion, but trying to guide those currents into safe channels, and to show that in her wide, tolerant bosom every legitimate form of Protestant Evangelical Christianity may find a home. . . . . We clergy, I know, are a privileged class; we are secured in our privileges by the law of the land in a way in which no other religious denominations are secured. But why are we privileged, and why are we secured? That we may do a great national work. And that is the aspect in which I wish to regard my work, and in which I hope all the clergy of this diocese are regarding their work; that we are not the ministers of a sect in any narrow sense, but the ministers of a Church which, by her constitution and in the discharge of her duty, ought to be as wide as the empire which has adopted her as the symbol of its Christianity, and which ought to welcome into her fold every one who will offer to co-operate with her. . . . I am very much obliged to you for the kind reception given to myself. Your kindness encourages me to go on with better heart than I should otherwise have in the great work that lies before me. I remember one of your newspapers said, in reporting my appointment to the diocese, that ten years hence would be time enough for eulogy. So let it be. I do not desire praise, but I am thankful for encouragement; and if ten years hence you tell me (if I live so long) that my work has been carried on in a spirit which has conduced to God's glory and the edification of the people committed to my charge I shall have reason to thank the Providence of God that sent me here."

The work which Bishop Fraser set before himself, from the commencement of his episcopate, lay, not so much in the direction of inventing new organizations, as of enlarging and quickening into more vigorous life the organizations already existing. He was far indeed from being negligent of the organizations of his diocese. He founded the Diocesan Board of Education, established a Bishop's Fund for Manchester and Salford, re-arranged the course of Confirmations, convoked Synods and Diocesan Conferences, revived the custom of Visitations, and formed a third Archdeaconry, that of Blackburn, from the northern part of the Archdeaconry of Manchester. Still, the prominent feature of his episcopate was not organization; for, although Bishop Fraser was an admirable and kindly critic of the organizations of others, yet he was not always successful in founding, and carrying forward to success, organizations of his own. His temperament was less that of the organizer than of the prophet—an impressive personality, a rush of energy, an overpowering magnetism of sympathetic will, a brave largeness of heart which evokes enthusiasm. It has been fortunate for Manchester that her first bishop was a builder—a strong, firm man who clearly conceived and solidly compacted the machinery of the diocese; and her second bishop a prophet, who called forth the heart of the diocese to realize the living mission of the Church, of which the machinery was but the symbol and the instrument.

In his first Charge, the Bishop said:—

"I do not court popularity; I know its dangers. I do not resent criticism; a public man must be prepared for that; but I do desire that you should give me credit, and that you should have grounds for giving me credit—whether you think I always act rightly or wrongly, wisely or foolishly—for a real desire to do my duty. I think I know what that duty is; and, according to the grace given me, I endeavour to fulfil it."

The manner in which "this real desire to do his duty" was carried into action sufficiently appears from the fact that, in the first three years of his episcopate, he made the personal acquaintance of upwards of 700 of his clergy; either preached or confirmed, or performed some other episcopal act, in all but 108 out of the 420 churches of his diocese; consecrated 26 new churches; held 160 confirmations, laying hands upon upwards of 29,000 candidates; superintended nine examinations for Holy Orders and (exclusive of those who had been ordained deacons elsewhere and of three or four candidates ordained by letters dimissory from other bishops) admitted 86 persons into the sacred ministry of the Church. In addition to these official duties, he delivered scores upon scores of speeches in connection with every variety of civic and social enterprise!

Few men possess the strength necessary for such phenomenal labour, and few dioceses afford the opportunity for its exercise. The physical configuration and social circumstances of Lancashire were both an assistance and a stimulus to the Bishop in his overpowering and conscientious "desire to do his duty." The area of the diocese is not large. The population for the most part is densely packed in a few great centres. Systems of railways cover the diocese with a network of steel. Every parish is easily accessible to the Bishop; and the Diocesan Registry easily accessible to every Churchman. And, if the compactness of the diocese is a great help to the Bishop, its social and intellectual circumstances are a greater inspiration still. From its lowest grade to its highest, and all through the great middle class which lies between the two, Manchester is a diocese calculated to stir a manly, earnest Bishop's heart to its deepest depths, and to call forth his highest and his noblest powers. The misery and degradation of its lowest grade animate the soul with a compassion resolute to leave no means untried for the alleviation of that misery and the amendment of that degradation. The spectacle of the surging multitudes of the working classes—men and women with hard hands, and warm hearts, and keen minds (upon whose character and conduct so large a part of England's future depends)—kindles a consuming desire to direct that conduct into the noblest channels, and to penetrate that character with the highest Christian principles. And the presence of immense wealth in the close neighbourhood of degrading misery, and upon the outskirts of surging multitudes, arouses a determination in every good man—especially when placed in a position of dignity himself—to do whatever in him lies to arrest the process of separation between the various ranks and classes of men; to cultivate among the rich a sense of responsibility towards the poor, and amongst the poor a sense of confidence in the rich; and to solve, in both directions, the difficult problem of the relation of the classes to the masses—a problem compared with which all other social and political problems fade into insignificance—by the proclamation of Christ's Gospel of the brotherhood of men. And, besides all this, Manchester is intensely interested in politics, in art, in the development of intellectual activity. As Mr. Gladstone said in offering the bishopric to Mr. Fraser, "Manchester is the centre of the modern life of the country." Some of the most notable battles of political warriors have been fought in Manchester. Nowhere in England can music and the stage find a more appreciative audience. The most remarkable of all collections of modern paintings has been exhibited in Manchester. The educational institutions of Manchester, from its primary schools through its magnificent Grammar School on to Owen's College (the home of some of the best learning and deepest research of the age), are in the first rank of the educational institutions of the world.

"Thought runs in Manchester," said Bishop Fraser, "almost with the quickness of an electric current from one end of the body social to the other. Life teems with an even superabundant activity. Discussion is frequent and energetic upon almost every conceivable topic. A Bishop of Manchester cannot, if he would, as long as he has health and strength, lead the life of a recluse."

. Nothing could have been more remote from the Bishop's practice than the habits of a recluse. He was incessantly preaching and speaking. Men are differently constituted; and Bishop Fraser's method of administering his diocese appeared to some to be lacking in quietness and spirituality. Yet, perhaps, according to his own conception of the spiritual life, few men have striven after "spiritual perfection" more ardently than Bishop Fraser. Accordingly he threw himself with characteristic energy into the Mission movement, although not fully approving of every detail of that movement.

Parochial missions are a distinctive feature of the reinvigorated life of the English Church. Few signs mark the greatness of the difference between the English Church of the last quarter of the eighteenth century and the English Church of the last quarter of the nineteenth century than the establishment and organization of parochial missions. At first parochial missions assumed the form of special services extending over eight or ten days. At these special services a series of distinguished preachers were invited by the parochial clergy to come and preach; sometimes upon a well-arranged and consecutive course of chosen topics; sometimes upon any topic which suggested itself to the individual preacher without any reference to the topics dealt with by his fellow-preachers. A mission of this character was held in Manchester in Lent, 1871. Of this mission Archdeacon Gore, who was one of the special preachers and a guest of the Bishop, thus writes:

"You ask me to recall a brief, but very pleasant, episode in my life—my visit to the Bishop of Manchester in 1871. It was an accident that I was his guest; he put a letter of invitation into the hands of the secretary to the mission, and, by my good fortune, it fell to my lot to receive it.

"The 'mission' idea was too immature in those days to allow of my saying anything of the Bishop's views on the subject. What we then took part in would scarcely be recognized as a mission now. Six parishes were selected, six days given to the work, and six preachers invited to preach a sermon in each parish. The sermon was followed by an 'instruction' not given by the preacher. The Bishop visited all the churches, one each night, and gave the 'instruction' when he was present. On the evening when he came with me, I was much impressed both by what he said and his manner of saying it. He took point after point of my subject, and put it to the people with a simplicity, a clearness, and a force which made me wish that the sermon had been more like the instruction. With singular humility and fidelity, if I may use such words, he introduced nothing new, but only commended what had been said. You can easily understand how this touched me at least, and, very probably, others also.

"Although I cannot speak of the Bishop's views on modern missions, I was not left in the dark as to his opinion of preaching. He craved for a preaching clergy—men, that is, who could really talk to hearts and souls. The way he used to speak has often since reminded me of Carlyle's words: 'That a man stand and speak of spiritual things to men; it is beautiful. I wish he could find the point again, this Speaking One; and stick to it with tenacity, with deadly energy, for there is need of him yet!' . . . Could he but find the point again, take the old spectacles off his nose, and looking up discover, almost in contact with him, what the *real* Satanas and soul-devouring, world-devouring Devil Now is.' Not in these words, but in this spirit and tone, the Bishop was always speaking; and surely no man ever tried more faithfully to act up to the thoughts which burned within him.

"But my delight that week—and it *was* delight—was in the man himself, pure and fresh from his country home, and still sighing for it—as simple as a child, absolutely boylike with his mother, and she well-nigh worshipping him. I said to her, 'Oh, Mrs. Fraser, you seem proud of your son!' I remember how instantly her answer flashed out, 'And have I not good right to be so?' The Bishop seemed to me to be ever bathing, so to speak, in memories of green fields and country folk; but yet he was throwing the whole force of his great character into the gigantic work which God had given him to do.

"I was never again so near him in thought and spirit, though his kindness to me never failed or flagged; but often, in the sadder days which came to him, my heart was made the sorer by knowing what manner of man it was that was called to suffer as he did. Well could I understand his hurried visits to Ufton Nervet, and his desire that his body might rest at last beside its quiet church."

A single extract from one of the Bishop's Mission Instructions in 1871 will illustrate the simplicity, the force, the practical directness which was characteristic of them all:

"These special services will have failed to produce the effect which it is hoped they will produce, if they leave the parish in which they have been held exactly as they found them; if they have merely drawn here and there a large congregation to listen to an attractive or eloquent preacher; if every one who has sat and listened to the Word of God as it has been delivered to him has not in some sense, and with some degree of sincerity, looked himself over fairly and honestly, and asked himself whether the life he has lived, and is living, and means to live, is the life that really is answering to the end of his being, and the purpose for which God created him and sent him into the world—whether it is the sort of life which will bring peace in the hour of death, and enable him to give a good account before the Great Judge of Assize. To every one of us, the richest as well as the poorest, the most ignorant as well as the most learned, God has committed certain powers, certain opportunities and influences which He has called upon us to use, and which He has left us free to use; which we can use either for His glory and in His service, or for the devil's service, or which in a certain sense we need not use at all, but can wrap up in a napkin or bury in the ground, thinking to ourselves, 'I don't do much good, it is true, but I don't do anybody any harm. I go to church; I do not go to public-houses or taverns, and even in my youth I did not go to dancing-saloons or betting-houses. I always keep myself respectable; I don't say I am very religious, or that there is much heart in my prayers, or that I ever make much sacrifice to bend my stubborn will under the influence of Christ's cross. I do not set myself up for having done much good, but I think I shall pass muster at the Judgment Day.' Let us not deceive ourselves; it is not enough not to have done any harm. God has sent us here to do some good, and the question put by the apostle is, that considering that these things shall all pass away, 'what manner of persons ought we to be?' The answer that different people give to this question depends mainly on the relation in which they believe this life stands to the life which is to come. Without pretending to prophesy about the details of the life to come, I think every one must be persuaded that what he is here, and what he has done here, will very much affect and modify what he will be, and what he will be expected to do, in the life hereafter. Some people have a notion—I cannot conceive where they get it from—that a sort of magical change will pass over them in the next life, and that they, who will see the glories of that kingdom, will not be at all like what they are here. My own opinion is that we shall be exactly the same there as here. I should not know myself if I forgot everything I did here. I believe the next life will be a continuation, a development, an extension, and a glorification of the life that now is, and that it will be its legitimate consequence just as the oak is the legitimate consequence of the acorn."

It was six years afterwards, in the year 1877, during the twelve days commencing January 27 and ending February 7, that the great Manchester Mission, memorable for the conspicuous and extraordinary part taken in it by Bishop Fraser, was held.

Before the commencement of the mission, however, there occurred an event which seemed most seriously to threaten it with division and failure. The Dean (the Very Rev. Dr. Cowie) had appointed the Rev. W. J. Knox Little as mission preacher in the cathedral; an appointment which appeared to some 'to imperil the success of the mission and to cast a gloom over the minds of those engaged in promoting it.' Alluding to this event in a sermon preached shortly before the commencement of the mission, the Bishop said:

"There is a false and a true sacerdotalism. If by sacerdotalism is meant that in the Christian Church there is a body of men set apart for special functions, and that no man has a right to take upon himself these functions unless he has been duly called and sent to do so, and that the blessing and power of Christ attend the ministrations of those so called, because their ministrations are ordained and commanded of God, then there seems to be nothing harmful or unscriptural in such sacerdotalism. But if by sacerdotalism is meant such sacerdotalism as that of the ancient Jews, whose priests had such prerogatives that no man dared have access to God except through them, such a sacerdotalism can have no place in the scheme of Christ's Gospel as it is shown in the New Testament. For what is our work as ministers of Christ's Gospel? It is to bring men to Jesus by persuasion, by example, by prayers, by entreaties, by labours public and private. What can be sadder than to read of men—apparently conscientious men—seeming to think that the truth as it is in Jesus, the truth by which men's souls are to be saved, their lives purified, their hopes brightened and their faith confirmed, is involved in vestments, in incense, in the biretta, in acolytes, in purple cassocks? And in Manchester, just when we are all hoping, for a while at least, to forget all minor differences, and to unite as a phalanx in the name of Christ against all the powers of evil, so mighty and so multiform, which are crushing us down on every side, some unkindly hand has managed to sow the seeds of discord and suspicion. I know not who is to blame, and I do not care to know. I have not read the letters which have been written on the matter —some of them, I believe, very bitter letters—but I do say, as Bishop of the diocese, that the circumstance is a most lamentable one. Are we for ever to present to those who do not wish us well the spectacle of a divided house? Is the taunt still to be levelled at us, 'See these Christians, how they hate one another?' Can we not forget our differences which, after all, are but minor differences, even for an hour?"

And again, in reference to the character of the mission, he said:—

"The mission we hope to hold is one of those times when we ought to declare ourselves on one side or the other. It is said our English nature is very undemonstrative. No doubt it is. We do not like the parading of our religion. For myself, I do not care very much about men saying their prayers in public places, and blowing their trumpet before their fellows, and looking about with a sour countenance which is meant to proclaim they are fasting. Silence, quietness, and the recesses of a man's own heart—these are the places where the great spiritual work is done, without any parade, without any ostentation, without any cant (which is a hateful thing), and without any solemn sanctimonious profession. Surely we can be real, we can be earnest, we can be loyal to the great cause without any of these things. There is in Manchester a sort of latent heat which comes out when the occasion is favourable for its development. Take the case of politics. Ordinarily we are calm enough, but at election times we throw off our reserve, and go forth, and proclaim ourselves, and wear our colours, and cry our cries. So let it be with the mission. Let it be an occasion for coming forth and proclaiming upon which side we are, whether Christ or the devil shall be our king; whether we will no longer connive at and be indifferent to the ravages of intemperance, of lust, of crime, of vice, or whether we will throw off our ordinary apathy in these matters, and for once throw in our lot with those who serve Christ by trying to lighten some of the burdens which oppress mankind."

The following letter shows the depth of the Bishop's anxiety for a blessing upon the mission, and the variety of the labours connected with the mission in which he himself was preparing to engage:

"To-morrow we begin the Manchester and Salford Mission. I am very full of anxiety about the result. There are a number of men of the extreme school—Mackonochie, Lowder, Boddington and others, who will be here, and in the present state of excitement I can hardly tell what they may say or do. To-morrow afternoon at 3.30 there will be a service in the cathedral specially for those engaging in the mission, clergy and laity, and I am to address them: pray that my thoughts may be guided aright. For the whole of the twelve days I expect to be incessantly engaged, mainly addressing large bodies of working men at the various great industrial factories, &c., of the town and neighbourhood—the mill-hands, mechanics, railway officials, omnibus and cab drivers, &c. I am even asked to address the people connected with the theatres, if they can be got together. One of the managers is quite favourable to the project. The work will be both delicate and difficult.

"Some result, however, of a permanent kind, I trust, will follow. I was at Bradford, in Yorkshire, last night—going there after my morning's work at Heaton Moor—and preached to a church full of a thousand people. The vicar, a truly earnest man, told me that the Bradford Mission had certainly borne fruit; and this encouraged me.

"My dear invalids are wonderfully well just now, though my mother is as helpless as ever; we are just getting her on to an air-bed to-day, which I hope will make so much bed-keeping less wearisome.

"You tell me I ought not to despond about my work; but you don't know all the difficulties, and all the things there are to depress and discourage one. I am naturally sanguine, but the work is wholly beyond my power."

Upon Saturday, January 27, 1877, the mission which had been so long expected and so anxiously prepared for, was commenced by the delivery, after the usual service in the cathedral, of an address by the Bishop to the clergy and others who had promised to help in the work of the mission. The Bishop selected as his text the words (Acts xviii. 9, 10), "Be not afraid, but speak, and hold not thy peace . . . for I have much people in this city."

Besides frequently preaching sermons during the course

of the mission the Bishop gave special addresses of a less formal kind to various bodies of people.

To Medical Students, he said:

"It is the function of medical men to deal with the body, and, as their investigations, analyses, dissections, or applications of the microscope do not carry them beyond matter, it is not altogether surprising that they should be tempted to think that there is nothing but matter in the world. I have read books by eminent medical men which teach very plainly that vital force is not all to be accounted for by any of the phenomena of matter, and I have not the slightest doubt that wise members of the medical profession will say that there are things in the world far beyond what they have discovered, or, perhaps, 'dreamt of in their philosophy.' Many old philosophers held that matter was inherently vile. The New Testament teaches us the dignity, I might almost say, the sacredness of the body. In all your dealings with the human body, never forget that the body is something for which Christ died; the body is for the Lord, and the Lord for the body. The thoughts and speculations of many materialistic writers, in these days, seem to carry them far away into dreamland; the dreams are anything but comforting, refreshing, or strengthening; but either sorely perplex the brain, distress the heart, or disturb the conscience. Against all the speculative theories I am content, for myself, simply to set the simple Bible story of the origin of man, rationally interpreted and rationally understood. I do not ask you to accept irrational interpretations, or to do violence to your conscience or your reason either. In these great parables, if they are parables, given in the first chapters of Genesis, we are told the relation of the human race to God and to the world; we are told of the unchangeable nature and subduing power of sin; we read the law of death with which medical men are perfectly familiar; and we have disclosed to us the power and promise which make it possible for frail men and women to live pure and noble and unselfish and worthy lives. On one occasion Christ said, 'Ye believe in God, believe also in Me.' He says still, Believe in God; believe in Me; and I would also say, Believe in yourselves. By this, I mean that you are not to think that when you die you will leave your bodies, as scientific men have done, to be dissected and then cast away on a dung-heap, and that that will be the end of all. I ask you, each and every one, to have faith in your destiny, in your work, in your capacities, and above all in your responsibilities. If men would only realize their destiny, their powers, their opportunities, and their responsibilities, how they would be rescued from the low, sordid, almost bestial lives which too many are content to live. Let me urge all present to live uprightly and to act up to their highest and worthiest convictions."

To Railway Employés, he said:

"The mission has been organized by and in connection with the Church of England, but you will be making a great mistake if you think the object of the mission is to proselytize. It is not to make more or better Churchmen, but if possible, by the help of God, to make more and better Christians. I certainly hope we shall make more and better Churchmen; but I should consider it no triumph, nothing to boast of, if by any word of mine I should draw away a pious or godly Wesleyan or Baptist from the communion to which he had belonged hitherto to the pale of the Church of England. I should not think such a thing a triumph or something to glory of. There is work enough for all religious men. There is work enough and to spare for them all in Manchester, without endeavouring to draw any one away from one religious denomination to another, except in so far as the spirit of God moves them."

To Cab-drivers, he said:

"The life of cab-drivers, whom I have come this afternoon specially to address, is a peculiar, and certainly, from a religious point of view, an embarrassing and perplexing life. They cannot often go to church: that is certain. Their time is very little their own. Their work is very hard. They have to rough it in all sorts of weather. When he gets home at the end of the day, a man must often be so tired and chilled that the only thing he can think about is to get a hot supper and hurry off to his warm bed. They are in all companies. They are at the mercy of every one who chooses to hail them. They must drive people to very queer sorts of places at times, and must often have very curious sorts of people in their cabs. Again, there are a great many bad habits in society, of which cabmen are the victims. There is the practice of treating with drink. Every time I see a cab at the door of a spirit vault, I know it most probably means that some one, who has been travelling in the cab, is treating the cabman to a glass of beer or gin. I am not going to condemn a man who drinks a glass of gin, or ale, after a long cold drive, though I doubt whether such refreshment answers its supposed purposes. Doctors say that it does not, but really lowers the temperature of the body instead of raising it. But I warn you, one and all, against allowing the habit of drinking to grow upon you by submitting to these occasional treats. When I consider the case of such men as policemen, postmen, and lamplighters, cab and omnibus-drivers, milkmen, and night-soil men, and others who are condemned to habits of irregularity and exceptional temptation, because they are ministering to the public comfort and well-being, I often feel perplexed: but at the same time I am wonderfully encouraged and sustained by reflecting on the inexhaustible resources of the love of God, and the manifold ways in which He can and does draw men's souls to Him. Although I have been in the habit of attending church twice a Sunday myself ever since I can recollect, yet I believe, and know, there are many men quite as religious as I who cannot attend church once on Sunday, or even once in the year. Society seems hardly to care a snap of the fingers whether these men who are ministering to their comforts are being helped heavenwards themselves or not. If a fashionably dressed young man with his hair parted down the middle, and a sixpenny Havana cigar in his mouth, were to hail a cabman at his stand, on a Sunday afternoon, to take him four or five miles out into the country, and the cabman were to say, 'Sir, I was just going home to put up my horse and get a chance of going to church, that is, if you can spare me,' in all probability the fashionable young man would come out with an oath, and say, 'Hang your church; drive me to Stockport.' This is the way in which society expects everything to minister to its convenience, and never stops for a moment to count the cost of ministering to it. If, any night, a poor lamplighter was taken suddenly ill, and the lamps in a particular street or quarter were not lit in consequence, would not there be a row next morning in the newspapers—letter after letter complaining of the administration of the town, and that, forsooth, society has to suffer, because a poor lamplighter has been taken suddenly ill? I say that society is extremely reckless. Just take the case of the milkman. When I go to church on Sunday morning, in whatever quarter of Manchester it may be, I find the milkmen running about the streets, doing the work which they usually do about seven in the morning, at any time from nine to one, just because people are lazy and like to lie in bed on Sunday morning, and do not care a snap about the milkmen's souls. These are things which society has to lay to heart and think about, and I should be most terribly perplexed if I did not believe that many roads lead to Christ, though all are up-hill, and not to be trodden without effort and self-denial. Now, just let me point out that cabmen, amidst all their difficulties, have also many opportunities. A cabman may sit on his box and say a prayer, or while he is waiting for a fare he can sit inside his cab, as I sometimes see them doing, and read something better than the *Sporting Life*; he could read his Bunyan's 'Pilgrim's Progress,' or his Bible, or something that would feed his mind and nurture his soul, and I do not think a customer would be slower to call a cabman if he knew him to be in his cab reading his Bible. Again, his mind may be employed with good thoughts, and these good thoughts and prayers will stand him in good stead when he is brought into temptation. I must again warn you against the sin of drunkenness, against the habit of profane swearing or the use of coarse and brutal language; and let me also plead with you to be merciful and kind in your treatment of your horses."

Of an address delivered to Slaughtermen, no record of which has been preserved, he himself, in one of his letters, speaks thus :

"The slaughtermen were really delightful, so hearty, earnest, ready to be reached, if one only spoke kindly and straight to them. When I talked to them of man's proper conduct towards woman, there really seemed to be kindled a spark of chivalry in their souls; and even when I spoke of what to many of them, I fear, would be almost a strange idea, the power and blessing of prayer, those strong, careless men were for the moment at least softened and subdued. They really gave me such an ovation as almost made me afraid of that peril, 'when all men speak well of you.' At any rate, I had another illustration of how the most neglected classes have that in them which can be reached if only we try to reach it."

But the addresses which attracted most attention were those which the Bishop delivered at two most interesting and impressive gatherings of the employés of the Manchester theatres. The first of these gatherings was held at the Theatre Royal, where the company of that theatre was joined by the company of the Queen's. The Bishop was accompanied by the Rev. J. A. Atkinson, M.A., Rector of Longsight (the secretary of the mission, by whom the arrangements for the Bishop's visits to the theatres were made), and was received on the stage by Mr. Sidney (the manager), Mr. T. Agnew, and Mr. J. Poole. The Address he delivered there, and one subsequently at the Prince's Theatre, were listened to with the most marked and respectful attention; and the singing was heartily joined in by almost every member of the Companies of the respective theatres.

"You can easily imagine," he said, "that it is with feelings very mingled, in which anxiety very largely predominates, that I have accepted the invitation to address you in this theatre.

"Those who know their Bibles—and all, I hope, know them more or less—will remember in the days of old that in a great Asiatic city, a seat of luxury and vice, a great preacher of the gospel once on a memorable occasion was advised by a message from his friends 'that he would not adventure himself into the theatre.' I fancy I must be the first Bishop of the Church of England, if I am not the first Bishop of the Church of Christ, who has ever addressed a congregation in a theatre. It was not that Paul was afraid of testifying to the Gospel of the grace of God anywhere or everywhere—it was not that he had any cowardly or selfish fears for his own personal safety or his life; he was ready when the occasion demanded to spend and be spent in the service of his Master, but in that theatre of Ephesus there was an excited and an angry crowd, not in the humour to listen to reason—their ears would have been deaf to the gentle pleadings of the Spirit of God—and he wisely yielded to the counsels of his friends and did not enter those theatre walls. I see before me those who are willing to listen, or else, I suppose, you would not be present; and, therefore, I have adventured myself into this theatre, hoping that by the help of God I may be enabled to say something to you which will profit you in what I feel—and I suppose in what you feel—is the delicate and difficult, and, I need not add, somewhat perilous work that you are engaged in doing. The fathers of the early Church were very severe in their judgment upon stage-players—the old fathers of an ascetic turn of mind, like Tertullian and Cyprian, denounced stage plays and stage-players in all forms of the most vehement language, and the early canons of the Church refused Baptism and even Holy Communion to actors until they had renounced their trade. I admit there was a difference. The theatre in the early days of the Church was utterly corrupt and degraded. Any one who has read the picture of manners to be found in the pages of Juvenal, and in those of later writers—in the pages of Gibbon, as to what a Roman theatre was in those days—can easily understand how men of earnest and somewhat over-stern minds would feel, that those who could lend themselves to such degrading exhibitions as were to be witnessed in the Roman theatres and amphitheatres could have no claim, no part nor lot, in the blessed work which Christ did for the world. I am amazed as I realize seeing you sitting before me. I am surprised at the gigantic dimensions of these large theatres, for there must be some three hundred people assembled before me. And I think that somehow or other Christianity should penetrate into the theatre. I remember how, in the old tale in the old book, the wandering tribes of Israel in the sandy deserts of Arabia, perishing for lack of water and grievously afflicted with thirst, came to a fountain where they hoped to slake their thirst, but found the waters bitter and well-nigh poisonous, and how Moses, taught by God, bade them cut down some wood that fortunately was close by and throw it into the bitter fountain, and the waters then became sweet and wholesome. The old interpreters said that the wood typified the Cross of Christ, which alone could sweeten the bitter waters of life and make them wholesome to those who drank of them. So I think that somehow or other the power of the Cross of Christ ought to be able to reach within the walls of the theatre. It would be, perhaps, an idle dream and a mere parade of words to say we could ever have a directly spiritual influence brought into theatres—though I am told that the recent Passion Play in Germany had a most directly Christianizing influence upon those who witnessed it, and that those who acted in it, although they were only common peasants, seemed to throw themselves into that wonderful exhibition with a realization of the great truths they were there to exhibit. Still, I do not expect that. I should be quite content if the wholesome and sound moral influence of Christianity, which makes us know and feel the value of purity and modesty in word and deed, and gesture and conduct—I would be quite satisfied if this could be found always to be the ruling principle of the Theatre Royal, Manchester, and of every theatre, whether royal or not, in the land. A great heathen teacher and philosopher, Aristotle, taught me that tragedy was a great instrument for purifying the passions—that through the influence of fear and pity it wrought out the purification of the passions. And I think no one will say who has seen any well-graced actor playing a part—a leading part—

in any of Shakspere's great tragedies, 'Lear,' or 'Hamlet,' or 'Othello' (though, no doubt, the incidents in the drama here and there verge on difficult and delicate points and the language of the age was somewhat coarse and gross), yet I think no one ever left a theatre where he had seen 'Hamlet' or 'Othello' well performed without in some sense or other feeling his whole nature elevated and strengthened, and, even if not spiritualized, at any rate the waters had been wholesome to him that he had drunk at. One thing you are to look to is that the parts you play are honest, pure, and worthy parts. I do not think that any player ought to be ashamed or afraid to refuse to take part in any drama which to any extent would compromise his proper dignity as a man or her proper modesty as a woman. If that resolution were in men's hearts and women's hearts too, the stage would be purified. There are those who think it would be better for society if theatres were swept away. That was once tried in England in the days of the Commonwealth, when what were called Puritan principles were in the ascendancy. Theatres were closed, and no one was allowed to see a play performed; but there came a terrible reaction—there came the period of the Restoration, there came the plays which are now never seen, which no actor would study, no manager would put upon his boards—plays of Congreve, Farquhar, Wycherly, and Vanbrough, and a woman (Mrs. Afra Behn) wrote a play which even men to-day would blush to read or see.

"The great Roman critic Horace tells us that those things which pass through the ear stimulate the mind much less than those things which are presented to the eye. I do not agree with those who say that it will be better for society if theatres are swept away. I believe that it will be infinitely worse for society. I do not want to abolish the theatre; I want to purify it. I want to make it a great instrument for providing healthful and harmless recreation to those who would always be seeking recreation. I have not the slightest wish to Puritanize society; I wish to purify it. We may preach until doomsday, but as long as God has given men the faculty of laughter and amusement, as long as men have oftentimes dreary hours to spend in an evening, which they find they cannot spend at home, they are sure to go in search of amusement, and of various forms of amusement; and I am not one of those who wish the theatre doors closed—I wish to see them open that they may present to those who go into them things that are lovely, and beautiful, and praiseworthy, and of good report. I hope it is not unreasonable to hope that the public taste may be improved. It is difficult, I know, to bring about a reform; but, if managers and actors in theatres will co-operate in the great cause of purifying the public taste, that desirable result may yet be achieved. I ask you honestly whether you can say that theatres in the last twenty years have improved or have deteriorated as places of public amusement and of public recreation? (Mr. Sidney: 'Yes; they have improved.') Well, I am glad to hear that. I have enjoyed the opportunity in my life of making to a slight extent the acquaintance of one or two actors. I remember in 1858, when I was employed on a Government Commission, I went to Sherborne in Dorset, and there I found, living in his own house and occupied with all good things—teaching the ignorant, going night by night to the ragged school—the great tragedian of the last age, Macready. Again, in 1865, when I was travelling in Canada, I met on a steamer careering down the St. Lawrence Mr. and Mrs. Charles Kean. I spent two or three days in their company, and I never enjoyed any person's company more. Last year I had the pleasure of meeting Mrs. Theodore Martin (Miss Helen Faucit) at Lord Egerton's at Tatton, and a more accomplished lady I think you cannot find. I therefore say that the stage need not necessarily be degrading to any one, and that it may be animated and pervaded by high and worthy motives. I do not think I ever was in a London theatre half a dozen times in my life; but the last time I was in one was about thirty-five years ago, when Mr. Macready and Miss Helen Faucit were performing in 'Othello.' I remember in those days the play bills used to announce at the Theatre Royal that 'His Majesty's servants will perform such and such a play to-night.' That was a mere phrase for describing actors at the Theatre Royal, which the King sometimes used to attend. But we are still His Majesty's servants, only the King whom we serve is not the King who lives in Windsor Castle or the Queen who holds drawing-rooms at Buckingham Palace, but the great King whom we have been singing about. He came into this world to redeem us and to sanctify every lawful path, and I will not say that the actor's path is unlawful. I will not put any obstacle or stumbling-block in your way, for I do not believe it is unlawful; but I do believe the actor is the servant of the King of Kings, and that the rules, maxims, and principles of the Gospel are bound to govern the singer, the actor, the ballet-dancer, the scene-shifter—every one who connects himself or herself with a public theatre. You ought to realize when you go to a play that you are His Majesty's servants, who are bound to present to other servants of the same great King something that will instruct them, and which, if it will not spiritualize them, will, at any rate, send them out unharmed and none the worse for what they have seen and heard. One of the saddest books I ever read was Mr. Herbert Spencer's work on the 'Morals of Trade,' in which he exposed the rascality of traders in their dealings one with another, and urged that the fault in that matter rested with society. If we ever get into the way of throwing the blame upon society, it is all up with us. If we do not recognize our personal responsibility, you may depend upon it we shall never be brought to any true sense of duty, and still less to any true repentance for sin. I am perfectly aware that there are all kinds of complicated interests involved in a great theatre. This theatre, I believe, to a certain extent belongs to a company, and it is said that companies have no consciences. I have been talking to some of the directors, and I know that they have a conscience, and that they wish to see the theatre conducted in all respects decently and in order. But it may be said, 'Society expects these things, and people won't go if you establish these maxims of propriety that you talk to us about.' I do not know how that may be, but I know that a great

G

number of people have scruples about going to theatres, because they are liable to see things they do not like, and which they do not want their daughters to see or hear. There is a great peril in that fact. Directors urge that they must pay a dividend—their 10 per cent.; the actor may say he does not like the part, but cannot refuse it, and a woman especially may say, 'I have the natural and maidenly feelings of a woman, and I do not like to pose myself before a great audience, many of whom are coarse and wanton men, who look upon me with lustful and lascivious eyes—I do not want to pose myself before them in an attitude and in a costume which degrade me as a Christian maiden in their eyes and in my own, but what am I to do? My bread depends upon it, and if I remonstrate I shall be told that somebody will be got in my place who will have no such scruples.' Well, I do not know how they are to get out of these things, unless there is more consideration on all sides—unless there is more consideration for the souls of men and women. I hope that by degrees certain things which I am sure every right-minded person amongst you laments at present—certain costumes, certain dances, certain interludes, will by degrees—it may not be done in a day or in a year—be abolished. I hope there will enter into theatres a spirit of higher morality, and that all will feel that the great principles of purity and modesty ought never to be compromised. I am always jealous of the influence of woman upon society. She has a special mission here, not merely to soften us, but also to purify us. If we men had had wanton mothers and wanton sisters, where should we have been? Oh, how our ears would have tingled when we heard their names mentioned. Anything which compromises the modesty or dignity of woman always excites strong feelings in my mind; and I feel sure that, when woman fails to keep her proper place in society, then society will go down with a run. I remember Juvenal said of society in his day, 'We are going down with a run.' Whether theatres are getting better or worse, I cannot say, but all our great cities are multiplying places of dangerous amusement which to a very great extent are corrupting old and young, and therefore I want to see what I would call legitimate places of amusement which shall stand like breakwaters amongst the surging waters of vice; I want to see theatres kept free from the taint which is spreading somewhat far and somewhat widely. You can do something in that direction. If I have spoken any word that has touched a chord in your hearts or awakened long dormant thoughts in your consciences, I earnestly pray that God's Blessed Spirit, Who alone can give the increase, will deepen that impression in your souls, and make the calling which you have chosen for yourselves, and against which I will not be thought to have said a single word, nobler and worthier, because purer and more Christian."

The address was received in the most solemn silence, and many of the audience were visibly affected during its delivery. There was a tendency occasionally to raise a cheer at some of the more popular passages, but the attempt was quickly checked. The audience having sung "Rock of Ages," the Bishop pronounced the benediction, and the company quietly separated.

The Bishop then proceeded to the Prince's Theatre, which was also crowded with employés and actors from every department of the theatre. His lordship was received by Mr. Henry, the manager, and Mr. Stephen, the stage manager, and conducted to the stage. After hymns and prayer, the former being sung to a full orchestral accompaniment arranged by Mr. Stanislaus, the Bishop delivered an earnest address, which was identical in many points with the one he had delivered at the Theatre Royal.

Of these addresses, Dean Stanley wrote to the Bishop:

"I so very much admire your address to the actors. You appear to me to possess the singular gift of going to the very verge of imprudence, and yet never crossing it. That, in your position, is almost perfection."

Among others to whom the Bishop sent an account of his addresses in the Manchester Theatres was the Baroness Burdett-Coutts; and, in the course of a few days, he received from her the following interesting reply:

"The duty, as it seems to me, which is laid on society is not to inaugurate new theatres, but to guide and direct public taste, and keep it pure and healthy. This is more especially within the province of those (and, oh, their power!) whose position almost necessarily exercises some influence on at least minor morals; and whose countenance would encourage both the managers and the members of the dramatic profession who endeavour to promote and maintain rules, decencies, good manners both before and behind the curtain. In this direction much might be done for the benefit of public morality and cultivation of mind and heart. All will admit, without fear of its being Puritanical, the objections to which theatrical representations are open—they are common wherever 'men do congregate,' even to places of instruction. Look, for instance, to evening schools; and these not always situated amongst the lowest. Then as to the profession itself—doubtless there must be many temptations in this calling, but so there are in many, perhaps all, others. On all these points I can touch very cursorily, and most imperfectly, far below the subject of your thoughtful consideration. No one can feel its importance more than myself, who love the drama and have found in it a source of unfailing pleasure, and a resource which nothing else offered.

"I have taken up already too much of your time, yet I must add some observations upon your letter in respect to a subject to which you give a wise and kind attention, and are inducing others to think also. Partial as I am to the theatre, I do not care for *Private Theatricals*, nor should I, as a rule, care to cultivate any taste for them. Of course I am only speaking generally. They may, and often do, offer harmless amusement and, in some circumstances, an easy and even useful recreation. But the profession of acting is a quite different thing from this dilettante pursuit. The one demands, to succeed in or follow in any degree, patience, industry, study, and often much hard work and privation. In private theatricals very different qualities are called into play—and I should rarely indeed wish to promote the desire to become the actor rather than the audience. It is one thing to follow a profession with its rules, restraints, and customs, and quite another to enter the same scenes unprofessionally. The expedient to get out of certain difficulties, such as by the adoption by lads of female parts, is questionable; and the habits and intimacies formed amongst amateurs place them, amongst themselves, on a quite different footing (unavoidably) to that occupied by the members of a company: also every wholesome check which an audience can afford is wanting. Pray excuse a long rambling letter with its feeble expression of feelings and opinions which, however, I entertain very strongly. I am, yours sincerely, my dear Bishop,

"BURDETT-COUTTS.

"P.S.—Mr. Irving is at present so engrossed with Richard that I have had no opportunity of naming the subject to him as I think you perhaps thought I would."

At the foot of this letter the Bishop pencilled the remark, "Good points.—Reformation of theatres best done by those who are eminent in the profession. Private theatricals to be discouraged, having the licence without the safeguards of the professional Drama."

Letters from all parts of the country poured in upon the Bishop in recognition of the "manly but discriminating" support which he had given to the Drama; and of the warm, tender, earnest manner in which he had preached Christ's Gospel to actors and actresses from the stage of the theatre.

LOUGHBOROUGH RECTORY, *February* 5, 1877.

DEAR BISHOP OF MANCHESTER,—Since my note will require no answer, I hope you will allow me to say that I read with great interest your remarks on dramatic entertainments.

My belief is that for the clergy to set their faces against all theatrical performances is a great mistake, and that rightly directed they are a valuable means of public instruction.

I always feel grateful to my father for taking me to the play to see a piece of which I forget the name, but in which a gamester was the prominent and ill-omened character, and I thought from that time, whatever other sins I may commit in life, I shall never be a gambler. No sermon will produce the effect of a harrowing scene on a sensitive mind,—

"Segnius irritant animos demissa per aures
Quam quæ sunt oculis subjecta fidelibus."

I am sure you will excuse me, my dear lord, for saying that I think your manly but discriminating praise of these things, as indeed all your utterances, are calculated to remove many prejudices. Believe me, with sincere respect, yours truly,

H. FEARON, Archdeacon of Leicester.

DEAR LORD BISHOP,—I hope your lordship will pardon me and not think me to be impertinent if I venture to express a sense of deep personal obligation at your recent bold and noble action at the theatres in Manchester. I have no right to express a single word to your lordship on the matter. I certainly should not think of doing so, if I had not some especial interest in the people to whom your lordship spoke. The principal dancer—solo dancer as she calls herself—at the Theatre Royal is well known to me. She is not very educated, but is one of the very nicest and best girls I have ever met with. She has been on the stage since she was ten years old, and during her career she has been the chief support of her mother and sister. I never met a more simple or gentle creature, and her sense of maidenly reserve and modesty is most acute. She wrote to tell me about your lordship's address, and this morning I have received a copy of the *Manchester Evening Mail* from her. It may be some satisfaction to your lordship to know that your gallant effort to speak a word in season to ballet-dancers is met by the warmest appreciation on their part, and that, in the person of one who has to pose herself before the public eye in this most dangerous calling, there does dwell the brightness of a spirit undefiled, and a heart true, tender, and pure as that of a little child. I beg once more to thank your lordship for your goodness to these poor people.

PRINCE'S THEATRE.

MY LORD,—Let me, as a hearer of your able discourse on Friday at the Prince's Theatre, beg leave to express my appreciation of the sentiments your lordship uttered, and also to ask permission to offer the accompanying drawing * which I trust may be personally interesting to you. Believe me to remain, your lordship's most obedient servant,

SCENIC ARTIST.

MY LORD,—From my heart I thank you for the noble work you have begun for the stage. I am much interested in the subject, as I have a brother who has made the stage his profession, and has married in the

---

* This drawing, a water-colour of the Manchester Cathedral, the Bishop hung in his drawing-room and highly prized.

same line. At the London Mission I endeavoured to get something done here, but without success; therefore, when I saw that your lordship had come forward and set the noble example, my whole heart overflowed with joy and gratitude. May God bless and reward you and bless your work. I have long thought that my mission might be to do something for those on the stage, but hitherto my efforts have been baffled. It is very difficult for a woman to know exactly what to do. I am trying again now, and just at this time of my renewed endeavours, to see what your lordship has done, was like a bright gleam of light across my path. Perhaps some day you will consider the question of how women may help their sisters on the stage, and I may read what you say.

Begging your lordship to forgive the liberty I take in writing, when I have not the honour of your acquaintance, and again heartily thanking you, I am faithfully and gratefully yours.

THEATRE ROYAL, LEICESTER.

MY LORD,—May I be allowed as a humble member of the dramatic profession to thank your lordship for the kind words addressed to the actors in Manchester and through them to us all. I am thankful that a class too often (especially I regret to say by ministers of religion) looked upon as pariahs and "outsiders" of society, should have been recognized by your lordship as worthy of Christian counsel and advice. When I read that your lordship had spoken *from* the stage I felt proud, but when I read *what* your lordship had said my heart was full to think how kindly you had recognized the fact that the stage in good hands is an advantage and not a curse to society. I cannot help thinking that much of the decline of the stage is due to the "snubbing" many of us get because we are actors. I myself have been refused admission to houses when seeking apartments, *because I was an actor*, for no other reason; and this is only one specimen of what members of the profession have to submit to. Your lordship will therefore understand how much that address will break down prejudices now existing. It will also cheer actors in their efforts (and they *do* try) to improve the tone of their profession.

I brought your address under my manager's notice and (with his permission) have taken the liberty of printing it on programmes, not I assure your lordship for advertising purposes, but in order that your liberal views may be circulated in this somewhat narrow-minded town, and I also propose to send copies freely to other theatres.

The Bishop's own feeling and opinion, in reference both to the general character of the mission and the special effort at the theatres, may be gathered from the following letters:

"Last night I addressed about seven or eight hundred of the employés in about twenty of our great drapery establishments congregated within the walls of the largest. I never spoke to a more attentive audience.

They seemed profoundly in earnest, and, as I spoke kindly and encouragingly, and did not forbid cheerfulness or amusements so long as they were pure, I hope that some of my words may have done good. With Coventry Patmore, ' I hold delight half discipline.' Paul bids the Philippians 'rejoice,' and I am not one of those who hold that, to be religious, you must be gloomy, or forswear anything that is good and lovely in the world; and so I tried to teach the people who are exposed to so many perils, that even in Manchester it was possible to lead pure lives."

"I quite agree with your estimate of the profanity of Mr. ——'s speech about the theatre. I thought it in very questionable taste; and I entirely differ from him in holding that what is lawful for a layman is lawful, or (to use St. Paul's words) 'expedient,' for a clergyman. This was one of the subjects on which I spoke earnestly to my young candidates for ordination the other day, in one of the evening addresses I always give them in the examination week. I may wish—and I do most earnestly wish—to purify the theatre; but I am not going to attempt that by myself attending theatres."

"It is unfair and untrue of Mr. —— to say that I 'recommend' the theatre. I certainly do believe that society would be worse rather than better—*i.e.* would be more likely to choose coarser than purer amusements—if theatres were swept away; but the whole tendency of my address was not to recommend the theatre indiscriminately, *as it is*, but to call upon the profession to elevate *it*, and the *actors*, and *society*, at the same time.

"However, notwithstanding what Mr. —— has said, I bear him no malice for it. He is too good-natured a man to be angry with; and I dare say when I meet him we shall be as good friends as we generally are. I, for one, however strongly I resent things at the moment, at least bear no malice. I have a hot and hasty temper, but not a sullen or vindictive one.

"Oh, that we could indeed see the dawn of the day of the Church of the future! As I read the pages of ecclesiastical history—those heart-rending pages of strife and controversy, of intolerance and cruelty, I almost feel as though the genius of Christianity had never, even yet, been comprehended."

"I am impulsive, and, people say, apt to make mistakes, and to say and do things that had been better left unsaid and undone. You may not, perhaps, regard my sayings and doings entirely without partiality; but at any rate you will look upon them without prejudice. The longer I live, the more I seem to see the need—if Christ's Gospel is ever again to become a power regnant in the world—that it should be proclaimed in all its breadth, largeness, and simplicity. If ritual would only drop into its proper place, I should not quarrel with it. I indeed prefer a solemnly ornate sermon; it seems to help my soul to soar. My quarrel is, when men forget the great law of *proportion*, and put that first which is only secondary, and even say that they cannot proclaim the first great sermon of God's love to man, without accessories which almost seem to make the power of the Gospel depend upon the tailor or the master of the ceremonies. I hope this mission will help to show men the 'more excellent way.' So far as I can judge, and as things have yet gone, God's blessing seems to rest abundantly on the work. There is a great 'hush,' as it were, in the air; men's lighter thoughts seem subdued and their more generous sympathies awakened. Congregations grow everywhere; in some of the churches they are overflowing; and all is being done calmly, and, I believe, wisely. Mr. Knox Little's addresses at the cathedral have been most soul-stirring. The crowds that gather at all the services (he preaches four or five times a day) are wonderful, and I hope he has taught people that a man may be a ritualist and yet have a tender and earnest care for souls. I hope he is not killing himself. He is not a strong man, and I have warned him not to overtax his strength; but his theme carries him away, and he forgets himself wholly in the message he feels himself sent to deliver.

"I have, myself, been mainly engaged with addresses to masses of working people—in numbers from five hundred to fifteen hundred—in some of the great iron-forges, mills, and factories. The earnest attention of the hearers is most remarkable. Oh, the fields are, if not white for the harvest, at any rate, ready for sowing the seed! Yesterday I had the most delicate and difficult business I ever undertook—to address the actors and employés at our three principal theatres. I hope you will be able to sympathize with what I said. I do so feel for all those actors, who by reason of their vocation are exposed to so many perils, and are (apparently) so little shielded. I want to see the theatre purified. It is useless to denounce it; that is only beating the air. But there is no reason why it should not become a place of pure and legitimate amusement. I don't know when I have been more touched, than when yesterday, after my second address, Mr. Henry, the manager of the Prince's, shook me by the hand, and said, 'Ah, you have spoken kindly to us; if all bishops would do the same, perhaps we should be better than we are!' There is a sort of Providence in these things. The hymns were not of my choosing; but were taken from the Rev. W. H. Aitken's hymns for a parochial mission; and one of those sung was Hymn 80, in which were these words—

"'For the love of God is broader
Than the measure of man's mind,
As the heart of the Eternal
Is more wonderfully kind;
But we make His love too narrow
By false limits of our own,
And we magnify His strictness
With a zeal He will not own.'

"This furnished me with the leading thought by which I tried to lead these poor players' minds to recognize and realize the 'love of God in Christ.' I have invited all the clergy of Manchester to a conference, as soon as the mission is closed, for the purpose of comparing experiences, ascertaining results, and getting to know what methods have proved successful: we must not let the iron, once heated, get cool again. If desires have been kindled, we must try to satisfy them. We shall be singularly dull and impassive if we have not learnt something from what we have heard and seen for the last week."

"I do not complain of being misreported; but sometimes, when very accurately reported, it is my ill-luck to be misunderstood. It may be remembered that a short time ago I ventured into the theatre for the purpose of addressing the stage-players and managers there, and I made some remarks, which I do not think the most perverse ingenuity could interpret into commending theatres as they are. The point of my remarks was, a recommendation to make theatres as I conceived they should and might be, so that people might go and receive no harm from them. In one of our amiable Christian newspapers quite a different interpretation was given, and a correspondent actually held me responsible for that fire at Higher Broughton, which destroyed a considerable amount of property belonging to Mr. Hazzopulo. Bishops are made responsible for many things; but I never knew one to be made responsible for the burning of a house before. It was alleged against me, that I recommended people to go to the theatre, that the servants of Mr. Hazzopulo went, the house was burnt in their absence, and therefore I ought to be made responsible for the financial damage. This is sufficiently amusing; but it only shows that you must be indulgent to poor bishops, and make some allowance for us."

Immediately after the mission the Bishop convened a conference for the purpose, "while impressions were still vivid, of ascertaining results, comparing experiences, and giving the opportunity of hearing what methods have been found most successful in the various departments of spiritual work with which the missioners have had to deal." The conclusions arrived at by the conference may fairly be inferred from extracts from a sermon preached by the Bishop immediately after the conference had been held:

"We have just passed through a period of more than ordinary solemnity—the twelve days of the Manchester and Salford Church Mission, with all its hopes and all its fears, all its encouragements, and all its anxieties. The mission period has passed away, and the preachers who have stirred men's hearts have returned to their own pastoral work; but there still remains what I call the hopes and fears, the encouragements, and anxieties. To me, as one who has moved about a good deal during the mission, it seemed a period of power and of conspicuous blessing. Good seed has been scattered freely, and has found entrance into many a heart; the question is, whether it has taken root there and will bring forth fruit. There was one peculiar characteristic of the mission which must have struck every one, and that was the entire absence of anything like unhealthy excitement or morbid tumultuousness of feeling. It was a kind of marked quietness, almost calm, that could be felt. Every one who is honest with himself, every one who searches out his own motives, and compares his resolution with his conduct, must be quite aware that there was a very grievous peril in all such work as that in which we have just been engaged. I will only speak of one special form of peril, which is the subtle one of self-absorption, by which I mean, lest you should come to think that the only thing that you and I have to do is, as the phrase goes, 'to save our own souls,' and lest, in the selfish endeavour to save ourselves from the general wreck, we should forget the duties we owe to others. Only yesterday a lady was telling me of an incident which occurred on board the 'North Briton,' fourteen years ago, when that vessel, in a stormy night, struck on a rock off the coast of Labrador. There were about three hundred souls on board, including a large number of troops, and all made up their minds to die. The lady, who was among the passengers, said there was an admirable spirit of resignation and of courage among all but one man, and he began to offer $100 for a life-belt, $160, $200, until at last he offered $1,000. He thought merely of saving his own miserable life, and did not care whether the other two hundred and ninety-nine were saved or not; but by the providence of God, without spending his thousand dollars, and without a life-belt, he and all on board got safely to land. If the souls of you whom I am addressing are actuated by a benevolent and Christian spirit, prompting you to service, and, if need be, to sacrifice, you will be saved. Have you ever tried to conceive what a wonderful change would be effected in the state of society, if we could root out the selfishness which exists. Religious selfishness, is, perhaps, the subtlest and the most dangerous. I venture to put it before you as a distinct and unquestionable Christian axiom, that the less you think of your own souls—that is, anxiously, fretfully and doubtfully, like a hypochondriac patient who is always feeling his pulse and putting his hand upon his heart to see whether it is regular, thus engendering the very disease from which he hopes to escape—and the more you think of your neighbours' bodies and souls the better will it be for yourselves, not only morally but spiritually."

CHAPTER V.

THE LANCASHIRE STRIKE.

The Bishop and Strikes—A Strike an Industrial War—Sermon on Strikes—Letter to Mr. Broadhurst—Causes of Strike—Proposed Remedies—Commencement of Strike—Letters and Sermon at Leigh—The Lock-out—The Riot—Letter to Weavers' Association—Sermons at Rishton and Halliwell—Proposed Compromise—The Bishop's Letter to the Manchester and London Press—Termination of Strike.

THE year A.D. 1878, the year of the great Lancashire Strike, was a year of special anxiety and indefatigable labour to Bishop Fraser. "This sad cotton strike," he said, "is on my mind night and day, and I don't think people half realize the magnitude of the issues which it involves." Everything which touched the interests and the progress of the masses of the people was deeply interesting to this Bishop of the people; and the Lancashire Strike set his whole nature on flame with desire to guide and help them by every means within his reach. Through the whole course of his life, the Bishop—intensely believing that Christianity ought to deal with men's present temporal affairs as well as with their future eternal prospects—had been a student of social problems; so that, when called upon to speak in the pulpit, upon the platform, through the Press, upon the topics of capital and labour, wages and work, associations of masters, unions of men, and similar cognate subjects, he commanded confidence; not only on account of his fairness of mind and largeness of sympathy, but also on account of the soundness of his knowledge and the thoroughness of his acquaintance with the issues at stake.

The great Lancashire Strike of 1878 was not, however, the first occasion, during his episcopate, upon which Bishop Fraser had exerted his influence in settling disputes between employers and employed.

In May 1871 he had pleaded against the strike threatened

by the cotton operatives in Oldham; in November 1872 he had counselled the employés of the London and North-Western Railway Company "not to be so foolish as to follow noisy agitators who had no stake to lose, but, in case of dispute with their employers, to choose men from their own body to talk over the matter fully and freely in a friendly spirit, thus avoiding the strikes which are threatening trade and becoming a very serious element of danger to society." In March 1874, and again in March 1876, he was chosen arbitrator between the house-painters of Manchester and their employers. In the spring of 1875 he had written his famous letter to the *Times* upon the lock-out of the agricultural labourers in the Eastern Counties, espousing the cause of the labourers: and in the following year he had been invited to arbitrate in a wage-dispute between colliers and their employers. In all these instances he had shown himself scrupulously just towards the capitalist and sympathetically generous towards the workman. He withheld his approval both from combinations of masters and unions of men; not because he was hostile to the principle of combination—a principle which, if rightly developed, is productive both of strength and sympathy—but because he believed that the *purpose* of these combinations, as distinguished from their *principle*, was a purpose of war.

Mr. Robert Little writes:

"It was my business as cashier to the secretary of the Manchester Conservative Club, at whose office the executive committee of the Discharged Prisoners' Aid Society held its meetings, to receive subscriptions. The Bishop, I believe, contributed to this society annually, from the commencement of his episcopate to the end.

"It was a time of severe commercial depression. Machinery was idle and operatives were starving. Bitterness was made more bitter by incessant strikes. Masters were furious. The Bishop came in to pay his subscription, and my principal stumbled on the theme of the hour. He informed the Bishop that the masters had it in contemplation to form a union, analogous to, and to cope with, the union of operatives. Suddenly there was a pause—he seemed thunderstruck—his face blanched and the cloud burst: '*It is WAR!!!*' then another pause, '*and I don't believe in war!*'"

A strike he regarded as an industrial war—a lock-out as a process of starvation or siege. And the same motives which prompted him to condemn international wars prompted him also to condemn industrial wars. He was ever ready to acknowledge that cases may arise in which war is essential, righteous, beneficent (and upon this topic he frequently quoted Professor Mozley's great sermon, Sermon V. in the volume of University Sermons). But, as he was keenly alive to the horrors of war, the heaps of slain, the desolation, the starvation, the agony, the wounded and the maimed, the sick and the dying, homes deserted, fields uncultivated, children fatherless, wives widows: so he anxiously dreaded the results of strikes and lock-outs, the alienation of masters and men, the gendering of bitterness and hatred, the insurrectionary violence of demagogues, the loss both to employers and employed, the triumph of riot and lawlessness, the sufferings of wives and children, the rancour which, upon one side or the other, must inevitably follow upon defeat.

The following extract from a sermon preached in St. Mary's, Oldham, in October 1877, shows in how truly sympathetic a spirit towards both masters and men the Bishop spoke upon the question:

"The Bolton strike is of this character: The self-actor minders are the people who are out on strike. They are in an association and receive payment from their society; but there are a number of other persons employed in the card rooms and elsewhere—men and women who are not in any society, and who are in the direst distress in consequence of this strike. I think I heard it said that a strike of 20 self-actor minders would throw out of work 200 pairs of hands. It is for these people who are in no association, who never received high wages, who probably never earned more than 18s. or £1 a week, and who therefore were never able to save much, even if of thrifty habits, that I plead. It is their case that touches my heart with so lively a feeling of sympathy. I confess I was delighted to hear two days ago at Bolton that there were many employers who were giving their people a dinner a day, and that others were giving them 3s. and 5s. a week for cleaning the mills and doing odd jobs of the kind, so that they may not be utterly reduced to starvation. But still it is a dire state of things. I was told that the distress and the trouble that now prevails—and widely prevails—at Bolton is a very pitiful sight; and if that is true of Bolton, where there are so many industries, how much more must be the distress arising from a strike at Oldham, where the people, I understand, are almost entirely dependent on the cotton industry. When I observe the way in which the Trades Union delegates at Leicester received the excellent advice given to them by Mr. Brassey with so much courage and sympathy, I do seem to see that there is a temper prevailing among the working men—and the same prevails among the employers—to do what is just and right, and to accept what is fair and reasonable. On a memorable occasion a French statesman—I can't call him a great statesman—said he went into a great war with a light heart. Within a few weeks he saw his country prostrate beneath the feet of the invader; and I think any one who at all attempts to realize the prospect of a two months' strike, and the tremendous loss of wages that will ensue, will feel with me that every method of conciliation and every instrument that can be used for coming to a right understanding should be resorted to, before what is practically a declaration of war between capital and labour is made. I cannot help thinking that if a man of intelligence and equitable mind such as Mr. Brassey were invited to come here and settle the question among you just now, as we are entering upon the winter season, a great amount of distress, the consequences of which we must all deplore, might, under God's good guidance, be prevented. I hope that you will not think I have travelled out of my own proper province, but I cannot help having my heart touched with questions of this kind, which, as the late Prince Consort said many years ago, really cut into the very quick of the life of this complicated thing we call English Society."

In the same spirit he wrote to Mr. Broadhurst, the Secretary of the Parliamentary Committee of the Trades Union Congress, from whom he had received a bound copy of its last year's publications, with a complimentary letter in recognition of his valuable speeches and letters on the Labour Question:

BISHOP'S COURT, MANCHESTER, *October* 25, 1877.

SIR,—I am very much obliged for the report of your Committee, and for the kind letter which accompanied it. I shall read the volume with great interest, as it touches upon many questions upon which I desire to be accurately informed. I will not deny that I take a profound interest in these social problems, which are second in importance to none as affecting the well-being of the community and our industrial future as a nation. Christianity, if it cannot solve them, yet ought to be able to help in their solution, by preparing the mind for a calm, unbiassed, and equitable consideration of the case in all its elements; and, in what you are pleased to say I have done in this matter, I hope I have not stepped beyond my province as a minister of the Gospel, in pleading that this is the temper in which discussions touching the rights of capital and labour should be conducted on both sides. It surely indicates that something is needed, when at Bolton it has just required a strike of nine weeks, involving severe distress and a loss of £90,000 in wages, to arrive at a settlement which might as easily have been arrived at without a strike at all.—I remain, sir, in entire sympathy with every really upward aspiration of the working people of this country, Your faithful servant,

J. MANCHESTER.

To Mr. HENRY BROADHURST.

The Bishop's sympathy did not confine itself to words; in cases of true need he was as ready with his purse as with his speech.

October 16, 1877.

MY DEAR CANON POWELL,—I am much concerned about this Bolton strike, both at its continuance and at the distress it appears to be causing amongst those who are not members of the Union. Surely some effort ought to be made to bring about a reasonable agreement between the two sides. Meanwhile, as a mark of my sympathy with those who are suffering apparently from no fault of their own, will you accept the enclosed cheque for £20 as a contribution to the funds of the local Relief Committee, which you told me when you saw me was being formed for dealing with such cases. Believe me to be yours sincerely,

J. MANCHESTER.

The Rev. Canon POWELL.

The course which the Bishop followed upon public questions often, as was natural, roused against him a spirit of violent antagonism; and, although he was fearless in following any path which he believed to be right, yet the tenderness of his nature made him sensitive to attacks; and, not seldom, when suffering from the bitter onslaught of some critic, the confidence of the people acted on his wounds like a soothing balm.

"I heard from a clergyman at Bolton yesterday, something that gave me unfeigned pleasure. He said: 'I am glad that, in your sermon at Astley Bridge last Sunday week, you did not take any side on the question of the strike: for I believe the men are thinking of asking you to arbitrate between them and their masters, as they say they can have confidence in your fairness.' These duties are not very pleasant or easy to discharge; but still I feel that I ought not to refuse the task when I am asked to undertake it. There are 10,000 pairs of hands unemployed in Bolton now, and a loss of at least £10,000 in wages per week; and this has been going on for three weeks or a month. Surely it is worth while, and not outside a Bishop's proper duty, to try to bring such a state of things to an end. I have been into Manchester and waited with a deputation upon the Mayor about an altogether different subject; but, having a few minutes' private conversation with him before my colleagues assembled, he told me that he thought of proposing to the joiners of Manchester, who have been out on strike for some ten or twelve weeks, to have an interview with himself and me, in the hopes that we might be able to suggest something that should bring the present unhappy state of affairs to an end. Whether we can succeed in this or not, I shall at least feel a satisfaction in the attempt; and confidence shown in this real way is an abundant set-off against any number of rabid attacks."

The Bolton strike, in the autumn of 1877—a strike which lasted nine weeks, and involved a loss of at least £90,000—was but a precursor of the more general strike which took place in the spring and summer of 1878—a strike in which 300,000 persons were immediately concerned, and which involved, in wages alone, a loss to the working classes of £75,000 a week. An intricate complication of causes led to the declaration of this industrial war. The state of the cotton trade was simply deplorable. There had been three bad harvests in succession; and bad harvests at home, although they temporarily stimulate the carrying trade between England and foreign countries, ultimately diminish the purchasing power of the masses of the English people. The price of wheat had risen, in two years, 20s. a quarter. Mr. Caird computed that, owing to the insufficiency of the harvests and various other causes, from 1872 to 1877, £160,000,000 more had been paid for foreign corn than in the previous five years from 1867 to 1872. Moreover, "the energy, ingenuity, and capital of civilized nations, especially of England, had been devoted for more than a quarter of a century to the development of the manufacturing branch of commerce, without any corresponding development of new markets for consumption; with the result that the power of producing manufactured articles had grown so great that whenever a demand for a commodity sprang up it was rapidly met," not only by the supply, but by an over-production of the supply, of that commodity. It was also alleged that, in times of prosperity and abundance, wages had been advanced, and hours of labour shortened, to an extent which could not be maintained in times of depression and scarcity.

Moreover, the impending gloom was not, by any means,

confined to the manufacturing industries of England. The whole world seemed menaced with catastrophe and distress. In the previous year gaunt famine had stalked through large districts of India and China, and South America, strewing its path with the emaciated forms of the dying and the dead. In North America commercial panics were frequent. Upon the continent of Europe the whole atmosphere of politics was charged with suspicion and alarm. The still unsolved Eastern Question was in an acute and critical condition. At home the people had not recovered from the ferment into which they had been thrown by the Bulgarian agitation. Mr. Gladstone had declared his conviction that Turkey should be dismissed from Europe "bag and baggage." Politicians were divided into Russophobes and Russophiles. The Jingo spirit (as it is called) was in a state of frenzy. The condition of Egypt was a condition of threatening insecurity. International uneasiness and want of confidence had, for the time, overthrown the foundations of commercial prosperity. The markets of the world were in a state of plethora and partial collapse. A less auspicious season could scarcely have been chosen by the people for the prosecution of an industrial war.

Neither party in the conflict disputed the fact of the depression of trade; their disagreement arose upon the causes of that depression, and the best means for remedying it. The masters contended that the chief causes were the political alarms which, by their operation upon markets, placed blocks in the ordinary channels of distribution; together with the height of wages which, by increasing the price of commodities, checked the process of consumption and so restricted the demand. The men, without denying the influence of political uneasiness, contended that the chief causes of the depression were the glut of markets consequent upon the rapid increase of machinery, and the excessive working of overtime, together with the adulteration of cotton cloths, which had not only degraded the *prestige* of English goods in the estimation of the world, but had also led to the establishment of cotton-spinning and manufacturing com-panics in the great emporiums of India and China. This antagonism of opinion concerning the causes of the strike was accompanied by an equally distinct antagonism of opinion concerning the best means for remedying them. The masters contended that by a reduction of wages the price of commodities would be lowered and the demand for them proportionately increased. The men contended that, by ceasing to adulterate their goods, the masters might restore the *prestige* of English manufactures in foreign markets; and by shortening the hours of labour, and so limiting the quantity of goods produced, the glut, caused by over-supply, would gradually be relieved. The masters, moreover, contended that foreign competition was an important element in commercial depression at home—a competition rendered all the more severe by the lowness of wages abroad; the men replied that any lowering of wages in England would only benefit the foreign consumer, and lessen the purchasing power of the people at home.

Between opinions so adverse as these, and held on both sides with unflinching tenacity, no compromise appeared to be possible. The strike of 1877 in Bolton had resulted in a five per cent. reduction of wages, not only in Bolton and its neighbourhood, but also in many other towns of South Lancashire, where cotton-spinning is carried on on a large and extensive scale. At the close of the same year the employers of North and North-East Lancashire proposed a similar reduction in wages of five per cent. The men pleaded that this reduction might be a while delayed in the hope of a revival in trade, and an increased activity among the looms and spindles of Lancashire. But inasmuch as trade, instead of reviving, became more generally depressed in the spring of 1878, the masters resolved upon a reduction in wages of ten per cent. To this resolution the employés very strongly demurred. They agreed to a reduction of five per cent., but entirely refused to accept a reduction of ten per cent., unless the reduction of wages were accompanied by a reduction in the hours of labour. At a mass meeting of cotton operatives, including power-loom weavers, overlookers, tape-sizers, twisters and drawers, winders and warpers, held on Saturday, April 13, 1878, in the Exchange Hall, Blackburn, to finally consider and decide whether the ten per cent. reduction of wages should be accepted or not, a resolution was passed, amid much cheering, and by an overwhelming majority: " That, in the opinion of this meeting, when the time of notice expires on Wednesday next (April 7), we refuse to work at the ten per cent. reduction of wages." An amendment, although supported by Mr. Birtwistle and Mr. Whalley, the Chairman and Secretary of the Wages Committee, to the effect that a reduction of wages by ten per cent. should be accompanied by a reduction of labour to four days a week; a five per cent. reduction to five days a week; and those working full time to receive full wages, was rejected with hissings and groanings. At this meeting representatives from many manufacturing centres, including Chorley, Darwen, Great Harwood, Clitheroe, Accrington, Church, Padiham, Burnley, Clayton-le-Moors, Nelson, Haslingden, Ramsbottom, Rossendale, and Preston, were present, and gave expression to their views. Upon the day previous to this meeting of the Men's Union, a meeting of the Masters' Association, presided over by Mr. Raynsford Jackson, had been held in Manchester, at which it was resolved that the ten per cent. reduction of wages should be uniformly enforced.

Thus began the great Lancashire Strike of 1878—a strike which, during its career, aroused intense bitterness between masters and men, caused widespread suffering, and entailed vast pecuniary losses upon both employers and employed. The Bishop's mind was filled, and his heart distressed, by the conflict. Upon April 20, he wrote:

"The strike is hardly a less important question than the war. It is said to affect 120,000 workpeople! Three of the leaders of the operatives waited upon me last Tuesday, but did not ask me to *do* anything. They wished me, however, to read an article from the *Manchester City News*, which they said exactly stated their case. They told me frankly that they had only funds to continue the struggle for a month; and what the issue will be it is impossible to foresee. There is to be a mass meeting of operatives held in Manchester to-morrow, the papers say. Amid all the abuse I get—and I assure you I get a good deal—it is at least some reward that these working people have some faith in me, as not being devoid of sympathy, fairness of mind, and common sense. This makes up for a good deal of unmerited abuse—charging me with sympathy with Ritualists, a desire to embarrass the Government, and what not besides—which at times I feel it rather hard to bear."

Upon April 29:

"I find that I am, much against my will, occupying some share of public attention, and a place in a leading article in the *Times* to-day. It seems that on Saturday the operatives on strike agreed to refer the question in dispute to a commission of arbitration, of which I was named the President. They had never broached the subject to me, and I am afraid that arbitration on such a difficult and complicated problem is 'above my might'; but I perhaps ought not to shrink from it on that account, if the misery that is certain to follow a strike could so be obviated. But I fear that the masters will not consent to arbitration, and the *Times* article, which is very one-sided in its tone, will tend to support them in that resolution. Now I hope you will not think me vain if I do feel a little pride in this mark of confidence. These encouragements help one to bear a good deal of discouragement."

Upon May 11:

"I shall be in the midst of the strike again on Sunday. The present state of tension cannot last long, though at present there are no signs of either side giving in, and the general lock-out begins to-day. I don't quite think it is a case for arbitration. The two parties to the quarrel must know much more about the real merits of the case than any outsider can do, and they ought to settle the difference by a reasonable compromise among themselves. It is difficult to get at the real facts and figures; but, so far as I understand the matter, I think that a reduction of wages, as proposed by the masters, is the only way of relieving the trade."

Preaching in Leigh parish church, on May 4, the Bishop said:

"The last two days I have spent in East and North-East Lancashire. I have been at Colne, Burnley, Padiham, and Accrington. In this district, as you are aware, a large strike prevails. Yesterday I saw strong men and women, strong boys and girls, what they call 'playing' in the streets of Burnley, Padiham and Accrington. They were all quiet, orderly, and well-behaved. I did not see anything that might be called a row. I did not see anything approaching disorder among these people. I saw them idle, and was told that eighty persons had applied to the Board of Guardians for relief, and had not been relieved. I was told that already the resources of many families had come to an end and their credit too. All this struck my heart most deeply and solemnly. I thought of those 120,000 men standing idle, and representing perhaps very nearly half a million of people. A worthy Baptist minister gave me a frightful description of the Forest of Dean, and he told me it was true, if people would only pay a visit to the coal and iron districts of the Forest of Dean or South Wales, they would see that the country had the appearance as if the scourge of war had actually passed over it. The whole of that country is becoming depopulated, and the remnant of the population is starving or half-starving. Lord Aberdare told me himself he did not think the iron trade would ever revive in South Wales. People say this is through the unsettled relations between capital and labour. If so, it is time these relations were readjusted upon a more safe and sure foundation. As things are at present, it is bringing ruin both to the people employed and to the capitalist. People are starving, and if the strike lasts a month in North and North-East Lancashire the month's earnings of the operatives, which, I estimate at £300,000 will be thrown away. That is something frightful to think about—at least it is to my mind. These poor people are suffering, and perhaps the masters won't recover the effects of the strike for years. I and the Rector of Burnley went into a house there the other day, and there the bailiffs were in for a paltry debt of £2 3s. The parties could not pay it, and in all probability their furniture will have to be sold to discharge the debt. That is only one sample of the distress which might become widespread. We ought therefore, I say, to pray for peace and for a restoration of those grounds of trust and confidence which used to prevail between master and man, employers and employed, and which just now seem to be somewhat rudely shaken. I am not here to suggest a remedy, but the fact is apparent on all sides that at present the cotton industry is not remunerative. Capital is not making a profit. There has been a gigantic development of what is called co-operative industry in Oldham, and some three years ago everybody was anxious to take part in it. Mills were built in Oldham by shares, and over a million and a half of money was vested in those mills. One mill was built at a cost of some £40,000 or £60,000, filled with machinery, and stocked with the requisite quantity of cotton to set it going. The parties who invested their money thought they were secured for the rest of their lives. Some of the mills paid a good percentage for a time, but others were built which had never paid a single dividend. About three years ago an aged couple who had saved over £200 invested it in a co-operative mill which was paying 28 per cent. I know that was true, because I saw a half-year's coupon, which showed 14 per cent. for the half-year. Well, this state of things did not last long. A change came over the cotton trade, and the shares for which the old couple paid £200 are not now worth £35. They rested assured in the hope of receiving £58 a year for life, but it has all gone. If there are no profits in a co-operative mill, surely the profits of a mill, managed by one capitalist, cannot be large. The fact is, as I have already observed, the whole of the cotton trade is not remunerative, and men and masters must face that fact. What is wanted is a restoration of confidence. In bad times, if one member suffers, all must suffer—the employer and the employed; and, if good times come again, the men will have a right to claim their old rate of wages. That seems a sensible and rational, and I may say Christian, way of settling the difficulty, which, if unsettled, will be of alarming consequences. If anything has to be done to bring about a restoration of that confidence, it must be done at once, as I am told the masters in East Lancashire are going to lock the hands out on Wednesday next unless the matter is settled. I hope wise counsels will prevail, and that no false notions of honour on the one side, or dogged obstinacy on the other, will prevent an amicable arrangement being arrived at. I hope the masters will be prepared to receive the men on fair and equitable terms, and I hope the men will not be too proud to go and ask to be received on fair and equitable terms."

It is characteristic of the hold which utterances of the Bishop, such as these, had upon the multitudes of the Lancashire people that, in this time of their anxiety and distress, they should naturally have looked to him as the rightful arbitrator and referee in their cause. By his knowledge of the details of the question at issue, he had won their confidence in his wisdom; by his outspoken fearlessness he had won their confidence in his courage; by his constant appeals to righteous Christian principle, he had won their confidence in his integrity; by his generous appreciation of their difficulties he had won their confidence in his friendship.

But, although the men desired the appointment of a Board of Arbitration "to be presided over by the Bishop of Manchester or any other impartial gentleman," the masters, who for some time had been working their mills at a loss, contended that there was no room for arbitration; and that the terms already offered to the men were the best which it was possible to offer. The refusal of the masters to submit the points in dispute to arbitration had the effect of hardening and irritating the temper of the men. The men charged the masters with wanton unfairness and a tyrannous lust for mere conquest in the strife. The masters charged the men with a wilful ignorance of the real causes of bad trade, and a self-interested docility to the fiery invectives of paid and noisy demagogues. It was war to the knife. The men appealed to the Trades Unions throughout the country for assistance in the strife; an appeal which was widely, and not ungenerously, met. The masters drew together in a compactly organized association; and, perceiving that the operatives on strike were maintained by the operatives at work, they resolved to lock out the workers until the strikers had yielded. Upon the 8th of May the members of the Masters' Association at Preston, where the operative spinners had resumed work at the 10 per cent. reduction, closed their mills; so stopping a large portion of the supplies by which the operatives on strike in the Burnley and Blackburn districts were being maintained. By this step at least 8000 persons were thrown out of employment; and, instead of being contributors to the Sustentation Fund, became a source of weakness and impoverishment.

The effect of the lock-out was instantly perceived in the deepening of the spirit of hostility between masters and men. In some instances, grave and simple, even pathetic, language was used. "We fear we are unable to cope with the organized force and power of the Masters' Unions, but we shall peacefully and quietly resist until starvation enforces submission." In other instances, their language was the language of excitement, of menace, of infuriated bitterness. Mobs thronged the streets. The evil-disposed among the masses fanned the flame of disorder for their own criminal purposes. In Great Harwood almost every factory window was broken. In Blackburn vitriol was thrown in the eyes of a landlord. In Preston, and other large towns, the authorities, apprehensive of serious rioting, had called in the aid of military force. The house of Mr. Raynsford Jackson, Chairman of the Masters' Association, was, with its contents, completely destroyed by fire.

Under these circumstances, seeing that arbitration was impossible, it was the intense desire of all good men to promote a spirit of conciliation. The masters were naturally exasperated by the excesses and wanton destructiveness of the mob; but the Bishop, from the first, knowing and respecting the true character of the majority of the people, steadily refused to allow that the lawless and brutal conduct of mobs of rioters was rightfully chargeable against the whole people. In almost every sermon preached at this time, he publicly expressed the opinion that

"the outbreaks at Blackburn would be found to be the work not of the better class of operatives on strike, but of what has been called the floating scum of our great cities, aided probably by a mob of reckless people, mostly young, of all occupations and of both sexes. I see that Lord Shaftesbury in the House of Lords, and the Home Secretary in the House of Commons, expressed the same opinion. It was also the opinion of two of the Manchester papers, the *Examiner* and the *Courier*. I came to that conclusion partly from what I had read hastily of the character of the outrages; partly from what I knew, or believed I knew, of the character of the better class of the working men in this great district; partly also because, having been in the strike district on the previous Sunday, I was full of hope when I saw the orderly character of the population of Blackburn, who were thronging the streets in all directions, innocently enjoying themselves, and, as their faces seemed to indicate, without one single thought of evil in their minds. I also knew how admirably the working class and their masters had behaved during that somewhat trying period of eight weeks' strike in Bolton. This morning I was having some talk with the station-master at Pendleton. He told me he had lived at Blackburn among the operatives for twenty years, and knew them well, and he felt satisfied that the better class amongst them would be revolted at the sad scenes that have taken place. I say I should be glad to be of the same opinion, but I confess that matters have assumed a somewhat different aspect since the first outbreak, and I think it is time, if the great mass of the operatives on strike would retain public sympathy, that they should show themselves guiltless of those discreditable acts of violence—that they should place themselves by some distinct act on the side of order."

"The general features of the strike," he writes in a letter dated May 17, "you will have learnt from the newspapers. It certainly is causing very serious anxiety, and though many people think that the worst is over, and that if the operatives kept themselves quiet for two or three days a settlement would be arrived at, yet, when the people are so much excited, the slightest spark may produce a conflagration; and, as an expected settlement did not take place to-day, many persons are feeling extremely anxious lest there should be a renewal of rioting and destruction of property to-night in the disturbed districts. Remembering how quiet and orderly everything looked in Blackburn last Sunday evening, I never was more taken by surprise than by the violent outbreak of Tuesday night. I think the masters were far too peremptory in their answer to the deputation of operatives who waited upon them to propose a settlement, and the two sides seem to have separated mutually exasperated. The feeling of disappointment was, no doubt, intensely bitter; and as Colonel Jackson is the chairman of the Masters' Association, and also, rightly or wrongly, is believed to have been the most resolute in counselling no concession, when ruffianism took possession of the streets, he naturally became one of the first objects of vengeance. I fear if he had himself fallen in their way, while their passions were at the hottest, his life would have fallen a sacrifice to their fury. They certainly displayed a most diabolical temper in the way in which they wrecked his house and property. I feel pretty certain, nevertheless, that the best class among the operatives have had little or nothing to do with these outrages, though they have not condemned them as I should have liked them to do. I think Lord Shaftesbury was quite right in what he said on the subject last night in the House of Lords. I said exactly the same thing in a sermon at Heyside, near Oldham, on Wednesday, for which the *Manchester Guardian* took me to task the next morning. I still, however, hold to my belief. The mobs are composed of the low population to be found in all our towns, with a large proportion of reckless young men and girls. I have looked through the lists of those apprehended for rioting, and they are almost entirely of this class. It is time, however, as Lord Shaftesbury told them in the Lords and as I said in my sermon at Heyside, that the great body of the operatives, if they would not have all public sympathy withdrawn from them, should show themselves on the side of order. There was to be a meeting of delegates at Blackburn at one o'clock, and Mr. Birtwistle said he thought a telegram from me, urging moderation, would do good. He had been able to get his own way hitherto, but the men had now broken away and could hardly be kept under any control; and the hands of those who wish for peace wanted strengthening. I declined to send a telegram, but said I would write a letter if he would undertake to go to Blackburn to deliver it (for it could not reach its destination in time by ordinary course of post). This he promised to do.

"I have been at Bolton every night this week (except Tuesday), and everything is quiet there. But strikes are threatened at Ashton and Oldham, and it is impossible to say over what area the mischief may spread. I hope, however, there will be two or three quiet days for reflection, and for enabling the better men to show the rest, who are more reckless and violent, how they are injuring their cause by all these outrages. No operative in his senses would burn a mill down; for it would be like taking the bread out of his own mouth till it was built up again. The worst feature of the strike in my eyes is that it shows that confidence is lost between the masters and the men. The men must see that it would be best to come to the masters' terms rather than adopt their own remedy, if only they could feel certain that the present rate of wages would be restored when trade revives."

The Bishop's letter to the delegates ran thus:

To the CHAIRMAN AND SECRETARY OF THE WEAVERS' ASSOCIATION.

May 16, 1878.

SIRS,—I understand that you are holding another meeting of delegates to-day, to see if it be not possible to come to terms with the masters in relation to this unhappy strife. I am afraid that the lamentable events of the last two or three days will not have made the settlement easier; but I do most earnestly trust the representatives of the operatives will look matters fairly in the face, and see to what issues the conduct that is being pursued is tending. Confidence is being destroyed, naturally bitter feelings are aroused, order has been rudely invaded, property violently attacked and wrecked, public sympathy is certain to be alienated, and, as a necessary consequence, a revival of better times rendered more remote and uncertain. Could not a proposition which is made in this morning's Manchester papers be adopted—viz., that the men should resume work for three months at least at the ten per cent. reduction, with confidence in the fair dealing of the employers that, if trade revives in that period, they should be entitled to the return of the old or any proportionate rate of the old wage? At any rate, whether the suggestion—which seems to me, in the face of the admitted depression of trade, to be a reasonable one—is entertained or not, I do hope that the most strenuous effort will be made to put an end to the present depressing state of things. I feel most deeply on this question, involving, as it does, not only the credit of Lancashire in the eyes of the nation, but the good name of the working classes, and the happiness of almost countless homes; and I trust I shall be forgiven for interposing myself, even for a moment, in your deliberations. I remain, gentlemen, your faithful servant,

J. MANCHESTER.

Messrs. BIRTWISTLE and WHALLEY.

In season and out of season, the Bishop, whose heart bled over the estrangement of masters and men, urged, with every plea he could devise, the cultivation of a spirit of mutual understanding and good-will.

Preaching at St. Peter's Church, Rishton, he said:

"MY FRIENDS,—I confess I do regret the present condition of things. When I was last in North-East Lancashire, the strike had just begun. No doubt the landscape looked bright. The brilliant rays of the sun were unspotted by clouds of smoke. I don't admire clouds of smoke coming from tall chimneys, and I think that factory owners might make less smoke if they would, but it indicates that work is going on, and that hundreds and thousands of families are enjoying contentment and competence. When no smoke comes from these tall chimneys, it means that there is a stoppage of work, and a stoppage of wages, that furniture will shortly have to be disposed of, that the clothes of the children will not be quite so tidy as they once were, they will be pinched and their stomachs 'clemmed,' and at last the man who once held his freedom dear will have to go to the Guardians of the Poor and tell his tale, and ask for a loaf of bread or half-a-crown to keep himself and his family alive. That is what it comes to. It is a terrible prospect before you. I don't understand how anybody, having human sympathy in his heart, can do otherwise than almost weep for this state of things. Our blessed Lord once wept for Jerusalem, because it knew not the time of its visitation. I don't know a sadder state of things than a great industry or a great people going to ruin, just because certain relations between capital and labour, which, I should think, might be readjusted somehow or other, have been disturbed. I saw the other day that the operatives paid me the compliment—I regard it as a compliment and an honour, showing that they have at least some trust in my impartiality and sense of justice—to suggest that I should act as chairman of an arbitration committee, to which the masters were asked to submit the dispute. The proposal was never made to me, and I have never opened my lips on the subject before now. I should not like to undertake the task. I don't feel that I have the requisite knowledge; it requires a very intimate acquaintance with the details of a large and complicated industry, in order to determine on some equitable basis how these matters should be arranged. I was asked, some four years ago, to be arbitrator between the House-painters of Manchester and their employers; but that was a simple matter. The great and complicated interests of the cotton trade are vast and important, and I am not sure that arbitration would succeed in dealing with the matter. Still, the principle of having a congress to settle differences is recognized by Scripture; and, if a man has a quarrel with his brother, he is directed to go out with his brother and settle it with him alone. That which is the wisest policy between nations, the wisest course between man and man, might even prove to be the wisest course in this case. I don't think the workpeople of Lancashire have any reason to mistrust their employers, and I don't believe the employers have any desire to wrong their people. There does seem to me to be a want of mutual confidence, and until that mutual confidence is restored I am afraid no compromise in the matter will be effected. I don't pretend to have followed the whole controversy and discussions through all their details, but, from what I have seen reported of the interviews between the operatives and the masters, I confess it has seemed to me that the language which has been used on both sides has been rather too much of an ultimatum. If they would leave out such expressions as—'This is the last thing we will offer;' 'This is the last thing we will accept;' there is room for an approach. If instead of saying, 'This is the last thing,' they said, 'This is our ground,' 'This is what we propose for consideration;' they could look at it, and fairly deal with it, and it would show that both desired the common interests of both sides; then there might be a fair and reasonable, and impartial and equitable conference. I cannot help thinking that reasonable men ought to come to some conclusion which would be an escape from the present difficult state of things. The difficulty is frightful. Here you are in the third week of the strike. Probably the loss in wages will be £100,000 or £150,000. It was said that if the strike had been complete there would have been 120,000 hands out of work, and this would have represented a loss of £120,000 per week. If this is the state of things, how long is it to go on? What is to be the end of it? What was the end of the Bolton strike? Did any of you read the letter of Dr. Watts in the papers yesterday? It seems to me, that unless you make up your minds somehow or other, and bring this question to a satisfactory, reasonable, early settlement, you are involving the country in terrible consequences. I cannot look with a calm eye on the prospect before us. If it had been the beginning of winter, instead of summer, I know not what would have been the consequences. Even as it is, distress has been caused; and the distress that will yet be caused, I am sure, must be most serious. I have no right to interpose myself, and don't wish to interpose in such a sense as to make a rule. I am not going to say whether the operatives or masters are right. You would not wish me to say anything of the kind from the imperfect knowledge I possess. The question is far too serious to be trifled with. No false pride, no jaunty bounce, no saying, 'I will gasp and die in the street rather than give in,' ought to interpose to prevent a reasonable and just settlement of this grave question. With these remarks I will leave the question to your wise and sober judgment. I have spoken not as a Lancashire man, because I am not one, but as an Englishman who desires to see fair and just feeling prevail among all parties. I wish to lift up my voice against war, whether it is between nation and nation, or between employer and employed, and I believe this nation only can prosper by acting on the apostle's maxim—'Esteem all men, fear God, love the brotherhood, honour the King.'"

Preaching at St. Peter's Church, Halliwell:

"It is thought that if we can turn out the children of our schools so that they can read, write, and cipher, it is all that is required. But does that power make men intelligent? It does not follow that because we have developed material resources during the past half century, with such wonderful scientific results, that the world is becoming more intelligent. I do not call a strike or lock-out an act of intelligence. A strike is a civil war between capital and labour. It cannot be called an act of intelligence for the operatives of Lancashire to lose during their nine weeks' strike £700,000. Then, again, take the riots—another uncomfortable feature. Were the riots likely to bring about a better feeling in the minds of the masters, and cause them to open their mills when their property was being destroyed? Although no machinery was destroyed, yet let us suppose that all the mills in Blackburn and Accrington had been destroyed (and it is possible when the streets are in possession of beardless boys and reckless girls), would you say that such persons were acting under the influence of reason? I think not. If England became a scene of anarchy and social chaos of that kind, all the joy that makes life worth living would be gone. Let me exhort all Lancashire people to read the Lord Chief Justice's remarks when fulfilling his painful duty of sentencing those foolish, misguided men who burnt Colonel Jackson's house. The Lord Chief Justice pointed out that workmen had no right or power to compel an employer to pay for their labour the price that they chose to set upon it. Labour has a right to make its own demand, and the capitalist has a right to consider how far he can meet that demand. This seems to me simple political economy and divested of jargon."

A compromise of 7½ per cent. reduction was proposed, but came to nothing. The Bishop's pleadings, however, with the masters to manifest a spirit of kindliness and good-will, and with the men to publicly dissociate themselves from the brutalities of outrage and riot, were more effectual. The Masters' Association, on its part, adopted a resolution suggested by Mr. Alderman Pickop, that, "if the operatives resumed work at the 10 per cent. reduction, the masters would be prepared to meet them in three months' time for the purpose of considering whether the condition of trade justified a return to the old wages." The men, on their part, issued the following earnest appeal; an appeal reflecting the highest credit upon their class:

"'Good name in man or woman is the jewel of their souls.' To the operatives of North and North-East Lancashire,—Brothers and Sisters in distress,—We address you once more as men labouring under a sense of the deepest responsibility for every word now said by us in this grave crisis. We appeal to you to listen and reflect. We counsel you only for your good; we have no other interest in this struggle. A great calamity has befallen our districts; riots ending in crime of the blackest character have existed in our midst for days. This vagabondism we disclaim and condemn. We are compelled by every sense of self-respect and decency to deny the slightest impression that such lawless and brutal conduct serves in any degree the cause of labour. Security is the twin sister of industry. Without peace labour can never enjoy plenty. We could have continued the struggle against your employers with a fair chance of success, but we cannot and will not struggle against the forces of order and the well-being of society. There is not a man amongst you who would grant to a ruffian with a brickbat what he had previously denied to persuasion and reason. How many of us workmen would discuss and debate with our houses sacked and our wives and families in danger? We know it is not the fair average Lancashire man or woman who has done this mischief. In all periods of agitation the dregs of society come from their dark recesses. Rapine commences with them, and fools follow. Fathers, with sons, remember in the midst of these new dangers your lads may be easily tempted. Mothers, with daughters, we ask your help to restore peace. In conclusion, we appeal to you, fellow-workmen, to assist by all the means in your power in restoring peace and order in the disturbed districts, and so contribute to win back the good name you have so long borne for patience under suffering and respect for the persons and property of your employers and neighbours.—(Signed,) THOS. BIRTWISTLE, Secretary, East Lancashire Weavers' Association; JOHN WHALLEY, Secretary, Blackburn and District Weavers' Association; E. ENTWISTLE, Secretary, Darwen Weavers' Association; LUKE PARK, Secretary, Preston Weavers' Association.—Blackburn, May 20, 1878."

But although a better spirit began to appear between masters and men, although outrages and riots were diminished, although conferences assumed a more conciliatory tone, yet the strike and lock-out continued with their attendant and rapidly increasing misery and distress. Good men on all sides exerted themselves to bring the unhappy, the disastrous contention to a close; and the Bishop addressed to the editors of the Manchester and London press a sympathetic, fervid, yet well-reasoned letter; a letter of a tone and quality such as too seldom falls from the pen of a clerical writer; a letter illustrating the keen, instructed interest which the Bishop took in large human questions, especially questions affecting the welfare of the industrial classes. Such letters as this both reveal the secret springs of that great hold which Bishop Fraser had had upon Lancashire, and also indicate one of the directions in which the Church, and pre-eminently the Bishops of the Church, must labour if, in the modern age, their influence, not only over the ecclesiastical few, but over the non-ecclesiastical many, is to be deepened and intensified.

THE STRIKE AND LOCK-OUT.

SIR,—Is it beyond the bounds of hope that either or both of the parties to the present unhappy struggle in North and North-East Lancashire will listen to one more appeal, which, as a Bishop of the Church of England, bound by his office to promote peace and good-will among men; as a resident in Lancashire, having under his eyes the poverty and sufferings sustained for seven dreary weeks, and threatening to be indefinitely prolonged; and as an Englishman, deeply interested in everything that concerns the well-being and prosperity of his country, I venture to make to them?

I do not come forward in the character of an arbitrator, or even of a mediator. I have felt and said from the first that no outsider can understand the complications of the cotton industry so well as those who are themselves engaged in them; and that the solution of the present difficulty must be looked for, not from arbitration, but from conference, conciliation, perhaps from compromise. Even if I had been vain enough to suppose myself competent to play the part which in some of the earlier proposals of the operatives they were ready to assign to me, the determined resolution expressed by the Chairman of the Masters' Association, in his replies to Lord Bateman and the Mayor of Burnley, would be quite sufficient to tell me that arbitration is a method of settling differences which, on the side at least of one of the parties to the conflict, would not be entertained.

But the strike has now lasted seven weeks. The delegates of the men, in their last manifesto, compute that by the operatives on strike, numbering with their families 300,000 people, already £525,000 in wages—or £75,000 a week—has been neither earned nor enjoyed; and, the funds at their disposal being exhausted, they are now making an appeal to the trades of Great Britain and Ireland and the public generally to support them in the struggle, which they represent as an effort of the federated employers to crush in detail the trade organizations established throughout the United Kingdom for the protection of labour against capital. In other words, 300,000 people, who might be maintained by £75,000 honestly earned in wages week by week, are to be sustained on a niggard and precarious charity, in order that this industrial war may be (as I have said) indefinitely prolonged.

Meanwhile, the angry passions inseparable from such a state of things are making themselves felt on both sides. "It is sad to observe," writes to me an earnest clergyman from one of the towns where the struggle has been the severest—"it is sad to observe the bitter feelings that are gradually springing up; and the hardest words do not come from the mouths of operatives only." A speaker at a meeting at Stockport is reported to have said, "If the operatives were compelled to succumb tomorrow and make peace, it would be of only short duration. If they had no reasonable hope of success in the present struggle, they had at least shown their strength, and prevented the attempt in the future of a further reduction."

Now this is a foolish way of talking, and a dangerous and mischievous condition of feeling. No display of strength can prevent a future further reduction, if such reduction is necessary as the only way in which trade can be carried on at a profit. If the operatives think that any man will either put or keep capital in a concern which yields him no profit, they are more ignorant than I can believe them to be of the first principles of politico-economical science, and of the common motives of human nature. And if peace, when made, is to be of no long duration, and further reductions, should they become necessary, are opposed with the same weapons and the same determination as the present one, it requires no prescience to foretell the future of the cotton industry of Lancashire. It will become as much a thing of the past as the manufacturing prosperity of Tyre.

In the interest of labour as well as of capital, I would invite the attention of both parties to certain phenomena which have come within my own knowledge or observation, and which I regard as typical. The iron trade of South Wales has disappeared, and as Lord Aberdare told me, in his judgment, is not likely to revive. The look of the country is described to me by those who have seen it as being as desolate as if it had been overrun by a foreign foe. I was told two days ago by a man, himself once a miner and now the coachman of a Wiltshire friend of mine, who has friends in the smitten district, that the people are emigrating in all directions—as he expressed it, are being sent off by shiploads. "What is the cause of this?" I asked, wishing to ascertain the man's views of the case. "Oh," he said, "the strike; though I don't know what they struck for, for they were earning, many of them, £2 10s. a week; and twenty years ago, when I worked in the pits from five o'clock in the morning to seven o'clock at night, it was only with a 'scrabble' that I could make my pound or five and twenty shillings." At any rate, whether my informant's view of the case is correct or not, here is a district, once the home of a thriving and remunerative industry, now reduced to the condition of a wilderness.

A month ago I travelled up to London with the managing director of one of the largest engineering works in Manchester, himself well known as a man of the highest intelligence and capacity for business. "What are you doing?" I asked. "Not much," he answered. "We have reduced our number of hands; and I don't know how much longer we may have anything to do for those who remain. We have just had to refuse an order that would have been worth £45,000." "Why?" I asked, with some surprise. "A foreign railway company invited us to tender for twenty locomotives. We offered to build them for £2,200 each; the company would only give £2,000. There was not much profit to be got out of the transaction, but to keep the men employed we were willing to have undertaken it if we could save ourselves from loss. So we called the heads of the departments together, who are all working by piecework, and asked them if they would help us to accept the order by reducing in fair proportion the wages that were being paid to them, so as to leave some small margin of profit to the shareholders. They to a man refused, and we had to decline to enter into a contract which would have been worth £45,000." I am not able to estimate how much of this sum represents the loss in wages to the men, whom it would probably have kept in constant employment for half a year. It may now have gone into the pockets of some foreign competitor whose existence the great body of the operatives seem utterly to forget or ignore.

I was informed recently upon authority that seemed to me sufficient that Bolckow, Vaughan, & Co., are sending the pig iron which they have made into Belgium to be manufactured into girders, rails, &c., and to be re-imported into this country for use, simply because the work can be done quite as well and more cheaply there than here.

Mr. R. W. Dale in his "Impressions of America," published in the *Nineteenth Century* for April (p. 769), asserts distinctly that "in Birmingham itself merchants are importing from the United States such articles as axes, hayforks, and agricultural implements of nearly every description, sash pulleys, and small castings of many kinds, although it is estimated that freight and other expenses add 17 or 18 per cent. to the cost of the goods," while " the Lowell manufacturers, who are aghast at the prospect of free trade, are actually sending cotton cloth to Manchester, and in American retail stores cotton goods are marked at a lower price than that at which goods of the same quality could be sold in Liverpool or London." He expresses a "doubt whether, if the protective duties were swept away to-morrow, our own manufacturing industry would receive at once the stimulus which some sanguine persons might anticipate. Leeds and Bradford might become more active, but that the Lancashire and Birmingham manufacturers would recover their old place in the American market seems extremely improbable."

These instances and forebodings could easily be multiplied if it were necessary, but I think that what I have said is enough to show that the operatives' theory of the present depression of trade—that it is solely due to over-production—is not a complete account of the case; while, of course, if to any extent it is due to foreign competition, anything that enhances the cost of production at home—as working short time must do —throws the advantage still more into the hands of our competitors abroad.

Indeed, it is the one fact of this foreign competition so seriously imperilling our position as a manufacturing nation in the markets abroad, and even, if Mr. Dale's "impressions" are true, in the market at home, that presses itself home to my mind as the great motive that ought to stimulate both parties in the present strife to a speedy reconciliation of their differences. Whatever, in a moment of temper and resentment, either the masters on the one hand or the men on the other may say about their inability or their reluctance to enter into trade relations upon terms of mutual confidence,—the masters denouncing the tyranny of trade unionism, the men replying with an attack upon the "insatiable greed of the capitalists,"—it cannot be to the permanent interests of either party that the trade of this country should pass into foreign hands.

It seems a groundless and irrational fear in the mind of the operatives that the "federated employers are making" in this lock-out "the first of a series of attacks upon the different branches of trade organizations throughout the United Kingdom," with the object of breaking the whole system down. It would be an absurd idea to think that trade unionism, which is only a particular form of the principle of combination—the instinctive resource of the weak against the strong—could be put down by a policy of this kind. Even if temporarily defeated, it would be certain to rise again by its inherent vitality as a weapon of defence. But it is quite certain that of trade unionism, as of all weapons, both a good and a bad use can be made. If trade unionism is used to obtain by fair and equitable means fair and equitable terms from the employer for the employed, no just complaint can be made against it; if it is used merely to raise wages, irrespectively of the quality and the cost of the work done, often to the deterioration of the one and the enhancement of the other, nothing can be more indefensible, and in the long run more mischievous to the true interests of those who resort to it. The joiners of Manchester would have a sad tale to tell, if they told it wholly and truly, of the results of their eleven months' strike. Mr. Lloyd Jones, an uncompromising advocate of the cause of the working man, said the other day at the annual demonstration of the North Yorkshire and Cleveland Miners' Association: "During the many years he had advocated trade unionism he had always impressed upon working men that their first duty was union. He said that deliberately, not because he wished to see them banded together that they might oppress capital and injure the capitalist. If they made that a leading thought, or a thought even, in their union, their union would become an affliction to the nation, as it would be an injury to themselves." While Mr. Samuel Morley—and no employer could show a more enlightened interest in the highest welfare of his workpeople than this gentleman—writing to the Bristol Trades Council, said, "I believe trade unions have done good service in bringing workpeople to act unitedly, and so in many districts they have ceased to be a 'rope of sand,' and have been able to ensure better and more just consideration from employers, but they have also, by transferring all negotiations as to wages and conditions of work to middlemen, who have often no connection with the work generally—none whatever almost always with the particular employer —altered materially the character of the relationship between the two classes. There is, I fear, ceasing to be the intimacy between masters and men which existed some years ago." And, referring to the number of hours now worked per week, he adds, "I am clearly of opinion that unless some different arrangements are made, involving some concessions, the demand for English manufactures will gradually diminish. Unhappily, we know to our cost that some markets for certain classes of goods are gradually closing to us; and, while this is perhaps to be expected, I feel anxious before it is too late to try whether I can induce representatives of both sides, who have influence, to meet and consider whether some amendment in our methods of conducting these negotiations and other points seriously affecting the interests of the men could not be brought into action. English manufactures cannot be consumed in England alone, and I confess I tremble for the future of large numbers of English workmen unless some changes are made."

These are wise and weighty words, and trade unions must take care that in their eagerness to get the golden eggs they do not kill the bird that lays them.

The Bishop of Salford gave some excellent advice, equally applicable to all, in the sermon which he preached in Bolton last Sunday. He said we should have less to spend, and therefore we must spend less upon ourselves in eating and drinking, and other forms of what must be called luxury. A wise man said that "the prosperity of fools shall destroy them;" and we all lived too fast and spent too much in those years when we over-rashly thought that the good time would never end, but that tomorrow would be as to-day, and probably more abundant. The tomorrow has come, and has dissipated these dreams; and reasonable men who cannot command, even when they deserve, success will adapt their style of living to their means. Twenty-seven shillings a week instead of thirty during a period of prices which are being reduced in nearly all articles of necessary consumption does not mean starvation, nor anything like starvation. It may mean a limitation of expenditure, but it need not mean much more. To the agricultural labourer in the south of England the wages at which the Lancashire operative has struck would mean wealth which he has hardly imagined in his dreams.

The operatives' own remedy for the depression—viz., 10 per cent. reduction in wages and working four days a week—shows that they do not consider the reduction itself unreasonable, though, as I have already endeavoured to show, the recommendation to work short time indicates that they will persistently recognize only one cause of such depression. Short time might stop the glut, but it would operate to our disadvantage rather than to our benefit in the conflict with the foreign competitor; and I fail to see how a man and his family would be better off on 18s. a week for four days' labour than on 27s. a week for five days and a half.

I do not think that a false pride or a dogged obstinacy ought to prevent the men from returning to work on the masters' terms if those terms can be proved to be necessitated by the present conditions of trade. The masters say that they are working at a loss. Is there any reason for doubting the assertion, except perhaps in a few special and favoured instances? Can the joint-stock mills, in which so many of the working class hold shares, produce balance-sheets during the last two years exhibiting a profit? How can capital be compelled, or why should it be compelled, to go on working till it is itself exhausted? or on what principle can labour dictate to capital the terms on which it should employ itself?

I ask the working men of Lancashire to debate these questions among themselves, free alike from passion and from prejudice. There never, perhaps, was a greater crisis in the cotton industry—not the least important of the three great staple trades—of this country. The interests of the operatives are as vitally concerned in an equitable solution of the question as the interests of the masters. If we do not take care, Lancashire may become as forsaken of her greatest industry as South Wales is of hers. It is in the hope of contributing something to prevent a national calamity—as one desiring to see only what is fair and right maintained between man and man—that I have ventured to write the foregoing pages, which I must trust to your kindness to enable me to set before the world. *Liberavi animum meam.*—I am, &c.

June 8.   J. MANCHESTER.

The Bishop's private correspondence, at this period, is full of sympathetic allusions to the industrial crisis.

This sad cotton strike is on my mind, night and day, and I don't think people half realize its issues, so I was moved to write the letter to the Manchester people of which I have told you, and to-day I send you a printed copy of it. I enclose some letters which have reached me this morning encouraging me to believe that it will do some good. Mr. W. Hoyle is a cotton manufacturer and a great advocate of Temperance, he is also a very thoughtful and right-judging man. Mr. Joseph Thompson is a Town Councillor of Manchester, a Quaker, but one of our most intelligent and highly educated citizens. It is satisfactory to me to find such men approving the course which I have pursued; but their letters make the outlook, at any rate in the immediate future, even more gloomy than I had feared. It is a most critical moment in the industrial history of this country; and the slightest inclination of the scale looks as though it would pour all our boasted wealth into the lap of the foreign competitors. And this sad weather damps all hopes of a plenteous harvest, which would have relieved *some* of the darkness of the future. We can but leave the issue, with patience and faith, in higher hands.

To a WORKING MAN.

June 18, 1878.

MY GOOD FRIEND,—I am sorry you did not like my letter on the strike. I am sure I tried to be impartial. But I thought, and still think, that the operatives had not taken all the elements of the question into consideration—made no allowance for foreign competition—and that their conduct was not only inflicting lamentable distress upon themselves, but was running the risk of permanently injuring the trade of the country. Unkindly feelings, too, were growing up between the two parties, which, if allowed to develope and intensify, would be the parent, not only of much discomfort, but of much mischief in the future. I therefore wrote in the interests of conciliation; and, whether my letter has had any influence or not, I am glad to observe that the course I counselled is being followed. I did not attempt to discuss *all* the social questions of the day, and therefore made no reference to the land question, which was outside my argument. I am afraid it will be found that all classes have paid too selfish a regard to their own supposed interests, when they have had the chance.—Yours faithfully,

J. MANCHESTER.

But, as the darkness is deepest just before the dawn, so the gloom of the industrial crisis was thickest just before its close, and on June 17, within ten days of the appearance of his appeal in the press, the Bishop's heart was gladdened by the termination of the strike.

"This morning's papers," he writes, "announce the 'Termination of the Strike'—the most joyful announcement that has met my eyes for many a long week—and to-morrow, if not to-day, most of the mill chimneys will be sending out their puffs of smoke again, and something a good deal more than the crust of 'starvation' will be found in 60,000 Lancashire homes."

All good men had longed for, many had laboured to bring about, this happy result; but none had either longed or laboured more earnestly than the Bishop. His heart was rent by the hunger, the misery, the desolation which the strike and lock-out had caused: he dreaded, in the interests of humanity and Christian brotherhood, the estrangement and bitterness which these industrial wars fomented between employers and employed. Recognizing fully the right of combination both among masters and men for the promotion of common aims and ends, he desired to see these combined associations animated not by a spirit of hostility, but of friendliness and good-will. His mission was to set men *with*, not *against*, one another. He was a fine illustration of the truth of the Duke of Albany's noble utterance at Liverpool in 1884:—

"A mutual understanding of class and class—that, surely, is what we need. There have been times and there have been countries when—

"'Those behind cried, "Forward!"
And those before cried, "Back!"'

But in our age and in our country it is not so. Those whom Providence has placed in the front ranks of this great nation are desirous that those behind them should move onward as swiftly as they can, for we have learned that, along the ways of wisdom and virtue, we shall advance furthest if we all advance together."

No man upon the episcopal bench has toiled harder, and more successfully, to promote " the mutual understanding of class and class," a most royal aim, than Bishop Fraser. Genius has seldom displayed the splendour of its originality more conspicuously in practical life. As the Prince Consort literally discovered a new career for a Prince, so Bishop Fraser literally discovered a new career for a Bishop. His was "an original thought and a new position." Deeply spiritual, he was also deeply human. An "Ireland" scholar, he was less interested in Greek particles than in the progress of mankind. A devoted student of the Bible, his religion was the religion of comprehensive sympathy and noble conduct, rather than a religion of scholastic niceties and the pronunciation of Shibboleth. He was more than a liberal Churchman; he was a loving man. He pondered over the signs of the times, not as a dogmatical visionary, but as a rational, responsible citizen, well instructed in the civic, the industrial, the social problems which no other philosophy or religion appears so well adapted to solve as the Gospel of Christ.

Letters of grateful appreciation of the part he had played in bringing to a termination this industrial war poured in upon the Bishop from all sorts and conditions of men. One only, from his highly valued friend, Dean Church, will suffice as a type:—

THE DEANERY, ST. PAUL'S, LONDON,
Whit Tuesday, 1878.

MY DEAR FRASER,—I must write a line to tell you how my heart goes out towards you at the noble and worthy line you are taking in this dreadful Lancashire civil war. It makes me proud to have had anything to do with a Christian Bishop who sees so clearly and does so bravely what his Master's servant ought to do in these dangerous and perplexed quarrels. It is in modern England an original thought and a new position; and yet it is the true order of things. It is, of course, not every one who could venture thus to mediate and speak the truth. You have earned the right to do it; and now you are able to set a true example. God grant that your words may be fruitful! Ever yours,

A. W. CHURCH.

CHAPTER VI.

COMMERCIAL DEPRESSION.

Commercial Distress—The Panic—The Bishop's Letter—The Relief Committee—Indiscriminate Benevolence—Savings Banks—Social Christianity—Improvidence—The Elberfeldt System—Organized Charity—The Organization of Relief—Thrift—Commercial Righteousness.

The termination of the nine weeks' industrial war was not the termination of the distress and misery which that war had caused. In the course of the war the operatives had lost, in wages alone, nearly £700,000. In multitudes of instances, especially where families were large, this loss amounted to a reduction to beggary. Small shopkeepers were compelled to give large credit and were thus placed at the mercy of usurers; clothes and furniture were pawned without hope of redemption; enforced idleness increased opportunities for drinking; the habits of extravagance, waste, and unthrift contracted in days of prosperity, found the bulk of the people unprepared for seasons of scarceness and adversity. Hundreds of families, which for years had been in receipt of upwards of £3 a week, were found not only to have made no "provision for a rainy day," but to be in debt on every side. Before the strike had lasted a fortnight, these families were thrown into the condition of paupers, soliciting relief from the Guardians of the Poor.

Moreover, the general outlook, instead of improving and brightening, grew darker and less hopeful. Every branch of industry, all ranks of tradespeople, seemed to be enveloped in the prevailing gloom. The case of the iron-masters and coal-masters became almost desperate. The Lancashire and Yorkshire Railway discharged a considerable number of servants, and lowered the wages of the rest. One of the largest brewers in Lancashire was compelled to put his men on half time. In Yorkshire and Warwickshire furnaces were blown out and forges stopped. In the great engine works at Crewe, the London and North-Western Railway put their men, numbering at least five thousand, upon short time. Markets and warehouses were glutted with manufactured goods. Persons, hitherto considered opulent, were reducing their establishments. Many sold their carriages. Where two gardeners had been kept, one was dismissed; hospitality sensibly diminished; the proprietors of hotels found their accounts dwindling into comparative insignificance. Panics were common, both at home and abroad. The failure of the City of Glasgow Bank had inflicted untold miseries upon thousands of persons in Scotland, and had penetrated England with a sense of insecurity. Failures grew common; each failure preparing the way for, and rendering unavoidable, other failures. The stoppage of the West of England Bank threw south-western England into a condition bordering upon consternation. A spirit of fear and trembling seized upon depositors. In Manchester the run upon building societies, notably the Queen's Building Society and the Victoria Building Society, was unprecedented. The amount withdrawn from the former society between Friday, October 11, 1878, and Wednesday, October 16, in sums under £50 was not less than £50,000.

Under these circumstances the eyes of the community were turned to the Bishop, the friend of the people, the just and wise counsellor of all classes; the man, who by his knowledge of economic affairs, and his absolute integrity in speaking of and dealing with them, had won the public confidence. In the height of the panic he addressed the following letter to the Manchester press:

Bishop's Court, *October 16,* 1878.

Sir,—On my return home last night—too late to get this letter inserted in your issue of to-morrow—I heard with regret that something like a commercial panic occurred in Manchester to-day, that a "run" was made by timid depositors upon one of our best-established building societies, while even more alarming rumours were being freely circulated. If unreasoning and unreasonable apprehensions get possession of the public mind, they may easily become the parent of a great and fast-spreading disaster. The prosperity of the country rests upon credit—I mean upon mutual confidence between man and man; and, if this foundation is rudely shaken, the building which rests upon it will certainly topple and fall. It does not follow that, because a Scotch bank appears to have been administered with culpable disregard of the ordinary principles of sound finance, that all banks and monetary institutions have been equally reckless in the use of their funds. The immediately available resources of no bank will bear up against unlimited pressure; and even the Bank of England would have to close its doors if all its depositors clamoured for a settlement of their accounts on the same day, or in the same week. And it must frequently happen that a bank's best securities are those which cannot be realized in a moment to meet the pressure of a panic. If a bank is believed to be unsafe or to conduct its business incautiously, we were foolish to entrust our money to it at all; but, if we have confidence in its administration and its solvency, the bank has a right to look, in the moment of a strain, for the support, the co-operation, and, above all, the self-control of its depositors. That rotten businesses should go down under the present conditions of the money market is to be expected, and for the future healthiness of trade it is better that they should do so. But, if the popular mind is possessed by panic, even the most solvent concerns may share in the collapse; and, though the ultimate realization of assets may be sufficient to meet all liabilities, the intermediate distress may be incalculable, and the credit of the country may sustain a shock from which it would not recover for years. The sound counsel of the old Hebrew prophet recurs to my memory in this as in all great crises—" strength " lies in " quietness and confidence."—I am, &c.,

J. Manchester.

With the approach of winter, the distress (in multitudes of instances so intense that, if unrelieved, it would have ended in starvation and death) deepened and spread. The weather was very severe; and, as always happens in hard weather, when food is scanty, sickness and disease wrought sad havoc among the over-crowded masses. In Manchester a Relief Fund was instituted to which most generous subscriptions were sent; but a difficulty greater than that of obtaining money presented itself, viz., the difficulty of discovering the most needy cases; of preventing imposture; and of avoiding the common abuses of philanthropy which so frequently foster pauperism. Unfortunately, too, the labours and anxieties connected with the industrial war, combined with the severity of the weather, and a constitutional tendency towards bronchitis, had placed the Bishop on the sick list, and compelled him, under medical advice, to remain a prisoner within doors at Bishop's Court. But, although he could, to his great regret, not attend the meetings of the Relief Committee, yet he watched, as his correspondence shows, all the proceedings with careful and sympathetic vigilance.

December 24, 1878.

The distress here, I fear, is increasing, and unless they extend their organizations—and I see they are beginning to do it—I fear it will become unmanageable. I deeply regret that this illness of mine quite prevents me from offering personal service. I wrote to Mr. Smith, the agent of the Provident Society, suggesting that the Committee should form a separate fund for the special relief of those who have been in better circumstances, but who now feel the pinch of poverty quite as keenly as the "poor." I have asked him to consult Mr. Oliver Heywood and Mr. Herbert Philips—two of our best men, *noble* fellows!—and, if such a fund is formed, have promised £50 to it. I shall be glad to add your cheque to this fund if I find it needed. I was led to make the suggestion by a letter which I received from a man who had been a commercial traveller, with a wife and five children, who had observed what I had said about the blankets, and who told me that they had been obliged to sell all their furniture, and had not one single blanket left, to buy food. Of course I can't tell whether the statement is true, or whether drink may not have had something to do with the result; but I have asked Smith to inquire into the case, and if he finds it deserving to give the man £2 on my account. There are a number of such cases; and therefore I suggested the formation of a special fund to deal with them. I have not yet received a reply. The money subscribed to the Provident Society now amounts to about £8,000; and about 3,500 cases have been relieved. But a much larger sum will be required if this weather lasts, and the distress continues spreading with its present rapidity. Most of the sums subscribed, I am sorry to see, are small—under £10. I am afraid this indicates that many who are supposed to be well off are feeling the pressure themselves; though many, I fear, do not realize what the suffering actually is.

December 26, 1878.

I am glad to see the hope expressed in the *Manchester Guardian* this morning, that the organizations which are at work are "breaking the neck" of the distress, and that the whole thing is getting under command. I do so much regret that the weather absolutely prevents me from engaging in active co-operation with the earnest and noble men who are throwing themselves into the actual work (like Oliver Heywood) with as much discretion as enthusiasm.

December 27, 1878.

Colonel Willis's letter (offering a donation) I am sure will gratify you. I never heard from him before, and only just remember the fact that he was my brother Alex.'s commanding officer nearly twenty years ago. How pleasant it is to find these unexpected evidences of Christian feeling! I have told him that *we* have no claim upon him, and perhaps Bedford or some other place has; but that, if he still wishes to dispense his liberality through me, I will gladly be his almoner, and that I have no doubt I can find, by the help of good Mr. Smith, a fitting object for his bounty. I enclose one of Mr. Smith's reports about a case into which I had asked him to inquire, which would just be a proper object. It is just this class of cases for which I wished a special fund to be raised. The advertisement which Mr. Oliver Heywood sent me was the response to that suggestion. I have promised another £50 to that special class of sufferers, and I will gladly devote your generous cheque to the same object. There is no immediate want of funds, for I see this morning that the subscriptions amount to £10,700, and up to Monday last they had only spent £3,000. But the organization is now covering nearly the whole of Manchester, and I expect they will soon be spending £3,000 a week. Happily the weather shows signs of breaking this morning; a gentle thaw is setting in; and with a milder temperature the distress will be considerably lessened. I am glad that the thaw is so gradual; for I went to bed with an anxious heart last night, lest, if a rapid thaw came on, my roof should not prove watertight, as the spouts were blocked with frozen snow, and I should find a general shower bath of a very unwelcome kind descending through all the ceilings of my upper floors. Fortunately my apprehensions were needless, and as the roof is getting lightened of its load every hour, and no harm has happened yet, I hope none will happen.

January 3, 1879.

I went to the relief depot to-day, and I must say that the people that I saw crowding round the doors were not at all the sort of people, judging by their looks, that I should care to relieve; they seemed people whose distress was entirely due to improvidence and intemperance, and whom I should like to have seen sent to the tender mercies of the Guardians. I believe a change of administration is to be introduced to-morrow, and I told the Committee I thought it was high time. According to the Mayor's estimate there are 45,000 people being relieved in this town; at Glasgow, with a larger population, and I should think with an equal amount of distress, there are only 30,000. I don't complain of the numbers, but I fear that the improper people are getting the relief, and the worthier objects are unnoticed and unknown. I think they are working the thing much better in Salford, in connection with the same central organization and out of the same central fund, but with three independent local and one independent general committee; and yet, even there last Tuesday, I heard accounts given of the tricks and malpractices both of relief-recipients and of tradespeople, which made me see what a careful eye and firm hand were needed to help to keep all things straight. Only think of one woman getting from a shopkeeper a pot of potted salmon for her shilling relief ticket! One of the most active members of the Manchester Committee, Mr. T. H. Birley, told me that he never felt before so strongly as he feels now the absolute necessity of some such organization as I have all along been suggesting, on the model of Elberfeldt, to meet a crisis of this kind.

Events like the trade depression and the social distress of this period brought out, in singular prominence, the distinguishing feature of Bishop Fraser's episcopate. By natural constitution, by his experiences as a commissioner, above all, by the power of his deepest spiritual convictions, he was intensely human; a citizen of the Pauline type, a Bishop who was less an ecclesiastic than a man. At the annual meeting of the Manchester and Salford Savings Bank in January, 1874, he said:

"Social questions have always taken a rank in my sympathies and estimation, not only far above political questions, but even, I may venture to say, far above ecclesiastical questions. By this I mean—and I do not wish to be misunderstood—that, without in any way relaxing my hold on what I believe to be the great truths of Christianity, I still feel that the great function of Christianity is to elevate man in his social condition. Therefore, I think my business as a Bishop is to do what I can, by example and precept, to diffuse everywhere the great principles of sobriety and thrift, and to take my chance as to whether my own particular community of the Church of England gains or loses thereby. I care very little for the dominance of this or that ecclesiastical party; my prayer for all who hold and propagate the Truth being that they may be blessed with the success they deserve. I do think that an institution like the Savings Bank is one animated by a Christian spirit, embodying a Christian principle, and such as should command the sympathy of every sympathetic Christian man."

The might of the influence which Bishop Fraser exercised over Lancashire largely sprang from the fact that his interest "in social problems was far above his interest in ecclesiastical questions." He was never weary of re-echoing the counsel of the reformers, "to keep to the Bible and the Apostles' Creed, letting divines, if they like, dispute about the rest." As Bishop Latimer borrowed his illustrations of the principles of Christianity "from the plough," so Bishop Fraser applied the principles of Christianity to the home, the factory, the exchange. He made Lancashire feel that Christianity was intended by Christ to leaven and ennoble all the relationships of life—relationships between parents and children, husbands and wives, masters and servants, employed and employers, trades unions and masters' associations—to speak out the honest truth both to the improvident poor and the extravagant rich ; to stimulate, but at the same time to organize, the distribution of benevolence.

In sermons and speeches, Bishop Fraser enforced and reiterated his convictions upon these great social, Christian, questions.

St. Peter's Church, Ashton, November 3, 1878:

"We have all been living too fast—all spending too much money on things which do not profit—rich and poor alike. Perhaps extravagance strikes one more in the working classes than in any other class, because it is more manifest; but all alike are spending too much money. In coming to Ashton this morning, I travelled with a lady who told me that she had visited a small village in the north of Lancashire which I know very well, and in which no rich people live; and she said she visited the village draper's shop, and found it hung with sealskin jackets, the lowest price for which was twelve or fourteen guineas each. She asked what sale there was for jackets of that kind ; and the shop-keeper replied that the girls in the mills bought them and bought them freely. The girls could no doubt get as good a jacket as they required, neatly made, for two guineas, and there would be ten or twelve guineas for the Savings Bank, to be put by until a rainy day. These are things to be considered."

The Savings Bank, Manchester, January 3, 1879:

"With regard to the present distress, upon which I should like to say a word or two, I am terribly afraid that, unless we have an almost immediate improvement in the state of things, the organization of the Provident Society will break down under the burden that has been put upon it. I was told only the other day by a friend of mine, who went to offer help, that one of the committee said, ' We have gone on a week, but if this is going to last for a month I don't know how we shall continue.' And there were some unpleasant facts mentioned on Tuesday by the Salford Committee. It was said that, in many cases, relief tickets were very much abused, that they were frequently honoured at public-houses, and that in shops articles were given in lieu of the food specified on the ticket. One ticket-holder, I am told, had taken potted salmon in lieu of the article specified on the ticket, and other cases of abuse were mentioned. A man who had been in receipt of 35s. a week at a dye works in Salford was thrown out of work in consequence of the temporary stoppage of the works through the bursting of the pipes, and three days afterwards he went to apply for relief!! There are a number of such cases, and unless we have an organization established on something like the Elberfeldt system the ground will never be properly covered. The amount of imposition we are liable to, whenever a pressure comes, is more than any of us are aware of; and, such being the case, more harm than good is being done by the money spent in charity. There are many, many cases of real distress which do not see the light; and if all who really wish to put their shoulder to the wheel to relieve the deserving distress, and to leave those wretched, reckless cases who do not deserve charitable relief, and who really have no claim upon our sympathy, to the Poor Law Guardians, I think that some good will have been done; whereas, at the present moment, I am in grave doubt as to whether, in the long run, we may not have been doing as much harm as good."

The Chapel of the Blind Asylum, Old Trafford, January 5, 1879:

"We see before us in Manchester at the present time, a sight which is enough to make one weep tears almost of despair. On Friday, from the Manchester and Salford Savings Bank meeting, I went to the temporary premises of the District Provident Society in Windmill Street; and in one of the upper rooms saw a contrast of modern nineteenth century civilization. On one side of the long distributing table were men—and I believe there are hundreds such—endeavouring by the exhibition of Christian sympathy and Christian action to show to the poor and needy, and even to the intemperate, the reckless, and the improvident, that there were those who cared for their bodies; and there is, at any rate, a real work being done when peoples' bodies are being cared for. But as I stood for half-an-hour watching the distribution of relief, I realized the difficulty of the work. People come forward who, it is plain to be seen, are not proper objects for Christian charity; having brought poverty upon themselves by drunkenness, improvidence, sloth, or something of that kind. I said some time ago that, if a crisis came upon Manchester, we should be quite unable to meet it; because we had no organization except the poor law system, and I called attention to the Elberfeldt system, which is really what is wanted in our great and dense populations, in order to meet, with any effectiveness, the actual phenomena of poverty. I would be the very last person to repress for one moment the emotions of benevolence; and yet I feel most acutely and clearly that there is no more difficult thing one has to do than to exercise a wise, salutary, and discriminating benevolence. A gushing benevolence I do not believe in. I trust nothing will be done out of mawkish and foolish charity. You may provide so many children with dinners every day, but are you certain that, by so doing, you are not relieving many intemperate parents from the responsibility which belongs to them of providing food for their children, and thus enabling them to spend more money upon drink for themselves? I deprecate all that sensational and indiscriminate charity which is doing so much mischief everywhere, and only aggravating the pauperism which it so feebly and spasmodically attempts to relieve. My first and last cry is, 'Let us organize and consolidate our benevolence.' I say that I believe you will, if you are Christian men and women, copy the example and precepts of the Great Teacher of Galilee, by going about the world with tender hearts, glad to give, ready to distribute; only making sure beforehand that your giving will help none but really deserving or really unfortunate people."

St. John's Church, Hurst, May 29, 1880:

"There are poor in England to-day just as wretched as Lazarus. In ninety-nine cases out of a hundred I fancy it is from their own fault, though I know that in some cases inherent weakness of constitution, and other causes over which men have no control, bring them to the sad state in which they are found—that sudden misfortune overtakes people, and that rich men become poor, and poor men poorer. It goes to my heart when I think of my own happy, sheltered, and prosperous lot, and when I read, as I do every day, some half-dozen appeals from every part of the country, not half of them true; yet not less saddening —telling of the sad lot of those who, if our conditions were measured by our deserts, deserve to be as comfortable as one's self. I quite admit there are great difficulties in the way of benevolence. What is called 'indiscriminate charity' does more harm than good, and is a foolish habit, which generates a great deal of hypocrisy and lying. Every one who tries to do good ought to take the further pains of seeing that he *is* doing good. It was said of Archbishop Whateley that he gave away in his life £40,000 in charity, and yet never gave sixpence to a man who accosted him in the street. That may seem rather hard, but it is my own rule pretty much. Deserving tramps are, I am afraid, very few and seldom to be met with; and I say again that, if we wish to do good, it is our duty to see that we do it, and not be content with bestowing a shilling here and there to any one who may ask it."

The organization of Christian benevolence is a problem which has exercised the thoughts of the Christian leaders of every age; and so far, especially in large towns, with only partial success. The larger the unit of the area "which takes charge of its own poor," the greater the opportunity opened to deceitful mendicants, because every increase of area means a lessening of personal acquaintance with the population; and the fundamental condition of the wise and beneficent distribution of benevolence is a personal knowledge of the circumstances of the recipients of that benevolence. To be a true helper to the needy, it is essential to *search out* * the cause of those we do not know. It was this great law of Christian economics which turned Bishop Fraser's attention to the Elberfeldt system—a system which he frequently explained and commended.

Old Trafford, January 5, 1879:

"The Elberfeldt system was adopted about twenty years ago, when the population of Elberfeldt was 50,000. The town was divided into manageable blocks of houses, and 300 volunteers distributed themselves into working parties; each party taking the oversight of one particular block, and making themselves acquainted with the condition of every family within that block. When the plan was begun, out of a population of 50,000 there were 4,220 paupers, and in 1876, up to which time the latest returns were made, the population had grown to 90,000, but the pauper list had fallen to 1,200. Here is a machinery which supersedes the poor law, and which has reduced pauperism."

The Cathedral, Manchester, October 28, 1877:

"With regard to Manchester, it seems to me that there is plenty of money and plenty of benevolence, but the benevolence wants organizing, and the money wants distributing. What we seem to require is some organization on a Christian basis. In such a work we could bury all sectarian animosities; and I cannot but think it would do good if an English Churchman and a Roman Catholic, or a Wesleyan and a Unitarian, would go to two and two on errands of mercy. The organization I wish to see is of this kind. I assume the population of Manchester and Salford to be from 450,000 to 500,000. Of that number, perhaps, one half live in circumstances under which supervision would be inexpressibly valuable. They would be living in 40,000 or 50,000 houses. That being so, I think an association of 500 members would be able to deal with them. Two members might take the oversight of 200 houses, or 1,000 people. The districts might vary in extent according to the character of their population. I would like to see each district visited once a week. No doubt there might be some risk, but can you tell me of any noble cause which can be maintained without risk? If a man is afraid of infection, or slinks back from typhoid fever, do not let him go; but, if willing to trust God with his life, or feeling that life is nobly laid down for the sake of his brethren, let him trust God, as medical men have to do, and go forth, paying special attention to those localities where the spirit-vaults, and dram-shops, and brothels abound. Those are the parts that want supervision, and, if the city were divided into manageable districts, two wise men might say of each: 'We will undertake to visit it once a week, we will soon find out the bad houses, and soon know the causes of distress and

---

* Job xxiv. 16.

poverty; and will report all cases where money will avail to remove them.'
I consider that a sum of £10,000 a year would suffice to meet the needs of
such an organization, and I do not think that Manchester would refuse to
find the necessary funds if the cost were even £50,000, if it could be
shown that by it we could prevent those terrible instances of destitution,
degradation, disease, sorrow, suffering, and shame which are a perfect
reproach to what we call our nineteenth century civilization. With reference to the persons who are to perform the work, I do not anticipate any
difficulty in getting the required number. I understand there are 2,000
young men who are members of the Young Men's Christian Association.
What nobler work could they have? Then there are about 3,000 young men
members of the Manchester Athenæum; and, considering these things, I
cannot but think that there is material enough which only wants to be
enlisted in this great work of charity. I would like to stamp the Cross of
Christ broad and deep on the work. There should be no sectarianism, no
priestcraft, no 'canting,' as men went about their work, in the name of
religion—there has been too much of that, and instead of doing good, it has
done an enormous amount of harm—but there should be energetic action
and wise and loving ministrations in the spirit of the Lord Jesus Christ."

The Bishop's private correspondence abounds in references
to the same topic.

December 24, 1878.

"I never wished to make my 'Elberfeldt' organization denominational,
or to connect it exclusively with the Church of England. I named it to
several of our most energetic and benevolent laymen, and they agreed with
me in the main outlines of the scheme; but everybody for the last year
has been too anxious about his own private business, to give time or spirit
to new enterprises. But good comes out of evil; and this distress is com-
pelling the formation of local organizations and district committees, which,
as a leading article in *The Guardian* said, 'it is to be hoped may become
permanent.' I am always inclined to wait for opportunities, and it was
because I thought the opportunity was come, that I tried to take at least
one more step onwards."

January 11, 1879.

"The Elberfeldt system is really, I think, 'coming to the fore.' My
speech at the Savings Bank, and my sermon at Old Trafford, on Sunday,
have called renewed attention to it. Mr. Herbert Philips is the Chairman of the Committee of the Provident Society, and one of our very best
and most liberal men. I have cheerfully put myself at his disposal. I
referred him to an article in the last July number of *The Contemporary* for
the best exposition that I know of the Elberfeldt system, though written by
one who prefers the system pursued in the Atcham Union, in Shropshire.
The only feature, or at least the chief feature, that I wished to introduce
from Elberfeldt, is the division of Manchester into districts under a body

K

of volunteer supervisors, who should undertake to make themselves acquainted with the condition—moral, educational, industrial, social—of every family living in their district. In fact, if you have the number of *The Contemporary* at hand, it is the principle stated in pp. 689-691 that I wish to impart. Apparently it has been introduced into Berlin, where they have 1,000 visitors for the poor; and are establishing bonds of sympathy, based upon actual knowledge, and of help showing itself in wise and practical methods, between the classes now sundered by terrible chasms of mutual ignorance, and sometimes of mutual antipathy. I ask for 500 workers, and for a fund of £10,000 a-year. When we have raised in a few weeks £15,000 to meet the present distress, there ought to be no *pecuniary* difficulty; and Herbert Philips' acknowledgment that now we are only making a 'scrambling attempt' to deal with the evil, ought to show people the need of organization. But I think the idea *is* taking possession of people's minds, and though the process is slow, one must not be too impatient."

January 21, 1879.

" There is no craze so difficult to deal with as the craze of philanthropic enthusiasm, which can or will only see one side of a question, and sets you down as a Laodicean, or something worse, if you do not see things in exactly the same light."

December 26, 1879.

" I am afraid we are discovering now the mischief we did by the almost indiscriminate relief of last winter, when we spent that £26,000 on relieving 40,000 persons. The weather is scarcely so severe, trade is better, and work is much more plentiful, and yet the number both of indoor and outdoor paupers relieved by Boards of Guardians is very largely in excess of what it was this time twelvemonth. The Manchester Guardians adopted a very strong memorial to the Government on Wednesday, in which they traced the mass of pauperism that prevails to the excessive facilities for obtaining drink which are placed in the way of people; and called upon the Government to take some effective steps in providing a remedy. In default of a proper organization, such as I have kept suggesting for the last two years, I am at my wits' end what to do, and I relieve no case into which I have not previously inquired through the agency of the District Provident Society. Without that aid I should be imposed upon, and be doing mischief right and left."

The result abundantly testified that the Bishop's fears of the pauperizing effect of the almost indiscriminate relief administered by the special fund in the winter of 1878-9 were far from being groundless. For in succeeding winters persistent efforts were made by the improvident sections of the people to obtain a renewal of relief. "These efforts," writes Mr. Herbert Philips, in an admirable sketch of the history of the Manchester and Salford District Provident Society, 1833–1885, "reached a climax in 1884, when, just as a remarkably mild winter was approaching its end, a very determined attempt was made by a body of men in irregular employment to force the Mayor to invite subscriptions and establish an organization for their relief." The avenging spirit of pauperization ever waits upon the careless distribution of unenquiring relief. Unless "the cause is searched out," generosity is guilt.

The difficulty, however, lying in the way of the organization of Christian charity is the difficulty of securing a sufficient number of Christian workers who will "search into every cause" with diligence and discretion. So long ago as 1833 the Manchester and Salford District Provident Society attempted, following the example of a similar society in Liverpool, to organize the relief of Manchester and Salford. About 800 visitors were required; but only about a quarter of that number were found to give their services, and many of these soon fell away. Yet, surely, there are thousands of Christian men who, as the Bishop said, "have nobler views of life than *merely* to have a stable full of hunters, a yacht lying in the Menai Straits, or a moor in Scotland;" thousands of earnest *young* men willing to give one evening of every week to definite work for their poorer brethren—only they need guiding and training how rightly to work in a well-organized method. Perhaps when ecclesiastical controversialists have settled the momentous question of clerical clothes, they will have leisure to consider the minor matter of the wise organization of Christian benevolence!

There were other lessons also which Bishop Fraser impressed upon Lancashire in connection with the commercial distress of 1878–9, besides the dangers of unenquiring benevolence and the need for the thorough organization of Christian charity. "I think," he said, "one of the great things we should strive to promote is the habit of frugality and of providence among all classes of our population." Over and over again he emphasized the need of this self-respecting thrift.

The Exchange Hall, Blackburn, February 28, 1879:

"I certainly wish that the great bodies of the working classes of this country had learnt more thoroughly than they seem to have learned as yet, the important lessons that are contained in the simple old English word—thrift. I do not mention it as a special fault of the working classes that they are unthrifty. I am afraid it is a general fault of Englishmen. Certainly, I believe that the late period of prosperity was a period which encouraged all people to become extravagant, and, I am sorry to say, selfishly extravagant. At the same time, I will say that the working classes, who are by far the most numerous, certainly are those who, it seems to me, most imperatively need to learn the lessons of thrift. Let me illustrate what I mean by one or two very obvious examples. Take the case of early marriages. One of my clergy the other day told me that he married a lad of sixteen to a girl of fourteen years. What do you think of that? I have also heard that it is a very common thing for young people in Blackburn to be married before they are twenty-one. A case was told me, about an hour ago, of a man who was going to be married, but he had not a very large stock of furniture or a large wardrobe, for he said he should have to borrow the coat he went to church in. Now, we will take an opposite case. I suppose I am not exaggerating when I say that in prosperous times there must be many a young man of twenty-one years of age, who, if industrious, could be earning 25s. a week. If he lived alone, and had nobody to keep but himself, I imagine that he could feed, dress, and lodge himself respectably for 15s.; thus saving 10s. a week. That is £26 a year, and if he postponed his marriage until he was thirty (and I really think that is pretty nearly soon enough, seeing that I am considerably over thirty and not married yet) that young man, instead of having to go to a friend and say : 'Let me have a coat to be wed in,' would be able to go to the bank and draw out £300. This is a practical point, which I think young men, and young women too, might lay to heart. I will now take another case ; Professor Levi has calculated that the net annual sum earned as wages by the labouring classes of the country, is about £450,000,000 ; and the sum spent by them on tobacco and intoxicants in the year is about £200,000,000. Now, how much better it would be for them, and for their wives and children, if they smoked and drank less in proportion. The other day I was sitting on the Salford Relief Committee, when there were 900 applicants for relief, and out of that number 460 were from the building trade. Of that 460, 200 were skilled artisans,—masons, bricklayers, joiners, painters, and plasterers. It was only the third week of the distress, and in that short time skilled artisans, who had been earning 9d. an hour as long as they had work, were asking for relief. Such things are terrible."

Manchester and Salford Savings Bank Association, January 26, 1881:

"Habits of thrift must be instilled early if they are to be effective, and I quite agree that real thriftiness is an important factor in all true education. Whilst I am glad to join in the direct and open crusades against the terrible evil of intemperance, I have always felt that indirect assaults upon that vice are perhaps more likely to be successful than the direct ones. It is because I feel that the habit of thrift is amongst the most powerful of weapons in this indirect assault, that I always feel so strongly about thrift. A thrifty man likes to have a comfortable home, which I think is the most powerful counter-attraction to the public-house or the spirit-vault. Such a man, too, likes to wear decent clothes, and though I sometimes lament to see young people tricking themselves out in costly finery, still that is better than spending the money in the public-house. There is, I believe, a growing desire among the people for decent clothes. It seems to me the people, as a people, are better and more comfortably dressed than they were forty years ago, and this I attribute to some extent, to increased habits of thrift. Thrifty habits, again, enable people to enjoy more health—full and more legitimate recreations. I wish we had more facilities for healthful recreation; but we are moving in that direction. All these things have an important bearing upon the evil of intemperance, and I think that all these efforts, made on various sides, are signs that things are after all not so bad as they were. The very fact that in our different centres so many gentlemen are willing to devote their time and leisure to almost every good work, may be taken as a sign that there is a growing sympathy between the different classes which constitute the commonwealth—the want of which, I believe to be one of the causes of the anarchy and disturbance that prevail across the Irish Channel at the present time."

The commercial distress gave the Bishop also an opportunity of frequently speaking upon another subject—the need of commercial righteousness.

Christ Church, Pendlebury, September 7, 1879:

"These signs of the times—this commercial depression, these anxious faces of our poor farmers, looking upon deluged fields, and seeing the crops they hoped to garner in their barns sweeping down the torrent—these signs speak to me as plainly as though every word were syllabled in tongues. I do not expect to see in my time the earth removed from its place, or the sun turned into blood; but there are signs enough around and about us to make us feel that these are anxious times, that somehow or other things have got out of joint, and we know not how they are to be put back into position. These signs on earth tell me that we, the English people, have been building prosperity on very insecure foundations; other nations will not now buy of us, because we have sent them, in years gone by, when we were passing through a fleeting time of prosperity, such rotten, worthless goods. We have been in far too great haste to get rich—not by honest industry, but by some financial stroke of luck; and, as a consequence, we have lost the tenderness of conscience which once marked English men of business, and English manufacturers. Mr. Robert Lowe has said that 'the principle of competition is the salvation of human society.' But to me, the spirit of competition, when it runs wild and breaks loose from all restraints of common honesty, leads to all that wretched adulteration and 'shoddyism,' which is one of the curses of the day. These signs of the times also tell me of the mischief wrought by competition; by strikers, by sham prospectuses, insecure investments, betting, gambling, and drinking, by tricking practices making themselves felt everywhere. The fact is, we have as a nation, to a large extent, forgotten God. Take the dishonesties practised in trade for instance. Is shoddyism 'jannock,' as Lancashire people say? Is it truth? Is it righteousness? The spirit of shoddyism has spread itself into all departments of trade in England. My belief is that only righteousness will, in the long run, establish commercial success."

The following testimony, kindly supplied by Mr. James Smith, the Secretary of the Manchester and Salford District Provident Society, shows how thoroughly Bishop Fraser's personal practice was in accord with his public utterances in the matter of painstaking benevolence and well-considered charity. Up to the time of the Bishop's death, Mr. Smith was the almoner of the Bishop's private charity. All applications to the Bishop for personal help were sent on to Mr. Smith, with full power to deal with every case on its merits, irrespective of whatever religion the applicant might be. No limit was placed upon Mr. Smith as to what he should do in each case; he had full power to do whatever he thought needful and right to meet the necessities of the case. These applications for help came to the Bishop from every class and religion of the community. Not unfrequently did the ministers of various denominations, in distress and want, come to the Bishop for his help and advice. Often, too, the Bishop sent pecuniary assistance altogether unsolicited. He had a favourite way of coming to Mr. Smith and saying:

"Smith, I fancy So-and-So is in trouble (*i.e.* some poor clergyman or minister). I have not said a word to them about their circumstances; but from the abject look of the wife, and the anxious, care-worn look of the husband, I fancy they must be in want; will you, by some means, get an interview, and if your ideas are at all confirmed in what I suspect, try to thrust this into their hands (a £10 or in many cases a £20 note), and under no circumstances let them have the slightest idea, directly or indirectly, who sent the money."

Hardly a week passed over without the Bishop paying one of these visits to Mr. Smith. It was not, therefore, a matter of surprise to find, when his accounts were examined after his death (for he kept even his charitable accounts with scrupulous fidelity) that during the fifteen and half years of his episcopate Bishop Fraser had distributed £31,535, an average of £2,000 a year—*i.e.*, nearly half his official income —upon various objects of Christian benevolence.

CHAPTER VII.

CO-OPERATION—SOCIAL SCIENCE.

The Co-operative Movement—Co-operative Congress—Co-operation and Agriculture—Co-operation and the Church—Social Science—Population of Cities—Education—Gradation of Schools—Health—The Interment of the Dead—Thrift and Providence—Recreation—Social Science and Religion.

THE Co-operative movement is one of the most remarkable industrial movements originated within the last fifty years. Its root-principle is to give the buyer a share in the profits of the seller, and the seller a means of obtaining ready-money from the buyer, by an identification of the interests of both. In its further development it aims at identifying the interests of masters and servants, employers and employed, by the process of converting the working-classes into their own capitalists. Co-operation has hitherto accomplished better results in its distributive province of a buying-and-selling movement than in its productive province as a manufacturing enterprise. The fundamental articles of the creed of co-operation are few and plain. In an ideal co-operative store, the dealers at the store are also the owners of the store; no credit is allowed, all purchasers are cash purchasers, those employed at the store have an interest in the profits of the store; and the buyers divide amongst themselves any gains which accrue upon the business done. It seldom happens, however, that an actual co-operative store is conducted upon these ideal principles. In some stores the true co-operative creed is less fully practised than in others; but, in all, the principle of allowing no credit is adhered to, cash payments being invariably the rule. This, of itself, is an enormous gain to all classes; for the curse of the credit-system is among the worst curses of the people. It is hopeless to seek for either happiness or progress in any class which is unthrifty and in debt; and the credit system is both an encouragement to improvidence and a fosterer of debts. Without committing himself to every point in the co-operative creed, Bishop Fraser—himself among the most thrifty and provident of men, whose proud boast was that he never was in debt in his life, and had never known what it was to waste a shilling—fixed upon the thrifty and provident aspects of co-operation; and, in the interests of social happiness and industrial progress, strongly enforced these aspects upon public attention. He was also stimulated to greater interest in the co-operative movement by the fact that two considerable towns in his diocese, Rochdale and Oldham, were the largest spheres of co-operative action in England; the former town claiming the proud distinction of being the birthplace of the co-operative idea.

Upon April 23, 1878, the delegates of the Co-operative Congress assembled at the Co-operative Hall, Downing Street, Manchester, under the presidency of Bishop Fraser. It was a rare circumstance in the history of co-operation that a Bishop should preside over a co-operative congress, and that co-operative delegates should listen with eager minds to the economical counsels of a Bishop—a Bishop both glowing with sympathy and bold in criticism.

"I have looked," said the Bishop in his Presidential address, "into this Co-operative movement, and have taken a considerable interest in it, and I also wish it every success. I am not a co-operator myself, and I don't think in the whole course of my life I ever spent a single sixpence at a co-operative store; nor do I mean to desert my retail tradesmen as long as they serve me fairly. But other persons, who may be differently situated in external circumstances from myself, no doubt have thought, and naturally thought, that the principle of co-operation is one that would very largely help them in the conduct of the affairs of life; and, therefore, they have gone into it with a vigour which seems characteristic of Englishmen when they thoroughly understand what they are doing, and are thoroughly determined to make what they are engaged in a success. You have been working the system, as I understand, for something like twenty-six years, and in that time you must have found out its strong points and its weak points: and if you are not like—which I don't imagine you are—that foolish bird, which, when it is followed by enemies, has a habit of burying its head in the sand and thinking it has no enemies, because it does not see them—I hope you have more intelligence—and having found the weak points in your system, I hope you are endeavouring to correct them in the wisest and most practical way. I do think there is need for caution and prudence in developing this matter just now. You are perfectly aware that the conditions of our commercial industry are somewhat disturbed at the present moment; and that it is certainly a time when everybody should move forward with a certain amount of caution; for I am afraid some disastrous consequences may yet be in store for some of those particular co-operative developments in consequence of the rashness with which, during a period of great prosperity in Lancashire, co-operative enterprises of the productive kind were started. I remember three or four years ago when the cotton industry was supposed to be enjoying a prosperity which people erroneously supposed would be chronic, and permanent, and almost normal, that there was an enormous development of what I cannot but call the speculative tendency in developing the principle of co-operation. In the neighbouring town of Oldham, I remember hearing with astonishment, that there were at that time in course of erection something like twenty-five co-operative mills, which, when filled and furnished with machinery, would each represent something like £60,000 of good hard money; the money being more or less easily procured on the principle of loans; so that when you heard of a co-operative mill, as was the case some time ago, whose dividend was at the rate of 28 per cent. for the whole year, people thought that the whole of the capital invested in the co-operative mill was producing that amount of interest, and did not know that perhaps three-fourths of the capital was borrowed money which was only receiving 5 per cent. interest, and the other fourth receiving that very large and attractive interest. At the time when these co-operative mills were built, the enterprise I think took a very unhealthy and a very dangerous form—I mean the form of share-jobbing—which I venture to think is entirely distinct from the principle of co-operation. I heard of instances of young men who had not £10 in the world going in for shares in these mills to the extent of £200, and not knowing where they were to raise the money. I think that is a very dangerous instinct, for it seems to be an instinct in human nature which you cannot altogether efface, and one of the things which should be very carefully watched and very carefully restrained, and I hope that, whatever you do in the erection of co-operative mills, you will do nothing to encourage jobbing in shares.

"In the course of my travels in the eastern counties, a gentleman one day said casually to me, 'Have you heard of the co-operative farm at Assington?' I had not heard of it then, and I don't think many others had at that time, so I said 'No.' He said 'Go and see it:' so I went one day to see this enterprise which had been at work for thirty-seven years, and was the oldest co-operative institution in the country. Its history is very simple. In the year 1830, Mr. Gurdon, the squire of the village, thought he would like to let some of his land to a body of working men, who would farm it on the principle of co-operation. In the year 1867 the population of Assington was 700, and the number of co-operators was fifty-six. There were two farms, one of 130 acres and the other of 112 acres. There were twenty co-operators on the smaller farm—they began with fifteen— and thirty-six on the larger farm. The smaller farm was commenced by fifteen men of the agricultural labouring class—a class that you will allow me to say is, I think, very unjustly depreciated in this country; a class by no means wanting in intelligence, a class by no means wanting in any of those qualities which go to make a man. The agricultural labourer is a man of few words, but of a great many thoughts. Well, fifteen of these men combined and undertook to take sixty acres of land at the usual rent. Wishing to give the experiment a fair chance the landlord trusted them with a loan of £400, for which they were to pay no interest for a certain time, and which they were to repay by instalments. When I saw them in 1867 they had paid off the whole loan of £400; they had increased their shareholders from fifteen to twenty; had increased their land from 60 to 130 acres, and were then paying £200 a year for rent, with the rates and taxes. That rate of progress, I think, would satisfy any landlord. I don't profess to be a perfectly competent judge of agricultural matters, though I know something about them, having lived the best part of my life in agricultural parishes; but all I can say is, that I went over the land, and it seemed to be perfectly clean, in perfectly good heart, and well farmed, the stock on the land being worth £1,200, so that I think you will see that the experiment has not been an unsuccessful one. I don't think these facts are generally known in the country, and I don't think, even yet, the public mind has awakened to the infinite service of creating a class that I think very much needs to be created, as a sort of intermediate link in our huge social disseverments. I think a class of co-operative agriculturists would be a most important and stable element in the commonwealth. In the first place, none of these co-operators were paupers, not one of them came on the rates of the parish. On the first farm I found four widows, who, by the help of their original industry were maintaining themselves without having recourse to the poor-rate. In agricultural parishes, where laying-by is almost an impossibility to the agricultural labourer, you know what is the gloom into which his widow and children are thrown, if unhappily his strength is cut down in the middle of his day. A great many of the clergy throughout the country have glebe lands. I had a glebe land in my last parish of 60 acres. I had a very good tenant, and did not wish to disturb him. He was a man who had worked himself up from the working class, and was thriving fairly. It was not good land, but he hadn't to pay a very high rent, and I think, on the whole, he got his bread and cheese, and he was content, and I was content; but I was determined that if anything had caused me to lose that tenant I would have tried that farm on the co-operative principle. Now, there must be many of the clergy who would be rendering a great service to the commonwealth, if they would deal with their glebe lands as Mr. Gurdon dealt with his. It is all very well to talk of our inexhaustible resources. I believe they are inexhaustible only so long as we enjoy the blessings of peace, but I don't know how soon they would be drained up if we went to war. With regard to these terrible strikes which cause so much distress as long as they last, and leave such misery behind them, I do sometimes live in the hope that, by the spread of the spirit which you have embodied in the co-operative movement, some of the relations between capital and labour will be better understood and more fully appreciated. I daresay there are faults in this matter on both sides, and there may have been a reluctance to look on the matter from what I call the intermediate point of view. People have looked upon it too much from the interests of their own class. That spirit runs through everything. My advice with regard to co-operative enterprises is, that they should be conducted on business principles; and, in order that the servants, such as secretaries of societies, may be delivered from temptation, books and accounts should be regularly audited by competent auditors. I was glad to see in the brief report which found its way into the newspapers, that my good friend the Rev. William Molesworth, in his sermon at the Cathedral, lifted this great question of co-operation up into its very highest sphere, and tried to teach those who listened to him, that you are really only exemplifying, in the secular department of human affairs, that important principle which I take to be almost the cardinal principle of Christianity. You are aware of those wretched controversies in which we are engaged just now. Some kind friend has sent me a letter, in which he said he had observed the tone of despair I had lately exhibited, and that I wanted my good archdeacons to come, like Aaron and Hur, to hold up my hands and help me to take a more cheerful view of things. Who can take a cheerful view of things, when people are splitting hairs (as they did in the olden days about the length of a vowel or a diphthong), about the length of the surplice? I am going to have a deputation this morning, I believe, to complain that the choristers' surplices do not come down to their knees. Really these puerilities take the heart out of me; seeing what I believe the Gospel of Christ has to do in the world. If we could only put down war, if we could only sow the seed of goodwill and peace amongst men, if we could realize the great bonds of brotherhood that make us sons of one great Father and heirs of one great common hope —*that's the Christianity which interests me.* And really, as to postures and the like, if people like them, let them use them; they rather irritate than please me. If people like to do all these foolish things that are being done, thinking they thereby promote the great cause of Christianity, I only sigh and say, "Let them do it." I only fear that there will come some reaction, when people will see that high sacramental theories and high sacerdotal theories break down under the pressure of temptation, and don't really help poor feeble struggling men and women to fight the battle of life with any force. I confess I do rejoice when from time to time men like Mr. Molesworth lift up their voices in our Cathedral pulpit, and proclaim the great principle of Christian brotherhood. You in your way, and according to your measure, are trying to teach the world that this great principle runs through the whole of our organized social and moral life, as it runs through our organized physical system. We are all parts of one great body, knit together under one great head, and, as Tennyson says:—

> 'Like a piece of art,
> All toil should be co-operant to an end.'

"And that end certainly ought to be the welfare (in the highest sense of the word), the physical, moral, social, intellectual, religious, spiritual welfare of mankind."

This speech is eminently characteristic of the Bishop. The speech does not keep strictly to its cardinal theme, which was co-operation; it wanders into the question of ecclesiastical ceremonies. Such wanderings are faulty in the orator; but they warm us towards the man. For, whenever he speaks, he takes us into his confidence and folds us to his heart. He is appointed to speak upon co-operation; but, within an hour, he has to meet "a deputation coming to complain that the choristers' surplices do not come down to their knees." The prospect of such a miserable interview "takes the heart out of him." By an effort he could have kept his heart-load a secret from the co-operative delegates, thus treating them as strangers; but, instead of this, he treats them as friends, taking for granted that, of their goodwill, they will not be uninterested in what is burdening him. Then, encouraged by their sympathy, he recovers himself and exclaims: "Let us realize the great bonds of brotherhood that make us sons of one great Father and heirs of one great common hope—*that's the Christianity which interests me.*"

But although, as the speech shows, the Bishop was not blind to the perils which appear to wait upon some (not indeed strictly natural) developments of the co-operative movement, neither was he blind to the great advantages of which the movement is capable.

At the annual soirée of the Failsworth Co-operative Society, January 29, 1881, he said:

"I have always watched with a great amount of interest what is called the co-operative movement; and so far as I can judge of the principles on which it is conducted, and the ends to which it aspires, the whole thing seems to me to be in the highest degree encouraging; and if England either is, or is to be, correspondent to the description of it that is given in the song about the land of the fair, and the brave, and the free; and if we are to have some pride in thinking of it, and to have a joy in its nobleness and feel honoured in its fame, I think these co-operative societies, which spread, to such a large extent, contentment, and all those other elements which go to ameliorate the condition of the great mass of the people, must be reckoned amongst some of the most potent influences of this generation to that end. I have noticed that in the course of the year the number of volumes in your library has been doubled, now standing at 2,735, and that 783 belong to the class of novels and works of fiction. I do not often read novels now, though when a lad I read almost every one that came out. Although a good novel is a very great refreshment, I have very little time for reading such works now, and I do not suppose I have read more than two new novels during the ten years of my episcopate; but when a man who is a great statesman, and has been a prime minister of this country, writes a novel, I suppose one is bound to read it, and I have read 'Lothair' and 'Endymion.' I do not know whether you have the latter fanciful work on your book-shelves or not, but I may say that I read it with a good deal of amusement and interest; and, though it is not a very satisfactory novel to my mind, I picked out two sentiments from it that seemed to me to be the two best sentiments in the book. One has reference to horse-racing, which it describes as the most demoralizing pastime practised in this country. The other sentiment is more germane to this meeting. I found in connection with a sort of socio-political discussion in one of the chapters (one of the interlocutors in which, I think, was a gentleman who was supposed to represent the young England of the future) the statement that we had not yet lost all the possibilities of our situation, that society had a great future and a vast horizon before it, and that the mighty spell that was going to work all this vast good for the great mass of the people of England was co-operation. Well, here you are trying co-operation. I think it is, in its principles, a better thing than competition. The latter though a very good thing in its way, and no doubt stimulating to men to do their best, still has connected with it many unhealthy motives, many rivalries and jealousies; and I am afraid sometimes it leads to practices which do not come up to a high standard of morality. The principle upon which co-operation is based is of an entirely different kind. It works on the principle that society, in a certain sense, is one great composite body. That is the idea, so far as I can understand it, that St. Paul put forth in one of his epistles, wherein he spoke of the Church as a Christianized society, and likened it to the human body. The three ideas expressed in the words liberty, equality, and fraternity are pretty well combined in co-operation."

This high praise of co-operation, and the declared preference of the co-operative over the competitive principle, did not go unchallenged, as the following letter from the Bishop shows:

"Manchester, *February* 19, 1881."

"Sir,—I beg to acknowledge your letter upon co-operation. For myself I have never spent a sixpence in a co-operative store, and, as long as I am well served by the retail tradesmen, probably never shall. But this does not prevent me seeing the advantages of these institutions to the working-classes in many departments of their lives; notably, in their reading-rooms, libraries, and educational classes, and, seeing these advantages, I cannot help wishing well to them.

"I also hold that the principle of co-operation is higher than the principle of competition; and though it may be, as you assert, that "the interests of those who practise co-operation are self-interested," still, if out of a self-interested motive a good result may be obtained, society has not much reason to complain. All trade is with a view to profit; and I suppose you would hardly claim for the association which you represent that, in their business transactions, they are actuated by pure philanthropy.

"There seems to me to be plenty of room at present both for the retail tradesman and for the co-operative store. You admit the latter has reduced prices, and led to a large increase of ready money dealing. If the competition were removed, who could answer for it that prices would not again rise, and the vicious system of credit return? Dignified neutrality is not the attitude I am wont to assume in any question which appears to me widely and deeply to affect the welfare of the working-classes. At the same time, in my appreciation of the co-operative movements, I should be sorry to say or do anything that would injure the retail tradesmen who sell good articles at fair prices. I have hardly ever in my life, unless I have changed my residence, changed a tradesman, and I am bound to acknowledge that I have hardly ever had a reason for wishing to change.—Yours, &c.,

"J. Manchester.

"Mr. Robert Dixon, *Hon. Sec.*
"*Manchester Grocery Trade Defence Association.*"

One or two further illustrations of the Bishop's interest in the co-operative movement, and its kindred associations, may be added.

Speaking at the Co-operative Hall, Downing Street, Manchester, November 27, 1882, he said:

"These co-operative institutions of yours are instances of the spirit which stimulates and penetrates a whole class or body of men. You first realize the wants of your class, and then, as those wants become more evident, you set about in a very sensible and practical way, to supply them. The great co-operative associations of Rochdale, Rossendale, and other places in Lancashire, have their science and art classes, their libraries, their news-rooms, their schemes of lectures, their concerts, and other forms of pleasing and wholesome recreation. And, in attempting to do all this, you are pursuing the interests of the whole class to which you belong; and at the same time are fortifying and raising the moral qualities and social virtues of that class. The utter abolition of the credit system greatly fosters thrift; the educational appliances develop intelligence; the lawful gratification of a pure and modest taste by which you minister to healthful recreation are on the right side in the great battle between intemperance and sobriety. And all these happy and humanizing influences gather round the co-operative associations of the working man."

At the Co-operative Union, Manchester, December 6, 1884, he said :

"The gigantic enterprise in which the co-operative body is engaged, shows, at least, what the wants and aspirations of the people are. They wish of course, and very naturally and properly, to get the best article at a moderate and reasonable price—a price which will leave a fair profit to the producer, and which will not bear unreasonably on the pocket of the consumer. But with their distributive depôts they associate various organizations for education, and moral and intellectual improvement. I have myself been a visitor to many of these institutions—those at Rawtenstall, Bacup, and Rochdale—and it has rejoiced me to see that, concurrently with the getting of the best goods at a moderate price, they aim at having libraries, reading rooms, science and art classes, and all the apparatus of education. It shows that as a body they appreciate the highest and best needs of the class to which they belong. I was present the other evening at a meeting in the ragged-school mission-room in Ancoats, where I had to address 800 men and women. The difference between the appearance of the body of people I saw at that meeting in Ancoats, and the appearance of such a body of people as I have seen at meetings in co-operative stores, is a living sermon on the difference that working men might make in their condition if they would only learn the lessons of thrift and temperance; without which no man has a right to expect that he will succeed, or prosper, or be happy in life. It is of great importance to indoctrinate the great body of the people of England with the idea that it is the bounden duty, and one of the great principles, of co-operation specially to elevate their own class. There is a great mass of people in this country whom Mr. Bright on one occasion called 'the residuum,' and who are the residuum just because they have not learned those lessons which co-operative people have learned and are trying to teach. There is nothing of greater importance to the country, especially when the electoral power is being placed in the hands of a still larger number of people, than that the great body who are the pith and sinew of the land should learn the moral, economical, political, and religious lessons which are the elements of our happiness, our prosperity, and our national well-being."

Preaching the annual "Congress Sermon" in St. Mary's Church, Oldham, May 24, 1885, he said :

"I feel that the pulpit is not the proper place to enter into an examination of the details of the co-operative system. But the principles of the system I believe to be thoroughly sound; and the movement has deservedly met with great success and prosperity. The principle upon which you have consolidated yourselves is implied in your name; you are co-operators, not competitors. You have associated together for purposes of mutual help; to encourage thrift and providence; to give men the benefit of cash payments; to promote educational and healthful recreation generally; and, in the largest sense of the word, to elevate the position of the working man. Can any one find a word to say against such objects as these? Even if co-operation has done no other service to working men, it has done an unspeakable good in insisting upon cash payments. On no other basis, as I understand the problem, can habits of thrift and frugality be really spread among that class of our people. I have spoken about their achievements, and I will now say a word about their critics and criticisms.

I have received, and have read with care, some communications on the subject which have been sent to me. One of these critics said in a pamphlet, 'Co-operators are a most estimable race of people, but they are keen as any one in the race for wealth and their devotion to Mammon.' "Co-operators will have need, I think, to be on their guard against this taint, to see that it does not reach them, for if it does it is pretty certain to corrupt. Their critics also say that co-operators have no independent auditors to audit their accounts, and that those accounts, as presented in their balance-sheets, are therefore not sufficiently trustworthy. To what extent that statement is true I have had no means of judging. It was accompanied with the remark that the Industrial and Provident Societies Act, while it recommends in very strong language the appointment of independent auditors, does not make it compulsory; and the critics think that, in the case of societies dealing with such large amounts of capital, and in which so many interests are involved, an audit by a Government inspector ought to be compulsory. I have not noticed any other criticism of importance, and I will only say, as your friend and well-wisher, that you ought to be sure you are honestly solvent before the world, and that the world sees and knows it. You ought also to be sure that co-operation is your true and primary motive, and not mere money-making. If these two principles are not kept in view, I prophesy that co-operation will not be permanent. I cannot call the co-operative mills—of which there are so many in this town of Rochdale—true instances of co-operation. They do not seem to me to differ from ordinary limited companies, except in the fact that the shares have been largely taken up by working men.

"While you, as co-operators, are doing permanent good to your country, I hope you desire to maintain the glory which has hitherto attached to the English name. I am not speaking of what some people call *prestige*, as, for my own part, I do not count that as worth much, but you must raise the name of England to something more sterling and true. The air is full of wild schemes. There are men of the type of Henry George going about the country, preaching that there will be nothing but poverty till the land is nationalized; but that is a mere idle dream. I believe if every man will try to do his duty towards his fellow-men in that spirit of brotherhood which the Holy Ghost has planted in the hearts of us all, we may look forward to the future calmly and without fear."

The co-operative movement is only one out of many movements bearing upon the progress and contentment of the commonwealth in which Bishop Fraser took a deep and sympathetic interest. Every question which touched the welfare of the community touched also his warmly beating human heart. His Christianity was not superior to considerations of drainage, of air and light, of architectural appliances. He preached the gospel of roomy houses, with an abundance of compartments and pleasant surroundings. He maintained that ignorance, and dirt, and disease were the foes of Christian progress; that education, cleanliness, and health were co-operators with Christ. It was not unnatural, therefore, that when the Social Science Congress met in Manchester in October, 1879, Bishop Fraser should be its president. No doubt it was a singular, a unique position for a bishop to occupy. No other bishop has sat in the presidential chair of a Social Science Congress, as no other bishop has sat in the presidential chair of a Co-operative Congress. Most bishops would feel themselves, and would be felt by others, to be out of place in such a seat. But to Bishop Fraser the seat was natural. Every man has his proper gift. And it is no disparagement to other bishops that Bishop Fraser was unlike them; and that his rare gifts fitted him for rare occasions. Had he been elected president of the British Association, on the ground of his religious sympathy with physical science, as he was elected president of the Social Science Congress, on the ground of his religious sympathy with social improvement, no one, except himself, would have been astonished. When Lord Norton handed over the bâton of his presidential office, at the Social Science Congress in 1879, to Bishop Fraser, he said that the Bishop was "the very man of all others in the kingdom most fit to hold it. No man understands the subject more thoroughly, and no man can give his opinions in more eloquent or impressive language."

A brief summary of his presidential address, at this Social Science Congress, will indicate the social topics which, almost daily, occupied the Bishop's eager attention.

"If anybody were to ask me what social science is, or how it is to be defined, I do not know that I could answer him; the less so as you have included in your range a department of art which in popular language is distinguished from science. I think the phrase 'social science' a misleading one, as claiming a measure of certainty for your conclusions, and a predictive power for your principles, which have not yet been attained; and I do not believe to be attainable. I remember, it is true, that Mr. Buckle maintained that social and political phenomena could be predicted; but when you examined his meaning you found that he only referred to that limited form of prediction which is implied in the calculation of averages, and which is something very different from the astronomical exactitude with which you can tell the very day, and hour, and minute of an eclipse.

"I invite you, then, to consider with me some of the problems involved in the social condition of great cities; and I shall illustrate my positions, as I severally take them up, mainly by facts and figures supplied by Manchester, about which I know more than about any other great city; not attempting any logical division or exhaustive treatment of the subject, but directing your attention to certain branches of it, which are not devoid of interest, and could even be treated picturesquely by one who had a gift that way, and are certainly of supreme practical importance.

(1) POPULATION OF GREAT CITIES.—"Within a radius of five miles from here, there is a population of probably 750,000, of whom 370,000 would be in Manchester, 170,000 or 180,000 in Salford, and the rest in suburban townships. For some of the necessities of social life, such as gas and water, these suburban districts are indebted to the great central municipalities, Manchester and Salford, with which they are locally connected; others, such as education and the relief of the poor, they provide for themselves; but still, for practical purposes, the whole may be regarded as one great, but imperfectly organized, community. It is already so large and so complex that I should regard with positive dismay the prospect of any considerable accession to its numbers and magnitude. The *distribution* of the population in these great industrial centres is peculiar and seems to follow a kind of law; and is an important element to be borne in mind when we are considering the social condition of the people. Things have undergone an almost entire change in the last half-century. Fifty years ago the wealthiest merchants in Manchester lived in the heart of the town, in streets in which to-day there is not a single gentleman's residence. Tradesmen lived over their shops, manufacturers found

existence tolerable under the smoke of their tall chimneys, surrounded by the cottages of their workpeople. The suburbs, which now stretch out their long lengths, or are dotted with handsome detached villas, on every side of Manchester, did not exist. Life perhaps was rougher and less refined; but there was more contact of class with class, more intercourse and sympathy between masters and men, fewer of those chasms across which we make so many futile attempts to throw bridges, and which constitute sometimes such insuperable difficulties in the way of large and effective schemes of social improvement. Now all these conditions are changed. You will hardly find one of our wealthiest men within two miles of his place of business or of the Exchange. The shopkeepers have migrated into the suburban townships. The centre of the city at night is a mass of unoccupied tenements. The working class and the poor still cluster thickly together in the murkiest and dismalest quarters of the town, with nobody, perhaps, living among them above their own social level, except the doctor and the clergyman; and though we are slowly trying, and to some extent successfully, to remedy the evil, in too many parishes, and those the very poorest, there is no parsonage-house, and the clergyman not unnaturally prefers to locate himself and his family where he can see the sun a little oftener and breathe a purer air. A large proportion of the working class, however, under the pressure of recent street improvements, which have been going on so extensively among us for the last ten years, have, like the rich and well-to-do, migrated to the suburbs, though not to the same suburbs; and, if the houses provided for them by speculative builders at the high rent of 5s. or 6s. a week, were a little more roomy and of a more solid construction, and were erected under stricter sanitary regulations, the change, no doubt, would be beneficial to all concerned. But, speaking generally, in these suburbs, the working class still dwell as a class apart, and are even further removed in distance from their employers than before. The houses have seldom more than two bedrooms, so that it is almost impossible to bring up in them a large mixed family with due regard to health and decency, and are often so flimsy of construction, and put together with such unseasoned materials, and erected with such supreme contempt of the recognized conditions of a healthy life. A change, which might have been of great social benefit to the class concerned, has been a change of very questionable advantage indeed. Still, these are the facts of the case in most of our great centres of population; and a most important body of facts, in their social consequences, they are. They are the conditions, partly physical, partly economical, partly moral, under which the problems of society are to be worked out, if possible, to their true solution.

(2) GRADATION OF SCHOOLS.—" Whatever may be the deficiencies of the Act of 1870, it certainly has not failed in its immediate object—the getting a large number of children to attend efficient schools. The next step onwards, which I think all the more earnest friends of education desire to see taken, is that which struck me so forcibly as the strongest merit of the

great American system of public schools, and which I recommended to the consideration of the Schools Inquiry Commission in the report on the American system which I addressed to them in the year 1865. I refer to the Gradation of Schools. Both Mr. W. E. Forster and Lord George Hamilton have recently expressed themselves warmly in favour of this feature of the American system. Mr. Forster says, 'In my opinion we shall have to grade our schools to give an opportunity to the poorer children to pass from the cheaper to the more expensive schools.' In my report, written in 1865, I said, 'The gradation of schools is just the strength of the American system . . . . . Any one with experience in educational matters will at once see that it is the one thing which our Elementary Schools have not, and which they most need.' With us, each school is a separate and disjointed unit; in the United States it is part of a compact, co-ordinated, homogeneous system. With us, when a boy has passed Standard VI.—a very low measure of attainment, if it is to be considered the complete intellectual outfit for life—his education generally stops; or, if it is to be continued, it can only be with difficulty, and at the cost of considerable sacrifices to his parents. In the United States he would pass naturally, and free of cost, from the primary school to the grammar school, and from this to the high school; and from this again, though not quite so naturally, because it is no longer part of the public school system, but yet without any insurmountable difficulty, to the University. Thus, to take an instance, in Boston, in the year, 1874, with a population of 357,000, as nearly as possible equal to that of Manchester, and with 56,684 children of the school age—*i.e.*, between five and fifteen—there were nine high schools, with an average enrolment of 2072 pupils, 1019 boys and 1053 girls; forty-nine grammar schools, with an enrolment of 23,863—12,471 boys, 11,392 girls; and 416 primary schools with 18,867 children—10,314 boys, and 8,553 girls, on the register; giving an average in all the day schools of 44,492, and an average daily attendance of 41,613 or 92·6 per cent. on the number enrolled. And this enormous school system was maintained, not, however, without some grumbling on the part of the ratepayers, at a total cost for all purposes, including buildings, of £373.000 for the year. And in this great and generous system, so generous that it may almost be deemed extravagant, the child who enters the lowest class in the primary school at the age of five may advance, if his parents will only keep him at school, through all the gradually ascending steps of the scale, till he reaches the highest class in one of the high schools; and I remember well the honest pride with which the admirable master of the Latin High School at Boston pointed to his head boy—who was hoping to proceed to Harvard University, with the help of that munificent liberality which is so characteristic of rich men in the United States, and which is scarcely ever withheld from real desert—who, he told me, was the son of an Irish labourer. You can easily understand how the possession of advantages of this kind reconciles even the humblest citizen to his lot, when he feels that his boy has the chance of becoming President of the United States, the very height of human ambition; or to put the idea in a more modest form, that in the great Transatlantic Republic there is a career opened to talents.

(3) HEALTH.—" Good health may be said to depend upon four primary conditions—a good water supply, good drainage, good air, well-constructed and wholesome houses. By the exertions of the two corporations, I believe that the death-rate in Manchester and Salford has been very sensibly reduced, and does not now exceed more than than 20 or 22 per 1000 under normal circumstances; and for some time past we have been wonderfully free from epidemic or infectious disease. The rate of mortality in Higher Broughton, the salubrious level on which I live, does not exceed 10 or 12 per 1000; while there are courts and alleys in Salford where it is as high as 60 or 70. The chief difficulty in dealing with these great and important questions affecting the public health arises from the fact that municipal bodies and local boards rarely attack the evil till it has become intolerable; and, when they do attack it, they find it encumbered with so many vested interests or acquired rights, that it is almost impossible to deal with it effectively, except at a cost which is enough to frighten them from dealing with it at all. It is this difficulty which has rendered the Act for preventing the pollution of rivers practically inoperative. With regard to the general water supply—whether for drinking or for household or manufacturing purposes—of our great cities, and, indeed, of the country at large, I am entirely of the opinion that it is neither right nor wise that the present hap-hazard system should be continued; that great towns, on the principle of 'first come, first served,' should be allowed to choose their collecting ground for themselves; and it has become, if we are at all to consult the interests of posterity, a peremptory necessity that England and Wales should be divided into districts by competent authority for the sufficient supply of wholesome water for the population residing in each.

"The sewage system of Manchester, which is rapidly advancing to completion, is well worthy of the notice of members of this Association. The chief produce of this system is a concentrated manure suited for agricultural purposes, of which it is estimated that from 20,000 to 30,000 tons can be produced in a year; and, if sold at the low rate of £2 a ton, would give a profit of 1s. 9d. to 2s. a ton. The gross annual expense of the night-soil department is between £60,000 and £70,000; and this profit, if attained, while it will dispose of refuse likely to be injurious to health, will also sensibly lighten the burden to the ratepayers. The air we breathe, and the purity of which is so essential to our health, both of body and mind, is chiefly affected by ventilation of our houses, and by the absence or presence of deleterious vapours and gases in the atmosphere. Smoke is not the only, nor, I am told, the worst offender in this respect. The chemical and particularly the sulphurous vapours that are given off, even when the smoke is consumed, are said to be more injurious to human life and more noxious to vegetation than those dense black columns of unconsumed carbon, which not only indicate our wasteful habits of consumption, but deface some of the most naturally picturesque districts in the land. Some few years back I was visiting the hematite ironworks at Carnforth, which at that time were in full operation. I was being shown over them by Mr. Barton, the manager. I noticed a thin column of white vapour issuing from the tall chimney; and I noticed, also, that the chimney itself was scarcely discoloured, though it had been discharging the duties of a chimney for many years. 'Do you never give off anything worse than that?' I inquired of my companion. 'Hardly ever,' was his reply; 'and the best of it is, our consumption of our smoke saves us £30,000 a year in fuel.' 'How is it, then,' said I, 'that everybody does not follow your example?' 'Oh,' he said, 'partly from want of proper looking into things, and partly because to produce this result requires a peculiar construction of the works, which, in the case of old establishments, may not be possible.'

(4) INTERMENT OF THE DEAD.—"I will now say a few words upon the provision made in our cities for the interment of the dead. On Friday last, I consecrated a portion of a new cemetery, provided by the Corporation, on the south side of Manchester, fully five miles from the centre of the city, containing 97 acres, at a cost, including the land, the fencing, the laying out, and the inevitable three or four chapels, of £100,000. It is very beautiful; but two thoughts occurred to me as I was consecrating the portion of it assigned to those who desire to be buried according to the rites of the Church of England. In the first place, this is a long distance for the poor to bring their dead; in the second place, here is another 100 acres of land withdrawn from the food-producing area of the country for ever. I do not think we always observe or calculate how much this area is being gradually contracted by the infinite number of works and processes requiring space, but not producing food, which are encroaching more and more upon it every year; nor to what extent the power of the country to support its population is reduced thereby. 'Jam pauca aratro jugera regiæ Moles relinquent.' In times of peace and plenty we can afford to be indifferent to this consideration; but I can easily conceive the existence of circumstances which would make this a very serious condition indeed. I feel convinced that before long we shall have to face the problem, 'How to bury our dead out of our sight,' more practically, and more seriously, than we have hitherto done. In the same sense in which the 'Sabbath was made for man, not man for the sabbath,' I hold that the earth was made, not for the dead, but for the living. No intelligent faith can suppose that any Christian doctrine is affected by the manner in which, or the time in which, this mortal body of ours crumbles into dust and sees corruption. I admit that my instincts and sentiments—the result, however, probably of association more than anything else—are somewhat revolted by the idea of cremation. But they are perhaps illogical and unreasonable sentiments. One does not particularly care to read in the papers how men of science stood, watch in hand, by the side of one of Siemens's cremation furnaces, and watched the process of destruction, and counted the minutes and seconds which it took to calcine the different members and tissues of which the body is composed. But Sir Henry Thompson has stated the case in a calm and thoughtful paper, which shows how little ground there

is for the somewhat morbid sentiments that, indeed, prevail in relation to the whole subject of the interment of the dead. There is another method which is popularly known as 'the earth to earth' system, which may be as efficacious; and, if so, would be preferred by myself and many more. All I call attention to is, that it is a subject that will have to be seriously considered before long. Cemeteries are becoming not only a difficulty, an expense, and an inconvenience, but an actual danger.

(5) THRIFT: PAUPERISM.—"How to encourage habits of thrift and providence, and at the same time to repress the tendency to pauperism and mendicancy, are two of the most important and difficult social problems presented by populations aggregated in large masses; and there are no questions in which a more careful discrimination is needed to arrive at a true estimate of the case. That there is a thriftless section in every class of society, from the highest to the lowest, there can be no doubt; and that, perhaps, nearly all members of all classes have in the last few years been living at a more extravagant rate than prudence can justify is probably true also. But, at the same time, there are many encouraging symptoms on the other side. Professor Leoni Levi estimates the earnings of the labouring classes in 1878 at about £420,000,000, of which £350,000,000 was received in cash, and £70,000,000 in board, lodging, clothing, and other requisites. He further estimates the difference in wages to the working class between prosperous and bad times to be as much as £50,000,000 a year; and he says that in the three prosperous years, 1871–73, the labouring class received some £70,000,000 a year, or an aggregate sum of £210,000,000, above the normal amount. In 1878 the total amount invested in the savings banks of both kinds in the United Kingdom, which represents mainly the savings of the working class, was £74,705,000, and, though this is an increase of £21,700,000 on the deposits of 1870, yet the Professor thinks this is but a poor account of the savings of the last eight years, during the greater portion of which, he says, the wages were liberal. But the Professor should remember that the savings banks only represent one particular form of saving, and act more as a kind of social barometer than anything else, indicating whether the tendency to save is on the increase among the people or not. I was glad to observe in a very recent return that even in this calamitous year (1878) the withdrawals from the savings banks have not exceeded the deposits by a larger sum than about £100,000. The working class have many other opportunities, and choose many other ways of investing their money than with either the Post Office or the Trustees' Savings Banks. A few years since, when not over far-seeing observers thought the tide in the prosperity of the country would never turn, more than £2,000,000 of money, almost entirely from the working class, was invested in a number of joint-stock cotton-mills with a limited liability in and about Oldham, and for some months that town and the neighbouring villages were as wild a scene of excitement in buying and selling shares as was Capel Court in the disastrous days of the railway mania. I am afraid that the investments have proved singularly unadvised and unfortunate; and there is perhaps no class that needs more earnestly than the working class to be

reminded of the wisdom of the Duke of Wellington's practical maxim, that the high rate of interest always promised in these attractive prospectuses means proportionate risk. I am told, also, that in Lancashire, and particularly in Oldham, a considerable and increasing number of working men live in houses of their own; and though I don't know, remembering the shiftings of manufactures and trading industries, and how valueless cottage property becomes except in connection with some large centre of employment, that it is a kind of investment I should be disposed to recommend very strongly to working men, still the fact of these investments is an evidence of thrift. There have been some counter-influences at work, it is true, in Lancashire, which, if one relied on the savings bank test alone, is the most thrifty county, or at least has the largest sum invested in the savings banks, of any county in England. I have heard thoughtful people say that the period of the cotton famine was, in a way that perhaps might not be expected, the most disastrous period through which the population of Lancashire ever passed. Up to that date a Lancashire operative had been ashamed to beg; and, though the best specimens of the class are ashamed to beg now, yet, under the operation of that principle of the Poor Law which refuses aid to those who have any resources remaining of their own, even steady people who saw their neighbours getting help at the very outset of the distress, and themselves at last reduced to the same level, became demoralized by the spectacle and seemed to lose their faith in the principle of providence. The Rev. W. L. Blackley, rector of North Waltham, Hants, has recently put forth a scheme which may briefly be described as a scheme of compulsory insurance, by which he thinks the independence of every man can be secured, and the curse of pauperism extirpated; and the suggestion has excited a good deal of attention, and from sanguine persons received considerable encouragement. He assumes that every young person—I am not sure whether he extends the system to females—could, between the ages of eighteen and twenty-one, lay by two shillings a week; that this sum should be paid to a national fund, secured by a national guarantee, and that, in return for a completed payment of £10, he should be assured until he reaches the age of seventy of an allowance of eight shillings a week while hindered by sickness from earning wages, and four shillings a week pension for every week he lives over seventy years. And he would secure this result by making this insurance compulsory. The arguments advanced in support of the scheme are ingenious and perhaps logical, but there is an inexorable logic of facts which I am afraid is against it; and the English people's notions of the functions of government must be considerably extended before there can be much chance of its being realized. We are endeavouring, taught by last winter's experience of distress and suffering, to revive the Elberfeldt system—a plan for organizing a systematic visitation of the poor. We have selected a conveniently situated block of houses near the centre of Manchester, and have persuaded an adequate number of volunteers to undertake the superintendence of it in suitable sections. A similar organization has also been started in the suburbs of Pendlebury, and, indeed, was partially at work during the relief operations of last winter. It is too early yet to speak of either success or failure. The result will entirely depend upon the zeal, and prudence, and perseverance with which the visitors discharge the duties they have undertaken. That some such organization is necessary if crises of distress are effectively to be dealt with, and if the richer half of the world is to know how the poorer half lives, I am absolutely assured. I am aware that it is becoming a popular doctrine among political economists that the true way to repress pauperism—which every one desires to do—is to rigorously apply the workhouse test. I paid a visit to my old Berkshire parish a month ago, and I found that, in the Union in which I was for some years a member of the Board of Guardians, the present policy was to diminish the amount of out-door relief by advancing money on loan, which is strictly required to be repaid. These repayments are sometimes obtained by putting on the screw, in the way the law empowers it to be put on, upon the near relations. I do not know that this policy in itself is a severe or an inequitable one, though it may easily become severe in its manner of administration. I was told that one—and that an almost immediate—effect of it was that it had very largely diminished poor rates.

(6) RECREATION.—"In the great panegyrical oration which Pericles delivered, nominally over the graves of those who had fallen in the first year of the Peloponnesian War, but really on the greatness of Athens, he considers that the city had a great claim on the gratitude and patriotism of her sons on account of the abundant bodily and mental recreations she had provided for them. I wish it could be said with equal truth that in England our provision for the refreshment and recreation of the people was so complete, that anything like a sense of dreariness, or even ennui, was impossible. 'I do not know any country in the world,' said a benevolent man to me, no longer ago than Sunday last—Mr. Clarke Aspinall, the Coroner for Liverpool—'where the amusements of the people are so few and so unattractive as here in England.' Here, again, is a most difficult problem. In the present state of artistic and intellectual education, the taste of our people is so coarse and unrefined, that it is almost impossible to prevent their amusements from degenerating into vulgarity and indecency. Mrs. Theodore Martin, with that generosity which is characteristic of her, is this very night performing in the Theatre Royal, as a mark of respect to the memory of Mr. Charles Calvert, who did so much, not in Manchester only, but in other towns, to uphold the character of the stage. I remember well on one occasion when I had endeavoured to show in public my appreciation of his efforts—for which, I am afraid, I got into the black books of many sincerely good but gloomy people—that, in acknowledging what I said, he told me what uphill work he found it, and how constantly his aims were defeated by the vicious public taste—not of the lower class alone—which preferred what was indelicate, and prurient, and corrupting. No doubt, our unkindly climate is unfavourable to many forms of out-door recreation, which are at once the healthiest and the most

accceptable to people living in a more genial clime. No doubt, also, we are making progress in the right direction, and the present generation enjoys much more leisure and many more opportunities for recreation than their forefathers did. One only wishes that their taste and appreciation of what is wholesome and beautiful enlarged with their opportunities.

(7) SOCIAL SCIENCE AND RELIGION.—" A final question remains, Can sound principles of social science—if such a science can be constructed—be impressed upon men's minds without an appeal to religious sanctions and religious motives? I frankly confess I do not think it can. The utilitarian philosophy is notoriously deficient in motive power. 'The peril of democracy,' said De Tocqueville, 'is its tendency to individualism.' But the great social doctrines of Christianity are all based on the idea of brotherhood. 'Do to others what ye would they should do to you.' 'Masters, render to your servants that which is just and fair.' 'Bear ye one another's burdens, and so fulfil the law of Christ.' 'We that are strong ought to support the weak, and not to please ourselves.' 'Look not every man on his own things, but every man also on the things of others.' These are some of the great principles, which, when they were first published, were indeed a revelation, which are happily the common property of all the churches now; and by which those churches, if only they were true to them, might regenerate the world. It is only, in my judgment, by the steady application of those principles to the practical details of life that society can be saved.

"The world is God's world, not the Devil's. Good is stronger than evil; truth than falsehood; right than wrong. There are remedies for each and all of these evils, if we know where to look for them, and if, when found, we have courage to apply for them. He, whose divine words have echoed from the Galilean mountains to the furthest limits of the civilized world, has taught us to 'seek first the Kingdom of God and His righteousness; and all other things' on which our hearts lawfully may be set, and which it is good for us to have, 'shall be added unto us.'"

CHAPTER VIII.

DIOCESAN SYNODS AND CONFERENCES.

Institution of Conferences—Diocesan Synod, 1874—Constitution and Purpose of Diocesan Conference—Religious Teaching in Day Schools—Temperance—Public Worship Regulation Act—Candidates for Ministry—Church and People—Definite Belief—Church of Rome—Ceremonialism—Ceremonial Innovations—Simplicity of Belief—The Church and Nonconformity—The Church and the Masses—Sermons—The Diocesan Synod, 1881—The Admonition.

AMONG the notable events of Bishop Fraser's episcopate was the institution of the Diocesan Conference. During the term of Bishop Lee's episcopate no Diocesan Conferences were held; nor did Bishop Fraser convene a Diocesan Conference immediately upon his accession to office; and when, in the autumn of 1875, the first Manchester Diocesan Conference was held, the Bishop was neither wholly favourable to the project, nor greatly hopeful that any decisive practical results would be gained from it. For, by a remarkable contradictoriness of events, Bishop Fraser, who, during his Lancashire life, appeared to be speaking incessantly either in the pulpit or on the platform, and whose utterances filled so large a portion of the columns of the Manchester Daily Press, was not naturally fond of speaking, and debating, and discussing. Before his accession to the episcopate he seldom appeared upon platforms; "I am not used to them, and I dislike them," he said. He always had refused to become a member of any clerical society, whose object was merely to debate and discuss. So far did his suspicion of the advantages of much speaking carry him, that during his life in Cholderton and Ufton he rarely consented to preach special sermons for charitable objects in other parishes than his own. His conviction was that a clergyman's greatest strength lay in quiet, steady work; in visiting from house to house; in attending to his schools; in penetrating his parish with the virtue of Christian example, rather than in the more showy, yet less abiding, work of speech-making and debate.

In the first three years of his episcopate, therefore, the Bishop convened no public conference of his clergy; although in each of those years he held, for definite practical consultative purposes, a private conference of the Archdeacons, the Cathedral Clergy, the Rural Deans, the Chancellor, and Official Laity of the diocese. At each of these three annual private conferences the subject of holding a general public synod of all the clergy of the diocese had been one of the foremost matters of consideration; and, in the end it was arranged that the rural deans should ascertain, so far as they could, the feeling of the clergy in respect to the desirableness of holding such a synod. As a result of these inquiries, the first Manchester Diocesan Synod was held on Thursday, November 26, 1874, in the Cathedral Church. The synod was preceded by a celebration of the Holy Communion, about six hundred of the clergy being present. In opening the synod the Bishop said:

"You are aware, my reverend brethren, what has been my motive for calling this synod of the clergy of this diocese. It was not my own original idea, nor at first, when it was suggested to me, did I receive it altogether favourably; but it has been pressed upon me as a duty that I owe to the diocese, in these somewhat difficult and perilous times in which the lot of the Church of England is cast, to call you together, not so much for the purpose of taking counsel, for that is rather the purpose of a conference than a synod, but for the purpose, first of all, of setting before you my own mind in relation to some of the more important questions which concern us in our ministry; and, secondly, for the purpose of ascertaining how far the mind of the Bishop is in accordance with the minds of the clergy, or, at least, the majority of them."

The following were some of the subjects upon which the Bishop set his mind before the clergy of the synod:

THE MAINTENANCE OF RELIGIOUS TEACHING IN DAY SCHOOLS.

"The majority of my brethren will admit that if the religious teaching in the day schools becomes diminished in quantity, or deteriorated in quality, the religious teaching in the Sunday school will be but a very poor compensation for the deterioration. I believe that Sunday school teaching, even more than day school teaching, requires a thorough overhauling. I must ask you to consider how far, as a body of clergy, you have the right to give yourselves a dispensation for neglecting your duties in the day school, on the ground that you throw your whole energy and your whole power into the Sunday school? With regard to the day schools I do not mean to say that a clergyman in a large parish can attend school every day, or even any great number of times, in the week, for the purpose of giving a lesson in religion to the children. But I think perhaps more might be done in this way than is done. Still I am not unreasonable enough to expect impossibilities; a man's own conscience must be his guide as to how he is to discharge this important part of his pastoral functions. I do most respectfully submit that there is no part of the ministerial office that is of more value and preciousness to souls than this bringing of the pastor's heart and pastor's mind to bear upon the training of the young. I feel certain that no time spent in the elaboration of sermons is a sufficient justification for neglecting to train the young in the day schools. I further submit this. The old philosopher, Aristotle, told us that *how* a thing was done was more important than the mere fact that it was done; therefore, if you cannot yourselves go into your schools as often as you could wish, you certainly ought, either in person or through your assistant curates, to visit them sufficiently often to make sure of two things—first, that religious teaching of a sound and effective character is really given; and, secondly, that it is given in a really religious tone. In this case the children will be more intelligent and more likely to satisfy the demands of the Government inspector in every department of their work just because their spiritual nature has been developed in the course of the training that they have received in the school. You are perhaps aware that the line of thought Mr. Matthew Arnold has taken with reference to the teaching of the Bible in schools is this. He says: Apart from the question of religious opinion, it would be nothing less than a national calamity for the only book in the world out of which children between five, six, and thirteen have any power of acquiring any knowledge of poetry, history, morals, and philosophy, to be cast on one side. That book is the Bible."

Temperance.

Upon Temperance, after observing that "temperance lectures are listened to for the most part by temperance people, who do not need to be lectured, and, therefore, do not reach the root of the question," the Bishop said:

"If you could establish a guild or brotherhood on temperance principles in your several parishes, and begin by enlisting young men into their ranks, and persuade them to be either total abstainers or to assist in promoting the cause of temperance, you would have gathered together a little source from which good would flow in all your parishes. You would also gain a hold on those young men which would perhaps make them pure and chaste as well as sober and temperate. I do not care by what name the organizations are called so long as they are formed, and I hope that you will all in your several parishes express to your people the strong feeling you entertain that this question of temperance lies at the root, not only of the prosperity, but of the material, moral, and physical condition of the nation. That is all I have to say upon the question. I hope that, whatever organization you may start, it will take a directly practical form."

THE PUBLIC WORSHIP REGULATION ACT.

"I hope I feel the very weighty responsibility that rests upon me as Bishop of this diocese in undertaking to bring before you this burning question of the Public Worship Regulation Act; and yet I feel that we should have met together this day for little purpose if, considering the circumstances by which we are surrounded, you went away without knowing clearly and unmistakably your Bishop's mind upon this distracting and most difficult question. I cannot in the least expect to carry the minds of all my brethren of the clergy with me in what I am about to say. To some I shall be thought to go too far, and to others I shall seem not to go far enough. I can assure you that I will not give utterance—or at least I will try to guard myself from giving utterance—to any sentiment which will needlessly give pain, or express any opinion which I have not maturely considered, or which I am not prepared deliberately to maintain. The Public Worship Regulation Act—or, as its fuller title runs, An Act for the better Administration of the Laws respecting the Regulation of Public Worship—has, I suppose, been the subject of more discussion, and, I might also add, of more misunderstanding, than probably any act which has passed the Legislature within our memory; but I wish to remind you, and, through the press, to remind others, that this bill or act does not touch, in one jot or tittle, the law of the Church of England, and that it is simply an act to facilitate modes of procedure against those who infringe the Church's laws.

"Before I proceed to consider in detail that act, I think it is of some importance to remind you of the very solemn obligations by which you are individually bound. Every clergyman whom I ordain, and every clergyman who is admitted to a cure of souls, has to make, before his ordination or institution, the solemn declaration that he accepts the Book of Common Prayer, and that he will conduct Divine service according to the order in that book prescribed, and none other. That is indisputably his moral obligation. By degrees the meaning of certain ambiguous rubrics in the Book of Common Prayer have become plainer, in consequence of the interpretations which have been placed upon them by the Court of Final Appeal. But in certain quarters the constitution of the Court of Final Appeal has not been approved of, and the extraordinary statement has been made that the Ecclesiastical Courts are so tainted with secular judges that no clergyman is bound to accept their decisions. I hardly think that any one present holds that view of their obligations. The main questions with which we are concerned have assumed, no doubt, within the last few months, a perceptible, and to my mind an unfortunate, difference of real significance. I remember mentioning in my Primary Charge that one of the most respected clergymen in my diocese, and a man who would not be considered a representative man of any extreme section—the Rev. Canon Raines—told me that from his ordination to that date he had always been accustomed to consecrate the elements of the Holy Sacrament in front of the Table. That is a mere matter of convenience and has no doctrinal significance; but the question assumes an entirely different signification when it is proclaimed that, unless what is called 'the Eastward Position' at the consecration of the elements of the Lord's Supper, and unless the Eucharistic Vestments, are specially allowed; doctrines which are felt to be vital and true, and no doubt dear as life to those who hold them, will be imperilled. If that is the true interpretation to be put upon this question, it becomes more embarrassing and more difficult to deal with; and it behoves you to look closely and deeply into the question itself to see what has been and is, from her public documents, the mind of the Church of England, and what seems to have been the mind of the Catholic Church of Christ in relation to this question. I am not aware that any other questions, in relation to the Public Worship Regulation Act, are likely to be so hotly contested as the two points I have noticed. It has been proclaimed with a loud voice that the business of every true Churchman is to bring about a Catholic revival, as though the Reformation and the principles of the Reformation were anti-Catholic; but when the matter is examined it is found to be not so much a Catholic revival that is meant as a Mediæval revival, and the ceremonies which are brought forward to be revived are mainly those which grew up in the twelfth, thirteenth, fourteenth, and fifteenth centuries, in the period which immediately preceded the Reformation; a period which our forefathers thought needed reform. I venture to claim for the Reformation of the Church of England and its principles—I have nothing to do with the motives of those who carried it out—the character of a Catholic revival, for the purpose of carrying the worship of the Church of England to the purest and most primitive times, and to get rid of those accretions which had grown up in the dark ages. And here I know that I may say something which may give pain to many who hear me, to some for whose personal character and sincere convictions I entertain the most profound respect. In these matters, however, it does not seem to me, as a Bishop, that, out of any personal regard, I should shrink from saying what is my own mind. And though I hope that I shall say what I am about to say with all tenderness, without any wanton desire to give pain to any single conscience, I must emphatically proclaim my conviction that the symbolism of Eucharistic Vestments and the symbolism of the Eastward Position, as we are now told we must understand them, are symbolisms of a doctrine that is not a doctrine of the Church of England, and which cannot be proved from Holy Scripture. I mean the doctrine that the ministers in the Holy Sacrament are discharging the functions of a proper priesthood, and that what we offer to God is a propitiatory sacrifice. If, in ministering the Holy Sacrament of the Lord's Supper, we offer a propitiatory sacrifice, what is the act by which we offer it, and when is the moment of offering? It was a question upon which my predecessor entertained a strong and, I believe, a sound opinion, that the word 'oblation' used in the prayer for the Church Militant did not refer grammatically to the offerings offered and placed on the Holy Table, but only referred to those offerings and devotions which are ordinarily understood as 'alms.' The reason for that interpretation is sufficiently plain. Then we come to the consecration prayers. In the Romish Church one of the great ceremonies is the elevation of the host; but in the Protestant Church we are prohibited from elevating the paten or chalice. Therefore I am at a loss to know what is the act when, in the celebration of the Holy Communion, I am supposed to be discharging the functions of a sacrificing priest. These are questions which we all ought to consider, and make up our minds about, before we vindicate or claim for ourselves a position or vestments that are supposed to indicate the sacerdotal character of the act with which they are associated. I think if you are honest with yourselves, and honest with your people, there will be no great difficulty in finding out what the mind and spirit of the Church of England is. No doubt there have always been two great parties within the pale of the Church. Hooker, in his fifth book of 'Ecclesiastical Polity,' says—'In receiving this holy ministry it matters not to me what these elements are in themselves; it is enough for me to know and to feel, "Oh, my God, Thou art true; oh, my soul, thou art happy."' This I take as the mind, and the sober, rational mind of the Church of England. Let us not attempt to be wise above that which is written, nor attempt to multiply ceremonies beyond the limits of justification. Above all, it seems to be our bounden duty as ministers of a national church, while we are zealous for the truth, to take care that what we call 'the truth' is not merely our own prejudice or opinion, and to see to it that every word we speak, and every act we do, has for its direct object the edification of the people committed to our charge. The most glorious title we can bear is the same with which St. Paul contented himself—a minister of God to men. The whole congregation of Christians is called a sacred or royal priesthood; but I cannot put my finger upon one single passage in Holy Scripture where the ministers of the New Testament are described by the word *hiereus*. And, as to priests, you know yourselves that, after all, whatever meaning may be given to it, it involves no higher functions than this, that by the exercise of spiritual power we bring people to Christ."

The Training of Candidates for the Ministry.

"I must acknowledge with pleasure that as a rule candidates who come before me, though no doubt young men of different spiritual temperaments, different degrees of spiritual development, are on the whole satisfactory. I should not ordain any one of whose general seriousness of purpose and general competency to discharge the duties of the ministry I was not fairly well persuaded. These young men are under the personal influence of myself and my chaplains, only for a few brief days, and, though I do the best I can to help them to realize the character of the work they are about to undertake, yet I wish my senior clergy employing curates and giving titles would remember what a very serious responsibility is laid upon them by so doing. I am afraid in more than one case I have incurred the displeasure of some of my clergy because I have declined to allow them to grant titles. I hold myself alone responsible to God in those cases. It is absolutely necessary if a young curate is to become an accomplished and effective clergyman that he be well trained. If incumbents give a title to a young curate, it seems to me that the incumbent is just as much bound to teach the curate how to do the work to which he is called as a joiner would be bound to teach an apprentice his trade. A young curate should not be left to follow his own devices; and if he sees the services conducted slovenly or irreverently he will, in a very short time, become equally careless and slovenly. It is a very good plan for a minister and his curates to meet on the Monday morning, as is done in some cases, to talk over the work of the past week, and map out the work of the week to come. By doing this the clergy would be rendering an unspeakable service to the Church of Christ, which in these days seems to need nothing more urgently than a supply of wise, and earnest, and faithful ministers."

The Relations of the Church to the People.

"It is asserted that the working classes are not under the influence of the Church of England, and perhaps not under the influence of any other religious body outside. It is said that the Church of England possesses the wealthy classes; the Nonconformists the tradesmen; and the artizans and mechanics stand outside of all religious agencies. This ought not to be; and, therefore, if any clergyman is conscious that his church is empty, or not filled as it ought to be, he is bound to ask himself the solemn question, How is it, and am I responsible? Some churches are filled and crowded and others are empty. In some cases this arises from the neglect of past years, and the neglect of past years cannot be recovered or atoned for in a brief space of time. It is not only a full church, however, we desire to see, as we know that churches may be filled by influences more or less meretricious, and which do not reach the fountain of spiritual life. I think that every pastor of souls ought to set before himself clearly the question whether his ministrations are really developing the spiritual life of his people. There is no question of more supreme importance than that we should not only make the ministrations of our Church wide, but also make them effective. I hope that we all desire to see our Church maintained as a national Church, and that not from any selfish or mercenary motive, but because we believe the cause of true, sober Christian religion would suffer much in the land if her witness was withdrawn, or in any way delivered with any more faltering tones than now. It is all very well for those who wish to liberate us from State control to tell us that we would be much more free to act and to adapt ourselves to circumstances if we were disestablished than now. I do not believe that myself for one moment. I believe that disestablishment would mean to a great extent chaos; and it seems to me that the only body who would gain by the disestablishment would be that great aggressive spiritual power which has lodged itself so strongly in our midst, and which would occupy a tenfold strength if the organization of the Church of England was destroyed; and, inasmuch as we are told that our dangers as an Established Church are not from attacks without but from dissensions and controversies within, it does seem to me that we have the greatest possible need to cultivate, so far as we can, consistently with our conscientious convictions, loyalty to the Church and brotherhood among ourselves."

In a letter to a friend, speaking of the Synod, the Bishop writes: "The Synod was, perhaps (as *The Manchester Examiner* described it), ' a little tame.' I hardly know why, but I think it will have done us all good. It will also have shown the world that we clergy can meet together, and even discuss ' burning questions' without flying at one another's throats."

But the principal result of the Diocesan Synod of 1874 was the convention, in the following year, of the first Manchester Diocesan Conference. Both the constitution and purpose of the conference differed from those of the synod. The synod was composed exclusively of clergy; no layman was admitted to take part in its deliberations. The members of the synod consisted of the entire body of clergy, licensed to officiate in the diocese, numbering over 600, whereas the clergy of the conference numbered only 153, of whom 38—the Bishop, the Dean, two Archdeacons, four Canons Residentiary, 21 Honorary Canons, nine Rural Deans, were official; and the remaining 115 were elected. The clergy, however, formed but a minority of the conference. The conference consisted of 426 members, and of these 273, or nearly two-thirds, were laymen. Nor was the conference more essentially different from the synod in its constitution than in its purpose. The purpose of the synod was to give the Bishop an opportunity of setting his mind before the clergy. The purpose of the conference was, in addition to this, and perhaps more than this, to give both clergy and laity an opportunity of expressing their mind in the presence of their Bishop.

In opening the conference (which assembled in the Town Hall, King Street, Manchester, after a celebration of the Holy Communion in the Cathedral Church), upon Thursday morning, November 4, 1875, and was attended by 143 clergy and 200 laymen, the Bishop said, after explaining the purpose of the conference:

THE VALUE OF DEFINITE BELIEF.

"With the vast conflux of opinion that circulates all round us, I think it is of extreme importance that Churchmen should recognize distinctly, and proclaim distinctly and firmly, though tolerantly and charitably, to others, what the ground on which we claim to be a National Church really is. As a National Church we stand, as it were, as the Church of England has always seemed to stand, at a middle point between two opposing currents of opinion. There is an opinion, that no man belonging to a Christian congregation ought to be called upon to say, 'I believe.' The very idea of creed, or of tests, is said to be alien from the spirit of Christianity, and that nothing more is required than that every man shall be fully persuaded in his own mind. I venture to say that is a foundation of sand—upon which it is perfectly impossible to build, and to organize, a religious community such as the Christian Church. If any man can say that in any period of the Christian Church a creed was considered a thing that might be dispensed with; if any one will tell you that Paul himself did not lay the same foundation which the Church of England lays to-day—one Lord, one faith, one baptism, one God and Father of us all—if that can be proved, we of the Church of England must be prepared to say that the organization to which we cling as dearly as we do to life is antiquated and out of harmony with the spirit of the age. But we believe that the religion of the Lord Jesus Christ—as we have it represented to us in the Church of England—fully satisfies the conditions that are and must be the essentials of a Church, in doctrine, in form of worship, and in government; and that the creed of Christianity is the only thing that can hold its own steadily, when almost all opinions are drifting widely on a stormy sea."

The Church of England and the Church of Rome.

"There is an abiding protest, which, as a branch of the great Catholic Church of Christ, I conceive we English Churchmen are bound to maintain, and bound to maintain perhaps to-day with even more energy than has been necessary for any time during the last twenty-five years—the abiding and undying protest against the pretensions of the Church of Rome. I cannot conceive any branch of the Catholic Church which has so widely departed from Catholic practices and principles as the Church of Rome. Those who read ecclesiastical history—we who have in our hands the records of the ancient councils—know that in the great Council of Nicea there was not the slightest idea of any supremacy, still less any autocracy, in the Church of Rome, and, though in the later councils primacy among peers was granted the Church of Rome, on the ground that she was the Imperial City, in another Council the second place was given to the great ancient Church of Constantinople, on the ground that she had the same title to be reckoned the mother of churches as the Church of Rome. It should be remembered that a diocese is a unit of the Catholic Church. The National Church is an aggregate of dioceses, compacted together by those providential circumstances wherewith Almighty God seems to have surrounded all of us. We feel that we in England have a right to maintain our ground as against the Church of Rome. We feel that the Bishop of Rome, when, twenty-five years ago, he took upon himself to divide this country into twelve dioceses, was guilty of an inexcusable act of schism, which the Council of Nicea would not have tolerated for a moment, for it was one of their canons that to avoid confusion there never should be two bishops in one city. I ask whether that council would have recognized a Bishop of Manchester, and across the water a Bishop of Salford. It is an intrusion of a proud, imperial, despotic Church into a province she had no right to claim. We are here occupying the ground of an apostolic organization. I believe even the Church of Rome will not dare to repeat the Nag's-Head story, and say that our bishops and priests have no legitimate succession. We are here with the Prayer Book, which certainly will stand comparison in respect of its antiquity and its piety with any manual the Church of Rome can put into the hands of its members. We are here taking our stand upon these great primitive creeds, maintaining the creed of the Apostles and the creed of the Councils of Nicea and Constantinople, consisting of the essential foundations of the Christian faith, and not those novelties and modernisms which have been added continually to the ancient creed of the Bishops of Rome. We have a right to take our stand upon these, as we consider them to be primitive and fundamental principles. We are, I hope, in charity with all men; we don't grudge any increase which Almighty God may please to bestow upon other religious agencies, who work outside our pale, and who, so long as they can symbolize with us in doctrine and in feeling, we wish to work with us hand in hand. But we do feel that in the Church of England we have an abiding assurance against the flux of modern opinion on the one side, and against the arrogant pretensions of the Church of Rome on the other; and I think the nation, before they commit themselves to any policy of denationalizing their church, should consider, solemnly and seriously, what tremendous issues in both these directions which I have indicated would be involved in that policy of denationalization. At any rate, let us who are Churchmen feel that there is one duty imposed upon us, I will not say higher than all others, but imposed upon us as Churchmen, which we are bound to endeavour to discharge. We are bound to make this Church of ours sink deeper, even deeper than she has yet sunk, in the hearts and affections of this nation. We are bound to get rid of those selfish interests which have too often been allowed to creep in and to mar and spoil the beauty of our Church organizations; we are bound to look at things from the point of view of men who feel that they have received a treasure handed down to them of which they are stewards for the national weal; and, using it in this sense, for the nation's good and not for our own, we will pray God *Ecclesia Anglicana esto perpetua*."

The success of the first Diocesan Conference; the opportunity it had afforded, especially to laymen, for the full expression of opinion upon controverted points; the evident interest taken in its proceedings by both clergy and laity; the plank supplied by the Conference in the building of a bridge across the gulf which threatens to sunder the clergy from the laity—these, and similar causes, had removed any misgiving Bishop Fraser felt at first in reference to the wisdom and utility of Diocesan Conferences; and it was with full sympathy that he convened the Second Conference upon Wednesday and Thursday, November 21 and 22, 1877. In his opening address, the Bishop said:

"I do not like the word 'ritualism,' because it is vague; and, of course, there is ritualism and ritualism. Every man who conducts divine service after a prescribed pattern is a ritualist as much as the man who conducts service after a pattern fashioned in his own mind. But, upon the principle that *edification* is the most important thing, and the thing with which we have most need to concern ourselves—I want to raise the question: 'Does an excessive attention to ceremonial edify?' St. Paul distinctly recognizes the principle of edification. I want you to compare that with one or two things that seem to me to be creeping in amongst us, and which I, for one, very earnestly deprecate. I refer, for instance, to the recitation of the Communion Office in a tone that is not heard many yards from the Holy Table. I heard the other day of a case of that kind where a person sitting not many seats from the holy table said that the whole service was perfectly inaudible. Now, it is perfectly true that in another great branch of the Christian Church, where that office is conducted in a tongue 'not understanded of the people,' the people yet know the order of the service, and they are taught that all depends upon the intentions of the priest, and that if they only accompany his acts with their own books and devotions they may be thereby edified. I do not deny that principle. I only say that it is not the principle of the Church of England. The principle of the Church of England is not that the congregation are edified by the intentions of the priest. It is a service in which everybody is supposed to join, and it is their united sacrifice of praise and thanksgiving. And I venture, therefore, to say that an inaudible performance of the Holy Communion Office is not a method conducive to the edification of the people. There is a remarkable utterance, the truth of which no one will gainsay, in the part of the Preface to our Prayer Book touching ceremonials. It is this sentence, which must be familiar, I should hope, to you all. After speaking of certain ceremonies which had been, by the wisdom of our reformers and revisers, swept away, the Preface says: 'Christ's Gospel is not a ceremonial law (as much as Moses's law was), but is a religion to serve God, not in bondage of the figure or shadow, but in freedom of the spirit; being content only with those ceremonies which do serve to decent order and godly discipline, and such as be apt to stir up the dull mind of man to the remembrance of his duty to God by some notable and special signification whereby he might be edified.'

"There are certain things done amongst us to-day—I hope I shall give offence to no one by speaking my mind plainly—which I cannot conceive rational men doing, or rational men liking to see. At the same time we must make allowances for a change of tastes. No congregations are actually standing to-day where they stood twenty-five or even ten years ago. Only yesterday I heard of a congregation, generally reputed very stiff in what are called the old Protestant ways, where they had just begun to chant the Psalms at evensong. And I maintain that all that really conduces to edification is permissible and lawful within the broad limits so wisely allowed by the Church of England, and, where variations not contrary to her mind are introduced for the purpose of edification, no one wishes to forbid or even to curtail them. But remember what I have said about edification. Edification does not mean the exaltation of the minister. It means the spiritual improvement of the people. I have drawn a distinction between innovations or variations which I have called contrary to the mind of the Church, and innovations or variations which commend themselves on the ground that they contribute to the greater edification of the people. It is, I suppose, an innovation that a hymn is commonly sung between the Litany and the Communion Office. In our large and populous parishes it would be almost impossible to comply with the rubric of having the Sacrament of Public Baptism administered after the Second Lesson at morning or at evening service, and that would be a variation. But no one can say that these variations are contrary to the mind of the Church of England. They are really introduced either for the purpose of giving variety to the service, or for meeting reasonable demands, without any derogation to the sacraments, in the conduct of worship. And then there is the question of lawlessness. I am aware of the subtle arguments by which it is attempted to be proved that the new ecclesiastical courts are something different in kind from those by which the 'due order of this realm,' in matters of this nature, used to be ascertained and enforced. But this distinction is inappreciable by ordinary minds, and was long ago denounced by Augustine. Augustine is commonly considered the great doctor of the Western Church, but I find that his authority goes for very little with those who claim primitive antiquity for their practices. There is a remarkable passage—I have quoted it more than once since I have been Bishop—in St. Augustine's letter to Januarius, in which he touches upon this question of ceremonies, and he says there can be no rule safer for a godly and a prudent man to follow than to adapt himself to the usage of that Church to which God's Providence has made him belong. And he adds that these innovations—it is a remarkable passage, which leads one to think that Augustine might have been living in the middle of the nineteenth century—are mostly introduced by young men—who go abroad and see fashions different from those they left behind them at home; and the more different they are the better they like them. Augustine goes on to say that these young men come home and reckon nothing as binding upon them but what seems right and fitting to their own minds. I ask you if that is an altogether inapposite description of the temper very largely prevalent in England at the present day? I need not tell you that an organized and orderly society becomes impracticable if such a principle is allowed. I need not conceal from you that we do not claim for our Church exemption from imperfections and abuses; but these have been wonderfully diminished of late years, and a healthy public opinion will diminish them, I hope, still further. I will mention two abuses urgently needing amendment—the abuse of patronage, and the pew system. What we need in these, and all other questions, is to get rid of narrow, selfish views; and to regard the Church as a great national institution to be used for the highest purposes of the nation. If we are true patriots and true Churchmen, no small personal interests will be allowed to stand in the way of needed ecclesiastical reforms. I appeal to the more generous and liberal sentiments of you all. Conserve all that is good and beneficial in this great institution; remove fearlessly and firmly all that is mischievous or obsolete. A leading Nonconformist minister—Mr. Guinness Rogers—tells us, in an article in the last number of the *Nineteenth Century*, that it is an idle dream—indeed, an impertinence, almost an insolence—for Churchmen to imagine they will ever again win back Nonconformists; that they know when they are well off, and do not wish to return to the house of bondage. Well, if so, let us dream the dream no more, and turn our attention nearer home and set our house in order, and make the Church as strong, by making her as useful and as comprehensive, as we can. There are certain things which it is right and wise to do whether we gain proselytes by doing them or not. It is always right to follow after the things which make for peace, and whereby one may edify another. These things, I hope, we may do without exciting either envy or opposition. In conclusion, though these conferences cannot actually effect much, they help to generate public opinion on matters affecting the Church, and that opinion should be large, liberal, generous, tolerant. We feel that we have inherited a great trust, and we desire to discharge ourselves of it in the highest interests of the Commonwealth, and as men acting in the sight of God."

In summing up one of the discussions, the Bishop said:

"To say that the wearing of a black stole is the same thing as adorning yourself with all sorts of ornate vestments in embroidered patterns of silk and satin, never seen in the Church of England since the Reformation, is pushing the argument to an extreme. Then, again, it is said that the bishops are breakers of the law as much as the other clergy, and somebody has said that things will never be settled, or in a comfortable state, until a bishop has been brought into court and, perhaps, put into Horsemonger Lane Gaol in the same cell as that occupied by Mr. Tooth. The statement that bishops on certain high days in cathedral churches, and in collegiate churches, should wear a cope was not a judgment nor part of a judgment. It was an *obiter dictum* in the course of a judgment, and, I think lawyers will bear me out in saying that *obiter dicta* in the course of a judgment do not carry the same weight as the judgment, and it was an *obiter dictum* which formed no part whatever of the ultimate decision which received the sanction of the Crown. If the law requires me to wear a cope—though I do not like the idea of making myself a guy—and although I do not think that the congregations who attend the parish church of Manchester would be in the least degree more edified in my ministrations because I put it on than if I wore the ordinary vestments, yet, if such is the decision of the Court of Appeal, if I am brought into court and compelled to do it, I will, though with a reluctant mind, but as wishing to obey the law, wear it."

In a letter, dated November 19, 1877, the Bishop makes allusion to his having used the expression, in reference to wearing the cope, " I do not like the idea of making myself a guy."

" By-the-by I am almost afraid that I exceeded the limits of episcopal propriety in using that word 'guy.' It is a sort of slang term, and I *hate* slang; but it came into my mouth at the moment, it exactly expressed what I felt, and so out it came. But I regretted it the next moment; and yesterday I got a severe anonymous letter from Hastings rebuking me for using it. Perhaps it was below the dignity of the occasion; but yet, slang or not slang, it exactly expresses the fact."

Three other Conferences were held during the episcopate

of Bishop Fraser, viz., in 1879, 1881, 1883; but as the discussions at these Conferences travelled, for the most part, over the same ground as that occupied by the Conferences of 1875 and 1877, it is unnecessary to reproduce at length the Bishop's utterances at the later Conferences. A brief abridgment will suffice :

Simplicity of Belief.

"The Primitive Church, the Church in the earliest days, the Church which formulated the first great creed, did not define the great articles of the Christian faith. They were left in all their simplicity, and as long as men say that they believe in God the Father, God the Son, and God the Holy Ghost, that they believe in the communion of saints, the forgiveness of sins, the resurrection of the body, and the life everlasting, I, for one, am not anxious to push these men into corners and tell them to define these articles, and say, 'If you don't define them as I define them, you are a heretic, and are to be cast out of the Church.' I don't think this is the way to promote Christian unity and Christian brotherhood."

The Church and Nonconformity.

"I confess I want to welcome Nonconformists back again to the Church, and to see the Unity of Christendom ; and I have pleasure in proposing to the Conference the following resolution (which was unanimously carried) :

"'That this Conference desires to promote a friendly recognition of those of our dissenting brethren who will consent to meet us on the ground of our common Christianity, and expresses an earnest wish to cultivate friendly relations with them, and to co-operate with them on any possible platform of Christian work. That, in the opinion of the Conference, it is desirable that the Convocation of this province should consider the question of the comprehension of Nonconformists, with a view to devising the best means of terminating our dissensions, and establishing essential unity and working harmony between all sections of earnest Christian people in the land.'"

The Church and the Masses.

"One of the difficulties that presses upon us all is how to make the Church, in the truest sense, national—how to get at the hearts of the masses of the people. A gentleman was speaking to me only the other day of a conversation he had had with a layman who is very probably among us now. The layman asked my friend this question: 'Do you really think that the Church of England has got the heart of the working classes of this country?' Some of you doubtless would say 'Yes'; some would probably shake their heads and have a doubt about it; some would say 'No'; but I am quite sure we shall all agree that there is no more important work for the National Church to do than to gain a firm hold of the hearts and affections of the great masses of the people. If the Church of England does not do that, cannot do it, or will not try to do it, then, without aspiring to be a prophet, I will say that the knell of the Church's doom is very nearly on the point of sounding. I deprecate most earnestly, and I hope all present, whether clergy or laity, will deprecate most earnestly, the intrusion of the congregational principle to the subversion of the parochial. I am quite sure that, if the clergy take more pains with their congregations than they do with their parishes, they are not doing the work which was committed to them when they were instituted to their parishes. When I institute a clergyman to a new parish, I commit to him 'the cure and government of the souls' of the people of that parish. That is his obligation, and that is what he undertakes to do; and if a man neglects his parishioners in quest of a congregation, whether rich or poor, I say he is doing all he can to prevent the Church of England ever becoming a National Church.

"I am quite certain of this—that wherever there is an earnest minister, backed up by an earnest and loyal laity, there is a blessed work, owned by God, going on; and there, I am sure, there is no hostility on the part of the people to the Church of England. I have now nearly completed the tenth year of my episcopate, and I have consecrated about 90 churches, ordained about 300 clergymen, and confirmed more than 100,000 catechumens! What is needed is that clergymen should be in more direct contact and sympathy with the people. Though I always endeavour to place myself en rapport with the laymen, and try to ascertain what their feelings and opinions are, yet it has been remarked to me that bishops are 'up in a balloon,' and do not know what is going on in the lower earth. We, the clergy, ought not to live 'up in a balloon,' away from the cares and interests of our fellow-men: but, by every legitimate means at our command, to cultivate sympathy and contact with the people amongst whom we live."

Preparation of Sermons.

"Now, with regard to the preparation of sermons. I am afraid you will think I am giving very bad advice to candidates for Holy Orders when I tell them not to spend too much time upon the preparation of individual sermons. When people tell me that they spend six hours one or two days a week in preparing their sermons, and that they have no time for reading, except by sacrificing the preparation of these sermons, I think that this is a bad way of ever becoming either pastors or divines. I say less preparation and more fervour. I feel certain that the language of imagery, similes, metaphors, and quotations of texts, with which some sermons are stuffed to repletion, is really a hindrance to the effect of such sermons upon the congregation; and I am sure that those of you who are in any measure students, reading day by day and week by week some profitable course of theology, ought to be qualified to stand up almost at any moment, and, without any elaborate preparation, to speak words to your people which will profit and edify them."

That the Conferences, under the wise, bold, and ingenuous presidency of Bishop Fraser, maintained their hold upon the interest of the diocese is clear from the following letter:

October 17, 1879.

The Conference has come and gone, and all passed off with an unusual amount of smoothness, considering we were not afraid to handle burning questions. Of the 446 members, about 320 attended, and, though the attraction of Lord Salisbury's meeting drew away a good many of the more politically-minded laymen to-day, large numbers were present throughout both days. The debates were well sustained, and were, I thought, listened to with great interest. The afternoon was occupied with an animated debate on Sunday recreation. Opinions were very much divided, too much so to make it desirable to take a vote or pass any definite resolutions.

But, besides instituting Diocesan Conferences, now common in the English Church, Bishop Fraser (stimulated by the unhappy controversies concerning vestments and ceremonies which were embittering Churchmen and exposing Christianity to scorn) took a bold and unusual step, in order to exalt his diocese, if possible, into a model of ecclesiastical harmony and Christian temper. The bold endeavour redounds to his honour; its partial failure was, in no sense, his fault. On November 11, 1881, the Bishop summoned a Diocesan Council to assemble in the library of the Manchester Cathedral. The Council consisted of the Bishop, the Dean and Chapter, the Archdeacons of Manchester, Lancaster, and Blackburn, the Honorary Canons of the Cathedral, the Rural Deans of the diocese, and Mr. Chancellor Christie. The subject laid before the Council was the present ceremonial difficulties besetting the Church. After careful deliberation, it was resolved to recommend to the Bishop that he should summon a Synod of the clergy for the purpose of delivering his decision upon the questions at issue, and then issue his decision as a Pastoral Letter, or Admonition.

On Friday, November 25, 1881, the Synod assembled in the Cathedral Church. With the exception of some thirty or forty men, the entire body of the licensed clergy of the diocese, arrayed in their academical robes, were obedient to the summons of the Bishop, and almost covered the central floor of the Cathedral. After a choral celebration of the Holy Communion, the Bishop entered the nave, and, taking his seat in a chair placed upon a daïs erected in the middle aisle, repeated a few collects ; and then invited the clergy to join with him in the recitation of the Apostles' Creed— " that great profession of faith which unites us to the Church of the ages gone by, and is the faith we have to hand on to those ages which are yet to come." After the recitation of the Apostles' Creed, the Bishop said :

> It seems to me that nothing less is involved in these unhappy controversies, and in the proportions to which they are growing, than the continuance of the Church of England in her high and responsible position as the one united and established Church of this nation. She is being shaken to her very foundations, and men, with far too light a heart and without any real appreciation of consequences, are crying with a recklessness which is simply painful, " Let the ruin of the present system come." If such men think that under any new system, which with due regard to actual phenomena it is rational to conceive, they will enjoy more freedom even in reference to the secular power than they enjoy now, I venture to prophesy that they will find themselves mistaken. For they will have to reckon with the great body of the English laity, who may be anything but disposed to grant this unlimited freedom to their clergy, or allow them to regulate all spiritual and ecclesiastical matters after their own will, and wherever there are trust deeds or covenants, or anything partaking of the nature of a contract, there the Courts of the State in cases of dispute will certainly be appealed to, and as certainly, will not be slow to interfere. A case that recently occurred between a Nonconformist minister and the trustees of his chapel at Huddersfield will illustrate what I mean. This consideration has been brought before men's minds again and again, but even yet it does not seem to have received sufficient attention. Instead of gaining greater liberty for our practices or our opinions in a disestablished condition, I fear we should find that we had put upon our necks a yoke that might easily become one of intolerable bondage.

* * * * * *

> The famous rubric round which the heat of the controversy gathers is by no means so clear and unambiguous as it is sometimes thought to be. It has to be interpreted by the facts of history, as well as by what are called the " obvious " rules of grammar. Not only certain lawyers of the present century, but history " read a *not* into it " for more than two hundred years. Speaking generally, it was neither enforced nor obeyed during that long period of time. Nor would it be easy to enumerate with any certainty or precision what were the ornaments of the Church and the ministers thereof, which were " in this Church of England, by the

authority of Parliament, in the second year of King Edward VI." It is plain that Bishop Wren did not think the rubric so clear. Commenting on the rubric as it then stood in the Prayer Book of Elizabeth, in which it first appeared, he says, " But what is now fit to be ordered herein, and to preserve those (ornaments) which are still in use, it would be set down in express words without those uncertainties which breed nothing but debate and scorn. The very words, too, of that Act, 2 Edward VI., for the ministers' ornaments would be set down, or to pray to have a new one made, for there is somewhat in that Act that now may not be used." And Wren was one of the Revisionists of 1661; and it is not a little surprising that with these views he consented to the rubric's publication in a form so likely to mislead. Indeed, almost every word, certainly every clause, in the rubric has been the subject of the keenest controversy. " It doth seem to bring back the vestments," said the party represented by Baxter; and if you read the Bishops' reply to this question you can hardly suppose, if you can give them credit for being honest, fair-dealing men, that they had any such intention. I, for one, should be sorry to impute it to them. Nor is it easy to put any ordinary grammatical sense on the phrase " shall be retained," as applied to Edwardian ornaments, which certainly had not been in general or anything like common use from the time of the canons of 1603, and in all probability not for forty years before. If you disregard history and facts in interpreting an historical document, you may say that the rubric is clear; but this is not the way in which historical documents are generally construed; and, taking the historical facts connected with this rubric into consideration, it seems to me that there is not a rubric in the Prayer Book the real obligations of which are more doubtful, or upon which the Bishop has a juster right to interpose with his authority between those who " take it diversely."

Nor, indeed, is this all. For it is not merely the use of questionable "ornaments" that is complained of and has become the fuel of controversy, but the manner and way in which they are used, and the continued and increasing growth of new and strange ceremonies which accompany their use. It is not merely that a chasuble is worn at the celebration of the Holy Eucharist, but that it is put on and taken off at a peculiar time and in a peculiar manner, and with divers and ceremonial accompaniments. Sundry ministrants and sub-ministrants or servers, variously clothed and variously employed—sometimes to swing the censer, sometimes to light the altar candles, sometimes to " receive the priest's biretta and place it on the credence," sometimes to ring the sanctus bell— all help to introduce a ceremonial which is, as I have said, new and strange to English Churchmen, and which I say advisedly, even if it were lawful according to the order prescribed in the Book of Common Prayer, which we have one and all solemnly declared that we would follow — as I am convinced it is not—certainly ought not to be introduced in any church on the mere fancy of the minister or of the congregation, of whom very probably only a minority are parishioners, the Bishops never being so much as informed or consulted about what is being done. Some amongst us are rapidly exchanging our old form of Episcopalian polity for a Congregational Presbyterianism without any of its constitutional safeguards.

* * * * * *

Surely, religious men, even if their interpretation of the rubric was as certain as it is precarious, should feel that this is a case to which Tillotson's famous maxim "Charity before rubrics" applies, and might consent to abandon even some cherished practices at the earnest request of their Bishop and for the sake of the peace and strength of the Church. And if we could only stop the violence of extreme partizans on both sides, and put an end for ever to all pretexts for invoking the assistance of the law to remove grievances, what would now be gained to the cause of peace, and charity, and unity! And is it not here, again, that the voice of the Bishop, pleading with his clergy in behalf of these great interests, may legitimately be heard?

For, my brethren, do we in truth realize the situation? While we are loud upon platforms, defending our own position or denouncing our brethren who differ from us, our parishes, many of them, are not half organized, our churches often are not half filled. While we are fighting about the shape, or name, or use of a vestment, the lighting of candles, the mixing of a chalice, and saying that thus only can we maintain the liberties of the Church, or set forth a theory of the Sacraments which is a theory only, and has never been defined as an article of the faith, the atheist teacher is at our doors, undermining the faith of our people in the whole scheme of the Gospel, in the character and revelation of God, in the great doctrine of a life beyond the grave, and in all that seems to me to constitute the only effective basis for virtue and morality. I do not at all know to what extent these destructive doctrines have spread or are spreading; but I do know that the lives of the mass of our own people are only nominally Christian, and that the greatest enemies of the Cross are those who bear the name, but follow neither the teaching nor the example, of the Crucified. It is against this "organized hypocrisy," this hollow, delusive formalism, that the voice of every true preacher of righteousness needs to be lifted up loudly and with an ever-increasing emphasis; for the canker of this unbelief is eating deeply into the very lives and consciences of our people. You all know it as well as I. And can we do this effectively if we are fighting among ourselves?

And so, "if by the grace of God, it may be," let us, as the clergy of a diocese, show to our fellow Churchmen elsewhere that we are not blind to the "signs of this time." Let us be prepared, if need be, to make some sacrifices of individual theories or preferences—none of them touching any fundamental article of Christian belief—on the altar of "peace, unity, and concord." Let us at least try to put an end, at any rate for a while, to these unhappy, distracting, embittering ritual controversies. I am about to suggest to you a way in which this may be done without the sacrifice of a single principle dear to Churchmen, and to admonish you to follow it. In setting before you a maximum standard of ritual, I by no means call upon you all, or all at once, to rise to that standard of the maximum. In many parishes it may not be expedient even to attempt to rise to it. But in all parishes it is not only expedient, but right, that there should be no neglect or even careless observance of plain, unambiguous, and important rubrics; and, further yet, that every attention should be paid to the decorous, orderly, and reverent conduct of Divine service in all churches. I visit churches at times in which it does not strike me that much, if any, attention has been paid to the imbuing of the congregation with habits of reverence; in which, for instance, the collection of the alms is still very unseemly; in which the habit of kneeling is almost unknown; in which much more might be done than is done to make the administration of the Sacraments—and particularly of the Sacrament of Baptism, so strangely neglected in comparison with the minute attention sometimes bestowed upon its great companion ordinance—solemn, instructive, and edifying. Because I would reduce excesses of ritual, it must not be supposed that I sanction, or am even indifferent to, slovenly, irregular, irreverent ways. It cuts deep into every instinct of worship in my nature when I see such things. Let not our zeal for what we deem purity of faith degenerate into fanaticism, and lead us to think that there is no place for what is fair and beautiful, and even, with due regard to the great law of proportion, for what is grand and "magnifical" in the service of the house of God (1 Chron. xxii. 5).

With this, I hope not too long, preface, I proceed to read to you the Pastoral Admonition that I purpose to issue to the clergy of the diocese.

The Admonition.

"It being a recognized principle among Churchmen that the voice of the Bishop, speaking authoritatively, with the aid of his proper diocesan advisers, should be regarded by all the clergy of his diocese as sufficient to secure from them that 'due and canonical obedience,' to which every clergyman is bound by the oath which he takes when licensed to the cure of souls, or admitted to a benefice; and whereas divers usages and ceremonies, which, if ever generally observed at all in this Church of England, had certainly been in abeyance for at least 200 years, have recently been revived or introduced in certain congregations without any proper ecclesiastical sanction or authority, whereby the minds of many Christian people have been disquieted, and consequences have ensued, much to be deplored by all who have the true welfare of the Church at heart; now, I, James, by Divine permission Lord Bishop of Manchester, having called into counsel and deliberation the Dean and Chapter of my Cathedral Church, and the Honorary Canons of the same, and the Chancellor, Archdeacons, and Rural Deans of the diocese, and having duly considered with them the dangers that threaten our Church from the long continuance of the present distracting controversies in matters ceremonial, do hereby make it known to the clergy of my diocese that it is my Admonition to them, as their Bishop, that, until it shall be otherwise ordered by lawful authority, in public worship in their churches, and specially in the administration of the Holy Communion, they do not exceed the limits of the ritual now practised and allowed, or which may hereafter be allowed, in the Cathedral Church of the diocese; and, inasmuch as it cannot be pretended that any essential truth or fundamental article of the faith is involved therein, I admonish and charge all who in their conduct of Divine service have gone beyond these limits to reduce their ritual accordingly; and, furthermore, I direct that no alteration in, or addition to the existing or accustomed ritual of any church be made (except so far as may be necessary to bring such ritual within the limits prescribed by this Admonition) unless and until the consent and sanction of the Bishop has been obtained for the same. To all which admonition and direction I desire my clergy to conform themselves with a 'glad mind and will' for the sake of the peace and unity of the Church, and in the interests of that charity which is the 'true fulfilling of the law,' and 'without which whosoever liveth is counted dead before God.'

"Given under my hand this 25th day of November, 1881.

"J. MANCHESTER.

"All which may He who is the Author of Peace and Lover of Concord bless and prosper to the edifying of Christian people, to the well-being of His Church, and to the glory of His most Holy Name, through Jesus Christ our Lord. Amen."

A few extreme persons, in both wings of ecclesiastical parties, and from exactly opposite poles of opinion, protested against the Bishop's Admonition; but the great body of Churchmen accepted it with a glad mind, believing it to be an earnest, statesmanlike effort to set at rest a controversy which paralyzes the energies of the Church, exposes it to the scorn and sarcasm of the unbeliever, and distracts the attention of Christian men from greater and more serious perils. "Tremendous, unquestionably," wrote the *London Guardian*, "is the responsibility of those who, at such a crisis, choose war and refuse all peace or even truce, especially for things which, by the confession of all, cannot for a moment touch the essence of the Word or the Sacraments, and, therefore, cannot fundamentally affect the basis of truth or the spiritual life of the Church."

Speaking of this Admonition in his last Charge, some three years after the Admonition had been issued, Bishop Fraser said:

My Admonition of November 25, 1881, was, with so few exceptions as hardly to require notice, received by the clergy with the respect which, I will venture to say, was due to it. It was a step taken not without much previous consideration and care. It received the approval—the all but unanimous approval—I think there were only three dissentients, and those not pronouncedly dissentient out of a body of forty-two—of a Council composed of the Deans and Canons of the Cathedral, both residentiary and honorary, the Rural Deans and Chancellor of the diocese, whom I convened to consider its terms before solemnly promulgating it to the clergy in synod formally called. I required the clergy to consider the ritual of the Cathedral Church, as then publicly practised and allowed, the standard of the maximum of ritual for the diocese. In that ritual, neither what are called "the vestments" were worn, nor were candles lighted ceremonially, nor was the chalice mixed nor incense used, nor, so far as I was aware, was anything done, or attempted, which went beyond the limits allowed by law. If this standard had been frankly accepted by all, it would have secured a service of worship edifying, reverent, beautiful; and it would have cut off all pretext for litigation, and all reasonable grounds for suspicion and heart-burning. It was frankly accepted by almost all. In two or three instances it reduced a ritual which had gone beyond lawful bounds, and I dare say caused some little sacrifice of feeling to those who made the reduction, but who, I trust, have been repaid by the consciousness that the sacrifice was made for the sake of the higher interests of the Church. But in far more numerous cases it has helped clergymen, who have long been waiting for an opportunity, to raise their services from the level of baldness, if not of slovenliness, to something more akin to decency and order; and I believe that the general result has been a considerable increase of the spirit of reverence and devotion, so far as these can be influenced by external things, in the congregations of the diocese. And, though it still pleases hostile critics in newspapers to describe the experiment as a complete failure, to those who know the actual results it will seem to have been a success far beyond what I dared to expect or even hope for.

One observation remains to be added to the narrative of Bishop Fraser's Diocesan Conferences. By universal consent he was not only an able, wise, and good-tempered president, but he had a remarkable facility for encouraging and eliciting the opinions of those who differed from him. He could give and take with absolute good temper and cordiality. Those who frequently attend clerical gatherings, especially clerical gatherings assembled under the presidency of a bishop, are familiar with the unduly subdued tone of one body of the speakers, and the unduly exaggerated tone of the other body. At such gatherings the great majority of the clergy simply sit still, saying nothing. Of those who take part in the proceedings, there is often an air of unreal hostility among those who differ from the Bishop; and an air of unreal deference among those who agree with him. The speeches on both sides are pitched in a strained and too high key; and the observant onlooker feels the absence of spontaneity, naturalness, fresh and open utterance. The peculiarity about Bishop Fraser was that, in his presence, all this unreality utterly vanished. The clergy felt at home. They knew they were risking nothing by opposing him; and gaining nothing by agreeing with him. He spoke right out, and they also spoke right out. From the first, the Bishop established a perfectly candid system of give-and-take. Probably no body of clergy ever felt more happily and confidently free with their Bishop than the Manchester clergy felt with Bishop Fraser. They understood and respected each other in their widest differences; and at the Diocesan Conferences the singular spectacle was not unfrequently witnessed of the Bishop's friends contending against the Bishop, and the Bishop's adversaries contending for him. Everybody felt absolutely easy and safe; and, therefore, even when the discussion grew hottest, its tone was natural, unforced, without any strained exaggerations either of concord with the president or disagreement from him.

"A special feature," writes Chancellor Christie, "of the Bishop's character as shown in the administration of the diocese was the encouragement which he gave to the free discussion by the clergy of all matters affecting the diocese. Meetings of the clergy in the way of synods or conferences had been extremely distasteful to Bishop Lee. When they met for the election of proctors for convocation, he never would permit any discussion, and would never consent to hold diocesan conferences; but Bishop Fraser wished that every matter should be fully and freely discussed, and he was most anxious that his own personal views, or what were perhaps supposed to be such, should never in any way interfere with the free expression of the opinions of others, or with the decision arrived at. He was desirous on every possible occasion to obtain a knowledge of the views of the clergy, and was never in any way offended by the expression of opinions opposed to his own. He showed this especially at the meetings of the Diocesan Conferences and at the annual meetings of the Archdeacons and Rural Deans, which were held in July every year at Bishop's Court, and, except in matters where he was conscientiously unable to do so, he was always ready, even too ready, to give up his own wishes and his own views, in matters of mere expediency, to those of his brethren, with whom it was his great desire to work in the most harmonious manner."

"My clergy have just as much right to their opinions as I have to mine," was his frequent remark; and few things wounded him more keenly than the supposition that he could show favour to those who agreed with him rather than to those who differed from him. One of his invariable counsels to candidates for ordination was: "Never make for yourself, or allow others to make for you, a party in your parish." And it would have grieved him to the heart if there had been a "Bishop's party" in his diocese; or if he had felt that any of his clergy, whatever their opinions or views, could have imagined, with just cause, that they would not receive fair play and equal sympathy from their Bishop. Bishop Fraser loved "to think and let think." Within the limits of the Prayer Book he encouraged the utmost liberty of thought and independence of action. No clergyman who was earnest, hard-working, and loyal to his ordination vows, had any reason to fear speaking out his full mind in the presence of the Bishop, however divergent from the Bishop's views his own views might be. To all his clergy of every school, Bishop Fraser sought to be a just and loving Father in God.

CHAPTER IX.

LAMBETH CONFERENCE—CONVOCATION—CHURCH CONGRESSES.

The Lambeth Conference — Convocation — The Ornaments Rubric — The Athanasian Creed—Christianity and the Masses—Church Congresses—Sheffield Congress—The Church and the Stage—Brighton Congress—Impure Literature—Newcastle Congress.

"We, Bishops, taken individually," wrote Bishop Fraser to a correspondent on February 17, 1879, "are not exactly a stupid lot of men; but when we meet as a body under the presidency of the Archbishop of Canterbury, it is surprising how small the practical outcome always appears to be." Similar sentiments, frequently occurring in the Bishop's correspondence, reveal one of the most strongly marked characteristics of his nature. He was not at home in all places, equally and alike. In some spheres and atmospheres he felt himself a stranger, chilled and silent. He was at home in a working men's meeting at a Church Congress, but he was not at home in the Upper House of Convocation. He sat almost daily, for weeks at a time, upon committees for the relief of distressed operatives; but he sat only for a few hours on committee in the Lambeth Conference of Bishops in 1878. He would probably have been a familiar figure in the House of Commons, if he could have entered there; but he was very seldom seen in the House of Lords, where he possessed a seat; and, in the course of his episcopate, he spoke in that august assembly only twice. These circumstances are strongly characteristic of the man, they reveal both the limitation and the largeness of his nature.

For Bishop Fraser's nature was quite large enough to be stirred to its depths by the world-embracing greatness of assemblages like the Lambeth Conference of 1878.

July 19, 1878.

"Stanley wished me to stay," he writes, "at the Deanery, to meet the 'Black Bishop,' who (by the way) is a very bright-looking, intelligent man, realizing (as Stanley said) the description of the Song of Solomon, 'I am black but comely.' But I said I could not consent to turn his house into an hotel; and he himself upon reflection added, 'Well, perhaps, it will be best if you are going to say anything at the (Lambeth) Conference that it should not be known that you come from *here*.' Oh, he is a splendid fellow!"

July 26, 1878.

"I can't tell you half I have got to tell you about the grand service we have just come from in St. Paul's—90 bishops, 800 or 1000 communicants—the spirit admirable—the Archbishop's parting words like a blessing indeed. Everybody seemed spiritually refreshed, though the trial of the body was severe, for the service lasted three hours!"

July 27, 1878.

"The Lambeth Conference has ended in a way and in a spirit, which has made the heart (I think) of every one of us full of joy. Last night, the discussion being on the question of Ritual and Confession, the clouds were dark indeed, and there was a very threatening appearance of a storm; but it seemed as though God had breathed a calmer spirit upon us all this morning, and, partly by moderate demands on one side and prudent concessions on the other, we at last agreed unanimously—or rather I should say with only two dissentients—to a conclusion quite strong on both these questions, for the purpose of bringing back, if they can be brought back by any influence, the extravagances of our younger men within the sober limits allowed by the Church of England."

July 29, 1878.

"I could only send you on Saturday a very hasty sketch of the service in St. Paul's, and since then you will have seen the accounts in the newspapers. Such a scene, I suppose, has never been seen in England since the Reformation. Upwards of 80 bishops, a congregation of 5000, and about 800 communicants. There was a Te Deum—though not a very effective one—after all. The service began with it, and ended with the Old Hundredth Psalm. The sermon, by the Bishop of Pennsylvania, was very unequal; parts of it were in the true American 'spread-eagle' style; parts were very eloquent, simple and pathetic. There was a considerable sprinkling of such phrases as 'blood-bought earnestness'; which to me are always offensive and nearly meaningless; and what were meant to be, perhaps, the finest parts of the sermon were to my mind the weakest. Still, on the whole, the effect was good; and the manner was less strained than the manner of American preachers is apt to be. The bishops who were present were very good specimens of the American episcopacy, and have left a very good impression behind them. I think also they will carry pleasant impressions back with them, for they have received a good deal of attention, which they appeared warmly to appreciate. Some of them visited Lincoln, others Lichfield, others Peterborough, and others Farnham; and they seem much struck with all they have seen. Some of them promised to take a look at me and Manchester, on their way home, but I can't answer for the promises being all kept. In the long procession which wound its way about St. Paul's on Saturday, my companion was 'the Black Bishop,' who was quite as much master of himself in all the exciting surroundings as any of the rest of us. The partings when the service was over were very warm and affectionate. Everybody seemed to hope that there would be another conference a few years hence; though all felt it was uncertain whether they themselves would be permitted to take part in it. Of the seventy-six bishops present in 1867, thirty have now passed away! The results of this conference will be made known to the world by the publication of the five reports of the committees, which the conference after much discussion finally adopted in their present form; prefixed to which will be the circular letter, signed by the Archbishop of Canterbury, of which I enclose the first rough draft. It was somewhat modified before it was finally adopted. That Encyclical of which I sent you a copy, and which was *not* adopted, was submitted by the Bishop of Lincoln, and no doubt was his composition. We all felt, I think, that *that* was not the sort of document that we should like to send out to the world. I dare say *The Guardian* of this week will contain a good deal upon the whole subject, though no publication of what actually took place is allowed. Something, however, is certain to ooze out."

But, although Bishop Fraser's spirit was large enough to be stirred, and his imagination fervent enough to be kindled, by the magnetic influence of a great assemblage of Bishops, gathered from all the continents of the earth, and united together in visible brotherhood in one solemn act of sacramental worship—yet he was far from being wholly carried away by the historic greatness and world-embracing fellowship of the assembly. The limitations of his nature restrained his flights of fancy and of thought. A religious poet, like Keble, would have mounted on wings amid the airy wonders of the scene; but Bishop Fraser had not the wings of a poet. He could not mount beyond the nether regions of practical life. In all things he desiderated "the practical outcome." In this quality, which led him to regard even great ecclesiastical events in their business aspect, lay one secret of his charm for Lancashire people. Their Bishop was practical and business-like; they understood him. He was a layman's Bishop, looking at things from a layman's point of view.

This desire for practical, measurable results strongly coloured his opinion of Convocation. He writes:

July, 1879.

" What Stanley says about Convocation is amusing, but I fear it is too true. It often astonishes me to find out how men, separately reasonable, become unreasonable and impracticable when acting in a body. They seem to be misled by what Bacon calls the '*idola specûs,*' the traditionary or conventional ideas which they have inherited, and which, though obsolete, they cannot or will not throw off."

August 1, 1879.

"The result of our meeting (in Convocation) has been very unsatisfactory. On the two great subjects submitted—the Ornaments Rubric and the Athanasian Creed—the Upper House voted (according to my judgment) the right way; but the Lower House would do nothing but leave things as they are; and, as the two Houses must agree before a vote can become an *Act* of the Convocation, nothing can be done. It is my hopeless task to persuade many of the clergy. They lend themselves passively to the leaders of a party and are impervious to reason. The Bishop of Durham has already made himself a power in the Convocation, and his speech yesterday on the Athanasian Creed was all that I could desire. If you see a report of Wednesday's proceedings, you will see what answer I made to Canon Hornby's argument of historic continuity. If historic continuity were a true reason, instead of a mere pretext, under which the sacerdotal and sacrificial doctrines may be introduced, it is valueless, from the simple fact that, if the historic continuity depends upon the vestments, it is hopelessly lost, as the vestments have never been in use, till the last few years, for two centuries. But I really have not patience to try and confute such arguments and theories."

The Bishop frequently addressed Convocation. For lack of space, however, a summary of three only of his speeches must suffice:

THE ORNAMENTS RUBRIC.

"I am surprised that, with those who so loudly proclaim against the Erastian tendencies of the present day, this rubric should find so much favour; for it is simply a product of Parliament, the result of the Act of Uniformity of Queen Elizabeth, from which the Lords Spiritual dissented, and as to which Convocation was not consulted. History is, perhaps, the best interpreter of statutes and rubrics. *Contemporanea expositio fortissime est in lege.* When Elizabeth's Commissioners—130 of them—made their tours into all the dioceses of England, with one accord, they destroyed chasubles, albs, vestments and every vestige of what they then considered was a relic of Popery. A similar thing happened in 1662. The bishops, in issuing their Visitation questions, never asked a single question concerning the doubtful vestments.

"It is extraordinary that, if the ornaments intended by the rubric be chasubles, albs, &c., they should by Elizabeth's Commissioners in 1559 have been destroyed, and by Charles's bishops in 1662 not even have been mentioned in their Visitation questions. What the true interpretation of the rubric is, I am not prepared to say. The existence of so much discussion is a clear evidence of the ambiguity of its meaning. But I think the rubric should be defined, the ornaments specified, and licence not allowed to escape under cover of ambiguity. In the interests of peace, and of the unity and progress of the Church the matter ought to be settled. The Church is not strong enough to bear the strain much longer. It is not gaining ground by these controversies. A writer in *The Guardian* charges me with attempting to destroy the lines of the Reformation settlement; but is the Reformation settlement to be concerned in a question, which is more a question of ecclesiastical fashion than anything else? As long as we have our Prayer Book, our Catholic Creeds, our Episcopal Organization, our Apostolic Succession, we have guarantees enough for maintaining the Catholic character of the Church of England.

"I want to see in our churches what sufficed for John Henry Newman, John Keble, Charles Marriott, Walter Carr Hamilton, for Samuel Wilberforce, and what sufficed, I believe, for all High Churchmen till within the last twenty-five years. I want to see no meanness or ugliness in the churches; and everything could be made seeming and beautiful with the accustomed vestments. The divines of 1662 were satisfied with them, and I am satisfied. If you choose to have the cope, to which, I believe, no ritual or sacrificial significance has been attached, I personally should have no objection. But against the tolerance of those vestments which symbolize doctrines which are not within the four corners of the Prayer Book, and which, in their present shape, have never been held even by the most advanced of High Church divines till within the last few years, I have made up my mind very decidedly; and I am quite sure that the feelings of the great mass of the people of this country are not with those who desire to introduce these things. In *The Guardian* of last week a paper was published containing certain returns from 887 churches within a certain radius of St. Paul's. Out of this number there were only 35 in which the vestments were worn.

"In my own diocese, where there are 476 churches, there are only 7 in which vestments are worn; and I think I have heard the Bishop of Liverpool say, that, in his diocese, which contains more than 200 churches there is only one case in which the vestments are used. I believe there never was a time in the Church's history, when there were grander opportunities for winning souls, and gathering together into one, the more or less fragmentary religious efforts of the nation, than lies, in the Providence of God, before the Church of England at the present time. But this opportunity will be lost, if, instead of breathing the spirit of our age, and studying the spiritual wants of the time, we go back into the middle ages. In a letter written by Dr. Pusey to the English Church Union he gave reasons why, at the beginning of the Oxford Movement, no thought was taken about vestments. He said, 'We have more serious things to do; we have to revive the faith of the nation.' In our day, these words are more than ever true.

"I cannot understand why the great historic High Church party in the Church of England should throw their mantle round these innovations. When the Oxford Movement began, submission to authority was its watchword: but now, if there is a vituperated and condemned body of men in England it is the bench of bishops. I ask you, would you, with your eyes open, wreck the future hopes of the Church, on which the eyes of Christendom are fixed to a large extent, for a chasuble and alb? Ecclesiastical vestments are often more an affair of tailoring and embroidery than of doctrine or principle. If these things are significant of doctrine, let us know what they mean; and we shall know how to deal with them. It is because I fear the controversy will continue so long as we have this ambiguous rubric, to which no definite meaning supported by historical evidence can be attached, that I ask this Convocation to accept the following motion:—

"'That in view of the doubtfulness attaching to any and all the interpretations of the rubric relating to the ornaments of the Church and of the ministers thereof, as it now stands in the Book of Common Prayer, and of the frequent litigation that has ensued therefrom, it is, in the opinion of the Convocation, expedient that the said rubric be expunged, and that, whether by rubric or canon, as shall seem best, a clear and distinct rule in this matter be established, conformable to the usage which, for the last 200 years, hath prevailed in this Church of England.'"

Upon the vexed and heated question of the recitation of *The Athanasian Creed* in the public services of the Church, Bishop Fraser's utterances in Convocation were no less plain and practical than upon the Ornaments Rubric. Brushing aside the tangle of academic underwood, the Bishop marched straight to the centre of the question with a firm, statesman's tread:

THE ATHANASIAN CREED.　　　*July* 31, 1879.

"I conceive that questions as to the date, or authenticity, or genuineness of the Athanasian Creed; or as to the accuracy or inaccuracy of its translation; or as to the desirability of a further search after manuscripts; or as to the mode of dealing with one of the principal difficulties of the case, whether by the addition of an explanatory note, or by the excision of the so-called Damnatory Clauses; or as to the increase, or reduction, of the number of times the Creed shall be recited in the course of the Christian year—do not really touch the issue, which is simply this—'Is the Athanasian Creed suitable for recitation in Divine service at all?'

"The Creed may be ancient—may be authentic—may be true—may be proved by most certain warrants of Holy Scripture, and yet may be unsuitable for use in the public service of the Church.

"Take the single instance of the Monitory Clauses. The Archbishop of Canterbury (Dr. Tait) has said, that 'nobody in the Church of England takes them in their plain and literal sense,' and much excitement has been raised by this declaration of his Grace. But, if people do take these clauses in their plain and literal sense, what need is there for that explanatory note which we are recommended to adopt, and which states that these clauses, contrary to their 'plain and literal sense,' are not to be understood as applying to those who 'from involuntary ignorance, or invincible prejudice,' are hindered from receiving the Catholic truths which the Creed declares. The language of the Creed itself makes no such exceptions; and I am, therefore, in common with the most highly educated theological minds, unable to accept or use its words in their plain and literal sense.

"The clergy are supposed to be bound to maintain the use of this Creed, because they have subscribed to the eighth Article. I do not see the force of that inference; it neither presses upon my conscience, nor convinces my understanding. Because I have declared my assent to the doctrines taught in the Creed, I have not committed myself to the further obligation of holding that the Creed is suitable for public recitations in the Church. There is sometimes an amount of quiet assumption in debating this and similar questions, against which I beg to enter an emphatic protest—I do not mean to use the word 'assumption' offensively, but simply in the sense of taking things for granted, which need to be proved. For instance, in a Memorial of the English Church Union to this House of Convocation, it is stated that 'any alteration or omission in, or any option for the nonuser of "the Athanasian Creed," or any portion thereof,' would give a shock to the confidence of many attached members of the Church of England 'in her claim to teach unfalteringly the whole truth once delivered to the saints.' Is it pretended, then, that the Athanasian Creed is 'that faith once delivered to the saints,' of which St. Jude speaks? or that 'Gospel' which Paul preached to the Corinthians, which they had received and by which also they were saved, unless they had believed in vain?—a Creed of uncertain date; doubtful authorship; precarious interpretation; not publicly used, as we use it, in any other Church in Christendom; which has never received the sanction of an Œcumenical Council? And with regard to that phrase of the eighth Article which asserts that this Creed, in common with the Apostles' and the Nicene, 'can be proved by most certain warrants of Holy Scripture,' no doubt there are degrees of certainty, and degrees also of importance, in the inferences to be drawn from propositions which Holy Scripture certainly contains. A great authority in the English Church—Richard Hooker—tells us that in any one truth all other truth may be by implication contained; but no one, I suppose, would maintain that the last inference in a long chain of reasoning (other than mathematical) is as certain and demonstrable as the first step in the reasoning; still less as the original proposition, the starting-point of the whole, which, may be submitted in the actual words of Scripture itself.

"There is a clause in the Creed declaring 'every person by himself to be God and Lord' which does not seem to be much modified in the proposed new translation 'every person severally is God and Lord,' which can only be received 'with considerable intellectual caution.' When a Creed contains doctrine of such subtle intricacy, and matters which even theologically educated minds are warned 'to receive with caution,' I cannot think that it is a document, as a whole, suitable for recitation in mixed congregations. In fact, this Creed illustrates, in a remarkable way, the manner in which the wit of man, aiming at a noble end, trying to pierce the cloud of darkness in which we feel we are enveloped, and through which we naturally desire to grope our way to higher and further and clearer truth—this Creed, I say, illustrates in a remarkable manner the way in which the wit of man has endeavoured to give, out of its own resources, a definiteness beyond what is given in Holy Scripture to *religious ideas*, by putting them into *theological terms*. Take, as an example, the use of the word 'proceeding' as applied to express the relation of the Third Person of the Blessed Trinity to the other Two. We know its origin —in the simple utterance of Christ—Τὸ Πνεῦμα τῆς ἀληθείας ὁ παρὰ τοῦ πατρὸς ἐκπορεύεται (John xv. 26). Would any one, if he had only this to guide him, maintain that this verb ἐκπορεύεται was designed to express the fundamental and distinctive idea in the relationship of the Holy Spirit to the Father and the Son? especially remembering, unless he maintains that he has a clear conception of a difference between ἐξέρχεσθαι and ἐκπορεύεσθαι—that Christ says of Himself, 'I came forth, that is, I proceeded from the Father,' ἐξῆλθον παρὰ τοῦ πατρός (John xvi. 28). Now I ask you to observe the process of the theological construction of dogma. The simplest—I know not whether it is the most ancient—of all the Creeds—that Creed which Jeremy Taylor wishes the Church had never gone beyond—contents itself with declaring 'I believe in the Holy Ghost.' The Nicene Creed, in its original form, ended with the same simple dogma. The Constantinopolitan Creed, with more development of doctrine, but still not going beyond the words of Scripture, declared its faith in these words: 'The Holy Ghost, the Lord, the Giver of Life, which proceedeth from the Father.' The addition of the *Filioque* Clause, which we, in common with the Western Churches have received, rent Christendom in twain; but even then left the idea of 'procedure' in its original indefiniteness, and did not attempt to 'intrude into things which have not been seen.' But mark the striking difference, not only in language, but in evident purpose, when you come to the phraseology of the Athanasian Creed: 'The Holy Ghost is of the Father and the Son, *neither made, nor created, nor begotten, but proceeding.*' Is there not, by the very force of this antithetical collocation of words, a manifest attempt to give—or to *seem* to give—definiteness to an idea, which, even when the attempt has been made, we all feel is, and must be, indefinite still? 'Who is this that darkeneth counsel by words without knowledge? Therefore have I uttered that I understood not;

things too wonderful for me, which I knew not.' Of course, religious ideas must be expressed in theological language, more or less precise. I do not join in the irrational cry against dogmatism. All systems of truth, physical as well as moral, material as well as spiritual, must rest upon an ultimate basis of dogma. But there are dogmas *and* dogmas; and there is abroad a spirit of dogmatism which is for being wise beyond that which is written, and delights to add to the number of theological propositions, which, at the peril of their soul's health, men are to be required to receive. Arguments in favour of the Creed have been constructed, upon the supposed peril of abandoning any of the Church's outworks at a time when the citadel of the faith is being assailed. My answer to such arguments is to ask a counter-question: Whether the Athanasian Creed really repels such assaults, or rather provokes them? Individual instances of course do not prove much; but I may be permitted to mention a case within my own experience. For thirteen years of my ministerial life I had charge of a rural parish of 200 souls. The one intelligent man in my congregation was the Squire. Whenever I stood up to recite the Athanasian Creed in his presence he did what George III. used to do, he sat down at once, closing his Prayer Book with an angry slam. And the pain this used to give me was poorly compensated by hearing the clerk and some fifty or sixty agricultural labourers reciting their alternate verses, from which I doubt if they received as much edification as they would have done from the more familiar language of the Apostles' Creed.

"I do not think that the Church's witness against Socinian and other doctrinal errors would be rendered one whit the weaker, by the omission of this 'Exposition of the Catholic Faith' from the public service of the congregation, nor even by its relegation to a place among the Articles—it need not be 'buried under them,' which the Rev. Francis Grey says would be the effect of such treatment. We might even leave it where it is, omitting the rubric which enjoins its use, and then we should be giving it the same place among our formularies that I believe the Greek Church gives it among theirs. The Apostles' Creed; the Nicene Creed; the Litany, supplicating God in the Triune name; the Communion Office, implying or stating the doctrine of the Trinity on every page; the glorious Doxology recited at the end of every psalm, which alone in some ages of the Church was considered sufficient to protect and hand on the primitive deposit, would surely be adequate to vindicate the Church of England's orthodoxy. I do not consider that the Church can fairly be charged with impairing or diluting Christian doctrine, or with making a feebler and more hesitating protest against error, because, governed by considerations of high expediency, she may think the Athanasian Creed unsuitable for public recitation, while still preserving it in its integrity among the muniments of the faith.

"I am told that this controversy about the Athanasian Creed is getting into the columns of the lowest class of newspaper, where it is being treated with far other than the reverence that the occasion demands. It is not likely, I fear, that the controversy will cease; and the question arises whether more harm or good is being done to the cause by its continuance. It is the tendency of unsatisfied demands to increase in importunity; and I can see nothing that can be gained by delay in this question but an increase of strife."

The relation of Christianity to the Masses was a topic of which Bishop Fraser's heart was full to overflowing.

CHRISTIANITY AND THE MASSES.

"The means of bringing Christian truth before those who do not attend public worship is a subject which, I cannot but think, concerns us deeply as ministers of the Gospel. I quite recognize the fact that there are large masses of our people who do not attend any place of worship. I do not think, however, speaking broadly, that Nonconformist ministrations are one whit more attractive than those of the Church of England. I do not believe that Nonconformist chapels, taken generally, are better filled with the masses of the people than are the churches of the Church of England. I believe also that there is a considerable exaggeration upon this question, arising from the fact that, while notoriously many of our churches are very empty indeed, it is forgotten that a large number are full to overflowing at all the services that are really attractive. It has got to be thought, indeed it is received by some almost as an axiom, that the people cannot be induced to attend church, but that they can be got into the mission-rooms. I am very slow to believe that fact; and, if I were compelled to believe it, I should do so with the greatest possible reluctance. I regard the mission-room as a poor and inadequate substitute for the church, and if it does not lead on to the church I consider it is rather a hindrance than a help. I am happy to say that I know a great many churches in my diocese which the people attend in large numbers. Anything more cheering and encouraging than the sight of the Sunday evening congregations in the Manchester Cathedral it is impossible to see; and at many other churches there is the same spectacle, showing, as I think, that when a suitable service is provided there is no indisposition on the part of the people to attend. With regard to the hindrances, I suppose we shall all admit that our services are very difficult of comprehension to uneducated and untrained minds. The very fact of people having to find their way about the Prayer Book to get at the Psalms, Collects, and any other Office which may be used, is a very serious impediment. I do not know how this is to be overcome; but I cannot help thinking that, if a little more instruction in the way of using the Prayer Book were given in the Sunday Schools, it would be a step in the right direction. The services are very often stiff by reason of our handling of them. There is no danger, I think, from the free use of the Prayer Book. I hope we all recognize that the soul of an artizan is quite as precious in the sight of God as the soul of a duke; and that any arrangement which makes it appear that the better-born are of more value than the working classes is wrong. The free and open system in churches does not always succeed; but I think, if it were worked with a real earnest spirit, it might be made to succeed. Another point is on a system that I cannot but feel is very mischievous, namely, the undue influence the wealthier classes possess in all parochial arrangements. There is, doubtless, an anxiety to get well-to-do churchwardens, and sidesmen, and other parish officers, all from the upper strata in the congregation. But the clergy do not go deep enough. Why not have the artizan or the agricultural labourer? I know parishes where this has been done—I do not know about the agricultural labourer, but where artizans have interested themselves in the Church and its work, and have been admitted to the offices of the Church with the happiest results. People are afraid that they will lose the pecuniary support of the wealthier classes, but I myself have no fear of that. We have no reason to fear that the masses of the people will be deficient in liberality for the support of the Church, if they could only be got to feel an interest in her, which it is the duty of the clergy to get them to do. You must not suppose that I am endeavouring to alienate the wealthier classes because I am seeking to secure the poorer ones; but I do say that the clergy have given them an undue influence in all their parochial arrangements.

"I now come to what is the most delicate, and, I think, the most important point of all. We are asked to consider how we can bring our people to receive Christian truth from those who preach. I candidly and frankly ask the clergy, whether the style of preaching too often practised in our churches has not been to a large extent an indisposing cause which has prevented many people from going to church. When the preaching is not attractive, the church is empty, and *vice versâ*. The sermons are too often over the heads of most people. If all could preach, like Charles Kingsley, sermons suited to all classes of people; or, like Mr. Spurgeon, who possesses those qualities which go to make a good preacher—wonderful power, style, language, illustration and fervour—the 20,000 clergy of the Church of England would soon become an enormous spiritual power in the land. The words of many sermons are too long, too learned; and also beyond the hearers in thought and idea. Another is that sermons are very often not on subjects that interest the masses of the people. They are upon some abstruse points of theology, or some defence of, or attack upon, ritual. These are things upon which the masses of the people do not think. Our sermons ought to touch the people on points of their daily lives. The people need to be taught and are willing to be taught. If preachers would select subjects which bear upon the duties of life, and which would interest the masses of the people, they would be able to draw people into the churches. The Bishop of Exeter said to me lately in London: 'How many souls has not preaching old sermons lost us?' Anything more pitiable than the spectacle of a clergyman reading from his manuscript, without ever lifting his eyes to look at his congregation, it is impossible to conceive. Lancashire people are in great dread of what is popularly called ritualism; but there is no body of people who more appreciate and enjoy a hearty, devout, and reverent service. I do not believe that what are called spectacular services are very attractive to them, or that they exercise any perceptible influence in the way of converting men's souls to God. It is not the thing they want; and they hold aloof from it. I believe that the power of preaching Christian truth in its grandeur, its simplicity, and with earnestness and sympathy to the masses of the people is, after all, the best means of bringing them, through Christ, to God."

From Convocation our story passes to Church Congresses. At the working men's meeting of a Church Congress, Bishop Fraser was absolutely at ease and at home. He took working men straight to his heart. He understood them, they understood him. One very remarkable feature of his character, however, comes into clearest prominence at these workmen's meetings. Perhaps no Congress speaker has ever been more popular with working men than Bishop Fraser; but his popularity was gained not by talking himself down to the level of the men, but by talking the men up to the level of himself. He spoke not as their patron, but as their brother. Moreover (and this was very characteristic), in meetings of working men he was the clergyman's advocate. In Convocation, and at those Church Congress meetings in which the clerical element predominated, he was the spokesman of the absent laymen; in working men's meetings he was the spokesman of the absent clergy. The generosity and chivalry of his nature seemed ever compelled to plead on behalf of those not present, or able, to plead for themselves. Had he been a frequenter of political meetings, he would, probably, have insisted with Conservatives upon the good points in liberalism, and with Liberals upon the meritorious aspects of conservatism. As a matter of actual fact, when he preached in a High Church, his theme often was the spirituality of the evangelical party; in a Low Church, the reverent orderliness of ritualistic worship; in a Broad Church, the indispensable necessity of fundamental dogmas. To Churchmen, he spoke of the sufferings and the courage of Nonconformists; to Nonconformists, of the immense advantages of an Established Church. An article in *The Guardian* describes this characteristic feature of Bishop Fraser very distinctly:

"The Bishop of Manchester is entirely a new element in Church

Congresses. His point of view is, to a great degree, non-clerical; and his mission appears to be, to make the clergy see what the lay world outside thinks about them and their sayings and doings. It is not altogether a gracious office to exercise, and it is no wonder that he provoked censure as vehement as the applause; but, it is undeniably a useful one; and it ought to be remembered that, in addressing a purely lay audience, at the working men's meeting, he took a very different line, entirely identifying himself with his brethren, and making perhaps the most effective defence of the clergy that has ever been offered to such a meeting."

The same honesty and independence of character which bade him plead to the farmer for the agricultural labourer, bade him also plead to working men for the clergy; not screening or palliating the faults of the clergy; but also not forgetting, or ignoring, their labours and self-sacrifices, especially in the cause of the poor. For this perfect honesty the working men honoured him. They felt him to be no sweet flatterer, but a sturdy, sympathizing friend. At Church Congresses he came to be called familiarly "the Working Man's Bishop"; a title which he, for a very characteristic reason, strongly deprecated.

September 30, 1878.

"I don't think I shall be tempted to speak at the Sheffield Church Congress, except at the working men's meeting, where I have promised, very reluctantly, to say something. I don't like being trotted out, as I have been at four congresses as 'the working man's bishop.' It is a rather invidious distinction which I do not affect."

That he was tempted, however, to speak at Sheffield, and yielded to the temptation, a descriptive account of the Sheffield Congress, in one of his letters, interestingly shows.

October 5, 1878.

"From looking upon Sheffield, as you pass through it by the railway, you would have no conception of its having such beautiful suburbs on the south and west sides. The Mappins live in a splendid house on the west, about two miles from the centre of the town, filled (but not extravagantly) with beautiful things, especially with pictures. I saw some very fine specimens of Turner, Wilkie, Gainsborough, Crome, Copley Fielding, Morland, besides the best representations of the more modern school. The Mayor is a well-educated, clear-headed man, of much decision of character, full of good sense and right-mindedness. I used very much to enjoy my walk down to town with him each morning after breakfast, the others preferring to go in the carriage. The Bishop of Ripon was their guest as well as our party; but he was called off by diocesan duties the following morning, so that we did not see much of him. He looked, however, *to me*, very, very far from well, and I could not but feel a good deal of anxiety about him. After dinner we went down to the evening discussion on intemperance, in which my old schoolfellow, Dr. Thomas King Chambers, whom I had not seen since our Oxford days, nearly forty years ago, spoke very sensibly, on the use and abuse of alcohol from a medical point of view. Canon Harper's speech was highly amusing, and was spoken with much emotion and evident sincerity; but of course the sense of the assembly was against him, and in some points probably he was not wise. Still, there was an underlying basis of truth in it all. The Archbishop sent a message to me asking me to speak; but I had nothing ready, and nothing new to say; and so I begged to be allowed to decline. The next day, Thursday, was a day of much interest and not a little heavy work for me. As you see *The Sheffield Independent* you will know the chief facts that occurred; and I need only add the few personal incidents that made the day one of special interest to me; and, therefore, I know will not be without their measure of interest to you. The opening discussion was on the attitude of the Church towards popular recreations; and it was delightful to me to see, with one or two exceptions, in how sympathizing a spirit the whole subject was handled. Mr. Brownlow Maitland especially delighted me. He is a splendid-looking man—come (as he said himself yesterday) of a martial race—about sixty or sixty-five years of age, tall, spare, dignified, with noble, refined features, and hair rapidly whitening; speaking at once with the emotion of deep conviction, and yet with entire calmness and self-possession. I did not speak to, nor was I introduced to, him; but I don't know when I have looked upon a man to whom I felt more instinctively drawn. The writer of one of the enclosed letters who talks of my 'dropping upon' Mr. B. M. has simply misread or misunderstood me. I could endorse every word he said. (By the way, I think what I said is reported better in *The Times*—though more condensed—than in *The Independent*.) I had no intention of speaking at all; but again a message came from the Archbishop that I must; and as the subject was near my heart, though I had made no definite preparations for a speech, I felt that I must obey. You will be able to judge for yourself to what extent I spoke wisely and temperately on a very difficult subject. You will see from his leading article that I did not convince the Editor of *The Independent* but I enclose a leading article from *The Manchester Evening News* which mainly upholds my view. *The Manchester Guardian* also in a leader this morning supports me. But I shall be prepared in due course, for the usual measure of abuse, from people who will persist in misunderstanding, and misinterpreting me. Bishop Ryan followed, as he generally contrives to do (though I like him and we are perfectly good friends), with a counter-reply; the ostensible object of which was Mr. Brownlow Maitland, but which I can see was also partially directed at *me*. I had, however, left the room and did not hear it. I went with Mr. Tooke and Mr. Mappin to see an armour-plate, 10 inches thick, rolled at Sir John Brown's works; and we also saw the beautiful process of converting iron into Bessemer steel. This occupied the hour that intervened between the morning and afternoon sessions. I had hoped to be free to prepare myself for the working men's meeting in the evening; but unexpectedly the Archbishop called upon me to take the chair at the discussion in the afternoon; as well as told me that I was expected to speak twice in the evening, as they had issued many more tickets than the Albert Hall could accommodate, and had been obliged to organize an overflow meeting in a neighbouring school-room which held about 1,000 people. Well, this scattered all my hopes and intentions of preparation, and I felt I must trust to the inspiration of the moment, which, somehow (though I don't know whether I do not sometimes run a risk by trusting it too implicitly) seldom fails me, when the subject is one in which I take an interest, or on which I have thought or read previously. So the chair I took, and presided over the debate on cathedral institutions; of course I had nothing to do but to listen, to call upon the speakers in order, and keep order. There was the stormiest discussion of the whole meeting that afternoon in the Albert Hall under the presidency of the Archbishop (who, however, as he always does, managed matters with great firmness and tact) on the subject of sisterhoods and women's work; but with me all was quietness and peace; though it must be admitted, the discussion was a little dry and dull, except once when Mr. Beresford Hope tried to put a little of what Disraeli once called 'Batavian' life and animation into it (the epithet, if you know Hope, is one of Disraeli's happiest and most incisive descriptions of personal characteristics. Of course it referred to the Dutch origin of the Hope family). Well, when I had done my duty as chairman, I went home to dinner, and that done, returned with the party to the 'Working Men's Meeting.' It was an astonishing sight, those 4,000 sons of toil gathered in that great hall. The Bishop of Ohio, to whom I sat next, at a later period of the evening, said, 'he had never seen anything of the kind in America,' and seemed quite penetrated by emotion at the spectacle. The Archbishop sent him a message requesting him to speak, to which he replied (I was told, by the Mayor, who heard him) 'I *dare* not do it.' It was indeed a sight to raise conflicting thoughts; but in my mind those of hope and encouragement largely predominated. I came a little late and was not in time to witness the Archbishop's reception, which I heard was grand; nor was I permitted to stay long; for I was hurried off at once to the schoolroom to address the 1,000 men who had overflowed there, and who were waxing impatient, thinking they were to be handed over only to those whom they did not much care to hear. So Tooke must tell you about the speeches of the Archbishop and the Bishop of Carlisle. The Archbishop is a massive man, and I rejoiced to see the hold he has got upon these Sheffield people. His whole conduct of the congress has been admirable, and it was easy enough to see the deep feeling which inspired him all through the proceedings, and especially at this great meeting of the working men. Well, you will see a summary of what I said at the schoolroom (where I spoke for about forty minutes), and a fuller report of what I said in the Albert Hall. I had only once been in Sheffield before, and so I was quite unprepared for, and for the moment almost unmanned by, the warmth of my reception. The speaker who preceded me, stupidly could not hit it off with his audience—was too solemn, preached a dreary sort of sermon, true enough, but not of the kind they wished to hear; and the people became very impatient, though he was slow in perceiving that they were not caring to hear him, and exhausted nearly the whole twenty minutes allotted to him before he sat down. The Archbishop, with great judgment, then interposed a hymn, which was grandly sung, and restored the audience to good temper and attentiveness, and I must say I never, *not even in my own Lancashire*, spoke to people apparently more intelligent and more willing to hear. Consequently, I was tempted to wander into fields of thought which, otherwise, I should hardly have dared to enter, and which (as he said in his closing remarks) almost frightened the Archbishop, till he put his glasses on and was reassured by the intelligent and attentive faces of the men before him. [This part of my speech is not well reported. In one important sentence a 'not' is omitted: 'I need *not* be called upon to deny any really ascertained truth of science: *if* it *is really* ascertained, and conflicts, or seems to conflict, with Scripture; it cannot be that there is any conflict (I said) between God's Work and His Word; it must be that I have put a mistaken interpretation on His Word.'] This is the substance of what I said; but I am made to say something very different by the reporter. Indeed, throughout this report (which, on the whole, is wonderfully well done, considering the short time at the reporter's disposal; for the meeting did not close till 10.30, and the paper was printed and in circulation before 8 next morning) you will have to exercise that wonderful faculty of yours of revision and supplementation and amendment. You will be amused at a little incident that happened in the course of my address in the school-room which came off first. I was reproving the spirit of envy of their betters which prevails to some extent among the working class, and showed itself very plainly in the Lancashire strike. And I said that a working man, if he has a tidy home, and a suitable wife, and children that are dear to him, need not envy a duke, and has all the elements of real happiness within command. When I spoke of 'the suitable wife,' a loud and hearty and good-humoured laugh rang through the room. 'What are you laughing at?' I asked, 'is it because you think that I, a bachelor, can't possibly know anything about wedded life?' upon which the laugh was renewed, if possible, still more merrily than before. Well, some mischievous spirit put it in my head to say, when silence was partially restored, 'perhaps it is not too late to acquire experience;' at which I thought the roar of laughter would have brought the roof down. When I presently had to make my way out through the dense crowd which packed the room, I felt the grip of a score or more of honest hands who would not part with me without this token of kindliness. So you may guess that I went back to my other speech, which was still to come, with a heart full of pleasant and encouraging thoughts. I have nothing more to say about the Church Congress; but I have come back convinced that, when in wise hands, as it was in Sheffield, it can be an instrument of much good, in spite of the sneers of *The Times*, in diffusing sound views of what the Church of England really is, and really desires to do, among the masses of the people; and I have come back also with the conviction that the heart of the Church is sound, and that it only needs that men should understand one another better, to love one another more. The Dean of Manchester made an excellent speech on Friday morning, on the subject of the spiritual life; the matter was good, and the manner temperate. Mr. Brownlow Maitland also came easily into the forefront in this discussion: and Walsham How's written address was admirable. The Bishop of Rochester opened the debate, but I was too late to hear him. I have no doubt that both Mr. and Mrs. Tooke will give you some interesting details; but I think I have said enough about the Church Congress for the present."

The limits of our space forbid that anything more than a very few brief extracts of Bishop Fraser's Church Congress utterances should be inserted. His remarkable sermon preached at the Nottingham Church Congress appears at length in the published volume of his University Sermons.

Sheffield Congress.

Though no doubt there is danger to us all, of adopting and acting upon a low standard of life, particularly in our relations to society; and though all of us are guilty of lamentable inconsistencies on this score, and are sometimes very different in the pulpit and platform from what we are in the drawing-room, the billiard-room, and other places of social resort; still, I could not quite endorse the sentiment, that the theatre must be abandoned or Christ be lost. Allusion has been made once or twice, and always kindly, to the part I took voluntarily, in connection with the theatre during the time of the Manchester Mission which was held in the beginning of 1877. That part was not of my own seeking; but when the secretary of the Manchester Mission said, "We have been thinking there is a body of people in Manchester who ought not to be entirely left out of consideration, and those are the people engaged in our theatres. Will you come and address them?" Well, I have a courage sometimes, the courage of my opinions, but more frequently I have the courage of my impulses, and when my impulses told me the thing was right to do, and that if I could bring, in any form, the message of the Gospel to these people who, perhaps, did not always hear it, or did not always have it presented to them in an attractive form, it was my duty, as Bishop of the diocese, to go. And I must say I never was more amply rewarded. Hanging on the walls of my drawing-room, I have a work of art of considerable merit. It was sent to me by the principal scene-painter of one of our Manchester theatres. It is a water-colour drawing of the Manchester

Cathedral, and, as he said, was a humble mark of gratitude for my sympathy extended towards himself and his fellow workers. As I was leaving the stage—for I had to speak to them from the stage of the theatre—the stage-manager grasped me by the hand and said, "Bishop! I thank you for the words you have spoken. You have spoken to us kindly, and if more clergymen would speak to us poor players kindly, and think of us a little better than they do, perhaps then we should do better than we do." A London clergyman working in a poor parish wrote to me a few days later to say that I had given some few grains of comfort to a "première danseuse" at the Theatre Royal, and how what I had said had helped her to struggle, at least, to do her duty as a true woman. He told me what the home life of this woman was; how she supported an aged mother and crippled sister out of her earnings as a "première danseuse." There are still just one or two more points of a practical kind, upon which I should like to touch. With the Ober-Amergau passion-play, as the centre of attraction to tastes and natures jaded by the London season, and resorting thither in search of some new sensation, I have nothing to say. But, on the other hand, I want you to remember the simple habits of these Bavarian people; and I believe it is to them—the simple peasants living in the mountain valleys—helpful in forming true and worthy conceptions of the great spiritual mystery which it attempts to portray. Then, again, I would say that the stage with us is very much what we make it. I had a discussion not very long ago with one of the leading directors of the limited company that own two of our great Manchester theatres, and I was speaking to him, as I have spoken plainly in public, upon the grave responsibilities that the managers of the great theatres incurred in putting before the public pieces of the character of "Pink Dominoes"; which has, I believe, been denounced by every respectable journal in the kingdom as an outrage on morality; but which is still represented, and is attended by thousands and hundreds of thousands in the land. What was his answer? He said "People will have it." And then there is another point of view. "It is," he said, "so much cheaper to put on the stage. What will you put instead?" "Give them a play of Shakespeare," I replied. "When Mr. Charles Calvert put 'Henry VIII.,' 'Richard III.,' and 'Henry V.' on the stage, crowds went to see them." "Yes," said this gentleman, "but it did not pay. It costs £3,000 to put a play of Shakespeare upon the stage; and if it were not for the success of our Christmas Pantomime, we could not afford to treat the public to entertainments of that kind. The fact is, the public demands spectacles rather than Shakespeare, and it becomes an expensive thing to put one of the great dramas on the stage; whereas out of the repertoire of our own theatre we can get up 'Pink Dominoes' for £40." It is simply a question of finance, and I do not think that fact is always borne in mind. But for the remuneration of the pantomime they would not be able to put Shakespeare's plays upon the stage. I had once been speaking of the pantomime, and a lady wrote to me in consequence of what I said, and asked "What am I to do? My children come home at Christmas, and they expect some entertainment. I take them to see the pantomime and they enjoy it; but, for the last two or three years, stage managers have introduced into the pantomime the ballet, and I am ashamed to sit in my place and to allow my daughters to see the ballet." She then asked me "What would you have me to do?" I am afraid I am not very good at giving advice, and some people would say that my advice was quite impracticable. So far as I remember the advice I gave was this: "My good friend, if you would only influence your friends, and persuade them to influence all they can influence, just to stay away from the pantomime for one single week, until that objectionable ballet be withdrawn, I think the evil you complain of would be cured."

It is simply this,—that we patronise the very things that in our more unctuous and professional moods we condemn. I am afraid that there is many a clergyman, who denounces the theatre loudly, who yet has not sufficient influence, in his own household, to prevent his wife and sons and daughters from going. Then what we have to deal with, first, is the hollowness of society in this matter. The heart of society is not sound on this matter. There are platform utterances which are very different from the practical maxims upon which we act. I remember well, in my old classical days, reading that the satirist Juvenal, who lived in the period of perhaps the greatest decadence of society at Rome, describes, in a memorable line, the demoralising influence upon some poor provincials coming in from the distant provinces of the empire to Rome, in order to pass the season there. "*Sic prætextatos referunt Artaxata Mores*," which, put into colloquial English, may mean "And thus they bring back to Sheffield the manners of Cremorne." And you, my friends, who represent what may be called perhaps the upper stratum of middle-class society in England, are to a great extent responsible for this. Many of you here, many in Sheffield, go to London for what is called the London season; and you have not the slightest scruple to include as many nights at the theatre in the fortnight, or the month, which you allow yourselves as you possibly can. I say, then, that you have no right to declaim against the theatre till you have, by some definite act of your own, tried to amend it. I do not believe that actors or play-writers wish to corrupt the age, but they are obliged by their very position to conform, more or less, to the demands of the age. It is you who demand, and they who meet that demand with the supply. And, therefore, I would just say this: we have, perhaps, been treating this disease, if it be a disease, too much as if it were functional, whereas it is organic. It is not the disease of this or that particular temper, or a natural instinct of the human mind; but it is that the whole fabric of society amongst us at the present moment has a leaven of evil working in it, of which some of us are not, perhaps, so much aware as we ought to be, and some of us who are aware of it, do not always take the wisest steps to prevent it spreading its virus in our midst. It does seem to me, my friends, that to you, the womanhood amongst us, belongs this great task of purifying the stage. If you, who are mothers, will not allow into your homes men who are known, whom your sons and husbands know, to be men of corrupt lives; if you young women will not allow fast and fashionable men to say to you things that they would hardly dare to say to a woman of the town; if, I say, you would surround yourselves with that fence which, by the blessing and power of God's grace, modesty can always surround itself with, a power almost immeasurable in its consequences could be brought to bear on the elevation of society. But I don't believe that the theatres ever will be purified till society has been worthily elevated, and I do hope and trust that the appeal which Lord Mulgrave and others make—according to their opportunities—to the leaders in society to exert their influence on the side of purity and virtue, will not be an appeal in vain. No doubt about it, the tastes of the lower classes are a little coarser and less refined than the tastes of the upper ten thousand; but I do not think, although it was a sentiment uttered by a great mind, there ever was a falser or more deceiving sentiment uttered, than that of Burke when he said—"that vice loses half its evil when it loses all its grossness." Vice sometimes, deprived of its grossness, becomes all the more mischievous, because it is all the more attractive.

I shall just say a few words on the subject of literature. No doubt there is much prevailing literature that is to be deprecated; but I thank Mr. Harry Jones for having brought us back to realities, and permitting us to believe, as I rejoice to believe, that in the class of people among whom he lives, and among whom I have seen with my own eyes *how* he lives, and what he is doing to improve their lives, things are not so bad as they seem to be, and as they are sometimes thought to be. I remember that once I did what was thought to be a somewhat hazardous thing. Preaching in Westminster Abbey the Sunday after the death of Charles Dickens, I could not let the opportunity pass without at least saying what was in my mind about the great writer. I remember a leading article in *The Times* a few days before had spoken of him as "the apostle of the people." I believe he was in a very true sense "the apostle of the people." I have read most of Charles Dickens's works, and, so far as I remember, there is not one single page, I doubt if there is one single sentence, stained with any impurity, or with anything that would suggest a vile, a vicious, or an unworthy thought. I believe that the literature of which he was the author has been pregnant with consequences of incalculable benefit to our people. It has made us see that there are simple virtues under rugged exteriors; it has taught the people the joys and blessedness of pure and innocent homes; it has taught them the great lesson of Christian sympathy; and though in all things Charles Dickens may not have been all we could have desired him to be, we are not his judges; and we do not know the circumstances of trial under which his life was passed. But I feel that England owes a debt of gratitude to its great novelist for what he has done to elevate and purify human life where it most needs elevation and purification. O my friends, if we would only endeavour, each in his own sphere, each within the range of his own influence, to make human life a little happier by making it purer (and I am quite certain that purity of life is the only condition of true happiness) then, far better than any speeches or papers read or delivered on this platform, however eloquent, earnest or true, will be that blessed influence you will carry back to your own homes in the resolution to make purer, brighter, worthier the society within the range of your own example.

Brighton Congress.

I have been asked to speak of certain dangers which beset working men —in common with all other classes on the intellectual and sensuous side of their nature—in connection with the more or less impure literature and degrading and degraded art, by which the moral tone of society is being greatly undermined. The evil grows, and is generated from many sources. One source is the Press, from which issues much wholesome food—and, I am thankful to believe, a large preponderance of wholesome food—but from which also issues much that can only be called poison. There is the studio of the painter and even of the sculptor, and, I am told, of the photographic artist. There is the theatre, from Her Majesty's Opera House down to the lowest penny gaff. There is the music hall, the casino, and the dancing saloon. All these are sources of the evil, and constitute elements in the danger of which I am speaking. It is the eye and ear, acting upon the bestial side of our nature, that are enslaved by the influence of which I speak. With many men and women the slavery is terrible. The whole man is held in bondage as by a legion of devils; and even when the chains are lighter we are only too sadly conscious of their weight and degradation. There are theories of human nature which push the ideas of human depravity to what I cannot but consider a somewhat dangerous extreme. All theories that finish at a dangerous extreme are likely to result in a terrible reaction, and the theory of extreme depravity seems to have led to a terrible reaction. In spite of the bestial side of our nature, which we all feel and recognize most heartily and readily, there is in us—at any rate, in the innocence of our childhood, and until the conscience has become seared and hardened—an instinctive revulsion from moral evil, and, however degraded we may have become, there is generally a chord of good in our nature which he who has a skilful hand can touch and find a response. There is no truth that for our own encouragement we need to bear more constantly in mind than this: that all men and women, however much the image may have been broken and defaced, are yet made in the image of God. Impurity is a mental disease, and I urge you working men to seek out noble opportunities and noble spheres of mental activity if you are tempted by this evil of impurity. The best of the heathen writers put much of our so-called Christian literature to utter shame. It is sometimes said by taunting men that the Bible is a coarse book; but the Bible deals with human nature as it exists, and human nature is too often a coarse thing. But I defy any man to say that any reading of the Bible leaves the impression that impurity is a matter of little account. If working men are looking out for authors in the various paths of literature with whom to wile away their leisure hours, there are in almost every kind of library writers who may be read without a single stain being left behind on the conscience, or a single thought that might not be remembered even in the dying hour. Walter Scott's novels, and even the story-books of Charles Dickens, as far as I remember, are not tainted with one single passage that would minister to gross profligacy or impurity; and there are ten thousand refined pursuits which men might follow, and keep themselves pure and unspotted. There is music with its most angelic power of purifying the soul, and there is the study of botany. In the town of Oldham the working men have established a naturalists' society; and nothing pleases me more than to see working men cultivating round their cottages little cottage gardens and spending their leisure time in this way (even sometimes on Sunday) rather than in places ten thousand times worse. I remember that when the Bethnal Green Museum was opened, some people made a mockery of the attempts which those poor folk made to receive the distinguished persons who were present at the opening. Some weeks after I myself went to see this museum, and I was profoundly interested to see the number of working men who were wandering through the courts of the museum intelligently enjoying the treasures of art and objects of beauty spread out before them. I am sure that if we only look for them there can be found in thousands of ways objects of legitimate beauty which could satisfy every legitimate desire of our souls. The working men of all countries are known as the proletariat, and they are supposed to be a somewhat dangerous class. I quite admit that the proletariat of the country, or the lower classes, are a dangerous class when they are discontented, when they have a right to be discontented, and when they are full of coarse and bad passions, which can only be kept down by fear; but I say at the same time, without one thought or reservation, than an honest, sober, thrifty, industrious working class is the very marrow of the nation. It is, no doubt, of importance in this country that the aristocracy should be pure and full of high aspirations; but I say it is of ten thousand times greater importance that the working class should be pure and full of high aspirations. I want you to realize your high position and value in the commonwealth. There is a danger which besets the working class in common with many other classes from sceptical as well as impure literature. I want you to remember that there is a vast difference between hypothesis and experiment. It concerns you far more to look forward to what you are to become than to look backward to what you have arisen from. I cannot entertain the idea that the Church and clergy are opposed to the true progress and enlightenment of the people; and I venture to say, after the efforts which the Church of England has made beyond any other religious body for the education of the masses, no man has a right to say the clergy are opponents of progress.

Probably few scenes in the history of Church Congresses have equalled the great scene at the working men's meeting in the Circus, Percy Street, Newcastle, upon October 6, 1881. Every part of the vast building was packed to its utmost capacity. Thrilling addresses had been delivered by the Bishops of Durham and Carlisle; when the Bishop of Manchester, amid vociferous acclamations, was summoned to address the meeting. After touching upon a variety of topics, he approached the central thesis of his speech: "Is Christianity a dead thing?" he asked. A voice from the great assembly, exclaimed. "God forbid!" "I thank the man who said that," answered the Bishop. "For I feared that some of you might have been carried away by secularism which, in its daring, says things about God and religion which it is awful to contemplate. The sacredness of the marriage tie, for instance, is sneered at. But, without fear of contradiction, I maintain that the greatness of England consists in its morality, and the morality of England has been built up upon the purity of its family life, and the man who breaks down that purity is an enemy to the human race. Will you, working men of Newcastle, pledge yourselves to resist this infidelity so destructive of domestic purity and domestic peace?" The vast audience rose to a man with the response:—"We will! We will!"—and the Bishop fairly broke down under the majestic emotion of the scene.

CHAPTER X.

CONFIRMATIONS AND ORDINATIONS.

Confirmations—Accrington Confirmation, 1877—Confirmation Addresses—Ordinations—Ordination Addresses—The Work of the Ministry—Notes of Ordination Addresses — Standards for Examination — Ordination Sermons—Cardinal Newman's Letter.

No department of Bishop Fraser's episcopal duties was, to himself, more interesting, and to others, more impressive, than his confirmations and ordinations. His whole strength of love went to this work. "It will be," he said to a friend upon accepting the bishopric, "at confirmations and ordinations chiefly that I think I shall be able to do good." Ever young himself, his heart ever yearned towards the young. As he stood to address a company of candidates for confirmation or ordination, his face was illumined with a sweet trembling light. You could see his breast heave, not with a consciousness of himself, but with a consciousness of the solemn importance of the occasion to the lives of his listeners. Sometimes a quiet tear would fall down his cheeks, and always his words and voice were eloquent with fatherly affection. His letters contain frequent allusions to his confirmations.

September 23, 1878.

Confirmations, when they become a mechanical repetition of the same thing, may grow tedious; but I do not find them to be so, and each occasion has some element of freshness in it which makes it different from others. The clergy also take great pains to have everything about the service lively and well-ordered, and the hymn-singing is always a great treat.

In these districts, where the people are mainly employed in large bodies in mills, I am almost—or almost always—obliged to hold confirmations in the evening at 7.30 or 8 p.m. People generally have got to take a great interest in the ceremony, and I generally have the pleasure of finding quite a full church, which gives me the opportunity of speaking a word that one hopes may be "in season," to many more than the actual candidates. Among the candidates yesterday was an old woman of eighty-six, who was determined to go through the whole preparation in proper manner, and insisted upon the vicar ascertaining that she knew her "Catechiz" with the texts.

Last week I confirmed about 1500 candidates, and am still going on night after night at nearly the same rate.

A most touching incident came to my knowledge on Sunday night. I had held a confirmation for a single parish, where the mission had brought forth much fruit. After the service was over, the clergyman asked me, "Did you notice that man about fifty-five or sixty that you confirmed?" I said, "Yes; I was struck with his attentive and respectable appearance." "Well," said the clergyman, "that man has been one of the worst livers in my parish. He is a foreman of one of the gangs on the London and North Western Railway, and he heard your address to the men at Longsight Tank. When it was over, he said to one of his mates, "Some one has been telling the Bishop about me, for he has read my very thoughts."

I need not say that nobody had told me; but the man took the words home, thought about them, offered himself to the clergyman for confirmation, is now apparently quite another man, and the example of his conversion—in his case, so far, a very true and real one—the clergyman tells me is most valuable to others. I did not hear this story till the man had left the church, or I should have liked to have spoken to him a few encouraging words.

November 18, 1878.

My confirmation at Leesfield was especially interesting. There were 245 candidates; and the church, which will hold 1100 people, was crowded in every part. Ten of the girls came from the parish of East Crompton, and it was touching to see them come up with their little knot of black crape on the top of their white confirmation caps in token of respect to their late pastor Mr. Meredith, who was justly and deeply esteemed by his people. I could not help noticing the fact, in my second address, as equally gratifying to me in respect both of *him* and *themselves*. These warm-hearted Lancashire people have such nice ways of showing affection where they really feel it. Poor Meredith's death—he was only thirty-four—was put down by the doctor to typhoid fever, and that to a cold caught at Canon Raines' funeral when the weather was terrible.

In connection with another confirmation, Canon Lloyd, the present Vicar of Leesfield, relates an incident, illustrative of the Bishop's observant interest in the candidates. It was the Bishop's general rule to confirm the candidates two at a time. A chair being placed for him on the chancel-steps, the candidates came up and knelt in pairs for the laying-on of the Bishop's hands. Upon one occasion two candidates who were coming together to the Bishop's chair, and who, by their mutual likeness, were obviously sisters, chanced to become separated. The Bishop, without any prompting, observed this; and when the first sister reached him, he stopped, called up the other sister, and bidding them kneel down together, laid his hands on both at once, thus gratifying the deep desire of both the sisters' hearts. A trivial incident: but characteristic of Bishop Fraser, and making an enormous difference to those sisters in the retrospect of their confirmation.

Similar incidents, small, yet pathetic, abound in the Bishop's correspondence. On one occasion, having been invited by the Mayor of Manchester to meet General Grant at a banquet, and having a great desire to converse with the General, but being prevented from attending the banquet by a confirmation, the Bishop was greatly disappointed. The next day, however, he received from one of the confirmees a grateful letter for the help conveyed in his address, and writes: "The letter quite consoled me for my disappointment. It is more part of my work as a bishop to help a struggling soul than to accept a mayor's hospitality, or to converse with a famous general." Upon another occasion, having held a large confirmation in Rochdale Parish Church, he discovered, on going to the Vicarage, that one of the servants had not been well enough to go to church, and at once said to Mrs. Maclure, the Vicar's wife, "I will confirm her in the drawing-room, if you will get the household together." Indeed, he was always willing to go any distance to confirm an invalid in a sick room, and always felt that such confirmations were peculiarly solemn. In one of his letters, he says:

May 8, 1877.

Oh, how slight are all the world's hopes, and promises, and prospects, besides those simple truths on which faith feeds, and which—God be thanked!—are as truly and fully the portion of the peasant in his cottage as of the queen upon her throne. How this thought, when one reflects upon the actual facts of humanity, enhances the blessedness of the Gospel.

CONFIRMATIONS AND ORDINATIONS. 207

I have had one or two cases for confirmation lately, which have made me feel this—oh, how strongly! One of a young lady of nineteen, who has been laid on a bed of constant pain for three years, with disease of the hip-joint from which she is never likely to recover— a perfect miracle of patience and gentleness. Another an old woman— at least a woman of sixty—in humblest circumstances, who has been bed-ridden twenty years, and who wished " the Bishop would come and confirm her"—a pattern of humble and yet most true and intelligent faith.

These things that come in one's way from time to time are *my* "Evidences of Christianity." What is there else that can give peace and patience and hope like this?

In one of his addresses, the Bishop said: "There are people in the world, who, as they make themselves merry with the ordinances of the Christian religion, also make themselves merry with the ordinance of confirmation." But to the Bishop the ordinance of confirmation was among the most important, most fruitful, most solemn ordinances of his great office. He took a personal interest in all the arrangements; often himself making choice of the hymns, and publicly announcing his preference for small confirmations, that the confirmees might feel themselves individually observed, not lost in a crowd; and that the service might be orderly, decent, quiet; not bustling, noisy, ineffective. In his confirmation duties, as in all other things, the last person he thought of was himself. So entirely did he place himself at the disposal of the people that he not only instituted evening confirmations, and confirmations in small parishes, and special confirmations in his own private chapel, and in the homes of the sick, but often, in the manufacturing districts, he held *two* confirmations on one Saturday afternoon, going afterwards cheerfully home to his work for Sunday. Once, when Canon Maclure gently remonstrated with the Bishop that he was wearing himself out, the Bishop made the noble reply, "Maclure, these confirmations must be, not when I want them, but when the people can do with them."

The effect of this readiness on the part of the Bishop to place himself at the disposal of the people, supported as that readiness was by the diligence of the clergy, was most noteworthy. In his last Charge, delivered in 1884, the Bishop says:—

"The number of candidates for confirmation has been steadily rising year after year, till in the year 1883 it culminated in the large number of 16,354, the largest number, I should imagine, which has ever been confirmed, in these last days, in one year by a single bishop with his own hand. The figures of this year are not quite complete, as I have four or five smaller confirmations still to hold; but they will probably amount to nearly 13,000. In the single rural Deanery of Bolton I have this year confirmed 3050 candidates, and from one parish in that deanery, St. Matthew's (Rev. C. Cronshaw, Vicar), I have received 302 candidates, 122 *of whom were males*. These figures show what zeal and diligence will do."

In a similar spirit of complete self-surrender, the Bishop never hurried over a confirmation, or went through the service as a perfunctory routine; but gave much time to it, always allowing an interval in the service for silent prayer, and showed an interest often described as "intense." The addresses (of which he always gave two, one before and one after the rite) were plain and practical; but never failing to unfold the meaning, and to emphasize the duties and the privileges of the ordinance. At a confirmation held at Accrington in 1877, the Bishop said:—

"It is one of the particular offices of a bishop to confirm. But when I say that, don't let me be supposed to mean that what is called the grace of confirmation—by which I mean its spiritual use to the soul—comes from the bishop. There is a grace in confirmation, when it is earnestly sought; but it is quite easy for any one of you to empty confirmation of its grace and power, and to make it a most unprofitable and irreligious form. If you come here in a wrong state of mind, not having thoroughly realized what you have come to promise, and having no intention of keeping what you promise, and no desire for the gift of the Holy Ghost, why, it is not at all likely that the gift you do not value will be given. But if, thinking and feeling it a very solemn thing to come here to-night and, in the presence of God—for though we cannot see Him He is here— to say that you do now take upon yourself, and bind yourself with, that solemn promise which your god-parents undertook for you in baptism; and if, feeling your own weakness, your own unsteadfastness, and your own powerlessness to keep this promise in your own strength, you humbly, and believingly, and lovingly, and obediently, seek from God the grace which He alone can give, and in which, and by which, you can be enabled to stand true to this your promise—then, I say, that no one need suppose that confirmation is a mere empty, external superstitious form; every one may readily believe that it is an ordinance of the

Church which the apostles instituted, and which God has certainly blessed, and which He will bless to you as He has done to others, to the strengthening and refreshing of your souls. The grace of confirmation does not come from me. Bishops don't go about their dioceses wishing people to believe that they have in their hands a gift to bestow; and that all that people have to do to receive the gift is just to say the two simple words 'I do'; and then kneel down before the bishop, forsooth, for him to lay his hands on their heads. No bishop would desire you to suppose that is all you have to do to secure the blessing of confirmation. You have all been for some time past under a course of instruction from your proper pastors—men who have known you for many years. It has been their business, and I hope their pleasure and privilege, to lead you to think more and more of the service Christ expects from every one of you. They have taught you the love of Christ and what you owe to Him, not only for what He has done—for His death on the cross—but for what He is still doing; for that continual intercession for you that He is day by day making to His Father, at that Father's right hand; and they have taught you, I hope also, to expect, if your hearts are prepared to receive it, in and through this confirmation, the gift of the presence of the Holy Ghost in your souls, which alone is able to make you stand in the day you are tempted, when the devil is at the very door of your hearts, and when but for Divine grace and the help of the Holy Spirit you may be betrayed and fall. This is what you have come for to-day—to make a very solemn promise to God, a promise such as you have never been asked to make before, and the like of which you will never be asked to make again. You may be asked to make other promises. Men and women, when they come to be married have to make promises of mutual love, mutual constancy, mutual affection; but those are very different promises from what you have come to make to-night. You have come here to-night to renounce the world, the flesh, and the devil. What does that mean? Go out into the streets of Accrington to-night, and you will see plainly enough what it means. I venture to say that, if I were to stand half an hour in the streets of Accrington, I should witness many things which I should say at once were unseemly in a Christian man or woman. I should see perhaps, in those streets, drunken men, and loose or immodest women; I should hear from time to time oaths and blasphemies or indecencies. Those are the outward sins—sins of which St. John speaks as manifest beforehand, going before to judgment, bearing on the face of them the sentence of God's condemnation. But, as we all know, there are more secret sins, sins hidden from men, but seen of God. Well, you are come here to-night to renounce all these sins, feeling as Christian young men and women that they are things which you will have nothing to do with. Now, what do we mean by renouncing the flesh? We carry bodies about with us. St. Paul says those bodies are, or ought to be, temples of the Holy Ghost, and tells us, "If any man defile these temples, him will God destroy." And yet through the body, through the mysterious connection of the body with the soul, all sorts of evil thoughts,

P

lusts, and desires are continually rising within us; so much so that St. Paul, writing to the Romans, says, 'I know that in my flesh dwelleth no good thing;' and to the Philippians he states, 'I keep under my body and bring it into subjection lest by any means, when I have preached to others, I myself should be a castaway.' There are many sins which could have no power at all over us if we had no bodies—sins of which I suppose the angels of God are incapable—drunkenness, gluttony, pride, over-much dress and pleasure. To many a girl and boy, life would be a dull thing if they were not constantly seeking some volatile pleasure —a dance to-night, a visit to the theatre to-morrow, a concert the night after, an excursion to Blackpool when the summer comes round; and all these things, which, in moderation, I am not going to say do any harm, but which, when we think of nothing else, drive all true religion out of the soul. We should bear in mind what the Catechism tells us we ought to do. How we ought—what I am afraid many Lancashire lads and lasses don't do—to love, honour, and succour our fathers and mothers, and not give them saucy answers, not disobey them, not turn away when they are giving us good counsels; to keep our hands from picking and stealing; our tongues from evil-speaking, lying, and slandering; to keep our bodies in soberness, temperance, and chastity; not to covet other men's goods, but learn and labour truly to get our own living in the station of life unto which it has pleased God to call us. Remembering that these are the commandments of which our Lord Jesus Christ says, 'If thou wilt enter into life, keep them,' I think it is necessary that we should have them present to our minds when we are making the very solemn promise that you are presently to give; taking upon yourselves what in your infancy your godparents promised for you, accepting Christ's service, voluntarily following Him as your Master, fighting His battles against the world, the flesh, and the devil, and promising to be true and loyal to Him to your lives' ends. I have got very little to do. My laying my hands upon your heads won't work a charm on your souls. My prayer that God will defend you with His heavenly grace, and make you His for ever, and enable you to increase in grace until you shall go to His everlasting kingdom, will do you no good unless you can heartily say at the end of it, 'Amen, even so, Lord, be it done unto me.' If you really desire heavenly grace, if you really wish to become God's children, then the prayer will do you good, then that touch of the hand—an external sign—perhaps will do you good; but, above all, your souls must be ready and prepared to receive the gift of the Holy Ghost; and we know the Holy Ghost is never denied to any one who asks for Him and desires Him earnestly, for 'your heavenly Father,' says the Lord Jesus, 'will give His Holy Spirit to them that ask it.' But I don't want to weary you with a long address, I merely wish you to lay to heart two things—first, that your confirmation is no mere idle, superstitious form. You know it would have been quite useless for the woman to have touched the hem of Christ's garment if she had not had faith. She believed that there was grace in Christ which could heal her body and soul; but if she had gone in mere superstition, thinking that by the mere touch of the hem of His garment, and without faith and love, that a miracle would be wrought on her behalf, I'm afraid she would have been mistaken. As the apostles state, there were many crowded round our Lord, and they got no good by coming into contact with His garments. It was the woman's faith which made her whole. And so there will be a blessing to those amongst you who have faith to believe that the gift of the Holy Spirit will be given you; if you feel your own weakness, and desire strength from God, and humbly seek it. It would be making Christ false to His word if we believed that at any time when we come to God and ask His Spirit he would send us away with a refusal. The second thing I wish you to lay to heart is, that we don't come in any self-chosen, new-fangled way of our own, seeking this gift of the Holy Ghost; but only in the way in which Christ's apostles ordained that followers of the Master should come. We come to the same God —the God whom we trust will be present in our hearts is the same God whom the apostles worshipped, and why should we doubt for one moment that the same blessing as in the days of old was given to the children of Christ will now be given to us who are walking in the steps of the apostles themselves? I would impress upon you, as my children, to have faith and to have love, to be sincere and earnest in your promise, and then to be sincere and earnest in your humble seeking for God's most Blessed Spirit, which is the very choicest gift He can bestow on your souls."

"The effect of his addresses to the candidates for confirmation," writes Archdeacon Anson, "could not be communicated by any written report. It was the *feeling* and *manner* with which they were spoken which made them so interesting and impressive. The one word to describe that manner is '*fatherly*.' His advice was so simple and wise. His manner so touching. Very few of those who were confirmed by him will ever forget their confirmation."

Bishop Fraser's Ordinations, like his Confirmations, were most solemn and impressive. None of those who (like the present writer) have been ordained by him can ever forget the intensity, the spirituality, the manliness of the Bishop's ordination addresses—their freshness, their affection, their force. At an ordination, Bishop Fraser's whole soul shone forth; his robustness, his reality, his simplicity, his humour, his faith, his love, his zeal, his truth, his devoutness, his straightforwardness, all poured themselves forth in spontaneous, irresistible flow. Upon one occasion, in bringing an address to its close, he paused and said, "I have but one word more, my young friends, to add, *Be humble, be earnest, be real.*" In those three injunctions the whole man unconsciously described himself; and, having thus spoken, he bowed his head, subdued in silent prayer. To scores of men, now labouring in the vineyard of Christ, their ordination by Bishop Fraser has been a great conversion, or turning-point, in life. He seemed to possess, in a wonderful degree, the strong and original power of opening men's eyes to see the true nature of their ministerial calling.

Yet his ordinations were not of the nature of spiritual retreats. He lifted his candidates to mountain tops, but to mountain tops where breezes blow, not where silence reigns. His ordinations were very sturdy things; wanting, perhaps, in mellowness, but never in manliness. Archdeacon Norris, one of the Bishop's most loved and honoured chaplains, continually urged him to separate the examination from the ordination, and to make the days immediately preceding the ordination more spiritual. But the Bishop put the plan aside, contending that "examinations are not unhealthy for the soul," and that a "spiritual retreat was not in his line."

June 11, 1877.

"That idea of Canon Norris's about separating the examinations from the more spiritual preparation of the candidates for ordination, is one that he has been long harping on, but which I do not yet see my way to adopt. Three days of 'spiritual retreat' might be to many men a very *unreal*, and, if so, a very unspiritualizing thing. There is something not altogether unhealthy in the examination. The new plan would involve much more time and expense—two journeys, and two weeks' occupation instead of one. I don't think I should feel equal myself to the conduct of a 'retreat;' it is not in my line; and there are very few men who could conduct one with effect. I am not sure that one of my present chaplains could—altogether, I see so many difficulties in the way that, in spite of Norris's persuasions, I do not think I shall be moved to change our present plan, with which I have no reason to be dissatisfied."

"At his ordinations," writes one of his examining chaplains, "the Bishop showed his accustomed sense and vigour. There was no pretence of godliness, no unnatural strain; he would talk with the candidates in a hearty and simple way, in language free from formality; yet none of them somehow could have taken a liberty with him. He would speak homely and wholesome truths to them, as 'Do not proselytize;' 'Do not throw bombs among your congregations;' 'The New Testament is not a dull book;' 'Do not spend too much time over your sermons.' During an ordination it was wonderful to see what he would get through; all done too, as it seemed, with the greatest ease; he never looked fagged or bored. Other business was not put aside at that time. Every evening almost he gave an address from the pulpit to the candidates, for which address he could hardly have found time to make a special preparation. He was the readiest of men; he eschewed over-thought. All was as clear and transparent in his speech as in his character; he never sought what was strained and forced. He spoke to them from the heart straight to their hearts. He told them things of every-day life, of what had happened to himself, not things removed from daily practice. Each address was lively and entertaining, nothing dull or heavy; it was no strain to attend. He did not say what was expected to be said by a bishop, but what he, James Fraser, really felt; nothing was cut and dried; all fresh and vigorous with youthful life. There have been many good bishops in the Church of Christ in all ages; but he was a copier of none. *There was an individuality about him.* When the day was over, he would talk to his mother, a sensible, vigorous and fine old lady, who, though she did not deny that she regretted the days of the Berkshire parsonage, yet evidently had the greatest pride in such a noble son, a pride which she was at no pains to conceal. She too, like that son, had her *non-vult* and her *vult*; but the *vult* for her son's honour was far stronger than the *non-vult* for position. At times on those evenings his happiness would burst forth into an almost childish joy. And yet one day I remember his saying to me sadly, 'I am not fit for this bishopric; *I am not good man enough to be a bishop.*'"

The Bishop held three ordinations in each year; upon the Second Sunday in Lent, Trinity Sunday, and at the autumnal Ember-tide. Most of the examining was undertaken by the Bishop's chaplains, though the Bishop himself not unfrequently set some of the papers. As many of the candidates as could be received were entertained at Bishop's Court; the rest were lodged in houses hospitably set at the Bishop's disposal for this purpose by his neighbours. All the candidates had one or more meals with the Bishop each day during the examination, and attended service in the evening in the pretty little episcopal chapel erected by the Bishop within the grounds of Bishop's Court. At these services the Bishop usually delivered an address. These addresses were not written out in full, but were spoken, hot from the heart, with the aid of a few brief reminder-notes. To the private chapel reporters were not admitted, so that nothing more than the barest notes can be given of the addresses spoken there; but in the first two years of his *Lancashire Life*, before entering upon residence at Bishop's

Court, the addresses were delivered in St. Mary's Church, Crumpsall, and have been, in part at least, preserved by the diligence of reporters. Among the addresses thus preserved are happily included his three first ordination addresses, delivered in April, 1870.

ADDRESSES TO CANDIDATES FOR ORDINATION.—FIRST ADDRESS.

On some accounts it is to be regretted that admission into Holy Orders is immediately preceded by an examination; and yet an examination is necessary, because it would not do in these days to send forth ignorant and uninstructed labourers—men of ill-balanced minds, men of scanty or imperfect information—to deal with those mighty problems which are now vexing the thoughts of men on every side, and so we must examine you to see that you are intellectually furnished for the work which you have to discharge. Yet, when one remembers that the world was converted by men, many of whom were ignorant and illiterate; when one remembers the mighty things which have been done by the simple power of faith and love and a sound mind, one must not lay too much stress on merely intellectual attainments, because the danger of an examination is that it should absorb too much of your thoughts and cares at a time when it is especially necessary that those thoughts should be fixed on higher things than the satisfying of a bishop and his chaplains that you have acquired the knowledge necessary and proper for your work. I say there is a tendency and a danger in an examination to fix the thoughts too exclusively upon that examination, and to look to the satisfying of the bishop and his chaplains; and, if you are selected to read the Gospel when the Ordination Sunday comes, then that is thought a great achievement. Now, it is not so at all. The great thing you have to settle in your minds is that you are following the call of God, that you are seeking a work in which you can try to do God service, and intend devoting to that service all your best thoughts, and cares, and studies, so that you may be found a faithful and wise steward, able to give to that portion of God's household which shall be committed to your charge their portion of wholesome strengthening meat in due season. There is one thing which you will have to confess in relation to this calling. You will have to say that you believe you are truly called according to the will of our Lord Jesus Christ, in the due order of this realm, to the ministry of the Church. You ought to have no doubts of the validity of your orders as administered in the Church of England; you ought to have no hankerings after another ideal which does not belong to the Church of England. I am quite satisfied that the Church of England provides for every earnest man spiritual assistance; no one need go beyond her wide and moderate limits to seek, either for his own sake or the sake of the people to whom he ministers, any other kind of spiritual food than that which the Church of England in her doctrines and her formularies prescribes. You ought to be well satisfied in your own minds both as to the position of the Church of England as a lawful branch of the Catholic Church of Christ, and that you yourself can loyally, cheerfully, heartily, willingly, render unto that Church the whole services of your soul within these fair limits. It is not a narrow platform, it is a wide and generous one, but yet it has its distinct limits on both sides; and within these limits I consider that every loyal member of the Church of England is bound, in conscience, by his ordination vows to confine himself. I cannot understand how people can satisfy themselves, when they have taken these solemn vows upon them, in seeming to be hankering after some other ideal, some other pattern, some other standard, of Church doctrine or ritual than that which the Church prescribes. I dwell upon this just now, because, if ever there was a time in the history of the Church of England when it seems to me to behove its ministers to be wise and faithful, wary and loyal, earnest and zealous, it is now. This is not the time for exciting suspicion and mistrust by new innovations, however well meant, however honestly purposed; it is rather the time for walking in the old paths, and teaching our people what we believe are the true foundations of holiness and the spiritual life. I am sure there never was a time in the history of the Church of England when the people of the Church were readier to receive spiritual truths through the ministration of the Church, if those truths are preached to them in all their fulness and their faithfulness. I believe the people are yearning for spiritual food. Wherever a good, able man is in earnest, his church is full, and the congregation abounds in good works. I am sure it rests mainly with ourselves, under God's Guiding Spirit, whether our ministry shall be a successful ministry or no. To this ministry so ordered, so limited, with such noble opportunities of doing service to God and of edifying this people of England, you are to be called.

In his second address the Bishop said:

The treasure that will be committed to your charge is the flock of Christ; which He bought with His death, and for which He shed His blood. You will be charged never to cease your labour, your care, your diligence, until you have done all, according to your bounden duty, to bring all such as are, or shall be, committed to your charge to the knowledge of God. How are you to promote the spiritual welfare of the congregations and the parishes that will be committed to your charge? The first means is plain—you must win their confidence. To win the confidence of the people is the secret of all success in every department of life, especially in the work of those that have the charge of souls. That confidence is to be won by the use of the simplest means—by hard work, by sincerity, by innocence or harmlessness, and, above all, by personal holiness. You must catch people by sincerity, by straightforwardness, by earnestness, by zeal, by labour—not by guile or by anything unhallowed. You must not aim at popularity. There is no greater snare to a minister in the discharge of his duty than the aiming at popularity. To be a popular preacher, to be one who is sought after much in society—these things are terrible snares to him who would be a faithful minister of Christ. You will be popular, in the sense of dwelling in the hearts and affections of your people, if you show you are willing to spend and be spent for them; but if you run after that miserable thing, the wind of popular favour; if your aim and object is to be well spoken of by men, you will get a thing that is not worth the having. Another thing I desire to warn you against in your parishes is, that you should not aim to make yourselves the head of a party. The Church of England now is terribly torn by parties, which are biting and devouring one another. You are sent into your parishes to promote peace and godliness, and it is your duty to bring all committed to your charge into agreement in the faith, and in the knowledge of God. It is a sad thing in a parish when those who ought to work to one great end are turned aside from it by the desire, or the ambition, or what they may consider the necessity, of becoming the head of a party. Do you remember how Paul was careful to eschew those who were ready to attach themselves to parties, to anything that could possibly create a partizan movement? You will remember how there were people calling themselves, some by the name of Cephas, some by the name of Apollos, and some by the name of Paul, and how Paul asked them how they had made his name the name of a party, since he had preached nothing but Christ and Him crucified, and that Paul was not crucified? You see how anxious Paul was not to lend the influence of his great name to the formation of any party short of the party of the great family, the great brotherhood, called by the name of Christ. I venture to tell you that you will be measured by your work; what you are worth to your people is the value that your people will set upon you. That will be the case in this diocese, where people do not seem apt to be imposed upon by names, and have a strong tendency to test the value of everything. You will be tested by your worth, and if you are worthy the love of your people you will have it, and your work will become blessed and full of true satisfactions—satisfactions higher and purer than any other which a man can obtain. One other thing you must remember, that in all parishes, in all congregations, there are those whom the Apostle Paul called weak brethren—persons who have scrupulous consciences, and are ever ready to take offence. These weak consciences have to be considered; you must not needlessly task them nor ridicule them, but must deal with them tenderly, wisely, and carefully, so that these weak brethren may haply become strong. Preach not yourselves, but Christ, for the work of the ministry is to bring men to Christ, not Christ to men.

In his third and concluding address the Bishop sought to impress upon the candidates the great truth, that as a minister is in his heart so the effect of his ministry is; and that before a man can shepherd the souls of others he "must take care of his own soul."

I was speaking to you, on the first night of our gathering here, of the sense in which I thought that without any unreality, or any fanaticism, you might give a sincere answer to the question that I shall have to put to you to-morrow—whether you consider yourselves to "be inwardly moved by the Holy Ghost" to take upon you this holy office which you are seeking. Last night I endeavoured to lead your thoughts to another subject, and to help you to realize in what spirit, and in what way, you could best discharge your duty to the people who will be committed to your charge. To-night I desire to speak to you upon one or two points which are not directly related one to the other, but upon which I should not like you to go out of my hands before I had said at least one word of counsel to you. First, let me say a word about your duty to the Church at whose altars you will serve. You are bound, I think, to be perfectly loyal to that Church. Now, in being loyal to the Church of England, I think it is absolutely necessary that you should, as far as possible, detach yourselves from all the trammels of party, and know no other teacher, and call yourselves by no other sectional name, than by the name of Jesus Christ and by the name of English Churchmen. Nothing can be more narrowing, not only upon the intellect, but, I believe, upon the whole spiritual nature, than the influence of party. It generates an atmosphere that is especially unfavourable to spiritual growth; and I do not believe it is the least necessary. I am quite sure that, when the platform of the Church of England was first raised, it was not intended to be the platform of any party. If you read the Declaration prefixed to the Thirty-nine Articles you will see the king there expresses his satisfaction that those Articles have been acceptable to all parties, and that men who differ upon other points somehow or other manage to agree upon them. Of course, if you are to be above the influence of party, you must behave in a charitable spirit towards your brethren of all sections and all denominations. And I would especially entreat you in dealing with those who differ from you, some perhaps on sufficient grounds, and some, as it may seem, on very insufficient grounds, pray try and do not become polemical preachers or bitter controversialists. There is surely no necessity because we differ from our fellow-Christians, or because we do not belong to the same denomination, for thinking ill of them, or speaking ill of them, or depreciating their work. They may be doing good work for God as well as we, and I am sure I am giving you counsel that will tend to your own peace of mind, and to the furtherance of your work in your different parishes, when I ask you to try to cultivate all good relations, and to put all charitable construction upon the conduct of those who may happen to differ from you. But the most important thing of all which I would desire to press upon you to-night—oh! see to it—*is to take care of your own souls.* Do you remember the lament of one of the old prophets of Israel, who said that he had been made a keeper of vineyards, and yet had not kept his own vineyard? Do you remember the doom of the priest who was sent with God's message to the king, and who delivered that message, truthfully and fearlessly, yet fell a victim to his own disobedience, as the poet of the "Christian Year" reminds us?—

> "Alas, my brother! round thy tomb,
> In sorrow kneeling, and in fear,
> We read the pastor's doom
> Who speaks and will not hear."

Specially then, take care of your own souls; nourish them with all wholesome spiritual food—with strong meat, if you are able to digest it—at any rate, nourish them with the wholesome milk of the Word, so that you may grow thereby. Take care of your own souls by earnestness and constancy in prayer; by diligent study of the Word of God; by meditating in the silence of your own hearts, and in the quietness of your own chambers upon the spirit in which you are doing your work; by reviewing your own ways, and assuring yourself of the simplicity and integrity of your own motives; and, above all, by watching how the light of God is shining in you. That is the way in which you may hope to become examples to the flock, and to minister the Gospel of the grace of God to those who are near you, with power. And pray remember that not only must you look carefully and narrowly after your soul; but you must also keep a watchful eye over your life. The minister of the Gospel is not the same as other men. There are places where *he* should not be found where others may, perhaps, be innocently found. There are things in which he must not allow himself to participate which to others may be harmless. We are bound to keep a restraint upon ourselves. Things lawful to others may not be lawful, and, perhaps, cannot be expedient to us. You remember how St. Paul tells us that the deacons must be grave, sober men; and he mentions a number of qualities that if you read them you seem at once to mark the minister of the Gospel by his very outward bearing, his manner, his look, his walk, and his dress; as one who is set apart to a holy office, upon which he must not bring dishonour by even the semblance of a careless life. We read in the Acts of the Apostles of some who looked upon the holy men who preached the Gospel which we have to preach now, and took notice of them that they had been with Jesus; and you remember how the Apostle Paul tells us that he bore about in his body what he calls the marks, the brand of the Lord Jesus; and so, he says, we ought to take heed unto ourselves that we wear Jesus' livery, that Jesus' mark is set upon us, that we are doing our Master's work in no careless spirit, but bringing all things into subordination to it, and making it the first and primary business of our lives. You will have to give up much, my friends—much which the world calls pleasure, and sets great store upon. You are entering a profession in which you can hardly expect to become wealthy, where you may be thrown into some part of the earth where there may be few to notice, few to appreciate, your labours. You may have to encounter ingratitude, thanklessness, and those things which Paul had to encounter; where he loved, the less was he loved in return. But for every sacrifice you make for Christ, and for the people of Christ, I venture to promise you that, in inward contentment, in the satisfaction of conscience, and in the peace of your souls, you will be repaid a thousand-fold. After all, though it may not bring wealth, though it may not bring greatness, and though it may not bring the thousand things that the world counts precious, and which are precious, yet no work to which a man can put his hand is so noble as the work of ministering the Gospel of Christ, no rest like the rest that is earned by labour, no retrospect so unspeakably blessed as the review of a life well spent in so noble a cause.

Bishop Fraser never lost an opportunity of impressing upon men the true character of the ministry of Christ. In an ordination sermon preached two years before his death he exclaimed:

"Ah, young men, do not seek to magnify your office by claiming for it prerogatives which it never was supposed to possess till primitive simplicity got to be overlaid by the accretions of a later age! Come to men, if you would win them, as a prophet, an evangelist, a pastor, a teacher, rather than as a priest. Realize what are the spiritual needs of the age if you would minister to them. Not only the Church, but Christianity, not only Christianity, but the most elementary faith in God, is passing through a great crisis. Don't think you can satisfy men's perplexities, or restore their faith, by mumbling spells and charms like Scæva's seven sons at Ephesus. Address yourselves to their understandings, affections, consciences. I cannot conceive anything more reasonable or more noble than Paul's idea of the Christian ministry—an instrument in bringing men to Christ, that His gracious Spirit may play, like the breath of Heaven, on their souls. This is surely the most glorious work in which a man can engage. It must be done in no Sardian or Laodicean spirit. 'Stir up the gift that is in thee,' cries Paul to Timothy. 'Take heed to the ministry thou hast received that thou fulfil it.' So go forth, young man, clothed with a Divine office, strengthened by a Divine power. Go and try to preach to men of the unsearchable riches of Christ; go and minister the Gospel of the grace of God, not in its letter, which killeth, but in its spirit, which giveth life. Go and be living epistles of your Master, known and read of all men—go and spend and be spent for the brethren—go and work while it is day, and trust to Him Whom you serve for your reward."

These are burning words—words which sank deep into the young hearts that heard them, and which are still bringing forth fruit in the patient, manly, spiritual labours, both in town and country parishes, of many of those upon whom the earnest, inspiring, Bishop's hands were, in ordination, laid.

The Bishop's Ordination Addresses were (as has been said) commonly delivered from brief notes hurriedly jotted down on scraps of paper. A few of these Brief Notes are here given; not so much in the hope of exciting general interest in them (for, indeed, to many they will, through their brevity, be almost unintelligible) but for the sake of awakening echoes of sweet, strong, holy memories in the hearts of those who first listened to the addresses of which these Brief Notes are the germ. To those who were ordained by Bishop Fraser these Brief Notes, consisting sometimes of little more than a word, will, it is hoped, be precious and sacred.

"Don't establish an autocracy in your parish. Give to every one his due. Enlist as much co-operation as you can. Give all something to do. Earnestness the great secret of success. Your influence will be in proportion as you are seen not to be seeking it—but seeking something higher, not your own glory but Christ's. Need of getting acquainted with your people personally. Paul preached not only publicly, but from house to house. In labouring for Christ you will be best labouring for the Church. Don't be led away by the spirit of party. Don't excite mistrust by anything you do or say. If it be possible as much as lieth in you, live peaceably with all men. Importance of personal character and conduct. Familiarity with Divine things does not necessarily develop an increase of spirituality. Above all, be real and true. Form a true conception of your office—not from medieval sources but from Paul, from Christ. You cannot help others unless you have a consciousness that your own inner life aims at a high standard. Carefully and regularly study Paul's pastoral epistles to Timothy and Titus. They contain the very essence of sober, earnest, spiritual counsel—not to make so much a priest or a priestling—performing certain ceremonies, or even administering certain sacraments in which his own feelings and character are not concerned—but the prophet, the teacher, the evangelist, and perhaps the highest title of all, the pastor, the shepherd of souls (Ephes. iv. 11). Young men, I pray you to lay to heart these things, I am sure they are true and profitable. You naturally desire to be 'able ministers of the New Testament.' If so, 'make full proof of your ministry'—take home the warning of Archippus to yourselves. Now, more than ever, the fortunes of the Church, which I cannot but regard as essentially governing the future of religion in this country, depend upon the faithfulness, diligence, and blamelessness, of her clergy. It is we, rather than any outward force, who will destroy or sustain her. Personal influence, as Dr. Newman taught, is the great instrument of maintaining and propagating the truth. What might be achieved, if all were earnest, sincere, consistent, sympathetic, considerate, wise and true, is almost inconceivable. So far from the Church having put out and exhausted all her powers, in some directions they have hardly been tried. Go forth, young men, in the strength of your own good purposes, and with the power of the Holy Ghost, and let it be seen that you 'magnify your office,' by the way in which you discharge its duties. Fervour and earnestness. Danger of mechanicalism. Simulated fervour—an easy thing, but deeply perilous. Be the clergyman always, everywhere. Be loyal to your incumbent; frank with him. If this cannot be rendered, separate. Never lend yourself to a party in your parish. Stand, I won't say aloof from, but *above*, all party. Theological subtleties, on which religious parties are mainly founded, not of the essence of Christianity. Personal religion all springs from, returns to, one central fact, the nearness of the soul through Christ to God. Your religious influence over others will entirely depend on this. Try to quicken a Christian spirit and temper in the young. I don't ask you to be ascetic. I want to see you, in the truest sense, manly; but I beg you to be circumspect. Give no occasion to scandal of any kind. Be a scholar, at least a Bible and a Prayer Book scholar. See your people from 'house to house.' This is sadly too much neglected for the easier work of multiplied services or sensational missions. Bring your motives and your conduct often before the bar of conscience, honestly, not morbidly, and with the simple aim of doing your duty more perfectly. I do not wish to deny you proper healthy recreations—but, remember, these must be strictly subordinated to duty. Give no scandal and be on your guard here. And so go forth in the strength of the Spirit of God to that noble work which you have chosen and to which you now seek to be called.

"Now, when you go into your parishes, don't stand on your rights, but rather remember Paul's compassion for the weak brother. A thing may be perfectly right for you to do, and yet it had better not be done, for the sake of your people. When I went to Cholderton I took two horses with me, intending to hunt once a week or so. Having sent them to the village blacksmith to be shod, I strolled up after breakfast to see how he got on. The smith remarked, 'You've a nice bit of horseflesh here, sir.' 'Yes,' said I, 'I think they are not bad ones.' 'I suppose you mean to go hunting.' 'Yes, I think a day a week would be good for my health, as there is not very much work in the parish.' 'Well,' said the man, 'I'm very sorry to hear it.' 'Why?' '*Because, if you go fox-hunting, I cannot go and hear you preach.*' On hearing that I determined, sooner than that one man in my parish should have a stumbling-block placed before him, to *give it up*—and I have *never ridden to hounds since.*"

"Before you can proclaim the love, joy, strength in Christ, you must know of it yourselves. I beseech you do not mistake anything else for it: no ritual; no services; no music."

"Be sure upon this one point—even if you should be doubtful on many others—that you are seeking to win souls—to bring lost or straying sheep back to the safety of the fold."

"Avoid indolence and self-indulgence."

"Pay some attention to your dress, that, without being at all fantastic, it may be becoming a clergyman."

"It is useless, perhaps, to protest against smoking. Yet it is self-indulgent; and needs to be practised with considerable self-restraint. It is inconsistent to visit a dying man reeking of tobacco. Glad to see so many are abstaining from alcohol."

"Be sure you allow yourself sufficient time for prayer, and make your progress real."

"Be very careful of your conduct towards females."

"Avoid all appearance of evil."

"It would be well to have your time clearly marked out: so much for this duty, so much for that, and leave enough for study."

"Without being ascetics, unless with a special purpose for a time, be on your guard against the moral enfeeblements of society; particularly its amusements."

"Bodily exercise profiteth little."

"I won't lay down *rules*. I will simply say, 'Always remember that you are a clergyman,' and don't follow that new type which defies public opinion and preaches Paul's doctrine, 'All things are lawful,' without remembering the qualifying clause, 'all are not expedient.' In Church services I lay stress on one governing principle, *be in earnest*. You will then never be hurried, slovenly, irreverent. You will seek to edify. There will be an undefinable something which goes to the heart. F. Maurice 'prayed the prayers,' not 'said them.' Have a quiet, serious earnestness, but not intensity, which is apt to overdo and become wearisome."

"*Sermons.*—Don't be slaves of MS. Don't be ashamed to ask people 'Was I heard? Understood? Did I help you?' Paul talks of 'speaking into the air' (1 Cor. xiv. 9)."

The Bishop felt very strongly, and sadly, the lowness of the standard reached by many of his candidates in their knowledge, especially of the Bible and the Greek Testament.

"The complaint," he writes, "that I have to make is that candidates do not know even the documents (*i.e.* the Bible and the Prayer Book) from which they have to teach. They know (many of them, but there are also not a few bright exceptions) neither their contents, nor their characteristics, nor their proportions. I most sincerely hope that I shall not be under the painful necessity of rejecting any. But it will not do, in this day, to commit the ministry of the Church to unlearned or incompetent men. And, really, so little suffices, that I do not feel much compunction in 'plucking' a man who will not take the pains to master that little."

And again :

"I am afraid I have not a very brilliant set of men before me at this ordination. We are using the same examination papers that we used six years ago; and I find that the scale of marks reached by the candidates was much higher then than it is now. I am at my wits' end for a plan to secure from candidates an adequate amount of preparation. At present, the professional training of no body of men is so meagre and unsatisfactory as that of the clergy. And yet we are supposed to deal with the most momentous subjects."

In similar language he spoke, in the presence of both incumbents and curates, of clergy and laity, in the Diocesan Conference held in October, 1883 :

"I think there is a great deal to be said seriously about the sermons of the clergy. The young men who come before me for ordination are going forth very ill-equipped indeed to deal with the intellectual difficulties of the day.

"A clergyman who is in urgent want of a curate hears of a likely young man, takes him up and sends him to the bishop, who finds he has only been considering the subject of Christianity from a teacher's point of view for three months perhaps, and is lamentably ignorant of his Bible ; he has read very little theology, but he passes the low standard with which we are obliged to content ourselves because of the urgency and pressure of the clergy, and he goes into the parish and begins to preach. Perhaps during his whole diaconate he has received no guidance, nothing to direct him in his studies, and I am told that sometimes he has not even a word of counsel given him as to the sermons he shall preach. This is a very serious matter. I had laid down a series of six books to be studied by candidates for priests' orders during their diaconate. These books include Butler's 'Analogy' ; Davison's 'Lectures on Prophecy' ; Professor Mozley's 'Bampton Lectures on Miracles' ; Bishop Pearson on the Creed, and Hooker. With great reluctance on the part of myself and my chaplains, I have been obliged to reduce that list of books, and I have struck off Mozley's 'Lectures on Miracles,' but I have determined that those who come to me for priests' orders shall at least know their Bible and the Greek Testament.

"We must make it a serious thing ; for at present the majority of our young clergy are very ill-equipped to go forth and preach at once to their people, and I am not at all sure that it might not be a desirable thing for the bishop to refuse the licence to preach, which is now given as a matter of course, to any deacon he sends out until he is satisfied that he can preach a sermon."

But richer in results, than either Ordination Sermons or Addresses, were the *Conversations* which the Bishop held quietly and separately, with each of the candidates. Who that has been admitted to the tender, hallowed, sanctuary of one of those conversations can ever forget the event? It was an epoch in life; a veritable conversion, and turning, of the young soul to God. The Bishop did not always kneel to pray with each candidate, but every word he spoke was an inspiration as holy as prayer. Robust, manly, true, tremulous with sympathy, lofty-minded, intense with purpose, the words from his glowing heart have kindled a flame in the listening heart of scores of clergy upon whose brows his ordaining hands have been laid.

And, when the day of Ordination came, with what penetrating tones he read his portion of the service!

"I would especially speak," writes Archdeacon Anson, "of the great charm of his 'reading' the Address in the Ordination Service to the candidates for priests' orders. Often as I used to hear it, each time it came with a freshness, a force, a tenderness which gave some new impression deeper than before. The perfect naturalness of his manner, the quiet, varied, yet always solemn and sympathetic, tones, brought out to the fullest extent every meaning of the searching truths of the exhortation he was delivering."

"The Bishop's power to sustain the attention of his hearers when he read an address to them was very remarkable. An instance of this is seen in his first Charge. It was announced by the reporters, who had been allowed to see the manuscript, that the delivery of the Charge would take four hours. How I could possibly sit as I had to do in the face of all the clergy and keep my eyes open I could not conceive! We heard the clock strike four times, the actual time occupied was three hours and twenty minutes, yet I felt no weariness. The interest was never allowed to fail. I would gladly have continued to listen."

The Bishop felt intensely the importance of good and reverent reading in the services of the sanctuary, such as is commended in the Book of Nehemiah (viii. 8).

"I deprecate," he said in his second Charge, "the practice, which I think is gaining ground, of appointing laymen—unless they are well-educated laymen—to read the Lessons in church. Nothing is more important than that the Scriptures should be read with clearness, taste, feeling, and intelligence. The substitution gives very little relief to the clergyman; if he will reduce the length of his sermon ten minutes, he will redress the balance of things; and to have the lessons badly read is a very great loss to the congregation. It is true that every one cannot read as John Henry Newman used to read the Scriptures in his church of St. Mary the Virgin, in Oxford, when every word, uttered in simplest fashion, but pregnant with scholarly feeling, fell like music on the listener's ear, kept the great church spell-bound, and touched the heart with a strange sense of spiritual power. I am thinking of forty years ago, but I remember the effect as distinctly as if I had heard the voice yesterday. It is not every one who can achieve this; but every one can say the prayers and read the lessons as if he *felt* them, and as if he wished that his hearers should feel them too. There is no part of our ministry which it is more worth while to do as well as it can possibly be done."

This kindly allusion to old Oxford days was responded to by Cardinal Newman in a manner equally kindly.

THE ORATORY, BIRMINGHAM, *December* 3, 1876.

MY DEAR BISHOP OF MANCHESTER,—I write a line to thank you for the very kind words about me, which you have introduced into your recent Charge. It is a great pleasure to me thus to be remembered by you.

It was not my good luck to see much of you when we were Fellows of one Society—but I have always held a hearty good-will and friendly feeling towards you, have followed your course in life with much interest, and was pleased some time ago to find that, in a photograph of you in some periodical, in spite of the signs of hard work, I more than recognized your Oriel features,—I am, my dear Bishop, your Lordship's sincere friend and well-wisher,

JOHN H. NEWMAN.

The BISHOP OF MANCHESTER.

CHAPTER XI.

OBITER DICTA.

Religion—Formalism—Dogmatism—Comprehension—Benefits of Discussion—Ecclesiastical Drugs—Family Religion—Education—Denominational Schools—Sunday Schools—Prize-giving—Desultory Education—Education and Youth—Self-made Men—Education of Women—Eloquence—Power of Plain Preaching—Curates and Clerical Incomes—Improvident Marriages—Heredity and Marriage—Cookery—Church Choirs—Hymns—Hymns and Music—Country Parsons—High Art—Sunday Opening of Museums—Funeral Reform—Cremation—The Volunteer Movement—Temptations of Youth—The Opium Trade—Fashionable Religion—Following Christ—Personal Salvation—The Prince Imperial—Dean Stanley—Dean Stanley and Lord Hatherley—Death of General Garfield—Dr. Pusey—Death of Dr. Tait, the Archbishop of Canterbury—Death of the Duke of Albany—General Gordon.

A GREAT man is not made in a single day. Bishop Fraser was really made in the quarter of a century diligently spent in the country parishes of Cholderton and Ufton. In the industrious tranquillity of those country parishes he had sedulously cultivated the arts of human fellowship; he had stored his mind with information upon all sorts of subjects; he had brooded reflectively upon the questions pressing for solution in Church and State; and, when the hour of opportunity struck, Mr. Fraser was ready and girded to use it. Manchester was his opportunity, and, directly upon his arrival there, he began to pour forth, in unexhausted and apparently inexhaustible freshness, his full streams of sympathy with every department of human enterprise. Bishops (through no conscious fault, but through the tendency of their training, the limitation of their sympathies, and the environment of their office) are often interesting only to a single class, or a limited selection of classes. They are interesting to persons of an ecclesiastical temper, to newspapers with an ecclesiastical bias, to various branches of the religious community. But they are not always interesting to outsiders

—to the great secular, civic, commercial, literary, social world.

It was otherwise with Bishop Fraser. Everybody was interested in him, because he was interested in everything, and everybody. He had something to say upon every subject; not always something learned, nor, indeed, perhaps, always something discreet. But he was intensely human, intensely social, intensely civic. He was a Citizen and a Man—as well as a Christian and a Bishop; and, by the very range of his information and sympathies, he was brought into contact with individuals and bodies of men whom bishops rarely touch; and, in the end, came to occupy an almost unique position—the position of premier citizen and principal ecclesiastic—in the south-east of Lancashire.

The purpose of the present chapter is to gather together some of the Bishop's incidental utterances; utterances which, dropped by the way, shed clear light upon certain phases of his character—particularly upon that largeness of sympathy, that directness of speech, and that all-enfolding catholicity of interest, which were among the secrets of his attractive spell.

RELIGION.

"Sensuous sentimentalism, a sad experience tells us, gives no strength to 'stand in the evil day.'"

"A Church is strong and growing which is full of *living souls*, not of squadrons of drilled machines."

"The only instance in which the absolving power is exercised in the Apostolic age, it is exercised by the whole congregation of the faithful gathered together in the name of the Lord Jesus Christ, and not even by an Apostle alone."

"A dogmatic system is a different thing from a spiritual power. We may lift up our hearts and thank God religion does not lie at the bottom of a very deep and unfathomable well, but upon the very surface of human life."

"Philosophic Atheism only makes the cloud of life ten thousand times darker than it is; for, although they say every cloud has a silver lining, there is no lining to that cloud. If the Gospel of Christ is not given to the world for the purpose of teaching us our duty towards our fellow-men, and setting us an example which we ought to follow, then I do not understand what the Gospel means. Common trials ought to bring hearts together with a stronger sense of common interest."

"Religion, not as a phrase, not as a sentiment, but as a temper of the soul and a habit of life, becomes, when it is most needed, a pre-eminent source of peace and 'assurance for ever.'"

"That life is the most Christlike which is spent in the most constant exercise of such simple, natural, and, I believe I may dare to say, easy virtues as tenderness, compassion, considerateness, equity, reasonableness, and beneficence."

"The real thing is the life of the Spirit in the soul. He is a Christian who is living like Christ, loving Christ, and trying to do what he can in the world as Christ did. I do not deny that it is well to have our outward bonds of union, our one baptism, our one creed, our common worship, but all these things are useless unless there is the Spirit of Christ."

"It is indeed true in a multitude of cases—'Tout comprendre, c'est tout pardonner.' How many hasty uncharitable judgments would be suspended, if we only duly remembered this. I am one of those who believe 'there is a soul of goodness in' many 'things apparently evil'; and, unless we *know* all, it is safer not to *judge* at all. I *do* delight to think well of human nature."

"Religion consists less in solemn phrases than in right doings. Our religious opinions are to a great extent conventional. The religion which has been preached from many a pulpit in this land is a religion which, as it were, goes in mid-air; never touches the solid earth, never deals with any practical problem of life, never aspires to give a man direction in the way in which he ought to walk."

"Religion is a much deeper thing than mere impressions upon the tympanum of the ear, or passing impressions upon the emotional element in our soul. Religion goes deeper down into the roots of our lives; and if it does not make us better and purer, more unselfish, gentler, more forbearing, more patient and humbler, though we may have a most exquisitely trained ear, and most exquisitely trained voice, and though we may take pleasure in listening to the sermons or anthems, still it is as the prophet complained when he said, 'I am to these people nothing more than the voice of a trained singer, for they hear my words, but they heed them not.'"

"One has need to be constantly on the watch, to be struggling against the devils of hypocrisy and formalism, lest one's life should be a great organized lie. Let me warn you against the 'dead level' of formalism, of self-satisfaction, of Pharisaism, and of mechanical worship. In speaking of a certain district, a Bishop once said to me, 'There is a deal of religion there, but not very much morality.'"

"As soon as men begin to multiply dogmas, they begin to fulminate anathemas."

"There are four things we must cling to: belief in God, belief in Christ, belief in a Holy Sanctifying Spirit, and belief in a world to come. These are enough to elevate humanity, and to make it, in some poor sense at least, worthy of its high destinies."

"Let me ask you not to multiply dogmas. It has been an unhappy thing for the Church that she has felt herself compelled to multiply dogmas in order to meet the assaults of heresy. One of the greatest theologians in the English Church, Bishop Jeremy Taylor, in his treatise on 'The Liberty of Prophesying,' said it was an evil day for the Church of Christ, when she felt herself compelled to add to the simplicity of the Apostles' Creed 'curious reticulations of faith.' The Church of Rome fortifies her strange modern dogmas with 'If any man believe not, let him be anathema,' and even the Church of England in one of her Creeds, has said of certain persons holding certain views that they were to be accursed. Men of narrow minds, and limited conception of truth, are always for anathematizing those who differ from them."

"St. Paul did not care much about men being like-minded in matters of opinion. It has been made a reproach to the Church of England that she includes men of such different opinions within her pale. It must be (men say) an organised hypocrisy—that Church of England—when we find High Church, Low Church, Broad Church and No Church, all claiming to be included in the National Church. Well, in the political world we find different parties, but they are all recognized as belonging to one great nation. We as Churchmen differ where we may lawfully differ, and where differences may be lawfully tolerated; but how grand are the fundamental verities of the Christian faith compared with the wretched jangle of words, and the miserable theological squabbles which divide the Church almost into hostile camps."

"The truth comes out all the purer and clearer from having passed through a little public discussion, when conducted in fair temper, and with a desire on each side to make the best of its case, without dealing in an unfair way with the case of its opponents. England has become what it is, because people have differed so long that they have agreed to differ. So long as they remain differing, yet still willing to credit each other with an equal amount of public spirit, still desiring to promote the common weal—so long as this spirit pervades the community, we may have our ecclesiastical differences, our political differences, and our municipal differences, without generating—what is always a great calamity in any society—social and personal animosities."

"The Christian life is a growth. 'Be ye perfect' said Christ, 'as your Father in heaven is perfect.' He spoke, as Jeremy Taylor tells us, not of perfection in degree, but in part or in kind, just as a babe has the rudimental perfection of a man. The growth must be perfectly natural. In the present day they are trying to make men grow by means of drugs. Some are trying to do it by a sort of belief in magic. People are being taught that they can only get to heaven through the priest, and absolution of the priest. This is the use of drugs instead of food. Drugs may be necessary here and there, in cases of severe or inveterate disease, but men of ordinary constitution do not want drugs, but the healthful exercise and wholesome diet of sound Christian doctrine."

"I attach great importance to Family Religion. I fear the sense of responsibility on the part of the heads of families has decreased. I am afraid there is a very large number of families in England, particularly in the working classes, who never have family prayer. We make a great profession of our Christianity, of our Protestantism, of our 'gospel light,' but we might sometimes spend a week in a man's house and not know he was a Christian at all.

"I have noticed the little children here in Church this morning, and listened to their singing, and observed that they sung their hymns with feeling, softening their voices at the proper time, and also raising them at the proper time. I also noticed their reverence. When they came to the name of Jesus they slowly and reverently bowed their heads. I like all these sort of things. I like to see children trained in habits of obedience and reverence."

Education.

"The qualitative ought to prevail over the quantitative principle in education."

"There is nothing so important as the imbuing of our young people with good principles; it is not so much mere knowledge they want, as the inward working of their consciences, in order that they may see things as they are, and realize the manifold dangers by which they are beset by reason of this evil world. Sometimes the very mention of evil suggests thoughts of evil, and that is a most perilous thing to do. If we imbue our young with Christian principles, with a love of that which is pure, lovely and of good report, and a hatred of that which is wrong, we may trust them with much more confidence than now to withstand the seductions of the world. It would indeed be contrary to all we should expect from the harmony of the human organism, if an attempt to interest the affections, discipline the will, enlighten the conscience, should be proved to hinder, instead of helping, the development of the intellect."

"I am afraid, that we, in England, in our zeal for 'denominational education,' lay too much stress upon the adjective, too little upon the substantive. But in the petulant talk that is sometimes heard about emancipating schools from clerical influence, as from some obstacle to the extension of national education, it seems to be forgotten, that to that influence, and that alone, the vast majority of these schools owe, not only their health, but their life."

"We shall never have in England education such as we ought to have, and such as would be in the highest sense a blessing to the nation, until parents rise to a higher conception of their duties to their children than they do now. I am not thinking merely of their duty to send their children punctually and regularly to school. That is a very obvious duty, and yet a duty constantly neglected. What I want to ask is: Are parents careful to see that the example they set their children at home is a Christian example, an example which will really help them to grow up in the knowledge and fear of the Lord, and in favour with God and man?

"The old heathens had very right notions about the way in which a child ought to be trained up. They had great belief in a pure domestic education. One of them said, 'Let nothing unclean ever enter into the house where a little child is,' no drunken man, no quarrelling father or mother, no bad language, no careless, slovenly habits; let nothing of the sort be seen in the house where dwells the little child. A Roman poet has said, 'The greatest possible reverence is due to a child.' Some parents are wonderfully careless about what sort of things they say before their children. They seem to forget that the little children are listening, and that their characters are being formed by ten thousand insensible influences that surround them day by day."

"I never was one of those who apprehended serious dangers to the future of morals and religion from the setting up of School Boards, or the prevalence of School Board schools. As long as the general temper of the country is in favour of morality and religion, the Boards and their schools will reflect this general temper. And though I would not advise that a single Church school should be given up which can be efficiently maintained—and I think we ought strenuously to endeavour to maintain them—yet, rather than see the Church waste her resources in an ineffectual struggle against a more powerful rival, if it ever comes to that, I would recommend that we should turn our energies in another direction, and do our best to sustain and extend that zeal for morality and religion in the nation, which, if it exists in the nation, is certain also in its measure to exist in the schools. Schemes, and well-considered schemes, for religious instruction are being more and more widely introduced into Board Schools, for many of which I am glad to know that the excellent scheme of the Manchester School Board has served as a model; and for the present, at any rate, I see no reason for being disquieted. We will not fret about the morrow. Never was the distinct teaching of the Church Day School more required than it is now. It is needed to keep up to any serviceable mark of Christian efficiency the biblical teaching of our Board Schools. I tremble not only for the Bible lesson, but for the charming and blessed children's hymns, and for the simple prayer. It is my conviction that if there were in this country only Board Schools all these precious specialities of our English schools, heirlooms bequeathed to us by the Christian educators of the past, whom, in spite of secularist cynicism and detraction, I will dare to pronounce among the purest and greatest benefactors the English nation has known, would presently be done away. The badge-word 'unsectarian,' would harden into 'secular'; all savour of Christian love and tenderness would pass away from the schools; and then, indeed, England would find that it had paid dear for its School Board secularism, and might look with vain envy on the Christian system of Scotland, or even the denominationalized 'National' system of Ireland. If Dr. Rigg is a true exponent of the mind of Methodism, the cause of religious education is likely to have more supporters in that great body than it is supposed there are."

"For it is for the cause of religious education and not for the cause of denominationalism, that my anxiety is aroused. If School Boards would accept a definite basis for the religious teaching of their schools—if, instead of simply putting a teacher in a school with a Bible in his hand, and telling him to interpret it at his own sweet will and pleasure—a process which would be likely to generate the intensest and most variable sectarianism—they would accept the programme which Canon Melville developed in an extremely able paper read before the Church Congress at Leeds, of religious teaching based upon the doctrines of the Apostles' Creed, enforcing the Ten Commandments, and including the Lord's Prayer, I should care very little what became of denominationalism. The existing theology of schools seldom goes beyond this—very often does not come up to it; and no sane man could wish to indoctrinate the minds of children under thirteen with the asperities of controversy, or the distinctive tenets of Anglicanism, or Popery, or Methodism, or Nonconformity in general. I am afraid that Roman Catholics would not accept this basis; and Jews and perhaps Unitarians, might claim the protection of a conscience clause; but all other religious bodies in England surely might agree to sink their differences and meet upon this common ground. Some such plan would not dissociate the elementary education of the future from Christianity; and as, even under the amended programme of the Education League, the school-houses are to be retained, outside the hours set apart for ordinary instruction, by the denominations with which they are connected; abundant opportunities might be found for building up the children of each religious body in the faith of that body, upon the solid foundation of elementary Christian truth thus previously laid. At any rate, as I have said before, whatever be the attitude of School Boards towards the Church, I should be sorry if the attitude of the Church towards School Boards should become an attitude of hostility. Still more should I regret if Churchmen tried to infuse into School Board elections the bitter ingredients of political or ecclesiastical strife. What is needed on School Boards is men of liberal, yet decided, religious ideas; men practically acquainted with the phenomena of education, men who seek a place there, not for the sake of notoriety or for an opportunity of airing their own crotchets, but because they desire to contribute something to the general good. Men who get upon School Boards, not so much to promote education as to represent parties, are not the men whom I desire to see there."

"I deprecate most earnestly the semblance of antagonism between the managers of Church Schools and School Boards; and, with equal earnestness, I entreat the clergy to give effect to their loud protestations in favour of religious education by themselves watching, with a tender and constant solicitude, over that most important element of their instruction given in the schools. To talk loudly upon platforms of the unspeakable importance of religious teaching, and then to delegate it wholly to the schoolmaster, whose interest in the matter is *pro tanto* diminished now that the amount of the Government grant is not affected by the condition of the school in this respect; or even, as often happens, to the pupil-teachers, who are far too young to be able to give this branch of instruction with befitting reverence and thoughtfulness, would be a hollowness of profession, combined with a dereliction of duty, of which, I am sure, we should all of us be deeply grieved to be suspected. It is an especial source of pleasure to me, whenever I hear of the younger clergy—those fullest of strength and energy—giving themselves systematically and earnestly to this most important, and, in the highest sense, remunerative work. I believe that no part of a clergyman's labours redounds more to his own inward satisfaction, and to his ministerial success, than that which he bestows upon his school. It was my own uninterrupted experience during the twenty-four years in which I had the cure of souls."

"It is sometimes thought there is nothing easier than to teach children the Bible and the way of salvation; but this idea is quite wrong, for the teacher's work is one which requires great thought and preparation. The Sunday School—although rightly attempting to meet the difficulty arising from parental ignorance—has created by its own energetic action another difficulty which is a very serious one. The very efficiency of our Sunday Schools has been a source of weakness. It is lessening the sense of parental obligation. I cannot conceive a worse condition of things for the spiritual health of a household than for the children to feel that on the Lord's Day—the greatest of all days in the week—they are handed from the care of their parents, who are their natural teachers and guides, to the artificial care and guidance of their Sunday School teachers. I am quite sure that the most earnest and experienced Sunday School teachers acknowledge that it is a feature which is to be regretted in the relation of the Sunday School to the family; for I think the teachers do not desire to take the place of the fathers and mothers of the children. I hope the day will come when, instead of the children being taken to the church in charge of the Sunday School teachers, and placed in a most inconvenient, remote, and inconspicuous part of the church to amuse themselves by their own little contrivances, the parents will take them to the church, and let them sit by their side, so that they will be under the guidance and care of their parents in the Lord's house on the Lord's Day. When I hear of the breaking up of Sunday Schools into classes, I think to myself they could put a little more life into the work if, instead of a class of six, they had a class of twenty-five, and, instead of having a languid teacher, they had some one full of life and energy, who could keep the attention of the class and keep the scholars 'alive.' At the same time I acknowledge that, but for the Sunday School, the glorious Christian religion might have died out in the land during the last hundred years. The Sunday School has been one of the great instruments which we have had for doing good, although it is human and therefore imperfect. The imperfection largely arises from the fact that, in our crowded towns, the better educated people live away from the smoke of the centre of the town, and do not take the part in Sunday School teaching which they took fifty years ago. I was gladdened to hear that of Preston a contrary tale may be told; and I hope that in all our great towns the work of Sunday School teaching may be earnestly taken up by the best educated of the people. In my opinion every Sunday School teacher ought to be a communicant, and he or she ought to be in the Church an example of a devout and reverent manner. Every Sunday School teacher, particularly every female, ought to be a pattern of neatness and tidiness in dress, and ought to be known by their class as persons of irreproachable Christian life, consistent in their conversation, not one thing in the school and another out of it, not teaching a class in the morning, as I have sometimes heard, and attending music-halls or concerts in the evening. All that sort of inconsistency you must feel at once to be utterly alien and contradictory to the profession which you follow; and I do most earnestly entreat you to remember that, in taking that office, you bind yourselves by a solemn responsibility to try and set to those children an example of what Christianity is in life and conversation. If you are not doing that, you are doing more harm than good in becoming teachers, because, I venture to say, if there is one thing more than another that gives a handle to atheists and infidels, it is the inconsistent lives of some professing Christians. If atheists see people going to church, and to the Lord's Table, and making religious professions, who they know are not living religious lives, they say, and not unjustly in such cases, religion is an unreality and a sham. Therefore, while I desire to encourage you, I would also warn you most solemnly not to undertake the duties if you do not feel that you are throwing your whole spiritual powers into them. It is a very solemn thing to train up a young child. I do not know what you thought of that boy of eleven years of age who was tried at the Manchester assizes for the bloody deed of manslaughter. Mr. Justice Chitty happened to be at my house on the evening of the day on which he tried the boy, and he was full of anxiety about his future, and said he did not know what was the proper punishment to give the boy. He sentenced him to a month's imprisonment, and then to five years in a reformatory, hoping in that time his character might be changed. But the matter that most agitated Mr. Justice Chitty was the air which that young criminal gave to himself in the court, where he seemed to consider himself a young hero who was to be admired for having done that terrible deed.

"Let teachers see that their whole conduct is saturated with religious feeling, religious tone, and religious principle."

"There is a vast deal of sickly cant and sentimentalism expended on the subject of corporal punishment in schools; of course, like all other instruments of education, it can only be properly wielded by a master of temper and firmness, and should in all cases be considered as a sort of *dernier ressort*; but, if I had a son of my own, I would rather send him to a school, such as I went to myself, where the birch was avowedly used, than to those improved seminaries of modern enlightenment, which nominally proscribe personal chastisement, but really employ more vindictive, more degrading, more hardening punishments."

"There is a little danger in this prize-giving system; it seems to be a new disease, a kind of fever. When I was a schoolboy, in 1834, the custom of giving prizes had not grown up, and I only got one prize at school in my life, and that was given to me during my last half-year at Shrewsbury. I was lucky enough somehow or other to get to be the second boy in the school, and there were only two prizes given, one to the head boy and the other to the second boy. The ambition to carry off a great many prizes is a very natural thing, only I want to warn you of one or two dangers. In the first place, the reward is too immediate. You exert yourselves, and the return comes in immediately. You must not expect that your success in life will come as promptly after your exertions as your prizes have done. Success in life is due mainly to plodding industry. Moral qualities are very much more valuable in securing success than even intellectual brilliancy. Steadiness, truthfulness, and conscientiousness—these are the qualities which not only command respect, but also success, in the best sense of the word."

"When I passed through Oxford University—between 1836 and 1839—there were only two first classes, viz., literæ humaniores, and physics and mathematics; and, certainly, when I remember the great Englishmen who came out of both Oxford and Cambridge, and who adorn and benefit the State in almost every department of public life, as statesmen, lawyers, clergymen, and the like, I do not feel sure that the modern extension of the University system, though no doubt it gives a larger and wider area for the development of particular talents, turns out better men. In olden times you heard a man say 'first class in classics and mathematics,' and it settled his intellectual position. Now, we have half-a-dozen different classes; but I am not so certain that knowledge is increased. You know the greatest of living poets said,—

'Knowledge comes, but wisdom lingers.'

No doubt, knowledge is coming to-day at a fearfully rapid pace, but I am not quite sure that wisdom is increasing in a corresponding ratio. I have no doubt there is an immense deal of talent in England, but the present system of education seems to be increasing desultory instead of concentrated talents; and I think that desultory talents are the most unprofitable endowments a man can possess. If a man will not confine himself to a more or less limited sphere, I do not think he is doing the best for himself or for others in the station in which he is placed; and I do not think he will ever do anything for humanity. Speaking before a number of persons who are parents, I think what I say may carry a little weight with it, when I tell you that is not my opinion only, but the opinion of every competent schoolmaster with whom I have discussed the subject. I am quite certain that in our schools, up to a certain age, the important thing is not how many things a child learns, but how well and how thoroughly each learns what he is set to learn. I know that the modern doctrine of commerce is that quick returns make the greatest profit; but it is not so in the discipline of the intellect. Many of our greatest geniuses have been men in whom, up to a certain period of their lives, there had been no genius discovered at all; and it was only by their going on, in a systematical method, that, at last, their genius seemed to flash out and to illuminate the whole world.

"Journeying to London with a Manchester man, we chartered a cab at the London terminus. I always take note of the number of the cab in which I ride, and I said, audibly, 'Seven thousand and fifty.' My companion said, 'Is that how you read those figures?' I replied, 'Yes; how do you read them?' 'Oh,' he said, 'we should call them seventy-fifty in Manchester.' You will see at once which is the quicker method, and so it seems to be in other things. If a man is not rapid, he is thought nothing of in the commercial world—that is the general tendency. Well, but there is a very good proverb, which, translated from the Latin, runs, 'Make no more haste than good speed;' and I am a little afraid that this intellectual rapidity suggests a good deal of looseness of thought—a good deal of carelessness of action, and I do not think it is by any means a satisfactory test of intellectual achievements. Pope says,—

> "'A little knowledge is a dangerous thing,
> Drink deep or taste not the Pierian spring.'

It is not a little knowledge which is in itself dangerous; no knowledge is dangerous as such—it only becomes dangerous when the little bit is magnified into a great deal, and when the possessor trades upon the ignorance of others, and upon the presumption that he himself possesses knowledge."

"It seems to me that the young men of to-day expect to start in life about the point where their fathers leave off; they expect to have their hunters and moors, and drink champagne, I do not know how many days in the week; to smoke cigars at fabulous prices, and to employ the most fashionable tailors. I do not see that these things contribute to the greatness and stability of the nation. If parents desire to see their children grow up useful and worthy members of the great compact English society, and to make them worthy of their country, they must train them up in habits of honesty and simplicity, perseverance and thoroughness. This is the moral aspect of education; and education is useless if it is not moral."

"No one is more glad than I to see any man rise by his own honest and laborious efforts in the social scale, because I, myself, have risen to my present position through having made good use of my opportunities in youth. And I will say, what I am never tired of saying, and that is, that if men would only use the opportunities that are so freely placed within their reach for the cultivation of the faculties that God has given them, there is no reasonable height of promotion or social advancement which men may not hope to reach in this free country of ours.

"I was much struck, as I visited a National School this afternoon, to see in one class a little girl, who, I was informed, was the daughter of a man who died worth £100,000, which he had made by honest industry; and whose feeling was, 'I will have my children educated on the same level as the children of my neighbours.' Well, there was that girl making her first essays in learning on the same bench with the children of the village; and Mr. Huth mentioned to me that, when he went to school, he sat between the son of the Prime Minister of Nassau, and the son of the man who mended his (Mr. Huth's) shoes. We have not got to that state of things, but we are fast approaching it. I am afraid that with this great advance of learning there will come the same sort of feeling which was prevalent about fifteen years ago in the United States of America, namely, that manual labour is a degradation, and that working with the hands is more or less a disgrace to every man—a feeling which results in the production of so many labour-saving machines. At one time the negro was the man who did the dirty and hard work; now they are getting Chinamen to do it. Mr. Gladstone said, about two years ago, that the time was coming when brain-power would be of less value than hand-power. I hope sincerely that this advance in education is not going to indispose Englishmen for the honest, even laborious, work, which God in His providence may place before them."

"I am terribly *arrière* in some of my ideas upon education, and I am continually getting into 'scrapes' with the softer and sweeter sex. I am always saying something which is not palatable to them. I am extremely anxious that women should be able to develop to the very utmost whatever powers God has blessed them with; but I distinctly recognize that men and women have different duties to discharge in life. I am not one of those who think that men and women are to be handicapped in the great race of life, and I do not think that we should encourage some of the distempered ambitions of some women. I have a distinct opinion as to what is a woman's proper place, and I have a distinct opinion as to what is a man's proper place; and I think they are happiest, and best, and most useful, so long as each discharges the proper duties of his or her station; and I cannot but say that I am not particularly anxious to see young girls come up to receive prizes on platforms whether from a bishop or an earl."

Preaching.

"Some people follow after eloquence. I do not believe much myself in eloquent preaching. I have heard what are called eloquent sermons, and they have passed through my mind without having the slightest effect upon me. I have heard beautifully rounded periods, exquisite rhetorical declamation, well-chosen tropes and metaphors, carefully set passages of poetry—all this I have heard; and I have listened to elaborate disquisitions upon some points of theology—very trenchant logic; very loud denunciations; I have heard all these things, but they have not touched my heart. Have we not felt the simplest utterances of an earnest man, whom we can respect for his life and work's sake, go into our heart and soul with greater force? If so, we have felt what is meant by the kingdom of God being not in *word*, but in *power*.

"The preaching of the Word of God is not meant to tickle the ear, or please the fancy, or to invite complimentary criticism. In these days those who preach have a great many temptations to think far more of themselves than of the message they have to convey. They like to see their sermons—well, I can honestly say I do not like to see my own—get into the newspapers and be circulated through society; and they think that that makes a reputation, and brings them under the bishop's eye, and that, if they have the reputation of being eloquent preachers, they will get preferments, and so forth. All these thoughts and motives, no doubt, are natural, but they are dangerous. The question for us to consider is, not whether people think we are eloquent, but whether people believe we are in earnest, and whether people can look up to us as examples of Christian life."

"After preaching last Sunday in a country church, I dined with a parishioner, whose wife, a charming lady, said to me, 'I sat under you rather nervously this morning, for I remember how you attacked us two years ago for our expensive bonnets and silk dresses. I have laid what you said to heart. I have not had a new bonnet this winter, and the dress I wear is two years old.' 'I am glad,' I replied, 'my words had such an effect. Your dress seems able to carry you through the winter, and you will have money to spare for other purposes.'"

Curates and Clerical Incomes.

"There are, no doubt, enormous difficulties just now in the way of making an adequate provision for the spiritual needs of our growing population, and I, as Bishop, know only too well the straits to which the clergy are often reduced in providing their parishes with assistant curates. The result of this is that a very large number of persons press into the Church with hopes which, I am afraid, often prove illusory—persons with small means, and sometimes with no marked qualifications for the work they wish to do. Sometimes they come in at a late period of life, when the first energy of youth has passed away, and I am bound to say that such persons do not, on the average, make very successful clergymen; but bishops find the greatest possible difficulty in refusing them, because they are pressed upon them so strongly by incumbents. I have laid down a rule in my diocese to decline to accept any candidate for Holy Orders who has passed thirty-five years of age, believing that, in so doing, I am preventing bitter disappointment. I have adopted another rule, and have acted upon it uniformly up to the present time, and that is, that whatever preferment falls in my way I will distribute among my own clergy, and I will never go out of my diocese if I can find there a suitable man for a vacant post. Still, I am bound to say that it is a most difficult thing to find suitable men for difficult posts. I have 250 curates at work in my diocese, but, if I had a difficult post to fill, I would have to reduce that number very considerably before I could put my hand on the proper man. I think you will rarely find a curate of fifteen years' standing who has the qualifications that really make a successful clergyman. I must beg leave to call the attention of the clergy also to this simple fact, that the clergy exist for the parish and not the parish for the clergy; and I feel bound, in the exercise of my episcopal responsibilities, not to put a man into any parish because he is poor, because he is married, or because he has a large family, unless I feel that that man will do his duty to the parish. I think, without getting to anything like a general system of equality in these matters, that some redistribution of incomes will become imperatively necessary, and, if it is thought that the bishops should come under the operation of the movement, I will have nothing whatever to say against it."

Marriage.

"Two young people are married and have a family. I would ask to what extent have those young persons, either before or after marriage, realized the responsibility in which they stand to their children? Did the young man, when he fell in love with the young woman, do so because he thought she would make him a faithful and loving wife, and be a careful and diligent mistress of his household, and a wise and firm mother of his children? Or was he caught by a pretty face, or a fashionable style of dress, or some of those utterly worthless attractions, which do not last sometimes through the honeymoon, and which make him find out, when too late to rectify the mistake, that he has married some worthless, heartless, silly thing, who has got no idea of the duties of life, and has never been instructed how to discharge them. And I would say to the young women, when they say 'yes' to the young man who courts them, 'What do they look at?' Do they consider whether that young man will make them a happy home for the rest of their lives, whether he will be staid, sober, industrious, and loving? Do they consider whether he is an exemplary fellow, or one with a tendency to intemperance, known to be a jovial companion, a frequenter of free-and-easies? I think that the young woman who marries a sot, a drunkard, or a spendthrift, must, if she has wisdom at all, see the consequences; must see the misery she is laying up for herself, a future full of sadness and sorrow. What can we expect from improvident marriages? Girls often do not inquire what sort of man they are keeping company with—whether he is drunken or sober—before they consent to become his wife? If he was in the habit of spending his time in dancing-saloons and such amusements, and took her with him when he was courting her, then she was encouraging such habits; and what right has she to expect that he will make a good husband or a good father? Girls should look a little further forward, and know what a man's character is before they take him for better or worse."

"Modern science has apparently come to the conclusion that there is a great deal more in the principle of heredity than it was formerly willing to allow. It is said that intemperate parents transmit to their children the tendency towards intemperance, and it seems to be getting generally realized that the principle of heredity, in the transmission of disease, ought to be most emphatically impressed on people's minds. I am afraid that a great many marriages are entered into very lightly which never ought to take place; for medical men will tell you that, where there is a constitutional tendency towards consumption or insanity, there nature herself seems to put a barrier, and to say that such marriages ought not to take place. If there is to be an utter neglect of manifest sanitary laws, we must expect to have growing up amongst us an unhealthy progeny; and I, therefore, think that parents ought to be strictly on their guard to prevent attachments springing up between young persons who are unsuitable in the respect I have indicated."

COOKERY.

"For my own part, though I hope I can appreciate a well-cooked dinner, my tastes are of the simplest kind. I hope it will not be thought that because we are paying a little more attention to cookery that we are pandering to epicurean tastes, which would launch people out into further extravagance. On the contrary, I cannot help hoping that cookery instruction will have a strong tendency to diminish what I do feel is the very extravagant outlay which, in many households, is lavished upon things about the kitchen. I trust progress will be made against those foolish opinions which, I think, have taken possession of a great many people's minds, that the way to treat their friends hospitably is to incur expense for their entertainment which the entertainer cannot afford, and which, perhaps, obliges the postponement of the tradesman's bills, when such payment is urgently required. It is, I think, absurd, and it seems to me vulgar, to measure hospitality by what it costs. I cannot help thinking that a school of cookery will in time imbue people's minds, and especially the minds of young housekeepers—and young ladies who will be housekeepers in the future—in such a manner that a more rational and, in all respects, a more agreeable state of things may prevail amongst us. I do not think that a *menu* of twelve dishes adds in the slightest degree to the real pleasure with which we enjoy a dinner. I do not myself profess to be superior to the pleasures of the appetite, as it is a part of one's nature, for which therefore one is hardly responsible; but the pleasures of the entertainment do not depend so much upon what is provided as upon the company one happens to fall amongst. I believe that a good deal of happiness and comfort depend upon the culinary art, and that a little attention bestowed upon what is not an unimportant department of human life might tend to sweeten, in some of its elements, domestic relations, and make husbands and wives, fathers and daughters, live in rather more pleasant circumstances."

Church Choirs and Music.

"It must be remembered that frequent and familiar intercourse in Divine things does not necessarily produce a devout or spiritual tone of mind. No!—the religious service runs into special danger of becoming a mechanical service, and every one who is at all familiar with our cathedral services knows of this peril. I ask you, therefore, as members of church choirs, to try and do everything to the glory of God, realizing His presence and endeavouring to do your very best because you are doing it for Him. I find there is a habit in my diocese, and I hope also in other dioceses, of gathering the choir in the vestry for one moment in reverent prayer before they take their places in the church. This habit seems to be adopted for the simple purpose of helping choirs to realize that they are going out into the direct presence of God. At the same time I have seen even this done in a mechanical rather than a devotional manner, and it is one of those things which require carefully watching over lest it should degenerate into a mere spiritual form. Then, again, if I may say so to the choirs, do have your music ready before you take your place in church. Nothing is so distracting as to see, while the first or second lesson is being read, the choir getting something ready, not listening to the Word of God as it is read, but thinking infinitely more about the singing. And one sometimes sees little boys during the service going from one side of the church to the other—to the leader or some one in connection with the performance. I use that word, for under the circumstances it is a performance rather than an act of service. Do, therefore, have your music ready, that everybody may listen to the Word of God, instead of making yourself anxious as to the next part you have to take in the musical service. I am quite sure it is not so easy to realize the presence of God in the sense that I believe David realized it when he wrote—if he did write it—the 150th Psalm, when he calls upon us to praise God in the Highest, to praise Him for His noble acts, to praise Him according to His excellent greatness, to praise Him upon the lute and harp. Then, again, let me ask the choir to think upon the influence they exercise upon the congregation, and to remember that the solemnity, the seriousness and devoutness with which they do their part, spreads over the congregation and makes it realize that it, too, is engaged in an act of worship. A choir placed in the chancel, and vested in surplices, may, if without reverent and devout conduct, have the worst of influences upon the tone of the people with whom they are worshipping. Therefore I say to you, you are bound to be demure and serious in your looks not giving way to any whispering or fidgeting. You are bound to do your part in solemnizing and spreading a true devout spirit through the congregation in which you minister. I know there are some churches where the congregation come to listen to the music (I have one such in my mind, where they sit while the anthem is sung), and, except that it is Sunday instead of weekday, there is nothing to distinguish it from a concert in the Albert Hall, or an opera in one of Her Majesty's theatres. As you know, it was an old sarcasm that in these churches it is 'Let us sing to the praise and glory of the choir,' rather than to the praise and glory of God. Do not attempt in your parish churches, particularly in small churches—for a small parish cannot be very musical—do not attempt more than your resources amply justify you in attempting. It seems to me to be the very height of absurdity to try and imitate the ritual of a great cathedral in a humble parish church. For instance, I venture to say that I think anthems are hardly ever edifying to ordinary rural, or even ordinary urban, congregations."

Hymns and Tunes.

"It is highly important that good taste should be exercised in the choice of hymns. I do not know whether any of you had the opportunity of attending any of the services of the American Evangelists, so called—I mean Messrs. Moody and Sankey. Well, the harmony between the hymns that were chosen and the address that Mr. Moody was delivering was among the most telling parts of the service. Was Mr. Moody speaking of the grace of Christian courage, he would say to his partner, 'Mr. Sankey, let us sing "Hold the Fort:"' or of the way in which the Holy Spirit is bestowed upon those who seek it, 'Lord, I hear of showers of blessing, Thou art scattering full and free;' or of the unsearchable riches of Christ's love and His redemptive power, "Safe in the Fold."' And in this there was a harmony which people felt and realized, and they passed from address to hymn, and from hymn to address, without being conscious of those jars and concussions which we feel when our services are imperfectly adjusted. And then, again, there is a strong unreality of language in many of our hymns. In many of the most popular there is an extravagance of language far surpassing the rhetoric of Chrysostom or Basil. One commences, 'There is a fountain filled with blood:' as though it were the chemical fluid of the Redeemer's veins which washed away sin. There is in others language, touching Christ's presence in the Sacrament, which goes even beyond the transubstantiation doctrine. A little time ago, at a children's service, the little ones were singing of heaven in these words: 'There is a garden blooming fairer than orchards bloom in May,' and those children would probably run away with the idea that heaven was filled with apple-trees, blooming as they do in the orchards of Shropshire and Staffordshire in the month of May. I cannot think that such words as these can help people to realize the character of God, or of the kingdom which is 'righteousness, and peace, and joy in the Holy Ghost.' We must not think that an elaborate service is in itself and by itself an acceptable offering to God; all depends on the temper in which it is rendered. And, remember, God is not dealing with us as a congregation. He has not accepted, and He is not expected to accept, and He never does accept, worship in the mass. He knows every heart, and hears the voice of every heart. He only accepts as much as is sincere, and He rejects, however true in time, however carefully modulated in expression, everything that is false or unsubstantial. Oh, those are words worth pondering over which Keble wrote for Palm Sunday—

> "'Lord, by every minstrel tongue
> Be Thy praise so duly sung,
> That Thine angels' harps may ne'er
> Fail to find fit echoing here;
> We, the while, of meaner birth,
> Who in that divinest spell
> Dare not hope to join on earth,
> Give us grace to listen well.
>
> "'Then waken into sound Divine
> The very pavement of Thy shrine,
> Till we, like heaven's star-sprinkled floor,
> Faintly give back what we adore;
> Childlike though the voices be,
> And untuneable the parts,
> Thou wilt own the minstrelsy
> If it flow from childlike hearts.'"

"I consider that many of our hymns are very foolish, and give people materialistic ideas, and such hymns should be studiously avoided. Another class of hymns is full of spurious sentiment. They describe us as being wretched here, and as anxious to get out of the world as fast as we can, whereas I do not suppose there is a single person in this congregation who wants to get out of the world. All such hymns are false and spurious, and can do nobody any good who sings them; and, if it is something we do not believe and cannot throw our hearts into, then we had better not sing it. It has been said, 'Let me but make the ballads of a people, and I care not who makes its laws,' and on the same principle I might say, 'Let others make the Church's creeds if I may make its hymns.' I find many erroneous conceptions and beliefs flying about in the world, which I think are distinctly traceable to the false teaching of hymns. Men do not rectify their ideas by the Word of God, but allow them to enter into their ears through some melodious tune. In this way they have got many spurious ideas. It is quite easy to push the music of the church too far. I have heard of a church in London to which people go for two reasons—for the preaching, which is said to be eccentric and clever, and has a tendency to startle rather than edify; and for the music, which is of a highly cultivated kind, but not at all devotional. I have also been told that the congregation sit during the anthem, and that their behaviour is most irreverent.

"I think a great deal more attention should be given to the choice of tunes, and we ought to select the tunes which best suit the words. What we want is to infuse a little more earnest feeling into our singing; we do not want our choirs to think only of showing how much voice they have got. I wish all choirs to remember that they are discharging in every sense a ministry of the Church of Christ, not a ministry of sacraments, but a ministry of song; and it is because I regard it as a ministry that I think the clothing of choirs in surplices is a right thing. It seems to impress upon them that they have a ministry to discharge, and any one who pretends to have a ministry in God's house, in whatever capacity, should remember that he is undertaking a solemn and responsible office, and that all his ordinary conduct ought to be in harmony with that office. It is a disgrace to any chorister, or anybody else who holds any office in the Church of Christ, to be guilty of drunkenness or any other act of immorality. I often wish that choirs would take pains to get their music ready before the time of service. I have noticed, and I think it is the result of carelessness more than anything else, that while the lessons are being read the members of the choir are bustling and getting ready for the chants, and while they are so engaged it is impossible that their thoughts can be going up to God."

Country Parsons.

"There is a very special blessedness in being a country parson, and indeed some of the greatest men in the Church of England chose that mode of life for themselves. Richard Hooker, who wrote the great treatise on 'Ecclesiastical Polity,' and other standard books on divinity, lived, at his own desire, in a quiet country village in Wiltshire. Then, again, three miles from Salisbury, at Bemerton, their dwelt the sainted George Herbert, who wrote a famous book called 'The Country Parson.' In our own times one of the most beautiful books of Christian teaching is John Keble's 'Christian Year.' He was a country parson, and a fellow of the same college to which I belonged in Oxford. He retired to a country village in Hampshire, not far from Winchester, where he ministered among simple country folk, not only by his preaching, but by the example of his Christian life. The great blessedness of being a country parson I remember well. I have had two country parishes myself. In the first there were but 190 people, and in the second 360; and when, in the providence of God, I was called to take the oversight of this great diocese, it was a great change. I was hardly prepared for it; but, though I have received nothing but kindness and help, my heart often turns to that smaller, and I trust hardly less useful, sphere when I was simply a country parson. The great blessedness of being a country parson is that one knows one's people, and is known to all. What is done by organization in large towns is effected by personal influences in country parishes, and direct contact in this manner is a great evangelizing power. There are difficulties, however, in a country parish which I ought not to pass by. There are often strong prejudices which have to be overcome. I think people are quite right in sticking to old ways, particularly if they happen to be good ones, and they have a right to require of any one who proposes a change that it shall be shown that the new thing is better than the old; but, at the same time, I know that country parishes are the home sometimes of prejudices that are not good, and of old ways that are not commendable, and sometimes the stirring breath of public opinion might do a great deal of good, might produce a great improvement. As one passes through the sweet parts of England and looks upon the beauties of nature, one naturally thinks that those who live there ought to be as pure and innocent as the things by which they are surrounded. One sometimes thinks that the devil never ought to get into these country parishes with his temptations and subleties; yet you must remember that the devil got into the Garden of Eden, and you know the disastrous consequence of his getting there. There is just as much need to guard against the devil in country parishes as in Preston, Wigan, or Manchester."

High Art.

"There is a great deal of nonsense talked about art nowadays. I have got perfectly sick of the rubbish that is talked about 'high art,' about 'æstheticism,' about things being 'too utter' and 'too too.' What rubbish! What stuff! That which comes before us in the name of art seems to me to be sometimes of a most corrupting and most demoralizing kind, and I beg leave as a Christian man as well as a Christian Bishop to protest against the desecration of art in this manner. I only hope that a manly and pure taste will be found to prevail yet among the masses of the people of England. In fact, I have found it to be so. In the summer I spent a fortnight in London, and refreshed myself now and then by going to see some pictures. I went one day with my wife to the National Gallery between the hours of twelve and two, and saw a considerable number of working people looking at the pictures there displayed. I noticed that they were almost always attracted by those pictures which to my uneducated mind have the most real merit, and are the most truly beautiful and most instructive; pictures of simple scenes, pictures by Reynolds, Gainsborough, Landseer—landscapes—pictures of homely, natural life and beauty. These seemed to be the pictures that attracted them, and I think it was a good deal better and purer taste than that exhibited by some of those connoisseurs whom I saw, in their dilettante way, criticising the pictures in Burlington House. So, again, if I take the stage, another department of art, I believe that corrupting dramas are those which often find most favour with what are called cultivated audiences, and that the masses of the people are much better satisfied with good homely dramas, such as 'Black-Eyed Susan,' which I remember to have seen when a boy, and which brought tears to my eyes. Those plays are the best which appeal to the best and most natural sentiments, and, from what I read in the newspapers, I conclude that that is the kind of play which is best liked by the working classes. I am not going to advocate the stage, nor even to defend it in its present condition. All I desire to say is, that in our pursuit of art we ought to try and follow what is really good, true, and pure, and not be led aside into an ignorant admiration of very questionable things, because we are told by gentlemen and ladies who pretend to be art connoisseurs that these are beautiful things, and we ought to admire them. I wish people would follow their own natural and simple tastes; and I cannot help believing that there is something very good in human nature, something that will not, if a man will only follow his natural and best instincts, allow him to gravitate downwards."

SUNDAY OPENING OF MUSEUMS.

"We, in the 19th century, have been a good deal imposed upon by that fine-sounding, but false, assertion of Burke's, that 'vice loses half its evil by losing all its grossness!' I do not know that evil is less evil by being wrapped up in a cloak and having its features hidden by a masque. We do not become more pure because we have become more prudish. There is a difference as wide as the poles between squeamishness and modesty. 'To the pure,' says Paul, 'all things are pure.'"

"I am one of those who have not lost their faith in human nature; and it is my belief that, under the combined, or at least the coincident, operation of many beneficent influences, the 'residuum' is steadily decreasing both in power and numbers. When our school system has developed itself into fuller adequacy to meet the wants of our population; when our various sanitary efforts have been crowned with more success than has attended them hitherto; when the people are better educated and better housed, I cannot but hope that the 'residuum' will visibly diminish. For it is not natural to a man to live a brutalized life; he was created with, and he has an instinct for, higher things; and it was not so much from natural predisposition as owing to the unhappy circumstances which surrounded great masses of our people in their younger days, when their character was receiving its bent and dominant impressions, that they found it so difficult to break away from old and familiar, and, I am afraid I must add, vicious associations. Still the fact that 30,000 people—for that was the estimated number—have been within the walls of this exhibition during the last thirty days, looking around, enjoying, and it could hardly be otherwise than impressed by, what they saw, is to my mind a fact full of hope and encouragement. The committee, I learn from the report, opened their exhibition on Sunday afternoons. This is a somewhat perilous subject for a Bishop to discuss in a mixed assembly of this kind; but, having alluded to it, I will venture to add that I am glad that the hours were so chosen as not to interfere with the usual hours of Divine worship. Some excellent people would regard even that as a desecration of the Lord's Day; but I hope they will not put me down 'as a heathen man or a publican' because I am not entirely of their opinion. Only two hours ago, I had a letter from a gentleman who described what he had seen, and who told me that if I had seen what he saw last Sunday afternoon in a large suburban parish not five miles away—the drunkenness, the profaneness, the grossness of conduct and language which marked the celebration of the local 'wake'— I should have wept at the sight of such things being done in a nominally Christian land. And when I know that such things are taking place, whether I can go the whole length with them or not, I must honestly say that I am not disposed, nor do I feel myself called upon by a sense of public duty, to launch any very vigorous protest against those who are attempting to provide—even on the Lord's Day, at suitable times—something that is purer and worthier, even if it does not succeed in lifting men's thoughts much above the world in which they live. People are not made saints, necessarily, by listening to sermons or singing songs about heaven. I would rather see men trying to do their duty and please God in that station of life, and in those relations of life, in which God's Providence has seen fit to place them. I cannot help thinking that many good people judge of these things too much from what I must call an unreal, or sentimental, point of view. We must look at facts as we find them; and instead of denouncing what we do not like, and doing nothing ourselves, let us be thankful for every effort which appears to contribute in any degree to that great march of progress—moral, intellectual, spiritual, individual, social, national—which I believe to be in accordance with the highest will, so far as we are permitted to know it, of the great Being Whom we profess to serve. I hope, in saying this, I shall not be misunderstood. I have never been able formally and publicly to advocate the Sunday opening of museums, art galleries, and the like; because I have always been perhaps too sensible of the perils of the experiment, and I have never seen how these perils are proposed to be safeguarded. High as are the claims and pretensions of art, it has not in itself, and necessarily, any moralizing or spiritualizing tendency. At the same time, I am not here to condemn what has been done in this direction by the promoters of this exhibition. On the contrary, I believe their motive is right; and so far as the motive is right I rejoice in its success."

FUNERAL REFORM: CREMATION.

"I do not know any customs more urgently needing reform, and reform of a practical kind, than the customs that have gathered round funerals in this country. I am not prepared to accept entirely the whole of the suggestions put forward—as, for instance, the abolition of mourning stationery or cards, which are at times a convenience; but with regard to scarfs, hatbands, and trappings of that kind, they cannot be abandoned a moment too soon. I am afraid that one gets into trouble sometimes with tradesmen, who are connected with the business of undertaking funerals, by advocating these reforms. I do not think, myself, that any advantage, in the long run, accrues to any class of tradesmen, by the community indulging in expenses which they really cannot afford to pay for. In a great many families the cost of a funeral is a very serious item just at the particular crisis at which it occurs. I do not believe it tells nearly so much upon the working classes as upon classes above them. Working men generally are in burial clubs. But there are other classes which do not belong to burial clubs. It is not considered 'the thing,' among many of these, to belong to such societies, and they have to pay the expense out of their own resources. Then there is the feasting, which very often is carried rather beyond the limits of moderation. I look at the drivers of hearses and mourning-coaches, and I cannot help fancying sometimes, that some of these extravagant habits at funerals have found their way into these men's faces. I do not say, of course, that these men are drunken; but they are exposed to peculiar temptations, which it is very difficult to resist under such circumstances. This eating and drinking at funerals is simply a gross violation, not merely of taste, but of all right feeling. If there is real sorrow in a house, when perhaps the head of the family, or the mother of the children, has been taken away, that is not the time for a crowd of people to go in and sit drinking whisky and water till all is blue. It is bad feeling, and to people of right sense the thing has only to be mentioned to be condemned.

"There is another thing that I might mention, and that is the absurdly extravagant sums that are spent upon monuments. I saw a monument the other day that cost £5000, and a more hideous thing it was impossible for eyes to look upon. I notice that Lancashire people like headstones to be three times the size of those in the south of England. When people spend £50, or £60, or £100 upon a monument, which may be only a monument of the bad taste of the designer; and still more when the epitaph records virtues and merits which those who lived with the deceased could never discover, I think they are going rather beyond the line. In these matters, we have to emancipate ourselves from the tyranny of custom and fashion. All we want is a little more independence and resolution to develop that latent opinion, which, when it becomes manifest, and takes possession of a large body, is perhaps the most irresistible force in modern times.

"I could not help noticing, as I came into church, the care which has been taken in the churchyard to decorate the graves of the lost loved ones; and I venture to hope the custom of doing up the graves of those you have loved, and placing your tribute of flowers upon them, will not die out; or be regarded as a foolish and extravagant expenditure of Christian love and affection. These flowers ought to teach us a lesson. They ought to teach us the lesson of Christian love. The flowers have bloomed in this neighbourhood under those gentle influences, rain, sunshine, and breezes, which are given by God, and all these influences should teach us lessons. The pure and fragrant flowers teach us that our lives are to be like them, pure and fragrant. It is not well to go and lay these tributes of tender affection on the graves of our loved ones, unless we know at the same time that the lives we are leading are not bringing any discredit upon the memory of those who brought us up, and left us with the last charge to follow the Lord Jesus Christ and to be true to Him."

"Strange things have come into men's minds with regard to what we ought to do with our dead, and that, instead of burying them, we ought to have them cremated. For my own part, I do not see that cremation interferes with the resurrection doctrine. My body will somehow crumble to dust, and it is enough for me to know that my personal identity, throughout eternal ages, rests with my Maker."

Address to Volunteers.

"What are the ideas that are associated with the British soldier? They are those of courage, loyalty, patience, steadfastness, comradeship, discipline, and organization—indeed, the idea of Christ's Church militant. You are none the less soldiers because you are volunteers, and are bound to exhibit all true soldierly qualities; bound to be brave and observe discipline; bound to remember the rules of comradeship. You know the difference between organization and disorder. I cannot but believe that the volunteer movement, which started into life twenty-one years ago, has done much, socially and morally, for England. It is not merely that the 250,000 men who have gathered round the volunteer standard are so much added to the military resources of the country, but, if they are true to their calling, they are so much added to the moral resources of the country. I believe a man becomes a better man if he goes through the discipline that makes him a good soldier. In all large bodies of men there are rogues and scamps, but I believe that in every well-conducted regiment there is a high feeling of honour, as well as of courage, which maintains what the French call *esprit de corps*, and which we might call the tone and quality of the regiment. The motto of the volunteer movement is 'Defence, not defiance.' If that motto were always remembered in England, and if it were always acted upon between nations, then would wars almost cease throughout the world. There are only two just apologies for any war. First, either it must be a war of self-defence; or, secondly, it must be a war undertaken to prevent, not a remote, possible, indefinite, imaginary danger, but an actual, present, or imminent danger. In illustration I will take two instances from our own history, but not from any recent period of it, for fear I might be said to be stimulating the political passions of the day. But, going back to the days of Queen Bess, there was the war against the Spanish Armada, which was one of self-defence. And there was the assistance sent out to the oppressed Protestants in the Low countries, who, under Alva and the Inquisition, were suffering intolerable tyranny, both of body and mind. If ever there was a just cause for which a nation might unsheath the sword and help another nation, it was the cause that shed the blood of Philip Sidney upon the field of Zutphen. If all the wars in which this country has engaged had been as pure in intention as these, her annals would have been, to my mind, far more glorious than they are.

"Just now I think most of discipline, which is the first quality needed in a soldier; for the whole of English society needs at present a little discipline to make it orderly and sound. There are great chasms in it; immense and manifold disorganizations everywhere. We want greater national unity amongst us, founded upon the high idea of patriotism. Who amongst you, if called upon to fight for his country, would think for a moment whether the man next to him, or his officer, was a Churchman, a Nonconformist, a Liberal, a Conservative? You would know there were higher interests than the interests of ecclesiastical party, and far higher interests than those of politics.

"When a man goes into active service, he must leave the comforts of life behind him, and endure hardness. I think we, as a people, must be prepared to endure a little more than we have been used to. We are living too easy, too luxurious, too selfish lives. It was said that Hannibal's soldiery, whom the Romans dared not meet, were enervated and demoralized by their winter quarters in Capua; and in our English towns many a regiment has been spoiled by its winter and summer quarters. Our tight little island is said to be impregnable, and our navy is said to be always able to keep off the foe by the help of the streak of silver sea. Our resources are also said to be illimitable, and our wealth unbounded; but we must bear in mind that it is 'righteousness that strengthens the nation,' and it is the spirit of the people that maintains the institutions and principles of the people. Do not imagine that because men have a fear of God before their eyes that they make either worse soldiers or worse citizens. Cromwell's Ironsides, although they said prayers, were not in the habit of running away on the field of battle. Havelock was no coward; Hedley Vicars sprang up at his post in the breaches before Sebastopol, and died with his men, doing his duty. It is an altogether false and ignoble conception of Christianity that represents it as only fit to guide the lives of silly women and children. He must be something better than a milksop who can keep himself temperate amongst the intemperate, pure amongst the licentious, able to master himself where others give a free rein to selfish desires. The man who would carry the banner of Christ amid the scoffs and sneers of the world, must be as brave as he who bore the colours of the guards up the slopes of Alma, and died when the summit of the hill was won. The soldier of Christ cannot be a coward."

Seeing Life.

"I am like the Psalmist, who said of himself, 'I once was young, but now am old.' But I do not feel myself old in character, or nature, or feelings even yet. I have a very lively recollection of my younger days, my school and college days, the life that I was leading between fifteen and five-and-twenty; and I hope I am, and always shall be, in very vivid sympathy with those who are exposed to the temptations, and need the safeguards, of youth. 'Seeing life' is a somewhat dangerous experiment, and it is a very misleading phrase. It merely means seeing the low side of life, the vicious side of life, and perhaps losing sight altogether of those qualities that make life really noble, and, in the highest sense of the word, worth living for at all."

The Safeguards of Youth.

"It is not always safe for young men, with an over-presumptuous confidence in their courage, to meet the devil face to face; you had better turn out of the way if you can, and find some angel of God unawares, who will lead you past the devil's lair. If you can get your minds and bodies possessed with worthy aims and healthy exercise, I think you will have a very great safeguard to keep you from evil. I would just touch upon another safeguard which I think is very potent; at least, I am sure it was with me, and I think it will be with any one whose heart is unsophisticated, and that is the gentle influence radiating from home. We may be far away from father, mother, brother, and sisters; but, after all, theirs are the tenderest images that we can ever conjure up in our fancies, and we should not do anything that would pain father, break mother's heart, or bring the blush upon sisters' cheeks. I would have you remember in your intercourse with young women never to say anything to them, or suggest anything to them, that you would be grieved for your sister to hear. And, then, do be careful in your choice of comrades and friends."

The Opium Traffic.

"Putting the question in the shortest compass, it seems to be mainly a question of political morality. The Indian Government is raising an income, which has been estimated at £7,000,000 a year, from a trade which may be described as one of questionable character. They are exporting to a country with which we are at present in friendly relations a drug which the Government of that country desire to exclude by reason of the mischief it is doing to its teeming population. It has become a question of high morals whether that is a defensible course of proceeding for a Christian nation to pursue. I honestly say that my conscience rebels against the traffic. I am but imperfectly informed of the facts bearing upon the question, but that is my conception of the actual bearings of it in relation to our duty towards the people of China. I believe that the China markets are almost the only markets that consume the opium products of India, and that the Chinese Government are opposed to their introduction into that country. We are strongly moved at home by the ravages of the drink traffic. We are adopting every remedy to stay them, and yet, by a sort of complacent Pharisaism, we are allowing, without any firm remonstrance, the Government of this country to do what they are doing in the way of poisoning and demoralizing the people of China."

The Man of Fashion.

"The Greek at Rome in the days of Juvenal was very like the man of fashion in London in the days of Queen Victoria. He was highly educated, had a taste for art, and was a great diner-out. 'The hungry Greek,' said the poet, 'will go anywhere for a dinner.' In these days, people are glad to invite the man of fashion to their tables; they are glad to listen to his conversation, but the result of his influence is degrading, not elevating. There never comes from him one single high thought, one single word betokening that he lives for an adequate and worthy purpose. The Greeks had, too, the cynical temper which scoffs and derides earnestness. The spirit of cynicism which is so prevalent in England to-day is of, all tempers, the most alien from the mind of Christ. The Greek had, also, the critical faculty. It is a high gift indeed to discriminate truth from falsehood, but he who would play the part of a critic has a difficult part to play if he would retain moral earnestness of character. That these gifts can be possessed by men who are morally debased is shown by the fact that the Greeks were indifferent to the great social vices. So are we. If the heart of this nation had not waxed gross, if its conscience had not become almost hardened, do you think we could sit down and confidently prate about the glorious privileges of our enlightened civilization and Christianity, when the people are spending 140 millions every year in intoxicating drink, and we are surrounded on every side by those terrible social evils, drunkenness, prostitution, commercial dishonesty and fraud? Religion in England, France, and Germany at the present day has got to be a matter of mere speculation. Educated gentlemen discuss these most solemn questions of religion after dinner over their wine and walnuts. Such persons have no firm grasp of truth, and consequently are wanting in elevation and steadfastness of purpose. Their lives are a mere tissue of inconsistencies. They are one set of people in the country, and another set of people when they go to town for the season. They are in one mood in church, and in another and contradictory mood when they are smoking cigars, or playing billiards, or following the hounds. It is not that they are differently engaged, but that they are different men. They care about little things because they have ceased to care about great things."

The London Season.

"People come up to London when the season is on, and what do they say? 'We have come up to London for the two months, and we are determined to go on enjoying ourselves and seeing everything that is to be seen.' But the enjoyment of which they speak is the turning of night into day; staying up all night to balls, parties, and so forth, and going to bed in the day; that is the enjoyment of the London season in this day. People say it is good for trade, this fashionable life; but I am not quite so sure of that. Of course there should be a legitimate and proportionate expenditure of wealth, and moreover it might be said to be a duty which was expected of society; but, whilst one can afford it, ten are made bankrupts by it. I should like to see the bad debt columns, and the unpaid bills of the tradesmen, and then to see how many shillings in the pound come from those who do pay. I heard the other day of a lady who gave £130 for a dress wherein to shine for one brief hour at Ascot; and while I have nothing to say about that, so long as it is a legitimate expenditure, I should like to know whether her charity was proportionate to her luxuries. How many good works are there at present crying for help, with little avail, because people say there is nothing to spend in consequence of trade being bad! But I think that, whenever the sun shines, the butterfly will always come out, and I have seen nothing to disabuse my mind of that idea during my present stay in London. There was a discussion some time ago between Professor Goldwin Smith and Mr. W. R. Gregg as to whether the luxurious possession of wealth was good for society and for trade. Mr. Gregg said it was, whilst Professor Smith decided to the contrary; and I confess my poor brain got a little puzzled over the arguments adduced. But my conscience told me that *luxurious* wealth cannot be beneficial for society in the long run. It is a hindrance to people who desire to live as they ought. Such people find they have so many expenses to meet in the fashionable world that they cannot subscribe as they would wish to charities and hospitals. They feel that their milliner's, jeweller's, draper's, and other bills, incurred so as to live in conformity with the world, prevent them from doing their duty. 'The fashion of the world passeth away,' says St. John; and that is verified at the present day, as you don't find the same fashions in two consecutive seasons. One fashion comes in before the old one is half worn out. But, as regards the changing of the fashions every year, I have said to myself the world may just take me as it finds me if it cares for my acquaintance. I must decline to be guided in my actions by mere worldly ideas. Of course, there is a certain amount of etiquette which every man and woman must observe. But when etiquette touches morals, and when the world's maxims come between me and my duty, then I say I am not bound to obey the world. Conscience must be the rule which every man, who would live a worthy life, must go by."

Following Christ.

"Some think they are following Christ when they are compassing sea and land to make proselytes to their own religious sect or denomination. Were we less anxious about our different denominational organizations; were we less anxious to promote the growth and expansion of our particular Church; a loftier tone and a more generous charity would characterize the Christianity of the age. Others think they are most truly following Christ, when they are contending, it may be to the very death, as fiery disputants for human opinions. Oh, what havoc have human opinions conspired to make of the simplicity of the faith! When I see the mass of human doctrines piled one upon another till they almost reach the very sky, and contrast it with the simple teaching of Christ or Paul, I am astonished to think what mischief the ingenuity of the human intellect has been able to accomplish in perplexing the clear path of duty, and in darkening knowledge with words. Others, again, think they are most truly baptized with the spirit of Christ when they isolate themselves from the world, and practise painful austerities and self-mortification.

"I remember some four or five years ago preaching, in the height of the London season, in a fashionable London church, and speaking somewhat strongly upon the frivolities of London society. When I got home I received a letter from a young lady, who wrote somewhat after this fashion. She said : 'Bishop, I think you were rather too hard on us at church last Sunday, in denouncing the frivolities of society. I feel them only too bitterly ; but please tell me how I am to escape from them.' She then detailed her daily life. It was after this sort—' We breakfast about ten. Breakfast generally occupies the best part of an hour, during which we read our letters, and pick up the latest news in the papers. After that we have to go and answer our letters, and my mother expects me to write her notes of invitation or to reply to such. Then I have to go into the conservatory and feed the canaries and parrots, and cut off the dead leaves and faded flowers from the plants. Then it is time to dress for lunch, and at two o'clock we lunch. At three my mother likes me to go with her while she makes her calls, and then we come home to a five o'clock tea, when some friends drop in. After that we get ready to take our drive in the park, and then we go home to dinner; and after dinner we go to the theatre or the opera, and then, when we get home, I am so dreadfully tired that I don't know what to do. Will you tell me how, when, and where I am to try and work for Christ?'

"I need not say that a life like that, so absorbing and so demoralizing, for it cannot be otherwise than demoralizing, prevents anything like true devotion to Christ. I could not, of course, tell the young woman to be undutiful to her mother, and I can only hope that God, in His own way and time, if He saw in her any real, earnest desire to serve Him, would find opportunities of usefulness for her. Our Saviour, with that wonderful consideration that belonged to Him, never demanded anything unreasonable. Some He has bidden to leave all and follow Him. Some He bids to go home to their friends, and there, within the circle of their own influence, declare what great things God has done for them. The way of the Cross, the way to Heaven, can never be the way of self-indulgence and self-pleasing, whether coarse or refined. It seems to me that a refined, self-pleasing, indulgent sentimentalism, with its pretty phrases, its exquisite propriety of emotion, with nothing endured, with nothing done, is one of the subtlest religious perils of the day. It is as the Son of God, come down from Heaven, that Christ said, 'Believe on Me;' but it is as the Son of Man, living a human life, that He said, 'Follow Me.' He showed how men might live in the world, and yet not be of the world; or, in St. Paul's phrase, how they might use the world without abusing it, and make life a nobler, purer, and holier thing."

Saving One's Own Soul.

"There are some people who think they are following Christ most closely when they concern themselves about the salvation of their own individual souls. No doubt his own individual soul is a matter of some importance to a man. No doubt, also, his bodily health is a matter of some importance to him; but if he is always morbidly feeling his pulse to see whether it beats evenly, and putting his hand on his heart to see whether it throbs steadily, or asking a doctor to apply the stethescope to his lungs, for the purpose of ascertaining whether there are not some incipient tubercles forming there, I am afraid he would fall unconsciously into that very state of disease which he had been so anxious to avoid. If people would but think less morbidly about the salvation of their own souls and go and work for Christ with a more absolute self-surrender, I believe the condition of their own souls would be ten thousand times more healthy and more secure than it often is. I do not find anything in the Gospel which tells me I am to be so very solicitous about the salvation of my own soul. The spirit of St. Paul, who would have been content to have been himself accursed from Christ, if by so doing he could have saved his brethren, was a much nobler, more generous, and more Christlike spirit than to be always, night and day, fretting oneself about one's spiritual condition. It is not a healthy thing, whether you go to a priest, as some recommend at the present day, to ask him to decide the matter for you, or are always yourselves probing into the condition of your soul. It is far healthier to go and do the work God has given you to do, and trust Him to take care of your souls. He will do it for you much better and more surely than you can do it for yourselves."

The Prince Imperial.

"Last Sunday I was staying with the Dean of Westminster, and all the country was saddened by the announcement of the death of the young Prince Imperial of France. The Dean had sent for an officer of the Artillery who had been connected with the Prince, for he wanted to know what the Prince was in his private life as a boy, and I heard the officer say that he was always a well-behaved young man. He used an expression which stuck to my memory, 'Of a pure life and of a clean tongue.' The Prince was also very fond of his comrades, and had a wonderful capacity for attaching his comrades to him. The Prince was a Roman Catholic; and, though Roman Catholics are of a different faith from ourselves, still we all hope to be saved through the same Lord and Saviour, Jesus Christ. The only thing left on the Prince's body was a little reliquary he had worn round his neck; but among his papers was found a prayer, almost the last prayer that he seems to have uttered or written. It was in French, but I will put it in English for you. It was this, 'Lord, if I must die, may I die in trying to save a comrade, and if I must live, may I live amongst the most worthy.' This throws a light upon the young man's character—a young man of twenty-three—that I wish every young man of twenty-three would be willing to emulate, and that all would pray to God in the same spirit. No matter what a man's religious faith, whether he is an English Churchman, or a Roman Catholic, or a Nonconformist, if he realizes his relation to God and to his fellow-men, he has realized the highest and noblest lesson of the Gospel of Christ."

Dean Stanley.

"I came here to-night full of hope that my dear, honoured, long-tried, personal friend, the Dean of this Abbey Church, would have turned the crisis of a dangerous disease. Last night's bulletin raised these hopes. Since 4.30 this afternoon, however, I hear that his attack—always menacing —has taken a most unfavourable turn. All things are in God's hands; and perhaps, even yet, in His goodness, He will avert what I should consider as nothing less than a calamity to this Church and nation. For Arthur Penrhyn Stanley let the earnest prayer be put up to-night by every one listening to me now. High—and justly high—in the esteem of the Gracious Lady who sways the sceptre of these realms; high in the esteem of all who are swaying the thoughts of the time—the poets, the philosophers, the historians, the men of science of the age; high in the esteem not only of members of his own Church, but of all Christians who, untainted by intolerance or prejudice, can admire a stainless, unblemished life, beneficent in his influence upon the society of this great city in which he moved, and which he graced; known to and trusted by the working men of England, whose true friend and counsellor he always tried to be, deep in the very heart of hearts of all his friends, without one personal enemy, dear with an inexpressible dearness to those of his own home, his kindred, his dependants, and every one who came within the reach of his warm heart and unstinting love, one asks involuntarily who can replace him if God sees fit to take him away? Pray for him, good people, while a prayer can yet avail."

Lord Hatherley and Dean Stanley.

"There have passed from the life of England, during the past week, two notable men: one a great layman, Lord Hatherley, ex-Chancellor of England, and the other, a great ecclesiastic, Arthur Penrhyn Stanley, my own dear personal friend. I suspect I was the last of Dean Stanley's personal friends who saw him as he was. No longer ago than the Wednesday before his death, I spent an hour with him, and never found him more genial, more simple, more childlike. Both the ecclesiastic and the layman have gone; but being dead they yet seem to speak. Both men illustrated the line of thought I have been endeavouring to lay before you, that the prophetic, or teaching, office of the Church is its highest office, that he who could proclaim Christ to man is the true priest of humanity, helping humanity to rise through Christ to God.

"Lord Hatherley was, I believe, for forty years a Sunday School teacher among the poor of Westminster—the Chancellor of England coming off the woolsack to take his seat among the poor working men's children on the Lord's Day to teach them.

"Let me tell you an anecdote which illustrates, in a remarkable manner, the temper of the man, and also brings into pleasant and gracious relief the character of our Queen. Lord Hatherley had a wife to whom he was devotedly attached. On one occasion when he had to visit Her Majesty at Windsor, the Queen, on the morning of his departure, said she wished he would remain another night at the Castle. He seemed distressed, and paused before giving an answer, and the Queen said, 'My lord, why do you hesitate?' He replied, 'Your Majesty, I have never been, since I was married, parted for four-and-twenty hours from my wife before.' The Queen, with that ready sympathy which is one of her most gracious characteristics, at once said, 'Oh, I won't keep you, then;' and whenever she invited her Chancellor to Windsor again, she was very careful to invite his wife to go with him. Is not that a sweet story, showing that, in spite of rank and education, the hearts of all classes beat alike in one respect?

"So, also, the Dean of Westminster, the great ecclesiastic, a man moving in the first ranks of London society, but never spoiled by it, a man of whom the Queen said the other day, that she grieved and mourned for him, feeling that she had lost an adviser and a friend, that man was as gentle and simple as a little child. He never felt happier than when he was taking a party of working men, 150 or 200, perhaps, round that Abbey which claimed so much of his interest, explaining the story of the great monuments placed there, and trying to make them feel in that simple way what a glorious heritage our forefathers have handed down to the Englishmen of to-day. And then he would gather them together in what is called the Jerusalem Chamber, and there spread his table for his visitors, and cared not how often this occurred. I believe that the seeds of the Dean's last illness were sown at a garden party—not a fashionable one, but a party of working men and women and children—which he was wont to give every year in the cloister gardens at Westminster, and at which he used to get Lord Shaftesbury, the great friend of working men, to present the prizes which he (the Dean) gave for the best window gardens. He used to encourage the poor of Westminster to take delight in such things. I hardly know whether the Dean's last words will make an adequate impression upon the public. The Dean had begun on Saturday afternoons a course of sermons on the Beatitudes. In great weakness he finished the fourth sermon a little more than a week before his death, and for his text on that occasion he took two of the benedictions together, 'Blessed are the merciful, for they shall obtain mercy. Blessed are the pure in heart, for they shall see God.' He illustrated his discourse from conspicuous monuments in the Abbey, taking sometimes one instance, and sometimes another, but I think that the Dean himself was the best instance of these two benedictions, for he was a merciful man, and as pure in heart as a little child. In some aspects of his character he was more like a little child than a full-grown man who had lived sixty-five years in the midst of this wicked world. In many aspects of its wickedness the world had never tainted his pure soul. No doubt he had his faults. In all his opinions I could not follow him; but I loved him as David loved Jonathan, and he has left behind, to me and to many, the great lesson that Christianity is not a matter so much of dogmatic faith (although, of course, it has its dogmas) as a temper, a spirit, a mind. When Paul spoke of 'the mind of Christ,' when he told people to be gentle as little children, to follow the meekness and simplicity of Christ, to be forgiving even as Christ was forgiving, Paul taught the same Christianity as Arthur Stanley taught. Let us read over those great benedictions which open the Sermon on the Mount, and see whether Christ Himself does not tell us that His religion is a temper—a bringing of the soul and the conscience into something higher, and purer, and more generous than the ordinary affairs of life."

s

President Garfield.

"It is by a spirit of self-devotion and self-sacrifice that every genuine ruler of men has won for himself the praise of being a good shepherd of his people. Why, and how, is it, that to-morrow morning every man, woman, and child in America will, in spirit, follow the bier of one man? Why is it that here in England, also, one man's death has touched us more deeply perhaps than any death in a high station which the younger ones amongst us can remember? Is it not for this simple reason that, more than any man perhaps of our generation, James Garfield seemed to us to have realized the idea of a good shepherd, giving his life for his people? I do not allude to the time when he placed himself at their head and rushed into the thick of the fight at Middle Creek that he might deliver his country from the curse of slavery. Nor was I thinking of the day when, with yet greater courage, he stood forth alone against an infuriated multitude, who wished to avenge Lincoln's death by violence, and calmed them with a few well-chosen words of Scripture. I point rather to what seems a grander and more deliberate effort of moral courage—I mean the good resolve to sacrifice, if need be, all his popularity; to brave, if need be, the wrath of some who called him friend, to exasperate numbers of secret enemies, any one of whom might take his life, in order that he might do what no other President of late had dared to do—purge the Civil Services of his country of a moral evil, of a corrupt system of patronage, which all good men deplored, but few had courage to withstand. Servant of God! Well done! Possibly He, with Whom are the issues of life and death, thought the work would be accomplished even more surely by his death than by his life—'he being dead yet speaketh,' and speaketh with far more power now than ever to a nation that has been learning, during these three months of prolonged agony, to love him with a daily increasing love. Everywhere he was honoured, revered, sorrowed for. Our gracious Queen, with that wonderful and touching sympathy which is so characteristic of her, has ordered—it is said to be quite an unprecedented mark of respect—that her Court shall go into mourning. He fell at the post of duty, seeking righteousness. It seems to have been the effort, the purpose, the dominant motive of his life, to do his duty. This was seen in him even as a boy, in his industry in helping his widowed mother on the farm in Ohio; in his thoroughness in study at college. The same indefatigable disposition marked his military life, and led to his determining, as soon as he was made President, to purge the political administration of his country. Politics in the United States are far too vehement. Men sell their votes for places as men in England—not the noblest Englishmen—sell theirs for pots of beer and half-crowns; and President Garfield was determined to put that down. He had opponents who called themselves Stalwarts, and one of these opponents was the man who shot him down, but he had done his work. He being dead yet speaks and influences. President Garfield died as all true men would wish to die—at the post of duty. Men like him are the men who keep the ideas of faith and virtue, duty and self-sacrifice, alive in the world. What would the world be without those ideas? To hold them up before the eyes of men, and bid men look at them, is in very truth to seek the kingdom of God and His righteousness; for the kingdom of God, as Christ was wont to speak of it, is not the home of sickly, namby-pamby sentiment, but of resolute endeavour, of strong and steadfast principle, of high and worthy aims. Ill will it fare with the land when earnestness and devotion to duty, purity of principle, and noble aim count for nothing in our estimate of public men. Thank God! cynicism is not yet canonized into a Christian virtue."

Dr. Pusey.

"On Saturday Dr. Pusey breathed his last. The movement in which he took so large a part took its name from him, though it was hardly he who headed it. He occupied a great and conspicuous position in the University of Oxford, and his great learning and high personal character were, perhaps, the reasons that led to his name being given to the party which gathered round him, rather than that of John Henry Newman. When I first went to Oxford, in 1836, Oxford was full of the feelings and opinions generated by that great movement. It carried most of the younger men at the time almost off their heads. The leaders of the movement were, no doubt, the most conspicuous men in the University, not only for their intellect, genius, and learning, but for their high personal character, the simplicity of their lives, and their sense of duty. I do not think it is a very wrong or mistaken feeling in a young man to look up to one older than himself, one superior in ability and position; and when he sees him living a high and noble Christian life, to be more or less attracted by it. I confess that the movement at that time had attractions for me, and if I have drawn back since, and hardly see things now as I did then, it is more perhaps because the movement has itself advanced than because I have receded. Dr. Pusey has died within the Church of England, but his great colleague, John Henry Newman, left our Church twenty-five or thirty years ago. He left, as he tells us in the Apology for his Life, in quest of a more infallible guide than he thought he could find in the Church of England. He has found one that claims to be infallible; but I cannot help doubting whether his keen intellect can be altogether satisfied with what he has found. Whether we think Dr. Pusey was right in all that he said or not, I would be sorry for the Christian faith, for the prospect of religion in England, if all men, of whatever denomination, whether Churchmen or Nonconformists, could not recognize and appreciate that simple, bold, earnest, and self-sacrificing life."

Archbishop Tait.

"The Church and nation have this day sustained a great loss by the death of Archibald Campbell Tait, Archbishop of Canterbury. He has died full of honours, if not full of years, for he was but seventy-one. Advent Sunday seems to have been marked by Special Providences

in the course of his life. It was on Advent Sunday, 1869, that he
gathered his family and servants around him, to receive what he thought
might be his last Communion. On Advent Sunday, 1878, he lost his beloved
wife, and on Advent Sunday, 1882, he has himself gone to his home. For
twenty-six years he has borne the burden of the episcopal office; twelve
years as Bishop of London, and fourteen years as Archbishop of Canterbury.
Thrice, at least, in his life, his cup of sorrow has been filled to the brim—
first, when he lost five children at Carlisle; again, after a long interval,
when there was taken from him his only son, his well-beloved, whose life
was just budding into promise; and last, just four years ago, this very
Advent Sunday, his heart still bleeding from its unclosed wounds, he lost
her, who for thirty-five years had been the partner of all his sorrows and
all his joys. Calm and dignified, both in manner and appearance, but
singularly simple, kindly, genial, and unaffected, he had the secret that
wins hearts and inspires confidence. To see him in the midst of his family
who adored him, in the home which was a sample of all that is best,
purest, and brightest in an English household, beloved and respected by
his servants, was to see him, perhaps, at his best and brightest; but
wherever you saw him, in the House of Lords, where his influence was
quite remarkable, or in the councils of the Church, you felt yourself in the
presence of a man who commanded respect by the simple power of his
great qualities. Persuasive, statesmanlike, far-seeing, courageous but not
uncompromising, he was the very type of a Christian prelate, suited to the
age in which God's Providence had placed him. I doubt if there ever was
an ecclesiastic in England who possessed so wide an influence over the
Christian laity. I do not know what it was that he exactly proposed to
himself as his aim; but the effect of his teaching and of his life certainly
was to make Englishmen regard their Church more as a national institution than as a clerical appanage; to break down those artificial middle
walls of partition which are ever being set up between clergy and laity,
preventing each from recognizing the other as co-ordinate members of that
great body of kings and priests, which is the true conception of the Church
of Christ; to bid us all labour, as he sought to do, not in the fields of
controversy, but in the great task of making the life of the nation more
Christian, more noble, more pure. I have said his influence was great,
and it well deserved to be. A great ecclesiastic, yet without a tinge of
ecclesiastical narrowness or pride; a true 'servant of the servants of God,'
in a far more real sense than that in which the title has often been
assumed; a loyal subject to the Queen, to whom, almost with his
parting breath, he sent his affectionate blessing; interested in every scheme
which had for its object the improvement or elevation of the people. We
cannot afford to lose the lessons of such a life. He being dead yet speaketh,
and, I trust, will long speak to the people in England. He seems to tell
us that God's service is a reasonable one, that in liberty hath Christ set us
free, and that doctrines of men are not to be raised to the level of doctrines
of God. He would speak to us, perhaps, if he had a living tongue still, of
the blessings and the rewards of obedience and loyalty, of unity and

charity, and would have us know that the true Catholic spirit is, not that which adds to, but that which holds fast by, the faith once for all delivered to the saints. 'Our master is taken from our head to-day,' and all true English Churchmen will know what they have lost by the death of Archibald Campbell Tait, Lord Archbishop of Canterbury."

The Duke of Albany.

"You will expect me to say something about the sad event, scarce two days old, which has touched every English heart, as though the sorrow which has befallen the Royal Family were indeed our own. The Queen has taken us all so much into her heart, and made us realize the incidents of that simple family life which she so much delights to lead, that we almost forget the Sovereign in the woman, and her joys become our joys, and her sorrows become ours too. The Queen knows that she will have our quickest, tenderest sympathy. And the Prince, for whom she and the nation mourn, had many qualities that commended him to all who could appreciate the gifts with which he was specially endowed. Prince Leopold was in sympathy with all the best and highest aspirations of the time. Gifted with a staid and sober wisdom almost beyond his years, he might by the influence springing from his exalted position have helped to guide them. For, though high, many of those aspirations are crude and incoherent, and they want a guide and disentangler. His last public speech, delivered at Liverpool, was a speech at once noble and most instructive. He spoke of the need of tempering the severity of social and economic laws by the spirit of sympathy and kindness. The last words of that speech were, that the progress of society was at once the most sure and the most rapid when all moved on together. He has died in the first prime of manhood—scarce thirty-one. There are some beautiful words, though they are not reckoned among the inspired words of God, which try to explain the perplexity caused by such a life of promise thus untimely closed. They are in one of the books of the Apocrypha: 'Honourable age is not that which standeth in length of time, nor is measured by number of years. But wisdom is the grey hair unto men, and an unspotted life is old age.' 'He pleased God and was beloved by Him. Therefore speedily was he taken away, lest wickedness should alter his understanding, or deceit beguile his soul. He being made perfect in a short time fulfilled a long time, for his soul pleased the Lord, therefore He hasted to take him away.' I do not say that this is an explanation, but it attempts to be one. At least the thought is consoling. We ought to be able to spare our dearest and best when God calls them; especially when their lives have been worthy and noble. Still, one cannot but marvel why some are suffered to live out their unprofitable and mischievous three score years and ten—ay, and even four score years—while others are taken in their career of inspiring example and usefulness. The only sure thing to rest upon is the strong conviction of faith that the Judge of all the world must do right; that this life is but, as it were, the ante-chamber of a far higher and nobler one, and that God has some work for His servants to do yonder even nobler and worthier than that He gave them to do here. That must be our hope and comfort when the young, and the good, and the highly-gifted die."

"Christ came, we are told, to heal the broken-hearted, and may He be present to comfort the hearts of our gracious Queen and of that poor young widow in this hour of bitter grief. Next to one, and, perhaps equal to another—one being when she was bereaved of her husband, and the other when she lost her tender daughter—this must be the bitterest bereavement our Queen has sustained. She will at least have the comfort of knowing and feeling that her sorrow is shared by her people. There are few, I suspect, who have not already thought of her in their prayers. It seems to me that never—at least in my recollection—has there been a more genuine and general outburst of national feeling than on this occasion. And why? Because he whom the Queen mourns was so gracious, so sympathetic, had such noble aims, was so full of promise, and for his years—he was but 31—was so wise. 'The best die young' was a proverb of the ancients, and he was among the best."

General Gordon.

"Gordon's soul seems to have fed mainly on two books—one, the Bible, which was his constant companion and study; and the other that wonderful treatise on 'The Imitation of Christ,' which was compiled at the end of the 14th century by the old monk, Thomas à Kempis, one of the 'Brothers of the Common Life.' 'The way of the holy Cross,' as the old monk called it, than which 'Thou shalt not find a higher way above nor a safer way below'—this was Gordon's way. Would to God it was every soldier's way! Other gallant men, whose names we all remember to-day, have laid down their lives for their country in this pitiable war, of which no one seems to know the object, and no one can foresee the issue. There were the two Stewarts—one of them Gordon's steadfast friend, the friend of his choice, whom he took out with him on his journey to Khartoum, and whom, with a rare spirit of self-sacrifice, he sought to place in safety, himself remaining at the post of peril; and the other, Herbert Stewart, than whom Lord Wolseley said there was not a finer soldier in Her Majesty's service. Then there were Earle, Eyre, Coveny, the adventurous Burnaby, who seemed in his most congenial element when his life was in his hand. All these, and many more true-hearted men, some of them comrades, I dare say, of the men of the Staffordshire Regiment here represented, have fallen at the post of duty to which their country sent them. They are like the three hundred Spartans who fell at Thermopylæ, over whose graves was placed the simple inscription: 'Stranger, tell the Lacedæmonians that here we lie in obedience to their words.' Apart from the sense of duty, Gordon had no love for war. His special love was for children. The man who was brave enough to lay down his life was the same man who spent his leisure hours in feeding and teaching gutter lads on the banks of the Thames. Grievous as was the sense of sorrow in every heart at the news of his death, we cannot call such a life thrown away. And, being dead, he still speaks. His voice will never be silent. It will go on speaking from the pages of history to generations yet unborn. It is the lives of such men as General Gordon which generate others like themselves. Yes, Gordon will live on in the pages of history as Nelson has lived."

"General Gordon was a remarkable instance of a man of the highest gifts and the most lowly ambition. If there was one thing that Gordon hated worse than another it was to get into the newspapers, to be talked about, or to get the praise of men. He absolutely dreaded this sort of thing, seeming to think that it would make him forget his humble position towards God. He never desired his name to appear in a despatch or to receive tribute from his countrymen or any memorial. He simply wished to go forth in the strength of the God Who, he believed, dwelt in him. He has left a name which will stand on the pages of English history as that of one of the greatest heroes of the 19th century. Men who live for lower objects—to amass wealth, to get rank or social position—perhaps call him mad, as Festus called St. Paul mad. Well, if to be somewhat different from the mass of the world, and to have a different standard of life and duty, make a man mad, perhaps Gordon may be said to have been mad. But it is a madness one wishes were a little catching, for the world would be all the better if there were more noble hearts, like Gordon's, animating men with a sense of what a blessed thing it is simply to do their duty."

This continual speaking of the Bishop's, upon every event and topic of the current day, called forth occasional criticism. But his own vindication is clearly expressed in a letter addressed by him to the editor of the *Spectator*.

SIR,—I accept your criticism in the friendly spirit in which I am sure it is intended. I only wish that you had told me how to escape from a necessity which seems to be imposed upon me like a doom. If I were to act upon your advice of "reticence," I should have to strike out all but a minimum of the engagements which crowd the pages of my pocket-book. Thrown by Providence, and by no choice or desire or seeking of my own, into the midst of an active, energetic population, with, probably, a dozen towns of more than 50,000 inhabitants within easy reach of Manchester, and at least three times as many so-called "villages," larger than most South of England towns, each with its various institutions, religious and secular, denominational and undenominational, in full activity, I am continually pressed with invitations to attend public meetings or to preach sermons for some object or other in almost all of these. As usual, three courses are open to me; I must either accept as many of these invitations as I can find time for, or I must make selections, which would certainly be deemed invidious and give offence, or I must refuse all. Rightly or

wrongly, wisely or unwisely, and claiming so far the right of selection as to give a preference to those which seem to fall most properly within a bishop's province, I have taken the first course, and with a result as unwelcome to me as it can be to any one else. If I go where I am invited I must speak, for I am invited for that, and for no other purpose, and if I speak, unfortunately for me, I am reported; and though I am perfectly aware that much of what falls from me on such occasions does not deserve the publicity it seems to attain, and which certainly I do not court, I cannot prevent reporters from reporting or editors from inserting what they please. If any one supposes that I have an unhealthy appetite which cannot be satisfied but with this kind of notoriety, such a person was never more mistaken in his life. So I trust, in charity, that those who cry "The Bishop of Manchester again" will at least remember the difficulties of the Bishop of Manchester's position. I would give much to be permitted, without sinking into uselessness, to hold my tongue, except on the rare occasions when I may wish to explain the motives that govern my conduct, and, when I do speak, to feel sure that my words would not travel beyond the audience to which they are addressed. But, situated as I am, and (it seems to me) no other bishop similarly is, will you or any other kind or candid friend tell me what I am to do? I am afraid, after all, that I shall be obliged to continue to act upon my own judgment, and, at the risk of offending, perhaps justly, the nicer taste of "cultivated people," try according to my lights to do the best I can for "the masses" by whom I am surrounded. I must submit with the best grace I can to the criticisms of the clubs and the literary world at large.—
I am, Sir, &c.,

J. MANCHESTER.

CHAPTER XII.

THE BISHOP OF ALL DENOMINATIONS.

Churchmanship—Simplicity in Religion—Worship—Reverence—Sympathetic Christianity—Intelligent Christianity—Interpretation of Scripture—Truth and Holiness—Comprehension—Absolution—The Holy Eucharist—The Priestly Office—Historic Churchmanship—Apostolic Succession—Establishment and Endowment—Disestablishment—Purchase of Livings—Voluntaryism and Endowment—Defence against Disestablishment—Church Reform—Nonconformity and the Church—The Bishop and Nonconformists—Religious Tolerance—The Bishop of the Jews—Testimony of Nonconformists.

At a meeting held in Manchester, in connection with the Missionary Exhibition, on March 11, 1870, a fortnight before his Consecration, Mr. Fraser said :

"I have noticed in one of the papers of this city a statement that it is not known to which party in the Church Mr. Fraser belongs. May I say I have never belonged to any party in the Church, and that I hope never to belong to any party. I think the Church of Christ is too grand an institution, and that the work of Christ is too great and comprehensive, to be frittered away in any partizan motives or by any partizan agencies ; and the thing above all others I desire to do, if I can do it, is, if God gives me strength and wisdom, to throw myself on the hearts of all good Christian people in this great diocese, to try to bring their Christian efforts into harmony of combination, and to give what little encouragement my position—not myself—may enable me to give to all Christian men and women who are endeavouring to do the work of Christ in a true Christian spirit."

This was one of the most notable characteristics of Bishop Fraser. Not by profession alone, but in actual fact and practice, he "belonged to no party in the Church." All parties alike could claim an equal share of his sympathy and support for whatever was true, just, lovely, in their system ; and all parties alike received equal reproof for whatever was faulty, extravagant, unreal. In a letter dated June 19, 1877, he writes :

"One of my great difficulties, and I dare say the other bishops have the same, is to allay the rabid 'Protestantism' (as it calls itself) which cannot see a single virtue in a Ritualist, but would hound and chase them off the face of the earth. Little as I like their proceedings, my sense of equity will not let me see good (even if they be mistaken) men unfairly treated. I have hardly any Ritualism in this diocese, and therefore I am bound to protect some of my best and most earnest clergy, whose work is being hindered because people choose to class them with the extreme party to which they do not belong."

There is, perhaps, no task which a man can set himself more difficult than the task of living a life higher than the life of partizanship, whether in politics or religion. As it is easier to be a politician than a patriot, so it is easier to be a Low, or High, or Broad Churchman, than simply a Churchman. Parties are one-sided, and make less demand both upon the moral and spiritual faculties than is made by comprehensive sympathy. Moreover, parties give large scope to the exercise of those deeply human feelings of antipathy, which comprehension seeks earnestly to restrain. The non-party man is, too, the butt of all parties. This was Bishop Fraser's experience; an experience, however, not untempered by the appreciative esteem and kindliness of moderate men of every school of religion and thought. In responding to a vote of thanks proposed by the Rev. Dr. Pope (Wesleyan) and seconded by J. K. Cross, Esq., M.P., at the opening of a bazaar in connection with the Bolton Children's Home, the Bishop said:

"One in my position has a great number of discouragements and disappointments. My predecessor in office said that when he came into Lancashire he had a skin, but by degrees it became a hide; by which he meant he had frequently to withstand the shafts of ridicule and unfriendly criticism. Still, these things do not move me. I go on my way, not pretending to be infallible, or that I do not sometimes make mistakes. Sometimes I say things on the impulse of the moment which I had better have left unsaid. It is a satisfaction, however, to be told by Mr. Cross that by this time Lancashire knows me, and though I will not take the full measure of the compliment that Lancashire honours me, still, if Lancashire will believe I am a man of average powers, who has a conscience, and who tries to do his work according to his lights in endeavouring to diffuse the broad principles of Christianity and of good fellowship amongst those with whom my lot is cast, they will about read my character and my aims."

Similarly at the laying of the foundation stone of the Oldham Infirmary:

"There is one thing which is especially interesting to me in this ceremony—it is, that it is one of those religious acts in which Christians of every denomination can join in perfect friendliness, and without compromising any one of their essential principles. Unfortunately it happens, perhaps through a necessity of human nature, that no two minds are constituted exactly alike, or, if constituted alike, they are trained under such different influences and circumstances that each man regards the same truths from a different point of view from his neighbour. So it is in religion, where, if possible, it would be desirable for all to think alike; all cannot and do not think alike. I for one cannot see any use in trying to ignore or blink these differences. They exist, and must be acknowledged; but whenever we can meet together, without compromising those principles which, as honest men, we all hold, whenever we can exchange the hand of fellowship in our Christian work, and whenever we can meet as common servants of one common Lord and Master, I for one do hail, and have hailed, and hope I ever shall hail, these opportunities, as giving me the means of broadening out my Christian sympathies, and widening the boundaries of my heart. I cannot see why Englishmen cannot differ on points of politics, on points of religion, and on points of municipal order without bitterness and without partiality."

In responding to the toast of "the clergy and ministers of all denominations," at the opening of the Manchester Town Hall, September 12, 1877, he said:

"Having had the luck or misfortune, as people may choose to think, to become the Bishop of this vast diocese—a task beyond my strength to discharge—I have yet been encouraged, during the eight years of my episcopate, with the most loyal, hearty, and sympathetic consideration from all denominations of Christians. I hope I do not arrogate to myself too much to-night in claiming to be the spokesman, not personally or officially, but the spokesman still, of the various denominations of Christians, which no doubt have representatives in this room. I am no lover of denominationalism in itself, I regret the schisms and divisions of Christendom, because I feel that the powers of Christendom are thereby weakened in doing the great things that Christendom has to do. But I accept this denominationalism as a fact—an almost necessary fact in a land of freedom of thought, civil and religious. Truth is many-sided, and, as Prince Bismark said to the pastors of Würtemburg not many weeks ago, 'no religious body has the right to assume that it has a monopoly of it.' I believe that, as people get educated, we may fearlessly put before them our respective claims, and it is not a mere idle sentiment, but a real, deep-reaching maxim, that truth is great, and with intelligent people will ultimately prevail."

This charity of religious toleration, so characteristic of Bishop Fraser, sprang not from any want of appreciation of the importance of the small matters of religion (upon which men differ), but from the profound conviction of the still greater importance of the large truths of religion upon which the majority of earnest-hearted men agree—truths such as earnestness, faith, sympathy, worship, Divine communion. Preaching at Lancaster Parish Church in August, 1875, the Bishop said :

"I believe that if all Christian men and women were thoroughly in earnest, if they lived and acted the Gospel which they preach and talk ; if they believed in the power of the Gospel in the same way as they believe in the power of water or steam, or of cotton or gold, they would realize to a much greater extent the truths of the Gospel, and they would live much better lives."

Again, in a sermon preached in June, 1879 :

"It is earnest men, moderate in tone and temper, with a loving care for souls, and without any foolish hankering after a medieval system of doctrine and ritual, utterly out of harmony with the spirit of the age, that will save the Church of England, save her by helping her to do the work that God's Providence is setting before her in that reasonable spirit, which, in the words of the preface to the Prayer Book, will commend the work to all sober, peaceable, and truly conscientious men."

Again, in a speech at Liverpool College :

"The heart of the English people is not turned away from the Church of their fathers, if only she will show herself a true mother to them. The spires of churches point to heaven and symbolize holy things. The towers symbolize strength ; and strength is a true symbol of the Church of England, which is strong in the love and affection of her children ; strong in her broad and solid foundations ; strong in her all-abiding and all-embracing sympathy ; strong also in the work she has done and is doing, and will for many years continue to do, for the glory of God and for the true prosperity of this nation ; and strong above all in her pure faith, which we hope will continue to abide in her."

At St. George's in the East, London, June 2, 1878, he said :

"A man is not a priest by being clothed with a chasuble, however it is ornamented. The true priest is he who has compassion on the evil, and on those who are out of the way. The whole Church of Christ is a royal living priesthood. Every man who helps to make this world purer and better is, in the highest sense, a priest of God. Mr. Ruskin might say it is foolish to talk like this in the East-end of London. Go and serve God, he would say, in green fields, not in crowded cities. But, wherever there is a spot brightened by human sympathy, there is green grass where men can sit down in fifties and in hundreds. Only a few can enjoy the dells and purling streams of Westmoreland. Most must live amidst masses of men, and it would be sad indeed if children could not laugh and play in crowded streets. In the dark courts of Manchester—and they have not such bright skies there as you have here in the East-end of London—I have heard larks singing in cages as merrily as when they soared aloft. Wherever men are pure and kind there can be brightness and joy."

At St. Elizabeth's Church, Reddish, August 4, 1883, he said:

"A simple worship may yet be a grand worship, and I will give you my own ideas of what really makes grandeur of worship. In the first place, a church must be full or nearly so, and any one who knows the difference between either ministering or worshipping in a church with the worshippers scattered thinly about here and there, and when a church is filled to its fullest extent, will understand what I mean when I speak of the grandeur of large congregations. The second thing that gives grandeur to worship is entire reverence. I am not sure that the clergy always set so fully as they ought to do the example of entire reverence. They chatter and move about, and do things which are quite unnecessary while the service is going on, and so, I am afraid, they make people forget sometimes that entire reverence is a grand element in worship. I do not want to see any prostration in the aisle with the face to the ground. That is not my notion. A simple, devout conduct—people standing where they ought to stand, sitting reverently when listening to God's Word, and kneeling when the Prayer Book tells them to kneel—that is what I call reverence. There should be an absence of all theatrical effect, and of everything that looks like tawdry display. I am sometimes shocked and startled at the incongruity of the things I see in churches—paper banners, for instance, do not make a church look more beautiful. Anything like tawdry display should be avoided if we want our worship to be simple and grand. I wish further to encourage hearty congregational singing, and full and devout responses. It was bad enough when the congregation left all to the clerk, and it is not much better now when they leave it mainly to the choir. It is sometimes said that congregational responses are apt to be discordant; but I could forgive the discordance for the sake of the unison and the power. Then, lastly, but greatest of all, let us try to so worship, that if a casual stranger comes into our House of God, when we are engaged in worship, and sees the spirit which prevails, he should feel himself induced to fall down and take part in the worship, and go forth acknowledging that God is with us of a truth."

At Poulton Church, December 9, 1882, he said:

"The Church is very far as yet from being put to those solemn purposes for which it was intended, and many congregations need this lesson bringing home to them that the House of God is a place of worship and a house of prayer. To many congregations it is a place where they can go to listen to an eloquent preacher, and that is all the people care for, and perhaps all the preacher cares for. Sometimes churches are made places of spectacle for music or gorgeousness. It is only here and there we find a congregation that has been brought up under better and happier influences. In some places people walk half way up the aisle of the church with their hats on, forgetting the reverence due to God. When one goes into a cottage or a drawing-room, he takes off his hat, and when we go into God's house we like to show that we know where we are. During prayers I have noticed that a great many people sit. Now I have never found any authority anywhere for a strong healthy man or woman to sit whilst praying. When you are in your own chambers you do not draw up a chair, sit down, and say your prayers. You go down on your knees, put your hands to your face, and try to keep out all other thoughts. Why, then, do you not do the same in God's House? You do not want to have earthly, worldly cares coming into your minds just at that time. Our Church directs that we should kneel, and kneeling makes a congregation more devout. I think, perhaps, we have got to think a little too much about postures; but there is such a thing as reverence. I confess that in going about the diocese I often miss reverence in congregations; there is earnestness of a kind, but not always that solemn, devout reverence in the presence of God which is so helpful to congregations, and the absence of which betokens so much that one does not like to see in such a place and at such a time. You ought to think of this. Devotion and reverence pass, as it were, as a thrill from one to another, and it is a spirit we cannot cultivate too much at present."

But Bishop Fraser, with all his passion for reverence and devoutness in worship, constantly warned his listeners against a merely mechanical reverence—those postures of the body which are unaccompanied by piety of heart and soul.

"The solemn question has often forced itself upon my mind whether the confessedly greater attention which has of late years been bestowed upon the services of the sanctuary has been accompanied by a commensurate growth in personal holiness. Of one thing I am quite sure—where there is true inner spiritual life, it will express itself outwardly in a reverent ritual; but I am not at all equally sure that a gorgeous ceremony is either a proof of, or will help to generate, that inward holiness, without which, in the ordinance of Divine worship, no man can really see God. There is no virtue in a religious service any more than there is virtue in a religious dogma in, and by, itself. It is a virtue in exact proportion to the measure in which we are penetrated, and governed, by its power. If anything can stifle all true spirituality of the soul, it must be the mechanical habit of uttering so many words, or taking part in so many acts of devotion, merely as a form."

"The mechanism of religion needs to be sanctified by the Spirit of God. It is only the Spirit that, entering into the mechanism of dry bones, can give life, and make men stand upon their feet, an exceeding great army. What we want to-day—above, beyond, and before all—is the spirit of a large-hearted, sympathetic, and intelligent Christianity."

Moreover, Bishop Fraser's hope of the ultimate comprehensiveness of modern Christianity was built not only upon the spread of sympathy among Christian people, but upon the admission of a larger, and more intelligent, conception, of the fundamental principles of the Christian faith. "Almost all the divisions," he said, "which have disfigured the unity of the Christian Church are to be set down to the inveterate habit of the human mind to treat verbal questions as if they were real." He yearned to get away from the surface questions of opinion which gender strife, to the deep foundations of truth which uphold piety. And in digging down to these foundations he was willing, for his part, to consent to the removal of every opinion and interpretation of theological schools not possessing Divine sanction. In thought and action he laid down for himself, and commended to others, the great and golden rule: "In necessariis unitas, in non necessariis libertas, in omnibus caritas."

At Liverpool College, 1878, he said:

"The spirit of inquiry has touched the question of religion, and has not been afraid to handle, and handle very freely, the Word of God; and I do not know that anybody ought to say that the Word of God should not be handled, and handled freely, so long as it is handled reverently. 'The truth shall make us free,' and no one feels so free as he who is seeking for nothing but truth in the inquiry which he is pursuing. It is impossible to deny that in many of our congregations of all classes—I will not say that a spirit of atheistic doubt prevails, but that a cloud of doubt has passed over thoughts and doctrines which at one time seemed perfectly clear. I speak for myself. There are many points of doctrine upon which reading, study, and reflection have made me think; and the outcome of those thoughts is, that I know to-day much less clearly than I thought I knew twenty-five years ago; and that I should be much less disposed to give a positive opinion to-day on many points than I should have been a quarter of a century since. I think that Protestants have dogmatized just as freely and just as absolutely as any other school of theologians. They have dogmatized far too peremptorily. There was a time when the literal interpretation of the cosmogony of the first chapter of the Book of Genesis was thought to be an undoubted truth, and when the days of the creation were said to be positively days of twenty-four hours. There may be some who hold that doctrine still; but it must be admitted that those views have undergone a severe revision, and I dare say that most of us, if we were perfectly honest, would say that, at the present moment, we are not prepared to give a dogmatic positive interpretation of the first chapter of Genesis. Paley told us long ago it would be the greatest of blunders to make Christianity answer with its life for an interpretation of which no one could pretend to say that it had the stamp of a Divine sanction upon it. The vital principles of Christianity are few—this is a point I am always anxious to insist on—very practical and very simple. To believe in a Father who made us; a Saviour who redeemed us; and a Spirit who sanctifies us; to recognize that there is a law of God, a very simple one, by which we are to govern our steps; and that in the effort to rule our way aright we have a help from God, which we have only to seek to obtain; and to believe in the resurrection of the dead and eternal judgment—this is the sum and substance of Christianity. If we can get people to lay hold on these truths, we may put on one side such questions as, 'Were those days of the first chapter of Genesis days of twenty-four hours?' 'Was the deluge universal or not?' 'Were the patriarchs' years years of 365 days or not?' 'Were those last verses of the Gospel of St. Mark the genuine product of the Evangelist or not?' 'Is that verse in the eighth chapter of the Acts of the Apostles genuine or not?' These are not vital points; and while I admit that, if, as some people tell us, the Christian faith is like a house of cards, it would be a supreme danger to allow doubts of this kind, even for a moment, to find entrance into people's minds, yet, as the Church of the living God is not a house of cards, but a house of solid materials, resting on a sure foundation, Christ Himself being the head corner-stone, we may treat with all charity the honest doubts of men, confident in the assurance that truth is great and will prevail."

Again :

"I have found in life that, where logical solutions are sometimes difficult, practical solutions, by the Providence of God, are easy. And if we will look at our religious difficulties, with a broad, clear, kindly eye, distinguishing between what is essential and accidental, between what we may gain even by losing, and what we must struggle to the very death to retain, we shall find, I think, that God's Holy Spirit now will not fail His

Church. It seems to me the only two things worth struggling for are truth and holiness. Men who care not for theological subtleties, men who revolt from the discussion of religious topics, in a partizan spirit, men who are sick and weary of controversy, will yet listen to the preacher who will point them to the love of God and try to persuade them to righteousness, temperance, and judgment to come."

Again, in a sermon preached at the Ormrod Memorial Church, Scorton, June, 1879:

"The Gospel is not a narrow Gospel, it is a broad Gospel; and therefore let us proclaim the love of God in Jesus, and the power of the Spirit to teach and soften the hard and stubborn will of every man. These are the messages that win men to Christ and cause thousands to amend their lives. The Church will become all the stronger, and gain more in the affections of the people, by being tolerant and large-hearted, open-handed and comprehensive, than by being bigoted, exclusive, and anathematizing. There never was a more splendid opportunity in England of working for Christ—the highest and noblest of causes—than that which God in His Providence is now presenting before us, the great, historical Church of England."

It was just this conviction of the splendour of the opportunity given to the Church of England in the modern age, which inflamed Bishop Fraser with indignation against those who, he conceived, were frittering away their rare opportunity in battling for dubious trifles, instead of contending for indubitable truths. In proportion to his devotion to all things deep and real was his abhorrence of all things superficial and false. Just because "his soul craved for earnestness and vitality," it also cried out against pretentiousness and shallow ceremonialism.

In some respects the views and teachings of Bishop Fraser were those commonly accepted by old High Churchmen. The Bishop held that the office of a priest in the Church was an office of Divine Institution; that the validity of orders depended upon Apostolic Succession; that the presence of Christ in the Eucharist was a Real, a Veritable Presence. On the other hand, these high views were in no sort mechanical, but altogether spiritual. Preaching on the great truth of Absolution at the Manchester Cathedral, April 3, 1881, he said:

"With regard to the benefit which persons labouring under a sense of sin may receive from a priest, no doubt a godly, sympathizing, minister may be of service to souls; but not your young priestling of twenty-five years of age, with no spiritual experience, airing priestly prerogatives. And the best and godliest minister has no power to release from that which is the real weight of sin. He may remove ecclesiastical censures, restore to communions and sacraments, but he cannot assoil the conscience, nor make the spirit feel itself free. For that, the minister must point the penitent to the Lord Jesus Christ, and to the 'blood of sprinkling which speaketh better things than that of Abel.' That he can and ought to do. It is the very secret, the crown and jewel of his priesthood, the end of his ministry, to point to that fountain open for sin and for uncleanness."

Again, in another sermon preached in the same year at the same place, upon the Eucharistic Service:

"The three great purposes of the Holy Eucharist are, that it is an act of loving remembrance of Christ; an act which is a great means or channel of grace; and an act whereby the Church, a little flock in the midst of an unbelieving world, tells out to all around that they believe in Him who died and rose again. What some people call the highest view of the Holy Eucharist seems to me to be the lowest. For instance, a multitude of ritualistic acts distract the mind instead of concentrating it, awaken sensuous feelings rather than spiritual ones, prevent a true discernment of the Lord's Body. While bells are tinkling, and censers are swinging, and acolytes are flitting about on their errands, now on the one side, and now on the other, and the priest is saying his office, so rapidly and in such undertones, that he cannot be heard, while the people are invited now to cross, and now almost to prostrate, themselves, the mind is distracted and the feelings are disturbed. I say emphatically, as your Bishop, that this has not been the usage since the Reformation, and if it ever becomes the use, which I do not think likely, I should regard it as a retrograde step, adverse rather than favourable to true and reasonable service."

The Bishop had used even stronger language upon this great, difficult, mysterious subject, in the earlier years of his episcopate. Preaching at St. Paul's, Heaton Moor, in January, 1877, he said:

"If clergymen teach the people to believe in a materialized conception of the mode of Christ's presence, they are going not only far beyond the limits of the true interpretation of Scripture, but far beyond the mind and spirit of the Church of England. What authority have they for saying that, by reason of a form of words in the consecration prayer, Christ comes and takes possession of a fragment of bread and a certain number of globules of wine, and in these forms passes into their souls? The only thing we need care about is the presence of Christ in our own hearts. I do not mean, of course, in the physical heart, I mean in what we call the soul or the spirit, that which realizes His presence. I maintain as strongly as any one can, the real presence of Christ in His sacrament, but I do not say that after the priest has said something Christ is there. I wait a while till all is finished, and then if I go away with the feeling that God's benediction rests upon me, if higher thoughts come into my mind, and godly resolutions have been strengthened, and purposes of a better life have been put into my soul; if I think of my Saviour crucified, risen, mediating for me and sanctifying me by His Spirit, if I experience all this, then I feel that I have received Christ in His Sacrament, and in the way in which Christ meant us to receive Him."

Equally definite, yet equally distant from both extremes, was Bishop Fraser's teaching concerning the nature of the Priestly Office. As he believed in the real Presence of Christ in the Eucharist, but not in a material presence, so he believed in the Divine character of the Priest's Office, but not in its sacrificial character.

"I once read in a religious periodical that a priest must have a special vestment, or he would no longer be distinguishable from the chorister. Have we come to that? that the tailor and embroiderer make a priest? In my opinion a priest is distinguished from a choir-man by his function, and not by his costume. Are we going to resolve the Christianity of this day into a rivalry of vestments? Does a man think that his administration of the Holy Communion, or his ministration of the Word of God, could be more effective to reach the people's souls, more effective to communicate the grace of God, if he wore a chasuble than if he wore a surplice? We have to ask ourselves the question, 'What is it makes a priest?' I answer in the words of Paul, 'The gift of God by the laying on of hands.' If men feel that they receive the gift of God concurrently with the laying on of hands, they have a right to feel that they are priests, sufficient for all those purposes which the Church of England demands her priests to perform. I say that we all ought to look more to what is the Church of England's conception of the priest's office. It is said to-day that the main duty is to offer Christ. Where is that phrase found? It is not a Scripture phrase. It may be found in some early Father, who used rhetorical language about the great Sacrament of the Holy Eucharist; but *I* do not think it would be found in any very early Father; and I do not think the Church of England authorizes her clergy to teach the people that Christ is sacrificed in the office of the altar. That was an error swept away at the Reformation. Offer Christ!! Christ Himself has done it once for all. He, as Great High Priest of the Church, by that one great sacrifice, oblation, and satisfaction, which He offered on the Cross of Calvary for the sins of the world, has rendered it a matter of utter superfluity that priests at any time thereafter should repeat, even in figure, that great and precious sacrifice. Enough for them if, through their unworthy ministrations, they could apply the benefit, and the power, and the grace, and the sanctification, of that sacrifice to the healing, and refreshing, and strengthening of people's souls. The duty intrusted to me when I became a priest was simply that I should be a minister, a watchman, a steward of the Lord, to teach, and premonish, and feed and provide for the Lord's family, to seek for Christ's sheep scattered abroad, and for His children that are in the midst of this naughty world, that they may be saved through Christ for ever."

It was Bishop Fraser's devotion to the Church of England which stimulated him to speak out, in words of boldness—boldness born of the jealousy inspired by affection—concerning the extravagances of ceremony, and errors of doctrine, into which a small band of clergy appeared to him bent upon tempting her. Himself a thorough, and thoroughly convinced Churchman, a student of Hooker, a loyal disciple of the Prayer Book, he burned with desire to save the English Church from being wrecked upon the rocks either of ecclesiastical fanaticism or intolerant dogmatism.

"If we are to maintain our faith and principles against the perils of the age, our Churchmanship must be intelligent and rational; and what I lament, as evidenced on every side, is the very general ignorance of the principles of the Church of England as they were established at the Reformation, among those who call themselves English Churchmen. There is a loud and noisy class of English Churchmen who throw up their hats and cry 'Hurrah for the Church,' on public occasions, who really do not know what their Church is, or what it is for which they cry hurrah, or throw up their hats. I would wish them to make themselves acquainted, from authentic and reliable sources, with the great history and principles of the National Church. I wish to urge upon Churchmen to make themselves more thoroughly acquainted with the Prayer Book, and also to study Richard Hooker's 'Ecclesiastical Polity.' The Church has to set out its faith and system against two opposite influences. These are, the predominating claims of the Bishop of Rome, and the more or less anarchical spirit of Nonconformity. I use the word anarchical, not in any disrespectful sense to the great body of Nonconformists; for I have a great respect for them. But the very essence of Nonconformity is the breaking up of an organized system. I will just state what I consider the five great fundamental principles of the Church of England, as they were established at the Reformation :—the sufficiency of the Holy Scriptures; the necessity of believing the Creeds, which contain the great dogmas of the Catholic Church; the independence of national churches; the necessity and validity of the Christian Sacraments; and the ancient threefold apostolic organization of bishops, priests and deacons. *Though people say the doctrine of Apostolic Succession is a Popish figment,*

I simply state it as an historic fact. It is as much an historic fact, as that Queen Victoria sits on her throne as the legitimate successor to her ancestors. In a day when religious opinion is in a state of chaos and utter confusion, Churchmen ought to know what it is they believe, and why they believe it. They cannot allow themselves to be considered a sect. They are not a sect. They are the ancient, historic, reformed Christian Church in this land."

Again:

"I do not wish to use hard words without cause. I can understand the principles of the three great Nonconformist denominations that have broken off—I think on very insufficient grounds—from communion with the Church of England. I say I can understand and respect their principles; but, in saying this, I do not mean to raise their credentials to a level with those of the Catholic Church. I believe fully—you will perhaps say I am *bound* to believe, but I believe without being bound, after the fullest and most candid examination I have been able to give the subject—that the Church can make good, not only a more ancient, but a more authentic, title for her ministry, and can claim not perhaps a fuller—for the measure of fulness depends, not so much on the title of the Church which gives, as on the faith of the worshipper who receives—I will not say then, can claim a fuller, but a more assured, blessing on her Sacraments. The man whom the apostle John found casting out devils in his Master's name, and who followed not with them, certainly had not as legitimate a commission as the Twelve or the Seventy whom that Master Himself chose and ordained, and sent forth armed almost with His own powers. Those who went out from the Church in the days of St. John, because they misliked some point in her doctrine or discipline, and established independent congregations of their own, had not the same guarantee to their work being of God, as those who received the gifts of the Episcopate through the laying on of Paul's hands, and who were left, the one at Ephesus, the other in Crete, to ordain elders in every city, to set in order whatever might be wanting, and to commit the deposit of doctrine which they had received to faithful men who might be able to teach others also. I do not wish to press extravagant conclusions out of the doctrine of Apostolical Succession; but where it exists, as a simple, ascertainable, historical fact, as in the Church of England, it is, upon a ministry possessing such a lineage, one authenticating seal the more."

Upon the vexed question of Establishment and Endowment Bishop Fraser's convictions were lofty and clear. Not for any selfish or sordid reasons (of these he was incapable), nor for the sake of social advantage or priority (for which he cared absolutely nothing), but in the interests of progress and religion, especially among the outcast and poor, the

Bishop advocated, with incessant fervour, the cause of Established and Endowed Christianity. He desired, not less for the sake of the Nation than of the Church, to uphold the unity of the national and the religious life. He desired that Church and Realm should stand together in the common warfare against iniquity—in the common defence and promotion of righteousness. He dreaded lest Disestablishment should foster among Churchmen keener animosities, stronger partizanships, greater ecclesiasticism, narrower teaching. He knew that Voluntaryism too often (though with magnificent exceptions) means Congregationalism (*i.e.* religious ministrations for the religious and those who can pay), whereas the ideal of the Established Church is the Parochial System—*i.e.* house-to-house visitation of all classes alike, poor and rich, irreligious and religious, goats and sheep, those in the way, and those out of the way, of salvation.

To a correspondent (Mr. George B. Birdsall), who wrote, asking his opinion about Establishment, and what were the best books to consult in forming an opinion on the subject, the Bishop replied :

"I am a friend of freedom (within proper limits, without which liberty degenerates into licence), but not at all of Voluntaryism, as that principle is commonly understood. If the endowments of the Church are swept away, I am satisfied that rural England will relapse into paganism, and that even in the poorer, and most densely peopled districts, of our towns, the ministrations of religion will be most imperfectly maintained.

"I hardly know to what books to direct you. There are, of course, the publications of the Liberation Society, but they are very one-sided.

"*The Financial Reform Almanack* gives the statistics of the Church of England."

Preaching at St. Mary's Church, Beswick, June 12, 1881, the Bishop said :

"In the interests of the nation, in the interests of religion, and in the interest of maintaining Christianity in the land, I should regret, with an exceeding bitter sorrow, if the establishment of the Church of England and its endowments were taken away. These old endowments were not the gifts of the State to the Church, but were the gifts of pious people in the olden times, some giving more, and some giving less. Thus we find some parishes much more richly endowed than others: whereas, if they were the gift of the State, probably all parishes would be endowed alike. The land out of which the cathedral and parochial revenues of Manchester come, was not bought by the parishioners, and was not paid for by them; but was given by Thomas de la Warr and others like him some four hundred years ago. These endowments, which maintain, on modest incomes, the clergy of the Church of England, the State has no right to seize, at least so it seems to me. They are public funds, I admit, and they are national funds, I admit, in one sense—that is to say, that those who hold them are liable to public authority and public opinion for the use of them; and they may be re-distributed and re-applied whenever it may be thought more beneficial for the great purposes for which they were originally bestowed. This has been done again and again in the history of the Church of England. But I seem to see that, if these endowments were taken away, in many parishes in towns, and in almost all country parishes, the Church and its ministrations would disappear, for men could not live on nothing; and I can assure you that, even at the present time, owing to agricultural distress, there is a very large number of clergy in the country who cannot get their tithes or rents from glebe lands, and who are at the present moment in rural parishes in Nottinghamshire, Warwickshire, Lincolnshire, and elsewhere, suffering great distress. I picture to myself, if that became chronic in all our rural parishes, and, perhaps, in many town parishes, the whole apparatus of the Church would probably be swept away, and the ministers of God would be found scarce enough. And that is a possibility which I cannot contemplate with anything like equanimity. I believe that, with all their faults, the nation cannot afford to lose the clergy of the Church of England. I believe that matters of infinite moment, causes of inestimable value to all that goes to make up the prosperity of a nation, would seriously lose their strength and their force if the great body of the clergy of the Church of England ceased to be. And therefore it is that I hope that Churchmen, and even non-Churchmen who still appreciate the value of the Established Church, will pause before they entertain the plausible theory of Disestablishment and Disendowment, and will not listen too readily, and too credulously, to those who go about persuading men that there is a glorious millennium of religious equality and spiritual development at hand, as soon as the National Church of this land is swept away for ever."

One of the best ways of defending the Establishment and Endowment of the National Church was, the Bishop felt, to explain their true origin and nature. This he never tired of doing. Preaching at the consecration of St. John's Church, Baxenden, June 13, 1877, he said:

"This church illustrates the way in which the Church of England was originally established and endowed. The help of the State has not been called in to-day. This church has been founded by the liberality of a private benefactress. It is the fashion in some quarters to sneer at what is called 'The Pious Ancestor' theory; yet those who have founded and endowed this church will, some 200 or 300 years hence, take their place among the pious ancestors who helped to establish and endow the Church of England. If any one asks you what the Church of England owes to the State, you won't forget the one million which the State gave to build churches in populous places, and another million to augment small livings; but, when you are asked how much the State has contributed to the establishment and endowment of the Church of England, you will reply, 'About as much as the State contributed to the establishment and endowment of St. John's, Baxenden, which we saw consecrated on the 13th of June, 1877.'"

Again, preaching at Didsbury Parish Church, August 4, 1878, he said :

"A patron, in presenting his nominee to a benefice, may be actuated by family or personal motives, but that does not prevent the Church being a National Church. The man, who is put in, is required to be a learned and a moral man, and, when he becomes the minister of the parish, his business is to serve *all the parishioners* in the parish. He is not merely the minister of a clique or a congregation, or of persons who pronounce Shibboleth in this or that particular way. He is bound to conduct Divine service in the Church, to baptize children, bury the dead, attend to the schools, visit the sick in his cure; and because these are public duties, or because these are what the nation has required of the ministers of the National Church, whatever may have been the motive that led to a minister being presented to the Bishop for institution, whether the highest conceivable or the lowest selfish, he becomes a minister of the National Church, and he is bound by all the obligations which are imposed upon that particular status. And, my friends, in the Sale of Livings (Didsbury had just been offered for sale) it is not your souls that are put up to auction. Your souls are not valued at £4 8s. a piece. It is nothing of the kind. It is merely the transference of the right of presentation. Your Bishop, so far as the law gives him power, must see that a proper minister is presented to have the care of your souls. They are not your souls that are offered for sale, and I think you can bear any amount of twitting or foolish sarcasm, from those who so misrepresent the sale of the advowson of your Parish Church. I know a case where an advowson has been sold, and next presentation bought, and where the incumbent is doing his duty thoroughly well—as well as any other clergyman in the diocese—because, remember there are certain checks in this matter. I do not like the system of buying and selling livings, because it causes scandal to scrupulous minds, and I respect that scruple. But I do say, as a matter of fact, the thing does not work out so very badly; and it is a marvellous thing, for which I am thanking God continually, that, in spite of all the scandals and abuses which are more or less inherent in all human institutions, and certainly from which the Church of England is not free, somehow or other, and I ask you to say how it is, the Church of England is living, and growing, and prospering.

"There may be said to be four kinds of ecclesiastical patronage. There is the official public patron; the individual private patron; the Crown; and patronage by trustees. There is also another kind of patronage—at least there are about four or five cases in the Church of England, and I am thankful to say there are no more—in which the parishioners have the right of appointing their own clergy. I have been asked, 'Why not adopt the congregational principle?' But the Church of England does not recognize the principle of congregations, and I should be sorry if it did. It recognizes parishes; and choice by congregation would be impossible in the Church of England, unless its constitution were utterly changed from what it now is. Clever writers, no doubt, can bring objections against every and all of these forms of patronage. If it is the patronage of the Lord Chancellor or the Premier, it is said to be political. If it is the patronage of the Bishops, 'Oh, it is nepotism.' If it is by trustees, they say it is partizan, and that the trustees put in men of their own way of thinking. And, though to some minds patronage by the parishioners might seem to be the freest from objection, I know of two instances where incumbents who were elected under that system were financially ruined by the cost of their election, and one was morally ruined. And, every time, the incidents have been those of a political election. In some cases public-houses have been opened, harangues have been expected from the candidates, addresses have been published, and canvassing has gone on all over the parishes. So you see objections can be raised to almost every conceivable form of patronage.

"The exercise of patronage is by no means an easy or a plain thing. It is surrounded by difficulties. If you will suppose that men have no consciences, and that they will undertake solemn obligations, with the deliberate and foregone purpose of not discharging them, then I will say that the system of patronage in the Church of England is rotten from the crown of the head to the sole of the foot. But, as a matter of fact, it is not so. I would like to see all appointments made probationary. Some people say, 'Let the people have a veto before institution;' but it is a difficult thing for the parishioners to go and hunt up all a man's antecedents, and I would rather that the first year of a man's appointment to a parish should be probationary, and at the end of the year, supposing that he were deaf, or had a weak voice which could not half fill the church, or were negligent, the parishioners ought to have some means of getting rid of such an incumbent—an incumbent who would be an incumbrance probably lasting many years. There would be no great hardship in it, because a man who was deaf, or ill, or infirm, or rheumatic, would not come. I would not allow, of course, any captious complaints to be made. I would not allow a man to be got rid of because he had a surpliced choir, or wore a cassock beneath his surplice, or adopted the eastward position. I should like to see a properly constituted Diocesan Council of laity and clergy assisting the Bishop in these matters. I should like the grounds of objection to be distinctly defined by law, and, if that were the case, I think parishes would have sufficient protection, and no harm would be done to any individual. That is my view, and I have mentioned it to several persons—laymen, members of Parliament, and others—who think there is a good deal in it; but I confess, as long as the notions of property attach so strongly as they do in the minds of men to ecclesiastical benefices, as long as a clergyman is supposed to be placed in an almost indefeasible possession of the freehold, and as long as people are so ready to grumble and murmur, and so slow to take definite action to relieve the Church of scandal and offences, I am not very sanguine that any effective remedy can be brought to bear.

"Again, let me ask you not to be led away—by brilliant writing, and plausible statements which need a little weighing before they are accepted—with the notion that the Church of England is a mere commercial institution, in which everybody is seeking, to make the most for himself and his family; and where public spirit, and high religious motives, and conscientious discharge of duties are never found. It is not so. The Church of England is a very great institution, its age witnesses to this. It is very well for people to say that the Church of England is Catholic, and Episcopalian, and Presbyterian, just as Government orders it to be. It is not true. That is not a true account. No doubt, in days of darkness, the Church of England fell more or less under the despotism of the Bishops at Rome. But, all through the ages of the Plantagenet kings, statute after statute was passed by the English Parliament protesting against the tyranny and usurpation of the Church of Rome; and at the Reformation the nation felt itself strong enough to cast off the yoke, happily retaining the Episcopal constitution of the primitive Church. It is true that for a brief period, during the Commonwealth, the nation abandoned the Episcopal order, and adopted for twenty or thirty years the Presbyterian, and it was during that brief period, I believe, that the parishioners of Didsbury elected their own minister, who, we are told, brought letters of 'godly conversation' from Blackburn, where he had been ministering before. But it is not true to say that the Government of the day makes the Church now Catholic, now Episcopalian, now Presbyterian. Whatever may be Cardinal Manning's hopes and expectations, the people of this country have never regretted the Reformation; and I do not think they show any signs of retracing their steps, or that they will ever throw themselves into what is falsely called Catholicism, but what is merely the modern doctrine and practice of the Bishops and Conclave of Cardinals at Rome."

In his experience as a country parson, and, upon a larger scale, in his experiences as a Commissioner charged to inquire into the educational condition of extensive agricultural districts, Mr. Fraser had enjoyed singular opportunities of judging of the comparative advantages and disadvantages, both to the religious and the national life, of Voluntaryism and Endowment—opportunities which greatly assisted in moulding the conviction of his later years. Preaching at Salisbury Cathedral on August 30, 1868, he said :

"The Church of England is at present maintained for a high national purpose—to keep alive the spirit of religion in this kingdom and people, to be the symbol of our Christianity, a standing witness against the tendency, inevitable in the natural man, to allow his spiritual interests to be absorbed by his material. She is maintained in her high estate, and for this lofty function, by the principle of endowments. Sweep this principle away, secularize, alienate the Church's present heritage, and you must fall back upon Voluntaryism. There does not seem to be here, as there so often is elsewhere, any third course possible. Now, I see that Voluntaryism is able to do, if not great, at least considerable things in towns and among dense populations; but it seems to me to be able to do only very feeble and insignificant things in rural and thinly-peopled districts. The religious communities that rely on this vaunted principle have, speaking generally, in country places no day schools for the education of the young, rarely even a settled ministry. They open their Chapels and their Sunday-schools on the Sabbath Day, and that is all. The 'daily ministration,' which in the Apostolic Church was thought a thing of some value, the visiting from house to house, such as Paul practised at Ephesus, and which is the secret of ministerial usefulness if offered to their people at all, are offered by, and seldom refused from, the clergy of the Church of England. Their children are taught, seldom with any designs of proselytizing, in Church schools; the clergyman visits and relieves their sick, christens their infants, joins their hands in holy wedlock, utters the last words of peace and hope over their graves. Where things are otherwise—I am speaking, be it understood, of rural districts—where there is a settled Nonconformist ministry, you will almost always find it in connection with the principle of endowment.

"Now, sweep away this beneficent principle—which, remember, has cost and is costing no living man a single farthing, by the maintenance of which no man is the poorer, and by the destruction of which few, if any, will be the richer, which is due wholly to the piety and liberality, not of the State, so far as I can discover, but of individual Christian men and women who charged their estates with these endowments centuries ago—and what do you do? You sweep away with it, and, I believe, you would sweep away for ever from this realm of England—from all sparsely peopled districts, which, however, in the aggregate make up a large proportion of our population—the blessing of a settled ministry, and with it all the blessings, to every rank in our complex social system, which a settled ministry implies. What, for instance, is to become of the education of the labouring class in country villages, if the clergy of the Church of England—the only body of men, I say it advisedly, who now interest themselves in it—no longer continue to devote both their time and money to the cause? I am happy to say that I stand as well with my people as any clergyman could desire or hope to do. We have no quarrels, no mistrust, hardly ever a difference of opinion. But they are not wealthy; and even if they had not been, as some people would say, *spoilt* by the vicious system of endowments, I doubt, if I were thrown for my maintenance upon their voluntary efforts, whether I could hope for an income of £25 a year. And I could not live upon that; it would be barely more than I am obliged to contribute every year to the support of my parish school."

But Bishop Fraser was too statesmanly and practical to expect, or even hope, that the Church would be permitted to continue as an Establishment unless, by her good works, she was strongly anchored in the affections of the people.

"The Church exists for the people as truly as the Sabbath was made for man. Her position is impregnable, so long as she stands on the solid foundation of popular appreciation of her usefulness. The English people are generous in their sympathies, ever ready to appreciate, even above its value, any effort that they think is really being made for their good. I would rather throw the cause of the Church of England on their large heart than on its supposed use as a bulwark to the Crown, or its supposed strength from its connection with the aristocracy. We have heard too much, I think, lately of this sort of argument, and neither Church, nor Crown, nor Aristocracy have gained advantage from it. The Crown rests securely on the loyal affection of her people to a Sovereign, whose conscientious discharge of her public duties is as conspicuous as are her private virtues. It is impossible to over-estimate what the moral tone of society in England owes to the personal character of the Queen. And, as for the Aristocracy and the Church Establishment, they will both stand as long as they are felt to exercise their high prerogatives for the public good. We must be worse than blind—we must be infatuated—if we cannot read the signs of the times. Churches as human institutions, as establishments, have fallen before, and will fall again. They have fallen, and, for purposes which no human wit can fathom, God has permitted their places to be taken by systems founded upon imposture, and which continue to propagate a lie. The Crescent of Islam now gleams in the burnished Eastern sky over many a shrine where once pointed heavenwards that Sacred Sign which of old so often led Christian hosts to victory."

Again :

"When the day of arraignment comes, as undoubtedly it will come, to the Church of England, the question she will be asked will be, 'What are thy works?' She will have to show, not only that she is a national institution, but a national blessing and source of strength, that there would be less light in the land if this candlestick were removed, less wholesome fruit for the nourishment of the people if this tree were cut down, fewer stays against the streams of infidelity, immorality, and ignorance, which already set in so strong, if these pulpits were silenced, these prayers and oblations made to cease, these schools secularized, and (as in Daniel's vision) there were set up instead upon our battlements the 'idols of the desolator.'"

While defending the Establishment, therefore, yet, in the interests of the Church, the Bishop was eager to welcome every well-considered Church Reform.

"My aim and object ever since I have been appointed Bishop has been to try and make our Church as national as possible. I want to throw open our pew doors; I want every abuse which is thought inherent or attached to our system cleared away. I want some limitation to the exercise of patronage. I should like to see an effective veto put into the hands of parishes, so that, if there were any attempt, on the part of a patron, to appoint an improper man to the charge of souls, they should have the power to interfere. There are many difficulties against which we have to struggle, and I call upon you, if you value your Church, to open your eyes wide whenever you see abuses in the system. You ought not to care what particular party proposes Church reform; you ought not to care whether it is brought in by the Conservatives or Liberals; but if it is a good measure, and likely to strengthen the Church, you should go in for it, and you also should determine not to rest till the Church has been cleared from every reproach that has been brought upon it."

In the course of his *Lancashire Life* Bishop Fraser thus proved himself to be the Bishop of all parties in the Church. Himself of no party, the good men of all parties, by the force of spiritual gravitation, were drawn towards him, for his simplicity, his earnestness, his religious truthfulness. The Bishop judged none, either of his laity or clergy, according to their party, but according to their works. He was equally hostile to dilutions of doctrine, to materialization of Sacraments, to enervation of feeling. He did not like superficial indifferentism parading itself as freedom of thought; or modern Sacerdotalism professing to be primitive Christianity; or fleeting sentiment usurping the title of saving faith. To him the Gospel was both a Creed and a Fact—but emphatically a Fact, and a Fact either powerful to elevate daily conduct, or not a Fact at all. To him also, the best candlestick in which to set the light of the Gospel appeared to be the candlestick of the English Church.

But, while the Bishop made no secret of his deep and ardent Churchmanship, he soon succeeded in gaining, in a very remarkable degree, the esteem of Nonconformists. This he accomplished by the exercise of profound and genuine toleration; not by any half-hearted and cautious trimming. He never sought to win the confidence of Nonconformists by first unchurching himself, but, just because he felt strong in his Churchmanship, he acted with warm and fearless charity towards Nonconformists.

"Nonconformists," writes Canon Lloyd, "especially were won by Bishop Fraser's large-hearted sympathy, and freedom from ecclesiastical or social pretension. Many who had been accustomed to regard a bishop in the abstract with suspicion, as a prelate and a peer, were disarmed by the heartiness with which he met them, and were glad to concede to him, of their own accord, the respect which his office would not have extorted. His relations with Dissenters were so amicable that a Nonconformist Mayor once described him as the ' *Bishop of all Denominations*,' and the phrase was often repeated. Doctrinally, he had little in common with the descendants of the Puritans, for his views were in substance those of the school of Hooker, modified by a sense of what he used to call 'the proportion of things.' His fellowship with Dissenters was widely different from that which has often led clergy of the Evangelical school to join hands with them."

Both his private letters, and his public utterances, bear witness to the method by which Bishop Fraser won for himself the proud and rare title of "Bishop of all Denominations." That method was the method of a good man's charity—not of a shrewd man's compromise. In a letter written when he had been seven years Bishop, he says:

"I did not accept the invitation of the Primitive Methodists to attend their Missionary meeting. Of course, one feels flattered by their kindly sympathy, but I never have been able to see my way to this particular form of liberality; and, while heartily wishing God-speed to every honest Christian effort, I only work with perfect comfort when I am working on my own lines and within my own legitimate sphere."

Again, speaking at Bolton, in June, 1877:

"Upon points where I am called to unveil the flag of my Churchmanship,

I am as staunch and strong a Churchman as is to be found in Her Majesty's dominions. But the fact that I am a Bishop of the Church of England ought not, I think—and if it did, I should be drawing very false lessons from the Great Teacher of my religion—to prevent me from holding out the right hand of fellowship, and from asking with my heart a Divine blessing upon every one, no matter with what particular religious denomination he is connected, who is engaged in the eminently Christian work of helping the widow and the fatherless."

In his Third Charge he says :

"The relations between the Church and the various Nonconformist bodies by which it is surrounded in these dense masses of population are variously described in the returns of the clergy. In one particular section of the diocese they are generally reported as 'hostile,' though the hostility seems to arise from political differences rather than from religious, every Churchman being *ex hypothesi* a Conservative and every Nonconformist a Liberal. I regret this introduction of political animosities into religious relations very profoundly. Men equally earnest for the cause of Christ may yet think differently on national questions; and as if the '*odium theologicum*,' where it exists, were not bad enough in itself, you try to mend matters by mixing it up with political rancour. In the district to which I refer, it is well known that partizan feeling, both in politics and in religion, runs very high. But elsewhere the relations between Churchmen and Nonconformists are generally reported to be friendly, and this state of feeling is, I am sure, one that we ought to try to encourage by every means in our power. A more cheering incident—a happier omen for future peace—has not occurred in this century, if ever in the history of the Church of England before, than that memorable address of the Nonconformist ministers at Leicester to the Church Congress assembled there, and the frank and kindly reception of it by the presiding Bishop. That was, indeed, an occasion over which a 'Te Deum' might have well been sung. An Act which has recently been passed by the Legislature may fairly be regarded as another step in the direction of promoting the same brotherliness of feeling. A correspondence, which appears recently to have occupied a good deal of space in one of our Manchester newspapers, but which I should not have seen but for the attention of persons who cut it from the columns in which it appeared, and sent it to me for perusal from time to time, and in which my doings and misdoings have been the object of a good deal of long-pent-up, but at last exploding, indignation, charges me with what in the eyes of the writers seems almost a deadly sin—with thinking not unkindly and speaking not unfavourably of Dissenters. I do not profess to love Dissent as such, but I have received innumerable kindnesses from Dissenters, and—amid our differences, which I regret—I desire to recognize the bonds of that common Christianity, which, in spite of those differences, make our hearts beat in unison as men engaged in the same great cause. Why should I abuse them? Why should I not try to discern in them, as in other Christian men, whatever there is of devotion to duty, of zeal for God and for righteousness, of spiritual-mindedness and fervency? The Church of England has no monopoly of these graces, nor would desire to claim one. Remembering how Nonconformity was made—no doubt, sometimes by self-will, and pride, and prejudice, and ignorance, but far, far more often by the Church's own supineness, neglect, and intolerance in days long gone by, of which we have not even yet paid the full penalty—though, as I have said, I love not the thing, I cannot speak harshly of it. I will not refuse to recognize and thank God for its virtues, and excellencies, and works done for Christ, wherever I see them. At any rate, it is in this spirit, and not in the spirit of estrangement or exclusiveness, that I am disposed both to pray and to labour for the reunion of the Churches."

Again:

"It is quite contrary to the constitution of my own mind and temper to regard a Dissenter as my natural enemy. I don't know how far I should be able to work *with* him in a directly religious cause, because I have never tried. We should, of course, have differences of opinion, and the ground on which we were working might cause them to emerge. But certainly I have never been disposed to work *against* him, nor have I ever been willing to credit—or I should rather say to *dis*-credit—him with any desire to work against me. 'We are of the same army,' once said to me a Nonconformist minister with whom I fell in at a place where two roads met—'we are of the same army, I believe, and are enlisted under the same Captain, though we do not belong to the same regiment.' 'At least,' I replied, taking up his metaphor, 'I hope we are fighting in the same battle on the same side—on the side of the Lord against the mighty ones;' and we drew together and talked pleasantly on matters of common interest till our roads diverged again.

"My Master's words to His over-hasty disciple warn me against attempting to forbid any man, whether lawfully commissioned, as I may think, or not, whom I find casting out devils in His name. And whoever brings personal earnestness to his work will have, I believe, power given to him by Christ to cast out devils; and there is no man that can do a miracle in His name, and then lightly speak evil of Him. But every one who knows the minds and moods of our rural populations knows also that the three great Nonconformist denominations are not those which reckon most adherents there. The more ignorant people are, the more they crave for excitement in their religion. Whitfieldism is more acceptable to them than Wesleyanism. The camp meeting, the revival, will always triumph over the calmer services of the chapel. And I need not, I hope, be thought narrow-minded or intolerant, because I don't like to find persons spreading about Richard Weaver's tracts, and telling people to look after their feelings rather than their lives; and, if they are of the number of God's foreknown ones, their conversion is sure to come, and when it comes will come irresistibly. I frankly confess I shudder at the moral effects of such teaching. It approaches too nearly that doctrine which Paul calls damnable—the doctrine which says, 'Let us continue in sin, that grace may abound;' and I should be sorry to see any people, transferred from the sober influence of the Church of England to such rank, such demoralizing, fanaticism as this."

Again :

"I, for one, give a large and broad meaning to that phrase, the Church of England, and I desire to see my dear Mother Church, which has been the Church of England for eight hundred years or more, and which I hope will be a Church for many centuries still, spread out her arms widely and fearlessly, and show herself ready to welcome all who will accept her ministrations, or in any way gather themselves to her fold. But, as a Christian Bishop, I consider myself open to do all I can to promote the interests of my Master's service, whether, according to my humble judgment, that service is being done by the hands of those who are called Churchmen, or by the hands of those who are called Dissenters. I do not mean to say that I consider the platform upon which Dissent is built as solid and as broad as the platform upon which the Church of England is built, otherwise I should be a Dissenter, and not a Churchman. But all cannot look at things exactly with the same eyes. All have not been trained under exactly the same circumstances. The lines upon which God has placed us—every one to do his duty—are not exactly the same lines; but all Christians are bound to have regard to their Master's warning to those very hasty disciples, who were for forbidding the man who was working the miracles in Christ's name, because he followed not with them. I confess my sympathies are broad enough, while I cling closest to my Mother Church, to bid—as far as I safely can, without compromising the ground which I feel myself most distinctly bound to maintain—to bid God-speed to every sincere, earnest, sober effort which is made—I was almost going to say, I cared not by whom—to extend the boundaries of my Master's kingdom."

Speaking to a gathering of Nonconformists, the Bishop said:

"I hope my own Church, the dear Church of England, will gain many of you. Perhaps you will allow me to say more than that, and you will not be offended if I, as a Bishop of the Church, say it—that I hope it will gain most of you. But all I can say is, if you, in your heart and conscience, think you can get more good to your souls under other ministrations than those of the Church of England, I would be the last Bishop in England to stay you from going where God's promptings lead you. I want to seek you by fair means, and not by foul means, nor by Acts of Parliament."

At a meeting held in the Town Hall, Manchester, January 16, 1883, the Bishop said :

"I belong to and represent a definite Christian organization, and there are certain things incident to that organization which more or less impede

U

one's perfect freedom of action; but I should think none the better of myself as a Churchman, and a great deal worse of myself as a Christian, if I could not recognize, and sympathize with, efforts made outside my own body to bring the comfort of the Gospel within the reach of the masses. I never would say a word to disparage the efforts made by any body of Christ's disciples. I do not think it is Christian, and I do not think I am bound by my Churchmanship to do it."

Toleration of this bold and hearty kind won the admiration and love of non-Christian, as well as of Christian, people. And a strange result followed, for, through his fatherly affection, Bishop Fraser came to be regarded as something more than the "Bishop of all Christian denominations." *He was Bishop also of the Jews.* No Jew felt more sympathy for his fellow-Jews, in their distress, in the years 1881, 1882; and no Jew worked more assiduously for the relief of this Jewish distress than Bishop Fraser. "Bishop Fraser made us feel," writes an eminent Jew, "that Christians worship the same God as we do, and recognize the Divine morality, taught at Sinai, quite as fully as we do." When a Committee was formed, in 1881, for the relief of the persecuted Jews in Russia, Bishop Fraser was elected Chairman, and presided, with scrupulous regularity, over its frequent business meetings. Mr. Alderman Baker, the Mayor of Manchester, declared, at a public meeting, that "he could scarcely summon language sufficiently eulogistic of the Bishop's bearing and conduct, as president of the Jewish Relief Fund." And the Bishop himself, in acknowledging the Mayor's commendation, narrated a circumstance probably unique in the annals of Cathedral restoration:

"Only this morning I had an interview with the churchwardens of the Manchester Cathedral, and they told me that a gentleman who did not wish his name to be known—a member of the Jewish persuasion—had offered to pay £150 towards their restoration fund to mark, as he was pleased to say, his respect for the Bishop. That gratified me exceedingly, and I only hope such kindness will not make me slack in the discharge of my duties."

In 1874, as Bishop Fraser was coming home from the Congress at Stoke-upon-Trent, a gentleman in the train introduced himself to him. He said he was a Jew, and asked a number of questions touching the Congress. He also accounted for his interest in such subjects by saying that he was a large employer of labour in Manchester, that he always deplored the negligence of religion by his workmen; but that since Bishop Fraser's coming he had noticed that, first his foremen, and afterwards the bulk of his workmen, had been roused to a sense of religion, which not only carried them to hear the Bishop wherever they could, but had further induced them to become regular worshippers.

"In 1882," writes one of his chaplains, "the Bishop acted as Chairman of the Committee for the relief of the persecuted Jews in Russia, and concerted with the Committee the best mode of distributing the money raised in Manchester for the relief of the sufferers. One old Rabbi met the Bishop in the street, and said: 'Oh, my lord, we pray for you every Sabbath in our synagogue.' In acknowledgment of his willing and able services the Jews sent him a letter of thanks with Munkacsy's picture of 'Christ before Pilate.' At the Bishop's death, to the expressions of sorrow and sympathy addressed to his widow, coming from the various communities of Christianity, were added addresses from the congregation of British Jews, from that of Spanish and Portuguese Jews, from the South Manchester Synagogue, from the Manchester Hebrew Congregation, from the Board of Guardians for the relief of the Jewish poor of Manchester. These addresses speak of 'the Bishop's brave denunciations of the wrongs under which their brethren had suffered, of his broad and tolerant spirit, and declare a hope that the lessons of love and toleration which he had taught by precept and example would tend to cement in closer union the bond of brotherhood between Jew and Christian.' There seemed well-nigh to be fulfilled the text, 'Where there is neither Greek nor Jew' (Col. ii. 11)."

Thus, while remaining a pronounced and definite Churchman, without abating or obscuring one jot of Anglican principle as set forth in the Prayer Book, and vindicated by classical Churchmen like Hooker, Bishop Fraser won the hearts of all sorts of worshippers by his tender sympathy and transparent manliness. A Nonconformist correspondent writes, that "at bazaars and sales of work in connection with various chapels it was quite a common occurrence that more photographs of the Bishop were sold than of their own ministers." Where he could not convince men of Church doctrine, he could at least show them Christian charity. We all need the lesson Bishop Fraser spent himself in teaching us—the lesson that Christ is greater than the Churches, and Religion deeper than religious differences. Nonconformists need the lesson as much as Churchmen, and Churchmen not less than Nonconformists. Nonconformity has done much to teach mankind the principles of civic and religious liberty; but the English Church may, with just and grateful pride, remember, that the most conspicuous illustration afforded by the nineteenth century of an intense Christian, whose tolerance embraced all parties, political and ecclesiastical, and whose charity blessed all denominations, was one of her own Bishops.

The following testimonies from Manchester Nonconformists set forth, with appreciation and discernment, both his attitude towards them and their attitude towards him. The Rev. Dr. Macfadyen, a leading Nonconformist Minister in Manchester, writes:

"The Nonconformists of Manchester joined in welcoming Bishop Fraser to his diocese, and from the first he, with his usual frankness, acknowledged their personal kindness. This mutual good feeling deepened as each party came to know the other better.

"In common with the entire community, Nonconformists paid a tribute of admiration to the features of his character, which such a community as that of Manchester pays eventually to all good men of all parties, and of all sects. His transparent sincerity, hatred of cant, willingness to look facts in the face, geniality, hopefulness, disinterestedness, large-hearted sympathy with every honest effort to help men, attachment to his mother, and love of simplicity, were not lost upon them.

"As he developed his ideal and realized it in part, they found it, on the civic side, more and more in harmony with their own.

"They sympathized heartily with him in every effort to promote civic and social progress, even though, in the exercise of individual judgment, they might differ from him as to some of the methods he advocated, and might disapprove of some of the things he did or said.

"It was a new thing to them to hear a Bishop say that he would rather stay in his diocese, than go to London to be a Legislator. They admired the boldness with which he confessed that, to secure education for the nation, he would part with some questions of the Catechism, and, even in a secular system of education, he could take his place as a clergyman. They valued highly his advocacy of the opening of the Universities to Nonconformists, and his expression of discontent with the Act of Uniformity. They endorsed his repeated attacks upon the compulsory reading of the Athanasian Creed, and his frequent expressions of regret that the Church of Christ had departed from the simple articles of the Apostles' Creed.

"And this admiration was only equalled by their surprise when, again and again, he maintained that the whole congregation is a royal priesthood, and that the Greek term for a sacrificing priest was not applied in the New Testament to any minister of Christ.

"But, pleasant as it was to be in union with him on such important questions, it was a higher pleasure to feel that we could speak boldly of our differences, as he and we did on so many questions on which there can be no compromise. Next to the pleasure of union is the joy of battle with a generous opponent. The Bishop never knowingly hit below the belt. The newspapers of the time would offer many illustrations of frank apology made by him when he discovered that he had unconsciously misrepresented an antagonist, or misconceived a fact.

"But beyond, and above, everything else, he was beloved by Nonconformists because they had confidence in his desire for Christian union. One of his first public appearances took the city by storm. Nonconformists could scarcely believe their own eyes when they saw the placard announcing that Bishop Fraser was to address a meeting in the Free Trade Hall on behalf of a mission, which was known to have no connection with the Church of England. They recognized the appearance in their midst of an ecclesiastical phenomenon. As he became known, it was clear that this was his declaration to the world, that he meant to cultivate Christian union, so far as he conscientiously could, and the advance he then made was, on the other side, gladly reciprocated. We have been familiar with other professions on this point which did not stand the test. Sometimes the platform is used as a good place to meet Dissenters, but the words spoken there are never acted out. Sometimes the meaning is honest enough, but it is attended by a patronage that is neither good to give nor good to receive. Sometimes they are made from a wish to proselytize, which could only stir resentment and make things worse.

"But in intercourse with Bishop Fraser we felt ourselves safe. In his bearing there was a freedom from arrogance, and an honourable dealing, pleasant to experience. He never concealed his preference for the system which he served so loyally, or his intention to advance its interest to the utmost of his power. But he was incapable of a resort to dishonourable means, and was always straightforward in aiming at his purpose. He was believed when he said that it was a pleasure to him to meet on common ground with those who differed from him, and was accepted on all neutral questions as their fit and proper leader. And this was the easier because it was seen and felt that he desired unity on Christian grounds.

"For my own part, I often regretted that his sermons dealt so little with the doctrinal and experimental sides of Christianity. In Manchester this kind of preaching seems to me to be specially needed. As one of our most valued leaders of thought said to me not long ago, 'the average Manchester Christian has never got beyond the Epistle of James.' He meant it for praise. I regard it as a weakness, and I regretted that Bishop Fraser did not oftener use his splendid platform for bringing out the side of Christianity which is most needed. But no one could know Bishop

Fraser and not be conscious that he was himself an earnest and devout Christian, and that his Christianity dominated his private life and directed his public action. It was this, more than anything else, I believe, that made it so easy on our side to work with him, and that led him in so many ways to show his affection for those who, in his judgment, loved his Master.

"When the news spread throughout the city that Bishop Fraser was dead, none grieved for the public loss more deeply than did the Nonconformists. I do not think that there was any Nonconformist place of worship in which his death did not call forth expressions of real sorrow, nor any pulpit from which hearty utterance of that regret was not heard. To myself, and to many besides me, now that he is gone into what Jeremy Taylor beautifully calls 'the all-reconciling world,' heaven is more home-like, because *he* is there."

The Rev. Stuart J. Reid, of Chislehurst, who from 1875 to 1880 was minister of the Broughton Congregational Church, almost opposite the Bishop's door, and who writes that "every Christmas brought some reminder of the Bishop's interest and good-will in himself and his work," says:

"From the moment Dr. Fraser first stepped out into the 'glare and whirlwind of publicity,' in a city which Mr. Gladstone once described as the 'centre of the modern life of England,' to the day when tidings of his sudden death fell like a bolt from the blue on that busy and vast community, which honoured and revered him, the Bishop of Manchester never lost his hold either on the classes or the masses of Manchester, and in a very sacred sense it is still true, 'deep in the common heart his power survives.' Within a few months of the end, he stated that he was charged, among other grievous sins, with thinking not unkindly and speaking not unfavourably of Dissenters, and he added, with that honesty and candour which were so characteristic of him, 'I don't profess to love Dissent, but I have received innumerable kindnesses from Dissenters.' Many a Nonconformist who does not profess to love the Established Church, nor to feel any special veneration for her Bishops, learned to think less harshly of the one, and more charitably of the other, through the light which was cast upon both, by Dr. Fraser's attitude and spirit. Not a few Dissenters, occupying obscure as well as prominent positions, could say with perfect truth that they had 'received innumerable kindnesses' from the genial and great-hearted Bishop. It is certain that no prelate of the English Church has ever won such enthusiastic reverence from all sections of Nonconformity. He was, indeed, as he has been justly called, the 'Bishop of all the Denominations.' Dr. M'Claren, of Manchester, speaking for the whole body of Dissenters, when the tidings of his death had shaken that city to its centre, declared only the sober truth, when he said, 'We ever reverenced the goodness and great qualities of the man. We all feel that the public life of this great city is sadly impoverished by the removal of a unique personality, which was the centre of union for many a good cause.'

THE BISHOP OF ALL DENOMINATIONS. 295

"What Nonconformists admired in Bishop Fraser was his genuine manliness, his transparent candour, his hearty recognition of what he deemed to be good and worthy, even in men from whom he conscientiously differed; and the zeal with which he threw himself into every movement, which sought to better or brighten the lives of the toiling masses amongst whom his lot was cast. There was in him not the smallest trace of priestly assumption or spiritual pride; indeed, his beautiful humility, and noble self-forgetfulness, can never be forgotten by any one who was privileged to know him even slightly. His religion was thorough—it ran right through him; it was practical—it came out in all he did and said. Men felt instinctively that the Bishop's ambition was to make the most of his singularly great and diversified opportunities, not indeed for any personal ends, but simply and entirely for the public good. In certain respects, to quote a homely phrase, the Bishop, by his very nobility and consecration, took the wind out of the sails of Nonconformity. The Lancashire operative who, Mr. Hughes tells us, told the Bishop that he would make a 'grand Methody preacher,' expressed, in the vernacular, the feeling that was uppermost regarding him, in the breasts of most Dissenters. On one occasion, my friend and neighbour, the late Rev. D. Jones Hamer, of Salford, made a somewhat unguarded allusion, at a public meeting, adverse to the Bishop, which the Tory press made the most of, animadverting on the speaker. The Bishop, with characteristic generosity, at once wrote to Mr. Hamer, repudiating altogether the sentiments expressed by the local papers, and assuring him that he did not doubt that he was animated in what he had said by the best of motives. Dr. Fraser delighted to get into conversation with people he met casually, such as fellow-passengers in the train. On one journey from London he entered very cordially into conversation with a young man who was a complete stranger to him, and when the train arrived at Manchester, instead of wishing his fellow-traveller the usual formal 'Good afternoon,' he inquired which way the young man was going through the city. When he found out that his home lay in Higher Broughton, he good-naturedly insisted on the stranger taking a seat in his brougham, and, whilst the latter still hesitated to avail himself of the offer, the Bishop settled the matter in his own cheery way, by grasping his fellow-traveller's portmanteau and handing it up to his coachman. The young man, though the Bishop did not know it at the time, was a Nonconformist, to whom Episcopal attention of this sort was not less startling than pleasing. Many Congregationalists in Manchester and Salford were greatly touched by the tender manner which marked Dr. Fraser when he found his way to the bedside of an old Congregational minister, and spoke to him, as he lay near the gates of death, with brotherly kindness and heartfelt sympathy. When a prominent Manchester Nonconformist, an alderman of the city and one of its foremost public men, told the Bishop of the harsh and uncharitable attitude of the Rector of the suburb in which he lived, Dr. Fraser laid his hand gently on the speaker's shoulder, and said, with deep feeling, 'Ah yes, it is very pitiful, One is our Master, even Christ, and all we are brethren.' It was because he never in his intercourse with Nonconformists stood on the pedestal of his exalted office, or met them on any other terms than those of Christian equality and brotherhood, that respect grew into reverence as time rendered more and more apparent the consistency, courage, and chivalry of one who was a born leader of men. Mr. Guinness Rogers—doughty champion of the Liberation Society though he is—spoke for the Nonconformist ministry when he said, 'Dr. Fraser never sank the man in the priest, or the Christian in the prelate, but sought, with the power which God had committed to him, to serve his day and generation. No Bishop ever won to such a degree the confidence and affection of all sorts and conditions of Nonconformists. Absolutely indifferent to the antiquated pomps of his office, the unconventional and fervid Bishop of Manchester spoke anywhere and everywhere on the current topics of the hour with a simplicity, straightforwardness, vigour, and courage, which carried his utterances far and wide, and made them more or less of a power in the life of the nation itself. He was intensely *human*, and people knew that he felt for them. The accent of sincerity, which was never absent from his speech, thrilled their hearts as the utterance of no hollow platitudes, however eloquently expressed, could ever have done. The beauty and sweetness of his character were continually replenished by the reality and depth of his spiritual life. He truly 'fought a good fight,' and did so on a perilous and exposed part of the battle-field of life, and there is little reason therefore to wonder that to-day, deep in the common heart, his power survives.'"

The Rev. S. Alfred Steinthal, M.A., Unitarian Minister, writes:

"It is not an easy task to put into the form of a letter the impressions left upon my mind of the life amongst us here in Lancashire of the late Bishop of Manchester, they are so varied and numerous. From the very beginning of his residence amongst us, he showed that genial sympathy towards all, and that kindly respect for those who differed from him, which won for him our high esteem and affection. He came to Manchester when very strong differences existed between the members of the Church of England and most Nonconformists on the subject of National Education. The National Education Union had its headquarters in this district, and had announced its intention of holding a meeting in the Free Trade Hall, at which gathering the Bishop was to speak. I well remember with what anxiety we looked at the papers reporting the meeting, and how pleased we were to find, that though he was not able to adopt our views as to the best method of solving the difficulties connected with National Education, yet he was not, like some men, thinking of upholding the Church's supremacy, but purely how best to promote the education of the children. He recognized with graceful courtesy the honesty of purpose shown by the advocates of the Education League. If the controversy had been conducted by all in the same generous spirit, there would have been none of the bitter feeling aroused, which unfortunately prevented the Elementary

Education Act of 1870 being as satisfactory a settlement as it might have been.

"The spirit which Dr. Fraser showed in this his first public appearance he maintained unto the end of his life. He always seemed more anxious to do justice to others, and to find the good there was in those who differed from him, than to secure a victory over them. His broad sympathy for everything which tended to the well-being of society made him willing to give his influence in aid of any benevolent plan which commended itself to his judgment; whether the promoters were Churchmen or not, never seemed for one moment to enter his consideration; and it was this forgetfulness on his own part of sectarian distinctions, combined with his unexampled readiness to act as leader in all the multifarious charities of his diocese, that made it natural for men of the most differing theological positions, always to apply first to the Bishop of Manchester, if they wished to have public support for any benevolent enterprise. He was the undoubted centre of the philanthropy of his diocese, and there is no Nonconformist who is not willing to allow that he well deserved the pre-eminence he had earned by the practical exercise of the highest of the Christian graces. But, just as he was ready to comply with the invitations given to him from all sides, so also was he ready to make use of men not belonging to the Church, when he thought they had any special qualifications for the particular work he had in view. I have known him write suggesting the initiation of plans to Nonconformists, keeping himself in the background at first, but joining in the work, when once it was begun, with his whole energy and zeal. He was a most thoughtful as well as liberal worker in charitable enterprise. He was not an indiscriminate giver. Manchester men well remember how he deprecated the multiplication of so-called charities, with expensive organizations; he was very desirous to prevent that overlapping of agencies which is productive of so much waste of money and of energy. I remember with what earnestness he entered on the advocacy of making one great Lancashire Fund for the relief of the Indian famine, instead of having separate funds in every town, and how glad he was of the success of the plan which he originated. He often spoke in favour of uniting kindred charities, and I am sure that, if his suggestions could have been carried out, the benevolent activity of the district would be more efficiently employed than it is to-day.

"Whenever he attended any meeting his rising was always welcomed by his audience, with the certainty that they would hear a speech in which manly sincerity, moral earnestness, frank simplicity, and the highest Christian principle would enforce attention and arrest sympathy. It always did one good to hear him; no matter what the subject was on which he spoke, he raised it at once by making it the expression of religious motive. But there never was any weak sentimentality in his utterance. I think it may be truly said of him that the general effect of his work amongst us has been to make men universally acknowledge that the very depth of his religious faith made him one of the manliest and purest of men we have ever been privileged to know. It is not for me to speak of him as a Churchman, except to say that he undoubtedly did much to take all bitterness out of the differences which exist between members of the Established Church and Dissenters. He did not underrate the importance of those differences, but he dealt with them, as with everything else, in the spirit of that charity which thinketh no evil.

"It is not possible to close this letter without referring to the winning influence he exercised by his genial sympathy in private. Busy as he must have been with all the intricate and multifarious duties of his high office, sufficient it might be thought to exhaust the powers of any man, he undertook with cheerful willingness a greater amount of general, social and philanthropic work, than almost any private citizen. But he in addition seemed to have his sympathy always alive for the private joys and sorrows of his friends. No sorrow visited the home, but his word of comfort came to cheer and strengthen the mourner's heart, and, more precious almost still, he knew how, with generous thoughtfulness, to increase any joy that might fall to a friend's share. I shall never forget, how once when he was away from home, enjoying a much-wanted season of rest, he sat down to write me a letter that I always cherish, speaking to me of one of the happiest events which has blessed my life, and making it still more rich by his kind words of congratulation.

"Excuse these hurriedly written notes. As I told you, I am just now overwhelmed with a multiplicity of engagements, but my reverent love for the memory of Dr. Fraser is so deep that I cannot resist your kind request to write a few lines of my recollections of him."

The Rev. Dr. Alexander Thomson, senior Congregationalist Minister in Manchester, writes:

"The only occasions on which I had the pleasure of meeting with the late Bishop Fraser were at public meetings of a religious or philanthropic character—generally those of the Bible Society and the Religious Tract Society—when the Bishop occupied the chair, and I was present as Secretary, or as one of the speakers. At such times there was, of course, very little opportunity for conversational intercourse; but I frequently could not help admiring the readiness and manifest good-will with which he made use of any opening to display affability to those with whom he came into contact. His whole demeanour and address were so simple and genial, so free both from stiff reserve, and from condescension, as at once to conciliate regard, and to suggest the thought—especially to the mind of a Nonconformist—how agreeably unlike he was to our ordinary idea of a high ecclesiastical dignitary. He was, indeed, one of the manliest and frankest men I ever met with. His manner at once made you feel at ease in his company, and removed any sense of uncomfortable restraint. The remark more than once fell from my lips, after returning home from such meetings, 'What a pleasure it is to meet *our Bishop!* He speaks to me just as freely as if we were old acquaintances, or as any of my own ministerial friends would do. He hasn't a particle of starch in him.'

His speeches were like himself, unaffected, straightforward, and practical, never studied for effect; but showing the pains he had taken to make himself well acquainted with the main points of the subject and the interest he felt in it, while avoiding all exaggeration, and aiming at an honest statement of the claims of the case. In listening to him one felt there was a charm in the transparent sincerity of the speaker, and in the plain good sense and kindly feeling he displayed, that was more persuasive than any elaborate rhetoric. And how admirably he would bring out—when it was appropriate—a distinct profession of those Christian beliefs which were the source of his strength and the inspiration of his life! I recall with pleasure two occasions in particular when he did so. The one was when he presided at a large meeting in the Free Trade Hall to promote the establishment of a Mission Hall for religious addresses to working men, in which Christians of different denominations, as well as our Wesleyan friends chiefly, were interested. While frankly affirming his preference for his own Church and its methods of working, he expressed his hearty approval of the object of the Mission in question, and his sympathy with its conductors, in so liberal and evangelical a spirit—reminding one of the Apostle Paul, whose language he quoted—that his words thrilled the hearts of all; filling us with thankfulness to God that a prelate—so truly apostolical in spirit—had been placed over this populous diocese. All who heard him that night needed no other proof that, whatever might be the case with others, he at least was in the genuine line of apostolic succession. The other occasion was at one of the annual meetings of our local Auxiliary to the British and Foreign Bible Society, when he referred to the doctrine of our Lord's Atoning Sacrifice as the vital centre of Revealed Truth, in a way most impressive and affecting, which showed how his own hopes rested there. I shall never forget it, for it deeply touched my own heart.

"My great regret is—especially now that he is gone—that necessarily I saw so little of him, our lines of movement lying so much apart; for he was certainly such a man as you rarely meet with, marked by an engaging individuality of character, combining elements of nobility, simplicity and sweetness, which drew one towards him by a strong attraction, and called forth at once affection and esteem. To have known him, though imperfectly and at a distance, I regard as a blessing, enriching and brightening the memory of past scenes. Even the sturdiest Nonconformist in this district might speak of him with pride as 'our excellent Bishop,' and we all lament that he was taken from us so suddenly and so soon."

Two remarkable letters may fitly close this chapter. One was written by a poor and obscure Wesleyan minister's daughter; the other by the great and famous Dean Stanley. Both letters brought messages from dying beds to the "Bishop of all Denominations," who, by the childlike purity of his spirit, the all-including charity of his affection, and the intense spirituality of his faith, held a place of sweet privilege, alike in the thoughts of the poor Wesleyan minister and the Dean's noble wife, as they lay at the gate of death.

> 2, MILTON PLACE, BROAD STREET, PENDLETON,
> *September* 21, 1880.

MY LORD,—If this be an intrusion, pray forgive me. I am not asking a favour—I will just state a fact and leave the rest to you. My dear old father (the Rev. T. G. Lee) lies, as you know, at the gate of heaven—in his own words, quoted from a hymn he loves—

> "I'm kneeling at the threshold,
> My hand is on the door."

He is just waiting to hear the "Come in." Ever since you were married, his one wish has been to see you and Mrs. Fraser together, and ask "God bless you!" The prayers he has offered for you will not, I think, be fruitless. The other day, Mr. Smith (St. Thomas's) gave him a kind message from you, and that revived the old longing, which only subsided because he thought it impossible—I don't *ask* this. I only wish to feel, when the memory of my dear one is all I have, that I left no effort unmade for his gratification. If you *can* gratify him, please let me have a line (enclosed is an envelope ready), as the *suddenness* might be too much; whereas, if I knew *when*, I could prepare his mind. To you and Mrs. Fraser I will not say *Excuse;* we are not able to keep a servant, and things are not as nice as in more palmy and prosperous days—but poverty for him will soon be over. Will you pardon this, from yours obediently,

> MARY A. LOVATT.

"The result was," writes Mrs. Fraser, "that we both went down at once to that death-bed, and there was the Bishop seen in all his humility and spirituality, kneeling by the old man's side, giving his brow a kiss of peace, and breathing sweetest words of faith, hope, and love, causing the dying man to exclaim, with lifted hands and streaming eyes, 'Nunc Dimittis!'"

> DEANERY, WESTMINSTER, *February* 1, 1876.

MY DEAR BISHOP,—I knew that, if you had happened to hear of the great change, you would be feeling for us. I thank you from the bottom of my heart.

On the night of your preaching, a sudden access of suffering came on, and from that time all hope fled. She has lingered, and lingers still, on the borders of life and death—her sufferings terrible to see—her mind and heart still the same. On one of the nights after she knew that she could not recover, she gave me this message for you, which I ought, perhaps, to have reserved for a future day; but as, when that day comes, I know not how I shall be able to write, and as you have spoken as you have, I send it you now. Ever yours,

A. P. STANLEY.

Her message was this. Tell the dear Bishop of Manchester that I bless his work—that I beg him not to leave you. I have always called him "my son," and I commend you to him. Tell him not to let himself be overborne by clerical prejudice. It is not likely (she said with a sweet smile), it is not likely that he will be—I only say this to encourage him not to be. Dear fellow! Let him continue, with you, to try to "enlarge the Church." She added a few words in playfulness, which I will give you on some future occasion, and then concluded: "But all the rest that I have said is quite serious."

I need say no more: you know how absolutely genuine are these wishes and hopes for you and for me.

How long she may be with us, or how soon pass from us, is quite uncertain. As I must still toil on in this sad world, I must ask you whether you will preach on one of the Sundays from April 27 to July 23, as I truly cannot. Yours,

A. P. S.

CHAPTER XIII.

THE CITIZEN BISHOP.

Religion and Politics—Bishops in Parliament—Clergy and Laity—Civil and Religious Liberty—Christian Socialism—Religion and Morals—Licentiousness—Purity—National Prosperity—National Decay—Christianity and Citizenship—Christianity and Patriotism—Christianity and War—Phœnix Park Murders—Assassinations in Ireland—The Irish Question—Greatness of Manchester—The Thirlmere Water Scheme—The Town Hall—The Bishop and the Press.

BISHOP FRASER'S conception of Christianity was preeminently ethical, yet he was no mere moralist. He saw distinctly, and held firmly, the sovereignty of the spiritual aspects of the Christian Faith. To him, the beginning and end of Christianity was God. Its source lay, as he said, in the Fatherhood of God; its saving power in Redemption through Christ, its daily strength in the Indwelling of the Holy Spirit. No one (as the last chapter shows) could have insisted more strongly that the supreme prerogative of man is the culture of his immortal faculties through the instrumentality of worship, prayer, meditation, and the Eucharist. But no one could, at the same time, have emphasized with more earnest insistence the fact that Christianity is ethical, social, civic; that it deals with man, not only as a spiritual being, but also as a moral, domestic, commercial, political being. Bishop Fraser believed intensely that no part of the life of man lies outside the scope and influence of religion.

"I wish," he said, "religion were brought down from the clouds, and made to move among men as a living power, fashioning their lives, governing their acts, restraining their tempers, and making them do their duty as Christians. Obedience to the law, submission to authority, the right use and true limits of liberty, the honour men are bound to pay to others, the loyalty and reverence due to the sovereign, are all classed by the old Galilean fisherman with the love of the brotherhood and the fear of God.

"I wish that the children in the schools—at any rate, the elder ones—were taught their duties and privileges as Englishmen. Just now I do not know that there is any more important subject to be taught the people than what their constitution is, and what they ought to be under it. They are never tired of throwing up their hats in favour of the great and glorious privileges of Englishmen; but they do not know what peril those liberties run when men can be got to give their votes for five shillings or even a pot of beer."

"It appears," writes a discerning critic in the year 1880, "to be Bishop Fraser's mission to reveal the application of the precepts of the Gospel to social and political life. He is not a great preacher in the usual acceptation of the term, but he is a preacher of homely, sanctified common sense. The source of Dr. Fraser's power lies in the vigour of his moral manhood, and in the catholicity of his sympathies with every influence within or without the Church which makes for practical righteousness. He is abreast of his times, and the broad, honest, earnest manliness of his tone of thinking and speaking chimes in with the advancing thought of the day. The Church which can multiply such men will be the Church of the future, and the cloud which threatens disestablishment will still remain for many a day no bigger than a man's hand if the clergy will lay to heart the obvious lessons of Bishop Fraser's busy and unselfish career."

One of the civic evils which Bishop Fraser most deeply dreaded was the identification of religion with any political party, although he deeply desired that all politics should be penetrated and purified with religious principle. He disapproved of the introduction of politics into religion, but encouraged the introduction of religion into politics.

"I want to keep a clear and distinct line between the Gospel of Christ and the wretched partizan politics which occupy far too much of people's thoughts and minds. Still I do want to see Christian influence spread farther, much farther, than it does. I do not want you to say, 'I must adopt one kind of principle in business, and another kind of principle at other times.' The principles that should govern a man's life at one time are the principles which ought to govern it at all times. Any variation from those principles, any undue attempt to take advantage of anybody, is acting as wrongly and as contrary to the principles of Christianity as can possibly be conceived. Can you doubt for one moment that Christianity is the one purifying and sanctifying influence in the world? Can you doubt it ought to penetrate into every department of human life? What a miserable thing it is when we find that as a result of our unhappy divisions there are departments of human life and activity that are withdrawn from the influence of Christianity."

"I most devoutly wish to see religion kept apart from politics. I do not like that which I find is the accepted maxim in Lancashire, that every Churchman is a Conservative and every Nonconformist a Liberal. It is a fallacy and a falsehood to introduce politics into religion, but certainly religion might interfere in the sphere of politics. Religion might make men conduct their political contests fairly; religion might come in and step before a man who is going to take a bribe, and say, 'Will you sell your vote for £5?' Religion might well come in and say to a candidate, 'Are you going to flood your constituency with drunkenness by opening the public-houses, and letting the people get drunk there?' Religion has got something to say in politics, and I think it should put before men a high and worthy view of the duty they owe, as citizens, to the State."

In an Address delivered at the Co-operative Hall, Downing Street, Manchester, November 27, 1882, the Bishop plainly declared what, in his judgment, should be the highest aims of politics:

"There are certain objects, social as much as political, which every true Englishman must have at heart—the progress of morality, under which, of course, I place the suppression of intemperance and licentiousness, the parents of more than half our crime, and of nearly all our poverty and wretchedness; the diffusion of a sound and suitable education among all classes; a wider and more equable distribution of whatever ministers to culture and to comfort; better relations between those two great classes, the employers and the employed; cheap and impartial justice—I don't believe that cheap law need necessarily be bad law; the maintenance, so far as is possible, of peace; increased facilities for healthful recreation; the substitution of merit for interest, as the highest claim of a public servant; fewer and narrower chasms between the social strata; these, and such as these, so far as they can be secured by political action, or by legislation, ought to be the public aims of every Englishman; and I am sure they are aims which Christianity should stimulate and foster."

Again:

"The Conservative looks back, the Liberal forward, and the Radical digs down to the root and spring of things. The Conservative is cautious, the Liberal is hopeful, and the Radical is daring. The Conservative believes in the wisdom of experience; the Liberal trusts in the tendencies of humanity; and the Radical, impatient alike of past and future, would clear the ground and make a new start. Each party has its merits and its demerits, its wisdom and its folly, its strength and its weakness. What the Conservatives call the teaching of experience may be only the unwisdom of immature age. It is foolish and perilous to trust the tendencies of humanity, if you make no attempt to guide them; and, on ground still cumbered with the *débris* of old institutions, the Radical will not find it so easy to plant and to foster his brand-new systems and ideas.

Still, as I have said, men will naturally ally themselves with one party or the other, according to their instinctive or acquired leanings. All I add is, do not be the bigots of a party, and do not forfeit the right to think for yourselves; and, if you feel that you cannot go along with your party, then act for yourselves. There is more importance in the cultivation of this independence of spirit than is sometimes supposed. Of course it may degenerate into a disintegration of those elements of cohesion by which alone great causes have been, or can be, won. The great peril to democracy, De Tocqueville thought, would be the development of individualism, the pursuit of selfish objects, or selfish ideas, rather than of the good of the Commonwealth. The mean between subservience to a party, and a proud and foolish spirit of self-assertion, miscalled independence, is not easy to hit; but if a man has a true love for his country, and a desire to promote its best and highest interests, he is not likely to err very far on either side."

Language such as this rarely drops from the lips of clergy, either in the pulpit or on the platform. Ecclesiastical politics are, for the most part, and on both sides, too frequently partizan politics. The organization of politics is clearly necessary; for only by the compact, solid, determination of a united body can great ends be achieved in the progress of the Commonwealth. As Bishop Fraser said: " Independence and individualism in politics may degenerate into the disintegration of those elements of cohesion by which alone great causes can be won." But the organization of politics is the business of politicians, each on their own side and within their own party, whereas the business of the Christian prophet is to seek to quench the evil in both parties, and to foment in both the flames of good. Let not the prophet, however, who sets before himself so large an end, hope that he will escape censure. His path on both sides is beset with the snares of misunderstanding. As the prophet sets his face forward and upward, he will encounter from both political parties in turn (as, in turn, he rebukes the narrowness and the bitterness of both) the shafts of ridicule and wrath. In his determination to raise politics above party, he will be accused by both parties of being "political." This was Bishop Fraser's experience. In a letter of January 5, 1878, he writes:

"The only vexation to me is, that people will not distinguish between politics and politics; and because one lifts up his voice in some great national question of peace and war, partizans, who identify the questions merely with the ephemeral fortunes of a government, denounce one as a 'political bishop!' I had an anonymous letter from Tamworth this morning, telling me I had better let politics alone, and explain the muddle which Christianity has got into. This, I have sometimes tried to do without leaving the other undone."

But, notwithstanding opposition and censure, the Bishop, strong in his integrity, pursued the equal path of true Christian politics. He greatly valued the possession of a vote, and constantly impressed upon men that a vote was an important trust capable of contributing to the achievement of noble ends. Nevertheless, as he tells us, he seldom himself voted. This abstinence was due not to any spirit of weak compromise (no one who knew Bishop Fraser would connect him, even in the remotest manner, with Mr. Facing-Both-Ways), but to the desire to keep himself free to speak, as Bishop, words of counsel and reproof to both parties, without difference or distinction. But, when politics widened themselves out into broad questions of humanity, when they touched some profound moral principle, Bishop Fraser sprang to the front as a Christian citizen. Careless of consequences, or of the opinion of men, he was very bold in any cause which he deemed to be the cause of public righteousness. The Bulgarian Atrocities, the Eastern Question, the Irrigation of India, the Opium Traffic, National Education, Marriage with a Deceased Wife's Sister, Sunday Closing, and the like, were all questions which seemed to him greater than party; on these questions, therefore, he spoke and wrote frequently and with vigour. But from minor questions—questions concerning party, but not involving any large principle — he kept himself severely aloof in determined silence. And, as he resolved, in the interests of a higher cause, to hold himself personally free from the entanglements of one-sided politics, so he frequently urged, with eager force, the necessity for the Church of England, as a great religious community, holding itself free also. The English Church cannot be both a political sect and a National Church—the appanage of a party and the religious representative of the Nation. If the English Church is to be national, her arms must open wide enough to embrace the whole nation. Upon this fundamental axiom, Bishop Fraser insisted without ceasing. Preaching at St. James's Church, Heywood, on April 25, 1880, he said :

"I am pleased to see the good temper in which the late general election has been fought by Lancashire people; and, now that the battle is over, I think it is time to return to the friendships of every-day life. There are people who seem to think that the Church of England is an appanage of a political party. I may refer to what I saw this morning in Manchester, where I noticed a large blue placard announcing that a Conservative meeting was to be held in a certain church school. I called the attention of the minister of the church to which the school belonged to the circumstance, suggesting that it was time the bill was taken down, as it might hurt some people's feelings to see it upon the school. The incumbent promised to see to it, and he said also that, before the schoolroom was lent, he told his people that if it was lent to the Conservatives it should also be lent to the Liberals as well, if they applied for it; but the latter had not applied. Now, I am of opinion also, that if schools are lent to one party, they should be lent to the other party as well. The Church includes Liberals and Conservatives, and some of you here present may be crest-fallen, while others may be triumphant; but I ask you to remember, in your differences, that you are all citizens of one great country, and members of one great brotherhood. The Church of England ought not to be a political Church, and, while I wish Churchmen to maintain their own political convictions, I would be sorry to see the pulpits of the Church used for political harangues, or her schools for political purposes."

In an address delivered at the opening of the Town Hall, Chorley, August 2, 1879, the Bishop, speaking upon the presence of Bishops in the House of Lords, thus made allusion to the character of his own interests in politics :

"I believe, as a simple historical fact, that bishops of the Church of England have sat in the Legislature of this country as long as there has been a Legislature. In the earliest days of the Plantagenet kings, bishops of the Church of England were honoured with a seat in English Legislature, and there have been times when the bishops of the Church, both in its pre-Reformation and in its sub-Reformation days, have done something for the liberties of England. It was an Archbishop of Canterbury who helped to wring Magna Charta from King John; they were seven English bishops who resisted the tyranny of King James; and though, perhaps, the political importance of the bishops is not as considerable to-day as it was 200 years ago, and, perhaps, the less often the bishops open their mouths upon strictly political subjects the better, still, I think that even now, the bishops are not altogether out of their place in the serene and tranquillizing atmosphere of the Upper House of the English Parliament. The bishops do not speak very often there, and I do not think it is desirable they should; but yet, if rare oratorical power could command listeners in the House of Lords, there is no one that has greater power in arresting the attention of that great assembly than the Bishop of Peterborough; if massive intellectual force could bring a question out in all its true proportions and magnitude, there is no one who can do that better than the Archbishop of York; and if there is such a thing as a grave, statesman-like habit, there are not many men of this generation who have more of the statesman-like mind than His Grace the Archbishop of Canterbury. As for myself, I am rather an infrequent visitor to that House. I have not taken my seat there once during the whole of this session, and only once during last session. I am, indeed, sometimes afraid that the doorkeepers may not know me, and that I may be turned back as a pickpocket. This is my misfortune, rather than my fault. My own diocese gives me so much to do that I have really very few leisure hours to spend in London, or to pass in travelling to and from London. But I will say this, that, whether bishops do much good in Parliament or not, I think that Parliament does a great deal of good to the bishops—I think it makes them understand the nature of difficult questions perhaps better than if they were more recluse in their lives and habits; and, though I am not a frequent visitor to Parliament, I am still thankful to be an unworthy member of it. I have hinted that I think bishops should not speak on purely political subjects, but there are politics and politics; and there are certainly great social questions which I think a bishop has a right to deal with. I should consider myself unworthy of my office if I used any influence I possess for or against any political party; but there are great political and social questions—in the highest sense of the word political—with regard to which, were I not to take an interest in them, I should be ashamed of myself, and ashamed of myself if I did not freely speak my mind upon them."

The view so naïvely stated, that "whether or not, bishops do Parliament any good, yet Parliament does bishops good," struck the Chorley listeners as both a novel and amusing view. But it was a view natural and true to Bishop Fraser. For one of the Bishop's deepest convictions was the necessity of bringing the clerical mind into full contact with the lay mind. The sundering, as by an unbridgeable chasm, of clergy from laity, he conceived to be hostile to the highest interests of both.

"The prosperity of the Church is undoubtedly," he said, "the prosperity of the nation. I have confidence in the people of England, and I believe, if the Church does her duty by the people, the people will do their duty by the Church. Let us make the Church useful. It is not by a selfish monopoly, but by the very widest diffusion, that any institution becomes really great and strong. I am sure that, if the clergy would only show a disposition to welcome the co-operation of the laity, there are many willing and energetic laymen ready to throw themselves into the Church's work."

But, in speech and example alike, the Bishop made it clear that, if the great world of laymen were to be interested in the work of the Church, the Church must, on its part, show a real interest in the affairs of the world; penetrating all affairs with the spirit of religion, not sundering the sacred from the secular, but hallowing the secular until it also becomes sacred. Every good thing, Bishop Fraser believed, is a gift from God.

"Look," he said, "at the well-ordered, temperate, civic freedom we enjoy! It is the gift of God's Spirit. I believe that every right and enlightened idea, whether in politics or religion, which has ever contributed to the progress of the nation has been put into the minds of statesmen by the teaching of the Blessed Spirit of Christ, Who, after all, is the great Teacher of all the world in all their duties—individual, social, political, and national."

The Bishop's ardent devotion to the Church of England sprang from this conviction, that the tolerance and comprehensiveness of the Church was a strong cement in the identification of the religious and civic life of the people; a great power in the promotion of the cause of religious and civic liberty. Preaching at St. John's Church, Farnworth, May 16, 1880, he said:

"People are beginning to realize that there is a spirit of comprehensive liberality and toleration in the Church which they would be sorry to exchange for the more stringent formularies sometimes put as a test of membership by bodies which stand outside of the Church. I have no belief that if the Church of England were swept away—Disestablishment and Disendowment accomplished—that there would be any gain to religious freedom. I believe there would then be an immense development of the sectarian spirit. In my diocese there are no unkindly relations between the clergy and Nonconformist ministers, and it seems to me that sympathy, brotherly kindness, and appreciation of what is good are the motives which should animate every Christian man; and, as Bishop of the diocese, my desire is to work with all who have these objects in view."

Again:

"Christianity is the best kind of Socialism, giving, as it does, every man his rights, but making him respect the rights of his neighbour also. Christianity teaches that the poor man as well as the rich man, the peasant in his cottage as well as the Queen on her throne, should all have their rights, and teaches them not to deny the rights of other men. 'Fear God,' said St. Peter, 'love the brotherhood, honour the king.' That is the code of a true social gospel, which teaches us to render to all men their dues. Society can only be based on a system of confidence. We have no right to live idle and useless lives. A useless life is as bad as—nay, worse than—death. One had better be dead than be living an idle, profligate, selfish, and useless life. Who wants a man to live his allotted seventy years in order that he may eat his three meals a day, fill his cellars with champagne, and take excursions when he pleases, if he cares not for those around him? Does such a man think he has no duties to his fellow-men, and the poor around him, and that he was only sent here to enjoy himself? Is the world any the better for our being here? If not, the sooner we get out of it the better for the world. An idle man or woman, who lives only for himself or herself, is not only an inutility, but, what is worse, is a curse. Such persons are only teaching others to lead an idle, luxurious, self-indulgent and self-pleasing life. God did not send man into the world for that purpose. No man ought to occupy a position in society who is not prepared to accept the responsibilities and to discharge the duties which belong to that position. No doubt the Gospel has been narrowed and is being narrowed day by day. We lay down comfortable theories of the elect, and are indifferent to the well-being of our neighbours. But that is not the Gospel; it is not Christianity. The Gospel is based on sympathy. It is love such as Christ's love that holds the world together."

The Bishop continually enforced the great law of human life, that happiness is not the outcome of wealth, but of work; and that material prosperity, unless founded upon moral and religious principle, is a curse.

Preaching at Manchester Cathedral in January, 1880, he said:

"The three crying evils of the day are intemperance, licentiousness, and debt. It was stated last week that nearly 60,000 bills of sale had been registered last year, and you know what a bill of sale indicates as to the financial condition of those 60,000 homes. These crying evils of intemperance, licentiousness, and debt are the direct result of immoderate and hurtful desires. I am told that there are tradesmen in Manchester, who can hardly hold up their heads by reason of the debts on their books, and I wish the wealthy, or seemingly wealthy people, would remember that it is an elementary principle of righteousness not to incur debts which they cannot pay. Another lesson, surely, which we have need to learn is, that we must be more industrious, as a people, if we are to thrive. We are afraid—at least many of us are afraid—of honest work; and yet there is nothing of which I feel more sure than that the future of the world, and, certainly, the future of England, is for the workers—for those who do not wish to eat the bread of idleness. There can be no doubt that there are a great deal too many idle and luxurious people in the world who acknowledge no law but their own pleasure, and refuse to recognize anything as a duty, or to help forward the progress of humanity."

Habits of licentiousness, the Bishop felt, were eating out the heart and strength of the English people. As a Christian citizen his whole soul rose in flames of indignant wrath against the vices which were destroying the roots of prosperity, progress, and felicity. Because he loved with all his heart the English people; therefore, with all his heart, he hated the enemies of the English people. The most terrible and dangerous of England's enemies he believed to be licentiousness. "The happiest men I know," he often said, "are those who are living the purest and the most useful lives." Preaching at St. Anne's Church, Manchester, March 1, 1883, he said:

"A word of digression may, perhaps, be pardoned on those Scriptures of the Old Testament which are sometimes accused of a grossness even amounting to indecency. No doubt, there are pages in them which some of us, judging from the mere point of view of literary refinement—a very different thing, however, from moral repulsion—might wish were not there; and we know what capital atheistic and infidel objectors of the present day make out of them. But this at least may be said: There is nothing prurient there; nothing to make vice attractive; on the contrary, if 'a spade is called a spade,' at any rate vice is painted in its true colours, and its hideous and repellent features stand out full and clear. No honest-minded man ever read even the coarsest page in the Old Testament, and thence gathered that God was giving him a 'licence to sin.' This is our answer to the infidel, and is a thing to be noticed and remembered. The story of the sin of David may be plainly, and even coarsely told; but at least it is not told without the sequel of David's repentance and of his punishment; and of the sad picture of his later days—one long, unrelieved, tale of shame and sorrow and suffering. Never was there a more mischievous and delusive fallacy than that of Burke's—great thinker though he was—that 'vice loses half its evil, by losing all its grossness.' Vice, described with the plainness of an Old Testament writer, is hideous to all; vice, disguised by the skill of a French playwright or novelist, becomes attractive to many. If drunkenness spiritually slays its thousands, licentiousness, I fear, slays its tens of thousands. And I do not desire that my words should be directed to those who socially belong to the working class alone. The rich and luxurious need restraint quite as urgently as any others. The trail of the serpent can be traced everywhere. Of nothing does the social atmosphere, which we are all breathing, need to be purified so much as of this subtle contagion of impurity. It penetrates everywhere. Our literature is full of it; our art, our amusements. It even lurks at times, when least suspected, hard by the very precincts of the sanctuary. It needs a manlier and more robust religion than that which is now too much in vogue to expel it utterly. The Spirit of God, playing freely on the nobler and more generous affections of the human soul, can alone do this. It is like letting the wholesome breath of heaven penetrate the chamber where we suspect may be gathering the poisonous fever-germs."

With equal plainness the Bishop spoke, in pulpit and from platform, against dishonesty in trade. Purity, he believed, was the only foundation of a great character; honesty the only foundation of a great commerce.

"If we do our duty, I am confident God will not forsake England yet; for I believe there is a future for her such as she has never yet enjoyed, a wider scope for usefulness, a larger empire, not in the modern sense of imperialism, for which I have no love at all, but in the sense of English energy, determination, patience, and perseverance. I hope that the name of English honesty in manufacture will spread over the face of the world; that by their exertions Englishmen will make the wilderness into a garden, so that it may be said in all countries, 'We owe this to England;' and, further, I trust that it may be said that we are a race of active, enterprising Christian people, whose word is as good as their bond, whose trade-marks can be trusted to be what they profess to be, whose cloth is not too heavily sized, whose articles weigh the proper weight and fill the proper measure, and who can be trusted in all their relations when they have given their word to stand to it."

Again, preaching at St. Peter's, Oldham, May 9, 1880:

"England has been anxious during the last six years as to whether our manufactures and our immense trades were going to Germany, Switzerland, or the United States. Some people have already foretold that the day of England's greatest prosperity in manufacture has passed away; and that she will never hold the place in the markets of the world in the future that she has held in the past. I do not know whether such people have considered that commercial prosperity depends upon moral causes. It is all very well for political economists to tell us that there are great laws which govern nations, causes which affect the demand and supply of labour, and all that sort of thing, and to fancy, when they have said that, they have got to the root of the matter. They have done nothing of the kind. Supposing any great product of British industry had occupied the markets of the world—China, Japan, India, &c.—creating a great demand for increased labour in its production, trade would be good, and wages high; but supposing the material deteriorated, and the goods of other producers were preferred, there would be a falling off in our trade, there would be too many hands, and wages would be lower. But what is it that has brought this about? Surely there must be a moral cause in our loss of trade. I was talking to a commercial gentleman the other day about cloth, and showed him the bag I used to carry my robes in—a bag presented to me by the widow of the late Bishop of Salisbury. Two years ago I bought a new bag, and gave a good price for it. I told the person of whom I bought it, to let it be of the best material he could produce, and yet, after only two years' wear, it is nearly as shabby as the one I threw aside after seventeen years' use. Everything nowadays is made showy and attractive; but foreigners who buy our goods may not want fine showy things, and when they get an article which looks glossy and appears nice, but does not wear well, they get dissatisfied with it, and go elsewhere for their purchases. For nearly every falling off in trade there is a moral cause. The prosperity of nations is not dependent merely upon the laws of supply and demand, and those things which political economists talk about. These are only secondary things. It is righteousness, not capital, that exalts a nation."

In Bishop Fraser's opinion one of the prime functions of Christianity was to produce good citizens. He had no sympathy with the selfish and degrading notion that the one business of the believer is, at any hazard, to get his own soul saved. He knew that numbers of persons in the morbid, engrossing, exclusive anxiety to "save" their souls, lost them. For him the nobler and the safer plan seemed to be —to lose and spend himself for others. In this way, he felt sure, Christ intended Christians to find, and gain, salvation for themselves. This is one of the keynotes of Bishop Fraser's life. Of himself he thought little, for others he strove much. Not his own salvation, but the spread of human sympathy and the promotion of human happiness, was his consuming desire. Hence he laboured to foster a kindly spirit between employers and employed; to elevate home into the blessed centre of daily delight; to purify politics; to show the true honourableness of trade; to increase self-control, soberness, and purity; to permeate social existence with the principles of the Gospel. To him Christianity was the chief factor in good citizenship, and good citizenship an inevitable fruit of genuine Christianity.

Preaching in the Manchester Cathedral to the Manchester Rifle Volunteers, February 16, 1879, he said:

"It is a common charge brought against Christianity that the virtues, the graces, the moral qualities which it develops, or helps to form, are not those which go to the making of good citizens; that it can produce saints, apostles, virgins, anchorites, confessors, martyrs, but not statesmen, captains, legislators, soldiers, patriots. The charge, I think, arises from a misconception both of the ideal function and of the historical action of Christianity in the world. It must be remembered that Christ's Gospel was not intended to be, and does not prove to be, a new and complete system, taking the place of the conception of life which had existed before; but rather a new set of principles, introducing themselves into the moral and social phenomena of the world, giving to men's aims a higher and a nobler range, sustaining those aims with purer motives and higher hopes, and placing before men's eyes, in the person of its Founder, the spectacle of a Divine life lived under the actual conditions of humanity. The duties of a citizen were sufficiently understood in the day when the Gospel first appeared among the moral forces of the world; not only among the Jews, with their Joshuas, and Gideons, and Davids, and Maccabees, but in Greece, with its Leonidas, Epaminondas, Aristides, Demosthenes; in Rome, with its Horatii, Curtii, and Decii. The spirit of patriotism burnt then with a pure and almost holy flame. The Spartan mother, sending forth her only son to war, with the parting charge, as she fastened the shield upon his arm, 'With this, or on this, come back to me conquering or dead,' has proved that, even in women's bosoms, the fire burnt as strongly as in men's. A true Christian patriot could not be an Alcibiades, a Coriolanus, a Cæsar. Even if suffering the harshest wrongs, he could not lift up his hand against his country, any more than he could strike his mother. But I venture to think, and to say, that a true spirit of patriotism, such as the Gospel permits and encourages, needs to be revived in England. Burke lamented, ninety years ago, that the age of chivalry was gone; now there is some reason to fear that the age of patriotism is going. Even among Volunteers the spirit of insubordination is said to be creeping in, and duty calls to deaf ears. Officers cannot, or do not, command; men will not, or do not, obey. Of course, this only implies that in a body of 250,000 all corps do not rise to the same level of discipline and military qualities; but it also implies the need of watchfulness, lest the spirit which gave birth to the movement should evaporate, and the movement itself degenerate into a plaything and a sham. Now, if you volunteer to defend your country in her hour of need, let me very earnestly impress upon you that unless you carry with you to your work the principle of obedience, and the principle of self-sacrifice—the two great principles, as I conceive it, of Christianity—

I take leave to say that your aid will be of no more value to your country than was the aid of Pharaoh, King of Egypt, to Judah in her hour of danger—'a staff of a broken reed, whereon if a man lean it will go into his hand and pierce it; so is Pharaoh, King of Egypt, unto all that trust on him.'"

The true attitude of Christianity towards war was another subject (as his sermons, speeches and letters abundantly show), which often filled the Bishop's mind.

Preaching at Holy Trinity Church, Hulme, on September 17, 1882, he said:

"I do not like the soldier's trade as such, and the errand on which he is sent forth must be distasteful to any man of a humane spirit and a Christian mind. But war, at times, is inevitable, and there are great qualities in the soldier which we love to see—courage, and what St. Paul calls the 'power to endure,' hardness, a sense of duty, of comradeship, of brotherhood. These are Christian graces, though you never can divest war of its horrors. To my mind, at least, it is terrible to think that harvest fields, and the labourers and the poor peasants, and the cottage homes in which dwell peaceful wives and children, must be ruthlessly devastated and laid low; for it is upon the masses of the people in an invaded country that the horrors of war chiefly fall. The kings and the queens, and the nobility, can find for themselves harbours of refuge, and be safe from the horrors of an invasion; but the poor peasant must stay where he is, and must see the iron hoof of the cavalry, and the level bayonets of the infantry, and the lumbering artillery devastating his fields, destroying his homes, crushing his hopes, and leaving nothing but a wilderness behind. And he who realizes these things must hope and pray that no necessity may ever be laid upon this country, either of maintaining a great standing army, or of being involved in great aggressive wars. We may well pray that, whenever we are called upon to go forth to battle, the cause may be righteous, justifiable, and true; and that this island, under the reign of our gracious Queen, may always be preserved from invasion and the horrors of war; for, say what you will, the soldier's is a terrible trade."

Again, at St. Anne's, Manchester, September 14, 1882:

"No doubt there is passage after passage all through the old Hebrew and historical Scriptures, where in times of great oppression, great wrong, or great tyranny, the spirit of the nation, as expressed by these prophets, seemed to rise up to the conception of God as a God of battles, Who went forth before their armies to war. No doubt, when war is waged, we surely have a right to believe that we can trace the movements of His hand in the phenomena we see. We have a right to believe that God is on the side of truth and righteousness. I know that cynical and unbelieving people say, 'What you call Providence is always found on the side of the strongest battalions.' Now, I have not so read history as to find God always on the side of the strongest battalions. I seem to see in many of those wars, especially those wars waged in the vindication of great principles against oppression, wrong, and tyranny, that God has joined Himself on the side of truth, and freedom, and righteousness. This is the most religious, and certainly the most Christian view to take, that God delights to make war cease in all the world, than that He delights to uphold, stimulate, and take part in it. And yet there are qualities in the soldier that are thoroughly and truly noble. In the true Christian soldier, and the true Christian sailor, I have seen many of those qualities which Christ has sanctified, and which I believe that nothing but the Spirit of Christ can produce in the soul of man. But this is the fair side of war, and the fair side of the soldier's life."

The Bishop's opinions upon the wisdom and righteousness of particular wars—opinions strongly expressed and adverse to the political party immediately responsible for those wars—often caused heated criticism. But his general declaration that war, notwithstanding its development of the heroic virtues of absolute obedience and self-sacrifice, is a horror and a scourge, coincides with the declarations of most of the greatest soldiers and sailors of all historic time.

Moreover, it was characteristic of the Bishop to feel strongly—especially in cases of suffering. He was a whole-spirited man, intensely sympathetic. The thought of misery, and distress, and wrong stirred his noble nature to its deepest depths. Because of the sufferings inflicted on the poor—wives made widows, children rendered fatherless, fields and homesteads devastated, industries destroyed—he hated war. All forms of war were horrible to him. During the Industrial War of 1878 he went from town to town, his face heavy with woe. Whenever he alluded to the Ecclesiastical Wars of Churchmen against Nonconformists, or of Churchmen against each other, his countenance was saddened with the gloom from his heart. And the Irish Question—which he held to be a bitter war—darkened with sorrow his whole being. At times he could think and speak of nothing else. On May 7, 1882, the tidings came of the execrable assassination of Lord Frederick Cavendish and Mr. Burke, in

Phœnix Park, Dublin; as the Bishop was on his way to preach at St. John's Church, Accrington. "When he heard the news," writes one who was near him, "he was like a wounded man, the assassin's horrible deed had stabbed him deeply through the heart." Ascending the pulpit, he said :

"I have changed my text, and also the subject of my sermon, through the terrible news I have heard for the first time since I set my foot on the platform of your station. That news almost unmanned me and disqualified me from conducting the service. I don't know whether all in this congregation will know what that news is. The Rev. J. Ormandy met me at the station and showed me a telegram to this effect. Yesterday afternoon, in broad daylight, Lord Frederick Cavendish, the newly-appointed Chief Secretary for Ireland, and Mr. Burke, Under-Secretary, were walking in Phœnix Park, Dublin. Lord Frederick could only just have landed, and they were both assassinated after a struggle, and both are dead. We must all feel stunned at this atrocious, wicked deed. It is not only that a young nobleman of high promise, of very high personal distinction, linked by the closest ties of friendship to our great Prime Minister, who had undertaken a responsible office full of the greatest difficulty, and also of the greatest peril, at a most momentous and critical period in this country's history, has fallen a victim to the assassin's dagger or knife. It is enough to have lost one such as Lord Frederick Cavendish, whom many of you know at least by sight; but there is something worse behind. It seems to make the English policy to do justice to Ireland, and to conciliate Ireland, almost hopeless.

"What are we to do? What can be done more than is being done? One was sufficiently shocked by the outrage the other day, when we saw that an innocent, elegant, and accomplished woman, driving home from church one quiet Sabbath morning by the side of her brother-in-law, was shot down by an assassin from behind a hedge. It was a horrid murder, but it was not altogether inexplicable. No one could suppose that the blood-stained murderers intended to shoot that poor defenceless lady. They were reckless in their deed of blood, and fired, not perhaps at random, but perhaps at the landlord who sat by her side. That was intelligible, though it is simply detestable to murder with any weapon for any cause; but Lord Frederick Cavendish must have represented the principle of English equity and English conciliation. No doubt there is a heavy amount of long arrears that Ireland may be said to have against England. One cannot read the story of England's conquest of Ireland, as it is called, with any satisfaction, if one is not lost entirely to all sense of justice and righteousness; but for the last fifty years, ever since 1830, so far as I have been able to read political history, the aim and efforts of all Governments in this country have been to do justice to Ireland, to right any wrongs that have been done, and, if possible, to repair them—

to equitably construe, and impartially administer, those laws which, when
so administered, are the basis of all society, the protection of life and
property. For the last fifty years Ireland has had no just cause for
complaint. Here is a young nobleman, who, I suppose, could not have
a personal enemy in the world, a man with a message of further conciliation to Ireland, murdered in a public place in Dublin. And this is how
the messenger of peace and conciliation, and dispenser of justice, has been
met. I hope the public spirit of the country is not so far extinguished
by political factions and personal aims that there will not be found another
of those spirited men to take the place which has been so sadly and dis-
tressingly vacated. For it is a terrible thing to be in an atmosphere of
assassination. A brave man will brave dangers almost unspeakable on
the field of battle, but there is a special kind of courage required to
work on, doing your duty while the pistol or dagger of the assassin may
be levelled at you from some unsuspected corner. You must all feel that
these are not only difficult but perilous times, perilous to all we hold
precious either in Church or State, whether in morals, religion, politics,
or society. I hope that those who aspire to be leaders of thought in
Ireland will, on the occasion of this tragedy, stand out and speak like
men. They cannot justify it, surely. We cannot believe that even a
righteous cause can prosper by the use of such methods. I hope that men
of authority, whose words are of world-wide importance, will measure
their words, when men's passions are so easily excited as at present. It
is difficult, in our calm society, to conceive what such things, as this
assassination, are. You see ordinary society so fair, so tranquil; life
appears so safe; your little children play in your parlours, and at your
house doors; you go to church on the Lord's Day, and send your children
to the Sunday School; we get our wages or pay them, as the case may be,
and perhaps to-morrow may be even more calm and peaceable. But forces
are lurking under, and beneath, this calm society, of terrible vitality—
forces which seem to select Ireland as the theatre for their manifestations.
One can hardly conceive of these terrible passions taking possession of the
public mind of England. Still, such things are not impossible. Some
of us can remember that, a long number of years ago, a Prime Minister
narrowly escaped assassination. Sir Robert Peel escaped, but his private
secretary, Mr. Drummond, was murdered. These are not the times to
either excite, or pander to, Irish popular feelings. This seems to be a day
when the bitterness of political partizanship ought to be mitigated, in the
face of the great crisis through which this country is passing. Whether we
are Conservatives or Liberals, whether we like the present Government, or
would see it changed for the Opposition, at any rate there is just now a
prior claim to patriotism than political partizanship. The country is in
danger, the integrity of the empire is imperilled. If we were all so false
and recreant to the claims of duty as some, I dare say we might say, 'Let
Ireland go.' If we did that, we should be false to our great traditions;
for whether we conquered Ireland justly or unjustly, whether we have used
the rights and responsibilities of the conqueror wisely or unwisely, ill or

well, at least we must accept the position; and, if there is one position and one responsibility that touches the Government of a free country more than another, it is that order is preserved, and life and property are safe. There is a danger about which I would like to say one word. Englishmen are somewhat slow to be excited, but when excited they are strongly excited, and in a moment of great excitement Englishmen have said and done things that, perhaps, in calmer moments they would not do. There is just this danger now, with the news of this terrible outrage, which seems to me to be the most terrible we have had in England within my memory. One cannot realize things that are very far off. One may shudder at the assassination of the Czar of Russia, almost in sight of his palace, shattered by dynamite in the midst of his guards. That was so far off that the excitement soon died away. Here we have a terrible outrage in our own country. It is just possible that the news of this terrible outrage may provoke a tremendous outburst of indignation in England, and things may be suggested, demanded, and done, which may neither be wise, nor right, to suggest, demand, or do. Do not let us lose our heads, because our hearts are affected. Justice, righteousness, and equity must still be done to men all round. We must make allowances for the blindness of the passions, and the ignorance which is next door to crime. We may not have done all we ought to do for Ireland, and I do not think we have; but it is a bitter thing, just at the moment we are trying to do all we can to make reasonable terms with Ireland, to see the way in which our efforts are met. Still, let us try to be calm. I little thought when I came here this morning to have to speak on this subject. I came to speak in aid of your schools, and how you should seek to train up your children in the school, and still more by the powerful influence of home. Do not let your faith in righteousness and justice, though it has been rudely shaken, fail you. Society is only prevented from becoming an anarchy by each man doing to his neighbour what he would that neighbour should do to him. That is the great fundamental principle of Christianity in its moral and social features. Leave this church this morning with this resolve in each heart, 'God helping me, I will do all I can for myself and my children to make England strong, to make England moral and honest.'"

Few men, suddenly made prostrate with grief, could, upon the spur of the moment, without preparation, have uttered so just and noble a plea. Nor, with all his gifts, could Bishop Fraser have uttered it, if long years of sympathy with every manner of distress had not schooled him for the task. It is the emergency which tests the man. This emergency showed the Bishop in his true colours, the well-equipped Christian citizen, hating wrong, glowing with sympathy, restrained in judgment, devoted to reform. From this moment to the close of his life the Irish Question was seldom absent from his thoughts.

Preaching at Holy Trinity Church, Hulme, February 8, 1885, he said:

"Is there, I would ask, any reasonable Irishman in the world—is there any one who can believe that English statesmen, or the English people, do not wish entire justice to be done to Ireland, and that the slightest trace of ancient wrongs—and there have been wrongs both ancient and numerous—should be effaced? All we are jealous of—and Irishmen ought to be jealous of it, too—is the integrity of the empire. If the empire were dismembered, would not Ireland be worse off as well as England? Why do not the leaders of the Irish party express their hatred of those dastardly attempts which have been made to create a reign of terror in England? What cause can be advanced by such a course? There seems to be an attempt to create a revival of that most terrible thing—race hatred—from which both nations have suffered surely enough in past years. Who can read the history of Ireland, in whatever age, remote as well as near, without horror, and pity, and shame? Why should we, by our violence and our crimes, delay the coming of better and happier times? Why should we sow the deadly seeds of race animosities, as though Celt and Saxon must ever be foes? Why cannot English and Irish live side by side in Ireland as in Manchester, recognizing themselves as citizens of one common country, desiring the best interests of all their sons?"

Episcopal utterances such as these seldom reach the public ear. Not that other Bishops are not less anxious than Bishop Fraser to penetrate political, and civic, life with broad Christian principles. But either they have not the gift so to express themselves as to catch the public ear, or their opportunities are fewer, and more limited, than his.

"Some bishops," said Bishop Fraser, in November 1882, "by circumstances which they did not cause, and cannot control (by their homes being placed in the country, or in some quiet, small, cathedral town), are separated from those who are engaged in the staple industries of the country. I have always counted it as my special good fortune, suiting my natural temperament, that Providence has set me down in a place where all the activities of life are in full force, and where, almost every day, I am brought into contact with some fresh phenomena of our strong national life. I thus learn far more than I can teach; but what I learn helps me, I hope, to teach with more directness, and force, and sympathy. It is a man's own fault—the fault of his vanity or of his supineness—if in Lancashire he sends words idly into the air."

All men are not gifted alike; there are many voices in the

world, and every true voice has its own signification. Not every bishop, however willing, could, like Bishop Fraser, enter the lists with Mr. Ruskin in a discussion upon Usury; preside over a Social Science Congress, a Domestic Economy Congress, a Co-operative Congress, preach a sermon to the British Association, the Church Congress, the Medical Association; act as arbitrator in a dispute upon hours of labour and amount of wages between employers and employed; give an address worthy of the attention of the learned staff of Owens College, and hold a gathering of Night-soil men in rapt interest; conduct a Parochial Mission, and authoritatively pronounce a judgment upon a Corporation's great water scheme; fill the University Church with eager auditors, and rouse a meeting of working men to a pitch of almost uncontrollable enthusiasm. But though all gifts are not equal, and success is therefore varied, yet a growing desire is evident among the clergy of all religious communities, to follow the example set by Bishop Fraser, and bring Christianity down from the clouds to the daily life of man. They desire no longer to float loftily as a balloon, but to dwell actively as citizens of a world which Christ died to make Christian.

One great motive which actuated Bishop Fraser in taking so diligent a part in civic affairs was the strong wish to induce other citizens of intelligence, wealth, and position, to come forward and take their rightful place—the place of duty and labour—in municipal life.

"In America," he said, "it is much to be regretted that the citizens who are the best able to serve the State withdraw themselves from political and municipal life, because they cannot tolerate the corruption and other acts by which success is to be obtained. I may venture to express the hope that, in Manchester, our best citizens—and there is no city in this empire that has better or nobler men ready to serve it—our best and worthiest citizens will come forward to take their place in our municipal affairs; in the management of which I am sure they will have the fullest confidence of their fellow-citizens."

As one means of inducing the best citizens of Manchester to offer themselves for municipal offices, the Bishop was wont to remind them that they were citizens of "no mean city."

In a speech delivered at the opening of the great Town Hall, on September 13, 1877, he said:

"I think the outside public hardly realizes the position Manchester occupies in this great English polity to which we all belong. I suppose it may be roughly said that Manchester is the centre of the interests—and of the very substantial interests—of something like 3,000,000 of people, if I include the adjacent large manufacturing towns, all of whom come under our influence. I presume that I am not understating the fact, when I say that one man in every eight, over whom the Queen of England reigns in this island, has interests, more or less vitally connected with Manchester."

Upon this greatness of Manchester and the vital needs of its teeming population, Bishop Fraser founded his defence of the Thirlmere water scheme.

"Dainty and witty gentlemen," he said, "leading a quiet life in London, indulge in cynical carpings at our expense, and tell us what a vulgar set of people we are with our Town Hall and the like; and that it is a thing not to be heard of, that one or two millions of people should fetch a prime necessity of life from a Westmoreland or Cumberland lake. But we have a right to stand up and claim our inheritance in England, and to say that two millions of people have a right to draw a prime necessity from any portion of the country of England to which they can get lawful access. I am surprised at the language used on this subject. We are told that our water scheme 'sounds very big, and very ugly, and very revolting; and England, with its lake scenery placed at the cruel mercy of such improvers as these, would be a country with the heart of rest and peace cut out of it.' Yet Glasgow has drawn its supply of water from Loch Katrine, and I don't know that anybody has said that the heart of rest and peace has been cut out of Scotland. Sir Joseph Heron has said to me, 'I wonder if you know where Thirlmere is.' And I suspect that many people may have gone into the lake districts, and may have returned, without having seen it. But because we are going to make it a lake of 750 acres instead of 355, and are going to supply a prime necessity of life to one or two millions of the Queen's subjects, we are attacked as if about to do a thing not to be tolerated in this country."

In a similar spirit of patriotic pride in the central city of his diocese, the Bishop warmly vindicated the erection of the great Town Hall, and the large expenditure it involved.

"The editor of the *Times*," he said, "tells us that, if we compare Manchester and Birmingham, Liverpool and Glasgow, with Florence and Dresden, Nuremburg and Venice, we must feel sadly that the art of acquiring wealth is not the art of spending it. Perhaps we may not be slow to admit that

Florence, Dresden, Nuremburg, and Venice are not Manchester, Liverpool, Birmingham, and Glasgow. Of course I know perfectly well which of these places are the pleasantest spots for the dilettante to spend his time in when he has nothing better to do than to look at beautiful pictures, and elegant relics of antiquity. No doubt the foreign cities stand upon a prodigious advantage in this respect, as compared with us; but, if you look at what constitutes the strength and wealth of a nation, you must multiply Florence, Dresden, Nuremburg, and Venice a hundred times before you get out of them towns like Manchester, Liverpool, Birmingham, and Glasgow. But it is said that we have been spending too much money upon our Town Hall. No doubt there has been a little extravagance in the matter. But there are extravagances and extravagances. There are some sorts of extravagances which are perfectly legitimate, and others which are perfectly illegitimate; and I say that a great stately building standing in our midst, as this building stands, at which I have seen our working people for months past gazing, in their dinner hour, with pride and wonder —I say you, the City Council, have done something of which you have a right to be proud, in erecting this building, and for which Manchester people have a right to thank you. Then, again, what has been the cost? I saw it stated the other day, in one of the Manchester newspapers, and I imagine the report was fairly accurate, that, putting aside the cost of the land, you have spent something like £500,000. Now I imagine that that is about the price of a first-class ironclad, which perhaps capsizes on her first voyage, or founders on her second, or blows up before she has got to sea at all.

" It does not follow that because we have built a great and stately Town Hall that, therefore, we are going in for extravagance in every department of life. As Bishop of this diocese I have sometimes felt it my duty to say that some features of our social life might be improved with advantage. We do sometimes spend too much money upon ourselves, our equipages, entertainments, and the like; and I hope the day is coming when people will be led to cultivate greater simplicity, which is a mark of greater refinement."

By thus heartily throwing himself into the civic life of his diocese; by the daily endeavour to Christianize political, municipal, and social affairs; by his civic pride and patriotic interest in every movement which made for the progress and well-being of the vast people of Manchester Diocese and Manchester City, Bishop Fraser earned for himself the splendid title, conferred by Mr. Oliver Heywood, of " *The Citizen Bishop*." And his own interest in others made others interested in him. His utterances were read by the people with increasing eagerness. Outside Manchester, critics said the Bishop " talked too much"; but within

Manchester, where he was intimately known and affectionately esteemed, the people never tired of his talking. He had not always something new to say; but he always had something clear, straightforward, and inspiring. He made no pretensions to be an orator, but the people recognized he was a man. Simplicity and manliness poured from his lips. "He does me good," was the common verdict of his listeners. The newspapers soon discovered in him an almost inexhaustible treasure-house. The people loved to read what the Bishop said, so the press reported him. In pulpit and on platform the Citizen Bishop was in touch with the people; and the Press, which is the mirror and measure of the people, gave to the people his sayings.

The Christian Church has scarcely yet arisen to a true conception of the power and utility of the Daily Press in the promotion of the cause of civic and social religion. The so-called Religious Press is often ecclesiastical, one-sided, prone to intolerance. Its papers are party papers, generally conducted for party purposes; but in Bishop Fraser the Press of all parties found common ground. He was reported with an almost equal fulness in papers of every colour, whether political or ecclesiastical. Himself belonging to no party, the Press of all parties published his utterances. Casting aside the small differences which separate men and churches, he inculcated the great principles upon which all are united in one—the principles of righteousness, truth, self-denial, nobleness. Loud fulminations are sometimes directed against the Press. But the lowest Press is never lower than the constituency which supports it; in many instances it is higher; and there are multitudes of people, outside the ministrations both of private and public religion, who owe every thought of goodness and worth which reaches them, to the direct, or indirect, teachings of the Daily Press.

An organ of such momentous influence as the Daily Press —capable of such powers of good—was not likely to be neglected or contemned by our Citizen Bishop. The Press was his far-sounding pulpit. For one person whom his speaking voice could reach, a hundred could be reached by his printed voice. But, though he honoured the Press as the strong Fourth Estate of the Realm, yet he never fawned upon the Press or flattered it. Of this, both by nature and upon principle, he was incapable. Towards the Press his attitude was just the same as towards every other organ and institution of the realm—the attitude of transparent integrity and unfearing manliness. The downward tendencies of some portions of the Press he severely reproved. "This new phase of Journalism," he said, "called 'Society Papers,' is invading all the sanctities of domestic life, and every kind of moral garbage is scraped together for the vulgar mind to feast upon." Again, in an Address delivered in the Edinburgh Philosophical Institution, November 2, 1877, he said:

"We believe in our newspapers; but can we trust them? Are we not, as persons who have not only a right, but a duty, to think for themselves, far too much under their influence? It used to be said, 'Beware of the man of one book.' It may be quite as truly said, '*Beware of the man of one newspaper.*' There are papers so intensely partizan, and so unjust and ungenerous in their partizanship, that I consider it a moral duty to myself, to avoid unnecessary irritation of temper, not to read them; and so I miss a good deal of the zest and piquancy of that downright bitter controversy, especially if it is flavoured with those personal jealousies or animosities, which so materially enhance the pleasures of life; which make breakfast so much more enjoyable when it is sweetened by a leading article, holding up to obloquy or contempt some one who may have crossed your path in life, or may be guilty of the unpardonable offence of holding opinions different from your own. I deny myself, so far as I can, these exquisite, but not wholly innocent, or wholesome, pleasures."

But, although there were some journals which the Bishop advisedly left unread, yet he was a man of many newspapers. He dreaded laying a narrow foundation for the fabric of his opinions.

"A man," he said, "who would form a full and fair opinion upon any complicated question at issue must go far and wide for his materials, and must study the point of view of more than one newspaper. The politician, or statesman, or publicist, who would guide the spirit of the age, who would appreciate, even if he cannot sympathize with, the desires and tendencies of the time, must go beyond what, in studied and Parliamentary language, are sometimes called 'the ordinary sources of information,' and will be very ill-advised, as well as ill-furnished, if he does not sometimes look to see what people are saying and writing in *Reynolds's Newspaper*, and the

Bee Hive, and the *Agricultural Chronicle*, as well as in the more stately columns of the *Morning Post*, the *Daily Telegraph*, or the *Times*."

Bishop Fraser was thus not less faithful in his reproofs of the one-sided narrowness of partizan journalists than of the one-sided narrowness of partizan politicians and ecclesiastics. But there was no Pharisaism in his censorship. It was the censorship of the simple, earnest, man: and men—*the Daily Press is only men veiled and anonymous*—seldom resent a manly rebuke which the conscience declares to be just. With the publishers and editors of many newspapers, Bishop Fraser was upon terms of the most cordial intimacy. The cause of human progress, refinement, and elevation, was a cause common to the best editors and the Citizen Bishop. With the pressmen of his diocese the Bishop's relations were always friendly and warm. One of these pressmen has kindly furnished the following sketch of the Bishop's attitude towards them, and their attitude towards the Bishop:

"Bishop Fraser was nowhere esteemed more highly than among the pressmen of Manchester. True, his advent in the diocese meant an increase of work, and especially of Sunday work, for them; but, whatever fault of much talking they might find with him, they loved him still. They liked him because he was so 'comeatable'; because of his manly, unaffected ways; and, even when they deemed it well to 'bottle' him, they 'bottled' him most lovingly. And 'James,' as they familiarly called him among themselves, had a liking for the reporters—always a smile and a cheery word for them, and now and again a hearty joke. His friendliness toward them was illustrated on the occasion of a dinner given by the Manchester Press Club to several reporters who were being transferred from that city to London. The Bishop had got to hear about the intended dinner, and he wrote to the Chairman (Mr. William Hewitson, of the *Manchester Examiner and Times*, the then president of the club), the following letter, which was read to the assembled pressmen, amid much enthusiasm:

BISHOP'S COURT, MANCHESTER, *December* 29, 1880.

"DEAR SIR,—I beg to offer the members of the Manchester Press Club my best wishes on the occasion of their gathering this evening to bid farewell, as I understand, to several of their colleagues who are exchanging work in Manchester for work in London. I desire that my good wishes may accompany them. I know how I am indebted to the Manchester press, not only for the faithfulness of its reports of what I say from time to time, but, on the whole, for the fairness and even generosity of its criticism. No public man has a right to ask for more at the hands of reporters and editors than that his words should be represented with substantial accuracy; and, if criticised unfavourably, still criticised without any desire or design of misrepresentation. On the whole, as I have said, I have little to complain of and much to be grateful for; and I am glad to have the opportunity given me of expressing my feeling towards the gentlemen who will be assembled at your meeting, and who so worthily sustain the character of the provincial press of England.—I am, dear sir, yours very faithfully,

J. MANCHESTER.

"In the month of May, 1882, there appeared in some of the English newspapers the following paragraph: 'A reporter has written to his Eminence, Cardinal Manning, inquiring whether Roman Catholic reporters (who, by the bye, are nowadays very numerous, owing to a special academy for their instruction in Ireland) would be permitted by the Roman Catholic Church to attend, for reporting purposes, Protestant, Atheistic, Socialist, or Republican gatherings. The Cardinal, in his reply, says: 'In reporting for publication, you are made to co-operate in their propagation by a material participation which, to a Catholic, is unlawful. To report, you must be present; and at such lectures no Catholic, even without danger of being hurt by them, ought to be present.' Mr. William Hewitson brought the Cardinal's letter and one or two collateral matters to the attention of Bishop Fraser, who, in reply, wrote: 'One knows the line that the Roman Catholic Church takes in these matters. Her rulers think that, by drawing a cordon of ecclesiastical discipline round their people, they make them safe. Protestant churches are not afraid to trust their people's consciences and right instincts. Each system, of course, has its dangers; but I am sure ours is the nobler, because the freer, the more generous. As a matter of duty, I cannot see that you are violating any conscientious obligation by simply *reporting*. If, judging for yourself, you found that this did your moral nature any harm, it would then become a matter of conscience, which no one could rightly decide but yourself, whether you should pursue such an occupation or give it up. For myself, I should be sorry to be pressed, by any circumstances, to pursue a calling which I felt was doing me moral harm. The question of 'writing up the views of a newspaper or other publication, while at the same time one's own opinions, both political and religious, may be of a different kind,' is of another order. I hardly see how a conscientious man could allow himself to do that. That seems to be a question of *honesty*—for surely there ought to be honesty in one's opinions as well as in other things.'"

The only quarrel that the newspaper press of his diocese had with Bishop Fraser arose out of a sermon, or address, in which he was reported to have said: "Look at the literature which is sometimes allowed to find its way to our drawing-room tables, the licence taken by even respectable prints, the cartoons which sometimes appear in *Punch*, where the idea is at least verging on the impure, if not actually impure." In a letter to *Punch* the Bishop made the following *amende*:

"What I meant to say, and what I believe I did say, was this: 'The light literature on our drawing-room tables, the engravings in our illustrated papers, even the cartoons of *Punch*, indicate that the tone of fashionable society, if not actually impure, is perilously near to the borderland of impurity. Nobody who knows the way in which your artists hold the mirror up to nature, and illustrate the foibles of the age, would charge them with ministering to impurity. Indeed, I have often admired the skill and the right feeling with which they have touched on delicate ground. But I was thinking of the general tone of that fast fashionable life which these pictures illustrate, and whose follies they so admirably expose. I deeply regret that I should have been misreported."

The last sentence of this letter was warmly resented by the Manchester press, it being pointed out that a man who was so remarkably fluent as the Bishop, could scarcely be always certain of the difference between what he said and what he meant to say. The dispute was happily terminated by the Bishop frankly withdrawing this sentence of his letter, and substituting the words: "I deeply regret that I should have failed to express my intended meaning." And he added: "I hope that the reporters of the Manchester press will now acquit me of any 'deliberate charge' against them to misrepresent either myself or any other speaker." Thereupon—to use the words of Mr. Alexander Paul, then of Manchester, and now of the *Daily News*—"the Manchester reporters immediately buried the hatchet, and renewed their attachment to the Bishop, who was a far greater favourite with them than any man could be expected to be who added so enormously to their work."

On one occasion, however, the Bishop did find himself misreported in Manchester; and it was a piece of misreporting which he enjoyed immensely. Speaking at one of the many meetings which he attended in connection with philanthropic movements—this particular meeting having to do with the waifs and strays of the city—the Bishop said: "We take tnese children out of the street, we clothe them, we tend them, we *watch* over them." In one of the next morning's papers the Bishop was made to say, "We *wash* them!" A few hours later he turned up at another philanthropic meeting, and the gentlemen of the press observed, as he took his seat on the platform, that his expansive countenance was lit up with an uncommonly broad smile. For a minute or two the Bishop had a merry conversation, picturing himself, armed with soap and towel, at a scrubbing-down of the unwashed juveniles of Manchester.

CHAPTER XIV.

THE BISHOP AND THE WORKING CLASSES.

Incidents in the Bishop's Relationships to the Working Classes—Modern Christianity—Modern Society—Classes and Masses—True Happiness—Religious Enthusiasm—Religious Fervour—Religion of Working Classes—Kearsley Colliery Explosion—Clifton Hall Explosion—The Bishop's Sympathy—Duty—Athletics—Luxury—High Aims—Bishop and Railway Men—Evidences of Christianity—Patriotism—Extravagance and Thrift—The Bishop and the Poor—Letters to Working Men—Church and People.

As in politics and churchmanship, Bishop Fraser's large citizenship and large Christianity could not narrow itself to the limits of a single party; so, in society, his large heart could not narrow itself to the limits of a single class. His affectionate nature embraced every sort and condition of men. Himself sprung from the upper middle class, a gentleman and a scholar, he was in his native element among the cultured and the well-born. But his sympathies ran, with a rush, beyond the bounds of his own class into the broad seas of human life. To the struggling and the poor, he was especially drawn by the resistless magnetism of compassionate tenderness. The darker and the heavier a man's lot, the more clear appeared to the Bishop the duty of endeavouring to lighten and to brighten it. Devoted to the peace, and beauty, and freshness of country life, he yearned over the multitudes closely crowded in ugly, noisy towns. From the first month of his residence in Manchester, this country parson, with a genial yeoman's face and a merry yeoman's heart, dedicated himself to the cause of the city-multitudes. He was everywhere; and always cheerily encouraging. Not in Manchester alone, but in Bolton, Preston, Rochdale, Oldham, and other towns in his diocese, he met the working people in special gatherings. Night-soil men, lurrymen, cab and omnibus drivers, policemen and postmen, colliers, foundry-men and mill hands, railway workers, and artizans of all descriptions, were often called together to meet their Bishop. He would sometimes address as many as two thousand employés during their "dinner hour." It was a strange and unwonted scene; the upturned faces of a crowd of hard-headed workmen, many of whom attended no place of worship, eagerly listening to the Bishop's simple gospel of practical Christianity; a Christianity for the fireside and the workshop; a Christianity of industry, truth, soberness, purity, brotherly kindness. At Gorton Tank, at Ashbury's Works, at the Atlas Works of Messrs. Sharp and Stewart, and at similar centres of industry, the Bishop, during his fifteen years of Lancashire life, addressed above 70,000 men. A graphic account of one of these assemblies is given in a letter received by the Bishop from a cobbler in the audience:

"I am no church or chapel-goer myself. But I went to hear you deliver the address in Johnson's Works, and when I was solicited to attend church regular by one of those zealous mission workers, I replied, that, if I attended church for the next year, I should never hear that grand old story, of which your lordship spoke, more plainly, more vigorously, more earnestly, or more eloquently, told. I have thought hours of the few words you spoke in that joiner's shop. I was expecting your lordship would have noticed the benches, saws, planes, chisels, &c., for, non-religious as I am, it struck me instantly as appropriate to the theme of that Grand Carpenter of Galilee which Holman Hunt has admirably depicted, and which you, in like manner, treated of. When you spoke of the curiosity you had to see one of those brutes who kick their wives, &c., your lordship little knew how many of such said articles you had in the little congregation before you. One of two men on my left remarked to his mate, 'There's a hot un for thee, Dick.' But Dick only coolly replied, 'Ditto, dirty cousin.'"

In addressing these meeting of working men, the Bishop preached no mere conventional sermon. "I do so hate," he writes in one of his letters, "those conventional sermons to fashionable congregations, upon whom you know beforehand you are not likely to produce the slightest impression. Give me a church full of Lancashire artizans ten thousand times rather, or a meeting of workpeople in a shed."

To workpeople the Bishop, with no roundabout locutions,

spoke forth his whole heart in plain and simple words. Mounting a chair or temporary platform, he proclaimed, what one correspondent calls, the "gospel of good common sense." His openness and fairness of mind made him a great favourite with the workmen of all creeds, and of no creed. In returning from one of these services, a workman thus addressed the Bishop: "Weel, awve bin to ear yo.' Yo' hit us 'ard, but yo' did it koind loike." This was just what the men felt. The Bishop was fearless in reproof of wrong, but he "did it koind loike." They felt that he was a fair and a just man—no respecter either of persons or of classes. Upon one occasion he had been giving the workmen at Ashbury's Works some plain counsels about "scamping work." Then, turning to the officials near him, the Bishop said, "Masters are equally capable with men of scamping work." This all-round fairness of utterance made the men feel they were not being condescendingly "lectured" by a patron, but faithfully counselled by a friend.

In his visits to the workshops the Bishop was generally accompanied by the venerable City Missionary, Mr. Jeremiah Chadwick. Indeed, Mr. Chadwick, or, as the Bishop generally called him, "Jeremiah," was the chief organizer of these gatherings. Many stories are current of the Bishop's relations towards "Jeremiah"; but the following are undoubtedly authentic. The Bishop and "Jeremiah" were in almost constant correspondence, and were so frequently seen together at workmen's meetings that the men used to say, "Yon comes t' Bishop and his curate Chadwick." Yet the Bishop did not know for years whether "Jeremiah" was a Churchman or Nonconformist. One day, however, clapping his hand on Jeremiah's shoulder, he said, "I have never in all these years, Jeremiah, asked you to what denomination you belong. What are you?" "I am an Evangelist," replied Chadwick. "That will do for me," said the Bishop. At the close of one of the outdoor meetings the rain began to fall: "Now, cannot some of you lend the Bishop an umbrella?" said Mr. Chadwick. "No, no!" rejoined the Bishop, "never mind me, Jeremiah, I should not be fit to be a Bishop if I was afraid of a shower of rain"; and away the Bishop went alone through the rain, with his fine manly step, to the station.

Addressing an assemblage of railway employés on September 26, 1879, the Bishop said:

"I understand through our common friend, Mr. Jeremiah Chadwick, of the City Mission, that you wish me to come among you a second time; and, though I am always reluctant to thrust myself forward on occasions of this kind, I feel that I cannot refuse the invitation that was brought to me. I came in grand style, being brought down in a saloon carriage of a special train, and with me were the chairman of the company and a goodly number of friends. I should be very sorry, however, for you to think a Bishop could not travel about in an ordinary train, or even a third-class carriage, if it were necessary. As I travel about my diocese, I do not, it is true, take third-class tickets—I would be thought rather mean if I did—but I frequently come back with third-class passengers whilst travelling in the Lancashire and Yorkshire district, and I never object to their company, but find them, when sober, civil and well-behaved."

Upon one occasion, some of these third-class passengers were shown into the compartment where the Bishop was sitting. In the crush the compartment became over-crowded, and, for want of room, a woman was obliged to sit upon her husband's knee right opposite the Bishop, who looked at her in keen and kindly amusement. "Weel," said the woman, "yo' need na' look at me as if aw wur doin' summut wrung. This is moi own mon, an a gud gradely mon he is an' no mistak'. Dunna think as I wud be sittin' on ony sooart of a mon's knee. Howsome'er my mon and me as bin to 'ear yo' praitch, an' yo' av praitched us a gradely gud sarmon." The Bishop, intensely amused, with a hearty laugh assured the woman he had never suspected her of anything wrong.

In a letter of August 20, 1878, the Bishop alludes to this incident:

"I got on very well at Leigh on Wednesday night. The church was as full as it could hold, and there was not a trace of ill-feeling. I must tell you when we meet some stories that will make you laugh at my adventures on my journey home. There was a crowd of people returning from the service, and they tumbled into the carriages without much regard whether they got into their proper class. I found myself with a very typical set of Lancashire men and women of the respectable mechanic or agricultural class in my compartment, and they were immensely amusing. The service was very effectively rendered, and my notes of the last Lichfield sermon came into use a second time. One of my old women encouraged me wonderfully with the assurance that in her opinion it was 'a very good sermon,' which at least meant that she understood it."

Incidents such as these put the people in good humour with their Bishop. They would often stop to speak with him on the road, or express their appreciation of his character in public gatherings. At the opening of Ordsal Park, the Bishop jocularly alluded to his frequent public appearances, and said he sometimes feared he talked too much. "Thar't a gud mon, onyow," broke in a voice from the crowd. Upon another occasion, a policeman stopped the Bishop in Strangeways, and said, "My lord, I've got an old father who wears the old-fashioned clothes, and his knee breeches are getting worn out; I thought if your Lordship had any of such articles with the gaiters, such as your Lordship wears, cast off and put on one side, they might come in handy. The Bishop entered at once into the matter, and said, "Well, I'll see, my man, what I can do for you when I get home": and next morning a bundle was put up all ready with his own hands.

In a letter dated April 29, 1878, the Bishop writes:

"The Vicar of St. Andrew's, Oldham, told me an anecdote which illustrates the kindness of heart of these Lancashire people, of whom be it known to you, the 'Owdham' people are proverbially supposed to be the roughest. It is my habit to carry my own bag, and a working man said to Mr. Sparling (the Vicar), "I did na loike to see th' Bishop carrying his own bag. It wur na reet. I'd half a mind to offer to carry it mysel'; but I was na washed, ye see; and so I was afraid to speak to 'im." I laughed, and at the same time thought that these rough people have still the feelings that we consider those of a gentleman."

A collier in Radcliffe, as he watched the Bishop walking down the street with firm, manly step, was overheard saying to his companion, "Eh, mon, yon's a gradely Bishop! What a chap he'd be for a hup and deawn foight!"

These simple stories are typical of the relationship existing between the Bishop and the working classes. It was the relationship of trusted friends. He entered into their character and their life. They believed in him and loved him. In him was no aloofness of officialism; in them no sense of distance or mistrust. Each clasped the other in the arms of a common Christian manhood. And thus, believing in their Bishop, the people listened to his words with attentive and obedient ears, as he reasoned with them of self-respect, self-reliance, self-control. Upon one occasion, the Bishop had been earnestly enforcing upon a degraded audience (shoeless, out-at-elbows, unwashed, uncombed) the Christian duty of bridling the tongue against the shameful habit of lewd jesting, of coarse swearing, of quarrelling at home. One of his hearers, specially addicted to cursing his wife, returned home, and ate his evening meal in silence. His wife, astonished at her husband's manner, said, "Hast lost thy tung, Dick?" "Noa," he replied, "but awve bin' earing t' Bishop, an' aw mean to owd my tung an' not cuss thee." Another came to the Bishop, after some months, neatly dressed, and said, "Sin' yo' towked to us abeeat cussin' and drinkin', awve given 'em up, an' as aw connot do nowt else to 'elp yo', an' aw want to 'elp yo in your wurk, aw'll cum and sing for yo' at yooar meetin's if yo'll let me." The Bishop's manner towards the working classes was ever genial and winning. "We must not attack these men," he used to say. "The Old Adam in them is too strong to be driven. We must draw them." And he did draw them with the cords of a man. Often he asked these rough men (unaccustomed to pray for themselves) to pray for him. And sometimes their prayer for the Bishop was the first prayer they had prayed for many years. One of them writes:

March 26, 1879.

DEAR BISHOP,—A poor man obeyed your request and prayed hard for you last night—he was put about at seeing you looking jaded, just like an over-worked willing horse; but it was not to be wondered at when he heard of the number of places of worship you have opened, and of the 90,000 little children you have received into the Church, besides preaching and speaking twenty-eight days a month with no "turn off" on Sundays, like any other mason, carpenter, or shopman, much less the warehousemen and manufacturers, who have the satisfaction of looking forward to "week end," and can each say, "Never mind being at it from six to six hard as I can—*week end's coming*, and I'll have from twelve or one o'clock on Saturday till Monday for rest and comfort."

Another writes, June 9, 1880 :

MOST REV. SIR,—I am afraid I have made a mistake in addressing you; but being only an *old Welsh working man*, and not accustomed to write to persons of high position, you will pardon me; but, as for respecting, revering, and admiring you, I shall not give in to any one. Your very plain manners and plain language—in your sermons, lectures, and addresses—quite delight me, and I pray that you may be endowed with health and strength long to live, so as to make your mark on the Church. Your openness of heart and liberal sentiments towards all classes are elements in your character which very few in your position possess—at least they don't show it; but you do, not only in word, but in deed, and by acting thus the Bishop of Manchester has gained to himself the character of Demetrius, who had good report of all men and of the truth itself. I read this morning of the great ceremony which is to take place at the consecration of Canon Ryle as Bishop of Liverpool. He also is a man whom I admire very much. I hope he will not lose any of that plainness of manner, which is so characteristic in him, after his elevation. He has been speaking very plainly of the bishops formerly by saying that if they were to *doff their lawn* and preach in earnest, and go more among the people, that six or seven of them would do more good than the whole bench, or something to that purpose. Now we shall see whether he will put those precepts into practice or not. But what I was going to say, and ask you, especially as you are one of the procession, Don't you think that less pomp and show would be more becoming upon such a solemn occasion? When we consider that God is a spirit, and dwelleth not in temples made with hands, nor is He worshipped with men's hands, but in spirit and truth, I fancy myself that the Great Being, in looking down from heaven upon such processions attended with such a gorgeous display of ceremony and formularies, that He says, "To what purpose is all this multitude of ceremonials and show? When ye come to appear before Me, who hath required this at your hand?" I look at all such pomposity as so very contrasted to everything related to our blessed Saviour.—Your very humble servant,

JOSEPH EATON (Bricklayer 71 years old).

In reply to this Welsh bricklayer, seventy-one years old, the Bishop wrote :

MY GOOD FRIEND,—I thank you for your good opinion of me, which I hope I shall never do anything to lose. I am this very day returned from the consecration of Bishop Ryle. I am as averse from anything like excessive ceremonialism as you can be, but there are times and places in which, in my judgment, a grand service where all is done reverently and in order is not out of place. Our Blessed Lord Himself, once at least, took part in a grand procession; and solemn services of a magnificent character certainly seem to have been acceptable to God in the days of pious Jewish kings. The consecration of a bishop is a public act of no slight importance, and ought to be done in a public manner, and a mean ceremony in a grand minster like that of York would have savoured of incongruity. I think if you had been present to-day you would not have been offended by anything that was either said or done, unless you are strict almost to the verge of a fanatic in your ideas. The good sense and right feeling which run through your letter will not allow me to think this of you; and if " God hath nowhere revealed that He delighteth to dwell beggarly," as our great English divine, Richard Hooker, has said, in justification of the erection of noble churches; so I think, within limits, and on just occasions, there is no harm, but the contrary, in putting such churches to a noble use. I am sure that all minds are not constituted in the same way, and all I desire is latitude and tolerance.—I remain, yours very faithfully,

J. MANCHESTER.

This courtesy in corresponding with cobblers and bricklayers, with all the fulness and sympathy due to equals, won their hearts. Yet the admiration of his few correspondents did not close the Bishop's eyes to the vastness of the multitude religiously dumb—the sad and toiling masses who never speak or write about religion. It was these thousands of thousands who never go to church or chapel—rough, yet honest, working men—whom the Bishop sought to train in the elementary principles of the Christian faith; and, as they did not go to listen to him in church, he went to speak to them in the workshop.

He was not satisfied—he was profoundly dissatisfied—with the conventional character of many Christian congregations. His was not the heart to feed itself fat, with the oil of self-complacency, over the bright and comfortable spectacle of churches filled with well-tailored and well-millinered congregations. His heart hungered, with a good shepherd's yearning, for the wandering sheep not sheltered within the Christian fold. Instead of contenting himself with what Christianity has done, he mourned over what Christianity has failed to do. He felt he was Bishop not merely of the worshipping few, but of the non-worshipping many. He wanted the goats to be saved as well as the sheep. Not only the thousands in the churches, but also, and especially, the tens of thousands in the streets and slums, he felt to be his people and his charge.

In an address delivered to the Church of England Evening Visiting Society in June 1870, he said:

"The great problem, which the Church of England, and all churches, has to solve, in the middle of the nineteenth century, is, how to reach the masses of the working classes. Churches have been built in this diocese of Manchester at a tolerably rapid rate since the diocese was formed. My predecessor, who, I expect, sank into a premature grave, under his aggravated labours, consecrated churches in his diocese at the rate of one in two months. I have been bishop of this same diocese barely three months, and I have already consecrated two churches, which shows even an increased rapidity in the work. Yet I feel that an infinitely more important problem than that of building churches is, how to fill them when they are built; and not only that, but also the problem of filling them with the proper class of persons. The great glory of the Gospel, when it was first preached, was that it was first preached to the poor, and the most conclusive argument which our Lord could bring in proof of His Messiahship to the Apostles, who asked Him for proofs of His mission, was that the Gospel was to be preached to the poor. And I take it that if any National Church or other Christian Community abnegates the primary duty of seeking to bring the poor and outcast within its walls, it cannot expect the blessing of God to rest on its labours, neither can it expect to extend and increase, even were it allowed to continue its miserable lethargic life. Last Sunday evening I was very much struck by a phenomenon which presented itself to my eyes in the streets of Manchester. I had been preaching what is called the 'school sermon' at St. Matthew's Church, Campfield, in one of the densest populations of this city. The church was filled to overflowing, and I saw from the newspapers that a good collection was made. I have nothing to say against the congregration; they were attentive and reverent; the services were hearty, and I believe a work for good is going on there. Yet when I left the church—it was my first appearance in a public capacity in that district—I saw gathered together a great miscellaneous crowd of roughs, outcasts, poor men in their working dresses, and women without bonnets—who are just the class which we desire to reach. These were outside, and the well-to-do class were inside. It seemed to me as though I had been preaching to the ninety-and-nine who needed not repentance, while the nine-hundred-and-ninety-nine poor ignorant people, living perhaps in a state of social savagery, were outside. In no other part of the world—not even in the South Sea Islands—could I have seen such a marked and painful contrast, as was presented to my eyes by the sight

I saw in St. Matthew's Church and outside it; and it struck me, if I was to be a bishop in a profitable sense, and the clergy working with me were to be profitable in a saving sense, that the class in the street more than the class in the church, was the class which we ought to reach; and we ought not to be satisfied with ourselves, or think we had done any work at all for Christ's Church, until that class was reached, and reached effectually."

Again:

"The religion of the mass of the world is nothing at all. It consists perhaps of paying so much per annum for a pew, occupying it with more or less regularity, and oftentimes in being angry with the apparitor for putting in some one else when they themselves have been late at Divine Service, and in saying with more or less fervency certain prayers. You have confessed your sins this morning. How many of you felt a single sin? You say that you have done many things that you ought not to have done. Have you made a resolution that you would not do such things again? You say that you have left undone many things that you ought to have done. Do you think what it is that you have left undone? I affirm that the religion which is professed by many is a huge piece of unreality, of insincerity, and hypocrisy. I feel myself that one has need to be continually on the watch, to be struggling against the devil of hypocrisy and formalism, lest one's life should be a great organized lie. I warn you against the dead level of formalism, of self-satisfaction, of Pharisaism, of mechanical worship, of the perfunctory discharge of obvious duties, and being satisfied because everything in the home and family happens to be comfortable. Is it all comfortable? Your servants are admirably behaved, your sons and daughters are all that you desire! Are you sure of all that? Are you sure that your sons are all you desire them to be? I am told that many young men in Manchester have a very different character from what their mothers and sisters think they have. How easily satisfied we are! We close the front door when the day's work is over, draw the curtains, and throw ourselves in our easy-chair, and see one child perhaps playing the piano, the wife knitting by the side of the fire, and the other members of the family pleasantly occupied, and everything is serene, and we say, 'This is civilization, this is Christianity,' while outside in the howling night are poor ragged souls, wandering in search of a home, thieves and drunkards, and the unfortunate women of Deansgate and Canal-street in Manchester, all plying their godless trade. What is that to you and me? We are at the fireside, all pleasant and surrounded with happiness, and we are saying, 'Peace, peace.' We say, 'Yes, these are the neglected classes.' Who has neglected them? I suppose the parsons must bear their share of the blame, and the people of the Church of England—the well-to-do, the educated, the rich—must bear their share also. They have not done their duty. A few days ago I received a letter from the wife of a clergyman in Manchester. Her husband's parish contains I do not know how many public-houses, several thieves' dens, and a great number of brothels. A poor woman who had fallen, but who, by the grace of God, had been enabled to rise again, undertook to join her in an attempt to reclaim some of these fallen women. This woman had an especial gift for addressing these poor women, and the work was apparently being blessed, when it was intimated to the lady that it was improper for her to be going about with a reclaimed prostitute; and that, if she continued so to do, she could not be received into society. With unctuous phrase and Pharisaic look, sanctimoniousness stepped in and said, 'We cannot receive you into our drawing-rooms, or among our family and friends, if you are keeping such society.' Such persons seem to forget that Our Lord Himself when upon earth was reproached for His friendship with publicans and sinners. On one occasion a bishop of the Church of England said to me (speaking of a certain district), 'There is a deal of religion there, but not much morality.' I would ask you who are present here, if you have ever found anything to come under that description—loud profession, but not corresponding morality? I ask you also—though it has been the fashion in certain schools of theology to decry morality—what is religion worth, if it does not purify the life?"

Bishop Fraser held strongly the belief that the miseries of the poor are largely owing to the selfish luxuries, the want of consideration and sympathy, of the moneyed class. At a meeting held in Association Hall, Peter Street, Manchester, October 25, 1881, he said:

"Society seems to have very little conscience. What with its impatience and its selfishness, it really is very reckless of the enormous cost at which its convenience and comfort are provided. The impatience of society, its inability to wait even for a moment when its desire for any particular object is excited, is one of the most unwholesome characteristics of the age we live in. The rush of modern life tramples down all the weak and helpless, while we speed recklessly to our own individual wants; and it is that, I believe, which is doing almost as much harm to society at large as the amount of vice which exists amongst all classes of society. 'Evil is wrought by want of thought as well as by want of heart.' I wish people would think a little, before they give their orders, as to the cost of those things to others—to their bodies as well as their souls, their well-being in every sense of the term. And then, as to the selfishness of society, so long as people are comfortable in their own suburban residences, and so long as they fancy and flatter themselves that their own homes, and their own boys and girls, are kept pure and unspotted from the world, they are ready to be very self-complacent with the pleasant idea that all is well without, because all is fairly well within. I think that the comparatively well-to-do classes of society need to feel much more acutely than they feel at the present time what a terrible accumulation of vice, misery, and suffering arises from a ministry to luxuries and wants, many of which could be easily dispensed with, but which they seem determined to have, let them cost what they will. We talk about our civilization, but I think it is not very much to boast of in England just now. I am afraid a great deal of our Christianity does not really go much below the surface, and has utterly failed to kindle in the hearts of a great many respectable and well-dressed church-going people, who have Bibles and Prayer Books, and who pay rents for their pews, any living, vital sympathy for the bodies or souls of their fellow-men."

Again, preaching at St. George's in the East, London, June 22, 1879, he said:

"However it may be with the East-End of London, I am not sure whether the West-End has any reason to plume itself on its superior godliness, whether the dukes and duchesses, the earls and countesses, the squires and knights and their ladies, are much more like what men and women ought to be than the costermongers and women of the East of London. No doubt at the West-End churches are filled; but, if we ask what fills the West-End churches, it is not certain that we can give a satisfactory answer to the question. I am not sure that they are always filled with people hungering and thirsting after righteousness, or with people who wish to know what the Christian temper and the Christian life are, in order that they may exhibit the one and live the other. It is all very well to attract people by a spectacular service and an eloquent harangue; but I was told the other day of a noted preacher who drew an enormous crowd to hear him under the dome of St. Paul's, and yet, immediately the service was over, the people rushed out asking who had won the Grand Prix de Paris."

The use of language so plain as this naturally brought upon the Bishop much public comment. Some extolled him, others blamed him. Some flatteringly contrasted him with his fellow bishops; others accused him of inflaming the masses against the classes. The Bishop's private correspondence shows that he himself was fully aware both of the peril of the flattery, and the significance of the accusation. In a letter of October 1, 1877, he writes:

"The letter headed 'Atrocities at Home,' was cut out of *Reynolds' Newspaper*, which some unknown hand sent to me this afternoon. It is just one of those compliments which I exceedingly dislike. I have no notion of being selected to the disparagement of my order, which contains men to whom, in all the higher qualities that adorn a bishop, I am not worthy to hold a candle. But it shows the importance of bishops neglecting to show themselves interested in the concerns of the people. *Reynolds'* is a democratic paper, which I am always glad to see when I can, because it has an enormous circulation, and it tells me what great masses of the working people are thinking and talking about. And nothing seems to me more important just now to the Church, as a national institution, than that her relations to the great body of the people should not be misunderstood, and that the poor, and 'they that have no helper,' should not suppose that bishops and suchlike have no care for them. Still, it is a delicate business, the difficulty being to avoid seeming, while wishing to be a friend of the people, desiring to set class against class. I did not escape the difficulty in my endeavour to say a word for the locked-out farm-labourers three years ago."

Bishop Fraser was, therefore, no cheap and noisy demagogue. The notion of setting class against class was utterly alien from his temper, which was, above all things, a temper of inclusive charity. But, to all classes alike, he spoke with transparent directness and plainness of speech, telling the rich of the utter selfishness of many of their luxuries; telling the poor of the utter selfishness of many of their complainings. In an address delivered to the railway employés at Peterborough, June 23, 1878, he held the balance with conspicuous impartiality:

"Oh, my friends, a working man wrote to me and said, if he wanted a thimbleful of drink, it is beer he gets; but, if a capitalist wants his drink, he has champagne. Do you suppose the happiness of life consists in the difference between beer and champagne; and that, because a man can put champagne on the table, he must be happier than you, who can only afford to drink beer? and because he has ten thousand a year he must be happier than you who have only five-and-forty shillings a week? There is a saying that every one has a skeleton in the house somewhere; and these skeletons are more likely to be in rich men's houses than in poor men's houses, because there are more places to put them in. A rich man cannot always make all things pleasant between himself and his wife, make his children obedient, keep away gout, cholera, or typhoid fever. The rich man may have been speculating in some foolish investment, have many sleepless nights, and wake one morning to find himself a ruined man. Do not allow your minds to run in this course. Friends, rise to a different conception of happiness than the distinction between beer and champagne, and ten thousand a year and forty-five shillings a week. Why, if a man has a house in which he feels as safe as if it were his castle, if he has employment which he is equal to, and brings him in fair wages, if he is wise in choosing as his wife a thrifty, clean, kind-hearted woman, and God has blessed him with little children to prattle, and tell him how they got patted on the head for good conduct at school, or gained a little prize for what they have done, then, if he has not the elements of true happiness within his reach, he is the most discontented man I ever met. Riches don't make happiness. It is the contented heart that gives the truest zest to life. In one of the public parks in Manchester there is a marble statue in memory of a gentleman who was for many years a representative of that city in parliament, Joseph Brotherton. He may be known here. I don't believe he owned a great amount of wealth, but he gained the confidence of his citizens, and when he died they put up a monument, and on it is simply this inscription: 'My wealth consisted not in the abundance of my riches, but in the fewness of my wants.' There is no greater harm a man can do to himself or society than increase his unnecessary wants. A rich man cannot now give a dinner without champagne; but his father was content with something simpler, and I don't know that his son's happiness is increased thereby. And you, working men, are not famous for thrift. Many of you, I am afraid, are marching along with those richer ones on this road to luxury, which, with many, is the same thing as the road to ruin. But, my friends, the man who is satisfied with simple pleasures—with the wild primrose, with the Virginian creeper, or the gilly-flower—that man is in the possession of the most abiding and permanent happiness. An honest spirit of independence is a thing I am sure every one ought to desire to see working men maintain for themselves and for their class. When I speak of a feeling of honest independence, I do not mean you should desire to be independent of God or your fellow-man. That is a most excellent book of Smiles's on 'Self-help,' but it wants a supplement on 'Fellow-help,' for we are dependent on each other for all the happiness in life which we enjoy. Mr. Ruskin, if he could have his way, would have us all located in some secluded spot far away from the whistle of the locomotive and the thud of the steam-hammer. There might be happiness, order, and prosperity in such a state of things, but not such happiness, order, plenty, and prosperity as we, in this generation, have been accustomed to. I admit that a tall chimney vomiting out thick volumes of smoke is not a great element in the picturesqueness of a prospect; but, when I associate with a tall chimney five hundred working men earning honest wages and living independently on a fair competence, enjoying the protection of the law, and able to give their children a good education if so disposed, I can see a bright side even to that gloomy picture; and, though I like the country as much as any man can do, I am not altogether dissatisfied at being thrown by God's providence in perhaps one of the dirtiest and smokiest towns in England. One wishes to see a well-ordered, sober, thrifty, and industrious class of working men in England. I quite admit that what we call the upper ten thousand do not always set the working men the highest example of thrift, honesty, sobriety, and the like, but we do not judge classes by exceptional instances; and, although the march of luxury has more or less seriously affected the happiness of all classes, still, the working classes being the largest numerically, it is they whom I ask, in their own interests and those of the country, to be sober, thrifty, well-ordered, and industrious. I wish so much money were not spent in drink. There was a little improvement last year. According to statistics carefully compiled, in 1877 £142,000,000 were spent in drink, and the year before £147,000,000, so that there was a slight reduction. Perhaps bad times might have had something to do with that. Half the sum spent is said to be due to the consumption of drink by the working classes. I am not going to deny the working man his beer, so long as it is wholesome and taken in moderation; but no one will persuade me that £70,000,000 might not be spent in a hundred better ways than in beer. And there is one other element in the happiness of men that I would like to see brought about. Do try and make those homes of yours homes pervaded by a Christian spirit, and homes which you can really feel to be homes for yourself, your wife, and family. Oh, my men, if you are married men, if you have children, do remember the duties you owe to that wife, do remember the duties you owe to those children. Never let a child of yours see father come home drunk, never let a child of yours hear father swear, never let a child of yours see you strike your wife, or hear a word of unkindness pass between you and her. Surely you can govern your temper sufficiently for that. As to temptations for drinking, most of you—unless you have given way to them for so long that they have become a kind of second nature—surely, in the power of Christianity, if you ask and trust more to prayer than to any pledge taken at a temperance-meeting, you can overcome that devil of drunkenness, though perhaps he is the hardest of all devils to overcome. I live among working men; I have always lived among working men. For the first twenty years of my ministry I lived among a population of agricultural labourers, now I live among artizans, and I am thankful to say I have always been brought into friendly and kindly relations with them both. I think I know, and I certainly can sympathize with, their trials, difficulties, and hardships; and I never feel myself more distinctly doing my duty as a Christian bishop than when I am trying to help them. But the thing above all I desire to see, and that every man must desire to see who has the well-being of England at heart, is, that the working classes in this country shall understand their own true interests, and that, understanding them, they shall adopt the best and wisest means of securing them for themselves and for their children."

As an illustration of "the kindly relations" existing between the Bishop and the people, even when they differed from him, may be mentioned an incident to which he himself referred at the Mechanics' Institute, Staleybridge, October 21, 1881:

"I do not know that I ever felt a compliment more than the compliment gracefully paid me last Tuesday, when three or four persons from Oldham waited upon me and said they were members of a club, comprising some seven hundred members of *all shades of political opinion, and of different religious denominations.* They were in the habit of meeting together and debating questions, and once a year they held a soirée, at which they were accustomed to be addressed by somebody to whom they were willing to listen, and just now, they said, 'You are the only person to whom we thought we should all agree to listen.' I appreciated the compliment, but could not accept the invitation, because, if I did so, I should be sure to be misunderstood."

Again, addressing a meeting in St. Paul's Schoolroom, Manchester, October 11, 1884, Bishop Fraser said:

"I desire to see prevailing in the conduct of all clergy, in dealing with the democracy, an endeavour to bind all classes together, and not to set class against class; but to make men feel that fair dealing and justice is the best way to ensure kindly feelings and tranquillity throughout the country."

Similarly, in addressing a vast assemblage of working men at the Sheffield Congress in 1878, he said:

"Each class has its own difficulties and temptations. And I want you, working men, to realize why it is we cannot help taking such a profound interest in you. It is not because your souls are of more value than the souls of any other classes; it is simply that, numerically, you are the most important class. When we remember that in our Lord's time, somehow or other, 'the common people heard Him gladly,' and now we can scarcely get the common people to come and hear us at all, it does seem to us that some of our machinery must be out of gear."

Again, at Oldham Church, December 12, 1880:

"The chief and most cogent evidence which Christ gave of His being the Messiah was, that His Gospel should be preached to the poor. Is the Church of England to do that, or leave it to Nonconformists to do? Does she not recognize it as her main duty? Is it not her most glorious title that she is the church of the poor, that by her constitution and theory she recognizes no social distinction, that her ministers are alike at the call of the poorest man and of the richest, and that they are bound to be ready to answer his call?

"This is not the day for privileged institutions or privileged classes to stand upon their privileges instead of upon the duties which these privileges imply and impose. What we need more than anything for success is faith, earnestness, patience, and perhaps more enthusiasm. I feel that in the Church we have too much adopted the old French diplomatist's maxim to the ambassador he was sending out to a foreign court: 'Above all, my friend, show no zeal.' We are too cold; 'high and dry' was the term applied to our teaching not long ago. We have let slip the great masses of the people because we have not succeeded in finding the talisman which would reach their hearts. Yet many a man like myself, having been amongst the working people, having been brought face to face with three hundred or four hundred at a time, having spoken a grain or two of common sense, and a grain or two of sympathy, knows that their hearts can and ought to be won.

"What the Church wants is the support of the people. The pyramid must stand on its base, not on its apex. 'Let us trust the people,' said Archbishop Tait. 'We must win the people,' said Bishop Magee. I echo those sentiments. Let us arouse a spirit of enthusiasm among the people. It is a nobler work to visit and comfort the poor, the sick, and the dying, than to embroider an altar-cloth, a cope, or a chasuble. Preach the intelligible Gospel, the Gospel that men and women can understand and apply and take hold of themselves, and which will assist in the discharge of their daily duties, not a mystical thing, consisting mainly in the reiteration of unintelligible shibboleths. Preach the intelligible Gospel—preach it lovingly, sympathetically, and exhibit it, if you can, in your own life and conversation. Be, in a word, a prophet indeed—for it is the prophet, and not the priest, who is to lead people's hearts—and then you will not wait long to see the Spirit of the Lord quickening what was dead and dry into life and cheerfulness."

The Bishop lost no opportunity of impressing upon his clergy the need of kindling in themselves, from the altar of God, the flames of fervid enthusiasm, and prophetic fire. The people are not saved by the keenness of a cold philosophy, but by the affection of an inspiring faith. Preaching upon this subject at St. Peter's, Little Oakley, March 30, 1882, the Bishop said:

"I do hope the clergy will never say they cannot reach the great masses of the people; for, if they do say so, they pronounce with their own voice the most fatal of self-condemnations. For what does it mean? That they are too gentlemanly, or too refined, or too cultured? or does it mean that they are too inactive to reach them? Does it mean that the people in the slums, the brick-kilns and the mines, and the excavators of iron-stone, must be got at by other agencies—Salvation armies, revivalist services, and the like—and that the Church is to leave to them the glory of winning out of the byways and lanes, the souls for whom Christ died? Why do these sensational agencies seem to succeed—I wish their success was more assured and permanent—while the clergy so often fail? It is because they are, or seem to be, more fervent. The ministers of the Church of England have many gifts and graces, but they too seldom have fervour, which, for the work they have to do, is, perhaps, the most needed of all. The common people rarely have subtle minds. Laboured expositions, an elaborated style, dogmatic precision, rarely touch and certainly do not affect or move them. They ask for some more potent tokens of the presence of the Spirit of God. Churchmen shrink, and rightly so, from extravagances, and lament to see some strange, and to them, startling things done in the name and for the cause of Christ. They naturally, and properly, like quiet, sober, and well-ordered ways. But all these things are compatible with fervour. If the clergy wish to reach the mass of the people—and to do so would be the greatest glory and stability of the Church—I venture to assert it will be never be done except by fervour."

But, although Bishop Fraser insisted thus strongly upon the necessity for fervour in Christian teaching, he was strongly opposed to all teaching which evaporated in mere fervour, and did not bring forth much fruit in the daily life. "To do one's duty in that state of life where God has placed us, is," he said, "in the highest and truest sense, the religion of Christianity. The real proof of people's religion is in their conduct. The man who tries to do his duty honestly, simply, and straightforwardly, is the man who has the best chance of getting near the throne in the Great Day." The Bishop often told his hearers very plainly that he desired to win them to Christianity, not merely because of its beautiful sentiments, and the delightsome feelings it engendered, but because "Christianity will be a comfort to you, a guide to you, and a strength to you, making you, both in character and conduct, better and nobler."

He believed also, very firmly, that among the working classes there was no inconsiderable amount of this sound and sober Christianity. Preaching at Oswestry, October 23, 1878, he said:

"Some one, who, I think, evidently does not know what he is talking about, describes the great body of working men of England as living in the world without God, and that a great mass of them never go to church or chapel. Perhaps it is true that a large number of them do not go to public worship as often as I could wish, or as would do them good. But it must be remembered that in many cases our churches and chapels do not very heartily invite them. No doubt our churches are becoming more free and open, and less victimized by appropriations than they once were; but still, even yet, the Common Law principle of the Church of England is not freely or fully recognized, that every parishioner has an equal right, according to his degree, in the Church which belongs to his parish. Then, again, I am afraid it must be confessed, that services, and perhaps sermons, have too often not been particularly attractive to the intellects, rough, shrewd, and keen, such as are mainly possessed by working men. Then, again, they to whom it is so easy to get to church with their wives and children, after leaving word with their cook or butler that lunch must be ready at one, and supper at nine, do not always make allowances for the difficulties which stand in the way of working men who do not keep cooks and butlers. The woman has to make the beds, and, perhaps, get the breakfast ready for a lazy husband, who lies in bed and expects to find a hot dinner ready for him at one or two o'clock. With well-to-do people it hardly needs any effort or self-denial to go to Church, and in many cases, perhaps, the hour or two spent in God's house on a Sunday is a convenient mode of passing time which might otherwise be rather awkward to dispose of.

"I believe there is an opportunity spread out before the Church of England to-day such as she has never had before in the sixteen or seventeen centuries of her history. I do not believe that the heart of the people of England is turned away from the Church of their fathers, if only she will show herself a true mother to them.

"Let the Church do its duty by the great masses of the people of England, and the masses of the people of England will do their duty by their Church. The strength of the Church of the middle ages lay in its being the Church of the poor; and the Church of the nineteenth century must win back the love and confidence of the poor. Mr. Joseph Arch must not be allowed to go about, and with any semblance of truth in his words persuade the people that the Church of England has always been the enemy of the poor. We must show that the statement has no foundation of truth, by labouring for the poor, and trying to bring them within the fold."

Two illustrations may here be given of the intensity of Bishop Fraser's sympathy with the sufferings of the working classes. The mining districts of Lancashire are unhappily familiar with great disasters—wives being suddenly made widows, and children orphans, by explosions in the mines. Two of these disasters during the Bishop's *Lancashire Life* were upon an appalling scale. The first occurred on Thursday, March 14, 1878, at the Union Brook Colliery, Kearsley Moor, when forty-three lives were lost. On the very day of the explosion, the Bishop wrote to the Rev. Charles Lowe, vicar of the parish in which the catastrophe had taken place:

MY DEAR MR. LOWE,—I am terribly shocked at the catastrophe which has befallen your poor colliers. I was glad to see that you were on the spot soon after the accident, discharging your duty in ministrations of comfort to the bereaved and sorrowing.

"I beg to send, through you, a contribution of £20 to the fund that no doubt will be raised for the widows and orphans of those who have perished I take it as a matter of course that a Relief Committee will be formed; and I hope that the money will be distributed simply in proportion to the necessities of each case, which is the only proper method of dealing with a great temporal calamity such as this is.—Yours sincerely,

J. MANCHESTER.

Upon the Sunday after the funeral of those who had lost their lives in this terrible accident, the Bishop went to Kearsley Moor, and endeavoured to teach to the sorrowing inhabitants, in a simple sermon at St. Stephen's Church, a few of the lessons contained in the sad, mysterious calamity:

"All these things would be inexplicable, and could not be reconciled with what we believe of the wisdom and providence of God, if this life were the all in all. But this life is not the all in all. An accident of this kind should make us feel our poverty and weakness. It calls forth strong and earnest feelings, and I can well believe that just now, at any rate, there are sobering and solemnizing thoughts pervading your minds, and that you have a deeper sense of your personal responsibilities. I am glad, indeed, to hear of the gallant band of explorers, headed by Her Majesty's Inspectors, who went down the mine at the peril of their lives; and also of the kindly aid given by neighbouring masters and workmen. I hope and pray that the lives of all here present will be purer and better; that you will think more of God; be more earnest and regular in your prayers; try to learn God's law more truly, and be found more regularly at Christ's Holy Table. I also hope that you will avoid running races and flying pigeons on Sunday; and, on the whole, I cannot help hoping and trusting that this awful lesson will not be thrown away. We see that, with all our skill, with all our constructive appliances, with all our ventilation, with all our scientific knowledge, yet, somehow or other, we cannot arrest God's hand when He sees fit to stretch it forth. We cannot say to God, 'I have surrounded myself with safeguards; my life is safe.' Our life is but a vapour. It hangs on the breath of God's will, and if He chooses to lift His finger all our contrivances are brought to nought.'

The second appalling explosion occurred on June 18, 1885, at the Clifton Hall Collieries, belonging to Messrs. Andrew Knowles and Sons. In this sad calamity 178 lives were lost, and there were left 366 widows and dependent relatives. The Bishop hastened, as soon as possible, to the scene of the catastrophe, that he might administer consolation and comfort to the afflicted and bereaved. He became also a member of the committee formed for the relief of the poor sufferers, for whom in Manchester and Salford alone a fund amounting to £27,512 was subscribed, the Bishop himself subscribing £100.

One great incident connected with this disaster—an incident of colliery life great enough to glorify humanity—deeply impressed upon the Bishop's mind the heroism of the working classes; a heroism attributed by him to the unconscious influences of Christianity. The incident cannot be better described than in his own noble, simple, touching words in a sermon preached the following Sunday at Christ Church, Marylebone, almost the last sermon he ever preached in London :

"Let me tell you in a few simple words a story which may, perhaps, do you more good than all I have hitherto been endeavouring to impress upon you. You have seen that we have had in Lancashire a terrible colliery explosion, in which 170 lives were lost. That explosion occurred at half-past nine in the morning, in a pit 510 yards deep. I did not hear of it till the evening, too late to go the spot. On Friday I went down to the scene, and I confess that the memory of it will never pass away from my mind. I saw a great, orderly, silent crowd. There were forty policemen, but they were not needed to keep order. There were weeping women about, there were ministers of Christ there trying to comfort them. I saw lying in two sheds sixty-six blackened stark corpses. They had mostly been recognized, but not all. One went about saying what few words of comfort one could to those who seemed to need it, and I think they seemed to feel that a bishop was not out of his place amongst them. But what touched my heart more than anything was to see a band of about a hundred men gathered together in little knots, perfectly silent, and looking perfectly resolute. I asked who they were, and what they were there for. They said, 'These are the volunteers who have offered to go down into the pit to rescue the bodies of those that are still lying there. They are waiting for their turn to be called.' They went down in drafts of ten or a dozen at a time, and remained underground as long as the fetid and unwholesome atmosphere allowed them. I need not tell you that men going down into a pit under those circumstances go with their lives in their hands. I was told that the only moment when there was anything like a symptom of disorder was when the dust and disturbance of the explosion had cleared away. There was a call, 'Who will be the first to go down the pit?' There was a rush to the mouth of the pit of men who were ready to go. Three, I believe, were at the first chosen to go as the first explorers, and one who saw them go says it was wonderful to see the calmness of their countenances. People who saw the first Christian martyr about to die, looking into his face, thought he looked like an angel. I never saw an angel, and I do not know what the face of an angel is like, but I think the countenances of those men going down silently and resolutely to what might be to them a pit of destruction must have had something angelic about them—perfectly calm, quite determined, resolute to do and to die if need be. A clergyman went with me, and I said to him, as I pointed to these men, '*Look there, my friend. You and I preach Christianity; these men have learned the practice of it.*' Men of that class, perhaps you may say, know nothing of the influences of Christianity. I do not know that. One of my own good clergy was going about there like a ministering angel, thinking of everybody but himself, and speaking words of comfort; and he told me that of those who were known to be dead twelve belonged to his Bible class, and four or five to his choir. These are the unconscious influences of Christianity. And what a loss it would be for the world if these unconscious influences of Christianity were swept away! I said to myself, these men, after all, are the best evangelists, and I am sure St. Paul would recognize them as true brethren, for were they not among those who counted their lives as not dear unto themselves, but freely gave themselves up for their brethren? This is what I saw two days ago."

It was this sympathy, manly and deep, with the sorrows, and losses, and difficulties, of the working classes which endeared the Bishop so closely to their hearts. Their bereavements were his bereavements; their hardships his hardships; their griefs his griefs. His heart beat with theirs. "I don't know how it is," he writes in a letter of March 25, 1878, "but I never feel more at home, nor more sure that I am usefully employed, than when I am among these kindly natured, intelligent working men, who, while they won't accept patronage, are so thankful for a little sympathy, encouragement, and advice."

"The Humane Society," writes Mr. Smith, of the Y. M. C. A., "for the Hundred of Salford, raised a fund for the purpose of presenting gold and silver medals to the heroes of the disaster, who risked their lives in going into the pit to save the lives (if any could be saved), and to bring up the dead. The Bishop looked forward to being present at the meeting which was held in the Mayor's parlour, in October 1885, but unfortunately, owing to sickness and failing health, he was unable to be present; but Mrs. Fraser was there, and it was on this memorable occasion that the words were elicited from the mouth of the Mayor, 'The Bishop is not only the Bishop of the Church of England, but of every Religious Denomination.'"

Bishop Fraser gave to the working classes not only warm sympathy, but also wise counsel.

A few extracts from his Addresses to the mechanics, artizans, and working people, will best show the sort of counsels he was in the habit of giving. Preaching in Manchester Cathedral to the Rifle Volunteers, most of whom were clerks and working men, on February 16, 1879, he said:

"The great peril of our day—a peril both to the Church and to the State, in fact, to every department of the Commonwealth—springs not from without, but from within; not from the strength and multitude of our enemies, but from our own chaotic disorganization, the peril of confounding anarchical licence and self-will with that divine yearning for freedom, and that noble spirit of independence which has done so much to form the national character of Englishmen. We need to revive in our own hearts the force of that spell that wrought such wonders in the hearts of Blake, of Chatham, of Nelson, of Wellington, as often as they felt the almost magic influence of their country's claims. It was the thought of his country—how he left her, or how he loved her—that filled the heart, and at last escaped from the lips of William Pitt in his bitter death-hour, when that sun of Austerlitz had set so gloomily and threateningly on the liberties of Europe. Surely it was nothing less than an inspiration that ran up that noble battle signal to the masthead on the day of Trafalgar, and has ever since inscribed it as his truest motto on the heart of every Englishman. The motive that has written so many gallant deeds on the page of our country's history has not been the quest of glory, has not been the propagandism of ideas; it has been simple obedience to the call of duty. The heroism that attracts us is of the simplest, least sensational kind. It is that of Philip Sidney on the plain of Zutphen, passing untouched the draught of water to the soldier by his side, whose dying agonies were even sharper than his own. It is such heroism as that of the gallant soldiers who nobly sank in the *Birkenhead* in Algoa Bay, so that weak women and weaker children might be saved. It is that of Napier, asking but for one day to get himself ready to proceed to the post of duty in India. It is that of Colin Campbell, calmly drawing out his thin red line which the Russian Cuirassiers, had they dared to charge so far, might have hurled to the ground. It is that of Cathcart going down to the 'valley of death' to reform his broken columns on the deadly day of Inkerman. It is the heroism of Hedley Vicars, a Christian soldier in every sense, springing up to meet death in an obscure sortie in the trenches before Sebastopol. It is that of Maxse, taking his lonely ride in the watches of the night through the enemy's lines, with only stars for his guide, to carry Lord Raglan's urgent message to the admiral to bring the fleet round.

"These are types of the character—samples merely taken at random—that have made England what she has been in the past, and must keep her true to herself in the future. These are tales that English mothers should never weary of telling to their children on their knees; tales that brace those who are no longer children with firmer energy and kindle their hearts with Divine fire."

To the railway employés at Gorton, September 21, 1879, he said:

"I have no fear of the future of England, if England will only to herself be true. If Englishmen will revive the old spirit of their fathers; if they will set before themselves steadily the claims of duty; if they will remember that God sent us into this world not to be idle and spend luxurious days; if they will remember the words of the old heathen poet, 'Labour conquers everything,' then I am not afraid for a country inhabited by a race possessing the great qualities of Englishmen."

In an Address delivered at the Leeds Mechanics' Institute, September 24, 1879, he said:

"I think the race is improving physically. I admire the athletic well-developed bodies of our young men, the graceful but not enervated forms of our young women. But I do not feel so sure of the strength and firmness of their moral tissue. I often hear men of my own age say one to another, 'Where will the young men who are to carry on the business of the country, its political business, its commercial and industrial business, come from, when those who are now bearing the burden have laid it down?' Of course, such a time will come, and are you, young men, ready to take up the burden and the responsibility when it comes to you? Are you preparing yourselves with any seriousness for the day when the future of this great and historical country will be resting upon you? I do beseech you to measure and weigh the two foundations of national glory —faith and righteousness.

"I have heard of balls in London this last season which have cost £5000, the rental of a good estate squandered in a single night, to enable 1000 or 1500 people to be crushed into rooms not large enough to hold half the number, the guests sometimes unable to make their way up the staircase, or to speak to their host and hostess. The foolish gaudy moths will flutter their brief season in the full glare of all this fleeting brilliancy. They will at last approach too near the flame, their pretty wings will get singed, they will drop, disappear, be trampled on; no one will ask after them, or shed a tear for them, or make more than a passing comment on the moral of their lives. The pace is too fast to allow of stopping to inquire after those who 'fall out by the way.' Yet 'luxury,' forsooth, is good for trade! If trade means bankruptcy, both of tradesman and customer, perhaps it is. If a nation, collectively, is possessed of high aims, and strives to attain its ends by the use only of worthy means, it will not lose its public spirit, its generous temper, its devotion to the call of duty. If any one says there is no scope for high aims, or worthy ambitions, or noble enterprises in the England of to-day, I say that man's eye is blinded to the most evident phenomena of his age. I can discern on every hand great causes crying out for defenders, for sustainers, for champions—to raise the tone of honour among men and women; to make the atmosphere of society once more pure and wholesome; to revive the morality of trade; to weld together once more, in a well-understood and well-balanced community of interest, the severed and almost antagonistic relations of employers and employed; to enlarge the sphere of action of reciprocal sympathy; to direct the wayward impulses of benevolence into carefully-

2 A

discriminated channels; to lessen the amount of drunkenness, and crime, and ignorance, and pauperism in the land; to do more than 'stand between the living and the dead,' which was all that the priest of old could do, and to play the prophet's nobler part; and, inspired with a true spirit of God, to 'breathe upon these slain that they may live.' These seem to me to be the calls that God, by the very manifest course of His Providence, is making to the English people, and to these calls I bid you listen, you men of Leeds!"

It was, perhaps largely, the manliness of his utterances which drew the people's heart towards the Bishop. Yet not the manliness only, but the depth and thoughtfulness also. For Bishop Fraser was not one of those speakers who think it necessary in addressing working people to shun difficulties, whether moral, intellectual, or religious; and to plausibly skim the surface of things. He had too much respect for himself, and too much respect for his hearers, to play the mere rhetorician. He boldly confronted all manner of difficulties; and with the candour of true courage frankly acknowledged that there were many phenomena both in morals and religion which completely baffled him. He had no cut-and-dried scheme professing to account for everything. But where he thought it possible by searching and reflection to understand deep things, he encouraged the most absolute freedom of inquiry and thought. He always paid his audience the homage of supposing that they were willing, and able, both to inquire and think. The homage of intelligence paid to them partly explains the loyalty of allegiance felt for him. The Bishop shirked nothing. He put grit into his utterances. He sought to win the people to Christianity by the strong, as well as sweet, reasonableness of it. He was more of a reasoner than a rhetorician; his aim being not to carry his hearers away for the moment, by a gust of words, but to send them home filled with food for long and quiet thought.

An instance of the Bishop's method is afforded by one of the earliest addresses delivered by him to the employés of the Lancashire and Yorkshire Railway Company at Miles Platting. One of the large worksheds was cleared out for the service, and about 2000 working men and lads attended.

"The meeting," writes an eye-witness, "was a sight to see. The Bishop, who had robed himself in his episcopal robes in a corner of the shed on the verge of the crowd, stood upon a temporary platform facing an eager throng of listeners, the bulk of them on the floor, but the flanks and rear of the great crowd perched upon dismantled railway carriages waiting for repair, in the Cimmerian gloom of the further parts of the shed. The men were in their working clothes, nearly all being dressed in their uniform of cotton slop, which, though probably white as driven snow when each wearer commenced his week's labour that morning, were already in many instances splashed with oil blotches and blackened with dust. Five out of every six eager upturned faces were grimy with oil and sooty; but probably Bishop Fraser never preached to a more decorous congregation either in Manchester Cathedral or St. Paul's. He spoke for nearly half an hour, and his audience, although for the most part they were closely wedged together in their standing position, or were perched uncomfortably upon carriage roofs, not only showed no signs of flagging in their interest, but throughout maintained a riveted and unremitting attention. At times, and for minutes together, they were so still, and every breath was so hushed, that the reporter, with his eyes and fingers engaged with pencil and notebook, could scarcely help fancying himself the only auditor of a voice sounding through an empty hall. Just before his Lordship took his place upon the platform, a local evangelist, who takes a leading part in the ordinary Sunday services, addressed the men. 'Now, lads, all them as can sing, sing out, and let us have a good hearty sing'—an appeal which afterwards was responded to in the most satisfactory manner. The Bishop was loudly cheered on his arrival in the shed, and afterwards on mounting the platform. His Lordship then read out verse by verse the hymn, 'Come let us join our cheerful songs with angels round the throne,' which was sung with great enthusiasm; after which the Bishop read the Confession, the Lord's Prayer, and a few Collects from the Church service. It was noticeable that while, at first, the audience did not appear prepared to take their proper part in the responses, after an example had been set them from the platform, they endorsed each petition by a hearty 'Amen.'"

The Bishop's method of dealing with an audience such as this—men whose faces and clothes were grimy with oil and smoke—is noteworthy. He did not deliver an extempory and unprepared address.

"There are," he said, "certain advantages in an extempory address and certain disadvantages. But I noticed at the recent meeting at Liverpool of the British Association for the promotion of science that when Professor Huxley, and Professor Tyndall, and Professor Lubbock addressed a large meeting of working men, they thought it more respectful not to deliver their thoughts in the crude shape in which they came uppermost to them in their minds, but to reduce them into writing, into a more methodical and also into a more compendious form; and so, on Sunday night, after my day's work, before I went to bed, I spent a quiet hour in jotting down on paper thoughts which long have been on my mind, which I am glad to have an opportunity of uttering in your ears to-day, and which I wish to utter in the most simple and intelligible form."

After this exordium the Bishop proceeded to deliver his written address.

"Some people say the revelation of God to man is a thing utterly beyond our experience. I do not know really that it is. Have we never heard a voice, which seems something different from any earthly voice, speaking to us at times in words of warning or words of entreaty, or words of encouragement—a voice that the boy Samuel heard when he was laid down to sleep that night in the temple, which at last he learned to recognize as the voice of God? Is there anything absurd or inconceivable in the hypothesis of revelation? As the Apostle Paul wrote in his epistles, God revealed Himself to man in many of His highest attributes; for instance, in his eternal power and goodness in the beneficent laws and operations of nature. The ideas of God that we derive from seeing what we see of His handiwork in the laws governing the universe are what we call natural religion. This natural religion, when apart from revelation, has been dim and weak, and has never been able to retain God in any perfect or sufficient conception of His character in the knowledge, the reason, or the conscience of man. So revelation was needed, if for no other purpose, yet for this, that the very idea of God should not be obliterated from the mind of man. So, revelation being needed, we have it. We bask in the light of it. Although we often do not recognize its influence, it is to the influence of Christianity that we owe all the main springs of our modern civilization; and if Christianity were swept away, that modern civilization would, before long, be found to be following in its train. Some people, who delight to trace contradictions and inconsistencies—of whom I am not one—say that the God of the Old Testament is different to the God of the New. I cannot see the difference, and I do not think that any dispassionate student of these two portions of God's Word can discover the difference. The one great revealed attribute of Almighty God, both in the Old and New Testament, is love. The one thing, and the only thing, that stands outside the pale of God's love, is sin. Nor is it only that in the Gospel is provided an atonement for sin, but further grace is given to conquer sin. Will any of you tell me that you must be, for instance, the thrall of drunkenness or the slave of lust, that you cannot speak the truth, although you desire to speak it? You know it is not so. Go down upon your knees—I don't say take pledges, for these are somewhat perilous things—but only let a man go down on his knees, and with an earnest prayer pray to break away from that sin which he feels besets him; let him weary not in asking, but pray to-night, pray to-morrow night, the night after, and whilst he prays, seek to keep out of temptation, out of the reach of the enemy, and I say grace shall be given to him, and he shall rise triumphant in Christian strength, and drive away the evil one. It is because we do not set about it in the right way that sin conquers us and leads us in its train as slaves. One special word I have to say to you. Your duties, I know, are such that your religious observances, even when you are most anxious to attend to them, must to a certain extent be few and irregular. But pray remember that religious observances are not religion. There is a great mistake, which is too current among all Christian people, that going to church is religion. It may, or it may not, be religion. Sometimes it may be the most irreligious act which a man does in the week. Religious observances are not religion, but only helps to a man's religion. Religion, as I have said, is a perfect abiding sense of duty to God. The pointsman, the porter, the stoker, or the engine-driver, who does his duty to his employers and to the public, and who does his duty to his family, may have rare and infrequent opportunities of attending church or chapel, but if he carries along with him into all his work a sense of duty to a Higher than any earthly power—that man's sense of duty shall, I believe, make up in the sight of God for the infrequency of his attendance at public worship. I do not know a better definition of religion than that which was given by the old Hebrew prophet: 'What does the Lord require of thee, O man, but to do justice, to love mercy, and to walk humbly with thy God?' Do not let my words be so far misunderstood as that I should be supposed to say that religious observances are of no importance. I believe them to be of the utmost importance. But I know that even the best disposed cannot go to church so often as you would desire to go; and so whenever you engage in a religious observance, I wish to say this—make it a real act of religious worship, and not of form. The form of godliness without the power is the most delusive piece of self-righteousness that a man can lay to the flattering and deceiving of his soul. So I say to you, be honest, be pure, be temperate, be truthful, be gentle, be unselfish, be ready to bear one another's burdens, and so fulfil the law of Christ; and whether you can attend church or chapel seldom or often, you have a right to believe that you are trying to lead, according to your opportunities, religious and Christian lives. He is the Christian, not who professes these graces, not even who prays for them, but who prays for them and wins them and practises them. I do not mean who practise them in church; that is not the place for practising those graces. You can hardly be dishonest in church; you can hardly get drunk in a church. That is not the place for practising graces; the place to show religion is in your homes, in your families, in your social meetings and gatherings. Do not be afraid of religion, my friends. Some people tell you that a religious man must go about with a downcast and gloomy face. That is not true; it is a libel upon religion. Religion was meant to save us in the world, it is true, but it was made to make us cheerful; it was sent to sweeten our lives, not to sour them; to make them joyous, not gloomy; to fill our minds with gladness, not to make us downcast, disquieted, or sad. What we need—you as much as I, and I as much as you—is to pray to be delivered from ourselves—from our low, carnal natures, from our fleshly appetites, from brutal passions, from sensual lusts, or grovelling desires, from all that our merely animal nature has a gravitating tendency towards; and Christ, in the power of His grace as Deliverer, will grant our prayer. And the aim of all our motives should be to stand fast in that liberty from the bondage of sin wherewith Christ by the indwelling gift of His Spirit hath made us free."

In after years, when the Bishop's engagements had exceedingly multiplied, and his powers of ready speaking had grown and ripened by much practice, he did not usually read his addresses to working people. But even to the end the character of his addresses remained unchanged. There was nothing of the merely plausible and superficial about them. He honoured the working classes by taking it for granted that they were intelligent, and by talking not only earnestly, but reasonably and intellectually, to them.

The foundation of his reasoning was generally laid upon the lines of Bishop Butler's classic work *The Analogy of Religion*, a book which, it is said, Mr. Gladstone reads once every year, and which Bishop Fraser constantly recommended to the attention of all classes of thoughtful men; from the clergy whom he ordained, to the artizans who frequently corresponded with him. In a letter written to an artizan in 1870 the Bishop says:

"You profess to be staggered by the difficulties presented to the reason in the scheme of revealed religion. If you will study Bishop Butler's *Analogy of Religion*, you will find that precisely the same difficulties present themselves in the constitution and course of nature, and though it is true that Bishop Butler's argument is addressed to deists—that is, to those who believe in a Divine Creator and Governor of the World—yet I think those who deny these will meet, in the visible phenomena of the universe, difficulties that are even more inexplicable upon the hypothesis of Atheism than they are upon the hypothesis of Christianity. In fact, there is no novelty in the arguments of modern secularists. They have been advanced, and to my mind satisfactorily answered, a hundred times in the course of the history of human thought; and the religion which has survived the attacks of Hume, Voltaire, and Tom Paine, will, I venture to say, outlive the attacks of Mr. Austin Holyoake, Mr. Charles Watts, and Mr. Bradlaugh. You must not put it down to timidity or misgivings about my principles that I am obliged to decline the challenge you have thrown down before me to meet one of your practised speakers in public debate upon the evidences or benefits of Christianity to the Church. I cannot conceive a subject more unsuited to public debate before a miscellaneous, and probably, in such subjects, even an untrained audience. Every one knows how much easier it is to put objections than to answer them, and to pull down than to build up. Besides, to press the arguments for and against Christianity into any limit of time, during which a public debate could fairly last, would try the patience of listeners, and would be simply to attempt the impossible. The evidence of Christianity is manifold and cumulative. Not only has each branch to be examined, but the might and value of the whole, when massed together, has to be ascertained. Besides, the work has been done. By Liebnitz, by Pascal, by Sir I. Newton, by Bishop Butler, by Paley, and by Davison, the evidences of Christianity have been examined, accepted, and vindicated. I have looked into the matter as profoundly as my faculties have permitted me for myself. I do not say that all difficulties are cleared away. The revelation in which I believe does not lead me to expect that they would be. But I recognize in Christianity, as a Revelation, the most probable and most complete interpretation of the moral phenomena that I see, and, as a Religion, the most potent remedy for the evils to which (even within the horizon of this present world) humanity is exposed. You first caricature and distort the features of Christianity, and then attempt to hold up the caricature you have produced to the ridicule and contempt of mankind. For instance, you say that disinterestedness is impossible under the Christian scheme, and in the face of such teaching as 'Do good, hoping for nothing again;' in face, too, of the central fact of Christianity, which I take to be the purest exhibition of disinterestedness that the human mind can ever conceive. In one sense men are often better than their principles; in another sense they are immeasurably worse. You take the low standard of morality by which many professing Christians are content to live, and convert that into an argument against Christianity. I respectfully demur to the cogency of such reasoning. I refer you, for an answer, to the Bishop of Peterborough's sermon preached before the British Association for the Advancement of Science at the Norwich Congress, and assert that the true character of Christianity is to be sought in the highest types of humanity, which it must be acknowledged to have produced, and not in the lower and average forms which it has nominally reached, but has failed to mould."

Lancashire people are not easy to win. They are blunt in the expression of their thoughts, quick to resent any assumption of superiority, formidable in their criticisms. But when once their confidence has been won, they will bear any amount of plain speaking with a trustful patience bordering upon enthusiasm. Bishop Fraser having won their confidence, they listened to him as he poured forth his stream of home-truths, not only without resentment, but with an affectionate inclination to yield their own will to his. The duty of thrift, and the unrighteousness of extravagance, were among the Bishop's most frequent topics of plain-speaking admonition. At a meeting of the depositors of the Savings' Bank in connection with the South Eastern Railway on July 13, 1881, he said:

"There is a character in an old Roman play who says, 'I am a man. Nothing human is strange to me.' And though I am a bishop I do confess to feeling an interest in human things, and in particular in human things which affect the larger classes of humanity—which interest the working classes of this country among whom I live, and move, and have my being. It was, I assure you, with no feeling of condescension whatever, but with a simple feeling of interest in what you are doing, that I came here to-day.

"I was travelling some years ago, and a companion said to me, 'Now, if you will excuse me, I should like to look over some papers I have here.' He began to take them out, and I saw they were prospectuses of several companies, financing concerns, stock and share lists, current prices, relating principally to our great provincial towns. I said, 'I suppose you are interested in a good many concerns?' 'Yes,' he said, 'I am; it is my line of business. I like finance.' 'Now,' I said to him, 'I am differently situated. I *don't* like finance; I like to save; and, when I save, I have always been content if I can get 4 per cent. for my savings. I have never changed a single investment that I once made.' 'Well, sir,' he said, 'you are quite right. I can only tell you that if I had got 4 per cent. for what I have financed away, I should be richer than I am.'

* * * * * *

"I am not going to repeat Franklin's motto, 'You cannot make an empty sack stand upright,' nor Burns' lines about the glorious privilege of being independent, because you will know these better, perhaps, than I do, and have had them quoted to you once or twice before; but I will say one thing in regard to this principle of independence, and Sir Edward Watkin, who is a Lancashire man, though he lives in Cheshire at the present moment, will bear me out in what I say. I have heard people remark that one of the worst things that happened for Lancashire was the cotton famine of 1861 and 1865; it rather changed, and not for the better, the character of a large section of the population. Up to that time independence had been a very great characteristic of Lancashire workpeople, but when that terrible and critical period arrived, this thing happened:—The drunken and thriftless man, who had never accumulated or saved anything, immediately fell upon the rates and got help from the relief funds, and made a pretty good thing of it from the beginning, whereas the steady, meritorious man, who had been saving and was proud of his house (there is a goodly expression in Lancashire: 'A house-proud woman,' *i.e.* a woman who likes to see her children well dressed, her furniture clean, and plenty of it) would not seek help in this way, but parted with one article after another, first a table, then a chair, till at last he came so low he was obliged to get relief; and then this thought, which I don't think was sound—though it is hard to reason with a starving man—came into his mind: 'I have been saving, and now I have come down quite as low as those who did not save; am I better off than this thriftless man?' I think there is no nobler class of men than a great section of the working classes of Lancashire, but I am told there has been a perceptibly deteriorating influence brought about by the famine upon this class. Well, now, I should argue with the man in this way. I should quite admit that it is very hard upon him, but I think, as long as a man has anything which he can call his own, he has no right to come upon his neighbour for maintenance. I should say to him, 'Those twenty years you have been living in comfort have been spent by your drunken neighbour in discomfort; you have had a happier time of it than he. You would be the man I should be the most ready to assist, if assistance were needed; I should be quite ready to put my hand in my pocket for you if necessary; therefore do not regret you learnt how to save when you had something to save.' Still I can quite sympathize with a man who has been trying to save, and suddenly finds some great disaster brought about by those wretched influences which occasionally disorganize everything in a country. I can quite sympathize with him if he resolves never to put by a penny any more, though it would not be wise. The Archbishop of Canterbury gave very good advice last year when he told the story of the two Scotch lads who were advised by their guardian to save something out of their income, whether it were large or small. I can with very great safety preach that doctrine, because I have always practised it, and never would spend all my income. I determined always to have a margin on the right side, and I can only say it has brought unspeakable comfort to me. No man is secure at any time in this troublesome world. My expenditure has always been within the limits of my income. For twenty-three years of my life I was the rector of two rural parishes, one in Wiltshire, the other in Berkshire. The earnings of the labourers ranged from 8s. up to about 10s., or at the outside 11s. per week. Why now, in London, a lad of fifteen earns much more than a Wiltshire labourer did at that time. In both these parishes I found the people were both able and willing to save. I continued in them a clothing club which had been started, to which the people contributed. The little sums of money saved were very acceptable when they wanted clothes, furniture, &c., and I gave them a premium at the end of the year of 5s. I found these people were able to pay 1s. or 2s. per month with a view of getting my premium at Christmas time, thus showing that the old adage is always true that 'where there's a will there's a way.' The principle of living strictly within your income is the only honest principle whether for rich or poor. I am afraid just now, from all I hear, that the difficulties of getting tradesmen's accounts paid are quite as many among the rich people as the poor; the rich are living beyond their income quite as much as the poor."

The Bishop's power of adapting himself, and his words, to his various audiences is scarcely less remarkable than his plain-spokenness. At Owens College, he sought to Christianize scholarship. Among the artizans, he sought to Christianize the laws and lessons of political economy. Among the destitute and abandoned, he sought to show that the Christian faith means sympathy—the sympathy of God expressed in the affections of man. On one occasion, after addressing a meeting of fallen women (with each of whom he shook hands after delivering his address), he wrote: "These poor wanderers are so much more interesting to me than the complacent Pharisees of all religious schools, who go through the world self-righteously thanking God that they are not as other men." Yes, sympathy was the Bishop's strength! Every one—from polished scholar to dirty gutter-boy—felt at home with him; and would accost him, with friendly greeting, on the road. When he went to address a mothers' meeting, the women of the place, with babies in their arms and shawls on their heads, would crowd to listen. Once, as the Bishop was coming out of church, having officiated at a wedding, a poor woman at the door, said, " I hope you tied 'em fast, Bishop." "Yes, I think I did, mother!" was the reply. As he was leaving the Free Trade Hall, Manchester, after a great temperance meeting, in company with Archdeacon Farrar, a little street-arab pressed up to the Bishop, and stretching out his tiny, unwashed hand, which the Bishop shook most heartily, exclaimed, " Good night, Bishop! good night, Bishop!" Among the working classes it was quite a common thing for fathers to talk to their children about " our Bishop." His name thus became a household word with a result which, occasionally, was amusing. At a Government examination of St. Barnabas' Schools, Oldham Road, the question was asked, "Why the Frazer River was so called?" Many hands were held up, and one fine little fellow answered, " After James Fraser, Lord Bishop of Manchester." ! !

Another characteristic story is related by the Rev. Thomas Betton, Vicar of St. Barnabas, Oldham Road:

"Mr. Betton had a short service about 10.30 P.M. with the 'night-soil men.' He overheard the men say, 'the Bishop won't come to us.' He went to the Bishop and said, 'I really feel ashamed to mention my object in coming, but I have been holding some short services with the night-soil men. It is a horrid hole, and the smell from the 'disinfectants' is by no means pleasant; but the men would like your Lordship to come to them, only the surroundings are such that I am ashamed to ask your Lordship.' The Bishop replied, 'Most willingly will I come. Poor fellows! they are men and fellow human beings, and if you go, why can't I come? When would you like me to come?' I mentioned the evening, when the Bishop said, 'I have four meetings on that day, but you come to me on the platform of London Road Station about 10.15, and I will go with you.' I told the poor fellows, who were something more than delighted. The Bishop was much fatigued. But at once he won their hearts. He said, 'My good men, I am glad to come among you; but I see you have been smartening up, I wish you had not, I would rather have come and been with you just as you usually are; but never mind, a little whitewash makes the place pleasanter for you.'"

The kind of plain, homely, tender, earnest address, which the Bishop was wont to deliver upon these occasions may be gathered from the following extracts from an address delivered at St. Paul's Mission School, Blackhorse Street, Bolton, July 1, 1870:

"I am sure there is no real peace or comfort in drink to the man who is given up to it. His house is not as happy, his family is not as happy, his wife is not as happy, as he would like to make them and her. Before I came up here, I lived in a country parish, among farm labourers, and when I went into their cottages, I could tell in a minute a home where the husband (and sometimes the wife) drank, and the home where there was sobriety and temperance; and if I were to attempt to measure the difference in the happiness of those two homes, I don't know by what expression I could describe that difference. A man does not need to live in a palace, or to eat off gold and silver plate, or to be clothed in purple and fine linen, to find out what happiness is. Happiness is a very simple thing, and, by the blessing of God, it is put as much within the reach of the poorest as within the reach of the richest. If a person only carries about with him a contented mind, and tries to do his duty in that station of life in which it has pleased God to place him; if he loves his wife, and she loves her husband, and both love their children and do the best for them; if they send their children to school, and know that they are getting on there, and they hear their little prattling tongues, telling how they have spent the day—I say, in that home you have the elements of happiness: they all centre round a man's own fireside. Happiness is not to be found in the spirit-shop or in the tavern—I don't think so, at least; and that struck me as I came from church last Sunday evening. I saw window after window brilliantly lighted with gas, and crowds standing around the doors. I knew what they were there for; I knew what those windows meant. I knew that within there was the devil of drink luring those infatuated men and women along that broad road which seems so pleasant, but which is so miserable, and which ends at last in the destruction both of body and soul. You know we are told there was a poor woman in our Lord's time out of whom there were cast seven devils—seven unclean spirits—who had taken possession of her. And again, in one of His parables, our Lord says that when an unclean spirit is driven out of a man's soul he tries to come back, and if he gets into the soul again, he brings with him seven other spirits more wicked than himself, and they enter in, and make the last state of that man worse than the first. Have you not known a man or woman who had two or three or even seven evil spirits? There is the devil of drink, there is the devil of foul language, there is the devil of lust, there is the devil of passion, there is the devil of selfishness; and sometimes we find that they all dwell in one human soul. Do you believe that that man's soul which is possessed by so many devils is a happy soul? Do you mean to tell me that the house where he lives is a happy home, that it is a Christian home, that it is a home that brings with it any blessings, or that it is associated with any happiness? You can't tell me it is so. And why should a man's home in England be of that kind? Why should we not all be living in happy homes? Why should we not all know what it is to say a kind word to our neighbour? Why should we not all know what it is to be at peace with God? Christ, Who came bringing—yes, those are the words—tidings of salvation and of mercy to us, told us that when He was gone, He would send Some One in His place, Whom He called the Holy Ghost the Comforter, Who should dwell in the hearts of Christian people, and give them the strength they need to gain the victory in the battle that every one has to fight against the world, the flesh, and the devil. I dare say some of you sometimes—if you have any thought about you—think in this way: 'Ah, I have never had the chance that other people have had. I was never looked after by father and mother when I was young, but I have been surrounded with all sorts of bad influences. I have not had a chance.' Well, it is true that some of us have not got the chance that others have, and I thank God that I have had so very good a chance of being brought up by a mother who looked after me; and I thank God, too, that His Providence has placed me under circumstances where temptation did not often come to me in any very terrible and powerful form, and I feel any amount of sympathy with those less happily circumstanced, who have not had God-fearing parents, whose homes have been homes of anything but Christian peace, life, and contentment, into whose ears there have been dinned oaths and blasphemies, and who have been surrounded by bad companions that have lured them into ways that, if left to themselves, they might not have taken. But still, when I have made all that allowance, my friends, I don't think that you ought to be the bond-slaves of the devil. Certainly, the Gospel does not tell you that you should. It is either the obstinacy, the hardness, or the despair of your own hearts, that tells you that. I don't know what besetting sin any of you may have—probably, you have all got one that besets you more strongly than another—but you could, every one of you, break away from it, if you only tried; and when I say, if you only tried, I mean that you must try in the strength of God. If you would only to-night, before you go to bed, go down upon your knees by the bedside—if you have a bedside to go down to—and open your hearts to God; if you would only ask Him to show you how you are living, to give you the help of His Spirit so that you might make your life better than it has been, oh! what a blessed thing it would be. But you must remember that it is no use praying only. Christ said, 'Watch and pray, lest ye enter into temptation.' You must not only go forth in the strength of prayer, but you must watch also. There is a companion with whom you have associated, and he has perhaps been a dangerous companion to you, and has led you on into ways in which it has not been good for you to go. Try little by little and break that intimacy off. Or there is the spirit-shop, into which you may have been lured night after night; try and pass by without going into it. If you can do it the first time, it will be easier for you to do the second and the third time. Don't expect to become a perfect Christian all at once. It is true that God does sometimes work miracles of conversion, but that is not common. We seldom see persons changed all at once from great sinners into great saints. The change is commonly gradual. But there will be a change—and you will find it to be a perceptible change—if you set to work in a honest, straightforward way; and be determined, and say to yourself, 'I won't be led any longer by devils that have only brought me on to ruin. My eyes are opened, and I will break away before it is too late. I will ask God to redeem me from iniquity, to send His Spirit into my soul, and to help me to engage in His service. And in the strength of that help, I believe I can and shall overcome the evil one.' Make the trial, my friends. Some of you perhaps will. And don't despair because you may find it difficult. Why, difficulties are sometimes what encourage us to make all the greater efforts. We don't care about doing a thing which is as easy as 'pat.' It makes the thing all the more pleasant and exciting—all the more worthy the part of men to do—to overcome difficulty. I ask you simply—Have I said anything to you that sounds unreal, or fanatical, or what the world calls 'humbug'—something in which there is no truth? If I have, don't attach that much of value to it (snapping his fingers). But if what I have said seems to be real—if you say to yourselves, 'There is some truth in what the Bishop says; I can see it partly '—why should you not try to give expression to that truth in your own lives? I fancy there are many before me who feel that the life they have led hitherto has not been altogether the life they should lead—that they have a desire after things better, things spiritual. Then why not try and do better, as well as wish? Good things do not come by wishing, do they? but they come by striving and trying after. If a man wishes to make a fortune, it won't come by wishing. He must set to work, and if he is a clever man, with a good head upon his shoulders, and if God blesses his labours, he will make a fortune. I have heard plenty of stories since I have been in Lancashire of men who have made large fortunes, but they have striven and struggled for them; they have not been easily cast down, but they have had patience —and that is what the Bible tells us: we must have faith and patience, and we must let patience have her perfect work. If you do that, in perhaps two or three years hence, you will wonder at yourselves to find what changed men and women you have become; how you that were weak have become strong; how you that were far from God, have been brought near; how you that never knew what it was to kneel down, have become men and women, earnest in prayer, and have found out the blessing, and the strength, and the comfort, and the power that lie in prayer. Well, my friends, I could stay here, talking for an hour longer, for there are thousands of things I should like to say on this opportunity, yet I cannot find time; but I do most humbly hope and pray that this endeavour of your faithful minister to gather around him here those who cannot perhaps be induced to go to church, as it is called, may be blessed at least with some fruits. I hope you will give him credit in what he does for sincerity, and for a simple desire to minister to the good of your souls. You can't suppose that he comes here, and that those that come with him, come here for any selfish purpose of their own, can you? They have nothing to gain themselves, but they simply come here to labour for your advantage. Your minister believes and hopes that he can do some little good to some of you; and I venture to say he feels as great an interest in your spiritual welfare as he does in the spiritual welfare of the wealthiest and most respectable member of his respectable congregation. I venture to say even more. I venture to think that if by his ministrations here one soul only could be brought nearer to Christ, if one soul only could be taught to see the error of its ways, and come to the Cross of Christ for strength and pardon, he would feel that all his labour would have been abundantly repaid, and there would be that joy in Heaven of which the Lord Jesus Christ speaks—that joy which thrills through the souls of the angels when they see one sinner turned from the evil of his ways, a joy greater than that which they feel when they see some ninety-and-nine respectable persons gather together who perhaps are needing in a much smaller degree to be brought to repentance—not that we all don't want to be brought to repentance, to be brought nearer and yet liker to Christ. Ay, bishops, and clergymen, and respectable people need quite as much to have the Gospel of Christ preached to them, and to be brought home to their souls, and to make them humble, and child-like, and kindly, and sympathizing, as any of you. We are all fallen sinners, as far as that goes; we all have but one hope; we all cling but to one Cross

—we with many advantages, you perhaps under many disadvantages. But I dare promise you this, because I promise it to you on the strength of Him Who can't lie—I promise you that if you will only strive to do your part, God will do His part. I will promise you that you are as dear to Him as any sons for whom Christ died; and I will promise you that you are all among those whom Christ came to redeem from iniquity, and to 'purify unto Himself a peculiar people, zealous of good works.' And now, my friends, I will only remind you that if you only trust in the promises which Jesus Christ has made, you will find you will have far more happiness in this world, far more happiness on your death-bed, and far more happiness in that Day of which the apostle speaks, and for which he tells us to look forward—the Day of the glorious appearing of the great God and our Saviour Jesus Christ."

Not only at public gatherings, but in private correspondence also, the Bishop sought to understand, and place himself in sympathetic communication with, the working classes.

One of his most frequent correspondents was Mr. Samuel Chapman, an intelligent cobbler, who occasionally communicated his thoughts to the *Manchester Examiner and Times* in letters signed, "An Ancoats Rough." To him the Bishop often wrote, prompted both by personal regard and by the feeling that Mr. Chapman was typical of a class which he earnestly desired to fully understand.

To Mr. Samuel Chapman.

October 14, 1870.

Sir,—I have been interested in the perusal of your letter of the 8th inst., which followed me to this place, where I am taking a short week's holiday. I think it is a great pity that the Church, either in the person of its ministers, or in the use of its buildings, should be used for political—*i.e.*, partizan—purposes, and I have not hesitated to say so in public, and in saying so have exposed myself to some obloquy, or at least to some sharp criticism. But I cannot interfere authoritatively in such matters, and must leave them to the good judgment and right feeling of those immediately concerned. The "system framers" and "doctrinaires," to whom I referred on the occasion which you mention, were simply the theorists, who, without any practical acquaintance with the subject, and ignoring all claims that existing institutions have established, think to dispose of all difficulties by a wave of the hand, or a stroke of the pen. At the time of the French Revolution of 1793, there was a certain Abbé Sieyès, who undertook to frame any number of Constitutions on the shortest possible notice, none of which, as may well be supposed, had much practicability in them. He is a type of the "system framers" I had in my mind. That *thought* should precede *action* is a principle that I never meant to deny. But even the Gospel, to which you refer, does not stand out on the page of the New Testament as a cut-and-dried system. It would never have adapted itself, as it has done, to the wants of human nature, if it had.—Yours faithfully,

J. MANCHESTER.

To the Same.

MANCHESTER, *August* 19, 1871.

SIR,—I read with much interest your letter of the 9th inst. Such letters help me to understand better than I otherwise should what the working men of Lancashire are thinking about, and therefore, by informing me, assist me in doing my work. I don't wonder that you, and men who think and observe, are staggered by the inconsistencies and hypocrisies of many so-called Christians; and much that is preached as Christianity is little better than a parody on the simple teaching of St. Paul or of Jesus of Nazareth. But we must not judge of principles or systems by their imperfect embodiment in human beings who profess to hold them, or have been brought up under them. We must try to form an estimate of them as they are in themselves. I think you will find that *all* moralities, political and social as well as religious, are included in Christ's teaching, and must be touched by the power of His Spirit to make them moralities at all. Doing what is right for conscience' sake—

> "Not with the hope of gaining heaven
> Nor of escaping hell"

(as a good old hymn has it), is the principle of Christianity.

With regard to French Communism, on which you ask my opinion, I could say much in its defence, if I believed those men who advocated it *were honest*, and were actuated by any other than selfish and sordid motives. Nobody could justify their excesses; but some of them, perhaps, dreamt noble, though wild and extravagant, dreams. One of the greatest social problems of the day is how to throw more bridges over the great and widening chasm that separates the very rich from the very poor. Happily for myself, I have never coveted money, and have always been content with what I had. I have more anxiety now that my income is ten times what it used to be, than ever I had; how to spend it, so as to do good and not harm.—Believe me, with very real sympathy, yours very truly,

J. MANCHESTER.

To the Same.

MANCHESTER, *February* 9, 1872.

SIR,—I generally read your letters with interest, and seldom without profit, even though our views probably differ widely on many points, and your mind seems proner to detect the defects and abuses of our social and ecclesiastical systems than to appreciate their merits and advantages. But you write frankly, and not unkindly; and as I want to know what people are thinking about, and how others look at phenomena which I, perhaps, may regard under the influence of an illusion, I read your letters, as I have said, with interest.

You know that I dislike any alliance between religion and political partizanship. Politics, in the higher sense of the word, are a noble department of human activity, and in this sense not only may be, but ought to be, governed by religious principles; but mere partizanship, the wretched questions which gender so much strife and bitterness, without having any tendency to increase the sum of human happiness or human virtue, is a very different thing. I am no politician beyond wishing to see good government established, equal laws prevailing, and intelligence universally diffused. Towards ends like these, every religious man not only may, but should, labour.

To the Same.

MANCHESTER, *February* 27, 1872.

DEAR SIR,—I thank you for your letter of the 25th, and for coming to my rescue against the Hulme indignationists (in a letter to the Manchester press). They say that *some* dirt, when thrown, always sticks; but I should think (in the opinion of the sensible part of the world) the amount of dirt thrown by these gentlemen which sticks is very small indeed. At any rate, I never feel in the least moved to reply to their attacks. I am not going to make myself a partizan, nor yet a persecutor, at their bidding; and if my general character will not sustain me, I must take my chance with other people who are misrepresented. At the same time, I have no sympathy with the especial ecclesiastical practices that are alleged to be in use at Hulme, though I will not help to throw a hard-working (even if mistaken) clergyman into the power of a pack of fanatical Orangemen, whose political creed seems to be their religion. I am fairly puzzled to know how to act for the best in your parish. I have no doubt there are faults on both sides, and all I wish to put an end to is, the bitterness and mutual recrimination that now prevails.

These broils in parishes, the offspring partly of folly, partly of obstinacy, fill me with anxiety and distress, and make me wish again and again that I had never left my quiet little village in Berkshire, where such anxieties were utterly unknown to me. I do not care for popularity (though at the same time I would not needlessly court blame); I shall simply try to go as straight to the point as I can, and leave my opinions and my conduct to be judged by fair-minded men.

I have not time for long letters, but I remain, yours very faithfully,

J. MANCHESTER.

To the Same.

MANCHESTER, *July* 19, 1872.

DEAR SIR,—I thank you for your letter. I have been out of the way of seeing much of the "adverse criticism of my words and actions" to which you refer. Judging, however, from what I *have* seen, I think my reputation may manage to survive it. With regard to *Punch*, I must say that the editor, in my judgment, deserves credit for the way in which he holds the looking-glass of truth up to the eyes of the world without reflecting much of its impurity. That he should be altogether immaculate is, perhaps, not to be expected; but he certainly (so far as I have seen) very rarely offends. It is very strange that people persist in misunderstanding one, when one says that the Church, as a Church, ought not to be made a political organization, or treated as the appanage of a political party, and that a clergyman is sadly out of his place as a political agitator. This is a very different thing from wishing to deny to any man, lay or cleric, the right of expressing his opinions on political subjects, or giving effect to those opinions by his vote. You must not suppose that the state of things in Hulme causes me no anxiety. But where parties are so strongly opposed, and the statements of one side are directly contradicted by the other, it is almost impossible for bishop, chancellor, or any one else, to interfere with any good results.—Yours faithfully,

J. MANCHESTER.

To the Same.

MANCHESTER, *November* 27, 1872.

SIR,—I thank you for your letter. I did not speak unadvisedly upon the points to which it relates, and I am glad (in one sense) to find my statements confirmed by your experience. That Sunday Schools are in a thoroughly unsatisfactory condition, in spite of their flourishing external appearance, I am (with great sorrow) convinced is the case; but as for calling them a "failure," that was the newspaper's heading to my speech, and no epithet of mine. I simply said that there had got mixed up with them many unhealthy mischievous influences (which I specified), which the teachers I saw before me, if true to their principle of doing their work as far as possible for God's glory, ought to try to cast out of their schools with all speed.

When you talk of "doubting Christian morality," pray let me draw your attention to there being a difference between *Christian Morality* and the *Morality of Christians*. You can hardly doubt, I should think, the morality of the Sermon on the Mount, or of the Epistle to the Ephesians, or of the Epistle of St. James. That *Christians* fall lamentably short of the standard of their own profession is what we must all admit with shame; but that our practice is inferior to our theory, or that there is much hypocrisy in the world (the thing, I suppose, that God hates more than anything else) is no reason for doubting Christian morality. The morality itself is one thing, the way in which it is practised is another.—Yours faithfully,

J. MANCHESTER.

To the Same.

MANCHESTER, *August* 25, 1873.

DEAR SIR,—I am afraid that most of my friends will be out of London at the time of your visit. But my brother, Colonel Alexander Fraser, may be there; and if he should be, and you will call and ask for him at the East India United Service Club, St. James's Square, he will do anything in his power to help you to get a sight of objects of interest. Happily, the things best worth seeing in London are open to the public without introduction. I should recommend you by all means, if you have time, to see Hampton Court and the gardens at Kew, and also the Crystal Palace at Sydenham, from the gallery of which (on a fine day) you get one of the most glorious views in the world. You will not find any Romanism in Bishop Butler, who was Bishop successively of Bristol and Durham in our own Church. But the argument of his great book is the common property of all Christians, and Professor Huxley has admitted its force to me. In Professor Tyndall's celebrated Belfast address there was, you may remember, an imaginary dialogue between a disciple of Bishop Butler and a disciple of Lucretius, which implicitly admitted the great force of Butler's argument.—Yours very truly,

J. MANCHESTER.

P.S.—If Colonel Fraser should not be at the Club when you call, you had better ask the porter whether he is in town, and when he is most likely to be found at the Club; and then (if it suits your arrangements) call again. I fancy the most likely time to find him would be about 10 A.M. He is at present staying with me, and I gave him your letter to read; and so he will know who you are when you call.

J. M.

To the Same.

MANCHESTER, *December* 7, 1872.

DEAR SIR,—As I have told you already, I have no power to prevent the application of schoolrooms to the purposes of which you disapprove (and to which I, too, regret to see them applied) by any exercise of authority as Bishop. But there is nothing I deprecate so much as the connection of the Church, as a National Institution, with any political party or political organization. I have recently refused to preach to some Orange Lodges solely on that ground, and you may depend upon it that my influence, such as it is, will always be exerted in that direction. And in the absence of authority, influence is the only power that I possess. I would remark, however, that parish schools, erected by voluntary efforts of Churchmen, are not "national" in quite the same sense as the Church, as an Institution, is; and I believe (and regret) that Nonconformist chapels and schools are freely used for political purposes. But there is no reason why Churchmen should follow a bad example.—Yours faithfully,

J. MANCHESTER.

To the Same.

MANCHESTER, *March* 20, 1873.

SIR,—I thank you for your letter, as for some former ones. In spite of an occasional bitterness to which you give way, and though we do not take the same views of all things and persons, I always read what you write with attention and interest.

You may depend upon it, that whatever influence I possess, shall be exercised in the direction which you indicate in your present letter, with the general purport of which I entirely agree. I wish to see the Church and the clergy divested of all partizan bias, and simply devoted to their proper office of bringing the Gospel home in all its simplicity and power, to the consciences and understandings of the people.—I remain, yours very affectionately,

J. MANCHESTER.

To the Same.

MANCHESTER, *August* 17, 1875.

SIR,—I was pleased to see your handwriting again. Your letters generally give me something to think about; and you are more considerate than some of my correspondents, who seem to think I have nothing to do but to "read, mark, and inwardly digest" what they are pleased to indite for my information. I suppose you refer to some report of words which fell from me at Darwen last Saturday. I have nothing to say against politics, as an old Greek understood the word, as the science of the relations and duties of man *as a citizen.* In that sense there can hardly be a higher or a nobler subject for human thought, and there would be no conflict between it and rational Christianity. But I was speaking of 'politics,' as they are commonly understood perhaps in New Cross Ward, and are exhibited in our municipal and parliamentary contests; and I need not tell *you* that a mixture of that kind of politics and religion is an unsavoury compound.

You talk of "bribery" and "intimidation" in the sense that Christianity appeals to our hopes and fears. It appeals to us, of course, as *men*; and, as all actions are followed by consequences, and our motives are largely influenced by our foresight of those consequences, I don't see how Christianity could address itself to us on other terms.

I wish you could read Bishop Butler's 'Analogy of Religion to the Course of Nature,' which I do not doubt is on the shelves of the Free Library in Every Street. You are quite competent to understand the argument, though it is profound and subtle, and I think the book would remove some of your objections and clear up some of your difficulties. —Yours faithfully,

J. MANCHESTER.

To the Same.

MANCHESTER, *May* 15, 1876.

DEAR SIR,—I was glad to hear from you again; and glad, also, to learn that you have an employment of a portion of your time, which, I should think, must be very congenial to you, and for which you are very well adapted.

I have merely recognized the fact that we are living in an age when the forces of democracy are præpotent, but I am not alarmed at them. They want guiding, doubtless; but the people are not unreasonable. I would, at any time, rather live under a democracy than under an oligarchy. One cannot but have *some* apprehensions for the future; but my hopes largely predominate over my fears.

If you send me anything to read again, pray don't think it necessary to prepay the return postage.—Yours very truly,

J. MANCHESTER.

To MR. JOHN POLLITT, *St. Mary's Road, Newton Heath.*

"I am sadly afraid that one of the elements that is contributing to diminish the influence of religion in the world just now is the extravagance and fanaticism of certain miscalled religious enterprises. An intelligent man, the editor of the *Northern Echo*, has taken me to task for saying, that I do not believe that the 'Strongholds of Satan' are going to be taken by storm by the Salvation Army. If the gospel of Christ cannot be made sober and rational, farewell to it as a wholesome influence on the soul of man. I am supremely indifferent to criticism, though I am not above learning from it anything it has to teach, even though it be severe. But here is a specimen, cut out of the *City Jackdaw's* 'caws' for this week, which, I confess, irritates me a little. 'On Sunday morning the Bishop of Manchester preached in the Eccles parish church on behalf of the Curates' Fund. There was a large congregation, more, we suspect, to see the Bishop, than from any idea of any spiritual benefit being reaped from his discourse.' Well, the sermon—whether weak or strong, eloquent or stupid, matters not—was on some elementary principles of *righteousness* which seem to be in danger of being forgotten by us, as a nation, as a trading community, as individuals. I wonder what the writer of the above caustic sentence considers to be 'spiritual benefit.'"

To MR. JEREMIAH CHADWICK.

MANCHESTER, *December* 9, 1882.

MY DEAR JEREMIAH CHADWICK,—I must write you a line to say how truly we—I and my dear wife—sympathize with you on the occasion of the death of your dear wife.

My wife went to see her in the infirmary less than a week before she died; and she seemed so cheerful that the news of her death came upon us quite with a shock.

I hope you will be able to make a home with some member of your family; where, I should think, you would be much more comfortable than you could expect to be if you lived alone.

We often think and speak of you, Jeremiah, and you have our sincere prayers that these latter days, which God still permits you to spend on earth, may be spent in calm and quiet peace and happiness. Such seems to be the most blessed close of a life of active service such as yours has been. Your wife is but gone before; and Christ has robbed the grave of its victory.

With my wife's kind remembrances, I am, dear Jeremiah, yours very sincerely,

J. MANCHESTER.

It was natural that the working classes, whose confidence the Bishop had thus so completely won, and whose hearts burned with affectionate trust in him, should desire occasionally to give vent to their enthusiasm in the presentation of some token of hearty esteem and goodwill. Once the employés at Ashbury's Works set on foot a penny subscription, and gave him a beautiful Bible. In acknowledging the gift the Bishop made the characteristic observation:—" Not only am I naturally pleased with the gift, but an additional pleasure is derived from the knowledge that *my aged mother* will be delighted that her son's first public testimonial in Manchester should have come from working men." Again, when the employés of the Manchester, Sheffield, and Lincolnshire Railway Company at Gorton Tank presented the Bishop with a large handsome Bible, and small Church Service, and Mrs. Fraser with a gold pencil case, as "a small token of their esteem and appreciation of his kind services," the Bishop said:

"Although I feel extremely grateful for this kindness to myself, and my dear wife, we both feel a little delicacy and embarrassment in receiving it, because it is so out of proportion to anything we have been able to give to you who have presented it. I would a hundred times rather preach to a congregation such as I see before me, than to the most fashionable congregation of the most fashionable church. The Bible I will preserve and cherish, with one given me some years ago by the workpeople at Ashbury's; while the Church Service I will carry about with me in going through my diocese. I do not know that any Bishop in the Church of England has more to boast of than I have in the possession of these three handsome presents."

Referring to these gifts in an Address delivered at the Diocesan Conference in the autumn of 1883, the Bishop said:

"I must say that I value nothing that I possess more than the Bible and Church Service presented to me by those simple working men. We have no reason to think that the working men are inaccessible to loving, sympathizing, Christian addresses delivered to them in a reasonable tone."

It is small wonder that Bishop Fraser, after his experience of the willingness of the people to offer him their cordial friendship; the earnest manner in which they listened to his plain, manly enunciation of fundamental Christian principles set forth, not in abstruse theological phraseology, but in the homely words of daily life; their frequent appeals to him in private correspondence to solve their doubts, and in public affairs, such as strikes, to arrange their difficulties; their invitations to preside over the Co-operative Congress, and other distinctively industrial assemblies; their almost daily manifestations of simple devotion to him, the trustworthy counsellor, the sympathizing friend, the plain-spoken censor of their faults, the stout-hearted champion of their liberties, the warm-spirited advocate of their virtues, the tender, pleading prophet persuading them to purity, truth, and heavenliness of mind—it is small wonder that, after an experience such as this, Bishop Fraser should have iterated and reiterated to the clergy of his diocese the wise and noble counsel of the great Archbishop Tait, "*Trust the people.*"

CHAPTER XV.

SECULARISM—SCIENCE—FAITH.

Atheism—Infidelity—Social Christianity—Religion and Science—Reason and Faith—Christianity and Atheism—Science and Conscience—Mr. Darwin—The Bishop and Professor Huxley—Religion and Knowledge—Bishop of all Classes—Belief in All Truth.

THE questions raised by Secularists interested Bishop Fraser deeply—chiefly because of their practical bearing upon the opinions and conduct of mankind. He often spoke upon these questions, with fairness of mind and temper (ever ready to acknowledge the sincerity of the motives actuating some Secularists and the integrity of their conduct), but with deep sadness and pain at the thought of the general tendencies of their teachings.

Preaching to the railway employés in Peterborough Cathedral, June 23, 1878, the Bishop said :

"I can understand that to people who deliberately set their face to work evil, Atheism may be an acceptable creed; to those who have lost all the noble instincts of their nature, to whom all spiritual elevation of soul is inconceivable—to them, the doctrine of Atheism may bring some slight morsel of comfort; but to struggling, earnest, zealous souls, to loving souls that are distressed and perplexed by the anomalies of this life, as well as feeling within themselves the germs of something better that may be brought to perfect fruit; to such souls I cannot conceive Atheism to be any thing else than the crushing down of all their best and noblest hopes and desires. Philosophic Atheism only makes the cloud of life ten thousand times darker than it is, for, although they say every cloud has a silver lining, there is no silver lining to that cloud—no passing gleam of sunshine to light up the utter darkness and despair that lies before it. No doubt even good men have drawn pictures that can only be called caricatures of God, Christ, and Creation; and the Gospel that has been preached from many pulpits has been often said to have been a gospel of damnation rather than salvation—a dark and dreary creed, of God being a sort of capricious father, Who has His favourite sons whom He pets and spoils, and leaves all the rest uncared for and neglected. But such a god is not the

God of the Bible; and I wish we would all take our ideas of God and Christ from the Bible alone, and not from Milton, John Calvin, or any other human teacher. I wish we could take our ideas of what we ought to do from the Sermon on the Mount, and those other great teachings to be found on every page of the New Testament Scripture. A philosopher like Mr. John Stuart Mill, looking out on the phenomena of society, may perhaps raise the question whether God is omnipotent, or, if omnipotent, whether He is benevolent, but I don't think any man, looking into his own soul, would have much doubt about the love or good-will of God towards himself. Is there any one in this congregation, who, looking over his past life, cannot trace again and again something which seems to be the very finger of God? and has it not been the finger of love, even if it was the hand of chastening? There are chastisements given in life, but it does not follow that God is angry with us, because He sees fit to correct us for our soul's health."

The Bishop's frequent addresses upon the natural tendencies of disbelief in God and the Judgment to come—however sincerely these results are repudiated by the earnest disciples of Secularism—drew upon him much correspondence. To a letter from Mrs. Besant, couched in most courteous terms, the Bishop sent the following reply:

October 11, 1881.

MADAM,—I did not say that "the doctrines of Secularism" which I indicated as "immoral," and as breaking down the sanctities of domestic life in England were openly proclaimed by atheistic or secularist lectures; but having mentioned the titles of atheistic lectures which I had seen placarded in Manchester, I asked, "What is the outcome of these doctrines?" I say advisedly, on the authority not only of the clergy, but of laymen who mix among the working classes and know their thoughts, that the sanctities of the domestic life are not valued by men who adopt the atheistic and secularist hypothesis. I have a letter this morning from a gentleman, Mr. W. E. Snell, in Edinburgh, who says: "Of course Secularists repudiate the sacredness of marriage." If men are taught that they have only to follow nature, they will interpret "nature" to be their own low, bestial nature, and will act accordingly. A book, that has been condemned as utterly immoral in its teaching and tendency—"the Fruits of Philosophy," for which, I believe, with whatever intention, you are responsible—is still publicly sold in the streets of Manchester, and was not long ago taken by a clergyman in Burnley out of the hands of a young unmarried female Sunday scholar, who was thus taking poison into her nature. In Manchester, not many months since, forty-seven men were apprehended by the police, engaged in the most detestable practices; and I say distinctly and firmly, that if men's faith in a God of righteousness is destroyed, and they are taught that there is no hereafter, and no account to be given of their lives here, these doctrines and their natural and necessary outcome, will destroy the moral health of life at its root, and make purity an impossible virtue. I feel bound to lift up my voice against these terrible issues, whenever I have the opportunity. The spreading canker of impurity in all classes of society—of which medical men sadly assure me—is the one thing that alarms me for the future of England.—I am, Madam, your obedient servant,

J. MANCHESTER.

In the firm conviction that *impurity* is one of the most alarming evils threatening the future progress of England, the Bishop continued to assail every influence which he believed was hostile to that strongest bulwark of morals—the Christian faith.

In a sermon preached at Emmanuel Church, Oswaldtwistle, July 16, 1882, he said:

"Christianity has its difficulties, and there are points on which we might desire, if we could have had our choice, that the revelations were fuller and clearer, just as we might desire that the days passing over us now, were less rainy and more sunshiny; but we cannot control these things, which are ordered for us by One Whom we believe to be wiser and Whom we know to be stronger than ourselves. And so, because there are difficulties in Christianity, I hope you will not give it up. There is sufficient light for a man to walk by, who does not deliberately choose darkness, and I am not going to try to escape from those small difficulties by plunging into and accepting the infinitely greater difficulties and perplexities of the creed of Atheism. Why God sends the rain when we want sunshine, why He sends or permits a pestilence when we want to enjoy life and health, I cannot tell; but to call upon me to believe that this wonderful universe, with its varied courses, and its wonderful controlling mechanism, these worlds upon worlds of space—to ask me to believe that all these things came by chance, and that I myself, with all the wonderful faculties with which God has endowed every human being, was developed by protoplasm from a germ, without any designing providence of God governing me, is asking me to believe what to my mind is absurd and impossible. And so, because there are difficulties in my faith which I cannot explain, I am not going to accept the infinitely greater difficulties of the creed of Atheism; for it does not make the theory of life easier, but a thousand times more difficult, to say there is no God, no Christ, no Holy Spirit, no soul, no life beyond. If I have one conviction in my mind deeper than another—and I only wish I could live in a more constant and habitual sense of it—it is that there is a God, and that I am responsible to Him, and that I shall have to give account of myself after what the world calls death, and that this kingdom to which I belong is a kingdom of righteousness."

At the Co-operative Hall, Downing Street, November 27, 1882, he said :

"I do not believe that the contagion of infidelity has reached the working classes, or is spreading among them more deeply or widely than it has reached, or is spreading among, the classes that are called socially and intellectually higher. The coarse attacks on the Bible and Christianity repel, rather than attract, and the working men are brought into too close contact with the facts of life to lose their heads in the presence of unproved, and perhaps unprovable, scientific hypotheses ; or to believe that this wonderful world, with all its adaptations and harmonies, came to be what it is by chance, or by the operation of a merely physical force, working under no control or direction of any superintending hand. There may be more intermediate links in the great series of antecedents and consequences than there were once supposed to be, but the logic of a working man's experience convinces him that there must be ultimately—no matter how remote in thought, but practically implied in every form of existence—a great First Cause. And to this idea, investing it with all those personal attributes with which Revelation has taught him to clothe the idea of Him, Who is the Creator and Sustainer of the world, he is not ashamed still to give the name of God. It is true the working man is said to be rarely found in the House of God. I cannot quite endorse this assertion, for certainly I see him there, and often in good numbers too. And if it is true, let us put the blame, at least in part, where it ought to fall. What have our church-builders and church-guardians done to make him welcome, and feel at home there ? No doubt the age of unquestioning faith is gone ; and in a time of universal inquiry, men are not so disposed to accept every statement of the preacher as docilely as they once were. But St. Peter tells us that it is very far from being a sign of unbelief that men ask for reasons for the faith we hold ; and no great harm will be done if it only makes shallow-headed men a little less venturesome in their assertions, and a little more moderate in their claims."

Again, preaching at Great St. Mary's, Cambridge, October 19, 1884 :

"On my way one day from the East of London to Westminster Abbey, I walked along the Commercial Road, as it is called, and the thronged thoroughfares of Whitechapel and Aldgate. I saw humanity there in many forms, few of them lovely. There was the street trader, plying his Sunday task, and the hundreds who had no Sunday clothes, and the shameless harlot, and the deadly spirit-vault, with its bar crowded with young and old, men and women, asking for poison, from end to end. And I asked, Can science or philosophy heal these things ? Nay, my thought was even sadder, for I asked myself, Can even Christianity, such as we know it, and have allowed it to become, heal them ? Could Sodom, could Egypt, could even the city where Our Lord was crucified, have shown sadder, more desperate scenes than these ?

"I am waiting to hear what the new philosophy has to say to these social facts, and, still more, what it means to do with them. Oh, you say, we will clear away these rookeries. The law has been passed long ago, and, if municipalities did their duty, the state of things had long since been mended. But these are not rookeries. The ways are spacious. I passed several blocks of model lodging-houses. Church towers and spires were to be seen on every hand. The spirit-vaults were the most bright and attractive of their kind. Yet here was a population on whom some remedial agencies are urgently needed to be brought to bear. For, indeed, science and philosophy are hardly safe amid such surroundings. 'The republic does not need chemists,' said a French terrorist, and sent Lavoisier to the guillotine. Oh, for prophets, I felt, as I gazed with a sad and ineffective sympathy, to guide these sheep, wandering as without a shepherd—to raise the slumbering hope, the higher motive, the worthier aim in the heart of each! for each heart, however debased, is still human, and made in the image of God. Oh, for more to answer to the loud call of the Bishop of Bedford, who, with apostolic zeal and indomitable energy, is labouring there, and whose one call is for men! Machinery will do much in every department of human activity which men used to do less exactly and more slowly. But they are men, and not machines, that are needed here. It is the prophet, with his large, free heart, that is needed, not the sacerdotal exclusionist, jealously guarding his supposed special prerogatives; a heart as large as Moses' heart, when he rebuked Joshua's ill-timed zeal for his honour with the memorable words, ' Would God that all the Lord's people were prophets, and that the Lord would put His spirit upon them.' At such a time, even if one like not their methods, one dare not rebuke nor try to hinder any who are working miracles or casting out devils in Christ's name. Surely they are for Christ, and not against Him. Instead, then, of finding fault with others, let us bestir ourselves. If we would not have the Lord come and smite the earth with a curse, let us see whether by Christian hands and Christian hearts something cannot yet be done to arrest the moral devastation of society. And if the battle goes against us, as it is possible it may, at least let us fall with our faces towards the foe, and with the spiritual weapons of our warfare in our hands. It is something even to have fought in Christ's name and for Christ's cause. Even in this nineteenth century, in the noble army of martyrs, ' yet there is room.'

"I have among my hearers a body of young men, who are the flower of the England of to-day, and the hope of the England of to-morrow. Young men, the problems of life, the vital problems, which touch the existence of individuals and of societies at its root, are vast and increasingly difficult. The ascertained and proved results of science do not seem to have made them easier ; and the unwarranted, but too readily accepted, hypotheses of science have but added to our perplexities. Whence came I? Whither am I bound? What is it proper and needful for me to do? Every one must feel that these questions, never easy to minds not content to rest upon the surface, have become increasingly perplexing when confronted with the fierce light of so-called scientific and philosophical inquiry, with theories of evolution and determinism, and a physical basis of morals, and all the other principles and conclusions of a materialistic philosophy. Men are not frightened now by what threw the poet back upon his own indestructible convictions:

> "'I found Him not in world or sun,
> Or eagle's wing, or insect's eye;
> Nor through the questions men may try,
> The petty cobwebs we have spun.'

"Men say to-day we are prepared for this; we don't care to seek because we know we shall never find. Have not masters in Israel told us that He is the Unknowable, the Unthinkable. Let us turn rather to our microscopes and laboratories, and there at least we shall find what is real and certain. Aye, turn to them, and if you have no power of seeing further than your eye will carry you, beyond visible results, crush out all that is human in your soul. For your theories of transmutation of energy, or the physical sequence of phenomena, will not analyse or account for the human heart, I do not mean the physical heart with its valves and wonderful apparatus; but what we call the human heart. These theories will neither dry a tear, nor call forth a smile. They will inspire neither love, nor hope, nor pity. And human life cannot live without these. Men can sleep, and feed, of course, but this is not life. Society is something more than a mere aggregation of machines. One seems to see scope there still for two great ideas—the ideas of faith and duty. Whencesoever I came, whithersoever I am travelling, the claims of faith and duty sound most imperious in my ear. I cannot, I dare not, ignore them. They solve at least some difficulties by pointing to a course of life, which, at any rate, is noble because unselfish, happy because pure, self-rewarded because content simply with the satisfaction of discharging duty. You may deem me a fool, as the Corinthians deemed Paul to be a fool, for saying that in Christianity, generously accepted, and reasonably applied, I still see the only true solvent of the immediate enigmas of life. It, too, has its mysteries, its hard sayings, even its deep shadows. Still there is Christ; there are words that we feel as we read them are words of eternal life; and our conviction is that of the disciples of old, 'If we forsake Him, to whom shall we go?'"

No conviction lay deeper in the soul of Bishop Fraser than the conviction, to use his own words, that

"Christianity is intended to unite and consolidate the world. The Gospel contains the true cure for all moral and social diseases. If any one wishes to see how Christianity deals with social phenomena, let him study the Epistle of St. Paul. The wisdom of the world, so self-complacent, fancying itself so profound when it is oftentimes so shallow, has devised plans more elaborate than Christianity. These have gone out, in the spirit of philanthropy, to redress the evil of the world, leaving Christianity behind. But although philanthropy is a very good thing when accompanied by Christianity, by itself it is always a vain, fussy, pompous, conceited thing, strutting about the streets, and saying, 'Admire me: I am philanthropy.' But philanthropy, apart from Christianity, is not going to do very much to heal the diseases of society."

What the Bishop desired was, that all things should be *Christianized*: philanthropy, political economy, physical science—all things. It was his most clear and earnest belief that every right feeling of man, every truth of nature, every fact of existence, could be enlarged and beautified by the inbreathing of the spirit of the Gospel. He laboured without ceasing to convince his hearers that, between true religion and true reason, it was impossible for any abiding hostility to exist.

At the luncheon given in connection with the laying of the corner-stone of the new buildings for Owens College, on Friday, September 23, 1870, in responding to the toast of "The Bishop and Clergy of all Denominations," the Bishop said :

"I have attended here to-day, I will not say at any inconvenience, but I must say with some apprehensions that I might be thought to be neglecting public duty. Some of you will know that this is my week for examining candidates whom I hope to ordain next Sunday; but it appeared to me that this was an occasion of sufficient importance to justify a bishop, even in the middle of this serious work, in coming here to express his wish that God's blessing may rest upon this institution. There may have been a time, perhaps not very long ago, when a Bishop of the Church of England might have felt uncomfortable in having his name coupled in the way in which my name has been coupled in this toast. But with my acquaintance of the episcopal bench, I may say that I do not believe that there is one member of it who would refuse to respond with cordiality to the toast which has been proposed, or if there be, I will say in the words of a noble earl who is the property of this county, in a memorable phrase of a speech which has almost become historical, 'If there be, I am not that one.' I do not claim to be more liberal than my neighbours, and I think there is nothing more despicable than pseudo-liberality ; but I do claim this for myself, that I love my fellow-men, and I very seldom find a person so disagreeable that when we have parted I can say to myself: 'I hope we may never meet again.' I do feel that it is desirable when we do meet, that we should bring out into the forefront those points upon which we agree, and not those upon which we differ.

"And further, I take a very large, broad, and comprehensive view of what is understood by truth. I believe that everybody who earnestly seeks to propagate the truth, to preach the truth in the largest sense of the word, is doing good, not only to his fellow-men, but is really labouring in the cause of Him Who is, first of all, the God of Holiness, but second to that, if second, the God of Truth. I will never believe that true science is contrary to true religion, or that true religion ought to be afraid of any legitimate consequences of true science. I know well, and the knowledge makes me speak with some tremulousness, that I am in the presence of those who are considered to be, and who have established their right to be considered to be, the ablest interpreters of the laws and phenomena of the physical and material world. I cordially welcome these gentlemen as teachers and propounders of the truth. I read their speculations with the profoundest interest, possibly with considerably more interest than they would bestow upon any speculation of mine. But I can listen to the president with profit and admiration while, with a master's art, he expounds his theories upon biogenesis and abiogenesis—which, when translated into the language of us poor people who sit upon the wall, I take to mean what is the best account of the wondrous phenomena of life. I can allow another worthy professor, who is sitting near me (Professor Tyndall) as much space and as much development for the faculty of imagination in the regions of science as he himself will claim. I can listen with interest to those other interesting and perfectly innocuous speculations which occupy the mind of another distinguished member of the British Association now present (Sir John Lubbock) as to whether we men who live in Manchester are deteriorated angels or developed savages. And when they all have done, I simply ask this at their hands—we only desire to be their collaborateurs in building up the great temple of Truth. The President of the British Association said in one of his speeches that when he was walking through the streets of Liverpool he could not help being struck with the phenomena that he there saw, viz., the contrast of luxury with poverty and vice. I ask him, and those who were with him, to say whether, after all these physical, material, and intellectual theories, which they hold, have been developed to the uttermost, they will solve the problem of the great moral and spiritual phenomena with which men are surrounded, and whether there is not also a place for us poor parsons as well as for men of science and philosophers? If they will only believe that we are not sceptics in disguise, or charlatans trying to palm off upon the world something that has been found to fail; if they will only believe that we want to tread, as they tread, calmly, step after step, where we find our remedies have succeeded, I think they will allow that we are searching after truth—the only truth that I care to find, practical truth; truth that will elevate man in the scale of being. I read yesterday a remarkable sermon—at least, so it struck me—which was preached on Wednesday, at the opening of the Social Science Congress at Newcastle, by a clergyman whom I am proud to recognize as a friend and chaplain of my own, in which he stated his belief that the great problem of the day was to correlate the Bible and the age.

Lord Bacon, in his preface to the 'Novum Organon,' hoped that he had accomplished the thing so long sighed for, a legitimate and permanent wedlock where there had been previously nothing but an unhappy divorce, between the *à priori* and the empirical methods of scientific inquiry. I can say 'Exoriare aliquis.' I do not care from whatever source it comes. I will welcome every means which is calculated to settle the disputed boundaries between religion and science, and show that both alike in their legitimate province minister to, and help to build up, the great temple of truth."

Of this speech, Professor Huxley said :

"I shall not soon forget the spirit-stirring speech of the noble prelate who sits upon my right—a speech which I shall recollect as long as I live. It embodied a spirit and a feeling which have not always been exhibited by men in his position. *O ! si sic omnia.* Had such men always filled the episcopal office, and had the same spirit always animated ministers as that which has been expressed by my friend who has just sat down, I incline to think there would have been no cases of antagonism between science and religion—an antagonism which does not really exist, but which is the artifice and creation of men. I say that that speech was better to me than even the generous wine with which one naturally fortifies oneself on an occasion of this kind."

Professor Tyndall said of it :

"If I have ever heard any speech with extreme delight, it was that of the Bishop of Manchester—and I cannot refrain from expressing my sympathy with every word of that speech. Such speeches as his tend to show that the difference between such men as he and the members of the British Association, who have been referred to, is at bottom but a difference of form and not of substance."

Sir John Lubbock said :

"I cannot help thanking his lordship for the manner in which he has spoken. Neither can I help remarking upon the change of feeling which now exists between scientific men and religious men—nay, I would not say religious men, but the clergy of this country, for I cannot admit that scientific men are not as religious as any other body of Englishmen."

In the course of a lecture delivered in the Albert Hall, Sheffield, November 24, 1880, the Bishop said :

"As a matter of fact, reason and faith are only two different attitudes of the human mind in relation to different phenomena. It is sometimes forgotten that the mind of man is an immaterial unit, and that it is one thing, not many; and although we have got into the way of dividing it into departments, and speaking of its different faculties such as will, conscience, affection, desires, understanding, and reason, yet, after all, these are only the efforts or acts of the same immaterial, indivisible thing which we call 'our mind,' in relation to different phenomena. We speak of our will, when we have to make a choice; of our conscience, when we feel divided between right and wrong; of our understanding, when we have to pause and consider whether we can accept certain propositions; of reason, when we engage in drawing conclusions from propositions; of affection, when we love; and of desire, when we fix our feelings, or our mind, on an object; but still, all the same, the mind is immaterial and indivisible.

"Philosophers and scientific men tell us that our bodily particles change. I do not know the exact period of time in which this occurs, but I have heard it said, that not one particle of my present body is the same as the particles of my body seven years ago. Whatever may be the strict period of time, all scientific men admit that there is a change in the particles of the body, that there is a waste of tissue; every thought which passes through the brain leads to a waste of tissue, and has to be repaired. But our personal identity remains unchanged. There is in us something different from the mere particles of our body, and that something we call our mind. The materialist cannot trace the connection of the body and the soul, or the relations of the material organization to the spiritual; but there is reason to think that the body with its soul or principle of life is different from, though associated with, the immaterial, immortal spirit which occupies it as a temporary home. There are two fields of phenomena in which men's minds exercise themselves, and upon which they operate—the field of necessary matter, and the field of probable matter; but they cannot reason everything out as they could a problem of Euclid. Even great physical theories are only accepted as hypotheses provisionally, so long as they account for phenomena. We cannot demonstrate these theories; we arrive at them by induction. It has always been a difficult thing to mark out the realm of reason and faith, or rather, how far in the realm probable matter may go, and where and when faith is needed as reason's necessary supplement. To inquire into mysteries too curiously is an abuse and not a use of reason, and an abuse and not a use of faith; and to assign the same authority to inferences which may be remote, that we assign to the principles upon which these inferences profess to be drawn, is an abuse and not a legitimate use of faith or reason. The ultimate human tribunal before which all truth as such must be judged, is the reason. In fact, it is the faculty of reason exercising itself with a moral force in the department of right and wrong, which are truth and falsehood in the moral sphere. It is said to-day that the demands of faith are such that the reason cannot possibly grant them. I cannot deny that something that calls itself 'faith' does sometimes make impossible demands, and even counts itself of a higher order when it succeeds in silencing reason's voice. I am not going too far when I say that all the extravagances of theology have come from this unreasonable faith, which after all is nothing more than what Bishop

Butler called that 'forward and delusive faculty, the imagination,' intruding into things it has not seen or heard, let loose without restraint, like a wild masterful steed without its rider. From these extravagances have come some sad and terrible reactions. There has come the reaction of Atheism, and the reaction of Agnosticism. They are the philosophies of to-day. They are fashionable; and some people say they are widely disseminating themselves. They may have disciples here, as they have probably in most of our great towns. There is nothing new in them. To use the words of Tennyson, they are 'old results that look like new.' They have been answered again and again; but they revive whenever the mind leaves sober and reverent ways to indulge in the pleasures of fanciful speculation. A modern writer has spoken of the belief in a personal God as an unverifiable hypothesis. I cannot attempt to prove the assertion. I cannot take God into a laboratory and analyse Him as we would analyse fire or water; but on the grounds of reason the belief in a personal God is the most probable hypothesis. Either there is a God, or there is not. There is no third course. The Epicurean hypothesis was that God lived afar off in the clouds, and did not take any interest in human affairs. That theory I at once dismiss. In the famous poem of Lucretius, translated by Professor Munro, you can see what the Lucretian hypothesis was. It was that everything that exists is made of a combination of atoms, which atoms are always moving through space. These atoms have hooks, and with these hooks the atoms catch one another, and thus is produced protoplasm, then amœba, afterwards the gorilla, and ultimately the fully-developed man. Now this is much less probable as a theory that appeals to reasonable man than the Biblical one. Our modern scientists are at issue on the origin of life. Huxley and Tyndall adopt the maxim that every living thing presupposes a prior living thing. They refuse the theory of spontaneous generation, but Haeckel and Clifford go in for it. They say: 'It is necessary for the completion of our hypothesis.' So we must get rid of the idea of God in the world, it seems, to complete the scientific hypothesis of a small knot of men; but philosophers as great as Haeckel and Clifford, men like Herschel and Clerk Maxwell, have said these atoms appear to be manufactured articles. You manufacture articles here in Sheffield, and every manufactured article presupposes a manufacturer. They do not come into existence by chance or evolution. Therefore, if men of science —such men as I can trust—tell me that the atoms have all the appearance of manufactured articles, then these atoms presuppose a manufacturer, or, in more reverent language, presuppose a Creator. Some people find fault with the Bible because God did not work a perpetual miracle by teaching the human race all things suddenly, instead of gradually, just as if you would teach a little child four years old in the same way that you would teach an older person. But they must remember that the Bible is not one book, but many. It is the literature of nations, and has been spread over many centuries. Its earlier books were written about 1500 years before the birth of Christ, and the latter ones about 100 years after that time. The Bible contains the progressive teaching of man. Whenever the development of the human race is mentioned in the Bible, it is mentioned as a revelation coming from God; and wherever its morality is spoken of, it is as the basis upon which the social duties of man are to be formed. Some complain that it contains passages that cannot be read to little children; but the Bible simply tells a true tale. Abraham did some things of which he was truly ashamed, and I should think he was ashamed when he turned Hagar out that day to please the petulancy of his other wife. Then there is a sad story of King David, but if King David—being a man after God's own heart—did those things, it is just as well that the world should know them. It is well that we should know the things that have to be guarded against. The Bible does not gloss over the sins of good men, any more than it exaggerates the sins of the children of the Devil. It is much more easy to destroy than to build up; and men nowadays very frivolously, between the puffs of cigars, determine whether there is a God or not. Then, regarding the matter whether the existence of God is capable of absolute demonstration, we must accept the conclusion of reason, whatever the consequences may be. Mr. Stuart Mill once delivered the opinion that he could conceive circumstances in which two and two would not make four, but five. But constituted as the human mind is, I think we should be obliged to accept the conclusion of the fifth proposition of Euclid, and the forty-seventh proposition of the same book, even though our whole theory of morals be subverted thereby. The two sides of an isosceles triangle must be accepted as being equal, even if the minds of men are disturbed by the fact. They must not go against the distinct conclusion of reason. But whether you are dealing with probabilities, or whether you are compelled to consider consequences, I ask you to answer this question: What would the world—what would society—what would human beings altogether become if these newly-furbished theories prevailed? They tell us there is no God, or, if there is, He is so far off that we need not trouble ourselves about Him. There is no hereafter. Frederick Harrison speaks about contributing to the progress of the race, and of an immortality five hundred years hence, and that all those will be remembered that contribute to the perfection of the race. But how many of you can take comfort in the fact that your names will be remembered five hundred years hence, as having contributed to that perfection? According to these ideas, we are mere automata acted upon by external forces—our will nothing but the reflex action of the muscle. God, if there be one, is a pitiless God; prayer is vain; the colours of good and evil are all blurred and mixed; there is no real distinction between right and wrong; there is no effective bridle upon the natural appetites; and there is no conscience sitting on her throne. These are the conclusions we are asked to accept. The only thing left us, says Professor Clifford, is to teach our children to be good. Upon his theory, I do not know how we can teach children at all; or, in fact, what goodness is, or how it is to be discriminated from vice and evil. But happily, these men are all better than their principles.

They say these things, but they do not live according to them. They do not bring up their children according to them. They bring up their children upon something distinctly like Christianity, though they call it another name. The very fact that they are obliged to recognize goodness, disposes of more than half of all their atheistic and agnostic arguments. I do not ask you to dethrone your reason even in the presence of mysteries; I only ask you to remember the restriction laid upon reason by its own limited capacities. The point I wish to insist on is that we have enough light, not to satisfy perhaps every speculative inquiry ; but to remove all reasonable doubts, and to guide us on the path of duty. Men can live by the light they have, and men can die, bravely and fearlessly, by the light they have.

"'More light,' it is said, were Goethe's last words. 'More light' I ask for, and more light I believe we shall get when our eyes are able to bear it. The last promise of revelation is, that we shall see God as He is.

"There never was a time when those who profess to be followers of the Lord Jesus Christ had more need to be united against the advancing foes of vice and unbelief, which threaten to submerge all goodness, all belief, and with it the whole structure of society. It is a lamentable thing to see men wasting their time and strength upon questions of an entirely subordinate character (or which can only be made prominent by running them up by strange and curious steps into latitudes where they properly have no place at all), when there are these great problems wanting solution, these great masses of people wanting to be won, and when the labourers in the great harvest field are so terribly few. I rejoice to think that the hearts of the working men of this country are waiting for an appeal to be made to them by those who really feel for them, who sympathize with them, who understand their position, can make allowance for their difficulties, and care for their souls."

Moreover, the Bishop solemnly and incessantly impressed upon all classes of the Christian world the supreme duty and the grave responsibility of adorning, in all things, the doctrine of Christ their Saviour.

Preaching at Ashton-under-Lyne Parish Church, October 30, 1881, he said:

"I have frequently had letters from Atheists and Secularists asking me if I could tell them in what ways the lives of a number of Christian people were better than their own. There is a terrible force in the argument, and I cannot consider it without shame in my heart, and the blood rushing to my head. I know that the drunkenness, lying, deceit, covetousness, and lust prevalent among nominally Christian people are a scandal and a disgrace, and I dare say there are men who have shaken off the belief in God and the love of Christ, whose lives are as respectable and decent as the lives of many Christian people. This does not prove, however, that the Atheist is right; it proves only that these nominal followers of Christ are wrong; and I put it to you whether the inconsistent, low-level lives that many professing Christians are leading, are not the greatest hindrance possible to the spread of the Gospel? If only we lived up to the standard of the Sermon on the Mount; if people could say of us now, as was said of the early Christians, 'See how these Christians love one another!'—how they help one another, how gentle, how meek, how generous, how forgiving they are!—the Spirit of Christ would become a mighty power in the world; and the greatest argument of the Atheist would be swept away."

And as the Bishop enforced upon Christians the responsibility of living Christian lives, thus commending Christianity to its adversaries, so was he careful to accord to Science, with ungrudging appreciation, the due meed of praise for its patient labours and brilliant achievements.

"I can recognize," he said, "as clearly as any one, the wonderful conquests of science. I am quite prepared to render science all true allegiance. The science of astronomy, *e.g.*, justifies itself by its power to prophesy. A science *must* be true that can tell what is coming to pass in connection with bodies so remote as Venus and the sun. There is no room for hypothesis or conjecture there. But the allegiance I render to science is not that of my conscience, but of my intellect. When science has proved her case, and established her laws and principles, my intellect must respect them; but they have nothing whatever to do with my conscience or my duty. The very idea of duty is outside the circle of scientific obligation, and the idea of righteousness is perhaps still further outside. Science cannot do for men what they most require; it cannot sustain them in the battle against sin; it cannot purify their hearts from passion or selfish motives. It may enable its student to conquer nature, but it cannot help him to conquer or elevate himself. Religion is not scientific (we do not go to the Bible in proof of scientific principles), and, on the other hand, it must be admitted that science is not moral, and we cannot go to treatises on science to learn our duty to God and man. The man of science may be moral or immoral, but it is not his science that makes him either the one or the other. The view which Paul took of European and Asiatic civilization was amply confirmed in every respect by contemporary historians and poets; and I ask, what chemistry, but the chemistry of the Holy Ghost, could so far have influenced that corrupt condition of society as to have raised aloft that high standard of moral and religious duty which now all civilized communities confess and admire? The code of morals of Christianity, instead of being a matter of idle discussion in the schools of philosophy, became a living power in the market and the home; and to live soberly, righteously, and godly, in this present world was felt to be the noblest, purest, highest, and happiest life for man."

The Bishop was no less generous in his esteem for scientific men than just in his appreciation of the conquests of science. In an address delivered at the Scientific Students' Association, at the Free Trade Hall, Manchester, April 27, 1882, he said:

"I looked to-day into Darwin's original and great work, 'The Origin of Species.' It is sometimes thought that when Mr. Darwin introduced biological science, he introduced a theory which would be subversive of those old ideas of faith, theism, and even of morality, upon which the social system of the civilized world had hitherto reposed; but, whatever may have been the conclusions of some of his followers, Mr. Darwin's system was a theistic, and not an atheistic one. In the last sentence of his 'Origin of Species,' Darwin used these words: 'There is grandeur in this view of life, with its several forms, having been originally breathed by the Creator into a few forms or one; and that whilst this planet has gone cycling on, according to the fixed law of gravity, from so small a beginning, endless forms, most beautiful and most wonderful, have been and are being evolved.' Whether the name of Darwin will ever occupy the same eminence, on the scientific roll, as the names of Kepler, Newton, and Laplace, it would perhaps be premature to say; but I am quite sure, so far as I am acquainted with Darwin's writings, that he has given no encouragement to that hypothetical school which is passing off, in the name of science, so many unproved conclusions, and is even asking us to surrender our most cherished beliefs in favour of unproved hypotheses."

This largeness and fairness of mind endeared him to all classes of the community. Christians recognized in the Bishop a splendid illustration of Pauline charity; non-Christians a noble example of the best human justice. No better instance of the Bishop's sentiments towards men of science and of their reciprocal feeling toward the Bishop can be adduced than that afforded by the banquet given, on July 14, 1880, by the Mayor of Manchester upon the occasion of the founding of the new Victoria University. In proposing the toast of "The Learned and Scientific Societies at Home and Abroad," the Bishop said:

"I am, unhappily, to my mind, a representative of views that are supposed to be most hostile to learning, and most afraid of science; and yet I am not afraid of any conclusions of well-authenticated science, nor hostile to true learning. It would be madness and folly to be either. Has not the poet said truly—

"'Who loves not Knowledge? Who shall rail against her beauty? Who shall fix her pillars? Let her work prevail.'

"I claim, as a Churchman, those great words, not merely for the Church which I represent, but for those great truths which all churches represent. We all have a right to bid God-speed to all sound learning and true science. It has been said that universities are the oldest institutions in the world, except priesthoods. Why is it that priesthoods are even more durable than universities? I may venture to hazard a doubt whether the prophecy that universities will survive priesthoods will be ultimately realized. Let us disassociate priesthood from priest-craft; let us believe that there are men belonging to all denominations who have a desire in their hearts to set conscience on her throne, and to tell men they are made for something higher than that which terminates with things that are seen. All I say is, that if universities ever survive priesthoods, whose mission is to proclaim moral and religious truth, it will be an evil day for universities and for the world. I am not afraid of any well-authenticated truth. It is an absurd charge to bring against divines or theologians that they never modify their own dogmas or creeds. Why, within my own memory, there have been half a dozen definitions of the first chapter of Genesis; and, simply recognizing the truth of the Great First Cause, we are waiting what you scientific gentlemen have to tell us as to how we may interpret the verses that follow. A philosopher, who, I believe, has not been displaced from his seat—I refer to Aristotle—has said that if the fact is evident, it is not necessary to give a reason for it. I think philosophy discharges her duty, or at least science, when she has put us in possession of facts; and I do not think that men of science have a right to turn it to a reproach against men of religion that they will wait awhile till all is perfect harmony in the schools of knowledge and science before they accept what seems to them at present, at least, to be nothing better than hypothesis. I picked up to-day, and I ventured to turn it into my somewhat rough English, a grand passage which I found in the preface to Lord Bacon's 'Great Instauration of Sciences.' He said, hoping that the new method of the inductive philosophy would be enabled to reconcile what he called the long ill-omened divorce that existed between the rational and empirical faculties, 'We humbly ask that human beings may never come into collision with divine, and that from our opening the paths of sense and the greater enkindling of natural life, nothing of incredulity or darkness may rise in our minds towards divine mysteries, but that rather by the pure intellect, cleansed from phantasies and vanity, and none the less acknowledging the authority of the divine oracles, all may be yielded to what is faith's due. And we would have all advised to remember the true ends of science—not merely for dilettantism, or contention, or contempt of others, nor for fame or power, or inferior motives of this kind—but for the service and uses of life; and that they do try to perfect and direct it in the spirit of charity. For from the lust of power fell the angels; and from the lust of knowledge men; but of charity there is no excess; and no peril ever came from it to angel or to man.' In conclusion, let me remind you that many distinguished prelates of the Church of England have occupied important positions in connection with the Royal Society, thus showing that theologians are not necessarily averse to scientific inquiry. These facts, I think, justify me in saying, with the poet—

> "'Let Knowledge grow from more to more,
> But more of reverence in her dwell;
> That mind and soul according well,
> May make one music as before.'"

To this brave and wise speech, according to Science her full rights, yet claiming for Religion her nobler sphere, Professor Huxley replied:

"It is ten years ago now since the right reverend prelate and I, by a very odd coincidence, occupied, as nearly as possible, the same positions as we occupy at present, viz., that the one proposed and the other replied to some such toast as that which his Lordship has just brought before you; and I recollect exceedingly well that the Bishop's speech was animated by the same catholicity of sentiment and broad appreciation of what science is doing in the world, that won for him the respect of all the men of science then present, however much we might doubt whether he comprehended our position or understood with what extreme tenderness we respect all faiths which as yet have done good in the world, or are likely to do good in it. I do not presume to say that the right reverend prelate has grown since that time. I do not think it would be possible to increase the measure of his liberality and of his charity."

In an address delivered to the students of Owens College, on June 26, 1879, the Bishop pleaded for the recognition by all thoughtful men of the claims of sound learning, whether scientific or religious.

"If you wish this college to take rank among the old universities, the students must not only think of being successful in their studies. I do not think the intellectual results of the old universities are more than half the advantage that is gained there. The moral and social influences of these institutions are not to be reckoned in a mercantile balance. Just now there are so many adverse influences abroad, so much to dissipate, not only the intellect, but the ἦθος, so much to demoralize and lower the tone of society, that sometimes one's heart sinks; and though I am quite sure there are noble young men and women who are trying to qualify themselves thoroughly for that part in after life which they may play, yet I am afraid —and I think there is cause for the fear—that there is a very large number of young men and women who really regard life, as I suppose we should all come to regard it, if we were merely a bundle of atoms held together for a certain period of time, to be decomposed and pass into other combinations, and there to have an end. If that is the true philosophy, I do not know who would care to live for anything beyond the present time. Still, there is something in this world that is worth living for. I made bold to say to some railway men the other day, that if Mr. Bradlaugh's theory were true, and Secularism were the guide of human beings' lives, still, there is a noble Secularism, as well as an ignoble one; and even if there were no life beyond the grave, it is better to live as Christ has taught us to live. Let me ask you most earnestly to see that what the old Greeks called the ἦθος—the moral tone, character, principles, language, behaviour, not only in the class but in the gymnasium—should be carefully looked at, and that a student of Owens College should almost be known by seriousness and earnestness, by high aspirations, by worthy living.

"Men who woo the muses, or pursue their researches in science year after year in the quietest and simplest way, who do not care for many changes of raiment, or for faring sumptuously every day—these men, I believe, get most of the true happiness out of life, as well as play the noblest part in it.

"No doubt the old universities were more or less overshadowed by a spirit of ecclesiasticism. No doubt they were much under the control of the priests; and I am one of those who think that it is the prophet, rather than the priest, who should guide the mind of the nineteenth century. I do not ask you to accept every theological definition or theory about God, but I do ask you to still cherish in your hearts a belief that there is a Personal God, to Whom you are responsible for your conduct. If it is possible to teach morality upon any other basis than the old accepted basis of the obligations of conscience, I want people to tell me what that new basis of morality is. I have not yet been able to discover it, and it is because I believe that in this nineteenth century the moral duties of society are infinitely more important to the well-being, and to the permanence of society, than any amount of intellectual research (though there is no need to disparage the one in trying to exalt the other) that I look with some discouragement upon that part of our modern system which seems to say because these things are doubtful and cannot be proved, because there are so many differences of opinion—though happily there are hardly any when we come to the roots and fundamentals—that therefore they cannot attempt to teach these things in their schools and classes."

Utterances such as these show Bishop Fraser in his true character—the character of the earnestly religious man, always ready to bid welcome to every fresh accession of knowledge, requiring only that the fabric of knowledge should be built upon the solid rocks of truth, not upon the shifting sands of speculation. Bishop Fraser was neither bigot nor sceptic; he was too spiritual to be a religious bigot, too profound to be a secularizing sceptic. This truth and intensity of character made him the friend of all learning and the prophet of all classes. He was as much at home when speaking at Owens College, or to the members of a Literary and Scientific Institute, as when talking to railway employés and night-soil men.

This all-roundness of the Bishop's interests and character is admirably depicted in a sketch of him by Professor A. S. Wilkins, of Owens College, in the *British Weekly* of March 25, 1887:

"The Bishop's interest was keen not only in elementary, but also in the higher education, alike for men and for women. Owens College and the Victoria University had no more generous supporter, no more sagacious counsellor. When the laity of his diocese (without distinction of creeds) gave him £1000 on the occasion of his marriage, he at once added £1000 more from his wife and himself, and founded therewith a classical scholarship at Owens College; and it gave him real pleasure to be told that the first Fraser scholar was the orphan son of an Independent minister. When the buildings of the University College of Wales at Aberystwith were all but destroyed by fire, a meeting was held at Manchester in aid of the fund for their restoration. The Bishop was in the chair, and himself gave a liberal donation, though he said at the time that, to judge from those supporting him, it was mainly a Nonconformist institution. What wonder that a Welshman present said: 'There isn't another Bishop on the Bench who would have helped us?' What wonder either that it was lamented by some—'the Bishop has thrown back for twenty years the Lancashire vote for Disestablishment?' Not twelve months after his death, a leading Nonconformist said in public: 'So long as Bishop Fraser lived, I wouldn't say a word for Disestablishment that might possibly hurt him; now I shall throw myself into the movement heart and soul.' The logic of this last utterance may be doubtful; there can be no doubt as to its significance."

Moreover, Bishop Fraser's genuine charity—his determined conviction that differences of opinion need not disturb the harmonies of good-will, his fairness of mind towards those who opposed him, his resolution to believe the best of every man—was a conspicuous and attractive feature of his character. In his Second Charge, he said:

"It is a foolish, as well as a coarse method of argument, to deny the possession of virtues, and even of lofty virtues, to those whom we call 'sceptics.' It is foolish, because if we refuse the name of virtues to qualities which the world, by a general consensus, recognizes as such, we weaken, instead of strengthen, the cause of Christianity.

"Nor do I think that they are effective advocates of this cause, who pile doctrine upon doctrine, and credendum upon credendum, deeming that the more 'curiously articulated' the symbol (to borrow a phrase of Jeremy Taylor's), the more likely it is to be a true expression of the faith which has been revealed. We may crave for dogmatic precision of formula, but it is unattainable; or, if apparently attained, it is illusory. The outlines of 'things not seen,' must, from the very nature of the case, be vague. Terms like 'person' or 'substance' in the Athanasian Creed, doctrines like that of the 'Resurrection of the body,' in the Creed of the Apostles, affect no two individual minds in the same way. If men were set down to define precisely the conceptions which the terms convey to their minds, you would soon discover, in some cases, how wide and significant those differences are. And if so, it is useless to contend that latitude in opinions is not to be endured. The glory of the New Testament—that which constitutes its title to be a 'law of liberty'—is that it sanctions and allows this liberty.

"Again, it cannot be denied that there have been modes of stating Christian doctrine, which have been singularly repulsive to the intellect, and still oftener to the conscience, of man. Take, for instance, Luther's doctrine of justification; or Calvin's doctrine of election; or the theory of indefectible grace; or popular explanations of the mystery of the Atonement. Men, with their glib tongues, have expounded these deep problems to their own supreme satisfaction in the pulpit, and have not known, sometimes have not recked, how many hearts they have hardened in the congregation, how many intellects perplexed, how many consciences revolted. If you would see how a doctrine full of mystery may yet be handled, so as to be brought into harmony with the analogies of nature and the moral phenomena of life, read Professor Mozley's 'Sermon on the Atonement.'

"And so, if the Church is to hold her place as the keeper and witness of religious truth to men, she must abate some of the pretentions she has made to certainty—I say nothing of claims to infallibility, which are monstrous—and must leave large room for differences of opinion in those she endeavours to gather within her pale. The variations of Protestantism, which have been a standing reproach from the days of Bossuet, have been the natural and necessary result of the illogical attempt to proclaim, on the one hand, the right of private judgment, which is indisputable and indefeasible; and on the other, to insist upon an identity of opinion on minute points of doctrine, which is incompatible with that right. Breadth of teaching, and tolerance of differences (where no moral error is involved), seem to me to be indispensable conditions to any religious organization which aspires to direct the religious thoughts of the age. There is, of course, another policy which is pursued with unwavering dauntlessness by the Church of Rome. That it will succeed, or is succeeding, where speculative thought has once been stirred, I cannot for a moment believe. Indeed, *ex professo*, it crushes speculation, just as it crushes historical inquiry; and tells its disciples that all they have to do, is to submit to be guided by the Church, and they are safe. I need not say that the policy of the Church of England is very discrepant from this. Requiring nothing to be believed of necessity to salvation, but those vital doctrines which can be proved by most certain warrants of Holy Scripture; taking her historic stand upon those ancient Creeds which have expressed the grand but simple faith of Christendom for more than 1500 years; warning us not to force particular texts to support irrational ideas, but to accept God's promises and God's truth in such wise as they be generally set forth in Holy Scripture; and leaving large margins for belief, or at least for differences in the expression of belief, she, of all living churches, is least afraid of having her credentials examined; she, with this freedom that she at once allows and demands, though the prospects of faith cannot be considered bright, even by a sanguine mind, has the least reason to quail before them. Believing that she is led by a Divine Guide, knowing that the stormiest sea can be stilled at His bidding, she can say, with the holy psalmist, 'Yea, though I am sometimes afraid, yet put I my trust in Him.'

"Men can argue against a theological formula; they cannot argue against a holy life. As long as there are evident tokens of correspondence between the religion we profess and the conduct we exhibit, and that conduct is high-minded, unselfish, pure, so long will the religion which is supposed to prompt the conduct be an influence in the world; but when the contradictions between the creed and the life are patent to every eye, and the religion in fact becomes an 'organized hypocrisy,' maintained only for selfish or sinister purposes, its influence, however great in the past, however capable of becoming great in the future, will become a thing 'which decayeth and waxeth old, and is ready to vanish away.'

"It requires some courage in a teacher, no doubt, to say, 'I do not know;' but we shall often have to say it. Our ignorance is far more extensive than our knowledge. We know the bearings of the city of God, and feel sure, when we are following Christ, that we are on the right road; but we do not know enough of the country through which we are travelling to be equally sure of the direction of every path, however alluring, that branches either to the right hand or to the left from the King's highway. The 'kindly light,' which is sufficient to save us from pitfalls leads us on, step by step, not always into realms of fuller knowledge— for those we are content to wait awhile—but into the sure ways of love and dutifulness. And yet obedience *is* knowledge; and the light seems to grow clearer as we advance, and at moments we yearn for no more than we have; our strength seems sufficient for our day. I do not deny the attractiveness of the study of dogmatic theology; and yet I sometimes doubt if it has conferred any conspicuous benefit upon mankind—if it has really made them wiser, stronger, or holier. One thing is certain; it was not as a philosophical system—though of course, it is capable of being philosophised—but as a rule of life, that Christianity conquered the world. Its propagators have not been the theologians, but the saints. It lives, not so much because it teaches, as because it sustains."

CHAPTER XVI.

MILES PLATTING AND CHEETHAM HILL.

Story of Miles Platting—Bishop's Refusal to ordain Mr. Cowgill to Miles Platting—Vestments, Incense, Mixed Chalice—Letters and Petitions in reference to Ceremonial at Miles Platting—Charges against Mr. Green—Principles involved in Miles Platting Case—Imprisonment of Mr. Green—Bishop's Letters to Mr. Green—Mr. Green's Replies—Correspondence with Mr. Gladstone, Lord Selborne, &c.—Bishop's Application for Mr. Green's Release—Vacancy of Living—Nomination of Mr. Cowgill—Issues at Stake—Bishop's Memorandum—Trial and Verdict—St. John's, Cheetham Hill—Statement of Case—Bishop's Letter—Mr. Gunton—Conclusion.

THE stories of Miles Platting and Cheetham Hill, though widely dissimilar in outward appearance, yet possess much community of inward character. In both cases the parties concerned were intensely in earnest, and were battling for what they believed to be fundamental principles. In both cases the accused clergy were warmly supported by the great majority of their congregations, and by a strong force of public opinion. In both cases the Bishop fought out the fight to its appointed end with a brave and manly heart, and without a thought of bitterness, claiming for himself, as Bishop, the right to be assured that candidates and nominees for benefices were loyal to the creeds and laws of the Church of England. In the one case, the Bishop was firmly persuaded that the constitution of the Church, and, in the other case, the foundations of the faith, were imperilled; but in neither case did he doubt the integrity of his opponent. In both cases it seemed like the irony of fate that one of the most large-minded and large-hearted Bishops of the age should be thrust to the front in a conflict *against* (as many thought) Catholicity and comprehension. And the two cases, taken together, show the firmness of the

Bishop's defence of the central truths of Christianity against ceremonial excess on the one hand, and doctrinal deficiency on the other.

The story of Miles Platting may now be told, after the lapse of years, without heat or partiality. In June 1869, some six months before Bishop Fraser's appointment to Manchester, Sir Percival Heywood had appointed to the incumbency of St. John's, Miles Platting, the Rev. Sidney Faithhorn Green. Mr. Green devoted himself with great earnestness and vigour to the work of his parish, which was poor and thickly peopled; but the ceremonial uses introduced by him soon attracted the adverse criticism of a body of his parishioners. Within a year of Bishop Fraser's arrival in Manchester, Mr. Green's practice of mixing water with the wine during the celebration of the Holy Communion was brought under the notice of the Bishop. The Bishop admonished Mr. Green to discontinue the practice, and Mr. Green replied (Jan. 23, 1871):

"As it is your decision that the water ought not to be employed as at St. John's during the celebration of the Holy Communion, I will endeavour to keep to the letter of your Lordship's admonition. . . . There are three alternatives open to me, but I have chosen that of submission, at any rate for the present. My poor father is afflicted with a mortal disease, and I should not wish the last few weeks or months of his life on earth to be embittered by my becoming the subject of a public prosecution. Such for me, personally, has no terror."

For three years after this, nothing noteworthy occurred in the development of the relationship between the Bishop and Mr. Green; but in the year 1874 a considerable number of letters passed between them, chiefly in consequence of the Bishop's refusal to accept, as a candidate for Holy Orders, Mr. Cowgill (nominated by Mr. Green to the curacy of Miles Platting) on the ground that Mr. Cowgill had refused "to recognize the obligatory character of the decisions of the Court of Final Appeal."

"Had your Lordship," writes Mr. Green (Jan. 28, 1874), "refused to institute Mr. Cowgill to a living, your rejection of him would have been intelligible; but, seeing that for years to come he can simply follow the lead of his incumbent, whoever he may be, and thus be learning wisdom by experience, it certainly seems to be a case for leniency towards hasty expressions. I write in the interests of the Church, which I have always longed to make comprehensive in the best sense."

The Bishop replied: "I do not feel that I can reconsider Mr. Cowgill's case till he has reconsidered his opinions, and brought them into harmony with the law of that Church which he wishes to serve." In return, Mr. Green suggested that "the best thing for Mr. Cowgill to do, will be for him to draw up a statement of his views upon Church and State, which shall first be submitted to a lawyer and then to your Lordship; for the words of the Act seem plain—'No person shall on, or as a consequence of, ordination, be required to make any subscription or declaration, or take any oath other than such subscriptions, etc., as are required by this Act." No *modus concordandi* having been arrived at between the Bishop and Mr. Green, Mr. Cowgill accepted an Assistant-Mastership at St. Chad's College, Denstone, and was ordained by the Bishop of Lichfield in the same year.

Another interval of three years elapsed, when it came to the Bishop's knowledge that vestments and incense were being used at St. John's Church. The mixed chalice had also been reintroduced, but this the Bishop seems not to have learned. The Bishop wrote immediately to Mr. Green, and received (May 17, 1877) the following reply:

"Your letter was a great shock to me. I had not thought of this (*i.e.*, the Bishop's unacquaintance with the matter). I am obliged to plead guilty to both indictments; but I had certainly thought that in these days of abnormal excitement the news would have reached you before. . . . We have employed the vestments at all celebrations of the Holy Communion, since last November. . . . What objectionable doctrine the vestment symbolizes I never could discover. All books say that it symbolizes Charity. This seems harmless enough. The idea we have in our church, however, is simply to add beauty and dignity to the services. If Christ be King of kings, we wish to worship Him as such. . . . As to incense, I have used it for the last six years precisely as I do now, for the purpose of perfuming the church, as Herbert recommends in 'Country Parson.' The effluvia from the chemical works are sometimes very disagreeable, and the church itself, moreover, is occasionally not very sweet, and incense seems to answer the required purpose of purifying it. I generally then burn a little incense when there is a choral or midday celebration, some time before the service begins. I do this also as a preparation for the service to be held. I never have used incense in any service. In this most trying neighbourhood, with absolutely nothing which can remind men of the beauties of Nature, where even common grass will not grow, and with a dismal uninviting Church, I have sought, I confess it, to press into the service of the Church everything which adds cheerfulness and beauty to it. My design has been to give the people something *to love*. . . . I think that people of the upper classes have no idea of the way in which the poor love the Church when they once grasp what to be a Churchman means. It is their *constant study*, it is in all their thoughts at work or at home, and I may say, even their recreation; for there are some, I believe, among us, in whom the words are literally fulfilled, '*He shall be satisfied with the pleasures of Thy House*.' . . . At an early choral celebration of the Holy Communion, I felt the tears running down my cheeks as I thought there were those who were desiring to stamp out this worship which was such a happiness both to me, and, above all, to those who enjoy it around me. But pardon me, my dear lord, that I presume to write to you in this way. Your letter is so very kind and considerate, speaking of what I see is an inevitable necessity so far as you are concerned. I must bow to my fate. There seems no alternative, but I shall always remember that in what has been the heaviest trial and affliction of my life so far, I received nothing but kindness and consideration at your hands."

It was no longer a question between the Bishop and Mr. Green. Public bodies like the Church Association and English Church Union took sides in it. The controversy now entered its second stage. On May 18, 1878, Mr. George McDonagh sent to the Bishop a petition signed by 320 parishioners of St. John's, Miles Platting, with a letter desiring that "his Lordship, as chief Shephard over us, will cause an inestigation, and Stop what is a scandel to our protestant reformed church. But we take higer ground, and Say if such teachings permeate the minds of the people, the Almighty Judgments have been and will be swift and sure" (Palm 94). The petition itself sets forth that "It is with feelings of deep sorrow that we now publicly testify to the propogation of false doctrine and deadly error by the Rev. S. F. Green, of St. John-the-Evangelist's, Miles Platting, Manchester . . . . and therefore pray that your Lordship will use the great power committed unto you, and irradicate this abominable idolatry, so that God's blessings may freely descend upon us." *

* The original spelling and composition of the Letter, &c, are preserved in the text as one indication of the character of the controversy.

To this letter and petition the Bishop replied May 20, 1878:

"I beg to acknowledge the receipt of a petition signed (you inform me) by 320 parishioners of St. John-the-Evangelist, Miles Platting, in which the petitioners publicly testify to the propagation of false doctrine and deadly error by the Rev. S. F. Green, the rector of the said parish, and call upon me to use the power committed to me to eradicate this abominable idolatry.

"I respectfully submit to the petitioners that, as no particulars, either of the idolatry or of the false doctrine and deadly error alleged, are given, I can take no steps, either by way of remonstrance or otherwise, against the inculpated clergyman.

"I have not counted the signatures to the petition, but I observe, upon a cursory examination of it, that whole families of five, six, and, in one instance, seven persons, have signed it at once, and that whole groups of signatures are evidently in one handwriting, and are not, therefore, the signatures of the persons whose names they profess to give. This fact very much weakens the value of the petition in my eyes."

The guarded character of this reply is probably attributable to the significant postscript appended to his letter by Mr. McDonagh. "P.S.—This and any correspondance ensuing it is purposed to make public.—G. McD." Such a postscript could not fail to have premonished the Bishop that the occurrences at Miles Platting were upon the brink of notoriety. The Bishop also may be pardoned for not having discovered "the particulars" of the petitioners' charge, seeing that the petition consists of eighteen pages, the first nine of which are occupied with signatures; then follow eight blank pages; and upon the last page come the charges.

"Mr. Green said in our house, in presance of us all, that he confessed once a month to a fellow Priest, and that he got more comfort therefrom than if he confessed to God. . . . and in a sermon, on the evening of 16th December, 1877, said, if a person died without recieving the Sacrament he knew they would go to Hell, and that their name was plotted out of the Book of Life; but that if a person took it they were safe."

These charges against Mr. Green were never substantiated, for the Bishop in a letter of May 23, 1878, said, "he must be excused from taking any further notice of charges made in so vague a way." Whereupon, May 27, Mr. McDonagh

2 D

wrote: "As we are but a body of working men, without the means of putting the public worship Regulation Act in force, there remains but the alternative of placing our case in the hand of the Church association." The Church Association took up the case, and upon December 2, 1878, the Bishop received a "presentation" duly signed by three parishioners. The matters charged against Mr. Green in the representation were (1) the mixed chalice; (2) lighted candles; (3) unlawful vestments; (4) kneeling during the prayer of consecration; (5) elevation of paten and cup; (6) placing the alms on the credence, instead of allowing them to remain on the Holy Table; (7) using the sign of the Cross towards the congregation; (8) consecrating so as to prevent the people from seeing him break the bread or take the cup in his hand; (9) unlawfully, and in a ceremonial manner, and as a part of the service, raising the cup; (10) a large cross of brass on the Table, or on a ledge immediately above the same, and appearing to form part thereof; (11) a baldacchino. It will be observed that in this list of charges the two counts of Mr. McDonagh's petition do not appear. Immediately upon the receipt of this "presentation," the Bishop wrote to Mr. Green:

December 2, 1878.

MY DEAR MR. GREEN,—I am sorry to have to inform you that a "presentation" by three parishioners, complaining of certain practices of yours in the conduct of Divine Service, has been made to me under the provisions of the Public Worship Regulation Act. The Act empowers me to stay proceedings, "after considering the whole circumstances of the case," if I think it expedient so to do: and nothing certainly can be farther from my wishes than ecclesiastical litigation in this diocese. It was the unanimous opinion of the bishops assembled in the Lambeth Conference, this summer, that no change in accustomed ritual ought to be made in a church against the admonition of the bishop: and, whatever may be your opinion of the authority of the Courts which decide ecclesiastical suits in this country, I hardly think you could refuse submission to a principle, so reasonable in itself, thus laid down. If you call at the registry to-morrow, you can see the "presentation" and the matters complained of; and I hope myself to be there at one o'clock, when I shall be glad to see you. It ought not to be difficult to you, as a point of principle, to submit to the direction of your bishop—under protest, if you please—in a matter of this kind; but if you refuse to do so, it seems to me that I have no choice but to allow the proceedings to go on. I should do so with infinite regret, but I have no alternative.

The Bishop also requested the complainants to give him an interview, but the controversy having now passed from the three petitioners to the Church Association, the complainants "declined to submit to the direction of the Bishop." In a letter, written five years afterwards, when the controversy was ended, the Bishop, alluding to this refusal of the complainants to submit their case to him, says:

"If ever such another case should arise within my jurisdiction, and the complainants refuse to submit their case to my direction, and I further know that some extraneous association, like the Church Association, is at the bottom of the business, I will put my *veto* on the proceedings. The interference of such associations between parishioners, clergy, and their bishop, is a great injury to the peace of the Church."

The interview with Mr. Green took place December 3, 1878, and was the turning-point in the course of the Miles Platting story. As when men stand at the parting of two ways, a single step makes all the difference in the after-journey; so was it at this critical hour in the story of Miles Platting. Single sentences were fraught with irretrievable issues. The present duty, however, is not to surmise what might have been done, but simply to relate what actually took place. An extract from the Bishop's call-book, under date December 3, 1878, records:

"Rev. S. F. Green, St. John's, Miles Platting: Would not see the 'presentation.' Declines to place himself in my hands, or to give up his practices. He said he did not think he should be saved if he gave up the mixed chalice."

In pencil underneath is written, as if in correction of the last clause, and to give Mr. Green's very words: "I should deny my Lord and imperil (or peril) my own salvation."

On December 20, Mr. Green wrote to the Bishop, in explanation of this assertion, that "no historical fact appears more certain than that the whole primitive Church regarded the mixed cup as part of the institution of the Holy Communion; and my conscience binds me to resist any attempt to tamper with our Lord's Institution."

The Bishop, at the interview, told Mr. Green that after twenty-one days, "the matter would be set beyond his power." Whereupon Mr. Green inquired: "Will you not exercise your discretion and stay the proceedings?" To which the Bishop replied: "How can I suspend an Act of Parliament in my diocese, *meo mero motu?* That's not what my discretion means." Thus the interview ended without any approach to agreement, and the Bishop received no further communication from Miles Platting till December 23, the date at which his right to intervene expired. Upon that day he received from Mr. James Wilcock, one of the churchwardens of St. John's Church, a letter "requesting the favour to present a petition from the Communicant members of the Church, relative to the proceedings with which the Rector, the Rev. Sidney Faithhorn Green is threatened." To this request the Bishop replied without a moment's delay.

December 23, 1878.

SIR,—I regret to say that the matter referred to in your letter of this day's date has now passed out of my hands as regards any discretionary treatment, and any petition presented to me by any party or parties in respect of it cannot in any way affect the course of proceedings. The Act follows a period of twenty-one days from the receipt of the representation for the bishop to consider "the whole circumstances of the case," and during that interval he has a discretionary power to stay the proceedings. I see by to-day's papers that the Bishop of Lichfield has just exercised this power in three cases in his own diocese; and by the happily wise readiness of the incumbent in each case to make the concessions required by the Bishop to bring the ritual of his Church within the limits prescribed by law, the Bishop has been enabled to stop litigation, and at the same time, I hope, to give satisfaction to those who appear to have had just grounds for complaint.

I should have been only too glad to pursue the same course; and for this purpose I had an interview with Mr. Green on the 3rd inst., in the hope that I might induce him to give up such usages complained of as were manifestly against the law—viz., the mixed chalice, the lighted candles, and the use of vestments—and that so, I might have felt myself justified in staying proceedings. As, however, he was absolutely immovable, and even refused to look at the 'presentation,' I was compelled to say, which I did with profound regret, that I had no alternative but to let the case go on, and as the next step has some time since been taken, as recognized by the Act, and the complainants have declined "to submit to the directions of the bishop," I am simply helpless in the matter, beyond being obliged to discharge those Ministerial Acts in giving effect to the Statute, which a mandamus from the Court of Queen's Bench would compel me to discharge, if I refused to do so. I may, and I do, regret profoundly the position of things, but I am in no way responsible for it. I cannot refuse to carry out an Act of Parliament.—I remain, Sir, yours faithfully,

J. MANCHESTER.

In due course the St. John's Communicants' memorial was conveyed to the Bishop, who, in acknowledging its receipt, pointed out that a large majority of the signatories were women, that some of them betrayed their ignorance in their handwriting, and that only about twenty-five per cent. appeared to be parishioners. To this it was replied that, in every place, the majority of worshippers are women; that it is hard to taunt the very poor, whose opportunities for self-improvement are limited, with ignorance; and that in all town congregations, a considerable element will be found to be extra-parochial.

But the importance of the Miles Platting case lies in the principles involved, not in the attendant personalities. Upon Mr. Green's side, the contentions were:—that the usages complained of were part of the inalienable inheritance of the Church Catholic; that they added dignity, beauty and richness (important elements, especially among the poor) to the worship of Almighty God; that the legal decisions concerning these uses were so contradictory, as to leave good room for large liberty and legitimate doubt; that it is unjust to punish those whose violation of the rubrics (if there be any violation) is a violation by reverential excess, while those who violate the rubrics by defect go unpunished; that the "aggrieved parishioner" is often a person who never attends, except for hostile purposes, the church with whose services he professes to be aggrieved; that the Public Worship Regulation Act is the enactment of Parliament, a secular body; that, therefore, it is no part of Church Law; and that, moreover, the courts which administer the Act are not Spiritual Courts. To these pleadings, the Bishop replied, that whatever his own sympathies and predilections might be (and they were always on the side of liberty), and however deeply hostile he was to the policy of associations like the Church Association, and notwithstanding his scanty liking for the methods or provisions of the Public Worship Regulation Act, yet the Act was an Act of the Legislature which he was bound both to administer and obey; that the *veto* empowering him to stay proceedings under the Act was not an *absolute* veto, but a veto *conditional* upon reason given; that he was unable to assign any reason which would in his opinion be held sufficient for staying proceedings; that, for all practical purposes, the Ecclesiastical Courts were Church Courts; that the citizen's plain duty, while using every constitutional means for changing a law of which he disapproves, is, to obey the law so long as it is the law; and that, finally, notwithstanding obscurities, the law concerning the mixed chalice, vestments, and altar-lights is discernible enough (especially when interpreted by history and long prevailing custom) to claim obedience.

The conflict at Miles Platting was the conflict of these opposing contentions. Both sides were earnest, and fully persuaded of the integrity of their cause. The issue of events alone could decide the question between them. In describing these events it is unnecessary to recount the slanders, outrages, bitterness, and fury with which the contest was darkened; it is needful only to recount the determining facts.

On June 14, 1879, the case came on before Lord Penzance; the charges were established, and in August a monition was issued to Mr. Green, who had not appeared before Lord Penzance, prohibiting him from using the ceremonies and vestments complained of. That monition was disregarded, and an order followed inhibiting Mr. Green from performing any services of the Church, or otherwise exercising the cure of souls. The inhibition was disobeyed. Mr. Green continued to officiate, using the ceremonies and vestments, which he had been admonished to discontinue, for upwards of a year. Mr. Green was then declared guilty of contumacy and contempt. On the 25th of November, 1880, Lord Penzance issued a *significavit* to the Court of

Chancery of the County Palatine of Lancaster, notifying to that court Mr. Green's contumacy and contempt; the writ *de contumace capiendo* was issued on the 9th of March, and on the 19th of the same month, Mr. Green was arrested and lodged in Lancaster Castle; the warrant for imprisonment being thus grounded not upon his ecclesiastical offences, but upon his contempt of court.

The spectacle of an earnest, hard-working clergyman incarcerated for contempt of a court which he conscientiously believed *not* to be a court with valid jurisdiction over his ecclesiastical practices was a spectacle which saddened the hearts of good and true men; and of none more keenly than of the Bishop of Manchester. But the question was, *how* to accomplish Mr. Green's release. Many suggestions were made, but nothing short of submission to the Court seemed to be effectual to procure that release; and this submission Mr. Green was resolute not to make.

Meanwhile, the services at St. John's Church were being conducted by Mr. Cowgill, who, in 1877, had, without the Bishop's licence, entered upon duty as Mr. Green's curate. In April 1881, the complainants in Mr. Green's case brought this fact under Bishop Fraser's notice, alleging that Mr. Cowgill conducted "the services with the same illegal ceremonies for which Mr. Green stands condemned." In a letter, dated September 2, 1881, the Archbishop of York wrote to Bishop Fraser, "not in his official capacity, but simply as a friend," that "the position of things at Miles Platting, *as described to me*, is somewhat of a weakness to us. One man is in prison for disobedience to the Court about vestments; and another man continues to use them with the Bishop's licence." To this letter the Bishop replied:

September 4, 1881.

The present Curate of Miles Platting has never held my licence (as you seem to suppose), but I have allowed him to remain, or, rather, have taken no steps to remove him, at the risk of being thought inconsistent, rather than occasion a scene of tumult, such as was witnessed at Hatcham, and does not even yet seem to have come to an end there. The congregation is largely a congregation of non-parishioners; they would resist to a man almost any change, and the parishioners have been estranged, and would not easily gather round a new man. As two years of inhibition expired on 9th August last, and at the end of three years the living becomes *ipso facto* void, I thought it best to wait for what seemed a natural termination of the embarrassment.

A little before this time, an effort had been made by the Archbishop of York, Dr. Thomson, to induce Mr. Green "to submit himself to the judgment of his own bishop," and suggesting that "there could be no dishonour or compromise of principle in such submission." To this, Mr. Green replied very civilly that, "he had refused that course (of obeying the ruling of his bishop) two and a half years ago, and saw no reason for retracting his refusal now." Hereupon, and in view of the impracticability of placing another curate in charge of St. John's before the voidance of the living, the Archbishop of Canterbury (Dr. Tait) wrote to Bishop Fraser:

September 10, 1881.

This, however, appears to me very necessary, if nothing else can be done, that it should be made perfectly clear that the difficulty as to Mr. Green's liberation arises solely from his determination not to obey his Bishop. May I suggest that it would be well for you to write a public letter to him calling upon him to leave the regulation of his service with you, and pointing out that the difficulties in the way of his release would disappear if he agreed to obey you?

In compliance with this suggestion, the Bishop wrote:

UFTON RECTORY, READING, *September* 14, 1881.

MY DEAR MR. GREEN,—You will, I trust, have no difficulty in believing me when I say that I have regarded the whole course of proceedings, which have resulted in your present imprisonment and separation from your parish and people, with the gravest anxiety and regret.

I could not but foresee the issue from the very first; the law was certain in the end to assert its superior strength over the individual who contested it.

It was with this knowledge that, at the interview which I had with you before these proceedings commenced, I so earnestly endeavoured to persuade you to bring your ceremonial practices within those limits which the law allowed, and which you yourself recognized, or, at any rate, did not exceed, in the earlier years of your ministry.

I said that you might throw all the responsibility upon me, and that in any explanation you might offer to your people, you could tell them that you made the concessions solely and entirely because your Bishop desired you to do so.

My efforts were ineffectual, and as, in my view of my office, I did not feel myself justified in interposing to protect a clergyman, however zealous and conscientious, who was openly and unquestionably breaking the law of the Church, as that law had been interpreted by tribunals whose constitutional authority both he and I had recognized when we were ordained—at least, which were in existence then, and whose jurisdiction we had both tacitly accepted—I was obliged, though with the greatest possible reluctance, to let the proceedings take their course.

I have had no opportunity of interfering since, and if I had attempted to do so, my interference probably would have been as ineffectual as it was at first.

But now that every appeal to reverse or stay the proceedings under which you have suffered has failed, it has been suggested to me by those whose authority I am bound to regard—the Archbishops of both provinces —that I not only might, but that I ought to, make one more effort to bring this painful state of things to an end.

I am told that if you would only consent to submit the regulation of the services of your church to me, as your Bishop, the Court by whose sentence you have been thrown into prison might be moved, by an arrangement with the other parties to the suit, to direct your release, a step which would be manifestly impossible so long as you determine to act in opposition to all constituted authority.

Surely you ought to find no insuperable difficulty in doing this. One of the practices for which you have been inhibited—the use of the mixed chalice, and which you told me at our interview you could not give up without peril to your soul—has been, not a fortnight ago, admitted by Dr. Pusey to be "non-essential," and does not come within either the terms or spirit of the rubric which deals with "the ornaments of the Church and the ministers thereof."

And this whole class of questions falls so expressly, by the very constitution of the Church of England, within the province of the Bishop, that I cannot understand how any conscientious scruple, in matters which no one can pretend touch the foundations of the faith, need create a difficulty in your mind.

Let me briefly recall to your memory your actual position in regard to your ecclesiastical obligations. You were ordained in 1865. The present Court of Final Appeal—its recent modification, half-a-dozen years ago, does not affect the question—was constituted, if I remember rightly, in 1832. You must have accepted this, therefore, as "the order of this Church of England," or, at least, as part of it, according to which you were "called to the Ministry of Priesthood." At the same time you declared that you would "reverently obey your Ordinary . . . following with a glad mind and will his godly admonitions, and submitting yourself to his godly judgments."

At your institution to the Rectory of St. John's, Miles Platting, in 1869, you declared that "in public prayer and administration of the sacraments you would use the form prescribed in the Book of Common Prayer, *and none other*, except so far as shall be ordered by lawful authority."

Without discussing the modern interpretation of the Ornaments Rubric, there are some of the usages for which you have been condemned—such as that of the mixed chalice, which certainly cannot be protected by that rubric—which are not in the order prescribed in the Book of Common Prayer, and from which, accordingly, you declared, on your admission to your present living, that you would abstain.

And as for the Bishop's right to interfere in a matter of this kind, it rests upon the simple and direct language of the Preface to the Prayer Book concerning the service of the Church.

"Forasmuch," says that document, "as nothing can be so plainly set forth but doubts may arise in the use and practice of the same, to appease all such diversity (if any arise), and for the resolution of all doubts concerning the manner how to understand, do, and execute the things contained in this book, the parties that so doubt, or diversely take anything, shall always resort to the Bishop of the Diocese, who by his discretion shall take order for the quieting and appeasing of the same, so that the same be not contrary to anything contained in this book. And if the Bishop of the Diocese be in doubt, then he may send for the resolution thereof to the Archbishop."

I must call upon you, therefore, as your Bishop, to put an end to a grave scandal which is causing grief to Churchmen of all parties, which is separating you from the parishioners, whose souls were committed to your cure and government; which is imposing hardships which no one desires to see imposed upon yourself and your family, and which, I am afraid, is likely, if prolonged, to lead to yet further distress and embarrassment, ending finally in your deprivation, by adopting the course so plainly indicated to you by an authority the spiritual character of which you can hardly dispute.

I would readily, if you preferred it, leave the "resolution thereof" to our common Metropolitan. He can have no prejudice in the case, and may be trusted to decide the issue on the broad ground of judicial impartiality.

The whole responsibility of any concessions you might be required to make would be thrown upon me or upon him. You would be doing what, I think, is demanded from you by the obligations which, as a clergyman, you voluntarily assumed; you would be restored to your people, among whom you would still be enabled to minister, without let or hindrance, "the doctrine and discipline of Christ" in all things which a reasonable mind would say are essential to their building up in the faith, or their growth in holiness; and if it involved a sacrifice, it would be a sacrifice made in the interests of peace, for which, says Bishop Jeremy Taylor, we are bound to be as zealous contenders as for the truth itself.

I most earnestly pray that you may be guided to a right mind in a matter vitally affecting, not your own personal interests alone, but those of the Church to which you belong, and in the hope that so it may be,—I remain, your faithful Brother and Bishop,

J. MANCHESTER.

P.S.—As the matter has become one of such wide public interest, there seems no escape from the necessity of publishing this letter, and your answer to it when received.

Mr. Green's reply, omitting the portions which were merely personal, ran substantially thus:

September 17, 1881.

My Lord,—It is indeed surprising to read that "the mixed chalice does not come within either the form or the spirit of the Ornaments Rubric." Dare any one deny that a cruet for the water was one of the *necessary* ornaments of the church in the 2nd year of Edward VI., far more so than even the organ for the music or the censer for the incense, for the use of water was then obligatory? And if there be a water cruet, how is that cruet to be used? Surely according to the unvarying tradition of the Church. Does your Lordship know that in condemning me for this you are condemning the generation of God's children? Do you think that Bishops Andrewes and Cosin, Wilson and Horsley, were unmindful of their ordination vows? In what a plight do you thus find yourself! Who would not rather say, "Sit Anima mea cum sanctis," rather than with the carelessness and neglect of a later age? You must surely know that Dr. Pusey's words in this connection mean that the neglect of the water *does not invalidate the Sacrament*. My Lord, when a clergyman has once realized that Christ instituted the Sacrament in wine mixed with water, and that the Universal Primitive Church by its practice recognized that this action of His was not fortuitous but designed, he will not begrudge the little extra trouble which a conformity to Christ's institution entails, and an attempt to hinder by violence a reverential exactness of this kind; will seem to him a monstrous disloyalty and insult to Christ.

Perhaps the most startling passage in your Lordship's letter is the following: "The Court of Final Appeal was constituted in 1832: you must have accepted this as the Order of the Church of England." Surely you must be aware that it was only by an oversight, as Lord Brougham himself acknowledged, that Appeals connected with the Church ever came before the Court at all. To read your letter one would suppose that Church *and* Realm is equivalent to Church *or* Realm, Lords *and* Commons to Lords *or* Commons. But I respectfully submit that it is absolutely impossible from the nature of things for the State to make an Ecclesiastical Court, or Court of the Church. How can people, not members of the Church at all, constitute a Church Court? I can conceive no greater abuse of words than to call a court in its origin and constitution extraneous to the Church an Ecclesiastical Court.

There is another important question which your Lordship has raised—that of obedience to Episcopal authority. Now I am thankful to say that I require no reminder of my duty in this respect, for I have ever held that there is no tie more solemn, as well as tender and affectionate, than that which ought to unite a Chief Pastor with his flock, whether priests or people. A right-minded priest will be anxious in all things to follow the least wishes of his spiritual father, and it will be a sore grief to him when, through any cause, obedience has to be refused. For, my Lord, all obedience to men is conditional. Above the Bishop is the Church and the Lord of the Church, and where obedience to the former clashes with the duty owing to the latter, obedience to the Bishop must give way.

My Lord, I cannot refrain from indignation that you should have asked me to give up my conscience into your keeping, and shift all responsibility on you. You can only have suggested such a thing on the supposition that in your estimation the things in dispute are of no moment; but if that be the case why, in the name of justice and charity, hand me over to be prosecuted at all?

One word more. Your letter threatens me with further consequences, and with deprivation. Be it so. *Malo mori quam fœdari.* What I am going to write now, I write in sober seriousness as before God—and not, I hope, as an empty boast. If the choice were given me between death, and whether I would subject our Master, Christ, and His beloved people at Miles Platting to the outrage that any mere outsider, living in open contempt of His ordinances, should order the Divine worship in His house; or, were the choice given me between death and the subjection of this glorious Church of England to Lord Penzance's Court—an insult which would not be tolerated by the humblest denomination in the kingdom—I trust by God's help I should not fear to die. I do not mention this as a great thing, but simply as the ultimate thing. The men of Rorke's Drift and Cabul surrendered their lives for what is a mere trifle in comparison.

The Bishop's reply, omitting the personal part, and recording only those portions pertinent to the principles involved in the controversy, ran thus:

September 21, 1881.

DEAR MR. GREEN,—My one desire is, if possible, to put an end to a state of things, which not only painfully distresses me, but is a matter of profound regret to all right-minded men. I wish, if it can be done, to see your prison doors thrown open, and yourself restored to your people and your duties.

There is one passage in your letter on which I build hope. You say that you "require no reminder of your duty, in respect of obedience to episcopal authority."

May I interpret this—my Chaplain, Archdeacon Norris, who is with me and has read your letter, thinks I may—to mean (1), that you hold your promise, and more than promise, of canonical obedience to me, as your Bishop, as binding on your conscience as ever; and that you are willing to return to your cure of souls at St. John's, Miles Platting, under the solemn obligation to me, as your Ordinary, which the oath of canonical obedience imposes?

And, if so, would you consent (2), if at any future time your judgment should differ from your Bishop's as to what canonical obedience requires of you, to accept the joint determination of the Archbishop of the Province with his suffragans? If you accept this interpretation of your meaning, then let it be the basis of a conversation between yourself and Archdeacon

Norris, who, by his own wish, proposes to see you to-morrow between one and two o'clock. The practical result at which you may arrive had better be committed to writing, to avoid the possibility of future misunderstanding.

If you accept my interpretation of your language, I should then be in a position to take whatever step may be possible for me to restore to you your liberty.—I remain, yours faithfully in Christ,

J. MANCHESTER.

At the close of the interview with Archdeacon Norris, Mr. Green wrote to the Bishop:

"I am at a loss to know why I should be required to assert that I hold my promise of canonical obedience as binding as ever. I certainly do say so *ex animo*—and have never since my ordination held otherwise."

This declaration of Mr. Green's the Bishop sent to Mr. Gladstone, stating that—

"It seems to me sufficient to justify me in asking whether you can request the Queen to exercise her prerogative of pardon and to release Mr. Green from gaol. . . . I do not know whether I am asking for a thing which can be done; but I am sure I am asking for what, *if it can be done*, would be a relief to many minds, and to my own among the rest. If Mr. Green would have submitted himself to me when these proceedings were commencing, I would gladly have interposed between him and his prosecutors; and it was only when he peremptorily refused to alter the practices, which had been condemned by a Court, the authority of which I felt bound to recognize, that I, most reluctantly, felt obliged to let the proceedings go on."

Mr. Gladstone at once put himself in communication with the Lord Chancellor and Home Secretary. Rumours also spread that Mr. Green had "submitted to the Bishop;" and were "popularly understood," writes Mr. Green, "as a concession of those principles for which I have been contending." Whereupon, "to prevent all possibility of misconception," Mr. Green wrote to the Bishop:

October 25, 1881.

(*a.*) By canonical obedience I understand obedience to the rules or laws of the Church, and that it is a part of the office of a Bishop to see that such rules are observed.

(*b.*) That if there be any rule (κάνων) of the Church unobserved by me, and the Bishop require me to mend my neglect, I am bound by my promise made at my ordination to obey him—and God will punish me if I do not.

(c.) That my obligation to obey the rules of the Church is, like the obligation to obey the moral law, entirely independent of whether the Bishop thinks it his duty to require obedience to them or no.

(d.) That should a Bishop order what is inconsistent with a rule of the Church in the name of some other power, we must obey the Church and take the consequences.

(e.) That there is a rule of the Church (the Ornaments Rubric) which orders lights, vestments, incense, and the mixed chalice, and that so long as it remains a rule of the Church there is no possibility of *canonical* obedience, in the strict sense of the words, except by conformity to that rule.

(f.) That with regard to things as to which there is no κάνων or rule, Bishops can hardly expect obedience in deference to complaints made by outsiders, and which are purely vexations.

I have written thus fully for the purpose of enabling your Lordship at once to cancel any intervention you may have exercised on my behalf, if such intervention be based upon a misconception.

The Bishop replied:

October 27, 1881.

MY DEAR MR. GREEN,—I should have replied to your letter by return of post, but that I have been to Cambridge, and only returned this evening. You have, of course, a full right to put your own interpretation on what you mean when you profess "canonical obedience." I would only observe upon your definition that by "canonical obedience" you understand obedience to the Rules or Laws of *the Church:* that *that* is not the language of the oath, which runs, "I will pay due and canonical obedience to *the Bishop* in all things lawful and honest." I had hoped—faintly, it is true, but most sincerely—that through the intervention of the Bishop there might have been a relief found from the present painful state of things; but with the limitations that you put upon your sense of the obligation of obedience I feel at once that this hope must disappear. I deeply regret it, as I had hoped that you might have been able to conform to your Bishop's admonitions without violating your own conscientious sense of duty.

To Mr. Gladstone the Bishop wrote:

October 31, 1881.

Mr. Green's view of canonical obedience puts an end to the faint hope I had previously entertained that there might have been a way found in which the Queen might have been asked to exercise her prerogative of pardon, without thereby weakening the constitutional obligations of law. Certainly, when I appealed to you, I did so on this ground. That appeal must now, at Mr. Green's own wish, be considered as cancelled.

In the course of another letter to Mr. Gladstone, November 7, 1881, the Bishop writes:

"In dealing with Mr. Green I take this ground: The interpretation of the Ornaments Rubric is uncertain. The custom of two hundred years is against the revival of the vestments. Their revival, on no recognized principle of ecclesiastical usage, cannot be left simply to the discretion of an individual minister or a single congregation. The revival has not had the sanction of the Bishops or of any ecclesiastical authority. The convocations have said that it ought not to be allowed without such authority. It is fraught with danger to the peace, unity, and higher interests of the Church. I, therefore, as your Bishop, call upon you on these grounds to discontinue the use of them. I think I should then be taking up ground that would have the best precedents in its favour. Augustine certainly says in his letter to Casulanus (Ep. 36): '*Episcopo tuo in hac re noli resistere, et quod facit ipse sine ullo scrupulo vel disceptatione sectare.*'"

At this time also, on November 25, 1881, after much anxious thought, the Bishop issued his celebrated Admonition to the clergy assembled in synod, as related in our Chapter on Diocesan Conferences. One of the objects of this admonition was to meet the difficulty felt by Mr. Green in submitting to Parliamentary Law in matters Ecclesiastical. An admonition from the Bishop himself, requiring that the maximum of ritual in his Diocese should not exceed the ritual of the Cathedral Church, was at least free from the objections raised against Parliamentary dealings with the ceremonies of the Church. When, however, Mr. Green declined to obey this admonition, the Bishop, with a sad heart, relinquished his last hope. "I really do not see what more you can do," wrote Archbishop Tait to Bishop Fraser. "Oh! how I wish you could have seen your way to comply with my admonition!" wrote the Bishop to Mr. Green.

The Miles Platting Story now enters its third and penultimate stage, the stage connected with Mr. Green's release from prison. This part of the story also must be recorded, like the rest, without reference to the contemporary clangour of words, the hot resolutions of party gatherings, the petitions of both clergy and laity on this side and on that. Two circumstances need only be noted. First, that the Bishop, with the same kindly inconsistency with which he did not remove Mr. Cowgill from St. John's (though ministering without his licence) also did not raise any objection to Mr. Leeds, in January 1882, assisting Mr. Cowgill, who was suffering from anxiety and fatigue. Next, that the Bishop, after declining in December 1878, to stay the proceedings, had no longer, in the eyes of the law, any power or status in the case. The law recognized only the complainants and the accused clergyman. Behind the complainants, however, by their own acknowledgment, was the Church Association; and "Mr. Green," writes Sir Percival Heywood, the Patron of St. John's, in a letter to Bishop Fraser, August 1882, "being a member of the (English) Church Union, has elected to be guided by that Society in his action hitherto." *It is impossible to understand the Miles Platting Story without distinctly remembering that it is the narrative of a struggle, not between two individual persons, but between two rival Ecclesiastical Associations; representing two antagonistic Ecclesiastical contentions.* In April 1882, the Bishop, being in Lancaster, wrote to Mr. Green, offering "to come and see him, to confer in a kindly spirit and with a sincere wish to find a door of escape from present and future difficulties." Mr. Green, however, declined the offer, and the struggle of the two rival Ecclesiastical Associations was left to drag its painful, weary length along.

Mr. Green's inhibition remaining in force for three years, the benefice of St. John's, by the operation of the Public Worship Regulation Act, became void—unless in certain contingencies, which had not happened. These three years having expired in August 1882, Lord Chancellor Selborne, who had taken a deep interest in the case, was of opinion, as he wrote to the Bishop, that:

"The proceedings have had their full and final effect in law. . . . and that, under these circumstances, it is no longer necessary, for any legitimate purpose of maintaining the authority of the law, that either the inhibition itself (for disobedience to which Mr. Green was declared contumacious and committed to prison) or the declaration of contumacy and contempt, or the imprisonment founded upon it, should continue in force, though they cannot be said to have so fallen to the ground as to be *ipso facto* determined in law."

But the question arose, *How* can he be released? Mr. Green not having submitted to the Court, the Court could not *proprio motu* discharge him. There must be some one to apply. If Mr. Green himself had applied, all difficulty would have been at an end. But such an application would have implied a recognition of the authority of the Court, and, if Mr. Green had been willing to recognize the authority of the Court, he need never have been imprisoned at all. Clearly he would not apply; yet, writes Lord Selborne, "it seems to be against all sound principle that the law should be made an instrument of keeping any man in prison (it might even be for the term of his life) not for any necessary purpose of justice, but only because he will not ask to come out." The promoters of the suit did not think fit to apply for a release. Indeed, to have done so, under the existing circumstances, would have been an acknowledgment that their whole proceedings had been an error. The only person left (seeing that the Law Officers had advised that "it would not be constitutionally proper for the Crown to interfere") was the Bishop. But the Bishop had no *locus standi* before the Court; he was not legally any party in the case. Moreover, as he wrote to Lord Selborne, October 17, 1882 (not because he felt any unwillingness to apply for Mr. Green's release, but in order to clearly forestall the difficulties),

"Sir Percival Heywood, the Patron of the benefice, has distinctly told me that Mr. Green has elected to be guided throughout in his conduct by the English Church Union; and that body, by the mouth of its president, has also distinctly proclaimed that it will treat deprivation by the Public Worship Regulation Act with the same contempt with which it has treated the Monition and Inhibition, and Sir Percival Heywood, in the most solemn language, declared at the Church Congress at Derby, that he did not and would not recognize Mr. Green's deprivation, but would assist him with all his power to maintain his rights as Rector of the parish as fully as before. If, therefore, Mr. Green were liberated from prison before the benefice is filled, he would come back to the parish, resume his old position there, claim and exercise all his old rights as incumbent. And, as Sir Percival has declared that he will not recognize the deprivation, of course he will not exercise his rights as patron and nominate to the benefice another clergyman for me to institute, who would then have rights against an intruder. The living must accordingly remain void till the right of nomination lapses to me; and as the notice to Sir Percival under 1 and 2 Vict. 106, 58, was only given on September 28, this event cannot occur till April 28, 1883."

Three days afterwards, however, the Bishop, having resolved to run the risk of all difficulties in his desire for Mr. Green's release, wrote again to Lord Selborne:

"I have had the opportunity, this morning, of considering your Lordship's memorandum with my Chancellor, Mr. Christie. I think I am not wrong in assuming, from the tone of the memorandum and of your two letters, that you are of opinion that I am the most proper person to make the application to the Judge of the Provincial Court of York for the release of Mr. Green. If this release is to be unconditional, I foresee the future difficulties which I have already indicated in my previous letters to your Lordship.

"But as I am as anxious as any person can be that Mr. Green's liberation should be effected, and my Chancellor advises me that, although I can in no sense be considered a party to the suit, I may properly make such application, I shall, on arriving in Manchester to-morrow, direct my secretary to take the necessary steps for that purpose."

On the 4th of November, 1882, the Bishop applied by counsel to Lord Penzance to direct the liberation of Mr. Green. The Bishop's motion was not opposed by the promoters of the suit, the application was successful, and Mr. Green was, the same day, released from prison.

Meanwhile the vacant living of St. John's had been sequestrated, as the law required, and the Rev. W. R. Pym, Assistant-Curate to the Rev. H. B. Hawkins, Vicar of Lytham, had accepted from the Bishop the temporary charge of the Parish.

The Miles Platting Story now entered upon its final stage. The Public Worship Regulation Act had asserted its authority; resistance by the clergy to enactments of the legislature had been proved to involve, in the ultimate issue, the penal consequences of inhibition, imprisonment and deprivation of benefice. But, to avoid the recognition of the right of Parliament to deprive an Incumbent of his benefice, Mr. Green resigned his living. The resignation, however, by Mr. Green (November 4), was five weeks later than the Bishop's announcement to the Patron (September 27) that the living was vacant under the operation of Statute Law. Here was another opportunity for divergence of opinion. *How* was the living voided? " By the operation of Statute," replied one party. " By the resignation of Mr. Green," replied the other party; but both parties agreed that the living *was* vacant, and on November 8, 1882, Sir Percival Heywood, the Patron, announced his intention of presenting to the benefice the Rev. Harry Cowgill; whom, it will be remembered, the Bishop had refused to ordain in 1874, on account of his utterances concerning the Judicial Committee of the Privy Council; and who, without the Bishop's licence, though with his knowledge, had officiated in St. John's Parish from 1877–1882. During these five years Mr. Cowgill had practised the same ceremonies for which Mr. Green had been inhibited and ultimately deprived.

The question now arose, whether the Bishop should institute to a living a man bent upon continuing the self-same ritual for which his predecessor had been compelled to forfeit it. Upon his side the Patron contended that Mr. Cowgill was a fit and proper person to be presented; that three beneficed clergymen had signed the Letters Testimonial, which was all that the Bishop could legally require in addition to the oaths of canonical obedience, etc., which Mr. Cowgill was willing to take; and that to require from a nominee to a living any promises not specified in law was an act of episcopal autocracy towards the nominee, and an infringement of the Patron's rights. Upon his side, the Bishop contended that it was unreasonable and injurious to institute to a living a nominee who would continue to practise the very ritual for which his predecessor had been deprived; and that any cause which was sufficient to lead to deprivation was sufficient also to justify the refusal to institute.

The following document—preserved in the Bishop's own handwriting, and entitled, "Memoranda by the Bishop of Manchester on the case of the Rev. H. Cowgill, refused Institution to the Rectory of St. John's, Miles Platting"—is a clear and concise statement of the Bishop's grounds for refusing to institute Mr. Cowgill:

"Mr. Cowgill has been officiating in the parish as Assistant-Curate since 1877. *He has never been licensed.* He applied for a licence, but the Bishop refused to grant one. The Bishop did not refuse permission to officiate, because he felt that the size of the parish required two clergymen; and, as he could not dispossess Mr. Green, the Rector, he did not think it right to refuse him the aid he needed in discharging his ministrations to the parish.

"For several reasons the Bishop did not think it necessary or desirable to use the power given him by Section 13 of the Public Worship Regulation Act to sequester the living during the inhibition of Mr. Green, and appoint a Curate-in-charge of his own selection. For (1) he preferred not to move, *pendente lite,* and thought it best to wait till he could act with full effect. (2) The way in which the Bishop of London had been baffled, under similar circumstances, at St. Alban's, Holborn, and the (late) Bishop of Rochester at St. James's, Hatcham, was not encouraging. (3) Mr. Green was in residence and possession, and was certain to resent any such act. (4) The congregation and the churchwardens (the latter and a large portion of the former *not* being parishioners) were certain to aid the Rector in any such resistance. *But it is not true that no notice was taken by the Bishop of these illegal proceedings.* It was with special view to the case of the five or six churches in the diocese, where similar illegal ceremonies are practised, that the Bishop, in a Synod of the clergy of the diocese, held on November 25, 1881, issued an admonition to the clergy, that in no case should they, in the ceremonial of their churches, exceed the standard of the ritual of the Cathedral—which admonition was specially sent to Mr. Green, at that time a prisoner in Lancaster Gaol, *though no attention was ever paid either by him or by Mr. Cowgill to its direction.* Other admonitions of a less formal character had been addressed by the Bishop to Mr. Green in 1871, and again in 1877.

"The special incidents of this case are as follows: September 27, 1882, the Bishop announced to Sir P. Heywood, as Patron, that the living of St. John's, Miles Platting, had become vacant by the statutory deprivation of the Rev. S. F. Green. Sir P. Heywood duly acknowledged the letter, but at a meeting of the working men's branch of the E. C. U. held at Derby, at the time of the Church Congress, he declared that, 'so help him God,' he would not recognize the deprivation. On October 24 the Bishop offered the charge of the parish to Mr. Cowgill, on condition of his reducing the ritual within the limits of law, and on the same day the living was formally sequestrated. On October 31 Mr. Cowgill declined to accept these terms. On November 2 the Bishop licensed the Rev. W. R. Pym to be Curate-in-charge during the sequestration; on October 28 the Rev. S. F. Green writes a letter to his late parishioners to the effect that, in order to save Sir P. Heywood from the cost and trouble of disputing the legality of the deprivation, he had placed his resignation of the living in his hands;

and on November 4—the same day on which an application for his release from prison was made to Lord Penzance, and he was, in fact, released—the Bishop received a letter from Mr. Green, saying that he had resigned. Of course the avoidance under the Statute having taken place on June 27, there could be no real resignation, and the Bishop replied to Mr. Green accordingly.

"On November 8 Sir P. Heywood, wrote a letter to the Bishop, in which he announced his intention of presenting the Rev. H. Cowgill, and on November 28 the formal document of presentation was sent to the Bishop's secretary. On November 22, 24, 28, the Bishop received letters from Mr. Cowgill praying for institution at the earliest date, in order that the parish 'might get settled down again before the season of Advent set in.' On December 2 the Bishop had his first interview with Mr. Cowgill, with the view of ascertaining, according to the 39th Canon, 'his worthiness for this ministry.' A second interview was held on December 13, and a third on December 15. Before the second interview Mr. Cowgill sent in to the Bishop's secretary a protest, to the effect that he being ready to comply with what he assumed to be the only conditions that the Bishop was legally entitled to require, the Bishop had no right to refuse institution to him."

In the course of these interviews, Mr. Cowgill had stated that he held "certain ceremonial acts and usages (*e.g.*, the use of vestments, of the mixed chalice, and of the lighting of candles ceremonially at the ministration of the Holy Communion), declared illegal by the highest judiciary tribunal, to be *not* contrary to the discipline of the Church of England; that he had practised them while officiating as Assistant-Curate of St. John's, Miles Platting; that he would give no promise or undertaking not to continue to practise them." The Bishop, moreover, asked Mr. Cowgill whether, if he should become rector of St. John's, Miles Platting, and his Bishop should admonish him to abstain from or discontinue the use of the practices in question, he would feel himself bound to submit himself to the Bishop's judgment according to his Ordination vow and the directions in the Preface to the Prayer Book "concerning the services of the Church"? This question, to which the Bishop attached great importance, and a satisfactory answer to which (as he said to Mr. Cowgill) would remove all his difficulties, Mr. Cowgill declined to answer, adding, that "having laboured with Mr. Green, whom he respected more than any man in the world, he should regard himself as worse than Judas Iscariot towards Mr. Green if he undid his work." "This," said the Bishop, "reduces the Declaration of Assent and the Oath of Canonical Obedience to a nullity." The Bishop felt he could not, consistently with his sense of duty, institute Mr. Cowgill to the benefice. If he had done so, besides the other reasons which he stated in his notice to the Patron, he would have been doing a signal injustice to Mr. Green, who would have been deprived for using the same illegal ceremonies which Mr. Cowgill meant to continue.

After consultation with Mr. Chancellor Christie, the Bishop, therefore, addressed to Sir Percival Heywood, the Patron of St. John's, the following letter, announcing his intention to refuse to institute Mr. Cowgill:

MANCHESTER, *December* 18, 1882.

SIR,—I deeply regret that from a sense of duty to the discipline of the Church, and in the exercise, as in the sight of God, of the "authority committed to me by the Ordinances of this Realm," I feel myself unable to institute the clergyman whom you have presented to me—the Rev. Harry Cowgill—to the rectory of the church and parish of St. John's, Miles Platting, of which you are the Patron.

I still more deeply regret that by selecting this clergyman—against whose personal character, however, I would be understood to bring no charge—you have placed me in a most painful position, and have left me no alternative.

The causes which led to the deprivation of the late Rector, Rev. S. F. Green, are notorious. Can I, without assisting others to trample on the law of this Church and Realm, and to defy all constituted authority, institute to the same benefice a clergyman who admits that he has practised there the same illegal ceremonial acts for practising which Mr. Green was deprived, and who, I have every reason to believe, means to continue and repeat the same illegal ceremonial acts, if and when he should be instituted to the benefice?

The illegal acts, with regard to which I have examined Mr. Cowgill, and to which I refer, are the wearing of illegal vestments—an alb and chasuble—the illegal and ceremonial mixing of water with the wine, and the ceremonial lighting of candles (or causing them to be lighted) at the administration of the Holy Communion in the church of St. John's, Miles Platting.

All these ceremonial acts Mr. Cowgill admits that he has done while acting as Assistant-Curate of the parish of St. John's, Miles Platting. He defends them on grounds the validity of which I cannot admit. And, though he declined to give any engagement or promise that he will not continue to do these same things in the future, he said that "I could not expect him to undo Mr. Green's life-work, and that he should consider himself as acting like Judas Iscariot to him if he consented to do so."

Mr. Cowgill, in a protest which he has handed in to me, claims that, inasmuch as he has fulfilled, or is ready to fulfil, all the legal obligations which the bishop is entitled to require—producing his Letters of Orders, and the Letters Testimonial signed by three clergymen of the diocese, and being ready to make the Declaration of Assent, and to take the Oaths of Allegiance and Canonical Obedience—I have no alternative but to institute him.

But I am not satisfied with the Letters Testimonial. In them the subscribing clergymen state that, "having had opportunities of observing his conduct," Mr. Cowgill "hath not at at any time, so far as they know or believe, held, written, or taught anything contrary to the doctrine or discipline of the Church of England." These clergymen are fully aware of the illegal acts which Mr. Cowgill admits that he has practised during the time that he has been officiating as Assistant-Curate of St. John's, Miles Platting, and that he practises them because he holds them to be lawful, and not contrary to the discipline of the Church of England, though the said acts have been declared to be illegal by the Court of Final Appeal in Causes Ecclesiastical. On this account, therefore, I am not satisfied with the Letters Testimonial.

With regard to the Declaration of Assent, which Mr. Cowgill says he is ready to make (in which he assents to the Book of Common Prayer, and declares that in the Administration of the Sacraments he will use the form in the said Book prescribed, *and none other*, except so far as shall be ordered by lawful authority), Mr. Cowgill has already made that Declaration when he was ordained, and yet it has not prevented him from introducing into the Administration of the Holy Communion forms not prescribed by the Book of Common Prayer, nor ordered by any lawful authority. The Declaration of Assent, therefore, as it would be taken by Mr. Cowgill, is no guarantee that he will not continue and repeat the same unlawful acts which he has practised hitherto, and for practising which Mr. Green has been deprived. With regard to the Oath of Canonical Obedience to the Bishop, Mr. Cowgill refused to answer the following question, when formally put to him : " If you should become Rector of St. John's, Miles Platting, and your Bishop should admonish you to abstain from, or discontinue, the use of the above-named things and practices, should you feel yourself bound to ' submit yourself to his judgment,' according to your Ordination Vow, and the directions in the Preface of the Prayer Book ' concerning the services of the Church ? ' " And lastly, when asked what he meant by " canonical obedience to the Bishop," he said he meant, " Obedience to the Book of Common Prayer ; " and, when further pressed that the Prayer Book did not prescribe the mixed chalice, and asked how he would act if the Bishop admonished him to give up that practice, he replied that the Bishop surely would never require him to give up what was part of the Institution of Christ.

And thus the Oath of Canonical Obedience, administered in one sense, but taken in another, is no security against the continuance and repetition of the illegal acts which Mr. Cowgill has hitherto practised in the Church of St. John, Miles Platting.

On these grounds, therefore,

1. That, during the time that Mr. Cowgill has officiated as Assistant-Curate of St. John's, Miles Platting, he has repeatedly and persistently violated the law of the Church of England, as declared by the supreme ecclesiastical tribunal of the realm, in wearing illegal vestments, and using a chalice in which water has been ceremonially and illegally mixed with the wine, and lighting, or causing to be lighted, candles in a ceremonial manner, and not for the purpose of giving light, at the Administration of the Holy Communion, and that he holds these usages to be lawful, contrary to the laws and discipline of the Church of England, as declared by the said supreme ecclesiastical tribunal;

2. That I am not satisfied, for reasons already alleged, with the Letters Testimonial produced from three beneficed clergymen;

3. That the Declaration of Assent and the Oath of Canonical Obedience, as understood and taken by Mr. Cowgill, are no security against the continuance and repetition of such illegal acts; and that I have every reason to believe that Mr. Cowgill will continue and repeat such illegal acts if he should be instituted as Rector of the Parish of St. John's, Miles Platting;

I feel obliged, after long and anxious consideration, and with deep reluctance, and only in discharge of what I conceive to be a solemn duty resting upon me to maintain the order and discipline of the Church, and the proper authority of the law, to refuse to institute the Rev. H. Cowgill to the Rectory and Parish Church of St. John's, Miles Platting; and I hereby communicate to you, as Patron of the same, this notice of my refusal, which I shall be obliged if you will acknowledge. I have expressly stated to Mr. Cowgill how gladly I should institute him, if I could only be convinced in my conscience, and according to my sense of the obligations belonging to my office, that I could properly do so.—I remain, Sir, your obedient servant,

J. MANCHESTER.

To Sir PERCIVAL HEYWOOD, Bart.

In the mind of Sir Percival Heywood this letter aroused very grave considerations. Was Mr. Cowgill being justly treated? Were his own rights as Patron being infringed? Were the wishes of the communicant members of St. John's congregation, who earnestly desired Mr. Cowgill's institution, not being unduly ignored? Was the Bishop not going beyond the limits of Episcopal authority in refusing to institute Mr. Cowgill? Were not the liberty and the Catholicity of the Church of England at stake in the matter? In order to try these issues Sir Percival determined to contest, in a court of law, the Bishop's right of refusal.

On December 22, the Bishop (having formally notified, three days previously, to Mr. Cowgill that he could not institute him to the living) held an interview with Sir P. Heywood, which resulted in nothing; and on the 26th Sir Percival wrote a letter to the Bishop, in which he stated that—

"he must either seek in a Court of Law to protect his right of patronage, or must ask Mr. Green to receive back the resignation which he had placed in his hands and to take his old place in the rectory from which, in generous consideration for me, he withdrew."

On January 21, 1883, the Bishop received a letter from Sir P. Heywood, informing him that he had directed his solicitors to vindicate his rights as Patron in a court of law; and on January 22 a formal writ of *Quare impedit* was served, and acknowledged the same day.

After the lapse of nearly ten months the case came before Mr. Baron Pollock, in the Queen's Bench Division of the High Court of Justice. For the purpose of laying his views before counsel, and particularly the grounds upon which he had acted, the Bishop prepared a Memorandum from which extracts have been copiously taken in the foregoing pages. At the close of the Memorandum occur the following remarkable words, setting forth the spirit in which the Bishop desired his action to be defended in the Courts of Law:

"*The Bishop hopes that counsel will be instructed to argue the case on the broadest possible grounds of obvious legality and common sense, and not entangle it in the smallest measure with mere technicalities, as he wishes the importance of the issue that is raised should be made intelligible to every one who wishes well to the principles of law and order, and the preservation of those principles in the administration of the discipline of the Church of England.*"

The case was so argued on December 10, 11, 1883, the Bishop's counsel being Sir Farrer (now Lord) Herschell and Mr. Jeune; the Patron's counsel being Mr. (now Mr. Justice) Charles and Dr. (now Sir) Walter Phillimore. After six weeks' consideration Mr. Baron Pollock, on January 22, 1884, delivered his verdict, the judgment being given, with costs, for the Bishop. The effect of this judgment was to leave the presentation to the living in the hands of the Bishop, by lapse; but he wrote on January 27 to the Rev. H. R. Heywood, a brother of the Patron:

"I am most anxious to meet Sir Percival on any terms consistent with my duty, and which may put an end to a state of things which from the very beginning has been the cause not only of much embarrassment, but of sincere regret to me. I have no wish to avail myself of the presentation. I would much rather accept a presentation from your brother, if only he will nominate a clerk who will conform to the law in matters of ritual, as that law has been authoritatively declared;"

—"the maintenance of which law," he wrote, January 25, to Mr. Oliver Heywood, also a brother of the Patron, "has been my only object in recent proceedings." Sir Percival, however, informed the Bishop that "he could not bring himself to suggest the name of any clergyman for the living." Accordingly, the Bishop collated, the rector chosen being the Rev. T. Taylor Evans.

Thus ended this celebrated case. During its progress many passionate outcries, on both sides, were evoked; and, perhaps, for all time, opinions may continue to differ concerning the comparative value of the various principles involved, and the best method of promoting them. Both sides of the story have been equally told, with all the impartiality of which the writer was capable, in order to make perfectly intelligible and clear the character and importance of the great principles at stake. It is pleasant to add, in the language of the Venerable Archdeacon Anson, who enjoyed, throughout this whole period, the privilege of close intimacy with the Bishop, that, "even to his most intimate friends, not a single unkind word ever fell from the Bishop's lips about Miles Platting."

The case of St. John's, Cheetham Hill, resembled, in its most important historic feature, the case of St. John's, Miles Platting. Its story may, therefore, be appropriately told with exceeding brevity. The living of St. John's, Cheetham Hill, in the patronage of the Bishop, became vacant in November 1884, through the acceptance by its Rector, the Rev. T. W. M. Lund, of the chaplaincy of St. Mary's Church for the Blind, Liverpool. When Mr. Lund's resignation was sent to the Bishop, it was accompanied by a memorial praying the Bishop to appoint, " as successor to their dear Rector," the Rev. C. F. Gunton, who for nine years had served as Mr. Lund's assistant-curate. This memorial, being signed by the whole body of Church workers, and almost the whole adult population in the parish, had great influence with the Bishop; and he would doubtless have presented Mr. Gunton to the benefice, but for certain charges laid before him impeaching Mr. Gunton's soundness in the faith. The nature of these charges will be easily understood from the following letter:

January 3, 1885.

MY DEAR MR. GUNTON,—I told you at our interview on Wednesday last that, being in grave perplexity upon the most difficult matter that I have ever had to deal with as a Bishop, I had done what seemed to be my duty, and laid the whole case before my Metropolitan, the Archbishop of York, and was waiting for his reply. When I had received it, I said you should hear from me again, and that it might be necessary for me to ask from you some clear and unequivocal assurances of your conformity to the doctrines accepted by the Church of England and required to be taught by its ministers. I laid before the Archbishop your Essay, read at the Manchester Clergy Society, upon the question, " Who is this Son of Man ?" Of this document the Archbishop says, " This Essay is one of two things: it is the production of one who strives to startle by a paradox a number of those who hold and teach the old belief, which he too holds, into a suspicion that he does not; or else he is prepared to bring down the conception of Christ to a Socinian level. I think that the latter is the true supposition; but either is fatal to his qualities as an Incumbent, appointed by the Bishop to take charge of a large parish. One idea runs through the whole; that the teaching of Christ is the operative part of the Gospel, and that the Personal Acts and Powers of Christ are not. Could you, after reading the Essay, feel sure that he does not mean to lower the conception of Christ below the standard of the Nicene Creed ? In my own mind I feel sure that he does."

This is the impression left by your Essay upon the mind of one of the clearest thinkers of the present day, utterly untainted by prejudice, and who cannot possibly have any *animus* against you. Such, too, as I told you, was the impression left upon me by what I described as "a most unbalanced Essay" . . . . How could I, even in deference to the most strongly expressed desire of an almost unanimous parish, and however much I esteem you for your personal qualities and zealous work, appoint to a parish of which I am Patron, as Bishop, one of whom it could be alleged, with any show of probability, that he held Socinian opinions of the Person and Work of Our Lord Jesus Christ? When, therefore, I am asked to appoint you to the Incumbency of St. John's—in addition to the evidence of fitness and desert which your nine years' honest work in the Parish supply—I have a right to ask to be satisfied upon these momentous points. A Bishop's appointment is scrutinized with very other eyes than those which scrutinize the appointment of an ordinary patron. In his hands is placed, to a certain extent, the guardianship of the faith as the Church receives it. No one can pretend that the Socinian explanation of the mysteries of Christ's Being is the explanation of the Nicene Creed, or of the Church of England. This is not a secondary or subordinate dogma, framed in a theological school and bearing its stamp, where, as upon many theological dogmas, a wide variation of opinion may be allowed. It is a foundation doctrine of the Christian faith. Jesus Christ is either a mere man, "differing," as you say, "from ourselves only in degree;" or He is, as St. Paul calls Him, "the Great God and our Saviour, who gave Himself for us that He might redeem us from all iniquity" (Titus ii. 13, 14), the Owner of the "Name that is above every name" (Phil. ii. 6-11). You have laid yourself open—partly by a lamentably incautious way of utterance, also perhaps from a desire to make plain to human reason things that, from their very nature, must lie beyond it, and which, though we may see analogies to them, we only receive because they have been revealed—to misconstruction. The misconstruction was almost inevitable, when, at the close of reading your Essay before the Clergy Society, you were asked, "Does Mr. Gunton, then, believe in the Divinity of Christ?" and you declined to answer. I am bound, therefore, under the influence of a solemn sense of responsibility, to call upon you to repudiate these inferences, which have been drawn, not unnaturally, from your words. Frankness is, I know, an essential part of your character. You are incapable, from any motive, of simulating what are not, or of dissimulating what are, your real sentiments. You will tell me frankly and without *arrière pensée* (1) Whether you accept the statements of the Nicene Creed about Our Lord Jesus Christ—that He is "God of God, Light of Light, Very God of Very God, Begotten not made, being of one Substance with His Father"—as *only* applicable to Him, and as teaching His true and essential Divinity; and (2) Whether you can *ex animo* subscribe to the Second and Third Articles of the Church of England. If you have been misunderstood on these points, you ought to be the first to wish to clear away the misunderstanding; and, on the other hand, if you cannot honestly say, "This is the foundation of my teaching about Him Who is at once the Son of God and the Son of Man," you will feel how impossible it would be for me, as a Bishop with any sense of duty, to nominate you to "the cure and government of souls" in a Church, of which this doctrine is one of the chief corner-stones. An unusual, and even an excessive, pressure has been put upon me; but if, unhappily, you should be unable to give me the assurance that I ask for, no amount of pressure would make me shrink from doing what, in that case, I should regard as my simple duty. I could not comply with the memorial of the parishioners and congregation of St. John's. May He, Whom Jesus said He would send "to guide His people into all truth," in this solemn issue direct both you and me! Yours ever faithfully in Christ,

J. MANCHESTER.

Mr. Gunton's reply to these questions failed to remove the Bishop's misgivings, and he finally decided, "notwithstanding the nobleness of Mr. Gunton's character," not to appoint him to St. John's, Cheetham Hill.

"But," he added, "I recognize his high qualities, and the ties of affection which bind the people to him. It has been a source of the acutest pain even to seem to sever these. I hope he will not feel less kindly towards me, or suppose that I feel less kindly towards him. He is the very man, when he has raised his teaching to the level of such grand passages as Colossians i. 9–29, to do good service in the cause of Christ and His Church."

Widely different, in many respects, as the case of Cheetham Hill is from that of Miles Platting, yet, in both cases alike, the critical and cardinal principle of *episcopal responsibility* was the principle at stake. In the case of Miles Platting, the Bishop considered himself the vindicator of the cause of law and order, as against anarchic excess; in that of Cheetham Hill, the vindicator of the verities of the Nicene Creed, as against doctrinal defects. Controversy was intensely painful to him—especially when the controversy was with earnest and devoted men. But, if great principles were involved, he did not shrink even from the miseries which controversy often carries in its train. Happily, in the case of Cheetham Hill, both parties, when the battle was over, generously resolved to forget the wounds inflicted during the strife. In a letter to the Bishop, of February 11, 1885, after the appointment of the Rev. St. Vincent Beechey to the Rectory of St. John's, Mr. Gunton wrote:

"Allow me to thank you for your kind letter which reached me yesterday: your words of trust in me dispelled a dark cloud and lighted my heart. With you I indeed pray God to guide me and reveal the way that is well-pleasing in His sight. It is a great comfort to me to feel assured of your good-will and blessing."

CHAPTER XVII.

LETTERS.

No element in biography is more important than letters—especially private letters to correspondents absolutely trusted. In such letters the writer unconsciously delineates himself. Even the most honest and transparent men are not quite the same in public as in private life. In public utterances, the judgment is in the ascendant; in private correspondence, the heart reigns supreme. In public, men appear as they wish to seem; in private, they appear as they really are. Not that any true man has two selves—one for open show, another for hidden use. The entire life of every true man is a single, organic whole—a single, homogeneous growth; always vitalized by the same principles, always aspiring towards the same ideals. But, in public, it is the man's intellect, his reason, his conscious aims, which are to the front. In private, the throne is occupied by the affections, the heart, the unconscious self. In public, men have a bridle on their lips; in private, their utterances run unrestrained and free.

In all Bishop Fraser's correspondence no single sentence has been found which, as far as motive and spirit go, might not be published with honour. He had not two selves; but one self. In public and in private he was the same. But in private the Man, as distinguished from the Citizen or the Churchman, shone forth most vividly. With the simple desire, therefore, of setting forth the Man, James Fraser, in all the freedom of his unrestrained, unconscious self, a considerable selection of his private letters is here given. These letters are arranged, not in reference to the subjects of which they treat, but in chronological order. Several letters already published are mingled with the private letters—either because of the inherent value of the letters themselves, or for the sake of some trait in the Bishop's character which, otherwise, might be left undepicted. But the reader will perceive at once, from the superscription of the letters, which are of a public, and which of a private, character. *The letters which have no superscription and no signature were written by the Bishop to Mrs. Fraser, after their engagement and previous to their marriage.*

To the REV. E. C. MACLURE.

February 10, 1871.

I shall be glad if the few words I dropped at Blackburn about the non-political functions of the Church do half the good you are kind enough to anticipate from them. They were drawn from me almost instinctively by the spectacle that I saw all round the walls of the room in which we were assembled, of nothing but Conservative flags belonging to the different Sunday Schools in the town, of the most pronounced blue and orange hues. It is simply monstrous (as it seems to me) that our young children, before they can possibly have formed a political idea of their own, should be taught to "love their friends and hate their enemies" after this fashion.

I rejoice in your appointment to the chairmanship of the Burnley School Board, and I hope you will guide its counsels clear from sectarian shoals. I am sure that, if they frankly tried to do so in the spirit of harmony, Churchmen and (at least, orthodox) Nonconformists might agree upon a common basis of religious teaching, sufficient for all the requirements of the case. But there are some (so-called) Churchmen who seem to me to do all they can, "not knowing what they do," to denationalize the Church, and to justify her Disestablishment and Disendowment by reducing her to the dimensions of a *sect*. There is a strange dementation amongst us; I trust that it is not a token that *Deus vult perdere*. —Yours very truly,

J. MANCHESTER.

February, 1877.

Really, the title "My lord" is quite too stately. Honestly, I always feel more or less uncomfortable when *any one* addresses me in this style. When I was Rector of Cholderton, I took pupils, and among them were two brothers, William and Herbert. William was one of the nicest, most affectionate-hearted, albeit wayward, lads I ever had to deal with. After going up to Oxford, where he did not do much good, he went out to the Crimea, and was mortally wounded in the attack on the Redan on September 7th, 1855. Before sailing, he wrote me a most affectionate letter, saying that the happiest and most innocent year of his life was the one he spent under my roof at Cholderton. His uncle, Col. ——, then lived at P——, and one of his cousins had just been ordained. William, who was always devising madcap freaks of a perfectly innocent kind, made up his mind that he would walk over from Cholderton to P—— (24 miles) to hear his cousin preach his first sermon, and return the same night. He started about four o'clock, and got into P—— church after service had begun, but in time to hear the sermon. After dinner at his uncle's, he set out on his homeward journey. If I remember right, it was in February, and a terrible downpour set in at nightfall. I sat up for him till one o'clock, and then gave him up, and thought his friends had wisely persuaded him to stay with them all night, and went to bed. But between 3 and 4 A.M. I heard him ring at the bell, and went down to let him in. Poor fellow! He was drenched to the skin; there had been no moon, and he had lost his way once or twice; he must have walked fifty miles in the day. However, we got him to bed safe and sound; and there he slept, there being no possibility of awaking him from 4 A.M. on Monday morning to breakfast time on Tuesday. This is a sample of his character. His brother Herbert was more staid and very nice, but I did not love him so much as I loved William.

William was one of the most affectionate, and (when I had to deal with him) manageable of boys. He was thoroughly truthful and most warm-hearted. I had at that time a favourite and very powerful bull-terrier; and it was quite interesting to see how fond William and that dog were of each other, and the tricks of various kinds that he taught him. On one occasion his fellow-pupil dared him to walk into Salisbury and back (a distance of twenty-two miles) between 12 o'clock and dinner-time (6). William only needed to be challenged to attempt anything. So away he started with his friend "Druid," and got to Salisbury. There he must needs go to the "White Hart" to luncheon, the dog accompanying him, to the coffee-room. He was very hungry, and he thought the dog must be hungry too, and between them they made a considerable hole in the cold beef. Unhappily the waiter came into the room as he was feeding Druid, so, when the bill came in, he found himself charged with "Luncheon for two, 4s." And we had a hearty laugh over his adventure when he got home, very tired and sore of foot, but within the prescribed time. This is only a type of his general character, which was as simple and natural as a child's.

There is nothing that more often causes me "vexation of spirit" than the line that the clergy so often take up in relation to their fees. I am sure it makes the laity think that they don't believe half they preach. In many cases the income of the benefice is an ample maintenance, though many poor clergy have hard work to scrape together £300 a year by means of fees. I never was a rich rector—my first living was only £275 a year, my last £420—but I have a satisfaction in feeling that I never put a fee into my own pocket in my life. I always applied them to some parochial object. You mentioned Mr. ——'s name in your last letter. Well, I shall ever regard him as one of the links in that chain of providences which have so wonderfully encircled me. I don't know how he has ever heard of me, unless perhaps he read my report on American schools. But he asked me to be one of the assistant commissioners in that inquiry which took me into Norfolk, and I suppose that the work I did for him, added to the work I had done for two other royal commissioners, first caused Mr. Gladstone's eye to light upon me and led to my being made a bishop.

I am so delighted to find that you have the element of a little of what I will call "righteous indignation" in your nature. I confess that conduct, such as Mr. A——'s, stings *me*, and I was glad to find that it rouses you to just resentment. I *do* hate little, mean, captious, fault-finding, hole-picking natures. I hope it is not wrong to do so. I would do them no harm. Only I cannot associate myself with them or work with any satisfaction in their company.

March, 1877.

It makes me half afraid, half angry, to see the formal mechanical way in which people do, what they call, their "Lenten penances," and then rush off, only with increased ardour, to their Easter festivities. Literal fasting does not suit me—it makes me irritable and uncomfortable, and certainly does not spiritualize me; so I have always tried to keep my Lents in the nobler and more healthful spirit of Isaiah lviii. I have kept them but poorly, after all; still, I am sure *that* is the true way of keeping them.

March, 1877.

How painful it is to share feelings without being able to *do* anything to help! One can *pray*, of course; and I do pray daily and earnestly for you all. But somehow or other—I hope it is no sign of imperfect faith—*mere* prayer *never* satisfies me. I always want to put my prayer into action, and into real living sympathy. The helplessness to alleviate sorrow, or to render aid where aid is required, always makes me feel so sad. I once learnt a very useful lesson from a very little child. When I came to Manchester I was asked to preach a sermon at one of the parish churches in that great city. I went down there and took a cup of tea with the clergyman, and was introduced to the members of his family, amongst them being a little girl of seven years old, who was on the tip-toe of expectation to know what a bishop was like. I don't know what she expected a bishop would be like, possibly something like a giraffe, or hippopotamus. After I had preached the sermon, the clergyman reported to me the amount of the collections, and said everybody seemed pleased but one person, and that was the little girl, who remarked to her grandmother that, "*after all, a bishop is only a man.*"

2 F

March, 1877.

I have just been bothered, and lost half an hour, with a good Israelite of German extraction, who wished to have my opinion about the advisability of giving a public lecture in Manchester recommending the study of Hebrew. These people, who ride their hobbies, are, it must be confessed, rather a bore. One can't put them rudely by, for they are well-intentioned, and one does not wish to hurt their feelings; but they waste a great deal of time. If this good man could have read what was passing in my mind, while he was telling me a long rigmarole story how, seventeen years ago, he taught a young lady Hebrew in 270 hours, he would have made his tale a good deal shorter.

March, 1877.

I should gather from ——'s letter that his own matrimonial experience has been unfortunate; but I am bound to say that my observation differs widely from his. Among my many married friends I hardly know one whose marriage I should characterize as a "failure." Men are sometimes such brutes (I can use no milder term), unfeeling, selfish, careless of the happiness even of those to whom they are bound by the tenderest ties. I have seen such instances, and they have always deeply touched and pained me. I shall often think of poor Mrs. —— in my prayers. It must be so hard for a warm and generous nature to be thrown back upon itself by coldness and want of sympathy.

March 25, 1877.

To-day I enter on the eighth year of my episcopate—an office of which the burden and sense of responsibility certainly do not grow lighter as the years roll on. I hope that my clergy have thought of me in their prayers to-day. Bishop Vaughan (the Roman Catholic Bishop of Salford), personally, I much like, and all our personal relations are friendly. In reply to a very friendly note which I received from him, I have told him that there is nothing less likely than that I should ever join his communion, as he (I dare say quite sincerely) hopes may be the case; that I *have* endeavoured to give a serious and dispassionate consideration to the "claims of the Church of Rome," and that the result has been an ever-strengthening conviction that the voice of Catholic antiquity, no less than the rights of conscience and a rational faith, are dead against them. At the same time, I have told him I don't deny the existence of some of the highest Christian graces in members of his Church, which, whenever I meet with them, always command my admiration.

March, 1877.

I have been burying this afternoon the wife of one of our best Manchester men. She was an admirable woman, and it was quite touching to see, by the faces of those gathered round her grave, the sorrow that her death had caused. The poor husband, to whom she had been the very sunshine of life, and who is the noblest-hearted of men, wrote me a very touching letter when I told him it would be a satisfaction to me to be allowed to officiate at her funeral; and when the service was over, though his heart was too full to speak, he grasped my hand in a way that was more eloquent than words. Oh, dear, what a comfort even a kind word is to sorrowing hearts, and yet how slow we often are to speak it! The longer I live, the more I seem to realize the privilege of being able to do anything that may lessen the sorrows, or augment the joys, of others.

March, 1877.

On Saturday I was occupying a very curious position. I heard a confession, though not exactly from a penitent. As I need mention no names I shall be disclosing no secrets, and the affair will amuse, if it does not interest, you. A lady, who told me she was thirty-five years of age, wrote to me to say she was staying with friends in this neighbourhood, was troubled with a somewhat serious difficulty, and wished to see me. So I fixed Saturday morning at 10.30, and punctually to the moment she came. I found that, being a Dissenter by birth, she had been for four years a Roman Catholic, having been converted by Father ———, who has since left the Church of Rome, and become almost an unbeliever in Christianity. The confessional revolted her, though, she honestly said, nothing was ever said to her there of the kind some people suppose, but she found herself surrendering her conscience and everything else to the priest. She joined the Church of England, and finding a parish in ———, where everything was to her mind, she offered herself to the rector for any work he might have to give her, and under his directions she superintends and teaches, apparently with very good results, a Day and Sunday School in an outlying hamlet. She speaks in the highest terms both of the rector and the curate. And now she is in this fix, about which she came to consult me. She is attached to the rector (who she believes never intends to marry), and the curate has made a declaration of attachment to her, and *I* am appealed to to tell her how to act. I could only tell her that she must be true to herself and to this love-sick curate, and that, come what might of her attachment to the rector, she must not lead the curate on with any false hopes. But just fancy the woman's supposing that *I* was the person to help her with counsel in such a predicament! She kept me two hours with her tale, which she told with great minuteness, giving me all the people's names, and, when we parted, thanked me, saying that her conscience was much lighter, and her way seemed much clearer than when she came. She left me, however, with no desire to be a father-confessor in many such cases.

April, 1877.

I officiated last Wednesday at the marriage of the youngest daughter of my secretary, a nice affectionate girl of nineteen, who is married to a surgeon here, a widower of about thirty-two, with I hope, in spite of the disparity of age, every prospect of happiness. Instead of the cut-and-dried exhortation of the marriage service, my wont is to say a few simple words out of my own head or heart (as the case may be) to the young couple standing before me; and this young girl, and her husband too, seemed both pleased and touched by what I said to them. When we were all assembled in the drawing-room (I was one of the last to return from the church) she came up to me, and in the simplest and most natural way possible, and in the presence of all the company, said, "My dear Bishop, may I give you a kiss?" Of course, I could not say her nay, and she kissed me as she would have kissed her father, and I could not help silently praying that her happy, guileless, trustful heart may never know a real sorrow or care.

April, 1877.

What with one thing and another, I have been nearly driven crazy this morning. For the last hour I have had a wild and stupid Irish curate with me, who wished me to accept him for priests' orders, but who, I found upon examination, knew nothing. He had no business to bother me this morning at all; but as he was here, and had walked three miles to see me, I could not send him off without attending to him.

April, 1877.

The story from the scene of war is simply sickening. One can only hope that some good may come out of all this evil and suffering, and though, in this case, I am all on the side of the Russians, one is glad to find that these great despotic empires are not so strong as they seem, and that, in the interests of freedom, and progress, and civilization, we don't seem just yet to be on the eve of the fulfilment of Napoleon's prophecy, 'that before the end of this century Europe would be either Republican or Cossack.' ... People are too careless to discriminate between what the French call *la haute politique*, when the voice of Christianity certainly may be heard, and the wretched war-cries of political partizans, when that voice as certainly ought to be silent.

May, 1877.

I quite echo your sentiment of not liking to let one's thoughts linger among tombs. Like Wordsworth's 'Little Cottage Girl,' I never like to think of those whom I have loved, and who are but gone before, as dead. I don't dislike musing in a churchyard; I often used to do so in the quiet one at Ufton, where I mean to lay my dear mother and aunt, and where I hope to lie myself, but it never was with feelings of sadness. There is a quiet holy joy in thinking of those who are "at rest from their labours," "and their works following them." (The two last stanzas of Keble's Meditation, in the 'Christian Year,' for the 25th Sunday after Trinity, are inexpressibly sweet and soothing, and it is thus that I like to think of death.) ... I never know which impresses me with deeper and holier thoughts, an innocent, artless child of five or six, or a venerable placid face of eighty or eighty-five. One learns much of "the mysteries of the kingdom of God" from either.

May 22, 1877.

I told —— (one of my clergy for whom I have great respect) the other day (he is a slight, mild-looking man of about 5 feet 6 inches), "I do so wish you were four inches taller. You know Lancashire people like a biggish man." He is a man of thorough goodness and earnestness, and he has a wife, I believe, who worked well in —— Parish in London, who is wholly like-minded. ... There is nothing touches me more than woman's trustfulness. I cannot think how men can be—as they often are—such brutes as to repay it with unkindness or indifference.

It is all nonsense, generally, for people to pretend they can't find time for this or that. I am as busy as most men, but when I can shake off fits of laziness, which (whether you will believe it or not) are much more natural to me than fits of industry, I always discover that there is time for anything I feel disposed, or know that it is my duty, to do. I sometimes give myself a special pleasure by sternly refusing to take my pleasures till certain other duties *de rigueur* have been done. I certainly think I enhance the pleasure of enjoyment when it comes.

* * * * * *

I have never got on my legs in the House of Lords but thrice. On each occasion I felt immensely nervous, and none of my efforts have been considerable. The best, which did command respectful attention, was on the University Tests Bill. But I am so rare an attendant there that I am never likely to feel myself at ease on that floor, and your audience is the most critical, the most unmoved, the most unsympathizing (unless you can really *compel* their sympathy, as only a few great speakers can) in the world.

You compare me to Charles Kingsley. Dear me! I haven't *half* his strength or great qualities. True it is, as the French proverb runs, "Il avait les défauts de ses qualités." Nature has bestowed upon him wonderful gifts, to which I have not the slightest pretensions. No, I am just a man, with a desire—I hope a laudable one—to be of some little use in his generation, and with this happy circumstance attaching to him (for indeed he claims no merit), that in the various posts in life where God has placed him—for he has never *sought* one of them—his efforts to be of use have been blessed with success far more than he deserved. When I say I never *sought* one of the posts in which I have been placed, I must modify my words. I *did* earnestly desire my first little living of Cholderton—it was only £275 a year gross income—simply that I might make a home for my dear mother. It was in the year 1847, when my youngest brother, a darling boy, was articled to a leading firm of attorneys. Some strain on his constitution—we thought it was some tremendous work he went through in connection with a contested election in which his firm was professionally engaged—proved too much for his strength, and he died in the autumn of 1847; and it was the greatest of joys to me that I had a comfortable, simple home to offer to my dear mother and aunt, in which we lived most happily for thirteen years—I taking a number of pupils in the while—till in 1860 we moved to Ufton, and in 1870 to Manchester. I admit I did covet Cholderton, not, however, so much for my own sake as for the sake of others, and no happier time could be spent by any one than the years I spent there. Some day I hope to revisit those haunts of my earlier years. I still retain the liveliest recollection of those good people, and I believe they have not forgotten me.

May, 1877.

I met Mr. Gladstone at dinner yesterday, and on shaking his hand and bidding him "Good night," I could not help saying, "I have never been quite able to forgive you for having put me where the work is so much beyond my powers." He pleasantly replied, "Well, I am afraid I am hardened enough not to repent, and you are the only person in the world who has *not* forgiven me."

June, 1877.

It was a treat to hear Stanley read that 4th chapter of 1 Samuel. The new Lectionary closes this beautiful chapter just before the touching incident of Phinehas' wife. But Stanley would not deprive the congregation of the treat. And it was almost enough to bring tears into the eyes. Oh, I am sure, when you know him, you will love him as truly as I do.

June 5, 1877.

Even granted that the Revisers of 1662 left the "Ornaments Rubric" as it is, in the hope that under its cover the vestments might be revived at some more favourable time—though I don't think this is a very reasonable hypothesis—they never could have meant that any individual clergyman was at liberty to revive these, and as much more individual ritual as he might think proper to select, merely on the suggestions of his own sweet will. They surely must have intended that the revival, if ever it did take place, should take place under lawful authority. As things are, anarchy seems to be the avowed end and creed of the Ritualist party: and nothing has grieved me more than to find Mr. —— (though he has always been a weak and unwise adviser) sustaining this principle with the weight of his personal character and great authority.

June 19, 1877.

" I send you some newspaper reports and one or two letters bearing on the events of the last week. The reports blunder, as they usually do with me. A reporter with whom I once travelled on the railway told me that I went at too great a pace for them. He said I was 'the fastest public speaker out,' and he told me how many words I uttered in a minute—I think he said 250, but of this I am not quite certain. Any how, I am afraid that my rapid utterance is too much for the reporters, and this accounts for the mess they generally make of my sermons and speeches: sermons more especially, because they often deal with topics that are out of their line. However, though their reports are full of blunders (some of which I have corrected), they will give you some idea of what took place. I have just cast my eye over the newspaper reports, before putting them up. They are even more poorly executed than usual, and you can see, as you read them, where 'I made the pace too fast,' by the inextricable confusion of thoughts and language into which the poor reporter has fallen. I quite dread to see the report of one of my sermons in the papers, for it travels round the country, and I am sometimes made responsible for the most grotesque things, which never entered my head, or found utterance at my lips."

July 3, 1877.

" I send you a report of my sermon at Lichfield, which makes me think a little better of *Lancashire* reporters than of late I have been doing. I hardly know whether you will be able to make even a glimmer of sense through the ridiculous nonsense they make me utter. I began to correct it, but found the task hopeless and endless. 'The rhetoric of Chrysostom and of Basil' is transformed into 'the rhetoric of Babel,' and so on.

" I have denounced the system of the confessional as demoralizing equally to priest and penitent; but, at the same time, it is a matter of exceeding difficulty and delicacy, and, if it were properly guarded, I think we need *more* spiritual and medicinal intercourse between ministers of the Gospel and individual souls, than less. I always think that our own Church has chosen just the proper mean course, though, no doubt, as was observed in the *Spectator* for June 16, p. 747, 'this is one of the many cases in which practically speaking, half-and-half measures are more dangerous than either extreme' . . .

" It seems to me that men form their opinions as though they were quite irresponsible for them, and, as Thucydides says, 'the investigation of *truth* is a thing on which they bestow no pains, simply taking up what comes readiest to hand.' In my sermon at Lichfield I touched upon another side of the same question, when I spoke of the perils to truth from the undue exaltation of opinions. Half the religious quarrels to-day are not about what have any right to be called 'dogmas,' or truths settled by competent authority, but about opinions which have thrust themselves forward, out of their proper sphere."

July 25, 1877.

"At 5 P.M. I went to the House of Lords, and was lucky enough to hear Lord Beaconsfield defend the Pigott appointment in that speech which I dare say you read in the *Times*. It was most skilful and masterly, and quite carried the House with the speaker. But it struck me at the time as being a little *too* complete—'Methought the gentleman did protest too much'—and it seems from what took place in the House of Commons last night that some of its statements are not altogether accurate. Still, it was a wonderful performance, and, though I do not admire the man, I could not withhold my admiration as I listened with rapt attention—you might have heard a pin drop in the House—to his polished sentences, his playful humour, his skilfully constructed arguments. It was a great intellectual treat, and even in the decorous and chilly atmosphere of the House of Lords, where all enthusiasm is out of place, was received with tremendous applause."

October 1, 1877.

"What do you think of the enclosed card of Mrs. ——? The lady called to-day, while I was taking an early dinner with the clergyman who has accepted the living of Heaton Norris, and left her card with the red-pencilled lines upon it, informing my servant that she would call upon me at the registry to-morrow at 3.30!! Strange things happen to me! I wonder if all she wants is to 'shake the hand of the liberal bishop,' or whether she will try his liberality in some other form. At any rate, you may be quite tranquil as to the results of the interview, which, if it comes off, you shall know next week. She is apparently an American lady, and I mistrust that species of the sex who visit Manchester; I have generally found them publishers' agents, who wish you to subscribe to some costly illuminated work, and of whom it is exceedingly difficult, without being positively rude, to get rid."

* * * * *

"At St. Mark's, Cheetham Hill, Manchester, I ventured to speak plainly (from John ix. 8) upon a subject of some delicacy to be handled in the pulpit, viz., the consequences of the transgressions of God's natural laws, and that these consequences are to be read as 'judgments' in the sense which our Lord has taught us to put upon such visitations, viz., as *warnings*. Of course I spoke principally of the way in which passion claims the right to override all law, civil or natural; and that, just as men claim the right to marry their deceased wife's sister or niece, so they disregard the physical consequences of marriages where the relationship of blood is too near, or even when insanity, known to transmit itself hereditarily, exists on one or the other side, etc. Everything is to give way to the simple phrase, 'Oh, the young people are attached to each other, and it would break their hearts to part them!' when, in fact, the attachment ought never to have been allowed to establish itself at all."

* * * * *

"It is not my habit to keep repeating my text, as some preachers do, but it was really the keynote of my sermon, which *was* a sermon, and would not at all have suited a 'platform.' The text I chose in the evening was made up of verses 3, 13, 15 of Job xiii. : 'Surely I will speak with the Almighty, and I desire to reason with God . . . Hold your peace; let me alone that I may speak, and let come on me what will. Though He slay me, yet will I trust in Him . . .' The clue to the argument of the Book of Job is the desire of the human heart to understand the ways of God, to discover the grounds of His actions, and to harmonize these with our human ideas of righteousness; the discovery that the problem is too vast for us to solve, contains more elements than we can put into any explanatory formula; the conviction still that this world, and especially the moral world, is not at the mercy of a brute force or mere arbitrary will, but that we have to deal with a Father—a Redeemer—One Whom we can and ought to trust under all circumstances, and even in our severest trials. This was the thought the text gave me, and which I tried to work out in my sermon, using the most striking illustrations that the phenomena of the day supplied me with. I asked whether we were not losing this trust in God, and replacing it by trust in the conquests of science, in the fancied security of our commercial and industrial relations."

October 16, 1877.

"After the game of football, which I enjoyed to see, and which went on till half-past four, we went to a concert given by the boys in the speech-room. The songs were mostly written by two of the Harrow masters, but required local knowledge to be thoroughly appreciated. The teacher of music, Mr. Farmer, is a complete enthusiast, who, as Dr. Butler tells me, has been of immense service to the 'morals' of the school, by his influence over the boys; and he made the entertainment pass off in a way that was a real treat to everybody present. At 7 P.M. the Head Master, who is the most hospitable of men (and, further, has the art of making the most exquisitely tasteful speechlets after dinner and on suchlike occasions), gave a dinner to about sixty old Harrovians, at which I was present, and the evening was concluded by a conversazione (no ladies though), with tea and coffee in the library, built to commemorate the Head Mastership of Dr. Vaughan. On the whole, I don't know when I have spent two happier days than those at Harrow. Everything seemed to smile; and the views from the different sides of the hill, and especially that from the churchyard looking south, are quite glorious. I seemed, when looking on those little active lads playing their games of football—which they do not play at Harrow in the savage Rugby fashion, but in a milder and more civilized way—to be almost a schoolboy myself again.

"I left Harrow at 10.30 on Friday morning, and ran up to town for two or three hours, returning to Manchester by the 2.45 train. I wanted to buy a handsome table for my drawing-room, but the only one coming up to my ideas was one for which they asked £45. I thought it would be too great a piece of extravagance; so I shall wait till I have time to make

another cruise among the shops in Wardour Street. The man told me
that this table to make new would cost £100, and it certainly was very
handsome; but I thought I ought to get what I wanted for £30, and with
so much distress about one I really felt I could and ought to forego a
luxury; so I have given up my table, and sent off to-night £20 to the
relief of the poor Bolton operatives, who are on strike and who are not in
any union, instead."

* * * * * *

"Mrs. —— called again on Saturday morning about twelve; she is a
magnificent lady, with a figure, I should say, a good deal 'improved' by
the dressmaker; Irish, as she said I should discern from her brogue, and
extremely gushing. The precise object of her visit I could not discover.
She certainly 'shook the hand of the liberal bishop,' and she did not ask
for any money. She only asked for two things, very different in kind.
(1) Could I do anything for a brilliant Irish cousin of hers, one Dr. ——
who is quite thrown away among the people at ——; (2) would I allow
my gardener to put up some cut flowers for an evening party at the house
of the lady with whom she was staying, if she sent for them on Monday?
and then, when I said I feared it would be out of my power to do anything
for her brilliant cousin, we parted with expressions of mutual regard. I
was away from home all yesterday, and I have not seen my gardener to-
day, to ask whether he had any flowers to send her or not. But I hope
he had, or my character will not stand as high as it did in the lady's
estimation."

* * * * * *

"One of the enclosed letters opens another scene in the play with Mrs. ——.
I hope I have now done with her. In my reply I told her that my views
about woman's place and rights in society were quite obsolete and old-
fashioned; that, having been brought up in the simplest of homes, by the
best of mothers, I had no wish to see women possessing or exercising the
franchise; and that I was afraid I could offer her no career in Manchester
for her diversified talents. Among them is not the talent for writing a
very fair hand; but I dare say she is a good-natured woman, who would do
some good in her generation if she only knew how. She has returned to
her talented and eloquent cousin at ——, in whose behalf she first spoke
to me.

"I am so glad you don't aim at such grand things as Mrs. ——. I had
so much rather hear of you going round to your invalids with your kindly
presents of 'game and fruit'; and your genial voice and sympathizing
smile. And I suspect that is the true woman's way of diffusing
happiness."

October 23, 1877.

"At Gloucester the storm had quite passed away, and then for the next
hour, till I got to Worcester, I gazed intently on, I think, the very loveliest
sunlit evening sky my eyes ever looked upon. To the right and left
were dark banks of cloud, so marked and figured that I often could not

feel sure whether they were clouds indeed, or were not really lines of picturesque wood-covered hills. And all between was what looked like a fair smooth ocean of sky, of the most exquisitely delicate tints—rose, blue, green—I ever saw. I really felt quite entranced. And I seemed to read in that bright sky the very emblem of the love of God; and I thought the sky, as it lay so calm and pure between those great banks of gloomy cloud on either side, witnessing still to the storm that had just passed by, seemed to tell of a peace and joy that may be found, even in this world, by those who seek for it. It was perhaps but a foolish fancy, but I can't tell you how it held me enchained for a whole hour, and I thought I could never grow weary of gazing with all my soul on that fair, weird scene."

November 6, 1877.

"Now I will tell you how I fared in Edinburgh. I never enjoyed a visit more. The people I fell among were most kind, and the weather, on the whole and for November, was not unfavourable. My host was Sir Alexander Grant, Principal of the University. He lives in Lansdowne Crescent, which is near the extremity of the new end of the town. He was an old fellow of Oriel, though junior to myself. He married a daughter of the late Professor Ferrier, and a granddaughter of Christopher North, a very sweet and accomplished woman. He also has his mother, a venerable and most intelligent old lady of 75, living with him, and there are six children. We had a pleasant party at dinner each day, and I met most of the intellectualities of Edinburgh: Bishop Cotterill, Lord Moncrieff (the Lord Justice Clerk), Sir Robert Christison, great in the medical world, an old man of 81, but full of vigour. Dr. Rainy, one of the ablest men in the Free Church, and Dr. MacGregor, the most eloquent preacher in the Establishment, Sir James Falshaw, the first Englishman who has been Lord Provost, Mr. Sellar, Professor of Latin in the University, and another old Oriel fellow, and many others. I conceived, from what I saw on these two days, a very high idea of the quality of the best Edinburgh society. It was too late to see anything of the city on the Thursday when I arrived; but under the admirable guidance of Dr. Sandford, of St. John's Episcopal Church, I utilized Friday and Saturday mornings, and saw everything, I believe, that deserves to be seen. The weather was too hazy to make it worth while to take the 'Queen's drive'; but all the other places that you mentioned, and many others, I saw. It certainly is a grand city, both in respect of what nature and of what man have done for it; but some few of the 'sights'—Holyrood, for instance—though full of interest, hardly came up to my expectation. One of the finest buildings there will be the new Episcopal Cathedral which Sir Gilbert Scott is building, at a cost of £120,000, out of money left by a Miss Walker, the nave of which, Bishop Cotterill told me, they hope to have finished by August in next year. It promises to be a very elegant building, 260 feet long, very lofty, and with three spires like Lichfield, the central and highest of which is to be 250 feet high. It will be by far the finest church, if not the finest edifice in the city, and Bishop Cotterill (who is an old Cambridge Senior Wrangler, and a very pleasant as well as able man) was, as he well might be, very proud in showing it to me."

* * * * *

"I am sometimes quizzed about not being married. How little my quizzers dream that I am engaged! It really is a great nuisance, that people who are doing nothing that they need be ashamed of are obliged to act as though they were, simply to avoid the gossip of a meddlesome world."

To W. R. GREG, Esq.

November 17, 1877.

MY DEAR SIR,—I thank you heartily for your letter. I am most glad to have my impression of your views corrected by yourself.* When one engages, to however small an extent, in controversy, one almost inevitably and unconsciously adopts a hard tone—at least, I feel that *I* do; but, to myself, I always separate the position taken up from the person who takes it; and nothing is more contrary to my nature than to condemn a man, *more theologorum*, as morally culpable because he holds opinions different from my own. It is a pleasure to me to know many men whose opinions are wide asunder as the poles from mine, whom I can unfeignedly respect for their personal character. I hope I am not guilty of an impertinence in saying that I reckon yourself among that number. And so my controversy with your opinions is limited to those opinions. How hard it seems to have to work out the problem of life, often in so much apparent darkness! How often Göthe's prayer—if it was a prayer—rises to the lips: "More light, more light!"—Yours most faithfully,

J. M.

November 19, 1877.

"First of all, there were my ordinary letters to read and answer; and then I could not but feel excited by the telegram announcing the fall of Plevna; and then Sir Henry Cole came by appointment at 10.45 to talk to me about the Domestic Economy Congress, which is to take place in May, of whose executive committee he has persuaded me to be the President; and then came in my Diocesan Chancellor (Christie) with a matter of business; and then it was time to walk down to Manchester on my usual Tuesday's business, and then at 2.30 I had to attend a great meeting in our Town Hall—the first yet held there, to hear an address from General Sir Arthur Cotton, and a great speech from John Bright on

---

* In his letter to the Bishop, Mr. Greg had said, "I do not abandon the *hope* of immortality: I only say it is unhappily unprovable. I do not think I ever said that I definitely *embrace* the doctrine of evolution, though I confess my opinions strongly incline that way."

the subject of 'Irrigation in India'—a subject which has always had a profound interest for me, ever since my brother Edward, twenty-five years ago, constructed, as first Assistant-Engineer under Colonel Smith, the Doval Canal, and used to write home letters full of interest, prophesying what English rule might do for India, if only the Government would turn its attention to canal-irrigation. Mr. Bright's was a great speech, and it was glorious to see the way in which he was received by the great audience —I suppose a thousand people—who filled every part of the magnificent hall. He lifted the question out of the low levels of party politics, and put it in its proper position as a plain national duty, too long grievously overlooked. I was called upon to move the vote of thanks to him, and Sir Arthur Cotton, and the Mayor, which I did as well as I could, and made one point which took with the audience, when I expressed the wish that the millions which had been sunk, never I feared to return, in Turkish bonds, had been spent in fructifying the arid, but not ungrateful, plains of India. I then attended for half an hour another meeting—the annual one of the Ladies' Sanitary Association—a very useful organization for diffusing sound and useful knowledge about health and domestic economy in the homes of the poor of Manchester; and then walked quickly home. At 7.30 I had to dine at the Deanery. On my table I found the enclosed sad letter from ——. I was full of the excitement of the great occasion in the Town Hall; and was quite unprepared for such sad news. How touchingly the tale is told! I don't think I have seen this poor boy for many years, and I have no recollection of what he was like; but I can see how the father's tender heart feels the loss. I must write to him to-morrow and express my genuine sympathy."

* * * *

"On Sunday nothing particular occurred except one thing, which in my experience as a bishop is unique. I was asked to preach without any collection for any object following the sermon! So I preached on the Gospel for the day, warning my hearers of the danger of fixing the mind upon things dim and speculative rather than on things clear and practical. In the afternoon there was a special service in the church for the school-children, and I spoke in a very simple way to about five hundred of them for about half an hour, just tracing their lives up, as they ought to have been from their baptism till then; and I was immensely pleased to find how interested even the smallest among them were. There was a whole seat full of little girls, none over ten, just below the pulpit, who gazed at me with all their eyes and listened with all their ears. It was, to use a favourite and good word of yours, very 'rewarding.'"

* * * *

"I am going to a dreadful dinner to-night, given by one of our wealthy people, a very generous and kind-hearted man, to all the official people connected with one of our Institutions. It is a very dense fog, and he lives miles away, so I hardly know how we shall get there. It will be a tremendous dinner of I don't know how many courses, unless he took my message, when he invited me, home to his wife, in which I besought her to let things be a little more quiet."

December 4, 1877.

"These huge entertainments are never much to my taste, but both the host and hostess were very kind and hospitable, and madam had at last taken my hint, and reduced the number of courses considerably. There were literally only two *entrées*, and about four sweets, instead of a dozen dishes of each as on former occasions."

November 19, 1877.

"That book of Maurice's on the 'Religions of the World, and their relation to Christianity,' is always my resource in questions like that about the salvability of the Jews; and still more that great utterance of St. Peter's in Acts x. 34, 35. As to Universalism, there are certainly passages of Scripture about the restitution of all things: 'God's will is not that any should perish'—'Christ's dying for all'—which permit, if they do not encourage, the hope that there shall be a final conquest of good over evil; and that, though sin, persevered in, unrepented of, must ever separate from God, there *may* be possibilities of repentance beyond the grave, of which we know nothing, and, therefore, had better say nothing. My chief objection to the Athanasian Creed—standing, as it does in this respect, in such marked contrast to the other creeds—is that it emphasizes in so very marked a way 'the everlasting fire.'"

* * * * *

"I spent the evening at the Athenæum, chatting with some old friends, and reading the new books and magazines. I read that book which did not interest you—'The New Republic.' The author is Mr. Mallock, a nephew of Mr. Froude. It interested *me* more probably than it would *you*, because I know most of the persons whose characters are delineated, but I could not finish it, and, though it is undoubtedly clever, it is wearisome and unprofitable reading. I don't know whether you remember enough of the book to care to know who are intended under the *dramatis personæ*. Dr. Jenkinson is Jowett; Mr. Luke is Matthew Arnold; Mr. Stubbs is Huxley; Mr. Stockton, Tyndall; Mr. Saunders, Professor Clifford; Mr. Rose, Pater, an Oxford man; Mr. Herbert, Ruskin; Lady Ambrose, Lady Amory, wife of the M.P. for Tiverton; Mrs. Sinclair, a Mrs. Singleton, of whom I know nothing; and Miss Merton is a person, who, I am told, with her mother, is employed by the Romanists to entrap unsuspecting or wavering women at ——. Stanley, I hear, is very angry at the book, for its satire of Jowett. Matthew Arnold is, I am told, not at all displeased at being represented as Mr. Luke."

* * * * *

"I am concerned that —— meets with discouragement at first starting at ——, but he ought to know that the conservative instincts of the bucolic mind are almost always more or less connected with the conservation of money in the breeches-pocket. He must not be down-hearted, but take courage from the Spanish proverb which says, 'All things are on the side of him who will wait.'

"These big tea-parties, are quite a Lancashire institution, as you probably know; and though I cannot describe them as in all respects very pleasant gatherings—for they are always frightfully crowded, and the atmosphere after a little time gets almost unbearable—yet, as instruments for creating sympathy and promoting good feeling, they cannot be despised."

To the Very Rev. DEAN COWIE.

MANCHESTER, *December* 15, 1877.

MY DEAR DEAN,—I cannot resist writing to you to express my profound regret at the language in which a clergyman of the diocese, and of your own rural deanery, thought it becoming to express his opinion of yourself at a public meeting held two nights ago in the parish of St. Jude, Manchester, as reported in the *Manchester Courier* of Friday, December 14. That differences of opinion exist within the Church of England is a fact, which it is not necessary either to disguise or to explain; as long as men are free to form opinions upon grounds which have wisely been left open, it must be so; but in criticising or commenting upon the opinions—and, still more so, upon the motives—of those from whom we differ, there are bounds which Christian charity—to say nothing of the courtesy which should exist amongst gentlemen—ought, unquestionably, to impose. I think that to the minds of all who are not blinded by prejudice or partizanship, those bounds will have been held to have been exceeded in the language that was used towards you on Thursday night. There are many points on which you and I differ, and differ widely; but I feel, as Bishop of the diocese, that I ought to protest against your being held up to public obloquy. I wish you to be at liberty to make any use you think right of this letter.—I remain, my dear Dean, yours most truly,

J. MANCHESTER.

December 24, 1877.

"You will like Mr. Robert Birley's letter. He is a younger brother of the senior M.P. for Manchester, and a noble fellow; so good, so modest, so devoted to duty. For some years past he has been one of my chaplains, and a more loyal man no bishop can have in that relation. He has good private means, and not very strong health; but he has chosen for his portion one of the poorest parishes in Manchester, where he lives and labours, beloved and respected by all. About four years ago I offered him a residentiary canonry in the Cathedral, which would have been worth £900 a year, besides the position; but he preferred to stay where he is, and where he has been labouring since 1861. His family is one of the noblest here; and I should think must have spent nearly £100,000 on the erection of churches, schools, and parsonages in the last twenty years. It is quite wonderful what they do.

"Just as I was leaving the steam ferry-boat, the other night, a respectable man, but quite unknown to me, who had apparently been in the church, came up to me and said: 'I wish to have the pleasure of shaking your hand, and thanking you for your sermon. You have preached, not only good gospel, but good common sense.' I never should wish any one to say anything more complimentary of my sermons."

January 6, 1878.

"Stanley has sent me his paper on Absolution, which I read last night. It is just after Stanley's nature, which (much as I like and love the man) is too easily satisfied with picturesque explanations. Robertson's sermon on Absolution, I remember, fixed my ideas years ago on the subject; and I have re-read it this morning. It seems to me far deeper and truer, and, in this sense, more philosophical. Stanley would get rid of the idea, and of the thing, or would render it into moral 'rebuke.' Robertson keeps both the ideas and the thing, and rescues it from magic, and gives it its true place, and use, and meaning. Do read Robertson's sermon over again, and I think you will see what I mean."

To Canon Carter.

January 12, 1878.

"I must, in deep sadness, write one paragraph more. This development of medieval ideas—this materialistic conception of the presence of Christ in His sacraments—this doctrine of the necessity of absolution by a priest in the case of post-baptismal sin—this invocation, now oblique, soon, probably, to become direct, of angels and saints—this interposition of the mediation of the 'creature' at every turn, what does it all mean? Whither is it leading us? That it is within the letter of the Prayer Book, no one can pretend. That it is in harmony with its spirit, few would assert. That it is 'Catholic,' in any true sense of that word, only the boldest would undertake to prove. The Bishop of Gloucester, in his recent Pastoral, says, that this tendency is to be especially noted in 'the younger clergy.' If so, one is tempted to ask them in the well-known words—

'Juvenes, quæ causa subegit
Ignotas tentare vias? quo tenditis?'

Will the answer be returned?

'Tendimus in Latium; sedes ibi fata quietas
Ostendunt.'

It must, I am sure, become increasingly difficult for many holding these views to stay comfortably within the limits, broad though these are, of the Church of England. Some openly avow that they *have ulterior aims!* Without wishing to lessen by a hair's breadth the long-sanctioned margin of tolerance and charity, it seems to become necessary for those who love their Church, who believe in the Catholic character of its faith and order, and in the sufficiency of the provisions it has made, for every true spiritual need of the human soul, to make a stand. Year by year, we are advancing in a direction which threatens to make a rational and scriptural faith impossible. Year by year, out of the undefined ill-understood misused word 'Catholic,' new and strange dogmas and usages are evolved. And the plea is, that to some these things are a great comfort. The same plea might be urged for dram-drinking. Etymologically, and truly, that only 'comforts' which *strengthens*. And I have seen nothing to prove to me that the new school of 'Catholic teaching' is producing men and women more imbued with the true spirit of Christianity, which is the spirit of love, and of power, and of a sound mind, than that old school of English Churchmanship in which I was trained and in which I hope to die.

"J. MANCHESTER."

February 28, 1878.

"There is more than a subtle and imperceptible difference between the two versions of Heb. i. 8. 'Thy throne, O God, endureth for ever,' is, of course, an ascription of Deity to the Son: but 'God (who is) Thy throne endureth for ever,' has, as you will see at once, another significance. There can be no doubt, that either version is equally borne out by the text; if anything, the latter has more to say for itself; but the so-called 'orthodox' are afraid if they admit it, even into the margin, one more text will be withdrawn which has been used to support the Divinity of our Lord Jesus Christ. But this is just that kind of timidity about the truth which half betrays the cause that it professes itself anxious to maintain. The Bible must be translated according to the *laws of grammar*, and not according to the assumed standard of orthodoxy."

March 18, 1878.

"I have been told that one of the chief motives in determining some young ladies to marry is the thought of the numerous wedding presents they will receive; and, certainly, the thing has reached portentous dimensions. I heard a lady sighing the other day, that when she was married, twenty-five years ago, not half such good wedding presents were bestowed; and were it not that her good husband makes her a handsome present on her birthday, and the anniversary of their wedding, she did not consider her drawing-room would be half furnished with pretty things! She has no family; so, perhaps, she may be allowed to 'vex her little soul'—though she is a very nice woman—about these trifles."

March 25, 1878.

"I laughed at your adventure at the bazaar, it was like all other bazaars, simply odious; if possible, more odious still, as a means of obtaining money for a religious or benevolent object. But such is the way of the world. Their success in these parts is wonderful. There was one in Manchester three years ago for an admirable institution—the Hospital for Sick Children, at Pendlebury, at which they raised £21,000! but, really, some of the artifices resorted to were disgraceful—pure gambling. I never will connect myself with them in any way, though hardly a month passes without my being asked to be 'Patron' of one in some place or other in the diocese. I received a letter to that effect to-day. The object is to clear off a debt incurred in the repair of the church and the enlargement of the school. I have subscribed once, and I must send them a trifle more; but with the bazaar I decline to have anything to do."

To a LADY CORRESPONDENT.

March 25, 1878.

MADAM,—I do not know that I can do much to satisfy your mind with regard to the existing order of things. I have not read my friend Mr. Arnold's address on Equality, and only know it through the review of it which appeared in the *Spectator* of March 2. The reviewer says that Mr. Arnold "never tells us what he means by equality," and that while (as he was sure to do) saying many telling things in a very telling way, he " falls a great deal too much into that French school of thought which regards equality as a thing which can be measured by law and protected by restrictions or bequests." Our feelings on this subject are, I suspect, very much influenced by physical temperament. I, for instance, who have had to work up my way to my present position (which perhaps is worth a great deal more in the eyes of other people than it is in my own) by my own efforts, and those consisting in simply doing the thing that was given me to do as well as I had ability to do it, and without any thought of ulterior consequences, have not found the world so wanting in sympathy as you seem to have done, and certainly have had no reason to complain that I have had to fight an unequal battle against favoured competitors. But, then, I have had few wants, am satisfied with simple surroundings (with a preference, certainly, for what is pretty to what is ugly), and as little disposed to set any value on pomp and dignity as any one, perhaps, in the world. Hence, possibly, my contentment with things as they are, as sufficiently good *for me*; though I do not agree with some philosophers that our world is " the best possible world," which it is superfluous to try to make better *for other people*. I can truly and heartily sympathize with any and every effort to make life purer and brighter, though at the same time I am certain that the prime *source of all purity and brightness is not without us*, BUT WITHIN. I have so far cast in my lot with those who wish to abate the unnecessary vitiation of the air we breathe, which no doubt presses most heavily on those who live in the slums, and accounts probably for the vast amount of intemperance that is the curse of our population, that I am a member of an organization in Manchester which has for its aims the suppression, by force of law, of all abatable nuisances of this kind. Believing, as I do, in the wholeness of man's nature, I quite admit that his *moral* and *spiritual* are largely affected by the conditions of his *physical* being, and that it is vain to preach sermons to men and women who live in styes, drink poisoned alcohol, and breathe a corrupted and depressing atmosphere. My simple counsel to you, though perhaps you will not thank me for it, is, "Do not crave for the impossible, but make the best you can of things as they are;" and that is best done by trying to make them a little better than they are.—Yours faithfully,

J. MANCHESTER.

" Mr. —— is one of the most vehement and bitter Radicals and Liberationists in this district. He is a wealthy man, and very liberal with his money; he has the courage of an English bull-terrier, combined with its fierceness. We have had some passages-at-arms together, for he is very fierce against certain institutions which I cherish; but, on the whole, I like the man, and I think he likes me. A letter of his appeared in the *Times* the other day, which perhaps needs an explanation. A certain Mr. A—— had published a coarse letter in the paper, in which he charged Mr. —— with being in the chair at a public meeting when a certain Dissenting minister made a very vulgar attack upon me which Mr. —— (so Mr. A—— said) had allowed to pass unrebuked. Now it appeared that Mr. —— was not present on the occasion, so he published his denial and sent it to me. I replied that I quite believed that he would not allow me to be attacked ungenerously, although in many points we differed so widely; and I said that only once had I ever thought that I had received an injustice at his hands, and that was when he charged me with a want of charity in relation to the relief of the Bengal Famine, because I said that the evil was so gigantic that I did not think it could be adequately met by private effort, but that the Government ought to undertake its relief.

"I tell you all this because I like you to see that, though these Lancashire people hold strong opinions, and express them strongly, they have generous hearts! The Church of England is supposed to have no bitterer enemy than Mr. ——, and indeed he has said some most unjustifiable things about her; but towards myself I have always found him frank and fair. He was most conspicuous in backing me up in the part I took last summer in relation to the Bulgarian horrors, which I am afraid are repeating themselves with all their former atrocity, while diplomatists are shilly-shallying in a way to make the blood boil.

"The only point that gave me an unpleasant twinge when I read Stanley's noble address was that on which the *Spectator* of last Saturday fastened, where he said that the highest and best notions of God are due to Spinoza. I only know Spinoza at second-hand, but he has always been considered the most philosophical expounder of the Pantheistic theory, which, in spite of its attractions for some minds of a very high order, has always seemed to me most inconceivable as an idea, and most depressing as a creed. Paul's grand conception of God being 'all in all' was surely something very different from Pantheism. But Stanley is rather too fond of these startling paradoxes; as again, when he represents Socrates on the same moral level as Christ. But for these extravagances he might be the great religious teacher of his age. Have you ever met him? To me he is one of the most delightful of companions, the most valued of friends. One does so mourn that that noble woman, a help so meet for him, has been snatched from his side."

April 13, 1878.

" You must not compare the work that I have been enabled to do with that grand and enduring work of which the noble man (the Bishop of Lichfield), just gone to his rest and his reward, laid the foundations in those islands of the Southern Seas, where his name will live in the grateful memories of generations yet unborn. I cannot tell you how I admired Bishop Selwyn, his simplicity, his devotion to duty, his largeness of heart, his entire freedom from petty, personal, unworthy motives. He must have made his mark as a man anywhere, and I thank God that he has made it on the Church of England. The recognition, in a wider sense than it was ever recognized before, of the Church's missionary duties, is entirely due, I think, to the new aspect he gave to missionary work, and the generous chivalry with which he threw himself into it. Both he and the late Bishop of Capetown were great bishops, but Selwyn's was the purer and higher character, to my mind; there was less evidence of a desire for personal, spiritual, or rather ecclesiastical power, which, even when the motive is noble, is a perilous ambition, and which betrayed Bishop Gray into more than one false step."

To the Rev. W. GATTY.

April, 1878.

"I cannot conceive what use a Liberationist lecturer, as such, could make of so obvious a truism as my statement that the Church of England is an abstract idea, materially and legally incapable of holding property. If anybody, I added by way of illustration, were to bequeath by will £10,000 to the Church of England, it would, I believe, be a void bequest, for there is no body with the legal entity of the name which could claim it. The property, I proceeded to argue, that is vaguely called 'the property of the Church of England,' is the property of various corporations, aggregate or sole, within the Church of England, and is either originally vested in those corporations or has been transferred to them. Of the former class are such corporations as the Ecclesiastical Commissioners or the Governors of Queen Anne's Bounty; of the latter class are the whole body of incumbents. You will not find a single acre of land, or a single pound of annual income, standing in the name or paid to the account of the 'Church of England.' The gist of my argument was to show the origin of what is called 'Church property,' for it is not strictly

'Church property' at all, but property conveyed by will or gift to particular corporations by private benefactors for the spiritual benefit of particular localities. I repeat, I cannot conceive how my dry matter-of-fact statement, which was merely made to clear away vague notions of Church property, can serve the purposes of a Liberationist. It is simply the statement of an indisputable fact, adverse, no doubt, to the theory that the State, as such, endowed the Church as such, but not otherwise bearing on the point at issue.

"Yours faithfully,
"J. MANCHESTER."

April 29, 1878.

"Have I ever told you of an eccentric old Yorkshire lady, a Miss ———, who was continually sending me the most extraordinary presents—fish of her own catching, butter of her own making, sponge cakes, cabbages, all packed together in a hamper, and the fish once or twice coming in a state of decomposition, which made it hardly safe to introduce them into the house? Well, this old lady left all she had to ———; a nice house and about £8000. My Chancellor told me that the rumour was that she intended to alter the will in my favour, but her quite sudden death prevented it. I told him that if such was the old lady's intention, so far as I was concerned, I was glad that she never executed it.

May 8, 1878.

"The only drawback to *my* satisfaction was that, on returning to the waiting-room, where we had left our hats and umbrellas, I found that some one had been there in our absence and exchanged umbrellas with me. It must have been a wilful piece of dishonesty, as the umbrella he left was not the least like the one he took away, being a shabby alpaca one, not worth 3s., while mine was a good green silk one, worth a guinea. I inquired of the hall porter, but could not discover the evil-doer, and had to go away digesting my dudgeon as best I could. Perhaps my hat, which was also a good one, would have shared the same fate if it had fitted, and if it had not been protected by its broad brim and rosette, which would have been noticeable on the head of the party who was the former owner of the alpaca umbrella.

"The 'inordinate love of eating,' of which the Head Master of ——— speaks, as a *vice* of boys, I am sure goes far to stifle the nobler and more unselfish instincts of their nature."

To the RIGHT HON. JOHN BRIGHT, M.P.

May 15, 1878.

MY DEAR SIR,—May I, without being deemed an intruder upon the sanctities of sorrow, venture to offer you this simple but heartfelt expression of my sympathy and respect under the heavy blow which has just befallen you. I have often heard your life described (not long ago by our common friend, E. J. Broadfield, whose picture of your household gathering together for family prayer, and yourself reading the 103rd Psalm to them, is one that will not soon fade from my memory), and I rejoice to think it is only a type of many homes in England still uncontaminated by that fashion-service and world-worship which seems to be almost eating out the old honest heart of the nation. And she, whom you have lost, was part of this picture, and I can understand what the blank must be, now that she is gone. As a fellow Christian man, I pray that God may comfort you, and that you may still be able to say, in those beautiful words which sank so deeply into E. Broadfield's ears, as he heard you read them a few weeks ago, " Praise the Lord, O my soul, and *forget not all His benefits.*"—With much respect I remain, my dear Sir, yours very truly,

J. MANCHESTER.

May 14, 1878.

"In Blackburn the alliance between Conservatism and the Church—*religion* not having much to do with the compact—is closer than in almost any other Lancashire town. I was not surprised, therefore, to hear that my late sermon (upon political partizanship) had produced some commotion, and that two or three persons of the shopkeeping class had told Mr. Baker (the Vicar) that they meant to be present, and that, if ' that political bishop' preached one of his Radical 'sermons, they would get up and leave the church. The Vicar did not tell me this beforehand, but afterwards he said he watched these people in the gallery, eagerly listening with their hands to their ears; but, as nothing was said to wound their susceptibility, they were graciously pleased to remain till the end."

May 19, 1878.

"The Thirlmere Scheme of the Corporation of Manchester is unexpectedly to be opposed in the Lords, and the Corporation wish me to say a word in its favour; and, that I may do so more effectively, they wish me to go to see the spot. So I am going with the Mayor on Tuesday, and shall spend Wednesday on the shores of the lake, returning home on Thursday. I have told them it is doubtful whether I can be in London when the second reading comes on; and, further, that I shall be of very little use as their advocate, for I never feel at home in the cold, unsympathetic atmosphere of the House of Lords. I have never ventured to open my lips there but twice, and then without much effect. But the Corporation will take no denial, and so I am going to do as they bid me."

May 25, 1878.

"The time I spent at Thirlmere was most delightful. In the first place, we were a pleasant party, consisting of the Mayor, Alderman Bennett, Councillor Harwood, and Mr. Hill, the Engineer of the Corporation, all of them most intelligent and kindly men. Then Wednesday was a very day of days. A more complete day for enjoying beautiful scenery could not be imagined. The rain that fell on the previous night cleared the atmosphere, and all the outlines of the hills were clearly to be seen; while the fresh spring foliage of the trees, the white fleecy clouds chasing one another across the sky, and reflected in the bosom of the lake, combined to produce a scene of such exquisite effect that I thoroughly enjoyed it. I was in the midst of it from 9.30 A.M. to 8 P.M., and flatter myself that I am thoroughly prepared to pronounce an opinion on the Manchester scheme. Whatever else it may or may not do, I don't think it will interfere to the serious prejudice of the scenery. The lake will be enlarged to more than double its present size, but it will still lie embosomed, as it now is, in the same hills, and the only difference that the eye will perceive ten years hence will be that the present expanse of meadow towards Dunmail Raise will be replaced by an expanse of water, still leaving, however, a sufficient extent of green margin to diversify the view and relieve the eye. I do not feel quite certain about the extent of foreshore there is likely to be. If we draw off 50,000,000 gallons a day, and there is a drought of seventy days—an almost unprecedented length in the district—the level of the lake will be lowered 18 feet, and there will be a corresponding amount of foreshore visible, according to the steepness or flatness of the bank. But it will be a foreshore, not of brown mud, but of dark shingle—such is the present foreshore of the lake visible in many places—and it will look not unlike a beach of the sea. I do not think it will be seriously unsightly, and of ordinary grass there will hardly be any visible. The question is, however, thrown back into some uncertainty by the Examiner of the House of Lords having decided that the Preamble of the Bill does not now correspond with the altered clauses which were introduced by the Committee of the House of Commons, and his decision will either be confirmed or annulled by the Standing Orders Committee on Friday next. It is rather hard that the Corporation should suffer and be put to expense for a fault that has been committed by the House of Commons, and not by them; but so it is."

June 6, 1878.

" I send you a letter of a certain Mr. ———. How strangely people are at the mercy of phrases! This writer is evidently of opinion that my Abbey sermon was not sufficiently evangelical, had not 'Jesus Christ and Him crucified' sufficiently for its theme, probably because the Sacred Name and the conventional phrases did not occur in every other sentence. He gives, however, but a sad picture of the spiritualizing influences of some of those East-end churches; it does not seem to occur to him that there are two ways of preaching the great doctrine which he thinks alone has power to 'lift men up,' and that somehow or other the mere using of phrases has not the power of 'drawing all men unto Him.' I suppose I must just write and acknowledge the communication, which is not made in an unkindly spirit."

June 16, 1878.

"We want a new cathedral for ourselves, though I fear, from the cost and difficulty of procuring a suitable site, we shall never get it; at least, not in my time. I confess I should like to see a worthy cathedral in Manchester. What we have is a fine parish church, and nothing more; and a great cathedral like York or Lincoln is, I do believe, a great educator and solemnizer of the religious feelings of the people."

June 21, 1878.

"I send you a letter which will interest you, from an old schoolfellow of mine, who is one of the editors of 'Hymns Ancient and Modern.' He is a thoughtful man, of strong High Church proclivities, but of large sympathies. It appears that, out of the profits from the sale of 'Hymns Ancient and Modern,' the proprietors make grants to poor parishes, which is a very noble way of spending the money. I shall not go with the least heart to the Lambeth Conference. These meetings and wordy discussions are not at all in my way. I rarely come away from them feeling either wiser or stronger. But of course, being in the boat, one must do what the rest of the crew do. I cannot, however, help my own individual feelings."

* * * * *

"We had a meeting to-day, under the presidency of the Mayor, in behalf of the Haydock Colliery Explosion Fund, and made a pretty good beginning. About £11,000 has been already raised, of which £1700 has been subscribed in Liverpool, and £1000 in St. Helens. The number of deaths seems now to be ascertained as 191, and there are 82 widows and 213 fatherless children. The widows will be allowed 5s. a week as long as they remain unmarried, and the children will have 2s. 6d.; the boys till they reach 12, the girls up to 13. It is then hoped they will be able to earn for themselves. You will read with interest the Archbishop's simple and touching reply to my letter of sympathy on the death of his son."

* * * * *

"I quite felt as you did at that church. There is a smell of sacerdotalism —in the offensive sense of the word—about all churches of this type, which always makes me long, as it did you, for the 'fresh air.' I dread the reaction that is sure to come. Men (and women too) will before long rebel, I feel sure, against the trammels of this spiritual bondage, and then will come some wild rebound. ——'s daughter has sent him a description of a service she saw, the ministering clergy looking like 'banner-screens,' and their robes or trains being held up by two 'ladylike' looking young gentlemen, clothed in crimson literally from head to foot; for, if I understand it rightly, they had crimson shoes. I suppose it was some very high festival indeed. And *this* is modern Christianity, which is to guide the ignorant, bind up the broken-hearted, and cure the ten thousand ills of modern society! Pshaw! !"

June 24, 1878.

"At 3 P.M. I started by the Great Northern Railway for Peterborough *via* Sheffield. It is not an interesting line of country, and I occupied myself with a book, having the compartment to myself most of the way. I got to the Palace, a quaint and interesting pile of buildings of various dates and styles of architecture, about 6.30, and was cordially and hospitably received. It is very charming to see the Bishop in the midst of his family. I think he has six children, three of each sex. The three girls and the youngest boy were at home. Mrs. Magee is characterized by much quietness and calmness of manner. She seems full of good sense and kindness, plays the mistress of the house with much grace, and is very and justly popular. The Bishop has the knack of saying sharp and caustic things, but to *me* nothing could be pleasanter, and, if my splintered tooth had behaved a little better, I should have enjoyed my visit exceedingly. But it was rather uncomfortable, and it would not let me eat much or sleep well. I had it attended to to-day on my return home; the splintered piece was removed, not much harm has been done, and all discomfort is gone. I had never seen Peterborough Cathedral, except in passing from the railway, before. It is *very* fine, in some of its features unique, and in an excellent state of preservation. The precincts, also, are very picturesque, and the service very nicely conducted. It was a grand service at which I preached. I suspect the number was over-estimated, but there were said to be over 4000 persons present, of whom about 1200 were employés of the two great railways (the Great Northern and the Midland) that have their centre in Peterborough. They came there to support the Peterborough Infirmary. There was a voluntary surpliced choir of 150 voices, and the organ was accompanied by cornets and trumpets, which had a very grand and inspiriting effect. I think the sermon satisfied the Bishop and Professor Westcott, who were among my hearers; and you would have been pleased if you had heard the simple, manly way in which the spokesman of the Committee of the railway men, who had arranged the service, came to me at the head of a deputation when all was over, and thanked me for having complied with their request. The people at the station, too, gave me a very cordial parting as I left this morning to return to Manchester. Altogether, I was very much pleased with my visit."

June 25, 1878.

"I have had such a delightful day! Leaving my bed at 5 A.M.—rather an effort to me—I started with Mr. Burder for Blackpool by a 6.15 train, arriving at 8.55. The day was glorious; the sea lay like a mirror, the air was most invigorating, fresh, and balmy. The hospitable mayor, who is drawing the Lord Mayor of London, in all his pomp, to Blackpool for three days on July 11, and who wishes me to come and meet him, had provided a luxurious breakfast. Then came a very satisfying Consecration service, at which the large church (holding 1200 persons) was nearly filled, and I preached on 'using the world without abusing it.' Service being over at 1.30, about sixty gentlemen sat down to a splendid lunch provided by the mayor; beautiful flowers and fruits, and exquisite viands crowned the table, while through the open windows came in the fresh sea air, and we looked over the calm expanse of water, and the long piers crowded with orderly pleasure-seekers. It was all most delightful. At 2.45 I took my return train to Manchester, and at 5.30 I was again at home."

July 6, 1878.

"The author of 'Philo Christus,' and the other volume, 'Through Nature to God'—I can't say I much admire either—reduces Christianity too much into a sentiment, and, instead of an historical basis, makes all rest upon what is little better than 'illusion' (the very word he continually uses); but Stanley tells me that he is a singularly *earnest*, and Bryce that he is a very *able* man; and in society he is specially attractive. I am sure he does not doubt the fundamental principles or ideas of Christianity; but I am afraid, like many, he is more or less at sea about his evidences and actualities. Oh, how one prays for more light to dissipate these darknesses, and settle these doubts, of good and earnest men who are seeking the truth and cannot find it! and how, as one beats vainly against the closed doors which as yet bar progress, one has to fall back simply on the great and consoling truth of 1 Cor. xiii. 12, or Newman's thought, 'One step'—and the next and nearest—'enough for me.'"

July 20, 1878.

"The Bishop of —— was very pleasant. I did not hear him preach, but I did hear him speak at the luncheon. He is one of those—a large class amongst parsons—who put on rather an artificial manner when they speak professionally, which always mars the effect to *me*. It is less pronounced in him than in others I have known; but even in him it is discernible, and, so far as it is, it takes away—to my ears—from the effectiveness of what is said. I hope *I* haven't got it 'unbeknown' to myself; and if, whenever you hear me speak in public, you discover the slightest trace of it, I shall charge you, on the love you bear me, to tell me of it; for what's the good of a wife if she wont help her husband to correct his faults?"

* * * * *

"The letter of Mr. ——, which I enclose, was prompted by an absurd paragraph in a Blackpool paper, which charged me with 'giving my encouragement and episcopal benediction to moderate intemperance,' because in a confirmation address, at Goodshaw, while I said, I did not mean to say there was any *sin* in drinking a glass of beer, or in smoking a cigar, I warned the lads how a taste for these things rapidly grows; how needful it is strictly to be upon our guard; and entreated them not to get into the habit of entering public-houses on any pretext, or even joining companies where much smoking is practised. These good people, like Mr. ——, are offended unless you denounce the very act of drinking ever so small a quantity, with fanatical vehemence, almost as the deadliest of sins. I never lose a chance of speaking to young people on the perils of intemperance; but, because I do it within the limits of reasonable argument, these worthy people set me down as Laodicean in the cause."

July 20, 1878.

"I have not read Canon Farrar's volume. The subject does not profoundly interest me, simply because I feel that all speculation about it rests upon surmise, and doubtful interpretations of figurative scriptures. But I *do* rest entirely on what Farrar calls the 'larger hope,' and the thought that God made or would permit the majority of mankind to be damned—'the gospel of damnation'—is to me simply unbearable."

July 22, 1878.

"On Sunday evening I preached at Manchester Cathedral. The heat reduced the size of the congregation, but they are always attentive listeners there, and I preached from our Lord's words in the 2nd Lesson, 'Not peace, but a sword.' I could not help being amazed by the apparitor turning round, as he was conducting me to my throne, and saying in a low voice, 'Mr. Councillor —— has come in all the way from —— (about four miles), to hear *your worship* preach.' I don't know who or what Councillor —— is, though I think he is a jeweller who has a considerable gift of the gab; but it was evident that the worthy apparitor thought that the communication would give me the greatest possible amount of pleasure. I can't tell you whether 'Mr. Councillor ——' was pleased with the sermon or not."

* * * * *

"I shall spend the rest of the evening here (at the Athenæum) skimming —as is my wont—the new publications, which these brief visits to London give me the chief opportunity of seeing. I very seldom find time to go to a Club or to a Library in Manchester, and so I fall rather behind the world in my knowledge of current literature.

"At Miss ——'s wedding, at which I officiated, an amusing incident occurred. A good many of the village folk had filled their pockets with rice to give the happy couple a parting benediction therewith. Seeing the carriage leave the house, with the coachman adorned with his white cockade, I suppose they thought it contained the expected inmates; so, as I drove rapidly through the lodge gates, I got peppered with a shower of rice, which I dare say would have been kept up if the good people had not suddenly discovered their mistake. I always notice that (at weddings) the bridegrooms are much more nervous than the brides, who go through it all with wonderful imperturbability, while the poor man looks as fidgety and bashful as possible."

July 29, 1878.

"I spent a most pleasant evening at the Deanery (Westminster). I expected to meet only the 'Black Bishop,' who is a very interesting and intelligent man, and the family party—Stanley, Lady Frances, and Miss Victoria Baillie. But, to my surprise and pleasure, I found staying there Père Hyacinthe and Madame Loyson, whom I had met there once before, two years ago, and with whom I was pleased to renew acquaintance. Unfortunately, he knows no more English now than he knew then, and the conversation had to be carried on entirely in French, and at conversational French, from want of practice, I am a very poor hand; and Stanley, though fluent, is not much better, for his pronunciation is a good deal worse than mine. I was made to describe the proceedings at the conference, which, on the last day, were of a very interesting character; and it would have made you laugh to see us. Stanley, and the Père, and Lady Frances, and Madame Loyson, and myself, with the 'black bishop' a little in the background, and Victoria Baillie engaged at a side table, nominally upon a photograph-book, but I dare say slyly enjoying the scene—and me, from time to time, at a loss for a word, or a term, or a phrase, and obliged to nudge Lady Frances, who kindly and readily supplied it. (It was like Lord Beaconsfield, in *Punch*, asking the French for 'compromise.') However, I hammered through what I had to tell somehow—sufficiently well, at least, to enable the Père to understand; and, when I rose up to take my leave, Stanley, who had much enjoyed the evening (as in fact, I think, so did we all), said to me: 'Vous avez eu une leçon excellente;' to which I could only reply: 'Oui, excellente pour *moi*; mais pour vous et les autres, je crains, très mauvaise et très ennuyante.' And so I said good night to them all, and betook me to my lodgings with the resolution in my mind that somehow or other I must set to work and acquire conversational French. I don't think my pronunciation is so very atrocious, and my vocabulary is fairly full; but it is the little turns and junctures where I find myself so much at a loss. Still, on the whole, I got through better than I expected, and they were all so good-natured and so amused, that I had no need of any *mauvaise honte* in the matter."

August 3, 1878.

"My modesty—of which you are so well aware—was almost overwhelmed by the unexpected compliment that the Home Secretary—who has always been extremely kind to me—paid me in his speech the other night (as reported in Thursday's *Times*) on the Bishoprics Bill, in the House of Commons. Well, I have just tried to do my duty, and that is all; and, if by so doing I have shown that there is any value in the episcopal office, I do not know that any man can have, or need have, a higher ambition than to be useful in his generation."

August 10, 1878.

"I send you the *menu* of the breakfast; you will see it was far too grand an affair for such homely dishes as 'trifle,' and for such unfashionable amusements as speculating who was to be the happy winner of the ring, and who the unlucky winner of the thimble. As I felt *my* portion secure, the absence of the mystic dish did not trouble me. I got a good deal of bantering from some of the ladies about my bachelor doom. One lady told me I must not go to the south for a wife! Another assured me that a lady of her acquaintance—since wedded—had told her that she would have accepted me if I had asked her! So you see what sport is made of a poor bachelor—even if he be hemmed in by all the dignity that surrounds a bishop—on such occasions."

* * * * *

"Garden parties are generally uninteresting affairs; but, when there are many well-known people present, a sort of interest can be maintained by acquainting oneself with their features. I heard Mr. Spencer Wells's praises sounded in the same key at Manchester. I suppose he is one of our most distinguished living surgeons. And I, myself, have more belief in surgeons than in physicians: physic has hardly yet passed out of the stage of empiricism, and seems to go upon no fixed principles; surgery is at least founded upon an exact knowledge of the human frame."

August 13, 1878.

"Perhaps you may like to read a letter from a worthy man here, Mr. ——, (who is a violent anti-vaccinationist, and who has gone to prison several times, rather than have his children vaccinated) in which he gives his opinion of the prejudices of the medical class on his favourite topic. I have declined, as you will see, to fall in with his programme of holding a conference of the clergy. I have not much doubt that vaccination is often hastily and carelessly applied, and without due regard either to the quality of the lymph or to the constitution and condition of the child: and, as far as this is the case, there is just ground of complaint. But it seems to me, in spite of Mr. ——'s array of figures—which can almost always be dressed up to suit a purpose—that no reasonable man can doubt that the scourge of small-pox has been wonderfully mitigated since Jenner's great discovery. I am glad you don't like the women of the Mrs. —— type. Some people tell me they are very charming: my good friend, ——, is, I think, wholly on their side; but I cannot get rid of my old-fashioned notion that God meant the sexes to pursue different careers, and there are many things which women attempt and claim to do in these days, which quite 'un-woman' them in my eyes."

August 20, 1878.

"I enclose another letter upon the subject of Unitarianism. The simple answer I gave him (and which satisfied him) was that a pious Unitarian might be saved on the principle of Acts x. 34, 35, but not by his Unitarianism. I thoroughly hold the doctrine of the 18th Article, that Christ is the alone Saviour, but that men may be saved by Him, who have never known Him, or may have only known Him imperfectly or mistakenly. If one could not have this hope for those of the human race who are honestly using such light as they have, Christianity would make me a most miserable man."

August 27, 1878.

"What a strange (and uncomfortable) phenomenon it is that people who can write and say such beautiful (?) things (as pious people call them) about religion, and the peace and joy in the Holy Ghost, seem to find so little of it for themselves, and seem such strangers to all they talk about! I suppose much allowance must be made for temperament; but to persons like myself, not much given to religious demonstrativeness, all this looks very unreal, and has a somewhat sickening effect.

"But I must say a word for Huxley and Tyndall, who, with all their errors (as I deem them), certainly so far as I have seen or known, are not profanely minded persons. I don't know where the quotations came from, or whether they are real quotations, but I think I can explain each. It might be that Huxley was scathing some pseudo-religious conception of God, which he may have said represented Him as little better than a 'pedantic drill-sergeant.' Huxley *might* have said that; I don't believe him capable of saying what Mr. —— attributes to him. And then Tyndall may have been replying to Professor ——, a very eminent Cambridge man, and who has taken a very strong position against the atheistic use of the atomic theory, and has said (though I confess I don't understand the remark, for I don't know who has seen an atom) that the 'atoms have all the appearance of manufactured articles'; in other words, that they imply a Creator, or at least a fashioner; and it may have been in reply to this argument that Tyndall used the phrase which sounds in your ears so objectionable, and would do so in mine, if I could be sure that he meant it as a dishonouring description of Him whom believers acknowledge to be God. But I don't believe Tyndall again to be capable of a wanton insult to other people's faith, even though he may not himself share it."

September 21, 1878.

"What a deal of misery people make for themselves by these unbending tempers! I wonder if you ever read Mrs. Marsh's novel 'Emilia Wyndham'; it must be twenty years since I read it, but it left an indelible impression on my mind, of the misery needlessly caused, when a husband and wife are too proud to open their hearts to each other. I almost forget the story; but the impression has remained as vivid as on the day I read it."

* * * * *

"My engagements for the week are:—To-morrow (Sunday) morning I ordain in the Cathedral, the Dean preaching the sermon. In the evening I preach at St. Matthew's, Ardwick, where the service is more to my mind than in almost any other church in Manchester. On Monday I go to Heywood in the evening. On Tuesday, as usual, I am at the Registry, and I have also an extra engagement at 3 P.M. at Owens College. On Wednesday I go to Burnley to distribute the prizes at the Grammar School; in the evening my remote Archdeacons and Rural Deans come to me, and I shall have a quiet dinner party of ten. On Thursday the whole body assemble here at 11.0, and, having spent the day in discussing various diocesan matters, we shall dine together at 6.0, eight-and-twenty strong, and finish with a service which is always a very hearty one, in chapel at 9 P.M. On Friday I go to Walsall, where I have promised to preach in the parish church, and I shall return on Saturday morning in time to take a confirmation at Worsley at 4 P.M. On Sunday week I shall be preaching in the morning at Longton; and in the evening at Farington—both places in the neighbourhood of Preston."

September 24, 1878.

"The Ordination really passed off very nicely. The candidates were an unusually promising set of young m n, and the musical part of the service is always rendered with admirable taste and feeling by Mr. Pyne, our cathedral organist, who is a son of the old organist at Bath Abbey. In the evening of the day, I attended with young Hornby—a son of the Archdeacon's, who had been ordained priest in the morning—a delightful service in St. Matthew's, Ardwick, where I had before me an enormous congregation, the church being filled to its utmost capacity. I was sorry, however, that I was not, what young men call, 'in very good form,' and I did not feel somehow as though I had any special message to deliver to them; but my subject was 'walking in the spirit, and so not fulfilling the lusts of the flesh.' I got the incumbent to let me have that beautiful hymn which so struck me in that church during the mission of 1877, 'Room for the wanderer, room.' That one verse—

> "'Room in the Church below,
> Room in the Church above
> For every soul that longs to know
> The depth of Jesu's love'—

to my mind, *is* the Gospel—is what makes it a 'message of glad tidings' at all.

"The Mowbrays—he and his two youngest children Edith and Edmund, who have shot up into a young man and young woman since I last saw them—arrived about 1.30 on Monday. They considerably lionized the Town Hall by themselves, and then came up here to lunch, spent a couple of hours, and then went on to Archdeacon Balston's to stay the night. Mowbray is an ecclesiastical commissioner, so I was anxious that he should see my house, now that it has become the Bishop's residence and that everything about it has been completed. He was pleased to express entire satisfaction, and thought I was far better off than many of my brethren, with their stately, but expensive, and often uncomfortable, palaces. I should be glad if one or two of my rooms, particularly the drawing-room, were a little larger, but, on the whole, I must not complain. Mowbray was particularly charmed with my dear mother's bedroom, which certainly has a look-out that would be called 'pretty' anywhere."

September 26, 1878.

" There is no doubt some truth in the general aims of Mr. ——'s book, but the way in which he works it out is most unsatisfactory. I spoke to him of my regret at the way in which he had handled the subject of miracles, and particularly the miracle of feeding the 5000, in the Appendix, and he said he should have been glad to recall those pages! What inexcusable haste, then, ever to publish them! But it is the way of the age: no sooner does a crude thought shape itself in the mind, particularly if it is startling and contrary to received opinions, than out it must come, as eagerly as if its author were an inventor hastening to secure a patent, lest he be anticipated by some rival."

October 12, 1878.

" Here comes a ring at the bell, and this time my visitors are Broadfield and Henry Irving, and a pleasant half hour's chat I had with them. Irving is a very striking and polished man, not in the slightest degree retaining any stage mannerism (as I remember Macready so markedly did) off the stage, and full of information. He told me much about the theatre that I was pleased to hear; and said distinctly, that but for the existence of such theatres in London as the —— and ——, the tone of the stage, particularly in the provinces, was high; and here, the plays in which he is taking part, such as 'Hamlet,' 'The Lyons Mail,' 'Louis XI.,' are all of a high class, which certainly would do no one any harm to see. The Baroness Burdett-Coutts is one of Irving's most enthusiastic patrons and admirers; and you may remember a letter in which she wished to introduce him to me a year and a half ago; an introduction which the then state of his engagements prevented me from availing myself of."

To the REV. CANON STOWELL.

October, 1878.

MY DEAR STOWELL,—Your note has inexpressibly shocked and grieved me. I wrote to our dear friend when you first told me of his illness; but I had had no answer, and I was hoping that all was going on well. There was something on my mind, about which I wished to ask you when we met at Sheffield; but in the hurry of other things I could not recall it at the moment, and the opportunity passed by. I know now that I wished to ask how dear —— was going on.

It grieves me sorely that I was not permitted to press his hand once more before he passed away. I hope the funeral will be fixed so that I can pay the last mark of respect *then*. If ever any man died at his post, doing his duty, dear —— has done so. There are many good works in Manchester and Salford—especially the Bishop of Manchester's Fund—about which I hardly know how they will be carried on without him. He was a man on whom I felt I could always rely, and who, though we differed on many points, was ever most affectionately loyal to me. I mourn for him with no ordinary feelings.

I do not know Mrs. ——, and feel a diffidence in writing to her; but I do wish that you would say to her in what high regard and affectionate esteem I held her husband, and how truly, how deeply, I sympathize with her in her bereavement.—Ever, my dear Stowell, yours in all sincerity,

J. MANCHESTER.

October 12, 1878.

"I was interested (at the Owens College dinner) in looking at the heads and countenances of these young men—of all religious denominations, and of all professions, ranging between the ages of twenty-three and thirty-five, or thereabouts; and I thought, 'Well, if this is a fair sample of the products of Owens College, there is nothing to be ashamed of; and I think before long it may claim its right to take rank among the recognized universities of the day.' I told them in my speech that I thought that perhaps their ambition was rather premature. I was well placed at the dinner between the President of the evening, Mr. Wright, a high Cambridge Wrangler, and Professor Balfour Stewart, one of the authors of 'The Unseen Universe,' who told me that he and his 'collaborateur,' Professor Tait, had another book in hand of the same purpose, but more popular in character, on the side of faith, against the materialistic Atheism of the day, of which he would send me a copy when it is published. He comforted me a good deal when he said he thought the tide had turned, and that scientific men were less ready to dash their theories against revealed truth than they had been."

To a LADY CORRESPONDENT.

October, 1878.

MY DEAR MISS ——,—I am afraid I cannot modify or retract what I said. I do think that many women are reaching after impossible things; that, if they could be attained, the fabric of society would be much less firmly compacted than it is now. Exceptions only prove a rule, and I regard the cases you instance as all of them exceptions. I still hold that a woman's proper sphere of duty and of influence, speaking generally, is the home, and that it is by doing her duty and exerting her influence there, that God intended her "to make the world a bit better for living in it." If a woman has no home duties, as may sometimes be the case, in God's name let her go out as Florence Nightingale or Octavia Hill have done, and fight against "the world, the flesh and the devil" in any sphere to which God in His providence seems to call her. But these will always be the *rare instances*. I did not say a word to depreciate the truest and highest cultivation of a woman's mind, and only wished to hinder her from dreaming impracticable dreams. If you think this wrong, I must bear your criticism and your censure as best I can.—Yours sincerely,

J. MANCHESTER.

November, 1878.

"I have seen this morning Mr. Ryder, the Registrar of the diocese, who is a great wanderer on the face of the earth. Where do you think he spent yesterday evening? With John Henry Newman—they were Oriel friends in days of old—at the Oratory, Edgbaston. He gave a delightful account of the old man—now in his seventy-eighth year—and said that he asked very eagerly after my work, and sent his kind remembrance to me. I shall always desire to keep a place in that good man's esteem."

November 16, 1878.

"I think you would like 'Les Misérables' if you read it. I don't know when I have been more charmed with any French book—for I read it in the original, and I don't believe there is any good translation—than I was with this; particularly with the first volume. It fell off very much afterwards, and became wearisome towards the end. But the character of the good bishop is beautifully drawn. I have no idea who was the original that sat for the picture. Here are one or two of the sentences I culled from the book, and have placed in my Manuscript Volume of extracts. 'Le suprême bonheur de la vie, c'est la conviction qu'on est aimé; aimé pour soi-même.' 'Personne vraiment respectable . . . remplie de la charité qui consiste à donner, mais n'ayant pas au même dégré la charité, qui consiste à comprendre et à pardonner.' After a description of a poor saintly woman: 'Il y a beaucoup de ces vertus-là en bas; un jour elles seront en haut. Cette vie a un lendemain.' These are nice; and the first expresses one of my happiest convictions."

November, 1878.

"Mr. —— is a good fellow, but quite out of his place as a clergyman. I am sorry to read that, since my time, he has doubled his stud of hunters, and doubled also the number of times per week that he enjoys that not very clerical pastime. Nobody used to be fonder of hunting than myself; but, like Cornish, I used to content myself with walking to see the 'throw off,' when the meet was in my own parish or within a mile or two. Cornish asks me what I did in the way of return-entertainments to these local grandees. Well, they were pleased enough to come and dine with us occasionally, but I never put on the table a grander dinner than my own cook could dress, and never attempted anything in the way of display. I think there is no greater mistake than to suppose that people will not care to come and dine with you unless you give them I know not how many entrées and different kinds of wine."

December, 1878.

"I send you a letter I think you will like to read from a Congregationalist minister, who had thoughts of seeking admission to the ministry

of the Church of England. It touches me to find how sensitive he is to
the little kindness I was able to show him in the matter, and I could not
help wishing to thank him for his friendly feeling. My terms were such
as to present some difficulties to him, and I did not like to alter them,
because you may as well have no rule at all as a variable one; but I have
offered to speak in his favour to the Bishop of Exeter, whose conditions
may be less rigid, if he wishes it. I am sure there are many Nonconformist ministers in his position, profoundly dissatisfied with the platform
of Nonconformity, and only too glad if an opening could be made for them
to escape from it. Our system is too unelastic to deal with such cases,
and, if they became numerous, I think it would have to be largely
modified."

December 21, 1878.

"I was immensely interested with Mr. Hoare's pamphlet on Buddhism,
and, like you, was struck with the points of contact between it and
Christianity. I quite think that your theory to account for the similarity
of *details*—so marvellous in some cases—must be the true one, and that
Mr. Hoare and others assign a much earlier date to the Buddhist
'Scriptures' (as he calls them) than they are entitled to. The coin-
cidences are such as almost to necessitate the inference that one system
borrowed from the other, while the internal evidence of the Christian
narrative absolutely precludes the hypothesis that Christianity has been
the borrower. The great underlying principle of all religion—faith in
God and love to man—no doubt came from the common source, the Spirit
of all truth. I believe there is a very interesting little volume on
Buddhism, by Mr. P. David, on the S. P. C. K. list, which I have not yet
read, but which I mean to get."

January 6, 1879.

"The consecration of the two cemeteries went off very successfully on
Saturday. My failure to appear on Thursday had evidently caused much
disappointment, as the two Local Boards in great force and a large con-
course of people had assembled. They were there again, however, on
Saturday, and a few frank words of apology from me seemed to make all
right. You would have laughed if you had heard the chairman of the
Leesfield Local Board (to whom I made my 'amends,' winding up with
the expression of a hope that 'I should be forgiven,') reply in his blunt but
kindly fashion, 'Well, we'll let thee off this once,' as though to tell me I
must be more careful in the future. We parted, in both cases the best
of friends, and though it was a nasty, foggy day, and at Leesfield I had to
conduct the service and make my address bareheaded, in the open air, I
took no harm."

January 14, 1879.

"I hope —— is putting by something for old age out of that good
income that she has. If she is making £100 a year, she might easily save

£50, and that would soon roll up into a nice sum. If you write to her, give her a word of counsel in this regard. I have again and again been surprised to find how often such advice is needed, and how many persons there are who do not seem to be extravagant or thriftless, yet who never seem to see the prudence of providing against a rainy day when they have the opportunity."

January 14, 1879.

Sir,—I am unable to attend the meeting which it is proposed to hold for the purpose of endeavouring to diminish the habit of tobacco smoking among young boys. It is an evil, and it seems to me, a growing one, which I have often observed and deplored. Whatever may be thought of the habit of smoking generally, I believe that medical authorities are universally agreed that it is physically most mischievous to young people under the age of thirteen. The moral effects consequent on the too frequent association of this habit with others of a pernicious tendency are not less hurtful to the character. It has often been a matter both of surprise and regret to me that parents seem so indifferent to both these classes of consequences to their sons; and, though I have no practical remedy to suggest, I hope the meeting which you are going to hold will help to fix public attention both on its proportions and its effects. It was stated in a leading article in the *Times*, a short time ago, that so sensible is the German Government of the mischief wrought by the habit on the constitution of growing lads, that in many towns the police forbid boys under sixteen to smoke in the streets, and that offenders against this regulation are punished by fines, or, in default of payment, even by imprisonment.—I remain, Sir, yours faithfully,

J. MANCHESTER.

January 27, 1879.

"Close to All Souls' Church, where I was last night, there is one of the Free Libraries, five of which are opened on Sunday from 2 to 9 P.M. Having ten minutes to spare, I had the curiosity, in company with my friend Jeremiah Chadwick, to look in and see what number of readers were collected there. There were not more than twenty; and I am told that the number, which at the beginning was about 800 in the day, is gradually falling off, so that a doubt is begun to be felt whether it is worth while to be at the expense of lighting up for so few. This is not a very great surprise to me, but I fear it will be a disappointment to others."

February 25, 1879.

"I *cannot* 'make long prayers.' To force myself myself to do so would be mere hypocrisy, or at best mere formalism; and I have given over the attempt. Never, I think, were my prayers and praises more truly earnest than now; not merely when I am formally on my knees, but a hundred times a day, I feel my heart rising to God in thankfulness for all that 'He has done to me.'"

March 5, 1879.

"I don't know whether you care for politico-economical questions; but, if you do, I am sure you will read with interest the two printed letters of Mr. Ecroyd's, which have gone a good way towards persuading *me*. I have again and again asked the question of politico-economists, without getting an answer: 'We require to import half our food supply; we pay for it with our manufactured productions, but how are we to go on paying for it, if those from whom we buy meat and corn will not take our iron and cotton and woollen goods in payment? and, if we can't pay for a foreign food-supply, how are our people to live?' It seems madness for all these foreigners to revert to a protectionist policy; but if they cannot be shown their true interest, and the superior advantages of free trade, each country producing and freely exchanging the products, whether raw or manufactured, that it is most suited to produce, I think we shall have to adopt some counter-policy in pure self-protection. At any rate, if the question interests you, I think you will be struck with the calm and dispassionate tone in which Mr. Ecroyd deploys his arguments."

March, 1879.

"Bishop Vaughan, the Roman Catholic Bishop of Salford, is an able and accomplished man, and when we meet on neutral grounds (which, however, is not very often) we always meet as friends, and I can get on with him much better than I can with some of our narrow-minded Protestant friends. By the bye, how generously and wisely Robertson always deals with some of the most salient points of Romanism—the worship of the Virgin, the Confessional, the Seven Sacraments! He shows how they are attempts (though erroneous and perverted ones) to meet some real wants of human nature."

March 8, 1878.

"I am sorry to notice the death of that poor Professor Clifford at the early age of thirty-four. One had hoped that in time he might have righted himself on the foundations of a rational and settled Christian faith. He began his thinking life as, and continued to be up to the time of his taking his degree at Cambridge, an advanced Ritualist. The recent phase of his thoughts on such subjects, except that it was almost outrageous for its sarcastic profanity, was what one might almost expect by the law of reaction on such a mind. The comfort in all such cases, is, that we cannot know the temptations of the inner man, and that the judgment is with One who does know all, and will make allowance for all. Such cases illustrate that quotation that I made from Professor Mozley in my Oxford sermon, how in some minds tendencies to unbelief are aggravated by the attitude of the Church towards the truth."

April, 1879.

"No doubt this earth, where man has not come in and spoilt it, 'is a fair place,' and we are given hearts to appreciate its loveliness. Here again we are in complete sympathy. No pleasure is so keen with me as the sensation of lovely scenery; and I feel that it is sometimes a selfish desire to gratify this feeling that makes me long to throw off the cares of an episcopate, and 'retire to some quiet spot where one may see God's gifts spring up from the mother earth,' afar from the noise of wrangling tongues. You will remember such was dear old Dr. Hook's continual longing also. I quite feel with you about the cottages of the peasantry in Cornwall. It seems to me the first duty of a landlord to see that the people on his estate are at least as well housed as his hunters and shorthorns. No doubt there has been great attention paid to this matter in the last twenty years; but some parts of the country are lamentably in arrears still. It was one of the features that struck me most in my commission work in 1867, and which I emphasized most strongly in the report I made to the commissioners."

April 4, 1879.

"What a contrast between different parts of England. Your description of the beauties of the Cornish gardens, and of the rhododendrons and camellias in full flower in the open air is almost beyond one's power to realize in these Northern Regions. I never saw the gardens and the country look more wretched; nothing growing or budding; everything brown and sere; and grave doubts whether the evergreens will recover the severe pinch this long winter has given them. It is enough to make one despair of one's garden—which really in May generally looks pretty—as one walks round the paths and sees rhododendrons, laurels, yews, looking as though they would never look green again. No April showers have come yet, and, as I have a small army of painters on the premises, I shan't mind if they defer their visit for a week or ten days; but certainly the outlook from the window of my usually pleasant morning-room is as dreary as anything can be this dull, leaden-skied morning, which is such a contrast to the two bright previous days."

April 15, 1879.

"I finished Stanley's volume of American addresses and sermons on Sunday evening. Some of the sermons are very beautiful—very characteristic. Did you see the report of the sermon on the Lord's Supper he preached in the Abbey last Sunday? There were some curious statements that he made about evening communions; and I mean to write and ask him what historical evidence he has that evening communions were the *rule* of the first and *second* centuries. No doubt they were common enough in the Apostolic age, but there, the evidence of their use, so far as I have been able to trace it, seems to stop. I confess I don't like them, though I have taken part in one or two that were very solemn and edifying; but I could never see why they should be denounced, as they are by those of the Ritualist school, as little short of a profanation."

April 22, 1879.

"I had a great deal of trouble (when at Cholderton) with ——'s husband, though I believe he had a liking for me at the bottom of his heart. He was one of the class of men who are sometimes described as 'their own worst enemies,' a man of violent passions of every kind, which he never took any pains to restrain, so that a generous nature became vitiated to the very core. His moral and spiritual history was just like that of King Saul. I remember his once telling me, after his wife had been reproaching him for his misconduct, and his own conscience told him that the reproaches were deserved (he met me in one of his fields, with a gun in his hands and a dog following him), 'Mr. Fraser,' he said, 'if I did not believe in a hereafter, I would gladly shoot myself as soon as I would shoot yonder dog.' I can't say his belief helped him much in regulating his life, whatever it might do in making him fear death. He was a strange compound of good and evil, and my heart grows sad as I think of him. I often fancy that some one else might have managed him better than I did."

April 26, 1879.

"On Thursday I went to London, travelling with the Dean and his married daughter, Mrs. Edward Romilly. I got there about 4 P.M. and made my way at once to the Lingens, but, finding no one at home and dinner not till 8 o'clock, I went and took afternoon tea with Mrs. A—— B——, where my cousin is spending a few days on her way to Brighton. I then called at the Bryces' in Norfolk Square, and then got back to my host's about seven. I spent a very pleasant, quiet evening there, no company being procurable on so short a notice. Both Lingen and his wife are special favourites of mine; they are so natural, so intelligent, so real, so simply and naturally good. They would wish me to make their house my hotel when I come to town, if I would consent to do so On Friday Lingen drove me down in his brougham to the Abbey by 10.30. The proceedings were of a very imposing character, and all went off well. I was not really wanted, for the Bishops of London and Ely presented the new Bishop, and all that I and the Bishop of Carlisle did was to stand on each side flanking the others while the presentation took place, just by way of telling the people that the Northern Province was the one immediately concerned. Westcott's sermon was a very grand one. What he claimed for the Episcopate was the spirit of counsel and the spirit of prophecy, and he indicated in a very striking way the Church's right to let her voice be heard and her influence felt in every matter that affects the interests of man. Every man has his proper gift of God, and whether his gift is of the highest, or only of the secondary order, he discharges his duty by faithfully exercising it under the guidance of his conscience and to the best of his ability. After the service was over—there were, I should think, 700 communicants, and we did not get out of the Abbey till 2 o'clock—we went back to the Jerusalem Chamber; and when thanking Westcott for his sermon, alluding to his claim for the Church to touch social questions, and to the existing great strike in the Durham coalfield, I said, 'Well, the Bishop will have this opportunity at once.' 'Yes,' said Westcott, 'but he must not improvise; he must only speak or act after full consideration.' Well, this is true; but, if he takes long to consider, the opportunity may pass away before he has spoken or acted at all. I went in to lunch with Stanley. He has of course seen a good deal of Lightfoot as a co-member of the New Testament Revision Committee. We were both agreed that, in all the high elements of the Christian character, a better Bishop could not have been chosen. I asked Stanley about the historical evidence that evening communions were the *rule* in the first two centuries; and he told me that it was a simple blunder in the report. What he said was, that for two centuries or more there were Churches —as of course I knew—in which evening communions were allowed on certain occasions. I had some talk with him about America. He agreed with me that there were not more than four fine natural prospects in the Northern States: the situation of New York, the Hudson River, Lakes George and Champlain, and Niagara."

May 3, 1879.

"The greatest and truest reproach, as it seems to me, that can be levelled against Romanism is that, though no doubt capable of producing a high type of saintliness in a few, it is utterly powerless—it does not even seem to attempt—to restrain the passions of the many. Certainly, the most ignorant and brutal part of our population are the Irish Roman Catholics, who at the same time live in the most absolute submission to their priesthood. Why, then, do these not mend their lives?"

May 5, 1879.

"We do not wish to 'create sins,' but we have a right to constitute our municipal law on the basis that we think best suited to promote family and national happiness. If people break this law (Marriage with a Deceased Wife's Sister), they must take the social consequences. Upon the question of 'sin,' we pronounce no judgment at all. That must be left to each man's own conscience. Mr. ——— is, I believe, a rich merchant who has broken the law himself, and finds most of the funds to maintain the agitation in this matter. The Norfolk farmers' petition is rubbish. What can they, as a body, care about the question? I believe it is possible to get up a petition in favour of anything. Some years ago I got a petition signed by four hundred people in and near ———, requesting me to restore a clergyman— who had been condemned to ten years' penal servitude for forgery, and was just let out of Portland on ticket-of-leave—to his benefice. The man was stained, according to popular rumour, with many other vices; but he had a genial, free manner, and hence the feeling in his favour. Needless to say, I did not grant the petition, and the man was afterwards convicted of another act of forgery, which enabled me to get rid of him altogether. He is still living at ——, and has friends who think him an 'injured innocent' still."

May 21, 1879.

"At Westhoughton, on Monday, I had one of my real enjoyments—a true Lancashire stone-laying. We walked two miles in a procession of 500 or 600 Sunday School scholars and teachers to the site of the new Church. I walked between the Rural Dean and Mr. Seddon, an old gentleman of 82, who had built the Parish Church, at a cost of £8000, entirely out of his own pocket. When we got to the ground there were 2000 or 3000 people of all classes gathered together, and looking on with that peculiar interest and eagerness which is so characteristic of Lancashire faces. Mrs. Makant (the lady who was to lay the stone, and who, with her sister, Miss Haddock, furnishes the whole cost, £6000), was there plainly dressed, serious-looking, and comporting herself throughout with a simplicity and unaffectedness that to me is the greatest of charms. And then I had to give an address, which was very well received, and then came the inevitable tea-party, and then my health proposed by old Mr. Seddon in language which my modesty will not allow me to repeat, and then a few words of thanks to me, and then we walked back, no longer in procession though, to the Parish Church, and the Confirmation at seven of 95 candidates, and then 'the plain supper in a quiet way' (which turned out to be salmon cutlets and champagne), and then the homeward journey and the sound sleep afterwards. It was altogether a most satisfying and encouraging day."

June 3, 1879.

"I have just had a kind of visit of inquiry from Mr. ——, whose two nieces were at the Cathedral on Sunday night, and told him that my cough was troublesome. (I can feel that it is getting rapidly better.) He had been in Oxford, and said, to my surprise, that it was both a hope and a rumour there that at the death of the dear Provost *I* was to be the Head of Oriel. I can't think how such an idea can be entertained; it is practically impossible. Nor, if it were likely, with nearly all my old friends gone, should I desire to return there and live almost as an alien in the land, and in the midst of new ideas, with many of which I have very little sympathy. No; when the time comes for putting off active harness, my hope will be to spend the evening of my days in some quiet, sequestered country home. My poor heart, when it gets vexed, as it sometimes does, at the folly and madness of the people, sets up such a yearning for that time to come.

"Manchester is really beginning to look very pretty. The last week has made such a difference, and the air the last three days has been charming. I fear the cold of this winter has killed a rather fine ilex, which stands opposite my front door. I hoped it was only a little late in putting forth its buds, but calling upon Mr. R. W—— to-day (a very pleasant, well-read man to talk to), I found him lamenting that six ilexes in his grounds had succumbed to the seven months' winter; so, I fear, mine has shared the same fate. But I shall wait another fortnight before I give orders for its removal.

"'The mad people seem attracted to me. Yesterday a man called to tell me he was all on fire, and asked me to 'intercede for him' and put it out. I have had no visit from Mr. —— yet, the 'possessed with a devil'; and I have not yet found time to send for Mr. ——, and inquire with what faithfulness he has kept his pledge, which was that for three months he would not touch alcoholic liquor except at meals."

June 6, 1879.

"I confess I share the feelings of any one who gets into moping ways, if he has not cheery hearts and bright faces sometimes near him. I think nothing is so delightful as nice people. They are even needed to make one thoroughly enjoy nature's fairest scenes. *I am not a child of solitude*, though all my tastes are quiet and homely. I am happy in having a crowd of valued friends, but I don't like to have them with me in a crowd; I prefer them, for perfect enjoyment a few, at a time."

June 10, 1879.

"There is an article in the *Times* of to-day describing the wonderful progress of the Roman Catholic body in the United States, where you would have thought that both the political inclinations of the country and the intelligence of the people would have effectively barred their progress. It is a wonderful system, with almost infinite capacity for adapting itself to circumstances. I had a visit to-day at the Registry from Colonel Shaw, who has just come to Manchester as United States Consul, and brought me a letter of introduction from Bishop Whipple, of Minnesota—the most apostolic man, I think, I ever met. He bore the same testimony to the growth of Roman Catholicism in his country, and said it was the only religious community there that practically had any organization at all. All these symptoms don't look very well for the future of humanity. It seems as though there would be a great struggle in which wild communistic views, superstition, and military depotism would be alternately contending for the mastery."

June 17, 1879.

"I had a very nice 'function' yesterday at the consecration of the Barton Cemetery. There was a very nice service and a very attentive and orderly assemblage of people. I made an address, which I think gave satisfaction to my hearers, in which I deplored these distinctions of Christianity, which were still maintained even to the confines of the grave, and said what I really felt and desired for the restoration of unity on the broad basis of what all hold to be the essential articles of the Christian faith. The Chairman of the Burial Board, who is a Dissenter, but a most excellent and generous man, warmly grasped my hand, and told me that he could not sufficiently thank me for what I said, adding, 'If all bishops would give expression to such sentiments, there would very soon be no Dissenters left.' Well, his kindly words at once comforted and saddened me—comforted me by their outspoken sympathy, saddened me when I remembered that by a large (though, I hope, a lessening) majority of the clergy such overtures of sympathy would be repelled."

July 1, 1879.

"So you have been to the Grosvenor Gallery and seen Mr. Whistler's pictures. Well, *I* have *read* of them; but I think it was —— who told me that there was one of these 'Nocturnes,' of which you could not possibly have told which was the right side up, if it had not been for two figures introduced into it, he supposed, for that very purpose. 'High art' seems to me a very conventional and fantastic thing, and, I quite agree with you, does not contain much that is conducive to the elevation of the people."

July 13, 1879.

"I breakfasted yesterday here by the side of Sir Thomas Wade, our Minister to China. I think you need not regret having given £5 to the Famine Relief Fund. He is a most intelligent man, and gave me a most interesting account of the country from many points of view. It seems impossible to say what that empire may not become in the next twenty-five years; and, if we are ever to lose our hold on India, the danger seems more likely to come from China than from Russia. The Chinese Ambassador in London (whose portrait is in the Academy) is said to be a most remarkable man, and to have his mind fully open to the accession of new ideas, while the natural resources of the country are so varied and abundant, and the industry and thrift of the people so great, that Sir Thomas Wade said that it was quite possible—indeed, highly probable—that our manufacturers will soon find themselves unable to compete with what the Chinese produce in their own markets."

July 21, 1879.

"Talking of the weather, I am sorry to say that here, as everywhere apparently, there is a return of 'rain, rain, nothing but rain,' and the prospects to the country are really becoming serious. As dear Cornish says, without wishing to be a great interpreter of God's dealings, there does seem something like a judgment, at least, in the sense of a solemn warning in it: and how the men of science empty such visitations of all their proper moral effect by saying, 'Oh, it is all the result of invariable physical laws.' At least there is a moral harmony and adaptation to these physical laws to the moral needs of the age. And this is all that I care that people should see and feel."

July 28, 1879.

"I took Cornish with me to Hayfield, and he was very useful there. When we arrived, we found the poor Vicar suffering agonies from a neuralgic toothache, and utterly unable to take his duty, though he got twice to church. Cornish, therefore, read the service, which he did charmingly. It was a very enjoyable day. The little manufacturing village nestles in a beautiful valley which runs up among the hills of the Peak country, one conspicuous hill closing it at one end. The people are simple and clannish, and the gathering of the inhabitants and visitors—the latter being chiefly Hayfield people, who had gone out into the larger world and prospered, and who come back on the anniversary sermon-day to show their affection for the old place—was enormous. I hardly ever saw a church fuller than this was at evening service. They have a curious way of showing respect to a bishop when one visits the place. Some twenty of the principal inhabitants meet him at the station, with tall white wands in their hands, and escort him in a formal procession to the Vicarage-house. And with this ceremony I am received. The collection last year was £71, this year £106, and the people were wild with excitement and pleasurable surprise; and nothing could exceed the kindly feeling they exhibited. It was altogether a scene to be witnessed, for I cannot describe it, and Cornish was highly amused at it all."

Bishop's Court, Manchester, *August* 8, 1879.

Sir,—I have an engagement on August 13, of a nature which will keep me at home, and a "mass meeting," however important and useful as a means of ascertaining public sentiment, is hardly the best place or method of debating delicate social questions. And I am hardly prepared to throw myself without reserve into the agitation for abolishing the punishment of the lash in the army. Officers whom I know to be not brutes, but humane gentlemen, have told me that they doubt if the discipline of a regiment can be fully maintained without it. It is a humiliating confession to make, for there is no doubt that the punishment is a degrading one, and ought never to be inflicted except in the most extreme cases, in which the man would seem hardly capable of further degradation. Much has been done, and is still doing, to raise the condition of private soldiers, and we may hope that the time will come when the sense of honour and loyalty and patriotism will so animate our soldiers that offences which alone could be thought to deserve an ignominious punishment will be no longer possible. Even now no good soldier runs any risk of this degradation.—I remain, sir, your faithful servant,

J. Manchester.

August 29, 1879.

"Nothing ever gives me more pleasure than to revisit old scenes with the heart full of happy memories, and nothing to disturb the present entire enjoyment of them. Sometimes, visiting an old haunt after the lapse of years, one finds that those who have had the ordering of things in the interval, having different views of the beautiful and the convenient from oneself, have altered, and modified, and re-shaped and re-arranged, till one hardly knows the old places again. It has not been so here (Ufton). There have been great improvements made in the house, which is half as large again as it was in my time, but everywhere else there has been no disturbing hand. The trees and yew-hedges, and the like, that I planted, and which had hardly *begun* to do well in my time, have since thriven wonderfully, and are now in the fulness of beauty and trimness, just in the state in which, when I planned and planted them, I hoped I might live to see them. I have been spared to do so, though not any longer as Rector of Ufton. Cornish and his wife seem profoundly happy, and have evidently well established themselves in the respect and affection both of the parishioners and the neighbours. They are keeping the place in first-rate order with a good staff of outdoor servants, and the place is all alive with chickens, and ducks, and pigs, and sheep, and cattle. Everything is just as I should have liked to see it, and it is a fair sight to see; and, as I gaze on it, I think how happy is the lot of the country parson, and, as I reflect upon his power of doing good, I say to myself, What an ill day it will be for the country if ever the said country parson, though there are here and there disagreeable and even haughty specimens of the class, is swept away."

August 30, 1879.

"C.'s factotum told me this morning he was 'right glad to hear what I said of them candles,' and was pleased to find that I 'had them Church views.' He is a very pronounced Protestant, and, when he once went to church at Macclesfield, told his master afterwards 'what good it had done him to see the minister *praich* in a black gown'— only another and opposite type of Ritualism!"

September 6, 1879.

"My plan (for inducting my clergy) is this. After a shortened evensong, I stand on the chancel step with the new incumbent by my side, and, having said what I deem appropriate to the occasion, I ask him those questions which are put to priests at their ordination, that the people may know what the ministerial obligations are; he then kneels down, and I place my hand on his head, saying the prayer which immediately follows the questions; and then I ask the congregation to join me in prayers for their new minister, which I select from other parts of the Ordinal. In this way (with two suitable hymns) a simple but effective service is produced, which always seems to interest those who are present."

September 10, 1879.

"I was very much pleased yesterday at the Registry to receive a visit from Mr. H. Birley, one of the M.P.'s for Manchester, and one of our best and most large-hearted men, in the course of which he said, 'Bishop, you have often taught us from the pulpit many useful lessons of simplicity of life, and I and many others feel that the time has come for putting those lessons into practice' (he has always been himself a man of simple life and manners). 'Can you suggest any plan, whether by association or otherwise, by which Manchester society can be influenced to adopt a simpler and less extravagant style of living and entertaining?' And I told him that I had no other plan but the force of example, and that if he and I, and others occupying foremost positions, would show the way, I have no doubt that many would be glad to follow, for I was certain that there were hundreds of people who were groaning under the tyranny of fashion, and who yet had not the courage to emancipate themselves; and I added that I was glad to hear that generally, and in spite of some notable instances the other way (as Mr. ———'s ball, to which my brother Alex referred), the style of entertainment in London last season was much more moderate, and that at dinner parties people were contented with much fewer entrées, and also with fewer sorts of wine. Yesterday, for instance, here, though the dinner was as handsome as needs be, there were only two entrées, three sweets, and three sorts of wine—sherry, claret, and champagne—enough, in all conscience, for anybody, but still a marked contrast to the style of entertainment that I have sometimes witnessed at rich men's tables.

"By the bye, we are to bring back with us from Nantwich this afternoon Walsham How, the new Bishop of Bedford, who is to stay here one night only. Lord ——— says the only bishop of Bedford he can recognize is the 'immortal tinker, John Bunyan.'

"Going down to dinner last night, he found he was walking before me, when, stopping on the stairs, he said, 'Come, take your proper precedence; I will yield to a proper bishop—a peer of Parliament—but not to those new bishoplings who are springing up like mushrooms everywhere to-day.' I don't think he has the least idea of there being anything spiritual in the office, and it is this tone running through his conversation which, in spite of its brilliancy, makes it to me so irritating."

September 19, 1879.

"The editor of the *Cumberland Guardian* returns, you see, though in a very friendly spirit, to the attack upon my 'pessimist views.' I have sent him a private letter, saying he misunderstands me. The pessimism of Schopenhauer says this is a thoroughly bad world, and this badness is necessary and ineradicable. I, on the other hand, say it is a good world; that the evil in it is all curable, and is to be regarded as God's wholesome method of discipline to bring us back to a recognition of, and obedience to, His moral and social laws. And I don't call this 'pessimism.' What the editor supposes to have been a quotation from Herbert Spencer was not one. It was simply the closing sentence of my sermon. I referred to Herbert Spencer's essay on the 'Morality of

Trade,' but I did not quote him. My good correspondent, Mrs. ——, misunderstands me also. I have never attempted to divorce faith from life, or this world from the next. What I have said is that *righteousness* is better than *orthodoxy*, which is all that some people mean when they talk of faith; but I have always held that *faith* (by which I mean trust in the love of God, and in the work and example of Christ, and in the power of grace) is *necessary* to a life of righteousness, and that the hypothesis of a next world is equally *necessary* to explain the perplexities and difficulties of this. One of my favourite texts, that I am always quoting, is 'Believe in God, believe also in Me.' It is true I have added, Don't speculate, as weak-headed people are fond of speculating, about the 'hereafter.' Do your duty here in this spirit of faith, and leave the rest in God's hands."

October 14, 1879.

"On Saturday I went to Bury. We had a splendid meeting—about 1200 in the room—most enthusiastic. Mr. R. N. Philips, M.P. for Bury, and a very popular man there, was in the chair. The only thing I regretted was that there was not a single clergyman present. Mr. Philips is not a Churchman, and is a Liberal, and though, I believe, they are personal friends, there have been passages-at-arms in public between him and the rector. Still, here was a society, with 9000 members and a capital of £100,000, and turning over in their (co-operative) business £250,000—a splendid example of what the public can and will do for themselves—doing also a good work for education in the town, and not one single clergyman of the Church of England was there to express sympathy. It is the way in which wretched political antipathies prevent the clergy from using their opportunities. Nothing could exceed the warm welcome the people gave to me, and that shows how they appreciate such little support and sympathy as I was able to give them."

October 20, 1879.

"To-morrow (Tuesday) I confirm at 7.30, at St. John's, Broughton. On Wednesday I consecrate a churchyard, and preach afterwards at an evening service at Peel, near Bolton. On Thursday I go out to Reddish, near Stockport, to consecrate a cemetery, and in the evening preach at St. Clement's, Longsight, on the occasion of opening a new organ. On Friday, at 2.30, the Bishop of Carlisle comes to distribute the Oxford and Cambridge Local Examination prizes, and in the evening, at 7.30, I confirm at St. Thomas's, Pendleton. On Saturday, at 7, I confirm at St. Stephen's, Salford. On Sunday I preach at Stockport parish church (outside my own diocese) in the morning, and in the evening of the same day at Heaton Moor. So I have a good week's work cut out before me."

To Mr. GEORGE CANDELET.

BISHOP'S COURT, MANCHESTER, *November* 22, 1879.

SIR,—I beg to acknowledge your communication, which I have read with respectful attention. I am quite aware that it is impossible to be precisely exact with statistics, and no doubt, in Mr. Hoyle's "Drink Bill," allowance should be made for excisable liquors exported (such as beer for India). When, however, all deductions have been made, there will still remain a frightful amount, which, to use your own language, has "found its way into the stomachs of the people."

No doubt, also, there are local anomalies in the relation of the number of cases of drunkenness to the number of public-houses, which could be properly accounted for by different causes, if each case were carefully inquired into; but I am amazed to hear you state as a general proposition that there is often the "least amount of drunkenness where there is the largest number of public-houses, and where there is the least number of public-houses there has been the most pauperism." I have never seen any statistics that would establish either of those propositions. Certainly where I see most drunkenness and squalor and wretchedness in the streets of Manchester are those parts of Great Ancoats Street and Deansgate, where I also notice the greatest number of spirit vaults and houses that sell intoxicants.

I do not at all commit myself to the programme of the Church of England Temperance Society's Bill, of which I heard for the first time the other evening, and some parts of it may be fairly open to your criticism; nor have I yet been able to satisfy myself how far the principle of compensation ought to go, nor upon what equitable consideration it ought to be based, but I go in strongly for one or two simple points:—

1. I think we have far too many drinking-houses, and that some effective means ought to be adopted for limiting their number.

2. I think that inhabitants and ratepayers ought to have some power in letting their voices be effectively heard in this matter.

3. I think the hours, in which places where drink is sold on Sunday can be kept open for such sale, should be diminished. With you, I trust much more to the effect of moral and educational influences than to legislation. As to the class of licensed victuallers, I have no word to say against them as a class; I suppose, like every other class—the clergy, if you like, included—it comprises men good, bad, and indifferent. Neither in my remarks the other evening, nor, so far as I remember, in a single speech delivered on the occasion, were they the object of any intemperate language. It was the system under which the evil has grown to its present gigantic dimensions, and the vicious habits of the people, which reciprocally foster and are fostered by the system, against which we directed our assault.

I have not a word to say against a properly conducted public-house, discharging its proper purposes. I feel that it is a convenience and a necessity with which society cannot dispense. But I have not the same opinion of a spirit vault. These I consider wholly unnecessary and wholly mischievous, and it is to them that I trace the poverty, the vice, and the crime, so far as these are produced by intemperance. I once used a strong utterance about them (viz., that I would as soon own a brothel as a spirit-vault), and I am not disposed to retract or modify a word of it.—Thanking you for the tone of moderation of your letter, I remain, yours faithfully,

J. MANCHESTER.

To *the* EDITOR OF THE "MAIDSTONE AND KENT COUNTY STANDARD."

BISHOP'S COURT, MANCHESTER, *November* 24, 1879.

SIR,—I think the question you have asked me had better be left to the judgment and discretion of the members of the club concerned. How can I, who am only too sensible of the comfort and value of an opened club on Sunday, when I happen to be in London, say that it is a wrong or inadvisable thing to open a working men's club on the same day? I do not for a moment say that it is; but, at the same time, I feel that the opportunity might be a help to some men, but a danger to others. Of course St. Paul's great maxim about "using the world and not abusing it" is appropriate here; but, when there is an opportunity of abuse, some men will use it for that purpose. The logical argument, I take it, is all in favour of opening; but other things have to be considered besides logical arguments, and unless I knew the temper of the members of your club, or at least the majority of them, I should not venture to give my advice on the subject. But my principle is, that I wish to see as much innocent recreation given on the Lord's Day as is consistent with its religious observances. At the same time, I feel that a liberty, which would be quite safe here, would be dangerous there.—Yours faithfully,

J. MANCHESTER.

December 8, 1879.

"The Mr. —— who wrote that curious letter about the 'lost tribes' called on me late on Saturday evening, having come, he said, expressly through the fog and bitter cold for the purpose. I don't know whether he was more surprised or mortified to hear me say that I did not feel the least interest in the question. 'What? Not if I could show you the very spot of ground on which your ancestor set his foot when he landed in Britain?' 'No,' I reiterated, 'not the least.' He could not believe his ears; but, when I again told him that such nevertheless was the case, with uplifted hands and an astounded look, he took his leave, doubtless deeming me the most phlegmatic and incomprehensible of men. I thought it was the only way to get rid of him. He had brought with him a thick bundle of papers, which, I suppose, contained the proofs of his theory, but my incredulity and indifference probably stopped him from producing them. The man—short, thick-set, about forty years of age—must be mad."

December 29, 1879.

"This terrible railway accident at the Tay Bridge has been hanging like a great weight about me all day. It threatens to be the most appalling railway accident on record, and I don't expect to hear to-morrow morning that a single life has been saved. It seems to have happened about 7 P.M. It was very wild and gusty here (though there was a brilliant moon), and Mr. Lund, at St. John's, Cheetham Hill, gave out, by special request, he said, of some one who had friends at sea, the beautiful hymn 'for those in peril on the sea.' At that very moment those two hundred souls must have been plunging through the chasm, down 130 feet, into the deep waters of the Tay. The very thought sends a shudder through me! It was remarkable last night with what earnestness and feeling the vast congregation—for the church was as full as it could hold—joined in the hymn."

To Rev. H. B. Hawkins.

Bishop's Court, Manchester, *January* 5, 1880.

My dear Hawkins,—What can I say in the way of comfort or sympathy under the terrible sorrow which I learn, for the first time, from the columns of to-day's *Times*, has just befallen you? It breaks one's heart to think that this is the sad termination of your many months' profound anxiety. Your well-disciplined mind, however, will regard it all as part, however difficult to read or to interpret, of the will of God, who we know is loving us even when He chastens. As long as your dear wife had the command of herself, her life was of the noblest; indeed it was, I fear, the intensity with which she threw herself into the Master's work, that disarranged the delicate balance of her mind, and for this last act no one could hold her responsible. You must not let your mind dwell on this. You will recall all that was pure, and lovely, and true, and of good report, in those earlier days of her wedded life; and you can never think of those days without feeling that she was a conspicuous example of one who "did not frustrate the grace of God." My whole heart goes out towards you, my dear friend, in this great sorrow. I have visions of a great happiness drawing very near to myself. Who knows how long it may be before they are overclouded? At any rate, I feel they make my heart more full of sympathy towards those who suffer; and my own joy is chastened and purified by the thought of the instability of all earthly things. Oh, how cruel at such times seem those who would rob us of our only light amid the darkness, that sure and certain hope of a life beyond the grave, which will clear up all mysteries, and wipe away all tears! If in this life only we had hope in Christ, then, indeed, at such times, and under such trials, we should be of all men the most miserable. But surely that sweet but troubled mind, having put off its fragile earthly tabernacle, is now at rest in Paradise with Him. Let this thought be your comfort and stay.—Yours affectionately, J. Manchester.

To the Very Rev. Dr. BURGON, *Dean of Chichester.*

December 17, 1880.

MY DEAR BURGON,—Don't be too despondent. Faith has not yet perished from the earth. I do not know so much about Oxford, but I sat next a young Cambridge man last night who cheered me greatly with his account of the tone of the majority of the young men there. You talk of Nemesis in the future. I sadly fear that what is befalling us now, the tone and tendency of which I like as little as you do, may be Nemesis on omissions and commissions of the past.

Did Oxford do her duty as "a place of religion and learning"—I mean her *full duty*—and has she a right to say that talents are being taken from her which she was using well? Nevertheless, my old friend, warm-hearted and generous, though vehement and almost fierce as ever, don't let thy spirit fail thee. Be a witness for truth, and above all for righteousness (for truth too often still lies at the bottom of a well, and is hard to be always clearly discerned), and let us believe of these things, "Magna sunt et prævalebunt." I send you a full copy of my charge. You won't be offended at the reference to you on page 64. There are points in which we differ; but, for the greater interests of the Church, I think we should be found fighting side by side. If you ever come northwards, pay me a visit. I want to introduce you to my noble wife.—Ever yours affectionately,

J. MANCHESTER.

To Rev. Canon MACLURE.

MANCHESTER, *Christmas Day*, 1880.

MY DEAR MACLURE,—My dear wife and I both thank you for the good wishes sent to us from the Vicarage, Rochdale. I hope that nothing will ever disturb such kindly feelings.

May all the best blessings of the coming year be on you and yours, and on all you put your hand to do.

God grant that the coming year may be one of greater peace and progress to His Church.

I believe with you that there is a kind of ebb in the tide, and men are beginning to find out how little there is in these extreme doctrines and practices to satisfy the hunger of men's souls. Oh that the spirit of Christ would guide us all to strive more for righteousness and holiness of life!— Ever yours sincerely (and with my wife's kind regards to you and yours),

J. MANCHESTER.

The following letter is published with Mr. Gladstone's kind consent:

(*Private.*)

10, DOWNING STREET, WHITEHALL, *July* 26, 1881.

MY DEAR BISHOP OF MANCHESTER,—Ten or eleven years ago (I think) you told me in the House of Lords that you looked to holding your See for ten years, and that you did not think you could stand the strain of it for more.

I put aside the thought of these words as to the practical intent: prophecy is so difficult about one's self or otherwise.

But it has lately been reported to me that you *now* cherish a feeling of this kind, and would gladly retire to some sphere of less fatiguing work. *Do you* desire it, and *can you* carry through the plan?

If you answer these questions in the affirmative, I shall be happy to submit your name to the Queen for the Deanery of Westminster.

But pray understand that I neither ask, nor even suggest, your retirement, and that this letter should be marked *nil*, unless it rests upon the basis of your own desire.—Believe me, with much respect and regard, faithfully yours,

W. E. GLADSTONE.

BISHOP'S COURT, MANCHESTER, *July* 27, 1881.

MY DEAR MR. GLADSTONE,—Your letter has been a great surprise to me, and has set my poor thoughts and feelings in a considerable stir. But I seldom take very long to make up my mind, where action is concerned, and in such matters I rarely find my second thoughts better than my first. And I do not feel what I suppose people mean when they talk of a "call" to Westminster. I do not think I have the gifts for it; that either the place would suit me or I the place. Certainly I could not fill it as dear Stanley filled it; that is not perhaps saying much, for I do not know the living man who could; but I doubt if I could fill it at all as it ought to be filled, according to my conception of its duties. I won't occupy your time needlessly by telling you why I think so; but the whirl of London society would be too much for me, and I am not sure that I could play my part as a minister of Christ there. Here, with many shortcomings and failures, the people seem to know me, and I them, and for a few years longer I hope to be able to work among them and for them. And then I should like to retire to some quiet resting-place, and spend among simple country folk the evening of my day. But, believe me, I am grateful, deeply grateful for this renewed mark of your confidence. I have done what I could to justify your sending me here. I am not sure that I should justify your placing me at Westminster. That your life may be long spared for the well-being of the country is the earnest and daily hope of —Yours most gratefully,

J. MANCHESTER.

To the Rev. Canon WOODHOUSE.

MANCHESTER, *August* 18.

MY DEAR CANON WOODHOUSE,—Many thanks for your kind and warm-hearted letter. Such testimonies of kindly feeling do one good. I am sixty-three to-day, but I can hardly realize it. Neither heart nor body seem to be so old. I have everything that I can desire here, so that

Westminster had no attractions for me. It did not cost me five minutes' thought to say "No," when Mr. Gladstone so unexpectedly offered it to me. For a few years longer I hope I may be able to work to some useful purpose here; and then I shall look out for some quiet retreat in which to spend the evening of my days.

May your future be bright, healthful, and useful. With kindest regards, in which my wife joins, to all your party.—I remain, yours sincerely,

J. MANCHESTER.

Colonel Shaw, United States Consul in Manchester, received the following letter from the Bishop:

MANCHESTER, *September* 27, 1881.

DEAR SIR,—Although I gave utterance to my feelings in regard to the lamented death of the President of the United States in a sermon preached on Sunday evening, which has been reported in the local papers, it might be expected from me, as the Bishop of the diocese, that I should convey to you, the representative of the United States in Manchester, the expression of the sympathy with which I am sure the hearts of all Churchmen are filled at the sad loss which your country has sustained. The character of General Garfield, as it got to be known, had deeply impressed the hearts of the people of England. No public man, in my memory, was ever followed to the grave with a more universal tribute of respect and admiration.

Let us hope that his influence will not die with him, but that his high patriotism and incorruptible integrity will long stand out as beacon lights to magistrates and statesmen, showing them in what spirit and upon what principles the true interests of nations are to be maintained.—I have the honour to remain, dear sir, your faithful servant,

J. MANCHESTER.

The Hon. Col. SHAW, U.S. *Consul, Manchester.*

To Rev. J. W. CLARKE.

MANCHESTER, *October* 16, 1881.

SIR,—In the excitement of the moment, when my feelings were strongly moved, I perhaps used, in the language you refer to, stronger words than would have fallen from me in a calmer season; but all I meant was that if a man's conscience, *when he has taken all pains to enlighten it,* plainly tells him that a certain course of conduct is his duty, he ought not to swerve from following it; being prepared, of course, to bear whatever consequences are involved. No doubt great mistakes are possible here; prejudice, passion, self-will, obstinacy, may all be mistaken for conscience; and nowhere is there greater need for that κρίσις, or "judgment," which Christ puts among the "weightier matters of the law"; but nevertheless I hold the view of John Henry Newman, expressed in his 'Apologia' on this subject.

What is a higher guide for us, in speculation and practice, than that conscience of right and wrong, of truth and falsehood, those sentiments of what is decorous, consistent, and noble, which our Creator has made part of our original nature?—I am, sir, yours faithfully,

J. MANCHESTER.

To the Very Rev. Dr. OAKLEY, *Dean of Manchester.*

January 19, 1883.

"I am afraid you give me credit for 'wider sympathies' than I ever possessed. I am a Churchman of the school and type of thought of Richard Hooker. I accept loyally and heartily the principles of the Reformation. I have no sympathy with those who decry those principles, or would undo that work. There is much in the teaching of the extreme party among us, about the Sacraments of the Lord's Supper, about the Invocation of the Blessed Virgin and of the Saints, about the power of the priest in Absolution, that I, for one, cannot distinguish from the teaching of the Church of Rome. I cannot bid this teaching welcome on the platform of the Church of England. Such doctrines were—at any rate, comparatively—unknown among us forty years ago; and, if they are widely spread now, it is because they have crept on stealthily step by step, till we are amazed to find the dimensions which they have attained. While we slept, men have sown tares.

"I yearn as earnestly as you can do for that 'better and brighter future for our Mother Church' which you foresee, if the policy which you recommend were adopted. I deeply regret that I cannot share those anticipations. Unless men will come back within the limits of the Prayer Book, as these were understood and accepted, until recent innovations blurred them, I can discern nothing for the Church but continued disquiet in the present, and disaster, probably destruction, in a future, only too threatening and imminent.—I remain, dear Mr. Dean, yours most faithfully,

"J. MANCHESTER."

To A CORRESPONDENT.

MANCHESTER, *March* 6, 1883.

DEAR SIR,—I am obliged by your letter. I must have expressed myself very incautiously, if my words fairly led to the inference that you tell me has been drawn from them. I know what has been done by the so-called "Blue Ribbon" movement in Rossendale and elsewhere; and I should be sorry to say one word in disparagement of it. But these movements have inevitably a large amount of excitement attached to them; and there appears to be, just now, great danger of strong but transient emotions being mistaken for that sober and steadfast spirit of religion, which alone can support a man under severe trials, or carry him through great temptations; and there is a fashion also prevalent, and not without its dangers, of marking, by some outward token—of which the "Blue Ribbon" is but one—that we have passed through these emotions, and may be supposed safe from the temptations of this or that particular sin. I therefore said that a true temper of religion would make a man sober and chaste, and pure, whether he "wore a ribbon at his button-hole or not"; but I should indeed regret if my words tended to discourage those who are working soberly and earnestly in the temperance cause. They were meant to direct not to dishearten them. I regard intemperance and licentiousness as the two great moral devastators of our time; but, if they are to be conquered, the resistance to them must be calm, steadfast, and unwavering.

You are quite at liberty to make what use of this letter you please.—I am, sir, yours faithfully,

J. MANCHESTER.

"Mr. —— was somewhat too severe and hard a man to 'win souls'; and his life had been too much engaged with 'the *temporal* incidents of spiritual things'—church rates, vicarial leases, Acts of Parliament, etc., to allow him scope for the 'weightier matters of the law.' Happily, these things have come to an end, and those who come after may thank *him* for having carried them through, and left them a freer and a nobler course. Every man has his own gift from God. May we all use our gift in the Giver's service!

"I think guilds or brotherhoods of young men—if they are kept clear of nonsense—are excellent things. It seems to be the only agency through which a parish priest can raise the tone of his young men into something like the purity and loftiness of purpose which becomes a Christian.

"Mr. —— is a very interesting and well-equipped man; but I thought he seemed to care more for *philosophy* than for *Christianity*, and for preaching, *i.e.* ἐπιδείξις, more than for parochial work."

The four following letters are of special interest, both because they are amongst the last letters Bishop Fraser wrote, and because each letter is illustrative of an eminent feature in his character. The first letter is addressed to the Rev. J. J. Swann, an earnest clergyman, with twelve children to maintain upon a curate's stipend, for the poor man never was beneficed. "Every Christmas day," writes one of Mr. Swann's sons, "for ten years the Bishop sent my father a cheque for £10; and that was his custom with other married curates in his diocese; and, in the spring before my father's death, the Bishop sent him £15 with which to get away to some seaside place, in the hope that the air would restore his health after a very painful operation." The letter is dated on the day of the son's ordination, and was written by the Bishop in the vestry of the cathedral immediately after the ordination, and sent by the hand of the son in the hope that it would cheer and encourage the father, who was suffering from a severe and painful malady which ultimately proved fatal. The second letter was written to Mrs. Swann from the Bishop's sick-room to support her with his sympathy and offers of help. The third letter was written to a well-known and greatly honoured Wesleyan minister, the Rev. Dr. Pope; the fourth letter (written three days before his death) shows the clearness of the Bishop's mind, and the reasonableness of his intense interest in human affairs, to the very close of his life. Thus, while the Bishop was occupied in acts of compassion for the needy; of sympathy with every brotherhood of Christians; and of large, intelligent devotion to the progress of humanity, the curtain fell upon the final scenes of his earthly career.

MANCHESTER, *May* 31, 1885.

MY DEAR MR. SWANN,—I think it will give you pleasure in your illness to know how thoroughly satisfied I have been with your son in his examination. He has passed *most* creditably, and I fully hope will make an excellent clergyman. It saddens me to hear his account of you. May God bless the means that are being used for your recovery.—I am, yours truly,
J. MANCHESTER.

MANCHESTER, *October* 6, 1885.

MY DEAR MRS. SWANN,—A letter this morning from the dean makes me fear that your husband's remaining days on earth may be few. For his own sake, in such pain as I fear he has been suffering, no one can wish that they should be prolonged, if all hope of recovery has passed away. But I should be glad if a word of sympathy from me could reach him before the last moment comes. For many months past he has been in my thoughts, and almost daily in my prayers. It was quite an exception if, in commending those who were suffering to God's pity, I did not think of him. My own gracious freedom from pain, even now that I am ill, makes me feel more deeply for those who are called upon, in God's mysterious ways, to suffer so much from which I am spared. May God be with him ever to the end, to strengthen, to comfort, and to sustain. I am sure friends will be raised up to you in this affliction; and all I will say for myself is, that if either now or hereafter I can be of any assistance to you, I hope you will let me know.—I remain, with my wife's true sympathy added to my own, yours very truly,
J. MANCHESTER.

Mrs. SWANN.

MANCHESTER, *October* 10, 1885.

MY DEAR DR. POPE,—I grieve to see, by the papers, that you are seriously invalided; and I should like to convey to you this expression of my concern and sympathy. I pray God that your illness is a removable one, and that you may not be permanently incapacitated for work that you have done so ably, and in so truly a Christian spirit.

I too am laid by—a clot of blood has formed in the subclavian vein—and I am ordered perfect rest for a while. It is a strange sensation to me, and I do not quite reconcile myself to it, when there is work calling aloud for workmen on every side. But such is the will of God concerning me; and He has been so gracious that I can commit everything to His hand.

I am so pleased that your brother has got so suitable an appointment at Oxford.—I remain, yours sincerely in Christ Jesus,

J. MANCHESTER.

P.S.—I had such a kind letter, the other day, from our venerable common friend, Joseph Hargreaves.

MANCHESTER, *October* 19, 1885.

DEAR SIR,—I have signed the enclosed paper with some reluctance.

My sole and single aim in joining in the demand for the suppression of the Opium Trade has been that China should be absolutely free in the matter to act as she deems best for the interests of her own people. To "suppress the trade" beyond that point seems to me politically and commercially impossible. Men will produce what others will buy; and it is quixotic to attempt to stop the flow of trade. When China can act freely with regard to the traffic, my hopes of what is possible of attainment are satisfied.—I am, yours faithfully,

J. MANCHESTER.

J. R. FINLAYSON, Esq.

CHAPTER XVIII.

HOME LIFE.

The Bishop's Devotion to His Mother and His Home—Miss Duncan—The Betrothal—Mrs. Duncan's Death—Domestic Economy—Constancy of Mind—Rumours of Marriage—The Bishop's Marriage—Dean Stanley's Address—*Punch's* Letter—Return Home—Home Happiness—Hospitality.

OF the many varied features of Bishop Fraser's life and character none shines forth in clearer beauty than his tender devotion to home. He was pre-eminently a home-loving man.

"I really cannot think," he writes, in one of his letters, "how people can care so much for the mere external (and too often illusory) elements of happiness, when all that really gladdens and brightens life lies within that magic circle which God's providence draws round each one to whom He grants the blessings of a *home*. . . . I have always held that home duties have the greatest claim upon us, and that nothing ought to displace them but the most imperious necessity. It is a pity that that good fellow —— is not more at home; his wife would be happier, his children would most probably have turned out better, and he himself would have done quite as much good in the world. We have a good man here in Manchester who acts much in the same way. His infinite schemes of private benevolence and public usefulness hardly leave him any time for his family, and they scarcely see him (I am told) from 9 A.M. to 10 P.M. I don't think that such an inversion of the natural order can be intended for us by God."

From the first dawn of childhood to the last evening of declining years, the centre of the Bishop's life was home. His father had died while James Fraser was still a child; but till the day of her death his mother reigned upon the throne of his affections. As flowers turn to the sun, James Fraser's heart turned to his mother, the light and joy of his whole being. His mother was his inspiration to industry; his first thought in success. At school and at Oxford he worked with all his might that he might gratify his mother. When he gained the Ireland Scholarship, and took his first-class, and was elected to the Oriel fellowship, it was to his mother he sent the first tidings of his victory. Her delight was his reward. The orphan son seemed to concentrate his whole energy to the service of his widowed parent. When absent upon his Commission work, he wrote to her constantly. At Cholderton and Ufton Nervet she kept house for him. He refused the Bishopric of Calcutta because he thought the climate of India would not suit his mother; and he could not go to India and leave her behind. His chief pride in going to Manchester was the thought of her gladness; and, when he chose a wife, his choice fell upon one whose life-long devotion to her widowed mother had been as true and tender as his own. Writing to Miss Duncan on January 6, 1878, about a year after his engagement to her, the Bishop said :

"Oh, what do we not both owe to God that He has given us good mothers. Whatever other happiness He may have in store for us, we should not have been *fit* for it without them. . . . It is beautiful and touching to see the natural affection of my aunt for my mother. My aunt never thinks my mother is rightly put to bed unless she has herself done the last titivations to her hair; and she sometimes sits up too long herself for this purpose. All the servants are as good and *kind* as they can be. A good mother and a faithful servant are certainly two great blessings for which to thank God."

His correspondence teems with allusions to his mother; especially at periods, which unhappily were frequent in her latest years, when her state of health caused him much anxiety and grief.

MANOR HOUSE, TETTENHALL, WOLVERHAMPTON,
June 20, 1873.

MY DEAR MR. PARKER,—I am sure you will be concerned to hear of my dearest mother's dangerous illness. She had come to visit some of our oldest friends at this house, accompanied by my aunt and my brother, Colonel Fraser, who had taken a short six weeks' run home from India. They had spent a happy eight days together; my brother had said his last good-bye, and the day was fixed for my mother and aunt's return to Manchester; the excitement of this leave-taking, I fear, proved too much. On the very morning of the day fixed for her return—last Friday week—my dear mother was struck with apoplexy accompanied by paralysis of the right side. She is still lying in a most critical state, so much so that I hardly dare to pray that her life may be prolonged. She can articulate "yes" or "no," but otherwise the power of speech has failed; and, though she is conscious, the doctor thinks the full power of her mind will never be restored. Happily, she is free from pain, and everything is done for her that medical skill and the kindness of friends can do. But it is a deep and bitter sorrow to me. For five-and-twenty years she has been the joy and light of my home, and I seem less able to do without her now than ever. She has been the very best and most devoted of mothers, and through all her life her one object has been to sacrifice herself for the good and happiness of her children. If she is taken from us, I shall hope to lay her body in that quiet churchyard at Ufton, which you know, and where I mean one day, when my work is done, to be laid myself. If I come to Bath in October for the Church Congress, which I am pressed to do, shall I be likely to find you there?—Yours sincerely,

J. MANCHESTER.

To the R v. CANON POWELL, *Vicar of Bolton.*

June 6, 1873.

"Both last night and the night before my dear mother had severe accesses of excitement, which I alone seemed able in some measure to appease. She is evidently much weaker, and I cannot conceal from myself that the end cannot be far off. Helpless, speechless, as she lies, I cannot wish that life should be prolonged under such conditions, and, heavy as the blow will be when it falls, I feel that I can part with her comforted in what I shall lose by the assurance of what she will gain. No mother was ever more worthy of the love and dutifulness of her sons. She has indeed done her duty by them all, and every thought associated with her memory will be a thought mainly of what we owe to her.

"P.S.—I can hardly realize what my future will be if it be God's will that I lose my mother. She has been everything to all her sons."

The Bishop's mother happily recovered—at least, partially—from this dangerous and threatening attack, but she was never again the same in spirits and health. The shadow of her approaching death always rested, after this paralytic stroke, upon the Bishop. It is wonderful to think of the brightness ever beaming upon his face, and the energy ever thrown into his immense and ceaseless work, while this shadow was hanging over his heart and home. For years he was the sole occupant of the lower part of his house; "my two invalids," as he used to call them, dwelling in a suite of rooms upon the first floor. The last thing the Bishop generally did before leaving home for a heavy day's work was to run upstairs and kiss his two invalids; and the first thing upon returning home, sometimes (as he acknowledges) "feeling very tired," was to go and kiss them again; to sing the evening hymn and say the evening prayer. The entries in his diary—for the Bishop kept a brief diary with punctilious regularity—make constant allusion to his "invalids."

"*Friday, May* 30, 1873.—A telegram tells me of my dear mother's illness. Fear it is paralysis. A later telegram gives no better account. Prepare to leave for Wolverhampton to-morrow.

"*Saturday, May* 31.— Leave by 9.30 train for Wolverhampton, arrive at 12.45. Find my dear mother very ill. Speechless, right side paralysed, semi-conscious. Dr. Crompton evidently has not much hope of a recovery.

"*Thursday, June* 5.—My mother has another access of excitement after dressing for the night, which passes off in an hour, and then she has a quiet night.

"*Wednesday, June* 18.—Leave Wolverhampton by the 2.57 train for Manchester, as my mother appears fairly well, and Dr. Best apprehends nothing sudden.

"*Monday, June* 23.—Better accounts of my dear mother. Sense returning to the paralysed hand.

"*Monday, August* 11.—My dear mother is brought home to-day. She accomplishes the journey beautifully.

"*Thursday, August* 14.—Leave home by 8.45 train for Carnforth, where I consecrate new church. Stay to luncheon. Address the men at the Carnforth Iron Works at 4.30; very attentive. Take tea with Mr. Barton, the manager. Get home by 9. Find my mother very low.

"*Friday, August* 15.—Sit two or three hours, cheering up my mother, to-day.

"*Wednesday, August* 20.—Read a good deal of St. Gregory the Great in my mother's room.

"*Wednesday, August* 27.—At home all day till the evening. Much of the time with my mother, who has a good day."

Thus the diaries continue year after year with varying sunshine and shade; sometimes the mother has a good day, then she is not so well, sometimes the aunt is a cause of special anxiety, then both "the invalids" are better. Meanwhile the bright, God-trusting Bishop—the man whose religion was a religion of faith, and works, and hopeful joy—eats his solitary meals, occupies his solitary room; bent upon cheering others, himself in solitude uncheered. Little did Manchester know, during these lonely years, of the true character of the domestic life of their joyful Bishop: the unresting man whose smile, and voice, and hand, and heart were ready to succour and encourage every honest worker, and every worthy cause.

Even at home the Bishop, though solitary, was not melancholy. He was surrounded by faithful servants, whose goodness to him finds frequent acknowledgment in his diary, and of whose comfort and pleasure he was constantly thinking. He tells how he enjoyed having a "servants' party"; how "the Shah comes to Manchester: all the servants go to see him: stay at home myself to keep house." He was considerate towards his servants, and his servants were intensely loyal to him. He could not bear to hear masters and mistresses decrying their servants. "There are exceptions," he said; "but good masters generally find good servants. *And besides I delight to think well of human nature.*" Thus, though the Bishop had occasional troubles with his servants, yet, in his loneliness, their affectionate loyalty was a pleasure and support to him.

Moreover the Bishop was no careless housekeeper. He was a house-proud man. When he took up his residence at Bishop's Court, the house required many alterations and additions to render it suitable for an episcopal residence. To every detail of these alterations the Bishop attended himself, inspecting the plans, overhauling the specifications, supervising the workmanship. Sometimes the workmen, taking advantage of his interest in the progress of the work, "bothered him for an allowance." Undaunted, however, by their familiarity, the Bishop insisted upon inspecting every joist, every drain, every gas-pipe. In the garden he planned the shrubbery and trimmed the plants. In the house he put up the blinds himself, nailed up the brackets for vases, hung the pictures, stored the wine. He paid all bills himself, and servants' wages. In the stable he was an authority, trying and buying his horses, looking after the bedding and the fodder. These details of house-needs interested him, and drew off his mind from the loneliness of his domestic lot.

Even in his bachelor days, too, the Bishop was "given to hospitality." He did not spread large and luxurious dinners. These he disliked, both on account of his preference for simplicity, and also because he felt that, with his "two invalids" upstairs, anything like banqueting would have been unseemly. But his diocesan officials, the candidates for ordination, and his more intimate friends, were ever welcome to his plain and hearty board. No one, indeed, whom he could find any reasonable excuse for inviting to remain, was sent at meal-time away from beneath his hospitable roof. Perhaps it was a young curate who had been to see the Bishop; the interview over, the curate would leave the house. But the Bishop finding it was one o'clock would run after him down the drive to the outer gate, calling: "Heigh! you must not go away like this. Come and have some luncheon." Then for half an hour the Bishop would sit and chat easily and helpfully with the young man; so sending him back with new heart and hope to his work in (perhaps) some crowded slum of a large town, where the earnest toilers find few opportunities of recreative social intercourse with their equals.

But it was not curates only who brought their troubles to the Bishop. Every one in a difficulty ran to the Bishop—priests and people, churchwardens and parishioners, clergy and laity, husbands in trouble with incompatible wives, wives in distress with reckless husbands, young men wanting to marry, young ladies perplexed with their love affairs, employers harassed with workmen, workmen depressed by their employers, religious people with their doubts, inventive people with their discoveries, literary aspirants with their effusions, even mad people with their hallucinations. If the walls of Bishop's Court could speak, many hundreds of strange tales of the hidden, inner life of Manchester could they tell, tales poured into the sympathetic ear of the Bishop. Often, too, when the house was still, the invalids and the servants gone to rest, would the midnight lamp of the Bishop burn on till 1 and 2 A.M., while he wrote letter after letter—twenty or thirty at a time—upon every kind of topic, social, political, and religious; often concluding his midnight correspondence, with none but God and the Holy Angels looking on, by sending £5 here and £10 there to the sick and needy, without distinction of sect or denomination.

A life so spent, though lonely, was not an unhappy life. No life of noble consecration to the happiness of others can be miserable. Every such life is a twice-blessed life: it blesses others, and it is a blessing also to itself. The secret of Bishop Fraser's happiness was this self-consecration to the happiness of others. He that seeks his happiness in self, loses it. He that seeks happiness for others, finds it for himself. Bishop Fraser is a splendid illustration of the operation of this wondrous law. When weary, by comforting his "invalids" he was refreshed; when solitary, he found society by going to visit some sick or dying friend, and praying at their bed. His diaries often tell of the inward help of these visits to himself.

Thus at home, and away from home, in the solitude of domestic life, and amid the stir of public duties, the Bishop went bravely on his way—never morbid, but always anxious about his "dearest of mothers." For four years after her first paralytic seizure in 1873, his anxiety was irradiated by glimpses of brightness and hope, but in May 1877 the gloom began to thicken more deeply around the much-loved form, and the strain upon his strength was very hard to bear. He writes:

May 8, 1877.

"Sunday was a great strain upon me; but happily, when I got home at 10 P.M., I found all going on fairly well. But I won't go through such a trial again. It would indeed be a bitter thing to me to be absent when the last moment comes; and it is not safe to be away from home, as I was last Sunday, from 8.30 A.M. to 10 P.M. So I have broken all present engagements, which made a demand of this kind upon my time, and must content myself for a while with doing the work that lies closer to home. The dear one has been less drowsy the last three days, but her mind has been more wandering. Dr. Crompton considers this a good symptom, that the pressure is passing from the brain. I am writing now at 11.30 A.M., and she has not awakened yet. She was talking incessantly, her maid tells me, till 5.30, in the happiest way, once even trying to sing a 'Kyrie Eleison,' which she did with a very firm and true voice; and then she fell asleep, and so remains. I hope when she wakes she will be much refreshed, for her eyes have closed very seldom, and then only for short intervals, for the last three days. It seems as though our prayers were at least answered thus far—that her last days and hours are calm and peaceful. That her time in this world will be *much* longer I cannot dare to hope.

"To think of the belief that the soul sleeps till the resurrection. All *my* hopes would be crushed by such a faith. I have often been puzzled by doubts and difficulties about the resurrection of the body, but never have had a faltering of faith about the undying nature of the soul."

May 9, 1877.

" I have no need to have the slightest fear for her future, for her whole life has been full of faith and self-sacrifice, and her wandering thoughts and words have shown all through how pure her soul has been ; but still it is such a comfort to me to think that the last articulate words she uttered, before this long sleep came on, were the attempt to sing, ' Lord, have mercy upon us'—her memory could not carry her beyond that clause, but she sang that over, her maid says, several times. She has been the very best of mothers—she always made our home so happy and joyous —she did so draw and gain the love of her children; and, now that all is to become a mere memory, my heart almost breaks under the trial. It is selfish grief, I know, but I can't help it. I should not wish this state of unconscious torpor to be prolonged, and I can't believe she will live through another night ; but it is hard to anticipate the moment when we will have looked on that sweet loving face for the last time. My dear aunt bears up wonderfully, but I dread the strain. They have through life been knit together with no ordinary bonds of sisterhood. I know that we shall have a place in your prayers."

May 15, 1877.

" My dear aunt, whose affectionate relationship to my mother you know, is wonderfully sustained. What may happen if my dear mother is taken first, I dare not think of, but at present her heart does not fail, and strength is given to her to minister, as she loves to minister, by her sister's bedside—perfectly happy if she holds one hand of the dear one in her own. A more devoted, self-sacrificing woman than this dear aunt of mine, I have never known ; she thinks of herself last, and a long way last of all. She was the sister who was always present when each of my mother's own children entered the world ; so we have, all of us, looked up to her as a second mother ; and she has proved herself one.

" I cannot tell you how fortunate I am in all my servants. Just now their kindness and attention are simply invaluable—one and all ; and my mother's special maid, who has been with her a little over two years, is a girl whose price, under these trying circumstances, is 'above rubies.' If she were her daughter, she could not wait upon her mistress more devotedly and watchfully."

2 K

November 16, 1878.

"I can't report much improvement in my darling mother. Her thoughts wander a good deal, but in such a simple, quiet, natural way, that it is quite touching to listen to them; and often I feel the tear silently stealing down my cheek as I sit by her couch-side, and look in her sweet placid countenance and listen to her innocent 'babbling.' She still looks and feels very strong, but it seems as though at last the mind were giving way, and there is a good deal of that sad, plaintive crying, which, she says, she can't help, but which happily does not betoken suffering either of body or mind. I believe she is perfectly free from pain; and at times her old love of fun comes up to the surface as bright and fresh as ever, and hardly a day passes without her saying something that causes a hearty laugh to us all. The transparent simplicity, and purity, and naturalness of her mind and character is what has shone out so brightly all through her illness whether in moments of consciousness or unconsciousness.

"What a mystery life is! Tyndall may well think that there are things insoluble by philosophy. Even one's religious hopes and convictions are sometimes staggered. If one did not know that one was in the hands of a Father, there are moments when even the strongest faith would almost break down."

November 18, 1878.

"I have nothing fresh to report of my dear mother. The mind certainly grows weaker; but, to me, it is quite beautiful, and deeply touching, to sit by her and watch and listen. All is so simple, and pure, and good. This morning I went in before starting to say good-bye. She had just finished her breakfast, which at first I did not perceive, till, on kissing her, I traced the scent of coffee in her breath. 'Have you breakfasted?' I asked. 'No.' 'Oh, yes,' I said, looking round and seeing the little tray with the empty eggshell on a side-table, 'you have! Why, your breath smells all coffee.' 'No,' she repeated rather persistently, 'I haven't.' 'Certainly,' I reiterated, 'there is the empty teacup and the empty eggshell.' 'Well, where is it gone then?' she asked, with quite a roguish expression of face. Her memory is weak, and her sight at times dim; but she is wonderfully placid, very manageable, and everybody about her seems to love her. It is a beautiful close to a very simple but earnest life of duty done. No children could possibly have had a better mother."

November 21, 1878.

"As I look back upon my own life, I can sadly remember many and many occasions in which I was wanting in dutiful regard to my dear mother; and my temper certainly at one time was not one of the sweetest. But age has at least had one good effect upon me, and I am not so impetuous and impatient as I once was; and I cannot be too thankful that this last long illness of my dear mother has given me the opportunity of repairing, and of being forgiven, all past undutifulnesses, though I cannot forget them, or help reproaching myself for them."

November 23, 1878.

"All is going on fairly well with my two dear ones. The mother has taken to rather more crying and wailing lately, but it does not seem to distress or exhaust her, and is no sign, I am sure, of her being in pain. She has much of the old fun still left. Last evening I was sitting by her, and she kept on crying; so I said to her, in a serio-comic tone, 'I wonder you are not ashamed to keep making that noise.' 'I can't help it,' she replied; but, nevertheless, the noise ceased. A minute or two after I had a rather violent fit of coughing. 'I wonder *you* aren't ashamed of making *that* noise,' it was now her turn to say, and she said it with a roguish archness that made me burst into laughter."

December 12, 1878.

"Surely, if humanity ever can be fit, my mother's pure, guileless soul is fit for the kingdom of God. What quiets her most is to hear read some of the more soothing portions of the New Testament, such as John x. or xiv. and Rev. vii. She will lie quite quiet while I read, and say something at the end which shows that the leading thoughts have entered into her soul, though perhaps not quite coherently, and have given comfort there. I do assure you it is a great privilege to me to minister to her."

For more than another year the paralysed mother lingered on, tended by her devoted, faithful son. But at length the end drew near. Early in April 1880, the Bishop wrote to a trusted correspondent:

"A serious change has come over my dear mother; and the end may come at any moment. I can now only pray that my dear mother may be taken to her rest quickly and without pain. She has long ceased to *live*; she has only existed; and now there is a possibility of suffering from bedsores, etc., from which may the 'good Lord deliver her.' At present she seems insensible to pain, and is as calm as an infant."

Upon April 27, 1880, she died a peaceful and a painless death. Not long before her death she sang (unconsciously, as it appeared to those about her; but who can measure the consciousness, lying deep beneath the physical surface of a departing spirit?) her favourite prayer: "Lord, have mercy upon us, and incline our hearts to keep this law."

2 K 2

Letters of heartfelt sympathy poured in upon the Bishop; many of which he answered with his own hand, in a spirit of brave and calm repose in the promise and the prospect of eternal life. Within a week he was able to write: "We are not sad. Why should we be? 'Blessed are the dead which die in the Lord' is the alone thought which drives all grief away."

To Rev. Canon Maclure.

April 30, 1880.

"I thank you earnestly for the sympathy that I know comes from an affectionate heart. There is no bitterness in my dear mother's death. All was most peaceful and painless. She ceased to breathe, and that was all. She had been so long unconscious of all that passed, that it seemed as though the spirit had gone long before, and all that was left was the mere physical life, to flicker down and at last expire. I bury her to-morrow in my dear old Berkshire country churchyard, where, some day, I hope to be laid by her side."

To Rev. Canon Powell.

May 2, 1880.

"I thank you and dear Mrs. Powell very sincerely for your kind words of sympathy. They, and the like words of many other friends, have been a great comfort to us; though, really, we are not sad. Why should we be? I laid my dear mother's body in my old Berkshire churchyard amid a crowd of old kindly neighbours, rich and poor; every memory she has bequeathed to us is full of blessedness; death came without a pang or struggle; of her acceptance by our Father for her Saviour's sake we have no fear. 'Blessed are the dead who die in the Lord,' is the alone thought that drives all grief away.

"My best of wives is the sweetest of comforters to my dear aunt, who is wonderfully calm, resigned, and sustained."

From the graveside of the mother so long and tenderly loved, we accompany the brave-hearted Bishop, the ideal son of an ideal mother, back to his home in Manchester. For some months that home had been, even in its deepest sadness, brightened by the presence of one who, to his latest hour, was the softener of the Bishop's sorrows and the enlarger of his joys. It was in the year 1867 that the Bishop —then Mr. Fraser—first became acquainted with Miss Duncan, the only child of Mr. John Shute Duncan, D.C.L., of Westfield Lodge, near Bath. Mr. Duncan, a native of Hampshire, having been educated at Winchester School and

New College, Oxford (of which society he was elected Fellow), was called to the bar at Lincoln's Inn, in November 1798. He did not, however, devote much attention to his legal calling; his temper of mind impelling him to the study of nature, and his ample means affording free opportunity for scientific pursuits. His brother, Mr. Philip Bury Duncan, D.C.L., also Fellow of New College, Oxford, was appointed Curator of the Ashmolean Museum; of which institution both brothers were munificent benefactors. It was owing to the joint efforts of the two brothers—whose hearts were strongly bent upon the social and religious advancement of their fellow-men—that the first Savings Bank in Oxford was established, and other movements of a social Christian character promoted. After the marriage of Mr. John Shute Duncan to Miss Welch, of Leck Hall, Lancashire, he removed from Oxford to Bath, where he and his brother maintained their honourable distinction in supporting every effort for the spread of scientific knowledge, social happiness, and sound religion, among their fellow men. They were among the chief founders and supporters of the Bath Savings Bank, the Mendicity Society, and the Bath Royal Literary and Scientific Institution. In the vestibule of the latter Institution hang, side by side, oil portraits of the two brothers, and underneath the portraits a brass plate with the inscription:

"In memory of two brothers, JOHN SHUTE DUNCAN, D.C.L., and PHILIP BURY DUNCAN, D.C.L., of New College, Oxford, and the City of Bath; who, with large minds and liberal hearts, did good continually, winning the gratitude and love of their University, their fellow-citizens, and their friends. . . ."

Among the published works of Mr. John Shute Duncan is one, entitled 'Collections on the Provisions for the Poor in various Times and Countries'; another, entitled 'Analogies of Vegetable and Animal Life'; and another, entitled 'Botanic Theology.' The very titles of these treatises indicate the character of the writer's mind and the direction of his interests. Upon his head sat the triple crown of knowledge, goodness, and religion.

Mr. Duncan died May 14, 1844, when his only child, Agnes, was not yet thirteen years old. To the nurture of this only child the widowed mother devoted her whole mind and heart, and it was with expressions of deep thankfulness and joy that, in the early part of the year 1877, she gave her consent to the betrothal of her daughter to the Bishop. To the Bishop his engagement was a source of great felicity. It brought companionship into his solitude, and shed a halo of brightness around his life. In his correspondence with Miss Duncan, he poured out his whole heart. His occasional weariness of unresting toil, his domestic anxieties, his official duties, the incidents of every day, the people he met, the speeches he delivered, the difficulties he encountered, the amusements he enjoyed, the aspirations he felt and cultivated —all were pictured with his quick and graphic pen. Copious extracts from these letters have been given in the preceding chapter, but a few others may be added here in further illustration of the Bishop's personal character and domestic interests.

May, 1877.

"I confess it has always been my hope, that I might not be compelled to wear this episcopal harness to the end. But my life has been such a course of special providences, that I am quite content to take no thought for the morrow, but simply to discharge, as best I can, the responsibilities of to-day. But I may frankly say, that I liked the pastoral life, such as was mine at Cholderton and Ufton, far better than the episcopal. Not but what I receive unnumbered kindnesses, and unnumbered encouragements. Still, it is too heavy a burden; and too much seems to depend upon the wisdom and character of one man, and that one in this case, in spite of all you are pleased to think and say of him, only too conscious of many incapacitating defects."

July 3, 1877.

"Everything about the See of Manchester is modern. I am the second Bishop, while other Sees have a roll of more than ninety prelates. So you must not expect a medieval palace as at Norwich, or Ely, or Salisbury; a plain, red-brick, characterless house is the one I live in, with pleasant grounds of three acres, and, for Manchester, with a very pretty look-out over the valley of the Irwell, which might pass muster with the 'Silver Thames,' at the distance from which I view it. Its fragrance also does not reach as far as me. The said house has six sitting-rooms, none of them particularly spacious, but lofty, apartments—and twenty bedrooms (including those for servants). I have added to it a chapel, and entrance lodges, which give the only episcopal character to the place which it has; and the whole, being surrounded with a good high wall, has the advantage, much to be prized in Manchester, of seclusion and privacy. Considering I am only two miles from the cathedral, I could not be domiciled more to my mind."

October 1, 1877.

"Dear me! Why will people make others miserable, when, by increasing the happiness of those around them, they add so much to their own! How wretchedly short-sighted is human pride and human selfishness. . . .

"I remember reading, years ago, a very powerful novel by Mrs. Marsh, which impressed upon my mind the perils of reserve and reticence between husband and wife so vividly, that I have never forgotten the lesson, and I really don't know any *domestic* lesson more thoroughly worth the learning. An affectionate wife's heart thrown back upon itself in silence and scorn, when its deepest wish is to be a comfort and help! It makes me very sad to think of it. As you have so often truly said, if our religion won't make us kind and gentle to each other, and cheer and brighten life, its most valuable qualities are lost. . . .

"For a man, I consider myself a miracle of prudence, and I never willingly run hazardous risks, or play tricks with my health; I am a moderate eater and drinker; I take plenty of exercise; I don't coddle myself, and I never smoke. . . .

"Under no circumstances, if we be but true to ourselves, can the future be dark save by a passing cloud, such as even the chosen 'Three' went through on the 'Transfiguration hill'; and passing clouds leave rich and rewarding experiences behind them, and help us to realize, more fully than perhaps we otherwise should do, the glory and the beauty of the 'perfect day.'"

February 5, 1878.

"Sunday was rather a hard day. I left home at 6.45, and caught a 7 A.M. train, which landed me at Blackburn at 8.30. The vicarage is one of the most hospitable of houses, the only fault I find with Mrs. Birch, as I tell her, is that she 'coddles' me too much; and she tells me that her servants say, 'they like to do anything for the bishop, but they never want to see Mr. —— again.' So I first of all got a good breakfast, and then went off two miles to preach my first sermon; then returned to dinner at 1.30; then preached at 3 in the parish church, which is a large one, to 1500 people, and again, after a pleasant tea, in the same church, at the 6.30 service, to upwards of 2000, the church being as full as it could hold; and then off home by the 8.30 train, arriving safe, and none the worse for the day's work, at about 10.30. The most disagreeable part of the whole was the early rising. I am never very fond of turning out in the morning, and to have to do so at 5.45 on a dark, cold, foggy morning, dressing by gaslight and shaving without hot water (for I don't like having one's servants up on such occasions), was the only unwelcome part of the day's work."

October 15, 1878.

"I *do* long for a quieter life—such a life as I had for those ten happy years at Ufton, but I hope I would not desert a post of obvious duty. I really do sometimes feel alarmed when I open my engagement book and gaze down the vista for the coming weeks, and wonder how I shall get through it all. But to no one has the promise of 'strength' proportioned to the 'day' been more signally verified than to me; and though I do at times long for those 'flashes of leisure,' which perhaps some day, when present duties have been done, we may be permitted to enjoy together, yet the work itself is my refreshment, and the generous sympathy that I meet with, wherever I go, sustains me in a wonderful way. Still, I can't forget that I am sixty years of age, and I have no right to count upon many more years of equal endurance. And, besides, I remember there are always as good fish left in the sea as ever came out of it, and this diocese requires the utmost energy, and concentration of energy, of a man in his prime, and old Aristotle taught me, when I read him, that the body is at its prime about thirty-five, and the mind about forty-nine. When, therefore, a man is a sexagenarian, he may be forgiven if he begins to think that a younger and more vigorous man, both in mind and body, would do the work better than he. But I am not meditating anything at present, only it does not infrequently flit before me, that five years hence, or thereabouts, it may be time to lay my (imaginary) pastoral staff down."

On November 18, 1878, Mrs. Duncan's spirit passed peacefully from earth. For fifteen years she had been blind; but, except for loss of sight, she remained to the last in full possession of bodily sense, and mental faculty, and spiritual vigour.

Upon receiving the announcement of Mrs. Duncan's death, the Bishop wrote:

November 19, 1878.

"At last the end has come. Thank God that it came, after all those hours of piteous moaning—so sad (as I know from my own dear mother's case) to hear—calmly, passively, without a struggle. I doubt not that the blessed 'happy look,' that you say the dear features—so deeply traced in my memory—now wear, is an omen of the happiness into which her pure soul has entered, at least one stage nearer the presence of the Lord. It is not—a death like this—a thing to mourn over. It is true all blows, however long foreseen, however long prepared for, fall heavily when they come; but when the heart recovers itself, and the voice of faith and hope once more makes itself heard, we can feel how much we have to thank God for, even when He takes from us those whom we have loved. We are spared their sufferings; and all that was pure, and good, and noble in them is one's still, an imperishable memory. 'Tis 'So He giveth His beloved sleep': 'tis so. He enables us, without a murmur, to gaze upon them while they are sleeping, and, even when the grave has hid all that is mortal from our sight, to preserve in our heart of hearts all that was sweetest and most lovable in them for ever."

Again, two days afterwards :

November 21, 1878.

"I quite share your horror of vaults. When my time comes 'to fall asleep,' I hope to be laid in that dear old churchyard at Ufton, where one day, I suppose, I shall lay the bodies of my dear mother and aunt. I had the grave made large enough to hold four coffins; and my idea then was that there might be room for those two dear ones, myself, and my brother Alex. But things have changed (and how much for the happier) with me since then—and so, when we, like David, 'have served our own generation by the Will of God,' we may still have what is mortal of us laid side by side till the Great Resurrection morn.

"When *lives* have been 'lovely and pleasant,' it is always a thought of comfort to my mind that even 'in death they are not divided'; and to make arrangements of this kind beforehand, far from having any element of horror or fearful omen in it, on the contrary, always exercises a tranquillizing influence on my feelings. It leaves one so much the less to disquiet oneself about, when the parting time at last comes."

The brightness of the Bishop's home was, therefore, not a flaming brightness, untempered by softening, chastening clouds. The happiest homes, like the most beautiful skies, are often chequered with clouds. This was Bishop Fraser's experience. His father's mining speculations; the death of nearly all his brothers; his mother's long illness; Mrs. Duncan's long illness and death; his years of domestic solitude—these were clouds in the Bishop's sky. Nor, as the following letter shows, was he wholly free from the trial of bodily sickness :

December 27, 1878.

"Christmas Day was fairly fine here. I walked down to, and back from, the Cathedral to attend the morning service. It was quite a refreshment once more to join in our beautiful service, reverently rendered in God's own house, after my five weeks' confinement. I, as the phrase is, 'celebrated' at the Holy Communion, and there were about one hundred communicants. My voice stood it pretty well, though I found the repetition of the formula of distribution was rather trying, and I feel that yet my voice has not got much bottom to it; so the 'miraculous prudence' will still have a sphere for exercise. There was a grand musical service in the afternoon, *à la* Sir Henry Cole, at which the bands of our two principal theatres volunteered their services. The Cathedral was crowded in every part, with a congregation mostly of the lower middle class, and the Dean told me that everything went off as nicely as possible. The service was evensong, interspersed with some of the suitable melodies from the 'Messiah,' and a collection amounting to £53 was made for the relief of distress. I did not myself stay for this, lest it should bring it late before I got home."

Yet, notwithstanding clouds, the Bishop's home was beautiful—beautiful with the brightness of simplicity, diligence, self-restraint, and absence of waste. At over sixty years of age, the Bishop could say, "I never wasted a shilling in my life." From his boyhood to his death he kept an account of all his expenditure with punctual exactitude. He felt just a touch of scorn for people who were too indolent, or proud, or abstract, "to attend to matters of fact like money." To the Bishop, money was a talent, like intellect or genius, to be enjoyed and utilized; a talent for which he was persuaded God would finally require an account. "As a parson," he said, "I feel specially bound to keep my accounts well, for parsons have a bad name in the lay-world as being bad business-men; though, for my part, I believe that parsons, taken man for man, are as good at business as any other class of equal number." And certainly no banker could have beaten Bishop Fraser in the keeping and managing of accounts. He loved "looking after things." No detail of expenditure, however commonplace, was deemed unworthy of his notice. Not that he was either a fidget or a niggard. He was merely brightly interested in all things, without any false or superficial dignity; and was thriftily careful upon lofty, happy, Christian principle. He was not economical that he might accumulate—though all through his life he "saved" upon principle a portion of his income. When he became Bishop his official income was £4200 per annum. "Of this," he said, "I spend a third, save a third, give a third." The last item he often exceeded, for, during his episcopate of fifteen years, his gifts in charity exceeded £31,500.

Another characteristic of the Bishop's habits, especially in domestic affairs, was his strong dislike of change. He seldom changed, and never without great deliberation, either a servant or a tradesman. When once he had selected a shop, he might be reckoned upon, if fairly treated, as a constant customer. Though a staunch supporter of the co-operation movement, he never dealt at a co-operative store, and publicly announced that he should be constant to his tradesmen so long as they continued to serve him well. This constancy of mind ran through the whole fibre of the Bishop's being; and was manifest in all things, from greatest to least. In one particular instance (of a somewhat domestic nature, yet perhaps not unworthy of mention in the story of his *Lancashire Life*) this constancy of Bishop Fraser's purpose had a singular and unusual result. As he never changed his tradesmen, so it was his boast that he never altered his investments. "I have never," he said, "changed an investment in my life." With great care he selected his investments; never coveting a high rate of interest at the risk of anxious insecurity. After his death his papers showed how he had retained through life the investments which in early days he had made at Oxford and Cholderton. But the most remarkable instance of this habit of not altering his investments had reference to his father's mining speculations. These speculations, at first, turned out so badly that, after the father's death, the widowed mother, with her seven children, was reduced to the restraints imposed by a limited income. Still the mother, under the influence of her son's counsel, left the investments unchanged; and, after many long years, the mines unexpectedly recovered themselves, and, at the time of his decease, the Bishop was the possessor of an ample fortune! Rarely, at least in the financial world, has the Spanish proverb, adopted by Lord Beaconsfield, been more conspicuously verified: "Everything comes to him who waits!"

In a year after Mrs. Duncan's death rumours of the Bishop's approaching marriage began to spread through Manchester.

Manchester, *November* 8, 1879.

My dear Canon Powell,—No; I *must* thank you and Mrs. Powell for your kind wishes, which I know come from cordial and friendly hearts. I think I have every reason to "count myself a happy man," and, when you know my future wife, I am sure you will say I have made a good choice. It has been an engagement of some three years' standing; but, as circumstances have been with both of us up to the present date, it did not seem possible to complete it. A year ago, however, she lost her mother, to whom she was as tenderly attached as I am to mine; and my two dear ones are in that happy state of painless calm, that I think I may venture to bring a wife home; and, if nothing unforeseen occurs, we shall probably be married early in the year. I don't wish the affair to become a matter of public gossip; but I *do* wish that my friends should know what is in store for me.—With many thanks to you both for continual kindnesses,—I am, yours very sincerely,

J. MANCHESTER.

When the marriage was authoritatively announced, the whole world of Manchester, without distinction of creed or class, prepared to rejoice with their Bishop.

December 19, 1879.

"I found out from Canon Pitcairn, whom I saw last Tuesday, and questioned upon the subject, that the clergy are steadfastly minded to make me some present; but it is not (as I was glad to hear) to take the shape of a carriage and horses. 'It is too late to stop the thing,' Pitcairn said, 'it must go on; and I am sure, if you read the letters, and saw the way in which the proposal was being received, you would be gratified.' Well, then, I ventured to express the hope that it would not take one other form. 'What was that?' he asked. 'Why, I hope you will not give me a pastoral staff' (I think this had been entertained, from the way in which he asked). 'Why not?' 'Oh,' I said, 'it would change the whole character of my life. I should always have to go about with an apparitor and a chaplain, which would be a great incumbrance; and besides, I am afraid it would offend a considerable number of people who don't like that sort of thing, and it would be also out of keeping with my whole idea of life.' 'Well,' he said, 'I am glad to have heard this expression of your feelings, which shall be duly regarded.'"

Not clergy only, but laymen of all classes from the chief magistrate to obscure toilers, joined in the general expression of heartfelt rejoicing. Shopwomen subscribed their shillings to make a suitable present to Mrs. Fraser, the working men provided their tribute to the Bishop. One woman wrote to Mrs. Fraser:

DEAR MADAM,—Will you please accept a dozen knitted dishcloths; they are such as I have used for many years, and prefer them to any other kind.

I know it is a poor gift, but in a large house the useful are as necessary as the ornamental, and are sent as a small token of my esteem and admiration of the Bishop's straightforward manliness in the work he is called to do. May you both be long spared to work for the Master, is the prayer, dear Madam, of yours, very respectfully,

A LANCASHIRE WOMAN.

Nonconformists were as eager as Churchmen to offer their congratulations, not only publicly, but in private letters. One Nonconformist wrote thus:

> MY LORD,—Although unknown to you, pardon me if I add a word of congratulation to the many you must have already received on your marriage. It would be an impertinence in me to refer to your kindly and good works, were it not that these have made your name a loved and honoured "household word" in our own home. Yesterday morning our first words at breakfast were good wishes for you and your bride; and at once our youngest children rushed voluntarily into the kitchen to ring the household bells. We are Nonconformists, but we often thank God for the good gift of the Bishop of Manchester, and we yield to no one in sincere wishes for your health, happiness, and usefulness. May God bless you and your bride.—I am, my Lord, with very much respect, yours faithfully,
>
> FRED. J. PERRY.

While, however, others were thinking of the Bishop, the Bishop was not thinking of himself. He was planning how he might best, and most wisely, extend, upon his wedding-day, some share of his happiness and joy to the poor and needy. Mr. Smith, of the Manchester District Provident Society, gives the following account of the Bishop's bountiful plans:

> "Some weeks before it was known that the Bishop was about to marry, he waited upon me, and said: 'Mr. Smith, can you keep a secret?' To which I replied, 'That depends, my Lord, whether it is worth keeping or not.' Then his Lordship said: 'Well; the secret that I want to repose in you is, that shortly I am about to be married, and on the morning of my marriage I intend to send you a cheque for £250, which I wish you to dispose of, not as charitable gifts, but as a wedding gift in some shape or form to any respectable and good people of any religious denomination whatever, whose clergymen or ministers may deem them worthy of being favoured with a gift from me on the occasion of my marriage.'"

This was carried out by a request, sent to every clergyman and minister of religion of every denomination in Manchester and Salford—that they would select from their congregation, some one or two individuals whom they would delight to honour.

In this way no less than eight hundred and fifty people were presented with a Scotch maud through their ministers with a handsome card, on which were the words:

"Presented to ——, by the Manchester and Salford District Provident Society, at the request and expense of the Lord Bishop of Manchester, on the occasion of his marriage."

During the progress of the arrangements for this presentation, the Bishop was so delighted with all that was being done—and in no case would have it classed as a charitable gift—that he told Mr. Smith not to limit the amount to the original sum fixed, viz., £250, but spend what was required, and, within some £2 or £3, £500 was spent on the object.

The Bishop's bounty, however, did not limit itself to these eight hundred and fifty poor people of Manchester. He remembered also the poor of his old parish of Ufton Nervet. Nor did he forget that large suffering class of "superior people" who do not proclaim their distress.

December 22, 1879.

"This morning, almost before I had finished my breakfast, I had a visit from Mr. Smith of the D.P.S., who, it appears, has had some conversation with Herbert Philips, a leading manager of the Society, about the money that I proposed to send them on our wedding-day. They suggest its distribution by the clergy of the poorest parishes in Manchester, in the shape of warm clothing among their people. I cheerfully acquiesced in the plan, only requiring that it should be distributed without distinction of sect, and I told Smith that I should send him £250 when the happy day arrived. I think this will be a much more satisfactory way of marking the day than by ordering, as in ——'s case, two tons of wedding-cake at 3s. 6d. a pound. I have told Cornish (Rector of Ufton Nervet), in acknowledging his letter, that I should send him £15 on the same day, and for the like purpose."

January 10, 1880.

"The Young Men's Christian Association have a fund, which they are distributing among the superior class of people—clerks and warehousemen—who have suffered as acutely as anybody in the late distress, but who do not proclaim their sufferings, and I don't think they are generally known. Besides, then, the £250 which I shall send to Mr. Smith, of the D.P.S., I shall send £50 to the secretary of the Y.M.C.A., for the purpose of showing sympathy with these people. The only other extravagance to which I suppose I must submit is to set the cathedral bells ringing on Thursday; and this I shall leave in the hands of Mr. Burder, who is always ready to do anything I ask him to facilitate matters. (He is coming to-morrow to meet Christie here at dinner.)"

The judicious manner in which the Bishop's £50 was expended among needy clerks and warehousemen is described in the following notice, which appeared in the Manchester Press, on the Monday following the Bishop's marriage.

"THE BISHOP OF MANCHESTER AND THE DISTRESSED CLERKS.

" On Saturday thirty-two joints of meat were sent to thirty-two families, containing in the aggregate 190 persons, with the following note from Mr. W. H. Newett, who has charge of the working of the Married Clerks' Relief Fund in connection with the Young Men's Christian Association: 'As to-morrow will be the first Sunday of the Bishop's married life, you will please accept this joint of meat for your family's dinner, provided out of his kind grant to the above fund.' Forty-four cases were relieved last week, chiefly by payment of rent, in order to prevent the break-up of households. It should be mentioned that, whilst careful inquiry is made as to the fitness of the recipients for help, no questions as to sect or belief are asked either of the applicants or their referees."

The Bishop's scanty personal preparation for his wedding is scarcely less characteristic than his munificent public generosity. He gave hundreds of pounds to others, but he expended very little upon himself.

January 9, 1880.

"I shall not bring my new portmanteau with me. They tell me that newly married couples are always 'spotted' by new portmanteaus. So I have had an old 'solid leather' one done up, which has stood me in good stead ever since I went to Shrewsbury as a schoolboy, stood all my Oxford journeys, crossed the Atlantic with me in 1865, and was with me that memorable week, in 1867, when I first heard of somebody. There is nothing, I see, like buying a good thing: this portmanteau has done my work for forty-five years, and seems to day as strong as ever it was. I sent it to be repaired and put in order by my saddler, and I am quite pleased by the way in which he has sent it home. The wedding presents still keep coming in. None has pleased me more than the 'tea cosey,' with its accompanying simple letter, from those three Ufton sisters."

The Bishop's marriage was quietly solemnized in St. Peter's Church, Cranley Gardens, South Kensington, on Thursday, January 15, 1880, at 10.30 A.M. Both the place and time of the marriage had been kept as secret as possible, the temper of neither the bride nor the bridegroom being favourable to ostentation and display. The Bishop's groomsman was his lifelong friend, the Rev. H. Pearson, Canon of Windsor. The wedding party was very small, consisting only of a few relations, a few very intimate friends, the two curates of the Church, and the "faithful Stone"—Mrs. Fraser's nurse and life-long friend. The marriage service was read by the Very Rev. Dean Stanley, an old and deeply attached friend of the Bishop; whose voice was more than once broken with emotion, while he threw into the familiar sentences of the service a wealth of meaning such as only the greatest readers, like himself and Cardinal Newman, seem able, spontaneously and without effort, to introduce. At the close of the service the following simple and touching address was delivered by the Dean—an address in which the warmth of personal friendship is sweetly blended with the benediction of deep religious feeling:

"This is a happy and Christian marriage. It is not only a blending together of two souls for the mutual society, comfort, and help of each; not only a constant giving and receiving of the purest happiness; but it is a new starting-point in life, a new starting-point of usefulness. 'Tis an encouragement to us to embark anew on the duties of life—a new pledge given, not merely as the philosopher has said, 'a new hostage to fortune,' but a new Christian pledge to God and man that former pledges will be fulfilled faithfully and well. It is the banding together of two lives for mutual strength and assistance — a partnership which will rejoice the hearts of both, and which, I trust, will be sanctified by the blessing of God. Each has secured a new second life, each will rejoice and sorrow as the other. None know so well as husband and wife the character of the dear one. None else can have such an interest at stake in the welfare, the fame, the grace, and the goodness of each other, as must be inspired by the thought of the indissoluble union with those in whose happiness and glory we ourselves become happy and glorious, by whose purity and strength we are made more pure before heaven and God. Many hearts of those who are absent this day are feeling with us and with you at this moment. Many devout aspirations, many Christian expectations, are being formed, and many humble prayers go up here and elsewhere that, with the new life now opening, blessings may spring up more abundantly in that rich experience known only to those who know what wedded life can be. We speak to you, and for you as well as to you. The day long expected has come at last, when you will now enter upon your joint labours. May you abound in every good and perfect work. Lord, forsake them not, but abide with them continually until they have shown 'Thy strength unto this generation, and Thy power to all them that are to come.'"

The simplicity of the Bishop's marriage was in keeping with his nature and whole way of life. In a characteristic letter contributed to *Punch*, and entitled, "A Bishop forgetting himself," the Bishop's simplicity is delightfully portrayed by one of those light pencils which have the rare gift of conveying, under the guise of amusement, a great and needed truth.

To Mr. Punch.

Sir,—I have long felt that Dr. Fraser, the Bishop of Manchester, was a highly dangerous person. He is always forgetting his position, and doing or saying something of a levelling and eccentric, if not an indecorous and even dangerous kind. One is constantly reading in the papers of his attending meetings at theatres, and club-rooms, and Mechanics' Institutes, and other haunts of the lower orders of an equally unconsecrated character, and making himself hail-fellow-well-met with the working men and other low persons whom he encounters at such places. Of course one understands at once that a Bishop of Manchester is in a difficult position. Still, I did not think that the degradation would have reached Dr. Fraser's domestic and family arrangements. I supposed that the man must behave like a Bishop at home, however he might comport himself in public. I grieve to find that I have been mistaken. Anything more indecent, for a Bishop, than his marriage as described in the papers, I never heard of. In the first place, instead of Westminster Abbey, or St. Martin's, or St. George's, Hanover Square, at least—or some other of what may be called the *comme-il-faut* marriage churches—his marriage comes off at a commonplace little district church in Onslow Gardens, that nobody ever heard of. The ceremony seems to have been sneaked through, as if everybody was ashamed of what was going on, or, rather, coming off. The church at which the ceremony was to take place was unknown to all but the Bishop's most intimate friends until a few hours before the time for which it was fixed, and the friends of the bride and bridegroom who were present numbered not more than a dozen. Did you ever hear of such doings? It is true there was a dean to read the marriage service, but then it was Dean Stanley; so Broad and Low Church that it might almost as well have been Mr. Spurgeon or Dr. Jabez Inwards. The clergy who assisted him were worthy of such a principal. They were actually a couple of curates! I must say I call such behaviour in a Bishop absolutely indecent! And the rest was of a piece. There was no musical service. The bride was in plain silver-grey satin—just like a quakeress—and seems to have had only one bridesmaid, if any. After the 'ceremony'—ceremony, indeed!—the Dean 'substituted' for the exhortation a private address to the Bishop and his bride of the most latitudinarian character. 'He felicitated them on their position as parties to a happy Christian marriage, spoke of the day as a long-expected one which had come at last, and congratulated them on the fact that, from many hearts of absent friends, prayers were being offered for their future happiness.' Did you ever read anything so loose and broad? And from a Dean to a Bishop! It more than makes one blush. It is enough to make one shudder. And this precious wedding-party seemed to have ended the ceremony as they began it—going back to a plain breakfast at the house of some nobody or other, and starting for Torquay by the afternoon train. I shouldn't wonder if they took a cab from where they breakfasted to the railway. In fact, there does not seem to have been a person of family or position mixed up in the affair from first to last. Of course we can't so much wonder at that, considering the sad way the Bishop has mixed himself up with the lower orders. But, still, he is a bishop, and one must grieve when a person of his class and calling, though only in a manufacturing district, can so lamentably forget himself.—I remain, sir,

ONE WHO NEVER FORGETS HERSELF.

After a brief month's holiday the Bishop with his bride returned to Manchester, there to enjoy till the hour of his sudden death his ideal of married happiness—the great gift with which, he often said, "Kind Heaven had crowned a life laden with goodness." For several months the aged mother still lingered on; tended now not only by the devotion of her son, but also by the affection of that son's wife, a true daughter to her. The aged aunt rejoiced with almost a mother's joy; for both his "old ladies" felt how thoroughly the Bishop deserved, after his lifelong fidelity to them, to be rewarded with the completed happiness of his home. They rejoiced, too, to think that, when they were gone, the Bishop would not be left solitary and desolate, the light of home quenched in darkness: little deeming that one of them—the aged and half-invalid aunt—would survive the fresh, strong, Bishop, and be nursed most tenderly till her dying hour by the Bishop's widowed wife. But, at first, no shadow of these impending sorrows lay across the brightness of this beautiful home. All was joy, and work, and love. The home life of Bishop's Court sent forth its rays of light and warmth into a multitude of other homes. Especially into the homes of the toiling clergy in crowded parishes was the sunshine of Bishop's Court poured. The birth of a child, the marriage of a child, the death of an inmate in the homes of his clergy, was generally the occasion for some communication of congratulation or solace from Bishop's Court. As the Bishop was the chief pastor, so Bishop's Court was the *central home* of Manchester. Not by an extravagant ostentation of hospitality, but by the simpler plan of untold sympathy, the presence and power of the Bishop's home-happiness was felt throughout the diocese. One of the greatest needs of modern England is greater devotion to home, and a stronger realization that the purest joys of which humanity is capable spring, and *can* spring, *only* from the fountain of the domestic relationships. Every fresh example of this great law of human felicity is a benefit to the race. It is part of England's favoured lot that the *First Home* in the realm has been, for half a century, consecrated to the illustration of this law of happiness. By her great and whole-hearted belief in the domestic relationships—relationships which death may darken, but cannot destroy—the sovereignty of Queen Victoria has become a sovereignty, not of dynasty alone, but of intense affection also. Similarly with Bishop Fraser, his simple devotion to his mother, his outspoken pride in his wife, his joy in home, did more to extend and deepen his influence among the Lancashire people, than either the dignity of his office or the power of his utterances could of themselves have accomplished. What Lancashire loved was less the Bishop and the orator than the MAN—the mother-loving, wife-loving, home-loving Man.

Moreover, the Bishop, although an uncompromising hater of luxury and extravagance, was yet generously given to hospitality. And what a genial host he was! How he ran to the door to meet his guests and attended himself to the details of their comfort! How the table, spread with simple bounty, seemed illuminated by the cheerful light of the Bishop and his wife! How the talk ran on, overflowing with an interest in all things, from grave to gay, from humorous to solemn! How he loved a story or a joke, so long as it was without malevolence! When he was tired with overstrain, or had some threatening of bronchitis, to which he was constitutionally prone, or had for a while lost his voice, how patiently and happily he would sit while his wife read aloud some newspaper, book, or magazine—dealing with the tidings and the problems of the day, or describing scenery (of which he was very fond), or sketching the life of some one he had known, or wandering into the regions of romance, or rising to the heights of poetry!

"A point," writes a correspondent, "no less characteristic is the entire unbending of his mind in leisure. Nearly the last time I saw him he was listening to Mrs. Fraser, as she read aloud Mrs. Ewing's 'Story of a Short Life.' He said afterwards that he was glad that he had not been obliged to speak to any one, for he could not have answered for the command of his voice, and, in fact, his emotion was evident."

But the sweetest hour at Bishop's Court was the hour of prayer. No laboured exposition, no lengthy routine of supplication, but a short passage from the Bible, with, perhaps, an occasional comment of pithy, devout, common sense; a few prayers so said that the power of every sentence came home, without parade of sanctity, to the inmost spirit of every one; and so arranged that all could take audible share in portions of them. It was a strong help to begin the day in the straightforward, manly, religious fashion in which it was always begun at Bishop's Court. "I shall remember to the day of my death," writes a visitor to Bishop's Court, "the way the Bishop read his family prayers. Young men have told me it was a memory and example which helped them in life." But no pen can better describe the home life of Bishop Fraser than the pen of her who, for the five last years, shared with him the beauty and the happiness of that life.

"*Home Life!* What a world of enchanting memories do the two words recall!—the daily round of noble work and occupation—the daily sunshine—the inspiring presence. First the cheerful breakfast, the rapid scanning of the daily paper—then the adjournment to the library—the consecration of the morning by the simple heartfelt prayers, and the reverent reading of the Word. 'How I love these little offices!' was the frequent remark. Then the prayers turned into action, the unvarying discharge of the daily correspondence as the duty to be first attended to, clear, concise, practical as to counsel; tender and loving n sympathy with the lowliest, forbearing with the most unreasonable, often interrupted, but never resenting, the sacrifice of self crowning all. Then (how the scene rises before me!) the hasty closing of the portfolio, everything in its place, not a letter left unarranged and out of its date, not a drawer closed in haste or confusion, a hasty glance at the clock not to be too late for the tram, the loving farewell—'Kiss the Auntie for me!'—never forgotten. 'Now I'm off,' and then, with a merry wave of the hand, the *bound* down that walk to catch the conveyance, full of joy and strength. How the tram-guards knew him! how they appreciated his kindly greeting! how the passers-by capped him! how pleased they were to see him often striding along with his sunny face and his cheery greeting! Those who know most can tell what the day's business meant—the round of meetings—the quick insight into the various financial interests of the numberless charities and philanthropic institutions of the city—the word of counsel, encouragement, warning. Churchmen and Nonconformists alike seemed to covet his presence and sympathy; he was as the life's blood circulating through them all. How he delighted to look in now and then at the District Provident Society, and have a chat with good Mr. Smith about the various cases of distress that pressed themselves on his notice, and which he would never relieve unless he was satisfied they were genuine (and how many proved the reverse!)—how rapid and complete was his discharge of business at the Registry on Tuesdays! Yet never too busy to lend a kind and courteous ear to those needing counsel or fatherly advice. What a joy it was to those in office to work under that bright command; so full of appreciation of the humblest service; so willing to give them all thanks and credit, and to take the lesser portion to himself! Then the frequent railway journeys, all accurately planned weeks beforehand, the exact time of the trains entered punctually into the engagement-book, so well known in the diocese —the sermon or address often thought out, and the heads jotted down, in the railway carriage, to appear as a finished composition an hour afterwards, the previous jottings often not adhered to, the inspiration of the moment often supplying abundant material, welling up warm and fresh from that big heart and thus going straight to the hearts of his hearers. How children loved him! how they stole on his knee! how they coveted his kiss! how servants rejoiced to wait on him! how genuine his acknowledgment of their smallest service! how he remembered every detail about the families of his clergy—remarked every new bit of furniture in their rooms, enjoyed the simplest fare, and repudiated all superfluities of entertainment! How stern he was when hearing of selfishness, neglect of duty, extravagance, impurity! how free to enter into the humour of the moment, to enjoy good stories, to listen to frank, unconventional remarks, to take in information everywhere! Thus the bright day passed—then the return home! the turning of the latch-key, the merry whistle, the joyous greeting, the abounding welcome—the rapture of the old Auntie as the footstep creaked on the stair. The cheerful recital of much that had been said and done during the day, then—'Now for business'—and down he would fly to answer the many letters that had arrived during his absence, till 7.30 P.M. brought the post and dinner. 'What have I done to be such a happy man?' was often the remark, as the easy-chair and the bright fireside ended the labours of the day. 'Sometimes I think the happiness is too great, but then'—and the dear face looked grave for a moment, and the voice dropped—' it's my way of giving thanks to God—being always happy—my cup overflows!' Then for the quiet enjoyment of books and papers *when* a leisure evening was permitted, all read and digested with marvellous rapidity in a way that astonished outsiders. No man was more abreast than he of all that was surging in the thoughts of men ; no heart beat more truly with all the associations of the age—none longed to be a greater helper, friend, and sympathizer.

" But enough and too much of these home pictures—' no skeleton in our cupboards, thank God !'—how *could* there be when such a Christ-like life was ever shining within ? Home, the best of all, nothing more wanted, craved for, the loves of the dear people outside, the love of God within, consecrating and ennobling every hour of the day."

CHAPTER XIX.

CLOSING SCENES.

Home Life—Wedding Gifts—Statistics of Diocese—His Lancashire Work—Premonitions of Death—Last Visit to Ufton Nervet—Last Letter—Last Illness—Death—Funeral—Ufton Nervet—Ufton Church—The Burial—After Death.

For five and a half years the full stream of this sweet home-happiness flowed brightly on. Now and again its waters were darkened by heavy over-hanging clouds. The dearly-loved mother died in the first half-year, and the life of the venerable aunt hung only on a slender thread. There were troubles, too, outside the home. The diocese which had been the abode of progressive work and general peace was torn and wounded by the thorns at Miles Platting and Cheetham Hill. The desire for retirement and rest grew deeper year by year in the breast of the brave and toiling Bishop. It was not, however, so much the weariness of work as the pangs of worry which tormented him. Longing for "the unity of the Spirit in the bond of peace," he found himself entangled in the meshes of party bitterness and ecclesiastical war; and the sweet memories of his former tranquil life as rector of a little country parish grew increasingly vivid and attractive. Gradually the unambitious longing "to doff the episcopal harness" hardened into a fixed determination, communicated only to his wife and most trusted friends.

Meanwhile, however, he marched boldly on, ceaselessly labouring, and greatly strengthened in his labours by the restful joys of home. The diocese, too, seemed to gather round him with an ever-deepening fidelity. The occasion of his marriage had been seized, both by clergy and laity, for the exhibition of sentiments of esteem and affection.

In these movements every political party, every religious denomination, every social class eagerly took their part. The clergy presented a handsome service of silver plate which the Bishop bequeathed to his successor in the See. A "Bishop-Fraser Scholarship" was founded at Owens College, a marble bust by Mr. Warrington Wood was placed in the Town Hall, and a portrait of the Bishop by Sir John Everett Millais, R.A., was presented to Mrs. Fraser. The address, accompanying the portrait, declared that

"Every interest of our common humanity, whether small or great, has had its claim ungrudgingly admitted, has commended itself to the Bishop's sympathy, and has received his most ready help. In him Lancashire has found not a bishop only, but a man overflowing with sympathy for his brother-men, whatever their politics, or their creed, or their station might be. And while by his liberality of opinion, his tone of moderation, his breadth of sentiment, his unvarnished and outspoken eloquence in the pulpit, the Church of England has gained immensely; that still wider and more general organization, which includes within its pale all good and faithful men, has been strengthened and enlarged by the example of unreserved sacrifice, of unwearying labour, and of 'cheerful godliness' which he has consistently set before us."

In acknowledging this address, the Bishop said:

"I have not laboured for popularity, though some people think I have won it. I have not shrunk from work, and I have wished that work to be not merely the varnish of superficial labour. . . . I cannot hope to please everybody; I have never attempted to do so. When I came here, conscious of my many deficiencies and disabilities, I determined that I would at least try to be honest and straightforward, to recognize good work wherever and by whomsoever done; and though I felt myself to be limited in my sympathies, and in some respects by my position, yet it is most gratifying to be assured that this tribute to one, however unworthy of so high a tribute, has been paid by persons of all political parties, and very many different views."

Such expressions of kindly feeling greatly cheered and upheld the Bishop. The ardour and success with which he continued his work may be measured by some statistics which occur in his last Charge, delivered less than twelve months before his death:

"Of the 492 incumbents of the diocese, 328, or 66 per cent., have been admitted to their cures by me—a wonderful illustration of that law of change which gives to none of us here a long abiding-place, and bids all do the work that lies before us while it is day; while the number whom I have ordained and sent forth into the ministry of the Church, in the period of 15 years, is 456. Of the 492 churches, I have either preached or held a Confirmation, or done some episcopal act, in 478. The aggregate population of the 14 parishes which I have not visited (with the exception of one parish of 4500, where peculiar circumstances kept me away), is under 5000; so that, considering that the population of the diocese has reached the huge total of 2,297,000, I have given opportunity to the great bulk of the people of knowing, at least by face, the overseer who is set over them."

These statistics may be further enlarged by information received from the Diocesan Registrar, Mr. E. P. Charlewood. During the fifteen years of his episcopate, Bishop Fraser consecrated 105 new churches, providing 60,196 sittings, of which 49,902 are free, besides consecrating twenty-one churches built in place of former churches, providing 15,573 sittings, of which 12,190 are free. The cost of these churches was £952,829. When Bishop Fraser came to the diocese in 1870, there were in it 681 clergy, of whom 396 were incumbents; when he died in 1885 there were 816 clergy, of whom 499 were incumbents. During these fifteen years the Bishop confirmed, with his own hands, 188,192 candidates, of whom 71,383 were males and 116,809 females.

Tabulated statistics, however, represent but a small portion of the great work which by incessant cheerful toil the Bishop accomplished in his fifteen years of *Lancashire Life*. He was the head and front of every movement intended for the advancement of progress and culture. He threw himself heart and soul into the cause of education in all its departments. He founded the Diocesan Board of Education, instituted the Diocesan Conference, established the Bishop of Manchester's Fund to provide means for Christian work in poor and densely peopled parishes. He also rearranged the diocese, dividing it into three archdeaconries in place of two; held frequent ordinations; answered with his own hand between 3000 and 4000 letters every year; preached in fifteen years no fewer than 2000 sermons, besides delivering very numerous speeches and addresses; presided over all kinds of committees; and gave his time and labour to the support of some dozens of charitable and other organizations. As Bishop Moorhouse (now Bishop of Manchester) generously said, at the unveiling of Bishop Fraser's statue:

"A vaster work, a more exhausting work, than that which was set by Dr. Fraser for a Bishop of Manchester, is not to be found in England. My great predecessor has taught the people of Manchester so great and true an idea of the scope of religious influence that there is no subject, save perhaps that of party politics, for which they do not look to their Bishop for light and leading."

It was, indeed, a magnificent conception of his office which Bishop Fraser had formed.

"Mr. Gladstone," wrote the *Spectator*, in 1876, " probably never did a better stroke of work for England, certainly never so good a one for the English Church, as when he recommended Dr. Fraser for the Bishopric of Manchester. Perfect simplicity, practical capacity, manliness of a high order, godliness of the most unpresuming type—these were the qualities needful to secure the popular influence of a Bishop of the National Church in the great metropolis of manufacture and commercial enterprise; and these qualities Bishop Fraser continues to manifest in higher and higher degree. A plain-spoken man, who has vigour and sense written on every feature of his fresh and open face—a man, who is as indifferent to the conventional dignities of his position as he is, on that very account, capable of using them to good effect; a prompt man, who seizes the first tool which comes ready to his hand for doing a moral work that must be done, whether it be a tool that the fastidious among his brethren or his clergy like to see him brandishing or not; a whole-minded man, who is incapable of dividing himself into two, and of keeping silence as a bishop, when he would feel it his peremptory duty to speak as a citizen; an earnest man, who never likes to say a word, which is the proper handle to a deed, without following it up by the appropriate action, and yet far too busy and sagacious a man to meddle in matters which do not concern the chief obligations of his personal or his official life, Dr. Fraser is just the bishop for a diocese which proverbially loves practical vigour, plain dealing, and hard work, better than any other qualities through which it might be possible to express the general characteristics of the Christian character.

"The Church of England would be much more nearly the true Church of the nation than it is if there were but many bishops like him. For, after all, what our clergy want is not so much learning—nor even piety, for they are usually full of piety as a class—but manliness. Bishop Fraser, and such as he, are the true leaven of the National Church and, while they remain to us, will secure the respect of English laymen for the Church."

But even the splendid strength of Bishop Fraser began to yield beneath the weight and magnitude of this ceaseless toil. In the early summer of 1885 he frequently complained of the heavy sense of dull fatigue. His doctor, a High Churchman, tried to persuade him to preach only once on the Sunday, and to attend the Cathedral in state, and give his benediction from the throne. He looked up laughing, and replied: "I don't do half the work you do. I know what you want. You want to put me in a mitre and cope to be stared at." So he continued to go about his work as usual till the 19th of August, when he started upon a short holiday, reaching his "dear old home at Ufton" at the end of the month. The story of this last visit to the peaceful home and country church he loved so well may best be told in the language of Canon Cornish, the Rector of Ufton Nervet, and for more than forty years the Bishop's tried and valued friend.

"On August 31, 1885, Bishop Fraser paid Ufton what was ordained to be his last visit. During part of the previous week, he and Mrs. Fraser had been guests of his old friends, Major and Mrs. Thoyts. On Sunday, August 30, he had preached twice in the parish church at Ufton, which had been rebuilt in the first year of his incumbency, as its rector; and which perhaps he loved the more, because he had been present when its foundation was laid, had watched its progress in building, and taken part in its consecration. The evening congregation was very large, as if drawn by a presentiment, unconscious to themselves, that they were to listen to him for the last time. On the Monday which followed, the Bishop and Mrs. Fraser came to the Rectory. After their arrival, a quiet walk to look on scenes familiar to him of old, and to greet a few men and women whom he remembered, closed the day till the dinner-hour. On Tuesday, September 1, we lunched with Captain and Miss Sharp, the tenants of an old Elizabethan mansion, formerly the abode of the squires of the parish. A few guests met him at dinner, among them two very old friends—the rector of the parish of Theale, and the vicar of Beenham.

"The next day, September 2, we made an excursion to Highclere. The Bishop had set his heart on this. In the previous year we had gone to Savernake Forest, and it had pleased him so that he then said: 'Next year we will go to Highclere.' And thus, spite of the day being damp and showery, and the remonstrance of Mrs. Fraser, we went. We were a large party; two carriage loads to Aldermaston Station. We then took the train to Newbury, and from thence posted to Highclere. When I sent the carriages home from Aldermaston, I proposed to the Bishop that one carriage should come for the ladies on our return, and that he and I should walk. To this he gladly assented.

"On Thursday, September 3, there was rain, and I have no record of anything we did, before the evening, when we dined with his old friends, Mr. and Mrs. Bland-Garland, and met his still older friends, Sir John and Lady Mowbray; Mr. and Mrs. Thursby were also there, connected with a Lancashire family of the same name, well known to him for their help and assistance in every good work.

"On Wednesday evening (to revert again to that day), Dr. Chase had joined us. Here there was a meeting of three old Oriel Fellows; and our talk naturally turned on Oxford as it was, as it is, and as it was likely to be. It also turned on one or two who were known to us. I had, on the June previous, seen C. P. Eden, the Vicar of Aberford, in Yorkshire, an old Oriel Fellow, who was then on what proved to be his deathbed, but retaining full mental power, and the strongly marked features of his amiable character. I also remember a little discussion, which arose from a fact which the Bishop mentioned, that he had sent to a man with whom we were all acquainted, who was known to be poor, a cheque for £20. This had been returned, though not unkindly. Had he acted kindly, in denying Bishop Fraser the pleasure of doing something for an old friend? On Friday we parted—Bishop Fraser and his wife to pay a visit in Gloucestershire, Dr. Chase to Oxford.

"On the day after their departure from Ufton, Mrs. Fraser's anxiety for her husband was awakened, and there arose a feeling in the mind of the Bishop that his hard work at least was over. The fatal blood-clot near the collar-bone showed itself. Frequent communications passed between us—at one time hope, at another fear was predominant. Fear, at least on my part, had given place to hope, when, on the evening of October 22nd, while I was entertaining some clerical friends at dinner, a telegram was placed in my hands, that suddenly, on that day, at mid-day, he had been called away. The shock was greater because in the morning I had received a cheerful letter from him—the last he ever wrote—written on the day previous. I have a fair amount of self-control. I made no mention of what had occurred to my guests till just before they left. They were kind and sympathizing, for almost all of them knew him. I then called in my servants, who knew and loved Bishop Fraser, to tell them the loss we had met with."

The Rectory and Parish Church of Ufton which were so dear to him are thus connected, in a way which is touching and interesting, with the memory of Bishop Fraser. During his last visit at Sulhamstead and at Ufton, he had seen most of his old friends. His last day of seeming health and strength was spent at Ufton, his last sermon was preached there, his last letter was written to his old friend the Rector. And now, when his life's labours are ended, he sleeps beneath the shadow of the church he loved so well.

Of his last sermons, Canon Cornish writes:

"There could have been nothing specially marked about them, or, under the circumstances, though having but an old man's memory, I should have remembered it. Characteristic they were in one sense; for they contained that homely advice which he was so wont to give to rural people—about their *home* duties as parents, children, husbands, wives. This I recollect."

The "last letter," written the day before his death, is instinct with general interest in human affairs, business-like capacity, sympathy and hope.

MANCHESTER, *October* 21, 1885.

MY DEAR CORNISH,—Your letter entertained us much—especially your account of your visit to Oxford. I am only sorry to hear of the continual depression of the agricultural interests. When will the lowest depth be reached, I wonder? It can't be very pleasant, with the growing luxury of the place, to find one's income reduced fifty per cent.

Do come to us as you propose, on November 2. We will try and not let you catch a cold this time.

The next week we shall probably go to London, where I have one or two engagements to fulfil—not requiring any great physical exertion—at the Bounty, the Ecclesiastical Commissioners, and a meeting of the governors of Shrewsbury School. I may also, perhaps, take the opportunity of consulting some eminent surgeon—Sir Joseph Lister is recommended—about myself.

I am making progress, I think, slowly in the right direction. I shall take the full time of rest ordered, but I don't at all expect that I shall find myself equal to the longer administration of this great diocese.

The dear Dean of Chester is very ill—Bright's disease, I hear; and is leaving home for the winter. People say he is not likely to return alive. Poor fellow, he cannot keep himself quiet; I told him plainly at York, last spring, that if he did not he could never live to another Convocation.

How did your political meeting go off? I can fancy Miss Sharp bursting with zeal. I hope the gong is hung and proves sufficient for its purpose. I think Catharine will not be at home when this reaches you. The wife sends all kind regards.—Ever yours affectionately,

J. M.

Men reveal themselves in sickness more clearly than in health. They may wear the cloak of an assumed self so long as they have strength to carry it; but in the days of weakness the cloak falls away, and the naked *under-self* appears. But

Bishop Fraser was not a man with two selves, with an inner and outer, an upper and under self. His was no veiled and cloaked character. He was transparent as the light, and shone with sincerity. His sickness attested this transparency even more clearly than his health. After the clot of blood had formed, and the pain in the swollen left arm had grown so great as to render medical aid necessary, he remained as bright and cheerful as ever. As in health he had girded himself with a high, yet natural, manliness to his labours, never posing as over tired; so in sickness he girded himself with equal manliness to the greater task of patient rest, never posing as over-stricken. When the doctors ordered him complete rest for two months he said: "I feel myself a great humbug, knocking off work when I feel so well. I am enjoying myself. These idle days are so pleasant. I know now how delightful my own home is. I never had time to thoroughly enjoy it before." "Am I not a great idle fellow, lying in bed this fine morning?" he asked of the old nurse, "dear old Stone," as he called her; "I declare you are spoiling me." Thus he could playfully wait as well as cheerfully work.

Yet amid all this brightness the shadow of death hung over him. Not that he was fully conscious that the end was very near. At least he gave no outward sign even to his dearest ones of such a consciousness. Perhaps, the weight of the thoughts which suggest themselves to the inmost souls of men in seasons of peril is bravely borne in secret, lest the tender hearts of the loved and trusted ones should be lacerated needlessly. But, whether or not he felt conscious of approaching death, he was firmly convinced that his *Lancashire Life* was over, and that the time had come for resigning the responsible office which for nearly fifteen years he had so faithfully and earnestly filled. In a letter written to his Diocesan Registrar, Mr. E. P. Charlewood, September 13, 1885, he says:

"I am not very well, and Dr. W. Roberts orders me complete rest for two months. I will tell you more about it when we meet on Tuesday. I must ask you to see and dismiss people who come on other errands;

but it will do me no harm just to drive down for half an hour at 1 o'clock, and take the institutions and other necessary things.

"What troubles me is a small clot of blood which has formed in some vessel near the left collar-bone, and impedes the circulation of the left arm. Dr. Roberts says that otherwise I am in perfect health; indeed, I look so, and he hopes that with care this trouble will disperse, but, for the present, he distinctly says I must consider myself an invalid, and that in the future I must 'remodel the work of the diocese.' This really means that I must give place to a younger man, for the reduction of work seems to me impossible.

"I tell you this frankly, and for your own information only. I must, of course, take my Ordination, and there are three churches ready, or nearly ready, to be consecrated. For the autumn Confirmations, I shall try to get Bishop Mitchinson, but I take what has happened as a warning that the *active* work of my life is done, and that the diocese of Manchester, with its vast interests, demanding the whole strength of a bishop in the fulness of his strength, must be handed over to a younger man.—Yours very sincerely,

"J. MANCHESTER."

It could not have been without deep and sharp pangs that Bishop Fraser came to the resolution to resign his See. For some time past, indeed, the yearning for a quiet country life had been growing on him. He had been growing conscious, too, of the diminution of his working powers, and he was not the man to hold on tenaciously to the dignities and emoluments of an office, when he once perceived that his strength was unequal to the discharge of every duty pertaining to that office. Still Manchester had become "very dear" to him. It was his "first, only, and beloved diocese." The people of Manchester had entwined themselves very closely round his heart, and the thought of leaving them was a daily grief and sorrow.

Yet, when Duty beckoned, Bishop Fraser followed; however thorny, dark, and steep, the path up which she led. The duty of resigning his See, in his eyes, was clear; and, however painful the thought of separation from Manchester, yet, in the interests of Manchester, he set himself firmly to endure the pain. Quietly and bravely he continued to fulfil such episcopal duties as were "of necessity": sometimes under circumstances of considerable physical difficulty —his last public act in the diocese being the consecration of The Saviour's Church, Bolton-le-Moors. Quietly and bravely also he continued to make all due preparation for the resignation of his See. He had entered into negotiations for a house in Bath, and upon the morning of his death had expected a letter concerning the transaction. "Heigh! has that letter from Bath come yet?" he said to "the faithful Stone," as she was leaving his room on the last morning, having just brought up his last breakfast. "Don't trouble yourself about Bath, my lord!" the faithful Stone replied. "You will die Bishop of Manchester yet." A strange unconscious prophecy, soon to be unexpectedly fulfilled!

Meanwhile the hours moved slowly, and not darkly, on. "People think I am better," the Bishop said to Mr. Charlewood two days before his death; "but I feel I am losing ground myself, I am troubled with a fulness of the veins in the forehead." Losing ground! The last sands of earth sliding away from his ascending spirit. Yet how calm and peaceful his spirit was! Rejoicing in the rest of home, surrounded by faithful servants, conscious of having *tried* to do his duty, proud of the affection of his diocese, sustained by the devotion of his wife, having wrought the work of a man in the spirit of a child—he waited, in tranquil hope, for either recovery or departure, as God should will.

A touching scene of the Bishop's closing days is tenderly described by the Very Rev. Dr. Oakley, Dean of Manchester:

"We were gathered for prayer and worship in the Cathedral on the Tuesday afternoon, two days before the Bishop died. The congregation was in the nave to hear the sermon from the Bishop of Sodor and Man, and that small choir, with its dim religious light, was occupied only by the choir and the clergy, and he stood in the seat which we call his throne. I had been struck before the service by some symptoms of decided weakness, and he did not himself disguise it. His aspect and expression caught my eye, and I noticed him with the keenest attention as we stood singing a hymn, and two thoughts crossed my mind. I had not seen him stand and look so like Millais' picture of him for a long time. He stood erect, like a dart, and was singing, as he could sing, with the simplicity of a boy; and, as I looked, the thought crossed my mind, 'Will he stand there and sing like that much longer?' And now we know! And the verse during which he attracted my attention was this, and it will do Manchester no harm to hear it—

> "'Oh, bless the shepherd, bless the sheep,
> That guide and guided both be one—
> One in the faithful watch they keep,
> Until this hurrying life be done!'"

Yet another closing scene. Two clergy called at Bishop's Court the day before the Bishop's death, accompanied by a little girl, daughter of one of the clergy, a golden-haired child of six years old. One of the clergy, noticing the Bishop's ailing arm, asked what the bandage meant? "Oh," he answered in his cheeriest way—"it is only to keep me out of mischief!" And when the friend replied, "We must not allow you to do so much preaching work away from home, you must have more restful Sundays," the Bishop said: "It is not the work which troubles me, but the worrying letters I get. I have had one this morning." Then his eye, which a tear had dimmed, rested upon the little child, and the sadness melted into a smile of happy love, and he led the party to the door, and dismissed them with words and looks of sweetest tenderness.

Another scene brings back across the space of more than eleven long centuries the fragrance of the sweet and blessed death of the Venerable Bede. Bede died translating the Gospel of St. John; and among the last meditations of Bishop Fraser were the Epistles of Ignatius, the Second Apostolic Father, "Captain of the Martyrs," probably a disciple of St. John.

"Shortly before his death," writes one, "I found him reading the Bishop of Durham's new volumes on the Apostolic Fathers, and dwelling with great pleasure on a passage in the Epistle of Ignatius to the Ephesians (vii.); 'There is one Physician, Flesh and Spirit, Create and Uncreate, God in Man, life in death, the Son of Mary, and the Son of God, first passible and then impassible, Jesus Christ our Lord.'"

This primitive Apostolic teaching, simple, personal, strong, the record of facts more than the reticulations of dogma, had been the inspiration of his life, and was his comfort under the shadow of death.

2 M

The last afternoon of the Bishop's life was spent in visiting an invalided curate at Higher Broughton, and in walking in the garden with Mrs. Fraser, discoursing happily of the events of the day. In the evening he was unusually bright, and Mrs. Fraser read *Kenilworth* to him, he being especially fond of the novels of Sir Walter Scott. After she had finished reading, he said: "God bless thee, my darling! What a happy day we have had!" The thought of his happiness was always present to his mind, and his cup of gratitude was always running over. "Everybody is so good to me. What have I done that everybody should be so kind? I don't deserve half the affection I receive." No day ever passed without some such expressions as these falling from his lips. Upon the last evening he seemed unusually overflowing with the happiness which wells up from the fountains of a grateful heart. He had a good night's rest, and in the morning—the morning of his death—when "the faithful Stone" came to attend to him, he talked happily with her of past days, of the *wonderful ordering* of his life; "of the goodness of God and his unmerited happiness;" then, affectionately grasping her hand, he said: "Dear old soul! you are everything to us both." After breakfast came the prayers and lessons with his wife— "one of those little offices of worship which he so dearly loved." The Psalm for the day was the 107th Psalm. "Oh that men would therefore praise the Lord for His goodness, and declare the wonders that He doeth for the children of men! When they cried unto the Lord in their trouble, He delivered them out of their distress. Whoso is wise will ponder these things, and they shall understand the loving-kindness of the Lord." Then he playfully dismissed Mrs. Fraser, "to write those letters, and I'll be with you in half an hour"—a promise predestined never to be fulfilled!

After his bath, as he was dressing, he was seized with the fatal stroke. The sudden intense pain in his head and neck seemed almost to overwhelm him. His last conscious words were words of manly courage: "I *must* bear it somehow." Almost immediately he ceased to be conscious, and at one o'clock in the afternoon of October 22, 1885, God set his noble spirit free. He passed through none of the slowly darkening twilights of a lingering and overclouded death. He sprang from light to light; from the light of the pure joys of earth, to the light of the still purer joys of Paradise. His simple, manly, thankful life could scarce have had a better, finer, happier ending! *Felix opportunitate mortis!*

> " .... His Master's call
> Found him prepared, full-panoplied for heaven.
> 'A good and faithful servant,' who had won
> The benisons of all, whate'er their name
> Or creed; giving his time, his health, his powers,
> To raise the fallen, rescue the downtrodden,
> And bind them in one bond of brotherhood,—
> Setting upon their brows the Seal of Christ." *

Upon England, the tidings fell with a shock of sadness in Lancashire, the sadness deepened into keen and personal sorrow. In Manchester especially, the sorrow darkened into the mourning of bereavement. It was as if the diocese had been a family and the father had died. Those who dwell at a distance from Manchester can scarcely realize the sense of desolation which gathered over the hearts of thousands within and near the city. A twelvemonth after his death a stranger on a tramcar in Higher Broughton asked a workman sitting by, if he "knew where Bishop Fraser had lived?" "Do I know?" replied the man. "You must be a stranger here. Ay, *everybody* in Manchester knew where the Bishop lived. That's the house," he said, as the tramcar passed by Bishop's Court, and the tears gathered in his eyes, as he added: "He was a great, good MAN." At the Manchester Exhibition in 1887, groups of persons might every day be seen gathered round Sir J. E. Millais' picture of the Bishop, tenderly and reverently gazing into his pensive face, or whispering together with a reverent hush their tales of his simple, manly *Lancashire Life*. "If there's

---

* Verses by J. B. Greenwood.

a saint in heaven, 'tis our Bishop, God bless him!" said one rough man, brushing a tear from his eye.

Length of duration is a test of grief, and these instances bear some witness to the strength of the hold which Bishop Fraser had laid upon the heart of his diocese. The lamentations over his death did not evaporate at his funeral. His memory still remains to multitudes a treasured and inspiring possession.

Those who saw his body after death record how "he lay in almost unearthly beauty, with a sweet smile on his lips, looking so young, so noble!" Yes, it has been truthfully said, that "in the faces of the holy dead, of those who have lived pure lives,—

> "'Before decay's effacing fingers
> Have swept the lines where beauty lingers,'—

there is a repose of almost angelic brightness."

It was so in the case of Bishop Fraser. Some poets have prettily imagined that the spirits of the newly dead linger for a while around the habitation they have left. If this were so, it would account for "the sweet smile which shone upon his brave and noble face"; for if, in life, the Bishop had succeeded in drawing men's hearts together, and inspiring them with high resolve, in death his triumph, the triumph of an all-conquering affection, was for a while complete. Few scenes have surpassed in pathos and ennobling influence the burial of the Bishop. As his life had been distinguished for the splendour of his simplicity, so his burial was distinguished by the grandeur of unostentation. By his will he had ordered that his burial should be without costly pomp and display, that his body should be taken to the quiet churchyard of his old Berkshire parish, and there laid beside the body of his long-loved mother. With tender reverence Manchester yielded itself to their great and simple Bishop's will. On the Monday after his decease the Bishop's body, in a plain, unplumed hearse, drawn by two horses, was taken from Bishop's Court to the railway station at London Road, followed by a single mourning-coach, with some half-dozen private carriages (one belonging to the Roman Catholic Bishop of Salford), and a procession of clergy. A halt of some two minutes was made at the Cathedral, whose muffled bells rang the soft sad music of a last farewell. The whole route, about four miles long, was lined with mourners, whose uncovered heads and stealthy tears bore witness to the general sorrow. Upon reaching the railway station the hearse was placed upon an open waggon, and the multitude of mourners, ere the train started on its southward journey, gathered round the loved and hidden form, and sang the glorious hymn, " Thy will be done."

Upon Tuesday morning, October 27, 1885, just as the noonday sun was shedding its glow of tender light upon the autumn foliage, the body of the Bishop reached its final resting-place at Ufton Nervet—his happy home for ten rejoicing years, his body's restful home till years shall be no longer. Ufton Nervet is among the most beautiful and peaceful of Berkshire villages. Its few inhabitants gain their livelihood by agriculture. "They look stolid," the Bishop, who was very fond of them, used to say; " but they have more sense than town-bred people think." In the village and the districts round are some of those stately homes of England where wealth is not wasted on rioting and luxury; but is consecrated to culture, goodness, and innocent delights. These stately mansions and simple cottages— each capable, notwithstanding difference of environment, of developing beneath its roof the ideal of Home—were the pleasant haunts of the Bishop in his Ufton days. For every child, and housewife, and labourer, and squire, his genial face had worn its smile of recognition. The charming rectory has been enlarged since the time of its occupation by Mr. Fraser. But his plain and simple room, which looks over the well-wooded meadows descending to the Kennet, and across the river to the climbing upland on the other side, is still the same. So also is the pretty garden, with its quaintly cut hedge of yew, beneath whose cool and tranquil shade the spirit of the cloister seems to dwell. The stables, too, whose inmates neighed in welcome of the cheery master's voice, are still unchanged. And the kitchen garden across the road, by whose sequestered pond the "two old ladies used to sit," and along whose grassy paths they walked, each with one arm twined in an arm of their strong tall son and comforter—still are there. So is the curious bench of stone built by Mr. Fraser from fragments of the former church, and proving, by its jumbled oddity, that its designer was not an architect born. The village school is also still unchanged, a simple room with simple furniture, silently attesting by its simplicity the conviction of the great Education Commissioner that the secret of education is not found in handsome forms and varnished desks and shining maps, and piles of various books, and display of extravagant apparatus. His common-sense instincts found place for their activity even in this one-roomed village school; for, as the school stands by the roadside, he ordered that all the windows should be in the wall farthest from the road. "I will not have the roadside idlers peeping into the school," he said; "nor the children's attention taken away from work by passing carriages and carts."

The church at Ufton was rebuilt in the early years of Mr. Fraser's incumbency. It is perfectly plain and simple—admirably adapted to the needs of its few rustic worshippers. But, though the present church is quite modern, yet a board upon the west wall connects the history of the church and parish with the life of England in the reign of Queen Elizabeth—for it tells how the Lady Marvin in 1581 gave "10 bushels of wheat to be made into good household bread, $12\frac{1}{2}$ ells of canvass at 1s. per ell, for shirts and smocks, and also $12\frac{1}{2}$ yards of narrow blue cloth at 1s. and 8d. per yard, for coats and cassocks. She did by her will charge divers lands and hereditaments at Ufton and elsewhere, with the payment of a sufficient sum of money to purchase the said wheat, canvass, and blue cloth, to be annually distributed about the middle of Lent." Side by side with this board hangs another board which tells, among other things, how "the Right Reverend James Fraser, Bishop of Manchester, formerly Rector of the parish, conveyed to the Provost and Fellows of Oriel College the sum of £500 in the Four Per Cent. Debenture Stock of the London and North Western Railway in trust to expend annually the interest of the same in the month of November, in purchasing warm clothing for twenty poor and respectable people of the parish to be chosen by the Rector at his discretion." The entire church, not only in its plain and reverent simplicity of plan and structure, but also in its adornments and furniture, is rich in suggestive memories of its famous rector and re-builder. The tiled reredos and stained glass in the eastern wall are his gift. Around the base of the brass lectern runs the legend: "In Loving Memory of James Fraser, D.D., Lord Bishop of Manchester (May 1886), Parish memorial." Upon the south wall, within the chancel, is a brass tablet with the inscription: "To the Honoured Memory of James Fraser, D.D., formerly Fellow of Oriel College, Oxford: for ten years Rector of this parish, afterwards for fifteen years Bishop of Manchester. Two of his nephews, Edward Alexander and Henry Pole Fraser, place this tablet in grateful recollection of the unfailing generosity and kindly watchfulness which ruled his private, no less than his public, life. He lies at rest near the western wall of the church which he loved. Born August 18, 1818, died October 22, 1885. He fed them with a faithful and true heart, and ruled them prudently with all his power (Psalm lxxviii. 72)." The walls of the church are enriched with texts of Scripture—chosen by Mr. Fraser himself, and indicative of the kind of inspired mottoes which, as holy lamps, guided his course in teaching, in action, in worship. Over the entrance to the church is written: *This is the House of God.* Above the door within the church, so as to be read by those going out: *Let that abide in you which ye have heard.* On the south wall: *God is a Spirit, and they that worship Him must worship Him in Spirit and in truth.* On the north wall: *Love worketh no ill to his neighbour, therefore Love is the fulfilling of the law.* Above the baptistery: *Of such is the Kingdom of Heaven.* On the west wall: *Watch and Pray. Let every one that nameth the name of Christ depart from iniquity.* Behind the organ: *Little children, keep yourselves from idols.* Above the organ: *Be strong in the grace that is in Christ Jesus.* At the entrance to the organ chamber: *Be ye followers of God as dear children.* Around the chancel arch: *Lay hold on Eternal Life.* On the east wall: *Glory to God in the Highest, and on earth peace, good-will to men. I am the Light of the world. I am the Bread of Life.*

Beneath the shadow of this Bible-honouring Church the body of the Bishop has found its sweet and hallowed resting-place. There were no conventional trappings, no money-purchased displays, no paraphernalia, at his funeral. Some scores of his friends came down from London to pay their last tribute of respect to the perishing casket which had contained the imperishable jewel of his great and noble spirit. Among these were some whose friendship had been the friendship of a lifetime; men like Dean Church, Dr. Chase, Sir John Mowbray, Lord Lingen, and Professor Bryce. From Manchester came many principal Churchmen, both clerical and lay, leading Nonconformists like the Rev. Dr. Maclaren, representatives of learning like Principal Greenwood and Professor Wilkins. As the coffin rested beneath the lych-gate it seemed buried in flowers; tokens of sorrow sent by poor and rich, Churchmen and Nonconformists. Among these tokens was an anchor of flowers from the members of the Greek Church in Manchester, and a wreath from the Jews. The body was carried by a company of chosen villagers from the lych-gate, underneath the ancient and magnificent yew which guards the entrance to the church, and placed in the chancel. The service was read by Archdeacon Anson, Archdeacon Norris, and Canon Cornish, and the benediction pronounced by the Very Rev. Dr. Cowie, Dean of Exeter, formerly Dean of Manchester. The little choir of female voices sang the two well-known hymns: "The King of love my shepherd is," and "Christ will gather in His own." It was noticed that, in the reading of the lesson, at the triumphant passage—"*when this corruptible shall have put on incorruption, and this mortal shall have put on immortality*"—the sunlight streamed through the windows of the church and rested, in soft, rich, glory, upon the flower-robed remains of the mortal, yet immortal, Bishop.

While the burial service was being said in Ufton Church a Service of Commemoration and Fellowship was taking place simultaneously in the Cathedral Church at Manchester. By the invitation of the Mayor of Manchester, members of Parliament, mayors of neighbouring boroughs, representatives of public institutions, magistrates and members of the Corporation, had assembled in the Town Hall, and marched in procession to the Cathedral. Within the Cathedral, men of varying schools of thought, of varying kinds of creed, of every condition and sort, were gathered to do honour to the memory of an earnest, large, and noble, life. Fallen women were there, rescued from a life of sin by the Bishop's sympathy, actors and actresses were there, night-soil men, artizans of every grade, students, scholars, ministers of all denominations, clergy of every party in the Church, politicians of diverse opinions—none felt out of place who had a genuine interest in any department of progressive human life, or in whose souls burned the lamp of desire for better, higher, holier, things. The Bishop's throne was draped in violet cloth and laden with memorial flowers. The service was conducted by the Dean (Dr. Oakley), Canon Woodard, and Minor Canon Elvey, and was intensely solemn and impressive; and, the Cathedral being too small to hold the throngs desirous to render their tribute of respect to the Bishop, simultaneous services were held in St. Anne's Church and the Church of the Sacred Trinity. The whole city seemed subdued with quiet sorrow, and almost every public man, of whatever creed or party, gave some expression to the sense of the people's grief. One hundred and fifty public bodies sent addresses of condolence to the Bishop's widow, and letters of sympathy poured in upon her from many corners of the land. A few of these letters are given in illustration of the manifold interests of human life, and the manifold sides of human character, which were touched by the Bishop's simple, straightforward, sympathetic, spiritual nature.

From the Archbishop of Canterbury.

ADDINGTON PARK, CROYDON, *October* 22, 1885.

MY DEAR MRS. FRASER,—The sad news which has to-night been forwarded to me to where I am staying, near Maidstone, fills me with sorrow and sympathy.

Your beloved husband was the only one of us who was prepared for this stroke, for he was always prepared. The tone of his last two letters gave me anxiety of the gravest kind, but I fully trusted that real rest, if he could take it without restlessness, would remove our fears.

It is too soon to hope that you yourself are not broken down by the very suddenness with which such energy and such love has passed from your sight, but it *has* only passed to some nobler region, and to mightier and to perfect Presences.

From the first time I saw him, more than twenty years ago, I have seen what it was impossible not to recognize, a character cut out and fashioned by God to a singular pureness, loftiness, and truth of purpose. And what fruit for God his dedicated ability and strength have borne in his most difficult of English dioceses, and *will* bear ever!

You will not for a moment fail, I am sure, in faith and love. The faith that resigns the few years to come of earthly companionship and blessedness is, when you realize it, the most perfect love both to him and to Him with Whom *he* is with a new perfectness. Let us strive to see all things as *he* now sees them. Our sorrow then will be full of hope, for it will be full of Christ.

Do not think I do not know how difficult it is to realize all this. But *it is true.*—Yours, in deepest sympathy for you, and for the whole flock which knew and revered him,

EDWARD CANTUAR.

To MRS. FRASER.

We, the Archbishop and Bishops of the Northern Province, request you to accept the expression of our deep sympathy with you in the death of our dear brother the Bishop of Manchester. He was endeared to us by his great kindness, his candour, his unselfish devotion to duty, and by that elasticity of mind and spirit which neither the cares of office, nor the advance of years, had power to abate. We held him not merely in respect for his high qualities, but in cordial affection. Nothing was more known to us than the unbroken domestic happiness of his later years; and our chief regret now is that that beautiful home-life is broken up. But there must remain to you, as to us, the recollection of intercourse with a noble and departed spirit, which will be a happiness to you for the remaining time of separation. We assure you of our love for your husband, and of our sympathetic regard for you; and we pray that God may speedily console you, and that you may see that even this chastening comes of love.

W. Ebor.
J. B. Dunelm.
H. Carlisle.
J. C. Liverpool.
E. R. Newcastle.
W. Cestr.
W. B. Ripon.
R. Sodor and Man.

From the Bishop of Durham.

Dear Mrs. Fraser,—It is indeed with the sense of a deep personal loss to myself that I write to offer you my heartfelt sympathy and condolence in your bereavement. It was always such a joy to see him, and his visit to Auckland will be long remembered, not by myself only, but by all here. On one of my last visits to the deathbed of my Uncle Trimnell, the conversation turned on your and his kindness to him.

I dare not pretend to offer you consolation in your loss. You will seek it where alone it can be found. But it will be some solace to you to remember that your sorrow is the sorrow of the whole Church.

This morning I received a telegram announcing the departure of the Bishop of Ely. Alas! "brother is following brother" only too quickly for us who remain behind.

May the God of comfort give you all comfort; yes, and all *joy* in believing.—I am, dear Mrs. Fraser, yours very faithfully,

J. B. Dunelm.

From the Bishop of Rochester.

My dear Friend,—He is with Jesus, and Jesus is with you. Try to give him up as the dearest sacrifice you can render, and peace shall flow into your soul.

My whole heart mourns with you and rejoices for him.—Your affectionate friend,

A. Roffen.

From the (Roman Catholic) Bishop of Salford.

St. Bede's College, Manchester.
November 10, 1885.

Dear Mrs. Fraser,—I have hitherto been unwilling to intrude upon your sorrow, more especially as you were aware of my public expression of sympathy and regret. But your kind note, just received, gives me the opportunity to tender to yourself directly my heartfelt condolence. I can never forget the nobility, the directness, and simplicity of your husband's character, and the sympathetic charm which played like sunlight on his countenance. The universal tribute of admiration must be indeed a great consolation to you. Though it will not heal the wound which can never disappear from your heart, it will, I trust, be soon as a soothing balsam under your dreary sense of loss. May God bless and support you under the heaviest trial that could be sent upon you.—Believe me, dear Mrs. Fraser, yours faithfully,

HERBERT, BISHOP OF SALFORD.

From the Very Rev. Dean BRADLEY.

DEANERY, *November* 1, 1885.

DEAR MRS. FRASER,—I can write one line now. I could not before. My heart was too full and too sore. I *could* not go to the funeral, and I buried a dear friend on Thursday. To-day I have said a fragment of what I have felt in the Abbey, and feel easier.

I feel as if I had lost one of my oldest friends. But I have no right to call him so. I never spoke to him till he once came and preached at Marlborough, in 1860, and it has been only from time to time that we have met. But somehow I have really loved him from the time I first met him, and have valued him more year after year. I rejoice to think that I never spoke or thought of him except with affection and honour.

How well I remember a conversation about him with Stanley, and a letter of his in which he spoke of him and Bishop Temple as the two pillars of the Church. I said but little to-day in All Saints' Church, but I put my whole soul into what I did say, and the attention was intense.

The loss to the Church is irreparable. I see no choice or prospect of any one *like* him being made a bishop; as Vaughan wrote to me, "there is no one like him."

I am sure, my dear Mrs. Fraser, you will forgive this short outburst. I am just out of the Abbey, and have no right to intrude on your sorrow. But, amidst the crowd of mourners for him, believe that one of the most sorrowful is,—Most truly yours,

G. G. BRADLEY.

From the Rev. Dr. MACLAREN (*Baptist*).

WHALLEY RANGE, *November* 17, 1885.

DEAR MRS. FRASER,—I thank you for your kind letter, which was delayed in reaching me by being incorrectly addressed. I hope you will not consider me intruding on your sorrow, if I avail myself of the opportunity which its receipt gives me, of saying how much I am indebted to you for letting me be present at Ufton. Many besides myself were grateful that you should have wished some one to be there from among Nonconformists, than whom none revered your dear husband more.

May I venture to touch upon more sacred ground? Perhaps the fact that I have the same solitary and dark road to tread as is appointed for you may be my excuse, if I say that, in my own sorrow, I have found many of the ordinary commonplaces of conversation crumbling away when I have tried to lean on them; and that there is only one thought on which such sorrow as yours can stay itself—the thought of the loving will of the Father. When we can say, "It is the Lord, let Him do what seemeth Him good," some faint beginnings of peace rise in the heart. I pray that the repose of a will yielded to the will of God may be yours, and, with much sympathy, I am, dear Mrs. Fraser, yours faithfully,

ALEXANDER MACLAREN.

From Rev. CHARLES VOYSEY.

WOODLAWN HOUSE, DULWICH, S.E.,
October 23, 1885.

DEAR MADAM,—No one can more sincerely grieve than I do for the loss to us and to this world of dear Bishop Fraser. I knew him not personally, but I was intimate with two of his dearest friends, Dean Stanley and Canon Pearson, and I therefore knew what the Bishop was to them. Of course his public career was an inspiration of the deepest esteem and reverence. I am very sorry for *you*, I am very sorry for the Church and country, that he has been taken from us.—I am, dear Madam, most faithfully yours,

CHARLES VOYSEY.

From Professor BRYCE.

OXFORD, *November* 1, 1885.

MY DEAR MRS. FRASER,—Will you permit me to do now what I did not venture to do in the first few days after the sad news reached me, say to you how deep and earnest is the sympathy which my sisters and I feel for you in this overwhelming sorrow? I cannot tell you half of what we have felt, and indeed even now we scarcely seem to realize the full extent of the loss, for every day brings to my recollection some new trait of nobleness and beauty in his character. I have never known any one in whom goodness and truthfulness and active zeal were so perfectly mingled. Though it was rarely, in this busy life which leaves so little time for the best pleasures, that I saw him, he was an abiding presence with me, he was a sort of standard to which we almost unconsciously referred; it was a comfort to think that so strong, and pure, and righteous a soul was always bearing witness to the truth, and labouring in every good work. He stayed with me once or twice when he came to London about nine or ten years ago and we came to love him as much as we had admired him before. Even the servants in the house seemed to love him, there was something so kindly and hearty in his manner; and what a pleasure it was when he remembered us, and brought you nearly every time when you were in London to see us!

Our hearts are very sore for you, dear Mrs. Fraser, but the thought of his noble life and mind, the recollection of his example, remain to help us all; if they do not console, they may help you to bear the suffering which our Father has sent, and look forward to that which his faith always saw.

Believe me to be, with my sisters' love and sympathy, ever sincerely yours,

J. BRYCE.

From Sir W. H. HOULDSWORTH.

NORBURY BOOTHS, KNUTSFORD, *November* 10, 1885.

DEAR MRS. FRASER,—I did not write to you in the midst of your great sorrow, for I knew you would be overwhelmed with letters. And I must not trouble you with many lines now. But the loss which we have sustained, in the unexpected death of our good Bishop, is to each one of us in this community such a *personal* bereavement, that it seems only natural and fitting in us to ask to be allowed to some extent to share in *your* sorrow. I am sure you know that we feel deep sympathy *for* you—but we also feel your loss *with* you. I am very sorry now I did not go to see him after he was partially laid aside. I often intended and often *arranged* to do so, but pressing engagements always seemed to come in the way, and I had not the least idea there was any danger.

I am very thankful I knew him. His character and example have been of much service to me. I can recall almost every public act which I was associated with him in, from the very first time I saw him in Westminster Abbey pulpit nearly twenty years ago.

His example and work will live long in this diocese, and I am quite sure that he has knit together the various bodies of Christians in Manchester in a way which will never be entirely lost. The congregation at the Cathedral on the day of his funeral was the best memorial, and he would have felt it almost the best reward of his work.

Excuse a very short and I fear inefficient note, but pray accept this expression of my sympathy and kindest regards.—Yours very sincerely,

W. H. HOULDSWORTH.

From Sir UGHTRED KAY SHUTTLEWORTH.

GAWTHORPE HALL, PADIHAM, LANCASHIRE,
October 23, 1885.

DEAR MRS. FRASER,—We hear with great sorrow of our dear Bishop's departure from among us, and from his great good work in Lancashire. We feel grieved for you and this early end of that *part* of your happy joint life which has been spent on this earth. But you will look forward —and meanwhile we must all try to feel thankful that he was spared a long evening of weariness, and powerlessness for that work which he loved. Can any end be more happy for such a man than to die at his post, after a warning, a call, and yet without a lingering time of weakness and suffering, trying to him and others?

His work in Lancashire for practical religion, for earnestness in the Church, and brotherhood among Christians, and for a manly, earnest view of the duties of life, has been grand. We shall cherish his memory—by "we," I mean Lancashire people of all classes and creeds—with affection, admiration, and reverence. His example must and will live, and the good he did by it will long survive him. "His works will follow him."

Pardon me, dear Mrs. Fraser, for intruding at such a moment with these expressions of feeling. If not now, they, and many like them, may be some comfort to you in moments when sadness cannot be repressed.

We too shall feel sad with you, and mourn the loss of a dear friend to Blanche, and me, and Angela—as well as the great public loss Lancashire and England suffer.—Believe me, yours sincerely,

UGHTRED KAY SHUTTLEWORTH.

From Professor PORTER, *Yale College.*

YALE COLLEGE, NEW HAVEN, CONN., U.S.A.,
October 23, 1885.

MY DEAR MADAM,—Excuse me, an entire stranger, for expressing the distress which I feel for yourself at the overwhelming sorrow which has come upon you in the death of your estimable husband, news of which has come to us to-day. I saw him intimately many times during his visit to America, visited him at Ufton, and was with him at Oxford in October 1866. I have since occasionally had letters from him, notably in a beautiful strain after his election and before his consecration as Bishop, again before his marriage. He was a just and good man, as discerning as he was gentle and loving. May the Good Comforter help you in your sorrow.— Very sincerely,

N. PORTER, *Professor of Yale College.*

From HENRY E. PELLEW (America).

KATONAH, N.Y., *October 23, 1885.*

MY DEAR MRS. FRASER,—The telegraphic message from the other side which reached us this morning, announcing the death of your noble-hearted husband, fills us with sorrow and bitter thoughts. I can scarcely bear to think of the loss which it occasions to the cause of religion, and the check which it will give to such a multitude of good works, centering in him as in a trusted leader. But God gave to him the splendid opportunity which he did not fail to carry out to the uttermost; and the regret which we all feel is, that the time was comparatively so short in which he was able to develop his wonderful gifts for the good of the Church, and of the people amongst whom he ministered.

From a Young Correspondent.

December 24, 1885.

MY DEAR MADAM,—Though I am a stranger to you, I most earnestly long to offer you my deep sympathy in your bereavement. I cannot express how deeply I was moved by the death of our beloved Bishop, and how I desired to tell you how earnestly I mourned with and for you. Words would not come to me at the time. I felt to the full *all* that has been written and spoken in his praise, and yet I long to tell you how much his words and example have been and *are* to me, and how I miss his presence on earth. If I feel this amongst a multitude of others, what must you feel, dear Madam, who are left alone! May God comfort and sustain you, for there can be no help in man.

I beg you to forgive me for writing—I feel impelled by gratitude and love to him to tell you how much he has done to help and comfort me. I never spoke to him, but very often I heard him preach, and I may truly say that his words went straight to my heart. He taught me the power of religion, and first made me *think*. Two years ago, in a time of deep sorrow, and consequent despondency and *doubt*, I wrote to him begging for his guidance. He was to me truly a father in God. His kind and earnest counsel cheered and encouraged me to take heart again. I read his letter often, though I know it by heart. They are the words of an Apostle, whose life was a faithful prayer before our eyes. Truly I thank God for knowing such a life to be a truth.

My sister and I were confirmed by him. Though we left the diocese of Manchester some years after, yet we never ceased to speak of him as *our* Bishop. He was indeed as a personal friend to us, as to hundreds of others. His boundless sympathy endeared him to all. We can never hope to look upon his like again.

> "May all love,
> His love unseen but felt, o'ershadow thee,
> The love of all his people comfort thee,
> Till God's love set thee at his side again."

I am, my dear Madam, respectfully and sorrowfully yours,

MRS. FRASER. H. P.

From a WORKING WOMAN.

Madam,—I hope you will please pardon the liberty I take in thus addressing you, but I am sure you will do so under the present circumstances; for I have thought so much about you since the dear Bishop's death that I felt as if I should like you to know a few of my thoughts, and, now that all the excitement is over, I feel as though I could think about him, and think of the many precious sermons I have heard from his lips. I have known him for the last nine years, and I am sure no one, only yourself, could have thought more about his death than I have done, and, although in a different station of life, I have truly felt for you and still do feel for you in your sad bereavement, and I hope and earnestly pray that God will give you strength and patience to bear your trouble bravely. It is very hard to part with those we love dearest on earth, but in the midst of your own trouble you do not forget the troubles and afflictions of others. I have read about your going to visit those who were suffering; that is like your dear husband, just what he would have done. I often think of words that I have heard from the pulpit at the Cathedral and other churches I have been to, to hear the Bishop; to me it was beautiful to read the papers, to hear what every one said and thought about him, for he was worthy of it all and more, for he was fond of the poor, and his heart was ever ready to respond to the sick and needy.

God grant we may all try to walk in his footsteps. I often think of the lovely piece that was put into the paper about the Clifton Hall Colliery explosion; I have it by me, and often read it and several little bits that I have cut out of the papers at different confirmations I have been to, little things that have touched me. I have also got the letter that you wrote just after the Bishop's death. I am sure I love you for his sake, and I hope you will still remain with us.

Madam, I hope, if I have committed any error in my letter that I should not have done, I hope you will please forgive me. I am only a cottager, but I have felt for you so keenly that I felt as though I should like to put my thoughts into words; although I can hardly express what I feel for you, it makes me feel rather afraid to write when I know you are so much higher in life than myself; but still I know you will forgive me when you know why I have written.

Madam, if you will please pardon me, I should so much like a photo of the dear Bishop and yourself; it would give me pleasure all my life to have you both to look at. One thing I would ask, and that is, if you will please promise me that you will not show this to any one at all, only read it yourself, as I am only lowly born and I know there are many mistakes; besides, other people may think that I should not have written to you, and I do not want any one, only yourself, to know what I have felt for you I ask you for these little mementos so that I may receive them from the loving hands of the one that was dearest to our Bishop on earth; and, should you not remain among us, I hope that some one will hear about you sometimes, that we may know how you are. I hope you keep quite well. Believe me, Madam, to be, yours very respectfully,

———————

Thus closed the *Lancashire Life* of Bishop Fraser, amid the admiration and sorrow of "all sorts and conditions of men." The story of his life (if the picture has been faithfully drawn, and the one aim of the biographer throughout the story has been to make the picture a *truthful* portrait, without minimizing defects and without exaggerating virtues) has shown him to have been a man fashioned in a grand and noble mould. The fire of humanity was set in his bones; his heart was too large, and his sympathies too expansive, to be confined within the limits of mere denominationalism or partizanship. Every denomination might say, "He belonged to us"; every party had some share in him. He was a Bishop of the Church Catholic, a brother of the human race, a citizen of the whole world. He did not know what narrowness meant. Even those who differed from him loved him, because his frank outspoken courage was blended with great sweetness and tenderness. When you met him you felt as if a ray of sunlight had fallen across your path. He was withal among the manliest of men; a fearless preacher of righteousness; loving orthodoxy much, but loving righteousness more; a man whose mind was all pure, so that he could speak whatever was in it without premeditation and without reserve; a man perfectly truthful all through; a man so full of sympathy that his face shone with the brightness of his heart; a man saddened by the thought of prevailing sin and woe, but firmly believing that the Gospel of Christ (whenever it is received in a true and simple way) is the power of God which saves from sin and brings a balm for woe; a man whose *Lancashire Life* has helped to make Christianity *live* in Lancashire.

His body rests in the quiet churchyard of his much-loved country parish, a peaceful spot, where evening after evening his grave is illumined by the kindly rays of the setting sun.

In the same grave rest also the bodies of his mother and his aunt. The spot is marked by two blocks of polished red granite, each surmounted with a cross. Upon one side of one of the granite blocks run the words:

HERE LIES THE BODY OF

HELEN FRASER,

THE DEARLY LOVED MOTHER OF
THE RIGHT REV. JAMES FRASER, D.D.,
BISHOP OF MANCHESTER.
BORN 31ST JULY, 1792. DIED 22ND APRIL, 1880.

"FOR EVER WITH THE LORD."
"HER CHILDREN CALL HER BLESSED."

Upon the other side:

ALSO OF HER DEVOTED SISTER,

LUCY WILLIM,

BORN 25TH DECEMBER, 1789. DIED 6TH FEBRUARY, 1886.

"LOVELY AND PLEASANT IN THEIR LIVES,
IN DEATH THEY ARE NOT DIVIDED."

At the head of the companion granite block is engraved a mitre, and at the foot the Arms of the See of Manchester, and upon the block are the words:

HERE RESTS THE BODY OF

THE RIGHT REV. JAMES FRASER, D.D.,

FELLOW OF ORIEL COLLEGE, OXFORD, 1840-1860:
RECTOR OF CHOLDERTON, WILTS, 1847-1860:
RECTOR OF THIS PARISH, 1860-1870:
BISHOP OF MANCHESTER, 1870-1885.
BORN AT PRESTBURY, NEAR CHELTENHAM, AUG. 10, 1818.
DIED AT BISHOP'S COURT, MANCHESTER, OCT. 22, 1885.

"THEY THAT TURN MANY TO RIGHTEOUSNESS SHALL SHINE AS THE
STARS FOR EVER AND EVER.
UNTIL THE DAY DAWN AND THE SHADOWS FLEE AWAY."

Close to the Bishop's grave is the grave of "the faithful

Stone," who died March 22, 1888. Upon this grave is a monument of polished grey granite, with this inscription:

IN AFFECTIONATE REMEMBRANCE OF

ESTHER STONE,

THE BELOVED AND TRUSTED FRIEND OF THE BISHOP OF MANCHESTER AND MRS. FRASER, AFTER A FAITHFUL SERVICE OF 54 YEARS IN THE FAMILY OF MRS. FRASER.

"WELL DONE, GOOD AND FAITHFUL SERVANT, ENTER THOU INTO THE JOY OF THY LORD."

"FATHER, IN THY HOLY KEEPING, LEAVE WE NOW THY SERVANT SLEEPING— FOR EVER WITH THE LORD."

But while the Bishop's body "sleeps in the Berkshire village churchyard," the city of Manchester contains two visible memorials of his *Lancashire Life*. The first of these memorials is a cenotaph in the Cathedral, with a recumbent effigy exquisitely sculptured by Mr. Forsyth—a living likeness in marble of the Bishop's form and face. A brass plate near this memorial bears the following beautiful inscription from the pen of the Very Rev. Dr. Vaughan, Master of the Temple, and Dean of Llandaff:

TO THE BELOVED MEMORY OF

JAMES FRASER, D.D.,

BISHOP OF MANCHESTER
1870 TO 1885.
A MAN OF SINGULAR GIFTS,
BOTH OF NATURE AND OF THE SPIRIT,
BRAVE, TRUE, DEVOUT, DILIGENT,
IN LABOURS UNWEARIED.
HE WON ALL HEARTS BY OPENING TO THEM HIS OWN,
AND SO ADMINISTERED THIS GREAT DIOCESE
AS TO PROVE YET ONCE MORE
THAT THE PEOPLE KNOW THE VOICE
OF A GOOD SHEPHERD
AND WILL FOLLOW WHERE HE LEADS.
THIS CHAPEL HAS BEEN ERECTED
BY HIS DEVOTED WIDOW,
MAY, 1887.

The chapel in which this monument is placed has been built by Mrs. Fraser in the eastern bay of the southern aisle of the Cathedral choir. Round the edge of the cenotaph is the following legend:

"In pious memory of the Right Rev. Father in God, JAMES FRASER, D.D., from Lady Day, 1870, to October 22, 1885, the faithful, diligent, and beloved Bishop of Manchester. This monument is erected by the clergy and laity of the diocese, and other friends, in the chapel built for it by AGNES his widow. After he had served his own generation, by the will of God he fell on sleep."

Day by day numbers of persons of all classes and creeds may be seen reverently and affectionately visiting this most beautiful effigy. For, as Bishop Moorhouse said, with no less generosity than eloquence, at the unveiling of the monument,

"In going backwards and forwards in my diocese, along the paths formerly trodden by the beloved feet of my great and saintly predecessor, I have met everywhere marks of his work, and proofs of his far-reaching salutary influence. Bishop Fraser's true monument is in the hearts of his people. In the deep and affectionate heart of Lancashire he holds a place apart. His name will be always remembered as that of a man who had found, in a singular degree, the art of making men love and trust him—as a man who spent his whole energy of body and soul to glorify God and for the good of his fellow-creatures; and I think that the sense of his loss is as keenly felt in many hearts in this diocese now as when first that sad message was flashed throughout this country that the Master had called him to Himself, and taken him to his rest."

The second visible memorial of Bishop Fraser which the city of Manchester contains, *is probably unique in the annals of episcopacy.* Like the first monument, this second monument was erected, not by the exclusive and princely munificence of wealthy magnates, but by the spontaneous offerings of a multitude of donors of every shade of thought, and every rank in life. But unlike the first monument, and unlike every other memorial of a Bishop, this second monument of Bishop Fraser is a bronze statue in an open square in front of a great Town Hall, where thousands of people pass and repass day by day, in pursuit of the varied interests of a surging city's commercial, municipal, political philanthropic course of life.

"It is a new thing," said the High Sheriff of Lancashire, Mr. Oliver Heywood, at the unveiling of this statue on Saturday, April 14, 1888— "it is a new thing which we are met to-day to do: a new thing, and yet a thing not appearing strange to us here assembled. I know of no other instance in which there has been erected on the public highway a statue of the Bishop of his diocese. I know of no instance, save one, in which I have seen a bronze statue of a Bishop. Down in the southern country, looking on the blue waters of a beautiful lake, looking also up to the white snowy mountains, there is a statue erected to the memory of Borromeo, the great Cardinal Archbishop of Milan."

But even Cardinal Borromeo's statue is not like Bishop Fraser's statue—in the heart and centre of a mighty city, identified for ever with the city's daily life. Nor is the position of the statue alone unique; its character is also without a parallel among episcopal memorials. Around its base the sculptor, Mr. Woolner, was commissioned to place three bas-reliefs: "representing, first, a Confirmation; second, an Address to men in a work-yard; and third, a visit to a Public Institution—thus setting forth the Bishop as the Churchman, the Citizen, and the Charitable Man." And upon the statue is engraved this memorable inscription:—

JAMES FRASER, D.D.,

Born 18th August, 1818;
Died 28th October, 1885.

Bishop of Manchester from 1870 to 1885.

"This Statue is erected by public subscription, to commemorate his character and work. His untiring industry, noble simplicity of character, large views, and kindness of heart, endeared him to men of all ranks and of every religious denomination. His example is worthy of imitation by all.

"The Panels on the sides of the Pedestal are intended to show the good Bishop bringing religion to the young, affectionate counsel to the workman, and gifts to the needy."

But the most unique part of the story of this unique statue remains yet to be told. Both the Mayor of Manchester who unveiled the statue (Sir James Harwood),

and the Mayor who initiated the work (Mr. Alderman
Goldschmidt) were Nonconformists—the former a Methodist,
the latter an Unitarian. The Honorary Treasurers were Mr.
Alderman Goldschmidt (Unitarian), and Mr. James Jardine
(Churchman). The Honorary Secretaries were Rev. Canon
Touge (Churchman), Rev. S. A. Steinthal (Unitarian),
Rev. Dr. Macfadyen (Congregationalist), and Mr. H. J. Roby
(Churchman). The programme of arrangements on the day
of the unveiling of the statue contains, among other notices,
the announcement that "The Old Hundreth Psalm" and
"God save the Queen" will be sung, that the statue will be
unveiled by the Mayor, and accepted by him on behalf of
the City, and that short addresses will be delivered by the
High Sheriff, the Lord Bishop of Manchester, the (Roman
Catholic) Bishop of Salford, the Rev. Dr. Macfadyen and the
Rev. S. A. Steinthal—a rare combination of the leaders
among Churchmen, Roman Catholics, Congregationalists,
and Unitarians, united to express their admiration of the
civic, philanthropic, Christian, toils of an Anglican Bishop!

It is a great and beautiful episode in the Church's history
—an episode fragrant with the perfumes of the primitive
Christian time when the followers of the Lord Jesus were
recognized by no Denominational Epithets, but simply as
"good men and full of the Holy Ghost." It is great and
beautiful that a Bishop of the Church of Christ, without
abating one jot of his principles, by his devotion to the
public good, and by struggling for that faith which (to use
his own language) "I believe to be the same in essence in
all Christian hearts, however different the outward form in
which it clothes itself," should have won all classes, and all
parties, and all creeds, to lay at his feet their wreath of
praise, and honour, and love.

INDEX.

ABSOLUTION, 274, 448
Actors, address to, 78
   letters from, 85, 86
Admonition, on Church ritual, 176, 415
Adulteration, a curse of the day, 134, cf. 97
Agnosticism, 386
   its conclusions, 387
Agricultural labourers, 139
Agriculture, might be worked on co-operative principles, 139
Albany, Duke of, 117, 261, 262
Altruism, 12
Amusements, public, 80, 154
———— attitude of the Church towards, 194
"Analogy," Butler's, 358, 371, 372
Anson, Archdeacon, 211, 224, 426, 536
Apostolic Succession, 165, 273, 276
Arbitration, 107
Arnold, Matthew, 158
Art, 245
"High Art," 475
Ashbury's Works, 331, 332
Assassinations in Ireland, 318
Assington, co-operative farm at, 138
"Association, Church," 400, 403, 405
Athanasian Creed, 186, cf. 28
Atheism, philosophic, 376
   attended with greater difficulties than belief, 378
   dependent upon mere speculation, 386
   its effect upon morality, 175, 377
   influence among working men, 379
Augustine, St., on ceremonies, 168
Authority of the Church, 31
—— Episcopal, 174–6, 410, 411, 438

BALLET, the, 199
   dancers, 82, 85
Banks, 121
Bazaars, 450
Beaconsfield, Lord, 440, 507
   novels of, 142
Belief, value of definite, 31, 164
——— simplicity of, 170
——— four essentials of, 228
Benevolence, should be discriminating, 126
Benson, Archbishop, 538
BIBLE, the, contains a progressive teaching, 387
   the Bishop's knowledge of, 34
   importance, and true object of Bible-reading, 35
   value in the education of children, 158
Birley, Robert, 447
Birley, T. H., 124
Birtwistle, T., 99, 105
"Bishop of all denominations," 265–301. See 286
Bishops, types of, 21
   the "perfect conception of a bishop," 43
   their varying opportunities, 320
   right of, to refuse institution to a living, 419
   in the House of Lords, 307
   interesting to various classes, 226
   "a bishop is only a man," 433
Bishop's Court, 61, 463, 494, 502
Blackpool, the Bishop at, 457
Bolton strike, 93–98
Borromeo, Cardinal, 550
Bradley, Dean, 540
Bright, John, M.P., letter of sympathy to, 454

Broadhurst, Henry, M.P., 94
Brotherton, Joseph, M.P., 17, 343
Bryce, Prof., on Fraser as a bishop, 21, 28, 48
—— letter to Mrs. Fraser, 541
Buddhism, 467
Burder, Mr. John, 511
Burdett-Coutts, Baroness, 83, 464
Burgon, Dean, 483
Burial of the dead, 151
—————— Bishop Fraser, 536
—————— customs, reform of, 247
—————— grounds, encroachment of, upon the country, 151
Burke, Edmund, quoted, 200, 311
—————— Mr., murder of, 317

Caird, Mr., 96
Calcutta, Bishopric of, refused by Fraser, 49, 491
Canonical obedience, 176, 412, 413
Cant, 73, 129, 234
Carlisle, Bishop of, 8, 471
Carter, Canon, letter to, 448
Cash-payments, the only basis of thrift, 145
Cathedrals, 456
"Catholic," misuse of the word, 448, 449
Cavendish, Lord F., 317
Ceremonial, when in place, 166, 337
Chadwick, Jeremiah, 332, 373
Chalice, mixed, 410, 411
Chapman, Samuel, correspondence with the Bishop, 367 *et seq.*
Charge, the Bishop's first, 157, 224
—————— his second, 394, 395
—————— third, 287 *et seq.*
Charity, private, of the Bishop, 122, 134, cf. 348, etc.
—————— Organization of, 122, 297
—————— its difficulty, 121, 123, 126
—————— pauperizing effect of indiscriminate, 127, 130
Charlewood, Mr. E. P., 5, 521, 527
Cheetham Hill, St. John's, case of, 427, 429
China, 475
Choirs, 241
 their ministry, 244

Cholderton, C, 438
Christianity. See also "Religion and Morality."
Christianity, a brotherhood, 140, 155
 a revelation and a religion, 359
 its double aspect, spiritual and social, 302
 the only solvent of the enigmas of life, 381
 comprehensiveness of, how to be attained, 271
 true "Evidences" of, 207
 unconscious influences of, 351
 vital principles of, 29, 272
 and citizenship, 313, 314
 — cowardice, 250
 — the masses, 170, 190, 346
 — politics, 26, cf. 303, 369, 436
 — social problems, 94, 125, 310, 380
Christian life, a growth, 229
Christie, Chancellor, 10, 172, 179, 418, 422
Church, Dean, 43, 118, 536
Church of England
 satisfies the essentials of a church, 161, 214
 a great national institution, 168, 282, etc.
 the church of the poor, 345, 348
 how established and endowed, 279
 its breadth, 229, 396
 — functions non-political, 367 *et seq.*, 431
 — fundamental principles, 276
 — mind as to the Eucharist, 161
 — principle of worship, 167
 — property, really belonging to particular corporations, 452
 — relation to the people, 162, 171, 190, 284, 345
 — relation to the Church of Rome, 165
 — relation to the Nonconformists, 170. See "Nonconformists"
 — true strength, 66, 268
 — system, parochial, not congregational, 171
Church of Rome
 aggression of, 165

INDEX. 555

CHURCH OF ROME—continued.
  claims of, 434
  its principle of worship, 167
  in the United States, 474
Churches, free and open, 347
Church-going, 76, 190
Churchmanship, a remedy for the times, 27, 164, 449
Churchmanship, ignorance of the principles of, 276
Church reform, 285
Citizen-Bishop, 22, 227, 302-329
  by whom first called, 323
Classes, need of mutual understanding between, 68, 133
  ——— separation of, 148
  ——— in the street, contrasted with classes in the Church, 341
CLERGY
  as a class, 3, 66, 202
  in the country, 244
  as business men, 506
  number of, in the diocese of Manchester, 521
  professional mannerism of, 458
  their office, 218, 219
  ——— duty of teaching the young, 233
  ——— duty of loyalty to the Church, 217
  ——— co-operation with the laity, 309
  relation to politics, 305, 307, 479
Clifford, Professor, 387, 469
COMMERCE
  development of the manufacturing branch of, 96
  panics in, 120
  and morality, 133, 312, 313
  — credit, 136, 143 (see also "Trade")
Common sense, gospel of, 332
Communism in France, 368
Competition, its evils, 134, 142
Condolence, letters of, to Mrs. Fraser, 538-546
Conferences, Lambeth, 181-183
  Diocesan, at Manchester, 163-166, 178, 399
Confessional, 435, 439
Confirmation, the Bishop's pleasure in, 204-207

Confirmation at Leesfield, 205; Bolton, 208; Accrington, 208
  in the evening, 204-207
Congress, Church, 192-203
  an instrument of much good, 197
  at Brighton, 201; Newcastle, 202; Nottingham, 196; Sheffield, 2, 18, 25, 29, 193, etc.
  Co-operative, at Manchester, 137; at Oldham, 145
  Social Science, at Manchester, 146
Consecration of Bishop Fraser, 53
Conscience, the basis of morality, 393
  duty of obeying, 485
  of companies, 81
  social, 340
  in reporting, 327
Controversies, ecclesiastical, misfortune of, 140, 173
  should be limited to opinions, 414
Conversion, usually gradual, 365
Convocation, 184-192
Cookery, 240
Co-operation and competition, 142
CO-OPERATIVE MOVEMENT, advantages of, 142, 143
  its principles, 136, 145
  educational influence of, 144
  criticisms on, 145
Co-operative congress, 137; sermon by the Bishop, 144
  farm at Assington, 138
  mills, 101, 138, 145, 152
Cornish, Canon, 476, 510, 523, 536
Cotterill, Bishop, 494
Cotton famine, its effect upon Lancashire character, 153, 360
Council, Diocesan, 172
Country parsons, 244, 477
Court of Final Appeal, 409, 411
Courts, Ecclesiastical, 160
Cowgill, Rev. Harry. See "Miles Platting"
  refusal of the Bishop to ordain, 398
  curate of St. John's, Miles Platting, 407
  nominated rector of St. John's, 419
Cowie, Dean, 73, 536
  letter of the Bishop to, 447
Credit system, 136, 143

Creeds, need of, 31, 164
——, Athanasian, 186
Cremation, 151, 248
Crusade, the modern, 40
Curates, 162, 238
Cynicism, 39, 251

DARWIN'S SYSTEM, not atheistic, 390
Death, state after, not a sleep, 497
Denominationalism, 267
Diary, kept by the Bishop, 493
—————————— Mrs. Fraser, 62
Dickens, Charles, purity of his influence, 200, 202
Differences, necessity of, 267
—————— without animosity, value of, 229
toleration of, 395
—————— should be governed by Christian charity, 471
Dignity, true and false, 5
Diocesan organizations, founded by Bishop Fraser, 66, 521
Discipline, need of, in English society, 219
Disestablishment, general result of, 163
its probable effect upon the Church, 173, 278.
—————————— upon religious freedom, 309
Dissent. See "Nonconformity"
Distress caused by depression of trade, 119
relief of, 122.
Divine service, decency and order in, 176
Doctrine, various modes of stating, 395
Dogma, value of, 30, 189, cf. 428
the process of its construction, 188
danger of multiplication of, 229
Dogmatic precision unattainable, 395
Dogmatism, growing spirit of, 189, 227, 253
Drink, consumption of, by the working classes, 344
Duncan, Mrs., 491, 504
Miss Agnes, 191, 491. See "Fraser, Mrs."
Duncan, John Shute, 501
Philip Bury, 501
Duty, claims of, 352

EARLY RISING, 457, 503
Eastward position, 160
Eating, inordinate love of, 453
Edification, the principle of the Church of England, 167
Edinburgh, society in, 443
EDUCATION, 230-237
the helpmeet of righteousness, 36
concerned with principles more than knowledge, 230
its debt to the clergy, 230
its moral aspect, 236
dangers connected with the advance of, 237
duty of parents, 231
religious, in day schools, 10, 157, 232
American system, 149
modern system of higher education, 235
at Ufton, 52
Fraser's early connection with, 23
Elberfeldt system explained, 127, 129
need of, 124, 126, 153
Eloquence, its dangers, 237, cf. 270
Endowments of churches, their origin, 278
Enterprise, great scope for, in England, 353
Enthronization of the Bishop, 54
Equality, 450
Established church, advantages of an, 278
Evening communions, 470, 472
Excitability of Englishmen, 319
Explosions, colliery, 318, 349, 456
Extempore speaking, 355
Extravagance, a general fault of Englishmen, 132, 152, 248
—————— among the working classes, 125
—————— when legitimate, 323
—————— the only effectual plan against, 478

FAIRNESS, general confidence in the Bishop's, 95, 102, 179, 193, 332
Faith and reason, lecture on, 384
Farmer, John, 441
Fashion, man of, 251

INDEX. 557

Fashionable life, its demoralizing tendency, 253
Fashions, 251
Fasting in Lent, 433
Fearon, Archdeacon, 85
Fees, the clergy and, 432
Fervour in the Church, 346
Formalism, "an organized hypocrisy," 175
FRASER, Right Rev. James, D.D.
"a Bishop of the Church Catholic," 546
"Bishop of all denominations," 286
"Citizen Bishop," 323
HIS LIFE
  early education, 5, 8
  preparation for the Episcopate 23, 226
  appointment to Manchester, 41
  consecration, 53
  first Charge, 157
  Manchester Mission, 72 et seq.
  Lancashire strike, 98 et seq.
  Lambeth Conference, 181
  president of the Co-operative Congress, 137
  ———————— Social Science Congress, 146
  Miles Platting case, 398 et seq.
  pastoral Admonition, 176
  marriage, 511
  desire for retirement, 519, 526
  death, 531
  a typical day of the Bishop's work, 445, 479
  a typical week of the Bishop's work, 462
  originality of his career, 117, 193
  work done during his Episcopate, 521
HIS CHARACTER
  approachableness, 334
  chivalry, 192, 295
  courage, 102, 155, 197
  devotion to duty, 67
  decisiveness, 11
  directness, 20, 50
  fairness, 95, q. v.
  frankness, 9
  geniality, 298
  happiness, 530

HIS CHARACTER—continued.
  impulsiveness, 10, 52, 197, 266
  inspiring, 14, 211, 324
  joyousness, 16, 206, 212
  observation, 15
  sensitiveness, 95, 100
  sincerity, 526
  sympathy, 12, 206, 298, 300, 316, 330, 351, 448, 495
  thoroughness, 295
HIS GIFTS
  practical, 183
  many-sided, 13, 22, 321, 362
  less those of an organizer than a prophet, 67
  wanting in poetic feeling, 20, 183; but cf. 443
HIS HABITS
  Bible reading, 34
  carefulness in keeping accounts, 135
  charity, 134, cf. 122, 394, 506
  dislike of change, 143, 507
  hospitality, 17, 495, 515
  love of country life and scenery, 49, 62, 71, 470
  love of home, 490, 514
  prayerfulness, 34; family prayers, 516
  self-denial, 442
  simple, but not ascetic, 19, cf. 512
  thrift, 137, 361, 506
  tolerance, 267, 271, 295, 382, 394
  work, 7, 52, 206, 437
FRASER'S relation to church parties, 26, 28, 273
Jews, 290
Nonconformity, 276, 277, 286, 291
ritualism, 36, 166, 174–6. See "Miles Platting"
FRASER as a chairman, 178
  in the House of Lords, 437, 454
  general confidence in fairness of, 95, 102, 179, 193, 332
  his income, 506
  his influence on the working classes, 335 et seq.
  his investments, 507
  his popularity among working men, 192, 374

FRASER, his relations with his servants, 494, 497
— "views," 273
FRASER, Mrs., the Bishop's wife
letters to, from the Bishop, 431 et seq.
devotion to her mother, 491
first acquaintance with the Bishop, 500
engagement, 502
marriage, 511
description of home-life by, 516
FRASER, Mrs., the Bishop's mother
extract from her diary, 62
last illness and death, 497-499
See 5, 34, 71, 374, 490, 492
Free Trade, 469
French, the Bishop's, 460
Friends, blessing of, 474

GARFIELD, President, 258, 485
Genesis, early chapters of, 75, 272
Gifts, a trust to be used for God, 71
Gladstone, Right Hon. W. E.
offer of the Bishopric, 41-47
—— the Deanery of Westminster, 484
and the Miles Platting case, 413-415
Glebe lands, 139
Gordon, General, 262
Gore, Archdeacon, 70
Gospel, the, must be intelligible, 346
"gospel of common sense," 352
"gospel of damnation," 376, 459
Grace, irresistible, doctrine of, 288
Grant, Sir Alexander, 443
Greatness, true, 14
Green, Rev. S. F., 398. See "Miles Platting"
Greg, W. R., 444
Gunton, Rev. C. F., 427-429

HAPPINESS, 363, 496, 503
—————— of the Bishop, 530
Harrison, Frederic, 387
Harrow, the Bishop at, 441
Harvest, importance of the English, 96
Hatherley, Lord, 256

Hawkins, Rev. H. B., letter of sympathy to, 482
Hayfield, anniversary at, 476
Health, public, its conditions, 150
Heredity, principle of, 239
Heroism, simply the performance of duty, 352
—————— of the working classes, 35
Heywood, Mr. Oliver, 122, 323, 550
Heywood, Sir Percival, 416, 417, 419
Home, happiness of the Bishop's, 515
—— devotion to, one of the great needs of society, 515
—— duties possess the greatest claim upon a man, 344, 490
—— —— the subject of the Bishop's last sermon, 525
—— life, Mrs. Fraser's description of, 517
Hornby, Archdeacon, 2
Horses, the Bishop's love for, 2, 221
Hospitality at Bishop's Court, 17, 495, 515
Houldsworth, Sir W. H., 542
How-Walsham, Bishop, 478
Hughes, Judge, quoted, 9, 4
Hunting, 261, 466
Huxley, Prof., 284, 392, 462
Hymns, choice of, 242
—————— Ancient and Modern, profits of, 456

IDLENESS a curse, 310
Impurity "a mental disease," its sources, 201
—————— the most terrible of England's enemies, 311, 378
—————— its treatment in the Old Testament, 311
Inconsistency the great enemy of Christianity, 234, 368
—————— an argument for Atheists, 389
Induction of an incumbent, service for, 477
Inquiry, the spirit of, 271
Insurance, scheme of compulsory, 153
Intemperance best dealt with indirectly, 133

Intemperance partly caused by vitiated air, 450
Interpretation of Scripture, 272
"Invalids," the Bishop's, 74. See also 374, 490
" Ireland Scholarship," 7
Ireland, 317-320
Irish party, 320
Irving, Henry, 464

JACKSON, Mr. Raynsford, 99, 103
"James," reporters' name for the Bishop, 326, cf. 23
Jews, the Bishop's relations with, 290
Job, Book of, the argument, 441
Judgment, private right of, 31, 395
" Judgments," 440, 475

KEAN, Mr. and Mrs. Charles, 81
Kingsley, Charles, 437
Knox-Little, Rev. W. J., 72, 88

LAMBETH Conference, service at St. Paul's, 192
Lancashire operatives, their orderly character, 8, 359
Lash, use of the, in the army, 476
Layman's work, considered as a training for clergy, 23
Lawful authority, 438
Lee, Bishop, 45, 65
——————— objection of, to synods, 179
Letter, the Bishop's last, 525
Levi, Prof. Leone, 132, 152
Liberation Society, 24
Liberty, intellectual, its value, and its excesses, 38
Liddon, Canon, 44
Life, the future, 72; effect of belief in, 471
—— a quiet, the Bishop's wish for, 504
Lightfoot, Bishop, consecration of, 471
——————————— letter from, 539
Lingen, Lord, 48, 471, 536
Literature, pure, value of, 200
Livings, sale of, 280

Lloyd, Canon, 65
London East and West-End churches, 341
Lonsdale, Rev. James, 50, 54
Lords, House of, 437, 454
" Lost Tribes." 481
Lubbock, Sir John, 384
Luxuries, spread of, 250, 340
——————— soon grow to be necessities, 17
Luxury, 343

MACLAREN, Rev. Dr., 540
Maclure, Canon, 59, 207, 483, 500
Macready, 81, 464
Mallock's ' New Republic,' 446
MANCHESTER
 City of, the centre of the modern life of the country, 41
 ——— Christianity in, Dr. McFadyen's view of, 293
 ——— Fraser's first speech in, 50
 ——— its death-rate, 150
 ——— its sewage system, 150
 diocese of, its character, 65, 68
 and district, population of, 65, 147
 Grammar School, 69
 Town Hall, 323
 see of, its modern character, 502
Manning, Cardinal, 327
Marriages, early, 132
——————— the Bishop's marriage, 511
Marriage-service, exhortation in, 436
Marriage-tie, sacredness of, 203
Martin, Lady Theodore, 81
Masses and classes, 68, 117
 Bishop's attempt to gain, 337
 must be reached by the Church, 170
Matrimonial experiences, 434
 brides and bridegrooms, 459
Matter, Christian view of, 75
Mauldeth Hall, 46, 61
McDonagh, Mr. George, 400
" Meditation among the Tombs," 436
MILES-PLATTING case, 397-426
 principles involved, 405
 a struggle between two rival ecclesiastical associations, 416

MILES-PLATTING CASE, History of—
A. First monition of the Bishop, 398
  petition from "parishioners," 400
  "presentation to the Bishop," 402
B. Interview between the Bishop and Mr. Green, 403
  refusal of the Bishop to exercise the veto, 404
  petition from communicants, 405
  inhibition of Mr. Green, 406
  imprisonment of Mr. Green, 407
  services continued by Mr. Cowgill, 407
  letter of the Bishop, 408; Mr. Green's reply, 411
  discussion as to canonical obedience, 412, 413
  "Admonition" of the Bishop, 415
C. Difficulties as to Mr. Green's release, 417
  application by the Bishop, and release of Mr. Green, 418
D. Vacancy of the living; nomination of Mr. Cowgill, 419
  Bishop's refusal to institute him; letter to the patron, 422
  action by Sir P. Heywood—verdict for the Bishop, 425
  appointment by the Bishop to the vacancy, 426
Mill, John Stuart, quoted, 387
Mind, the, an immaterial unit, 384
MISSION, the Manchester, 72–89
——— Bishop's anxiety about, 74
——— addresses to medical students, 75; railway employés, 75; cab-drivers, 76; slaughtermen, 77; actors, 78
——— concluded by a conference, 89
Missions, parochial, 69
——— ——— are an opportunity for declaring belief, 73

Missions, "instructions" at, by the Bishop, 74
Molesworth, Rev. W., quoted, 140
Money, 506
Monument to Bishop Fraser, and memorial chapel, 549
Moorhouse, Bishop, 532–549
MORALITY, Christian, different from morality of Christians, 370
——— and commerce, 133, 312, 313
——— and conscience, 393
——— and politics, 251
Mowbray, Sir John, 43, 536
Mozley, Prof., quoted, 93, 395
Municipal offices, their claim upon citizens, 321
Music should be proportionate, 242
——— choice of tunes, 243

NEWMAN, Cardinal, 220, 225, 259, 466, 512
"Newspaper," the man of one, 325
Newspapers, influence of, 324
——— and preachers, 58
——— their attitude towards Fraser, 23, 59, 328
——— partizan, 325; "religious," 324
——— "society," 325
Nonconformists, their feeling towards the Bishop, 392–4, 509
Nonconformist ministers, 467
NONCONFORMITY, 170, 190, 288–9
——— its principle, 31
——— its spirit more or less anarchical, 276
——— proper attitude of Churchmen towards, 217, 287, 431
——— and the sacraments, 277
——— in rural districts, 288
Norris, Archdeacon, 40, 212, 412, 536

OAKLEY, Dean, 528
Ober-Ammergau, passion-play at, 198
Office seeking, 33, cf. 437
Opinions, each man's right to his own, 11
——— undue exaltation of, 439

Opium traffic, 251
Opportunities, good use of, 236
Orangemen, 369
ORDINATION, training of candidates for, 162, 222–3
——— at Manchester, not of the nature of a retreat, 212
——— Fraser's addresses previous to, 211–14
——— notes of addresses, 220
——— the Ordination call, 215
——— "moved by the Holy Ghost," 33
Oriel, the Bishop a Fellow of, mentioned as a possible Provost of, 473
Ornaments Rubric, 174, 184, 411, 438
Owens College, 69, 392, 520
Oxford, Fraser's expenses at, 6
——— system of classes at, 235
——— modern tone of, 483
"Oxford Movement," 259

PANTHEISTIC theory, 245, 451
Party purposes, use of the Church for, 367
Party spirit, 217, 265
Patriotism, 314, 352
Patronage, Church, 168, 280
Pauperism, methods of repressing, 154
Pearson, Rev. Canon, 512
Penzance, Lord, 406
Personal influence, 57
Peterborough, the Bishop at, 457
Petitions, small value of, 472
Pew system, 168
Philanthropy, 382
Phillips, Mr. H., 122, 129, 130, 510
"Philochristus," 458
Phrases, complimentary, 10
Physicians and surgeons, 461
Plays, cost of production, 198
POLITICS, proper meaning of, 24, 26
——— highest aims of, 304
——— the various parties in, 304–5
——— and religion, 303, 369, 436
Political clubs, 25
Political economy, deals only with immediate causes, 313

Poor districts, personal visitation of, 128, 129, 131
Popularity, 215, 520
Population of great cities, 147
Porter. Prof., 543
Powell, Canon, 71, 500, 508
Prayer, 344, 365, 468
——— practice of, 33
Prayers, family, at Bishop's Court, 516
——— for the Bishop, 335
Prayer Book, preface quoted, 410
Preaching of Bishop Fraser, 21, 58, 191, 302, 331
Presence, doctrine of the Real, 274
Presentations to the Bishop from workmen, 374, 375
——— on his marriage, 518, 520
Priesthood, the office of, in the Church of England, 161, 273, 275
——— of the whole Church of Christ, 268
Prince Imperial, 255
Prizes, 235
Protestantism, 266, 477
——— variations of, 395
PROVIDENCE, Fraser's belief in, 33, 50, 88, 263, 433
——— in war, 316
Providence. See "Thrift"
Punishment, corporal, 234
Pusey, Dr., 259
Punch, 328, 370
——— on the Bishop's marriage, 513

RAILWAY employés, visit of the Bishop to, 333
Rapidity of thought, dangers of, 236
Reading, good, importance of in Church services, 224
Reality, the great want of Christianity, 268
Reason, conclusions of, must be adopted, 387
——— and Faith, 38, 384
Recreation. See "Amusements."
Reformation, The, "a Catholic revival," 160
Reid, Rev. Stuart, 295
Relief, organization of, 122 *et seq.*

2 O

INDEX.

Relief, mischief of indiscriminate, 130
RELIGION
  a matter of act and temper more than word, 228, 257, 303, 347
  often degraded into a matter of speculation, 252; or of formal observance, 339
  in families, 240
  and morality, 28, 340
  and politics, 303, 369, 436
  and religious observances, 357
  and science. See "Science"
  Fraser's influence in promoting, 291
  "natural religion," 356
Reporters and the Bishop, 326, cf. 439
—————— conscience of, 327
Reserve between husband and wife, perils of, 503
Responsibilities, personal rather than social, 82
Rest, not idleness, 55
Retirement, Bishop's wish for, 519, 526
Revelation, not a strange idea, 356
Reverence, habit of, 230, 269
  devout, not mechanical, 270
  in choirs, 242
Reynolds' Newspaper, 341
Righteousness, the Bishop's love of, 36, 483
  need of, in commerce, 133
  the true strength of a nation, 250
Ritualism, of two kinds, reverent and superstitious, 37
  its anarchical spirit, 438
  see 88, 166, 174, 266
Robertson, quoted, 448
Rochester, Bishop of, letter from, 539
Rogers, Mr. Guinness, 295
Ryder, Mr. T. D., 45, 466
Ryle, Bishop, consecration of, 336

SACERDOTALISM, of two kinds, false and true, 72
  cf. 37, 161, 456, 486
Sacrament of the Lord's Supper, not a propitiatory sacrifice, 161
Sacred and Secular, not to be distinguished, 22, 309

Salvation Army, 373
Saving, practice of. See "Thrift," 457
Savings banks, a social barometer
SCHOOLS, Day
  gradation of, 149
  maintenance of religious education in, 157:
  need for distinct Church teaching in, 231
  Sunday, 157
  and parental obligations, 233
School Boards, 231
  religious instruction in Board Schools, 232
SCIENCE
  agreement of, with religion, in the search for practical truth, 383
  Lord Bacon quoted, 391
  claims only the allegiance of the intellect, 389
  powerlessness of, to arrest God's hand, 349
  scientific theories, only hypotheses, 385
  "scientific temper" and religion, 38, cf. 465
  medical science and religion, 75
  social science and religion, 155
Secularism, 376, 381
Secularists, 358
Selborne, Lord Chancellor, 416
Self Help, and Fellow Help, 343
Selfishness, is not happiness, 11
—————— of society, 340
—————— of rich and poor, 342
—————— religious, 90, 254, 313
Self-satisfaction, peril of, 339
Selwyn, Bishop, 452
Sentimentalism, one of our subtlest perils, 254
Sermons, preparation of, 172, 232
  "evangelical," 455
Sermons of Bishop Fraser
  first in Manchester, 55
  after Manchester Mission, 90
  on strikes, 93
  at the Co-operative Congress, 144
  at Nottingham Church Congress, 197
  on confirmation, 208

Sermons of Bishop Fraser at Cambridge, on the relation of religion to the problems of the day, 379
Servants, 424
Share-jobbing, 138
Shaw, Col., 485
Sheffield, 193
Shoddyism, 134
Shrewsbury School, sermon at, 8, 33
Shuttleworth, Sir V. Kay, 543
Smith, Mr. James (District Provident Society), 122, 123, 134, 509
Smoke, consumption of, 151
Smoking, practice of, 468
Socialism, 310
SOCIAL PROBLEMS
   the Bishop's knowledge of, 91, 147 et seq.
   ———— interest in, 94, 124
   clue to the solution of, 117, cf. 68
   connection of Christianity with, 94, 125, 146, 310, 380
   condition of great cities as to
     (α) population, 147
     (β) education, 149
     (γ) sanitation, 150
     (δ) cemeteries, 151
     (ε) thrift and providence, 152
     (ζ) relief of pauperism, 153
     (η) recreation, 154
Social science and religion, 155
   ———— Congress, 146
Society, inconsiderateness of, 77
Spectator, letter from the Bishop to, 263
SPEECHES of Bishop Fraser
   first, in Manchester, 50
   on co-operation, 137
   on social science, 147
   before convocation, 184
   at Owens College, on science and religion, 382
   to actors, 80
   to volunteers, 352
   typical, to working men, 352–367
Speechmaking, the Bishop's early dislike of, 156
Spinoza, 451
Stanley, Dean, 47, 83, 182, 255, 257, 300, 438, 448, 460, 470, 472, 512
Statue of Bishop Fraser, 549

Steinthal, Rev. S. A., 296
Stewart, Prof. Balfour, 465
STRIKE, the great Lancashire
   its causes, 96
   conflicting theories concerning, 97
   proposals for remedying, 98
   the Bishop's opinion concerning terms of agreement, 100, 105
   history of
   reduction of wages, 98
   protest of operatives, 99
   proposals for arbitration made, 100 ; declined, 102, 111
   behaviour of the people, 100
   general lock-out, and consequent disturbances, 103
   the Bishop's efforts at conciliation, 106 : his letter to the *Times*, 110
   growth of a spirit of compromise, 109
   termination, 117
Strikes, The Bishop's experience in 92
   ———— attitude towards, 93, 94
   their effect upon other branches of the trade concerned, 93
   their effect upon trade in general, 101, 112
   Co-operation a remedy for, 140
   distress connected with, 93, 119
Success, the source of, 335
Sunday, observance of, 246
   opening of art galleries on, 247, 468
   opening of workmen's clubs on, 481
Synod, Diocesan, the purpose of, 157
   first, 157
   second, 172

TAIT, Archbishop, 260
   on the Miles Platting Case, 408
Tay Bridge accident, 482
Tea-parties in Lancashire, 417, 573
TEMPERANCE QUESTION, The, 158, 458
   frankness of the Bishop in dealing with, 10

TEMPERANCE QUESTION, The, proposals
  for effective legislation, 480
  blue ribbon movement, 486
Temple, Bishop, 48
Theatres, 78-89, 197, 464
  ———— only to be improved by
  public opinion, 199, 245
Theatricals, private, 84
Theologian, Fraser not a skilled, 20
Theology, Fraser's, spiritual rather
  than scientific, 28
  extravagances of, seen in Atheism
  and Agnosticism, 386, *cf.* 469
Third-class passengers, 333
Thirlmere water scheme, 322, 454
Thomson, Archbishop. See "York"
Thomson, Rev. Dr. A., 298
Thought, leaders of, their responsi-
  bility, 318
Thrift, 18, 132, 145, 152, 360, 361
Time, wasters of, 434
Tolerance, the Bishop's, 267, 271
  ———— within the Church, 273
  309
Tolerance towards Dissent, 288, 289
Tooke, Rev. T. H., 42
TRADE. See also "Commerce"
  general depression of, in 1878, 97,
  100
  condition of cotton industry, 101,
  115
  foreign competition in, 98, 112
Trades unions, 92, 102, 114
Tyndall, Prof., 384, 462

UFTON NERVET, described, 533-536
  the Bishop's wish to be buried at,
  436, 492
  the Bishop's last visit to, 523
Union, English Church 400
Unique experience of the Bishop, 445
Unitarianism, 461
Universalism, 446
Universities and priesthoods, 391, 393
  moral and social influence of, 392

VACCINATION, 461
Vaughan, Right Rev. Dr., Bishop of
  Salford, 434, 469, 539

Vestments, Eucharistic, 160, 169,
  184-5
  at St. John's, Miles Platting, 399
  ought not to be used without ecclesiastical authority, 415
Vice, 200, 311. See "Impurity"
Voluntaryism, dangers of, 278
  ———— ———— and endowment, 283
Voysey, Rev. Charles, 541

WANTS, unnecessary, harm of, 343
Wars, when justifiable, 249
  their relation to Christianity, 316
  industrial, 93, 108
Wealth, weakening effect of, 19
  if luxurious, not beneficial to society, 252
  disproportionate influence of, in
  parochial arrangements, 191
Wedding presents, 449
Wells, Mr. Spencer, 461
Westcott, Canon, 471
Westhoughton, stone-laying at, 473
Westminster Abbey, 19
Westminster, Deanery of, offered to
  Bishop Fraser, 484
Whalley, Mr., 99
Wilkins, Prof., on the Bishop's attitude towards social questions
  on the Bishop's interest in education, 394
Woman, dignity of, 83
  purifying influence of, 199
  position of, 237, *cf.* 464
  "rights of," 442, *cf.* 461
Work, Fraser's power of, 52
  the possibility of finding time for,
  437
Working classes, the Bishop and
  the, 330-375; kindly relations
  between, 344
  important because of numerical
  strength, 345
  heroism of, 350
  influence of, 202
  wages of, 152, 361
Workshops, the Bishop's visits to,
  331, 337, 355
World, The, is it good or bad? 478
Worship, is individual, not collective,
  242

Worship should be grand, yet simple, 269, *cf.* 176
"Public Worship Regulation Act," 159, 406

YORK, Archbishop of, on the Miles Platting case, 407
on the Cheetham Hill case, 427

Young men, the coming race, their responsibility, 353
brotherhoods of, 487
Young Men's Christian Association, 510
Youth, its perils and safeguards, 250, 251.

WORKS BY THE SAME AUTHOR.

OPINIONS OF THE PRESS.

GODLINESS AND MANLINESS.
(MACMILLAN & CO. 6s.)

The Author writes clearly and vigorously, with considerable felicity of phrase. Frequently the argument and thought are original and valuable.—*The Academy.*

Each Essay is practical, pointed, thoughtful, complete in itself, readable, reasonable, conclusive.—*The Saturday Review.*

The Author writes with reverence of spirit, thoughtfulness, and beauty of style. Some of the papers are full of charm.—*The Scottish Leader.*

In many of the Papers are very striking observations of a kind to quicken and strengthen faith.—*The Record.*

A book of a very high character. The thoughtful reader will find it abounding in thought and stimulating to thought.—*The North British Daily Mail.*

TRUE RELIGION.
(DAVID STOTT, LONDON. 5s.)

This book, written in epigrammatic style, should greatly interest those who think over their daily life.—*The Spectator.*

Contains many wise and admirable sayings. Is certainly ably written; the style forcible and pointed.—*The Scotsman.*

Not less manly and honest than scholarly and Christian.—*The Literary World.*

A very fascinating book.—*The Liverpool Daily Post.*

From first to last these Essays are interesting.

A volume full of suggestiveness and uncommon power.—*The Liverpool Mercury.*

BISHOP FRASER'S SERMONS.
(MACMILLAN & CO. 6s. each Vol.)

VOL. I., UNIVERSITY SERMONS; VOL. II., PAROCHIAL SERMONS.

These sermons are the Bishop's very own. They show his heartiness, vigour, simplicity, clearness, and force.—*The Guardian.*

We recommend to our readers these volumes to be read and re-read.—*Church Quarterly Review.*

We find Bishop Fraser at his best in these two volumes.—*John Bull.*

These sermons might well serve for models.—*The Literary Churchman.*

One feels, in reading them, breezes from the upper world breathing around.—*The Homilist.*

Bishop Fraser's strong individuality gleams through every page.—*The Family Churchman.*

These sermons are addressed by a man who thinks to men who think and feel.—*The Oxford Review.*

They show the best characteristics of the man as well as the preacher.—*The Cambridge Review.*

Those who read them will be thrilled again and again by memories of the Bishop.—*The Manchester Guardian.*

Emphatically among the sermons of the age.—*The Manchester Courier.*

www.ingramcontent.com/pod-product-compliance
Lightning Source LLC
Chambersburg PA
CBHW031935290426
44108CB00011B/562